The Facts On File
# DICTIONARY OF
# NAUTICAL TERMS

The Facts On File
# DICTIONARY OF NAUTICAL TERMS

## Thompson Lenfestey
*with Captain Tom Lenfestey, Jr.*

Facts On File®

AN INFOBASE HOLDINGS COMPANY

The Facts On File Dictionary of Nautical Terms

Copyright © 1994 by Thompson Lenfestey

Facts On File, Inc.
460 Park Avenue South
New York NY 10016


**Library of Congress Cataloging-in-Publication Data**
Lenfestey, Tom.
    The Facts on File dictionary of nautical terms / by Thompson
Lenfestey.
        p.    cm.
    Includes bibliographical references.
    ISBN 0-8160-2087-6
    1. Naval art and science—Dictionaries.    I. Facts on File, Inc.
II. Title.
    U24.L46    1993
    359′.003—dc20                                            92-31490

Jacket design by Linda Kosarin
Composition and manufacturing by the Maple-Vail Book Manufacturing Group
Printed in the United States of America

10 9 8 7 6 5 4 3 2 1

This book is printed on acid-free paper.

*To*
*Hatty*
*Harriet, Tom Jr., and Hudson*

# TABLE OF CONTENTS

# ILLUSTRATIONS AND TABLES

# FOREWORD

The sea embraces a wide variety of disciplines each with its own unique assortment of terms and usages. These terms differ not only from vessel to vessel, whether iron or fiberglass, sail or diesel, but between the trades in which they sail. The everyday usage of the Coast Guard or Navy sailor differs markedly from that of the merchant mariner, the fisherman, the yachtsman, and the ship broker.

In defining both general and specialist nautical terms, Tom Lenfestey has done a remarkable job of pulling together a wealth of information, much of which is not easily found even in professional publications. He has managed the difficult task of covering all the variants of the maritime field without getting bogged down in any one. As an interesting addition to the literature, Mr. Lenfestey flavors his definitions with examples of usage and, in the case of more unusual terms, their etymological roots.

With centuries of sailing and sailors behind us, and centuries more to come, no book can capture every nuance of the language of the sea for all time. But Mr. Lenfestey has done a fine job of offering a thoroughly practical and up-to-date guide to nautical usage for today's mariner.

K. B. Raisch
Chief Warrant Officer
USCG Barque *Eagle*

# PREFACE

More than 40 years have passed since the last new and comprehensive dictionary of maritime words and phrases was written. Since that time, marine construction and shipbuilding materials, maritime law, naval warfare, and marine navigation have all undergone profound change. The maritime shipping and transportation industries and the U.S. merchant marine have also changed significantly in the past quarter century. So, too, nautical usage has evolved, and many new terms have been introduced into the language.

The need for a new dictionary geared both to those with professional interest in maritime matters as well as to amateur yachtsmen and armchair sailors being evident, I approached Facts On File with the idea for this book. They recognized the place for such a dictionary of nautical terms and phrases and one that included not only definitions, but etymologies, usages, and parts of speech as well.

Today's nautical English is a curious blend of terms, the oldest of which were first spoken before Shakespeare's day and hold their original meanings now, and the most modern of which spring fully jargoned and acronymed from the desktop computers of electronics laboratories. And much of seamen's English comes directly to the language not only from other European maritime nations, but from Africa, Asia, and Oceania. As the sailor's work has changed, we have found it easier to find new meanings for old words than to create new ones afresh.

This leads to one of the delights and torments of the maritime lexicographer. Some writers would have you think that their favorite word came over with the *Mayflower,* but in many instances a little research demonstrates that the word in question is of 20th-century vintage. While one writer will work up a patently specious proscription on the word "boater,"

meaning boatman, another will take a positively belligerent stand on whether you "fake" or "flake" a line.

How much ink has been spilled in the controversy over whether to use "line" or "rope" is anyone's guess. But the evidence is pretty clear that "rope" was used throughout the ship until less than 100 years ago, and that "line" was used only for "cordage, smaller than ropes, and formed by two or more fine strands of hemp," in the words of Biddlecombe.

Few people would want—or dare—to fix the language of sea. But it is unquestionably important that any language be stabilized and codified to keep it intelligible. It has been my primary purpose to describe common usage rather than to prescribe correct usage. Nowadays, whether you use line or rope is a matter of personal preference.

However, there are many nautical terms that have several meanings, some contradictory, but so fixed that one must know them to use them properly. "Westerly," for instance, can mean from the west or to the west depending on whether one is describing an ocean current or the wind. A mariner ignores the difference at his or her peril.

Pronunciation is yet another area of partisan contest for the armchair lexicographer. An interesting example arises with the word "tackle." This frequently shows up in naval glossaries with the curious pronunciation of "tay-kl." Yet in all my years at sea and on seacoasts, as an enlisted man, Naval officer, and yachtsman—a "boater"—I have yet to hear the word pronounced except as it is said on land.

My own experience at sea has necessarily been a significant point of reference for both usage and pronunciation. I have frequently called on the ear and extensive knowledge of my son, Captain Tom Lenfestey, Jr. (U.S. merchant marine), who contributed a great deal of his time and effort over the years in preparing this work. I have also called on the help of many experts in different fields for their ideas on definitions and pronunciations. But the final decisions, and therefore any mistakes, are my own.

I would be remiss indeed if I did not express my appreciation to my wife, Hatty, for her assistance with the illustrations and her extensive help in proofreading the manuscript. Jessie Hall also spent interminable hours proofreading the manuscript and has my special thanks. I thank Hudson Lenfestey and Harriet Plyler for their support and encouragement. I especially want to thank Lincoln Paine, senior editor at Facts On File, who acted as my clinometer when I listed too far to port or starboard. His unflagging diligence and meticulous attention to detail as he went through the entire text has brought a better focus to this work and made it a handier reference than it would have been without his help. Thanks also to free-lance proofreader Carol Ferrari. And by no means least, I offer a word of thanks to Duchess for her unfailing companionship, wagging her tail when my frustration erupted into audible sounds and hand wringing.

As I have said, it is not my intention to permanently fix nautical usage, but rather to describe it as it is used today so that those who pursue the sea for their livelihood or for pleasure may use its rich and technical idiom with ease and understanding. *Festina lente*—make haste slowly—lest the language of the sea become the gibberish of the sea.

# KEY TO THE USE OF THIS DICTIONARY

Each entry includes the part of speech, pronunciation (when needed), and a definition or definitions. Examples of proper usage are shown when it is thought that such illustrations will help the reader better understand a word's meaning or its application.

Words that appear in boldface within the body of a definition derive from the defined term or are used in conjunction with that term but not deemed significant enough to warrant a separate definition.

"See" references (set off in small capital letters) are used to point the reader to other words that either illuminate the main entry or with which the main entry is frequently confused.

"Also" references (set off in italic type) are used for variant spellings or synonyms that are either obsolete or too rare to warrant a separate entry.

In nautical English, the spelling of a word is often an inadequate guide to its pronunciation. In such cases, a simplified pronunciation or a rhyming word is given in parentheses, for example: boatswain (pron. bosun).

Parts of speech are identified as follows: adj. = adjective; adv. = adverb; interj. = interjection; n. = noun; phr. = phrase; prep. = preposition; v. = verb.

Common abbreviations are shown in parentheses, but they are rarely given a separate entry of their own. Acronyms and abbreviations used in the dictionary are listed in the appendix.

# A

**A** See ALFA.

**aback** *adv.* With wind on the forward side of a square sail. The sails are said to be set aback when they are set to catch the wind to propel a vessel backward. When sails are flat aback, they are positioned so that the wind is nearly at a right angle to the foreside of a square sail. **To be taken aback** (or **caught aback**) is to be inadvertently in a situation where one's sails are aback, either through bad ship-handling or a sudden wind shift. Also *abackstays.*

**abaft** *adv.* or *prep.* A position toward the stern or the back of the vessel with relation to another object on the vessel but not behind the vessel. See ABAFT THE BEAM.

**abaft the beam** *phr.* A position bearing between 90° and 180° from ahead or relative to the ship's course. "The nun buoy is abaft the beam" means that the nun buoy is behind a line perpendicular to the keel at the ship's widest part, the "beam." See RELATIVE BEARING.

**abandon** *v.* To leave permanently. "To abandon ship." You do not abandon ship when you go on leave and intend to return. Abandoning ship is a permanent all-hands evolution, usually in the event the ship is sinking or irreparably damaged.

**abandoned (ship)** *adj.* A vessel that has been left behind with no one aboard and no one apparently looking after it, but still afloat. Under maritime law an abandoned ship on the high seas can be claimed by whoever finds it.

**abandonment clause** *n.* Clause in marine insurance that sets the conditions under which the owners of a ship may abandon a vessel to the underwriters, the conditions being capture, seizure, detention, and so on. See CONSTRUCTIVE TOTAL LOSS.

**abeam** *adv.* or *prep.* At a right angle to the centerline away from a vessel; being approximately 090° or 270° relative. A log entry might say that at 0421 Sombrero Light was abeam. See RELATIVE BEARINGS.

**abeam to windward position** *phr.* The position of a racing sailboat that is parallel to and upwind of another boat when a line between their two helmsmen would be more or less at right angles to their centerlines.

**aberration** *n.* In celestial navigation, the slight apparent change in the position of a heavenly body or the movement of the Earth during the period of the passage of light from the heavenly body to the observer.

**able seaman (AB)** *n.* The merchant service rank above that of ordinary seaman and below that of an officer.

**ablock** *adj.* Said of two blocks and tackle when both blocks are together, or "two-blocked."

**aboard** *adv.* or *adj.* (1) In or on a vessel, within the bulwarks. Before boarding any vessel as a guest, one requests permission to come aboard. The traditional greeting when a guest arrives is "Welcome aboard." Cargo is also said to be aboard. (2) The term also means near the vessel, usually with the intensifier "close." "With the dense fog, we had not seen the ferry until she was close aboard." In the same sense but with a difference, you might be told to lay the ship aboard the tanker for fueling; that is, take the ship close alongside the tanker.

**abort**  *v.* To curtail or discontinue a plan or mission. "We will abort fueling if the weather worsens."

**about**  *adv.* The other tack. Used as an idiom, "to come about" or "to go about." To come (or go) about, the bow must pass through the wind. A common exchange aboard sailboats goes as follows: Helmsman: "Ready about!" Crew members on port and starboard sheets respond: "Ready about." Helmsman: "Hard alee," as he moves the helm to leeward to bring the vessel to the other tack. "About" can also be used as a verb, as in the command "About ship."

**aboveboard**  *adj.* Above decks, without concealment. "We did not strike the cargo in question below, but kept it aboveboard."

**above-deck girder**  *n.* A stiffener that is run longitudinally between hatches outside the hatch coaming; provides longitudinal support and support for the deck.

**abox**  *adj.* A square-rigger term for being hove to, said of a vessel when the head yards and the after yards are braced on opposite tacks. When boxing engines, one engine is going ahead while the other is backing.

**A-bracket**  *n.* A strut at the stern that supports the propeller shaft when there is no keel extension for support. Also *shaft strut.*

**abrasion**  *n.* The act of rubbing or wearing away or the result of such action. Cordage or rigging so worn is said to be *abraded.*

**abreast**  *adv.* Side by side, generally connotes close aboard or alongside. The term is often used to refer to a ship or other object that is not on the ship but is beside it. It is also proper to say that the admiral and the captain walked down the quarterdeck abreast while the executive officer brought up the rear.

**abrid**  *n.* A bushing in a gudgeon. See GUDGEON.

**abroad**  *adj.* Hoisted. A flag is said to be abroad when it is run up a staff; a sail is abroad when it is bent on and extended. Rarely heard today.

**Abroholos**  *n.* A squall that is frequent from May through August between Cabo de São Tomé and Cabo Frio on the coast of Brazil.

**absent flag**  *n.* Square blue flag flown from a yacht's starboard spreader indicating that the owner is away from the vessel. Rarely seen today.

**absent without leave**  See AWOL.

**absolute contraband**  *n.* In admiralty law, a term applied to equipment and supplies ordinarily used in time of war.

**absolute humidity**  *n.* The mass of water vapor for a given unit of air.

**absolute motion**  *n.* The motion of a given object relative to a fixed point in space. See APPARENT MOTION.

**absolute temperature**  *n.* Temperature based on absolute zero, which is the zero value of the thermodynamic scale, $-273.15°C$ (0 on the Kelvin scale) or $-459.69°F$. Absolute zero is the point at which molecular motion almost stops and is the lowest temperature theoretically possible.

**aburton**  *adv.* Stowage of goods such as casks athwartships instead of fore and aft. Especially useful for the supplies of food and drink for the ship's company because the casks move less with the roll of the ship. Secured in this manner they are said to be stowed aburton.

**acceleration**   n. (1) In celestial navigation, the correction applied to mean time to convert to sidereal time. (2) Increase in speed or velocity.

**accepting authority**   n. An officer designated to accept delivery of a ship in the name of the government. In the U.S., this would usually be a naval district commandant.

**access opening**   n. Openings in any part of a ship's plating used for a passageway during construction or to gain access to a space after construction is completed. On small boats, the opening to the engine space is an access opening and is kept covered by an **access panel** that can be lifted or unscrewed.

**accident boat**   n. Small lifeboat kept swung out on passenger liners in case of a man overboard. The USCG designation is rescue boat.

**accommodation**   n. A cabin or stateroom equipped for passenger use.

**accommodation berth**   n. Permanent berth maintained alongside a wharf by a shipping company for its vessel or vessels that return to harbor on a regular basis.

**accommodation ladder**   n. Steps lowered over the side of a ship that form a stairway as opposed to a ladder or gangway.

**accommodation plan**   n. Drawings of a ship that show the arrangement of berths for passengers and ship's officers.

**accumulator**   n. (1) An elastic section in a line or chain, such as one towing a paravane in minesweeping. The accumulator prevents the line from parting

when something suddenly causes it to take a strain. (2) A storage battery.

**acknowledge**   v. To respond to the originator of a message that the message has been received and understood. The single word is often used at the end of a message as a request or demand for a response.

**aclinic line**   n. An imaginary line through the points on the Earth's surface at which the magnetic inclination or dip is zero. This is the magnetic equator, along which the magnetic needle remains horizontal. The magnetic equator ranges from about 15°S in South America to about 10°N in Vietnam. See AGONIC LINE.

**a-cockbill**   adj. (1) Said of yards with ends cocked up, or **topped up,** to clear a land structure such as a warehouse. Yards are also put a-cockbill in time of mourning. (2) When used of anchoring, the anchor is a-cockbill when it is hanging free of the ship, either when being let out or hauled in.

**acoustic clouds**   n. A cloud formation that muffles or deflects sound signals.

**Acoustic Data Analysis Center** (ADAC)   n. A computerized data bank of underwater sound characteristics maintained at the U.S. Naval Research and Development Center in Carderock, MD.

**acoustic mine**   n. A mine detonated by a ship's noise or a noise similar to that made by a ship.

**acoustic speed**   n. The maximum speed at which a submerged submarine can expect to travel without being detected by conventional sound detecting systems. See CAVITATION.

**acoustic torpedo**   n. Torpedo guided by sound, of which there are two types: (1) active, which seeks a target through onboard sonar generating pulses; when the pulse is received, the torpedo begins steering by the received sounds; (2) passive, which seeks a target through emissions from the target itself.

**across the tide**   *phr.* Meaning perpendicular to the waves. A vessel is said to be across the tide when it is being held in such a position by the wind instead of being allowed to lie downstream from the anchor.

**action information center**   See COMBAT INFORMATION CENTER.

**action report**   *n.* An account of an engagement with an enemy.

**active sonar**   *n.* Sonar that emits a sound and records the length of time required for its return to determine distance. See PASSIVE SONAR.

**active tracking station**   *n.* A satellite tracking system that operates by transmitting signals to and receiving responses from the satellite.

**act of God**   *n.* Term used in marine bills of lading and marine insurance and defined as any event that proceeds from nature and one that responsible authorities could not have reasonably foreseen. Damage due to lightning, hurricanes, or earthquakes is considered an act of God.

**act of man**   *n.* The action of the master of a ship in sacrificing gear for the preservation of what is left. This is an underwriter's general average term under which circumstances the interested parties are liable for their proportionate share.

**actual total loss (ATL)**   *n.* A term used in insurance bills of lading meaning the loss of a vessel to such an extent that it cannot be repaired or the materials necessary are not available.

**adjacent zone**   *n.* Term used for water beyond the limit of territorial sea that is claimed by a nation for customs enforcement, fishing rights, etc.

**adjustable pitch propeller**   *n.* A propeller so designed that the pitch can be altered fractionally to improve efficiency when going from saltwater to freshwater.

**adjustable skeg**   *n.* A support for a propeller that can be moved up or down to change the angle of the shaft and propeller.

**adjusting wedge**   *n.* Wooden wedge used in launching a vessel to raise it from the keel blocks to the cradle.

**adjustment of compass**   *n.* The compensation for the magnetic fields on a ship (from structural steel, engines, cargo, and so on) achieved by placing magnets and ferrous cylinders to cause a magnetic compass to read as accurately as possible. See FLINDERS BAR.

**admeasurement**   *n.* A legal term referring to the various determinations of a ship's dimensions, size, or capacity. For merchant ships, the USCG appoints an admeasurer. The naval services have their own teams perform the service. In England, merchant ships are admeasured under the supervision of Lloyds of London. These figures are the basis of all fees and licenses.

**admiral (Adm.)**   *n.* A flag officer in the U.S. Navy or U.S. Coast Guard ranked below fleet admiral and above vice admiral. From the Arabic *amir-al,* commander.

**admiral's barge**   *n.* Any boat in which an admiral or other high-ranking naval personage rides. An admiral's barge is usually considerably heavier and more comfortable than a gig or liberty boat. When Louis Lord Mountbatten was commander of NATO forces in the Mediterranean, he had a steam-powered barge with marvelously gaudy brass steam lines running along the sides of the vessel.

**admiral's watch**   *n.* The second dog watch (1800–2000) when the admiral traditionally strolls down to the navigation bridge to pass the time of day with the commanding officer.

**admiralty**   *n.* (1) A court with jurisdiction over all maritime matters; an admiralty court. (2) Maritime law governing U.S. ships at sea as provided by the Congress under the Constitution. (3) The United Kingdom's equivalent of the Department of the Navy.

**admiralty**   *adj.* Pertaining to matters of "admiralty" such as admiralty law, admiralty courts, and admiralty cases.

**admiralty court**   *n.* A court with cognizance of all maritime cases, both civil and criminal, including collisions, contracts for seamen's wages, action to recover possession of a vessel, damages or injury to cargo, salvage, pilotage, towing charges, charter parties, respondentia, bottomry, damages and trespasses taking place at sea, and so on.

**admiralty droits**   *n.* Proceeds from the sale of wrecks, derelicts, and enemy vessels seized by noncommissioned ships. *Droits* is French for rights.

**admiralty law**   *n.* The branch of law dealing with all aspects of navigation and commerce at sea. Collisions at sea, for example, come under admiralty law. Both civil and criminal actions that concern maritime activity come under admiralty law. See *Blackbook of the Admiralty* of 1190, the earliest codification of maritime law in England, before Magna Carta of 1215. The *Blackbook* was enacted in 1336. See OLERON, LAWS OF.

**admiralty sweep**   *n.* A wide turn by a ship's boat when approaching the ship.

**adrift**   *adv.* or *adj.* (1) Afloat and unattached in any way to shore or the bottom, and without power. (2) Loose, poorly stowed. See LUCKY BAG.

**ad valorem**   *adj.* Describes a duty computed as a percentage of the value of the cargo.

**advance**   *n.* The distance a vessel travels forward between the time the helm is put over and the time that the vessel's heading changes at least 90°.

**advance freight**   *n.* Cargo held as a deposit to cover a ship's payment for freight-handing charges. The advance is shown on the bill of lading and is insured by the shippers.

**advancement in rating**   *n.* Promotion of an enlistee to a higher grade, as distinct from an officer's advancement from one rank to another.

**advantageous current**   *n.* Current that flows in the direction of a vessel's heading.

**advantageous side**   *n.* The side of the rhumb line between two racing marks that provides a faster course to the mark because of wind or current.

**advection fog**   *n.* Fog formed when warm, moist air blows over a colder surface and is cooled below its dew point. This fog is most often encountered at sea and is often quite dense.

**adventure**   *n.* Small consignments of cargo sent aboard a vessel to be sold by the master or bartered for foreign merchandise. This was a little business venture masters formerly engaged in on behalf of family and friends. It is different from the underwriters' term marine adventure.

**adz(e)**   *n.* A tool with a blade set at right angles to the end of a curved handle used for shaping timbers.

**Aegis**   *n.* (pron. eejis) An integrated total combat system that enables combatant ships to engage automatically air-borne, seaborne and land-launched weapons simultaneously. In Greek mythology aegis was the name of the shield of Zeus, which was given to him by Athena.

**aerial**   *n.* Early word for antenna; it was usually a wire rigged between two mast trucks and was used for receiving and transmitting messages.

**aerodynamic force**   *n.* The force developed when airflow is deviated by the sails, wings, or foils.

**aerographer's mate**   *n.* An enlisted weather forecaster, petty officer in the U.S. Navy.

**aeromarine light**   *n.* A marine light, as in a lighthouse, having parts of its beam deflected to an angle of 10° to 15° above the horizon for use by aircraft.

**aeromarine radio beacon**   *n.* A radio beacon established for both marine and air use.

**affirmative**   *interj.* A term used in radiocommunication to mean "You are correct," or "What you have transmitted is correct." "Charlie," the name of the code flag for affirmative, is often used on the radio in place of "affirmative."

**affluent**   *n.* A stream that flows into a larger stream or lake. See EFFLUENT.

**affreight**   *v.* To charter a vessel for carrying goods.

**affreightment**   *n.* (1) A charter party. (2) The act of chartering a vessel. (3) The act of shipping goods by bill of lading. See CHARTER PARTY.

**afloat**   *adj.* Being buoyed by the water, as in "We are apparently no longer aground, but are afloat." Also occasionally used to mean "at sea."

**afore**   *prep.* An obsolete term for "before," something that is afore the mast is ahead of the mast.

**afoul**   *adv.* Entangled. Propellers can run afoul in heavy seaweed, and ships are said to be afoul when they collide.

**aft**   *adv.* Toward the stern. It is sometimes used as an adjective, though "after" is preferred. See FORWARD; RELATIVE BEARING.

**aft**   *prep.* Toward the rear. "The flag bag is aft of the mast" means that the flag bag is abaft the mast. When a preposition is called for, abaft is preferred.

**after**   *adj.* Located toward the stern, thus the after stateroom, the after gun mounts, or the after steering position. Usually it implies that there are others forward, but not necessarily. The superlative form is aftermost.

**afterbody**   *n.* (1) The portion of a vessel's hull that is aft of amidships. (2) The section of a torpedo that contains the propulsion and guidance systems, as distinct from the warhead.

**after brow**   *n.* The gangplank or walkway used at the stern when more than one is used.

**afterglow**   *n.* (1) The broad, high-arched radiance or glow seen occasionally in the western sky above the high clouds during later twilight. (2) The decaying luminescence of the cathode ray tube screen, such as for a TV or radar, when it is turned off.

**afterguard**   *n.* (1) The owner, skipper, navigator, and other officers aboard a ship who have accommodations aft. Those who are not called on to do foredeck work. (2) Used slurringly on U.S. Navy vessels to refer to members of the crew who stand by in the dry, warm spaces when work in the weather is being done. Earlier usage referred to members of the crew whose duties were to attend the aftergear.

**aftermost** *adj.* The superlative form of after, nearest the stern.

**afternoon effect** *n.* The warming of seawater by the Sun as it reaches its zenith, which can cause loss of sonar effectiveness.

**afterpeak** *n.* The compartment at the stern that is aft of the last watertight bulkhead. See PEAK.

**after perpendicular** *n.* An imaginary line that passes vertically through the intersection of the load waterline and the after edge of the sternpost. On submarines and vessels with similar sterns, the after perpendicular is the vertical line that passes through the points where the design waterline intersects the vessel's stern.

**after poppet** *n.* An upright timber used to support the stern of a vessel during launching.

**after steering** *n.* The emergency steering station near the stern of a vessel; in the event of damage to the main steering station, control of a vessel's movements is taken over by after steering.

**against the Sun** *phr.* A directional term meaning from right to left, counterclockwise; left-hand lay. The expression assumes you are looking south at the Sun's path.

**age of diurnal inequality** *n.* The time interval between the maximum semimonthly north and south declination of the Moon and the maximum effect the declination has on the range of tide or the speed of tidal current.

**age of parallax inequality** *n.* The time interval between the new or full Moon and the maximum effect of these phases on the range of tide or the speed of a tidal current.

**age of the Moon** *n.* The time interval expressed in days since the last new Moon.

**age of tide** *n.* The lapse of time between the moment of transit of the Moon at which a tide originates and the appearance of the tide. Also *retard of tide*.

**Ageton method** *n.* A navigation system developed by Comdr. Arthur A. Ageton, USN, that greatly reduced the time necessary to solve the astronomical triangle. It consists of a set of nine tables in nine separate books arranged for the computation of altitudes and azimuths from a dead-reckoning position.

**agonic line** *n.* A line on a chart connecting points on the Earth's surface where there is zero magnetic variation.

**agreed value clause** *n.* A charter term used in bills of lading that limits the liability of the carrier to a specified amount.

**aground** *adj. or adv.* Resting on the bottom and not afloat, usually by accident. A vessel is said to go aground or to run aground. When it is done deliberately as in an amphibious landing or when a small boat is run up on a beach, it is not said to be aground but to be "beached," "on the beach" or to have "landed." See AFLOAT.

**Agulhas Current** *n.* A portion of the South Indian Current that flows south through the Mozambique Channel along the eastern coast of Africa to the Agulhas Bank, then southward and later eastward.

**ahead** *adv.* (1) Forward of the bow, toward a position in front of the vessel. Another vessel or a landmark can be said to be ahead. (2) In signaling the engine room, ahead indicates that the engines drive the ship forward, as in "All engines ahead one-third." See ASTERN; RELATIVE BEARING.

**ahead reach**   *n.* The distance a vessel travels forward from the time it is at full speed until it comes to a stop after the engines have been reversed.

**ahead steering test**   *n.* A test of the steering during sea trials while using full power. The helm is put hard over in each direction in turn and kept in each position for about 10 seconds.

**ahead-thrown weapon**   *n.* A missile that is thrust forward by rocket power or is fired from a launcher. These are used especially in antisubmarine warfare (ASW). See HEDGEHOG.

**ahead-to-leeward position**   *n.* The position of a boat when it is parallel to and ahead of another boat to windward.

**ahoy**   *interj.* Used to hail either a ship or a person. "Ahoy on the tender." "Ahoy on deck." "Ahoy, my lads, the wind blows free."

**ahull**   *adj.* or *adv.* Used of a sailing vessel driven without sails with the helm lashed. A boat is ahull when all propulsion is removed or inoperative. Lying ahull, or "sailing under bare poles," is one method of storm management.

**aid to navigation**   *n.* Any signal device external to a vessel that is specifically intended to assist a navigator in determining the vessel's position or safe course, or to warn of dangers or obstructions. It is a general term for buoys, beacons, lighthouses, and other markers installed to assist navigators. A distinction is sometimes made between fixed piloting aids and offshore aids to navigation such as loran, SATNAV, and so on. Some authorities consider only charted aids to navigation to be covered in the term, but government publications, among others, recognize uncharted aids in navigation. An aid to navigation should not be confused with navigational aids, which includes charts, navigation instruments, and methods intended to assist the navigator.

**air**   *n.* The movement of air. "Light air plagued us during the entire race."

**air control ship**   *n.* A ship equipped or designated to control aircraft.

**air course**   *n.* Ventilation system along the sides of wooden ships created to prevent mildew and rot. The space is from 4 to 6 inches wide and runs longitudinally to give circulation in the frames, ceiling, and planking.

**aircraft carrier, attack (CV)**   *n.* A warship designed to support and operate aircraft, engage in attacks on targets afloat or ashore, and engage in sustained operations in support of other forces. Nuclear-powered carriers are designated CVN.

**air funnel**   *n.* An empty trunk through the deck that allows fresh air to pass below decks or into a hold.

**air group**   *n.* The aircraft assigned to an antisubmarine warfare carrier in the U.S. Navy.

**air hammer**   *n.* Hammer driven by compressed air used for riveting and chipping.

**air-independent propulsion system (AIP)**   *n.* A submarine propulsion system to become operative during the 1990s that will have the very quiet noise level of electric-drive systems with the sustained endurance of closed-cycle propulsion.

**air mass**   *n.* Air with similar characteristics in pressure, temperature, and humidity, overlying a large land area. There are two types, maritime (m) and continental (c); a further breakdown is tropical (T) and polar (P). Thus there are a continental tropical airmass (cT), or a maritime polar airmass (mP), and so on. Maritime arctic is rare because of the scarcity of sea water among the ice fields and land masses. Equatorial air is exclusively maritime and is therefore designated simply (E).

**air officer**   *n.* Officer responsible for aviation matters on a U.S. Navy aircraft carrier.

**air operations**   *n.* The control center for air operations on a U.S. Navy ship; also *air plot.*

**air port**   *n.* A porthole or circular opening in a ship's side for light and air.

**air scoop**   *n.* A device made of sheet metal or synthetic material that can be fitted into an air port on the side of a ship to scoop air.

**air search attack team**   *n.* A U.S. Navy antisubmarine warfare group consisting of a search aircraft and one or more attack aircraft.

**air strake**   *n.* The uppermost strakes of ceiling in wooden-hull ships. It is just below the sheer clamp, with a narrow opening between the top of the strake and the bottom of the clamp for ventilation.

**air surface zone**   *n.* A restricted area for use in antisubmarine operations.

**airt**   *n.* A Scottish word for any of the cardinal points of the compass.

**air temperature correction**   *n.* The correction necessitated when the air temperature is significantly different from 50°F at the surface of the Earth, at which temperature the *Nautical Almanac* has been standardized. The refraction of light (as well as of sound and radio waves) is greater at lower temperatures and less at higher temperatures. Except in cases of extreme temperatures, however, this correction is not usually applied unless results of unusually high accuracy are called for.

**ait**   *n.* (pron. ate) British terminology for a small island in a river.

**Alaska Current**   *n.* The counterclockwise current of the North Pacific, west and north of Vancouver Island, that follows the coast of Canada to Alaska.

**albatross**   *n.* Large sea bird with a wingspread of as much as 11 feet and found in the Southern Hemisphere. Sailors consider it very unlucky to kill them because they are supposed to carry the souls of dead sailors. "Why look'st thou so?—With my crossbow/I shot the albatross." *The Rime of the Ancient Mariner,* by Samuel Taylor Coleridge.

**alcohol-type foam**   *n.* A foam effective for fighting fires involving many water-soluble and some non-water-soluble cargoes.

**aldis lamp**   *n.* Hand-held electric light used at sea for signaling or spotting buoys.

**alee**   *adv.* On or toward the lee or leeward position; on a sailing ship, used to describe the position of the helm with respect to the centerline or amidships position. When coming about or tacking, the helm is put **hard alee.** See ABOUT.

**alert**   *n.* A period of time during which a signal warning of an imminent attack or other danger is in effect, as in a hurricane alert, an air (attack) alert, or a pollution alert.

**Aleutian Current**   *n.* An easterly flowing North Pacific current that lies north of the North Pacific Current. It divides to form the north-flowing Alaska Current and the south-flowing California Current.

**Alfa**   *n.* Phonetic word for the letter "A." In a single-letter signal, it means "I am undergoing a speed trial."

**alidade**   *n.* A bearing circle graduated into 360° fitted on a gyrocompass repeater with a telescopic sight mounted over it. Some alidades are mounted so that they stay pointed in the same gyrocompass direction until changed manually. The device is used for getting the bearings of other ships, landmarks, or other points. See AZIMUTH CIRCLE; PELORUS.

**alignment**   *n.* (1) The placing of two or more objects in a line. (2) The orientation of the measuring axes of inertial components of inertial navigation equipment with respect to the coordinate system to be used.

**alist**   *adj.* Said of a vessel "tilted" to one side, as in "The ship's alist to port."

**alive**   *interj.* Alert. "Look alive! The Old Man is watching from the bridge."

**all-aback**   *adj.* On square-riggers, for a ship to be all-aback was for all the sails to be positioned for the wind to strike their fronts, a maneuver to slow the ship. The position of sails when they are "in stays"; that is, the helm has been put hard alee, but the sheets have not yet been loosened to allow the sails to go to the other side. This is done to prevent the vessel from being "in irons."

**all back**   *interj.* The command to signal the engine room to put all propellers in reverse.

**alleyway**   *n.* Ship's corridor; a passageway, especially one on the first deck below the upper deck.

**all fast**   *interj.* Said when a rope has been made secure.

**all-fours**   *adj.* Said of a mooring with four cables used, two from the bow and two from the stern. "With very little room to swing, we used an all-fours mooring."

**all hands**   *n.* The entire ship's company. Under certain circumstances, those on watch are excluded.

**all-hands**   *adj.* Involving all members of the ship's company. Abandoning ship is an all-hands evolution.

**all in the wind**   *phr.* (1) All sails "luffing" from sailing too close to the wind. (2) The moment when, in the maneuver of coming about, the sails go from one side to the other.

**allision**   *n.* An obsolete term to describe the striking of a stationary vessel by a moving vessel; a collision.

**all night in**   *phr.* Expression meaning a full night's sleep without a watch. "After three stormy days, it was a relief to sleep all night in."

**allotment**   *n.* A part, or all, of a seaman's or an officer's pay that is sent to a relative, friend, or bank each payday.

**allowance**   *n.* (1) In racing, the time in seconds per nautical mile which a higher rated boat gives up to a lower rated boat. (2) The amount that the summer freeboard may be exceeded in freshwater, called the **freshwater allowance.** See PLIMSOLL MARK OR LINE.

**all-round light**   *n.* A navigation light on a ship showing an unbroken light over an arc of the horizon of 360°. See NAVIGATION LIGHTS.

**all sail set**   *phr.* As much sail aloft as the vessel can carry. "All sail set and drawing well." (Note that when using this idiom sail is singular.)

**all standing**   *adv.* or *adj.* (1) To be fully equipped: "The ship was ready with all standing." (2) To be stopped quickly: "To be brought up all standing." (3) "To turn in all standing." is to go to bed fully clothed. (4) Describes a vessel sailing before the wind with all sail set. (5) An all standing jibe is an accidental maneuver where all of the sails are caught aback.

**almagest**   *n.* An exhaustive chronicle on astronomy and geography, including early tables for astronomers worked out by Ptolemy in the second century B.C. at the first true observatory at Alexandria, Egypt.

**almanac**   *n.* An annual publication composed of various lists, charts, tables, and other information in a given field. See NAUTICAL ALMANAC.

**Almanac for Computers**   *n.* An annual publication of the U.S. Naval Observatory designed to facilitate the application of digital computers and small calculators to problems of astronomy and navigation requiring coordinates of celestial bodies.

**almucantar**   *n.* A parallel of altitude on the celestial horizon. See ALTITUDE.

**ALNAV**   *n.* A message intended for all U.S. Navy personnel.

**aloft**   *adv.* (1) In the rigging, above the upper deck. "The bridge must be notified before any man is allowed to go aloft." "You may lay aloft and repair the radar antenna." Aloft is always in the open in its nautical usage. You would not go aloft to a higher but enclosed deck, but you would go aloft to a crow's nest that is up the mast and protected from the wind. (2) Above the Earth. "The winds aloft were too strong for lighter-than-air craft."

**aloft there**   *interj.* A hail to men working aloft.

**alongshore**   *adv.* Close to shore; to sail alongshore is to sail near the shore. See OFFSHORE.

**alongside**   *adv.* Side by side and, usually, in contact with. "*Midway* has signaled that she expects to arrive alongside, starboard side to, at 1350" would mean that *Midway* will come alongside at the pier or alongside another ship. "Abreast" is slightly different and does not imply contact.

**alongside**   *prep.* A position alongside another, usually an enemy. "Sail our ship into a position alongside the French corsair so that we can sweep her decks with

a broadside and board her." In this sense, alongside of is sometimes used.

**alow**   *adv.* Rhymes with, and has same meanings as, below. (1) Low down. "Studding sails are set alow and aloft." (2) Below decks. "All hands! Lay alow!"

**alphabet code**   See PHONETIC ALPHABET.

**altar**   *n.* A step in a drydock now associated with support for the wale shores. The altars usually all but surround the vessel.

**alternating (Al; Alt)**   *adj.* Light phase description indicating a light that shows color variations, primarily between white, red, and green. See LIGHT PHASE CHARACTERISTICS.

**altitude**   *n.* The height above a given reference plane, above the Earth's surface or above sea level. For navigation, altitude is the angular distance above the horizon from 0° to 90° at the zenith (Z). All points having the same altitude lie along a parallel of altitude called an **almucantar**. The **computed altitude (He)** is the tabulated altitude interpolated for increments of latitude, declination, or hour angle. If no interpolation is necessary, the tabulated altitude and computed altitude are the same. The **observed altitude (Ho)** is the reading from the sextant with all corrections applied.

**altitude azimuth**   *n.* One method of obtaining the bearing of a celestial body by solving the astronomical triangle for the azimuth, or angle at the zenith. The altitude gives the zenith distance, the declination gives the polar distance, and the dead reckoning latitude gives the colatitude.

**altitude correction tables**   *n.* Found in the *Nautical Almanac,* give the compensating factors for correcting for refractive characteristics of the atmosphere if the temperature and barometric pressure are significantly different from the standard, 50°F and 29.83 inches.

**altitude difference**   *n.* The amount the computed altitude differs from the observed altitude using the Marcq St. Hilaire method. If the observed altitude is larger than the computed altitude, the altitude difference is measured from the assumed position of the observer toward the body. If the computed altitude is larger, the altitude difference is measured from the assumed position of the observer.

**altitude intercept method**   See MARCQ ST. HILAIRE METHOD.

**altitude of apogee**   *n.* As defined by the *International Telecommunication Union,* the altitude of the apogee above a specified reference surface serving to represent the surface of the Earth.

**altitude of perigee**   *n.* As defined by the *International Telecommunication Union,* the altitude of a perigee above a specified reference surface serving to represent the surface of the Earth.

**altocumulus**   *n.* A cloud formation from about 6,500 to 20,000 ft that anticipates a cold front. See CLOUDS.

**altostratus**   *n.* A continuous layer of clouds from 6,500 to 20,000 ft that follows a cold front and anticipates a warm front. See CLOUDS.

**ALUSNA**   *n.* U.S. Naval attaché. ALUSNA Berlin would be the U.S. Naval attaché in Berlin.

**always afloat**   *phr.* Charter party phrase that specifies the vessel in question must always be afloat and not assigned a berth in which she will be aground part of the time. Allowance is made for tide differences so that a boat may be brought to its slip at a time when the channel depth is high even though it may be too shallow part of the time, as

long as the berth is deep enough for the boat to stay afloat.

**ambient temperature**   *n.* The temperature of the air surrounding a given object.

**American Ephemeris and Nautical Almanac**   See ASTRONOMICAL ALMANAC.

**American Practical Navigator**   *n.* A two-volume publication of the Defense Mapping Agency Hydrographic/Topographic Center originally written by Nathaniel Bowditch. It comprises an epitome of navigation and navigation astronomy and provides tables for solutions of navigation problems. It is almost universally referred to among mariners as **Bowditch.**

**American whipping**   *n.* Term given by British sailors to the whipping of rope and reef knotting the ends at the center of the whipping before trimming.

**America's Cup race**   *n.* A match race series in which the *America*'s Cup is presented to the winner. The trophy, originally called the Hundred Guinea Cup, is named for the schooner *America,* the victorious (and sole) U.S. entry in a race held off the Isle of Wight, England, in 1851. U.S. boats successfully defended the Cup in 24 challenges over the next 132 years, until *Australia II* beat *Liberty.* The catamaran *Stars and Stripes* won the cup back for the U.S. in a controversial series in 1988.

**amidships**   *adv.* The middle of the ship, either lengthwise or widthwise, or both. "We took a kamikaze hit amidships." In this sense it would probably mean amidships lengthwise. "Put the boom amidships," would mean to put the boom on the centerline, parallel to the keel. It is used as an adjective in such instances as the amidships cargo hatch. See RELATIVE BEARING.

**amphibious** *adj.* Capable of operating on land and sea. From the Greek words for double life.

**amphibious assault ship (LHA)** *n.* A naval ship designed to embark, deploy and land elements of a landing force in an assault by helicopters, landing craft, and amphibious vehicles.

**amphibious command ship (LCC)** *n.* A naval ship from which a commander exercises control in an amphibious operation.

**amphibious force** *n.* A naval force and a landing force along with support forces, trained, organized, and equipped for sea-land (and sometimes air) operations.

**amphibious transport dock (LPD)** *n.* A U.S. Navy ship designed to transport and land troops, supplies, and equipment by means of the landing craft, amphibious vehicles, and helicopters that it carries.

**amphidromic points** *n.* The nodal points around which the tides oscillate and where the depth of the sea remains constant.

**amplitude** *n.* (1) The angular distance of a celestial body north or south of the prime vertical circle; the arc of the horizon or the angle at the zenith between the prime vertical circle and a vertical circle through the celestial body measured north or south from the prime vertical to the vertical circle. The term is usually used only with reference to bodies whose centers are on the celestial horizon and is prefixed E or W, as the body is rising or setting, respectively, and suffixed N or S to agree with the declination. Amplitude is labeled **true, compass,** or **grid** as the reference direction is magnetic, compass, or grid east or west, respectively. (2) The maximum value of the displacement of a wave or other periodic phenomenon from the zero position. (3)

One-half the range of a constituent tide. See WAVE AMPLITUDE.

**amplitude of pitch** *n.* The degree of a vessel's fore-and-aft motion in waves. See PITCH.

**amplitude of roll** *n.* The degree of transverse motion of a vessel in waves. See ROLL.

**anabatic wind** *n.* An ascending wind; a wind that sweeps up a slope. "The anabatic wind from the sloping roof caused the wind vane at the top to give faulty readings." See KATABATIC WIND.

**analemma** *n.* A figure-eight scale found on most world globes and sundials that indicates the Sun's declination and the equation of time. The word is the Latin for sundial.

**anchor** *n.* Any equipment used to grab the bottom and hold a vessel in place by means of cable, rope, or chain. Anchors come in many designs: Danforth, Navy, mushroom, stockless, plow, Dunn, Baldt, and so on. An anchor is said to be "let go" when it is dropped, and "weighed" when brought up. To "swallow the anchor" is to give up a life at sea and settle on shore. See GROUND TACKLE; SENTINEL.

**anchor** *v.* To use an anchor to hold a ship in place. "We anticipated the storm and anchored in the lee of Cape Sunion."

**anchorage** *n.* Any place suitable for vessels to anchor; places too deep or too shallow would be excluded, and areas of open water that are shallow enough to anchor in could be anchorages, albeit poor ones. A **quarantine anchorage** is one used by vessels satisfying quarantine regulations.

**anchorage buoy** *n.* One of several buoys used to mark a designated anchorage, as distinct from a mooring buoy.

# Anchors

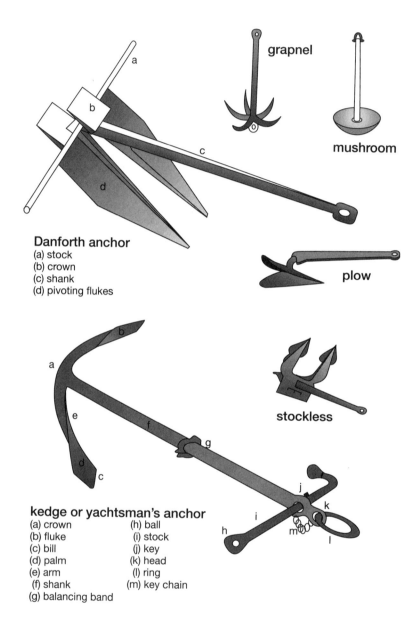

**grapnel**

**mushroom**

**Danforth anchor**
(a) stock
(b) crown
(c) shank
(d) pivoting flukes

**plow**

**stockless**

**kedge or yachtsman's anchor**

| | |
|---|---|
| (a) crown | (h) ball |
| (b) fluke | (i) stock |
| (c) bill | (j) key |
| (d) palm | (k) head |
| (e) arm | (l) ring |
| (f) shank | (m) key chain |
| (g) balancing band | |

**anchor ball**   *n.* A single round ball hoisted to show that a vessel is at anchor or aground.

**anchor bed**   *n.* The fitting on the bow of a vessel used to secure the anchor. See BILLBOARD.

**anchor bell**   *n.* The bell required by the *Navigation Rules* to be sounded during periods of reduced visibility when at anchor or aground.

**anchor bracket**   *n.* A bracket placed on a rail at the bow of a small craft for holding an anchor.

**anchor cable**   *n.* The heavy cordage or wire rope that attaches an anchor to a vessel to hold the vessel in place when the anchor is on the seafloor. See SENTINEL.

**anchor chain**   *n.* Stud-linked chain used for anchors.

**anchor chocks**   *n.* Deck fittings used for stowing an anchor; anchor chocks are not the same as bow chocks through which the anchor line is led. See ANCHOR BED.

**anchor deck**   *n.* A short forecastle deck used for stowing an anchor.

**anchor detail**   *n.* Crew stationed at the bow to handle ground tackle.

**anchor hoy**   *n.* Small boat or lighter used for carrying anchors and chains in a harbor, especially for placing and removing permanent moorings. "Hoy" comes from the Dutch word *hoie,* a small harbor boat used for carrying passengers and cargo short distances.

**anchor ice**   *n.* Ice formed at the bottom of the sea or lake that attaches itself to the bottom and stays there.

**anchoring berth**   *n.* An assigned place to anchor in a roadstead.

**anchor in sight**   *phr.* When weighing anchor, an expression to indicate the anchor is up, and followed by a report as to whether the anchor is clear or fouled.

**anchor light**   *n.* A light required under the *Navigation Rules* for anchoring when not in an established anchorage. Also *riding lights.* On smaller vessels, an all-round anchor light is sometimes inaccurately referred to as the masthead light because it is usually placed at the top of the mast. See MASTHEAD LIGHT.

**anchor pocket**   *n.* A recess in a bow for stowing an anchor to maintain flush sides while maneuvering around wharves.

**anchor pool**   *n.* A scheme for gambling on the time when the anchor will be let go.

**anchor rode**   *n.* The chain, rope, or cable attached to the anchor to hold a small boat. Some authorities consider the use of this word the mark of a well-versed seaman; it is actually more of a yachting term used in the United States. It is rarely heard in England and never heard in merchant and naval circles. Also *anchor warp.*

**anchor's aweigh**   *interj.* The report given to the bridge by the anchor detail to let the conning officer know that the anchor is just free of the bottom. The vessel is then considered underway, though it may not have "way" on. See UNDERWAY; WAY.

**anchor spring**   *n.* A stern hawser attached to the anchor ring in addition to the bow cable so that the vessel rides broadside to the waves or tidal current.

**anchor watch**   *n.* (1) One or several persons on watch and on deck during the night when a vessel is at anchor. The anchor watch is available to assist the duty officer especially in handling ground tackle to make sure the anchor is holding. A member of the anchor watch often sits on the anchor chain to feel the anchor if it should start dragging. See ANCHOR DE-TAIL. (2) An electronic term for setting the navigational systems to monitor small changes in position.

**anchor well**  *n.* A deck well for stowing an anchor.

**Anderson turn**  *n.* A man overboard maneuver. See MAN OVERBOARD MANEUVERS.

**anemometer**  *n.* An instrument used to measure wind force and speed, usually used in conjunction with a wind direction indicator or wind vane.

**an-end**  *adv.* On end. A mast is said to be an-end when it is perpendicular to the deck.

**angary, right of**  See RIGHT OF ANGARY.

**angle bar**  *n.* The bar that forms the gutter or waterway that leads to the scuppers.

**angle clip**  *n.* A short piece of angle iron or angle bar used for attaching beams.

**angle collar**  *n.* A ring formed with an angle iron.

**angle of attack**  *n.* The angle between the apparent wind and a boat's heading.

**angle of cut**  *n.* The smaller angular difference of two bearings or lines of position.

**angle of deviation**  *n.* The angle at which a ray is bent through refraction. See ANGLE OF REFRACTION.

**angle of entrance**  *n.* The angle at which a bow cuts through the water; it is the angle between the centerline and a tangent to the designed waterline at the forward perpendicular.

**angle of heel**  *n.* The angle at which a boat leans from the vertical at any given moment.

**angle of incidence**  *n.* (1) The angle between the horizontal chord of a sail and the airflow. (2) The angle of an underwater fin to the flow of water.

**angle of reflection**  *n.* The acute angle generated by the path of a reflected wave with a perpendicular to the surface at the point of reflection.

**angle of refraction**  *n.* The acute angle made by a refracted ray with a perpendicular from the refracting surface.

**angle of repose**  *n.* The greatest angle at which bulk cargo can tilt without shifting.

**angle of roll**  *n.* The angle between the transverse axis of a vessel and the horizontal. See ROLL.

**angle of yaw**  *n.* The angle between a ship's longitudinal axis and its line of travel as seen from above. See YAW.

**angle on the bow**  *n.* A submariner's term, the angle between the line of sight of an observer on a submarine measured relative to the target from an imaginary line extending dead ahead of the target to 180° port or starboard. The angle on the bow is critical when maneuvering the submarine into a position to fire torpedoes.

**angular distance**  *n.* Piloting term for the difference in degrees, between two directions, one being the reference direction and the other the given direction.

**angular distortion**  *n.* In cartography, the distortion in map and chart projections resulting from nonconformality.

**angulated sails**  See MITERED JIB.

**anneal**  *v.* To heat metal to a very high temperature and then cool it slowly to soften it so as to make it less brittle or to remove permanent magnetism. Flinders bars must occasionally be annealed when they acquire permanent magnetism and become ineffective.

**Annie Oakley spinnaker**   *n.* A parachute spinnaker with small holes to allow dead air to escape; named for the storied sharpshooter.

**annual inequality**   *n.* Seasonal variation in water level or current, more or less periodic, due chiefly to meteorological causes.

**annual variation**   *n.* The amount of change in the magnetic variation caused by changes in the Earth's magnetic field as it affects magnetic compasses. Annual variation differs from one location to the other and is indicated within the compass rose on navigation charts.

**annunciator**   *n.* A signal device used to transmit speed orders to the engine rooms. Also *engine order telegraph.*

**anomaly**   *n.* The angular deviation of a planet from its perihelion as observed from the Sun.

**answer**   *v.* Respond, said of a helm when it reacts to a movement of the rudder. A ship is said to answer the helm smartly.

**answering pennant**   *n.* The pennant used to acknowledge a signal. It has three red stripes separated by two white stripes.

**Antarctic Circle**   *n.* An imaginary line drawn approximately along latitude 66°33′S, the northern limit of the South Frigid Zone.

**Antarctic Circumpolar Current**
See WEST WIND DRIFT.

**antarctic convergence**   *n.* The narrow zone between 50°S and 60°S in which the cold water of Antarctica and

the warmer water of the Temperate Zone converge abruptly.

**antarctic intermediate water**   *n.* The cold antarctic water that sinks beneath the warmer water north of the antarctic convergence.

**antenna**   *n.* In electronics, any structure used to collect or radiate electromagnetic waves.

**anticyclone**   *n.* An area of relatively high pressure, generally circular. Winds tend to blow from high-pressure to low-pressure areas, but are deflected to the right in the Northern Hemisphere and to the left in the Southern Hemisphere due to the Earth's rotation.

**antifoulant**   *n.* Any preparation painted on a hull or other marine object, such as a pile or seawall, to discourage barnacles, teredos, grass, and other undesirable growths. On hulls, the antifoulant is often applied over an **anticorrosive finish** that prevents rust. Copper compounds are the most frequently used antifoulants.

**Antilles Current**   *n.* A current that originates in the West Indies as part of the Atlantic North Equatorial Current and flows north and joins the Florida Current north of Grand Bahama Island to form the Gulf Stream. See GULF STREAM.

**antinode**   *n.* Either of the two points on an orbit where a line in the orbit plane drawn perpendicular to the line of nodes and passing through the focus intersects the orbit.

**antipode**   *n.* A point on the Earth that is 180° from a given point. The North Pole is the antipode of, or is **antipodal** to, the South Pole.

**antipodean day**   *n.* A day gained when sailing eastward across the meridian of 180° or the International Date Line. Thus, a ship sailing eastward from east longitude to west longitude goes to a day that is one number less than before it crossed the date line.

**antirolling devices**   *n.* Any device that reduces a vessel's amplitude of roll, including the bilge keel or rolling chocks, "antirolling tanks," fin stabilizing systems, and gyroscopic stabilizing systems.

**antirolling tanks**   *n.* Baffled tanks designed and arranged to damp the motion of a ship using the free surface effect. Also *flume tanks.*

**antisubmarine warfare (ASW)**   *n.* Term for all techniques used against enemy submarines, including listening and tracking devices and weaponry.

**apeak**   *adj.* (1) Straight up and down, used to describe the anchor line hove to that point, but before it clears the bottom or is atrip. The man heaving around on the anchor will call to the boatswain (or boatswain's mate), "The anchor chain is apeak," or the captain will order the ship to be hove apeak so that he can weigh anchor when the signal is given. See ATRIP. (2) A yard or spar is apeak, or topped, when it is oblique to the mast.

**apex**   *n.* The highest point of a cone or triangle, or the maximum latitude (vertex) of a great circle. See DIRECTION.

**apogean current**   *n.* The weaker or neap tidal current that occurs when the moon is in apogee. See PERIGEAN CURRENT.

**aport**   *adv.* Toward the port side. "Put the helm aport."

**apostle**   *n.* A heavy timber or knighthead at the bow of a vessel, used for securing hawsers. Old usage.

**apparel and tackle**   *n.* Charter party term meaning ship's gear such as sails, rigging, anchors, and other general equipment.

**apparent**   *adj.* As seen, such as "apparent horizon." Apparent noon is when the Sun's center appears to cross a meridian; the true crossing precedes the apparent crossing by about 8 minutes.

**apparent horizon**   *n.* The point on the visible horizon where sea and sky meet, which is dependent on the refractive index and the height of the observer's eye.

**apparent motion**   *n.* The motion of a celestial body as actually observed from Earth. The absolute motion is computed taking into account the motion of the Earth—that is, as if the Earth were stationary.

**apparent noon**   *n.* The moment the Sun reaches the upper branch of the observer's meridian.

**apparent place**   *n.* A point on the celestial sphere to which a star or planet is referred by an observer on the Earth's surface. Also *apparent position.*

**apparent secular trend**   *n.* The nonperiodic tendency of the sea level to rise and fall or remain stationary with time. It is called "apparent" because it is often not possible to know whether a trend is truly nonperiodic or merely a segment of a long oscillation.

**apparent sidereal time**   *n.* Time based on the daily rotation of the Earth with respect to the equinox or first point of Aries.

**apparent slip**   *n.* The difference between the speed of the water propelled by a propeller and the speed of the vessel through the water, relative to a fixed point in the water clear of the wake.

**apparent solar time**   *n.* Time based on the **apparent Sun,** that is, the Sun as it appears in the sky. See APPARENT TIME.

**apparent time**   *n.* Time calculated with the **apparent Sun** as the celestial reference and the lower branch of a meridian as its terrestrial reference.

## Apparent Wind

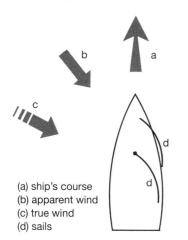

(a) ship's course
(b) apparent wind
(c) true wind
(d) sails

**apparent wind**   *n.* The wind direction and speed as it seems to be to an observer on a moving vessel. A vessel on a course of 000° at 10 knots in a wind from 180° at 10 knots would have zero apparent wind. The same vessel at the same speed and course with a wind coming from 000° at 10 knots would have an apparent wind of 20 knots from 000°. Also *relative wind.*

**appendages**   *n.* Protrusions below the waterline such as stabilizer fins that create wake and interfere with speed sensors that may be located downstream on a vessel's hull. Sensors should be located away from the wake of appendages when possible.

**apple stern**   *n.* Rounded stern, associated primarily with Dutch sailing vessels.

**approach, right of**   See RIGHT OF APPROACH.

**approach tack**   *n.* The tack that will take a vessel to a starting line, a mark, or a lay line.

**appropriated berth**   *n.* Berth leased by a shipping company for its regularly scheduled ships.

**appurtenances**   *n.* In admiralty law, a term that refers to tackle and equipment necessary to the proper utilization of a vessel for its designed purpose.

**apron**   *n.* (1) That part of a wharf that is on pilings beyond the landfill area. (2) The cargo-handling facility of a wharf or pier. (3) A gentle, smooth slope on the seafloor often found near groups of islands and seamounts. (Is sometimes called an archipelagic apron). (4) A curved timber fayed on the after side of the stem from the head down to the deadwood. It provides the surface for securing the hood ends of planking and strengthens the stem. Also *stomach piece.* (5) A sloping underwater extension of an iceberg.

**apsides, line of**   *n.* (pron. apsideez) The line joining perihelion and aphelion.

**aquaculture**   *n.* The cultivation of marine products, usually for human consumption. The cultivation of sponges and of the queen conch in the Caribbean Islands are two of many examples. Also *mariculture.*

**aqueduct**   *n.* A conduit or fabricated structure for carrying water, usually elevated to carry water by gravity. These are frequently noted on European charts.

**arch board**   *n.* A decorated plank across a vessel's stern that is sunk in the taffrail at the lower side and frames the stern ports or windows.

**arched squall**   *n.* Violent storm accompanied by a black cloudy arch.

**archipelago**   *n.* A large group of islands and interconnecting waters, closely related, that form an intrinsic geographical entity. When the islands are sufficiently populated they become an economic and political entity. By the 1982

United Nations Convention on the Law of the Sea, the boundaries of an **archipelagic state** can be determined with respect to a system of straight baselines.

**arch knee**   *n.* A molded timber that forms the upper face of the propeller aperture and is fitted between propeller post and rudder post.

**arc of the horizon**   *n.* Term used to define the angle through which a light is visible. Rule 21 of the *Navigation Rules* states that "Masthead light means a white light placed over the fore-and-aft centerline of the vessel showing an unbroken light over an arc of the horizon of 225°." Also *arc of visibility.*

**Arctic Circle**   *n.* An imaginary line drawn approximately along latitude 66°33′N; the southern limit of the North Frigid Zone.

**Arctic Current**   See WEST GREENLAND CURRENT.

**Arctic Ocean**   *n.* The world's fourth largest sea, approximately 5,400 square miles in area. The main passages to the south are Baffin Bay, the Denmark Strait, the Norwegian Sea, and, to the Pacific, the Bering Strait. The central surface in covered by a perennial drifting icecap. The three main ports are Murmansk, Russia; Prudhoe Bay, U.S.; and Narvik, Norway.

**arctic sea smoke**   *n.* Dense water vapor that rises from warm surface water when very cold air moves over it; it may rise several hundred feet, thus obscuring the horizon and landmarks while the sky is quite clear.

**ardent**   *adj.* An obsolete term to describe a vessel that needs a weather helm to keep from heading up into the wind; this is much to be preferred to a boat that requires lee helm to keep it from heading downwind.

**argosy**   *n.* A merchant ship, originally from the Aegean port of Ragusa, now Dubrovnik.

**argument of perigee**   *n.* The angle at the center of attraction from the ascending node to the point of perigee, measured in the direction of the motion of an orbiting body.

**Aries**   See FIRST POINT OF ARIES.

**arm**   *n.* The elbow of an anchor between the crown and the fluke. See ANCHOR.

**arm**   *v.* (1) To place tallow or wax in the cavity of the lead of a lead line for the purpose of bringing up a sample of the bottom. (2) To render a weapon operationally ready.

**armed guard**   *n.* Naval gun crews maintained on merchant vessels in wartime. (2) Any guard with a gun.

**armillary sphere**   *n.* The principal instrument of early astronomers. It consisted of a skeleton model of the celestial sphere with several movable rings that indicated the orbits of the various celestial bodies. It has been attributed to the third century B.C. Greek astronomer Eratosthenes, and the Chinese may have used such an instrument 2000 years B.C.

**arm of the sea**   *n.* A term for a comparatively narrow offshoot from the main body of a sea.

**armor**   *n.* Heavy protection against projectiles in ships and aircraft.

**armor belt**   *n.* An area of reinforced protection on the hull of a warship above and below the waterline.

**armor boxing**   *n.* Compartment enclosed with armor.

**armored cable**   *n.* Electrical cable encased in a protective sleeve.

**armored rope**   *n.* Wire rope with wire wrapped around each strand with a hemp core, used in salvage work.

**armor shelf**   *n.* The foundation plating underlying the **armor belt.**

**armory**   *n.* The compartment of a ship in which portable weapons such as guns are securely stored.

**arrest**   *n.* Temporary detention of a ship, for example, to be held pending settlement of a claim; quite different from capture.

**arresting gear**   *n.* The assemblage of cables, blocks, resistance cylinders, and so on, designed to stop an aircraft on a carrier deck without injury to craft or personnel.

**arrêt de prince**   *n.* (pron. ahreh duh pranse): The understood right of a belligerent to hold a foreign vessel in port to prevent its carrying news that would be of assistance to the enemy; international law is well established that the vessel's owners be reimbursed for any loss caused by such action.

**arse**   *n.* The bottom of a block opposite the hole in a block through which the fall is rove.

**Articles of Agreement**   *n.* The papers signed by crew members and ship's master that give the details of the crew's employment contract. Also *ship's articles.*

**artificial horizon**   *n.* A horizontal reference such as a level used when the horizon is not visible to the observer. Sometimes a level is attached to the sextant to serve as an artificial horizon; otherwise a dish of water can be used.

**ascending node**   *n.* That point at which a planet or comet crosses the ecliptic from south to north.

**A-scope**   *n.* In early radars, a cathode ray display used to measure target ranges and size.

**ASDIC**   *n.* The acronym for Anti-Submarine Detection Investigation Committee, the name given to a British sounding device used in searching for submarines in antisubmarine warfare before sonar was developed. See SONAR.

**ashcan**   *n.* Slang for depth charge.

**ash ejector**   *n.* Device used to force ash from coal-burning boilers through an opening in the ship's bottom by hydraulic pressure.

**ashore**   *adv.* On land. "The captain is ashore." Synonymous with the naval phrase "on the beach."

**aspect**   *n.* A British term for the relative bearing of one's own ship from the target ship measured 0° to 180° on either the port or starboard side.

**aspect ratio**   *n.* (1) The width-to-height ratio. With height the same, a wide boat is said to have a lower aspect ratio than one with a narrow beam. (2) The ratio of the length of the luff of a sail to the length of the foot.

**assigned frequency**   *n.* The center of the frequency band assigned to a radio transmitting station. Also *channel frequency; center frequency.*

**assignment clause**   *n.* A marine insurance term by which the person affected by the policy (the owner or beneficiary) is allowed to assign his or her interest in the policy to another person.

**assistant engineer**   *n.* A duly certified engineer responsible for an engine room watch.

**assume**   *v.* To establish a watch or a command when none has existed in the immediate past. If you assume a watch, you establish it with no predecessor to give you the current information. When a ship is put in commission and the new commanding officer is installed, he assumes command. See RELIEVE.

**astarboard** *adv.* Toward the starboard. "Put the helm astarboard."

**astay** *adv.* Used to describe the position of the anchor cable when being heaved in to the point that it is roughly parallel to the forestay but still holding. Today, more often, you will hear "The anchor is at the short stay." Also *astays*.

**astern** *adv.* The opposite of "ahead" or "forward." See AFT; AFTER; ABAFT; RELATIVE BEARING.

**astern** *prep.* Behind a vessel; 180° relative to the vessel's heading. "*Wisconsin* has taken a position astern *New Jersey*."

**astrolabe** *n.* A medieval astronomical device designed to determine the altitude of celestial bodies. The astrolabe was superseded by the cross staff.

**Astronomical Almanac** *n.* An annual publication published jointly by the Nautical Almanac Office of the U.S. Naval Observatory, and HM Nautical Almanac Office of the Royal Greenwich Observatory. This is an "ephemeris" that gives high-precision, detailed information on a large number of celestial bodies. It is arranged for the convenience of astronomers and is not primarily intended for use by navigators.

**astronomical day** *n.* A day as defined by the Earth's complete revolution with reference to a celestial body; the astronomical day begins at midnight. (Prior to January 1, 1925, the astronomical day was from noon to noon, 12 hours later than the calendar day.)

**astronomical equator** *n.* A line that connects the points having 0° astronomical latitude. Since the deflection of the vertical varies from point to point, the astronomical equator is not a plane curve, but since the verticals through all points on it are parallel, the zenith at any point on the line lies in the plane of the celestial equator.

**astronomical tide** See TIDE.

**astronomical time** *n.* Time formerly used for astronomical observations and calculations. In the 1925 edition of the *Nautical Almanac*, astronomical time reckoned from noon (0 hours) of one day through 24 hours was abandoned in favor of Greenwich Civil Time.

**astronomical triangle** *n.* An area on the celestial sphere bounded by the observer's celestial meridian, the hour circle passing through the observer's celestial body, and the vertical circle passing through the celestial body. See NAVIGATIONAL TRIANGLE.

**astronomic latitude** *n.* The angle between a plumb line at a point of observation and the plane of the celestial equator. The astronomic latitude is the result of observations of celestial bodies that is uncorrected for deflection of the vertical.

**astronomic longitude** *n.* The angle between the plane of the celestial meridian at the point of observation and the plane of the celestial meridian at Greenwich. The astronomic longitude results from observations of celestial bodies without correction for deflection of the vertical.

**astronomy** *n.* The scientific study of the universe beyond the Earth, especially dealing with, among other things, the size, constitution, motions, and relative positions of celestial bodies.

**astrotracker** *n.* A navigation device that automatically acquires and continuously tracks a celestial body in azimuth and altitude.

**asylum** *n.* A place of refuge or protection from the law.

**at anchor** *phr.* A term meaning anchor down and holding, or made fast to a mooring buoy or similar device, but not secured to a shore, bank, quay, or pier.

**ataunt** *adv.* With all masts standing and fully rigged, and all sail set.

**athwart** *adv.* Transversely, from side to side on a ship.

**athwart** *prep.* Across, perpendicular to the keel. "We found the whaleboat athwart the poop."

**athwartship** *adv.* or (less common) *adj.* Crosswise to the length or centerline of the ship. The seats in a canoe are athwartship. See RELATIVE BEARING.

**Atlantic Equatorial Current** See EQUATORIAL CURRENTS AND COUNTERCURRENTS.

**Atlantic range** *n.* The Atlantic coast of the United States.

**atmospheric pressure** *n.* The pressure exerted by 14.69 pounds per square inch, 29.92 inches of mercury, or 33.90 feet of water lift. Also *barometric pressure.*

**atoll** *n.* In the Indian and Pacific oceans, a somewhat circular island of petrified coral polyps that nearly encloses a lagoon. The larger atolls are often quite deep and long, affording excellent anchorages for large ships. A Malay word.

**atrip** *adj.* (1) A sail is said to be atrip when hoisted to the cap, sheeted home, and ready to be trimmed. (2) Describes an anchor when it has been broken out of the bottom; same as "aweigh"; rarely heard today.

**a-try** *adv.* Sailing or hove to under storm trysail. "We lay a-try while waiting for the storm to pass."

**at sea** *phr.* (1) To be on the ocean out of sight of land, on a "voyage." (2) A marine insurance phrase used to describe a ship that has left its moorings ready for sea even if it is still in the harbor. See ASHORE.

**attack cargo ship (LKA)** *n.* A naval ship designed or converted to transport combat-loaded cargo in an assault landing.

**attack center** *n.* The submarine equivalent to a surface ship's advance combat direction system.

**attend the side** *phr.* To be on the quarterdeck to greet important people arriving.

**attention to port** (or **starboard**) *interj.* Command given to topside personnel when a ship renders passing honors. Personnel who can be seen by the passing vessel come to attention and, if ordered, salute. See PASSING HONORS.

**attestation clause** *n.* A marine underwriter's term for a clause that certifies the policy has been signed by a duly authorized representative of the insurance company, thereby formally binding the company.

**aureole** *n.* The glowing portion of the corona of the Sun or Moon frequently seen through altostratus clouds.

**aurora australis/aurora borealis** *n.* High-altitude lights of many colors, known as the southern and northern lights, respectively, in the Southern and Northern Hemispheres. The phenomenon is thought to be caused by the injection of charged particles, especially solar particles, into the atmosphere. The scintillating beams of light move from the horizon toward the zenith. They are most frequently seen in the polar regions, but are also observed as far as the Temperate Zones. So little is known about this phenomenon that aircraft pilots are still asked to report their observations of it. Also *polar lights.*

**auroral zone**   *n.* The 10°-wide belt located an average distance of 23° from each of the geographic poles, the scene of maximum auroral activity.

**aurora polaris**   *n.* A high-latitude aurora borealis.

**Australia Current**   *n.* A part of the South Equatorial Current that branches off near the Fiji Islands and flows in a southwesterly direction to the east coast of Australia.

**Automated   Mutual-Assistance Vessel Rescue System (AMVER)** *n.* A system operated by the U.S. Coast Guard to provide important aid to the development and coordination of search and rescue efforts in the oceans of the world through the medium of a worldwide merchant vessel plot. The Coast Guard's information comes by way of standard broadcasting equipment in the participating ships.

**automatic   frequency   control**   *n.* The technique or circuit that automatically maintains the frequency of a receiver within specified limits.

**automatic pilot (or autopilot)**   *n.* Any of a number of electric or electronic steering devices for sailing and power vessels; automatic pilots sail a compass course. Large ships, with the exception of U.S. Navy ships, have automatic steering connected to a gyroscope. These devices allow the helmsman to attend to other duties in the pilot house. They also have greater steering accuracy and consistency than does a helmsman and require fewer people in the wheelhouse. See SELF-STEERING.

**Automatic Radar Plotting Aids (ARPA)**   *n.* A system by which radar is used for collision avoidance by automatically assessing the risk of collision. ARPA is now required on larger ships.

For such a system to meet the Inter-Governmental   Maritime   Consultative Organization's (IMCO) requirements, it must meet their standards for detection, acquisition, tracking, display, warnings, data display, and trial maneuver.

**automatic   radar   plotting   discs (ARPD)**   *n.* Devices mounted on vessels that automatically assess risk of collision. ARPD has been superseded by Automatic Radar Plotting Aids.

**Automatic Station Keeping (ASK) system**   *n.* A highly sophisticated drillship positioning system that employs surface and subsurface sensors to monitor wind, current, wave action, and other forces. These sensors are linked to shipboard computers that control the vessel's thrusters and keep the ship in position.

**automatic ventilating sidelight**   *n.* A sidelight or porthole that is closed automatically by a float when it is submerged.

**auxiliary machinery**   *n.* Nonpropulsion machinery used to power equipment not involved with the ship's movement through the water, such as the anchor engine, condensers, and feed pumps. Often simply called auxiliaries.

**auxiliary   power**   *n.* Additional or standby power, usually used with reference to a sailing vessel with engines. Under the *Navigation Rules,* a sailing vessel using auxiliary power is considered a power vessel and abides by power vessel rules.

**auxiliary   ribband**   *n.*   Auxiliary wooden strips running longitudinally, used temporarily to align transverse frames. They are auxiliary to the main ribbanding.

**auxiliary rudder head**   *n.* A second rudder head forward of the primary rudder head and connected by a yoke, used on vessels with insufficient beam to allow a normal tiller to be installed.

**auxiliary sailing vessel**  *n.* A vessel capable of being propelled both by mechanical means and by sails. See SAILING VESSEL.

**auxiliary tanks**  *n.* Tanks on a submarine located amidships and built to take full sea pressure; they are part of the trimming system.

**auxiliary vessel**  *n.* A vessel that is not primarily a fighting ship but is part of the fighting group, such as repair, fuel, supply, and hospital ships.

**avast**  *interj.* Stop. "Avast there! Where are you going?" " 'Vast heaving around!" Stop pulling. The term is generally used when continuing the action would endanger gear or personnel.

**average**  *n.* Marine underwriter's term that signifies damages or expenses arising from the perils of navigation in a marine adventure when a total loss has not been sustained. The loss is averaged equitably among the interested parties. The term also includes the adjustment made for goods that have been lost or thrown over the side. In a policy that includes the phrase **free of all average (FAA),** no claim for deterioration or partial loss is recoverable.

**average bond**  *n.* A bond or agreement given by the several owners of merchandise of a vessel with general average contract clauses; the owners pledge to pay their share of a loss and not detain the vessel and cargo to settle claims.

**avulsion**  *n.* The rapid erosion of shoreline during a storm.

**awaft**  *adj.* Afloat or adrift.

**awake**  *adj.* Old term meaning ready for use. A sail was awake when it was ready to be hoisted.

**awash**  *adj.* (1) Washed over by the waves. If a coral atoll is said to be almost constantly awash, the implication is that it is at or close to sea level. If the decks are awash, either the deck is close to the water (very little freeboard) or the seas are heavy and washing over the deck, and the vessel could be in danger of sinking.

**away**  *adv.* (1) To get a boat or a detail of men ready for a purpose. "Call away the damage control party." "Call away the barge." (2) An idiom used for direction. "Where away?" is the reply to a report that something has been sighted.

**away**  *v.* Word used to order something to depart. "Away the number 1 lifeboat!" "Away the gig."

**aweather**  *adj.* Toward the weather side. "The helm is aweather," meaning the tiller is toward the weather side. The opposite is alee.

**aweigh**  *adj.* Refers exclusively to the anchor and means that the anchor is just clear of the ground. When the anchor has broken loose from the ground and is clear, the man in charge of the anchor detail advises the bridge, "Anchor's aweigh." At that moment, the vessel is "underway," though she may have no "way" on. See ANCHOR'S AWEIGH; UNDERWAY; WAY; WEIGH.

**awning**  *n.* The traditional term for a canvas cover over a cockpit or deck area, used for protection from the sun and rain. **Bimini** is now the more fashionable word for smaller awnings of yachts.

**AWOL**  Acronym for absent without leave, unauthorized absence. This can mean that someone has stayed beyond his or her leave or that he or she has left without permission. The term has been replaced by "unauthorized absence" and "unauthorized absentee."

**axially increasing pitch**   *n.* Pitch of a propeller blade that increases from leading edge to following edge.

**axis**   *n.* (pl., **axes**) (1) A straight line about which a body rotates. The **polar axis** is the straight line between two poles of a body. The **major axis** of an orbit is the longer diameter of an ellipse or ellipsoid; the **minor axis** is the shorter diameter. (2) A set of reference lines for certain systems of coordinates.

**aye**   *interj.* An affirmative response. "Aye, Sir," means simply "Yes, Sir, I understand." "Aye, Aye, Sir" means "I understand and will comply."

**azimuth (Zn)**   *n.* The horizontal direction in degrees of a celestial point from a terrestrial point. Azimuths are measured from a reference direction, usually south, clockwise through 360°. Ships, aircraft, and other objects are identified not by an azimuth but by a bearing. The **true azimuth** is the true bearing of a celestial body based on a corrected compass reading.

**azimuth angle (Z)**   *n.* An angle measured clockwise in the horizontal plane between a reference direction and any other line.

**azimuth circle**   *n.* (1) A device placed over magnetic compasses and gyro repeaters, most frequently seen on bridge wings, with 0° through 360° marked on the circumference. The azimuth circle has a sight vane through which the watch officer can take bearings of celestial bodies and relate them to the true bearings on the magnetic compass or gyro repeater. It is fitted with an adjustable mirror so that it can be focused on celestial bodies. The "azimuth circle" is the same as a "bearing circle" with the addition of the mirror/prism system for celestial work. See ALIDADE; PELORUS. (2) A vertical circle that originates at the zenith and intersects the horizon at a right angle.

**azimuth diagram**   *n.* Graph paper used on shipboard to obtain the true azimuth of a celestial body, a fast but low-accuracy method of determining azimuth.

**azimuth tables**   *n.* Published by the U.S. Hydrographic Office as HO 260 and 261, they are volumes I and II of the agency's publications. These have been largely superseded by hand calculator methods, but for calculations of azimuth these give results with accuracy within one minute.

**Azores Current**   *n.* The slow, constant southeast branch of the North Atlantic Current and part of the Gulf Stream system. The mean speed is 0.4 knot, and the mean maximum speed computed from all observations above 1 knot in the prevailing direction is 1.3 knots. The Azores Current is an inner part of the clockwise oceanic circulation of the North Atlantic Ocean. Also *Southeast Drift Current.*

# B

**B**   See BRAVO.

**back**   *n.* Forward side of a propeller; the after side of the blades is the **face.**

**back**   *v.* (1) Said of the wind when it changes direction counterclockwise in the Northern Hemisphere. Also *back around; haul.* The opposite is to veer. Bowditch notes that U.S. usage applies only in the

Northern Hemisphere (with clockwise movement in the Southern Hemisphere called "backing"), while others use back to mean a wind moving counterclockwise in either hemisphere. (2) To move stern first. (3) To catch the wind with the sail on the windward side of the vessel. (4) To back a yard is to brace the yard so as to bring the wind on the forward surface of the canvas. See ABACK; BACK-WIND. (5) To reverse the engine(s) and propeller(s), as in the command "All engines back one-third." (6) To back an anchor is to lower a second anchor to the bottom with the shank secured to the cable of the first anchor. Compare with BACK ANCHOR.

**back anchor**   *n.* A small anchor to supplement the holding power of the main anchor.

**back and fill**   *v.* (1) To sail a ship to windward with a tide carrying the vessel to windward in a confined channel. When tacking is not possible, the vessel is allowed to back with the wind and then turn enough to catch the wind and sail forward on tide and wind until the opposite side is reached. This is repeated as often as necessary. (2) With steam and diesel ships the term relates to such situations as breaking through an ice field when the ship advances until forced to stop, then backs, stops, and goes ahead again.

**back a strand**   *phr.* A splicing term meaning to fill the score left open when one strand is removed with one of the opposite strands in a long splice. With a backhand splice, to back a strand means to tuck one strand helically around the opposing one.

**backbone**   *n.* (1) Cordage stitched to the back of an awning to which the crow's-feet, or reinforcements, are stitched. (2) The longitudinal assemblage of a vessel that includes the keel, keelson, stem, and sternpost.

**back cloth**   *n.* Triangular canvas panel secured to the jackstay of a yard in the middle to facilitate stowing the bunt of a large square sail.

**back down**   *v.* To reverse a vessel's engines.

**back easy**   *interj.* The command to ease a rope slowly and deliberately.

**backer**   *n.* (1) Flat, braided cordage secured to a yardarm inside the sheave and used for a base for reeving the earing of the head of a square sail. (2) A broad sennit nailed around a yardarm inside the sheave, fitted with an eye or thimble through which the head earing is then rove.

**back freight**   *n.* Freight charged back to the shipper after a vessel fails to deliver it at its intended destination and returns to the originating port. "To backfreight" is to return cargo or to turn away a ship or cargo.

**backhanded rope**   *n.* Rope with each of the strands twisted right-handed, the same direction as the yarns, with the strands laid together left-handed.

**backing**   *n.* The small stuff used at both sides of worming that fills the contlines of hemp standing rigging. The worming keeps out the moisture, and the backing helps to hold it in place. Also *sister worming.*

**backing angle**   *n.* A short piece of angle iron that reinforces the butt or splice of two angles.

**backlash**   *n.* (1) The amount of play in a gear or other equipment; the amount a part can be moved without moving an adjoining part. (2) Shocks attributable to play in steering equipment or other mechanical devices.

**back off**   *phr.* To slack a line or cable.

**back piece**   *n.* Backing on the after side of a wooden rudder shank.

**back post**   See RUDDER POST.

**back pressure**   *n.* The pressure on a piston on the return cycle of a reciprocating steam engine.

**backrope**   *n.* An after guy that secures the dolphin striker and counterbalances the force from the forward end of the bowsprit. See SQUARE-RIGGED VESSEL.

**backrush**   *n.* The seaward movement of the water from a wave that has just broken, the water itself being called backwash.

**backset**   *n.* An eddy, a surface current contrary to the main current.

**backshore**   *n.* (1) A timber used outside a ground way to hold a way in place during a launching. (2) That part of a beach that is usually dry at high tide and only reached by the highest tides.

**back sight**   *n.* An altitude observation of a celestial body facing away from the body; this is done when the horizon is obscured by land or another vessel, but only if the arc of the sextant is long enough to allow it to be done.

**back splice**   *phr.* To finish a splice at the end of a line by tucking the strands back from the end.

**back spring**   *n.* Spring line leading from the bow aft to a cleat or bollard on the wharf or pier. Also *after bow spring.*

**backstaff**   *n.* A device with which the user was able to turn his back to the sun to determine the sun's altitude by aligning the shadow cast by the sun on the backstaff with the horizon. It had two arcs so arranged and designed that the sum of the two was the zenith distance of the sun. This was later refined by the addition of a mirror that made it possible to observe other heavenly bodies. It was invented by John Davis in 1590 and was an improvement over the earlier cross staff. Also *sea quadrant.*

**backstay**   *n.* A stay that supports a mast and leads from the mast down and aft to the deck, another mast, or the vessel's side. See FORESTAY; JIB STAY; MARCONI RIG; RUNNING BACKSTAY; STAYSAIL STAY.

**backstaysail rig**   *n.* A jib-headed ketch with the usual mizzen replaced by a stump mast on which the backstaysail is set up.

**backstay stool**   *n.* Outboard plating on a vessel's stern to which the backstay is anchored; same as chain plates for shrouds.

**backstrap**   *v.* Used for a vessel that is precluded from making headway when there is ample wind to do so, as when sailing against the tide or current.

**back to battery**   *phr.* (1) Of guns, describes the position of the muzzle after it returns to firing position. (In modern guns, when the breech block is returned to its firing position, it is "in battery".) (2) Slang expression for personnel returning to duty after being ill or "out of action."

**backward ship**   *n.* A vessel due to be loaded sometime in the future.

**backward tip**   *n.* During launching, if the stern leaves the ways, but has not sufficient buoyancy in the water and the bow lifts clear of the ways, the stern plating can be crushed on the ways and the bow can be caught by the wind and thrown clear of the ways.

**backwash**   *n.* (1) The water and mud thrown aft by a boat's propellers. (2) The returning water of a wave after its uprush on the beach. See BACKRUSH.

**backwash**  *v.* To reverse the fluid flow through a filter to remove accumulated sediment that would reduce the efficiency of a pumping system.

**backwater**  *n.* Water held back from the main flow; water that overflows the land and is held in a pond.

**backwater**  *v.* In rowing or paddling, the action taken to stop the forward motion or back a boat or canoe by reversing the direction of the oar or paddle.

**backwind**  *v.* To trim a sail so that the air that strikes its windward side is deflected to strike the leeward side of the next sail aft. With the wind on the bow, backwinding the sails is a reasonable way to back out of a slip. See BACK.

**badan**  *n.* A small Arab sailboat used on the Gulf of Oman; the boats have straight vertical or knee stems and sharp sterns with false sternposts.

**badge**  *n.* A carved ornament placed on a ship's stern, and frequently including a port or a carving of a window. See QUARTER BADGE.

**badra**  *n.* An Australian double-rigged dugout used for fishing and turtle hunting by the natives of Lower Batavia.

**bad weather**  *n.* A legal phrase used in charter parties by which is meant weather that reasonably precludes loading, unloading, or working cargo with the equipment at hand.

**baffle**  *n.* Plating installed in a tank to slow or deflect the fore-and-aft or athwartship movement of fluids such as water, bunkers, and so on. Also *swash bulkhead; wash plate.*

**baffle area**  *n.* Area astern of a vessel and on both quarters, to about 30°, in which a sonar contact is most difficult to maintain because of the detecting ship's propeller noises.

**baffling (winds)**  *adj.* Confusing or shifting winds that make tacking and course changing continually necessary.

**bag**  *v.* To stow a sail in a bag.

**baggage master**  *n.* A member of the ship's crew in the purser's office responsible for storing passengers' luggage.

**bagged cargo**  *n.* Bulk goods, such as grain, carried in bags or sacks.

**baggy**  *adj.* Used to describe a sail that sags when the edges are taut.

**baggywrinkle**  *n.* The scruffy-looking padding used on shrouds to prevent chafing. Baggywrinkle is never used in the plural. Also *bag wrinkle.*

**baghla**  *n.* (pron. bagla) A lateen-rigged commercial vessel used in the Red Sea, along the coasts of Arabia and India, and in the Persian Gulf.

**bag lanyard**  *n.* Small line going through grommets at the top of a seabag or sail bag to secure its contents.

**bag net**  *n.* The name for all nets in which caught fish are funneled into a pocket, including trawl nets, shrimp nets, and so on.

**bagpipe**  *v.* To lay back a mizzen by bringing the sheet to the weather mizzen. The maneuver is used on square-rigged ships when tacking in light air by backing the spanker; this is done by hauling the weather preventer and spanker to windward to increase the turning moment.

**bag rope**  *n.* A strong line that runs from rigging to bulwarks of a trawler to prevent the net swinging in too far when the gear is hauled aboard.

**baguio**  *n.* (pron. bahgheeoh): A typhoon in the Philippines.

**bail**   *n.* (1) A half-hoop used for a handle on a pail. (2) Half-hoops used to support awnings. (3) The spreader used for the topping lift that secures an accommodation ladder.

**bail**   *v.* To remove water from a boat, usually by bucket.

**baillie rod**   *n.* A deep-sea sounding device. It consists of a steel tube about 2 feet long with a rounded top through which a movable steel rod passes. There is a double flap valve at the lower end to collect samples of the sea bottom.

**balance**   *v.* Submariner's term meaning to maintain depth with no way on by riding a density layer. Also *to hover.*

**balance**   *adj.* Said of a sailing vessel that tends to remain on course with little assistance from the helm. Such a vessel is said to be well balanced or in balance.

**balance canoe**   *n.* A canoe fitted with an athwartship plank used as an outrigger, most common in southern India.

**balanced jib**   *n.* A club-footed jib that extends forward beyond the bowsprit.

**balanced rudder**   *n.* A rudder with part of the blade forward of the axis of rotation so the water pressure on the main part of the blade is partially counterbalanced. The ratio of rudder forward to rudder aft is called the **balance ratio.** Also *equipoise rudder.* See UNBALANCED RUDDER.

**balance jib**   *n.* A Chesapeake Bay boatman's term for a club-footed jib on a sloop-rigged fishing skiff.

**balance point**   *n.* In what have become known as old-fashioned anchors, the point on the shank where the anchor balances; it is usually fitted with a pad eye. See ANCHOR.

**balance ratio**   *n.* On a balanced rudder, the ratio of the area of the blade forward to the area abaft the rudder stock.

**balance reef**   *n.* Reef in a quadrilateral mizzen or mainsail that runs diagonally from the leech cringle of the shortest reef to the throat of the sail.

**balance reef band**   *n.* Canvas backing that reaches diagonally across the quadrilateral spanker, or on a storm trysail that reaches from the throat to the clew, and along which the reefing points are arranged.

**balancing band**   *n.* A band on the shank of a stocked anchor near the center of gravity to which a shackle is fitted. It is used on anchors on vessels that are fitted with billboards. See ANCHOR.

**balancing ring**   *n.* A ring fitted to the balancing band on the shank of a stocked anchor, used for fishing the anchor.

**balandra**   *n.* A Philippine sailing dugout with plank sides and double outriggers.

**balandrita**   *n.* A sloop-rigged fishing boat used in Peru between the mainland and the Lobos Islands.

**baldhead cutter**   *n.* Sailing vessel with short cutter rig and no topsail.

**bald-headed**   *adj.* Said of a vessel that does not carry topmasts where one might ordinarily find them, as in a gaff-rigged schooner without topmasts. Also said of a vessel not setting topsails, for whatever reason.

**bale cargo**   *n.* General term for cargo wrapped in burlap or similar material.

**bale cubic**   *n.* The bales a compartment will hold in cubic feet. This is part of the vessel's trim and stability booklet. See GRAIN CUBIC.

**baleira** *n.* A whaling ship used on the coast of Brazil, built very light and fast under either sail or oar.

**bale sling** *n.* A rope spliced together at the ends, doubled and wrapped around a bale of cargo; one bight is passed through the other end so that the bale can be hoisted.

**balinger** *n.* (1) A sloop of war used in the 15th and 16th centuries by the English and probably the French, usually about 100 feet long, narrow and built without a forecastle. It was adapted from an earlier coastal trading vessel used on the Bay of Biscay. Also *ballinger.* (2) Name given to a type of trading vessel in the Philippines and Moluccas.

**bali wind** *n.* A strong easterly wind along the eastern end of Java.

**ball** *n.* (1) A shape or visual aid hung in the rigging of a vessel between sunrise and sunset as prescribed in the *Navigation Rules* to indicate the vessel's navigational status. A ball has a diaameter of at least 0.6 meter. (2) The end of the stock on early anchors.

**ballam** *n.* A type of dugout used on India's Malabar coast for hook-and-line fishing.

**ballast** *n.* Any heavy material such as lead, concrete, or water placed low in a vessel to increase stability. A vessel is said to be in ballast when it has ballast aboard but no cargo. "We were in ballast and rolling heavily. The boom ends were dipping into the waves." *A Ship's Log Book* by Frank Farrar. Pleasure vessels are considered to be in ballast by marine underwriters when they have no passengers or cargo aboard.

**ballast/displacement ratio** *n.* The ratio of a ship's ballast to her total displacement.

**ballast keel** *n.* In sailing vessels, a keel used to increase resistance to heeling by lowering the center of gravity.

**ballast passage** *n.* A passage made in ballast, especially a tanker.

**ballast port** *n.* An opening for handling rubble ballast.

**ballast tank** *n.* (1) Tanks used for holding water as ballast that can be moved from tank to tank or discharged via ballast lines. (2) Tanks used for varying trim and buoyancy as used on amphibious craft. See TRIM TANKS.

**ballistic bulkhead** *n.* Reinforced bulkhead designed to protect a vessel and crew from gunfire.

**ballistic error** *n.* The error in a gyro compass introduced by any change in speed or direction and causing a very small amount of mercury in the mercury ballast system to flow from one container to the other. **Ballistic damping error** is the temporary error that results from the damping of the oscillations of the spin axis.

**ball lightning** *n.* A phenomenon that occurs during thunderstorms when the discharge of electricity takes the form of a ball between 10 and 20 centimeters in diameter.

**balloon foresail** See SPINNAKER.

**balloon jib** *n.* A triangular sail of light material that is set between the bowsprit head and the topmast head. A balloon jib of a looser cut than a genoa and used on a broad reach. Also *ballooner.*

**balloon jib topsail** *n.* A light air racing sail set on the jib topsail stay.

**balloon sail** *n.* Any of a number of different cuts of large, light sails, especially headsails, used in racing and cruising when reaching or running. Also *blooper; chute; spinnaker.*

**ball plug**   *n.* A plug used in small self-bailing boats that uses a ball in a holder that opens by sliding aft when the boat is underway, releasing any water that is in the boat, but slides forward to prevent water from entering when the boat stops.

**ball vent**   *n.* A tank vent that is closed by a captive floating ball or plug when it is submerged.

**balok**   *n.* A lug-rigged one- or two-masted Maylay trading vessel used in the Lesser Sundra Islands.

**balsa**   *n.* Light wood used by shipwrights to pack bilge keels.

**balsa sandwich**   *n.* A method of making Fiberglas using balsa wood between layers of Fiberglas.

**Baltic bow**   *n.* A type of bow found on icebreakers and other vessels that frequently have to force their way through ice fields. The Baltic bow recedes sharply just below the waterline to allow the vessel to ride up over the ice and crush it by its own weight.

**Baltimore clipper**   *n.* A 19th-century U.S.-built schooner or brig-rigged vessel of 90 to 200 tons, characterized by its long, low hull, sharp-raked stem, and sharp-raked masts, and used for smuggling and the slave trade.

**baluk**   *n.* An open rowboat with six oars used for transportation in the waters around Istanbul. The oarsmen stand when rowing.

**banderole**   *n.* A streamer flown from the masthead as a wind vane.

**banding**   *n.* A strip of fabric sewn over the tabling of a luff, head, or foot. Also *strengthening piece.*

**bank**   *n.* (1) A relatively shallow rise in the seafloor located on a continental shelf, such as the Grand Banks off Newfoundland. (2) The shore at the side of a river.

(3) A rank or tier of oars. A **trireme** had three banks of oars.

**bank**   *v.* To partially smother the fire in a boiler by covering with ash and reducing draft when temporarily in port.

**bank blink**   *n.* A glow over white sand, snow, or an ice mass caused by the reflection of bright sunlight. See BLINK.

**bank cushion**   *n.* In a restricted channel, the counterforce that results from the increase in bow wave and pushes a vessel's bow away from the bank as the current throws it toward the bank.

**bank effect**   *n.* The tendency of a vessel in a narrow channel to be pulled toward the bank at the stern from the action of the propellers, which causes the bow to tend away from the bank. Also *bank suction.*

**bar**   *n.* (1) A bank of sand, gravel, shell, or mud in shallow water, either partially or totally submerged and identified by the seas breaking over them and marked by **bar buoys.** Crossing a submerged bar should be undertaken with caution if at all. (2) A unit of atmospheric pressure equal to $10^5$ newtons per square meter or 0.987 standard atmosphere. (3) A dark wall of cumulonimbus clouds on the horizon during a storm that may reach a force of 6 to 8; also *storm bar.* The barometer falls rapidly and winds become increasingly gusty.

**barber**   *n.* A strong, icy wind especially on the Gulf of St. Lawrence.

**barbette**   *n.* A stationary ballistic bulkhead on a revolving turret on a warship.

**bar-bound**   *adj.* The condition of a vessel when it cannot leave port because of insufficient depth of water over the bar at the mouth of the channel or harbor.

**barden**   *n.* The system of installing stanchions and angle-iron supports for shifting boards to keep grain in place during a voyage.

**bar draft**   *n.* Depth of water over a bar at mean low water.

**bareboat charter**   *n.* A charter party that leases a vessel to the charterer without a crew.

**bare sailing**   *n.* Sailing with sails hauled in too close.

**barge**   *n.* (1) In the U.S. Navy, a boat designated for official use by flag officers. "The captain rides a gig because it makes him feel big; the admiral rides a barge because it makes him feel large." (2) A vessel not equipped with a means of self-propulsion. (3) An open scow with flat deck.

**barge**   *v.* (1) To carry by barge. (2) In racing, to force oneself between the starting mark and boats to leeward. This can be illegal if it appears the barging boat, the windward boat, is failing to keep clear of leeward boats.

**barge, self-propelled**   *n.* A vessel with a relatively flat bottom and usually several times longer than it is wide and that carries its own propulsion plant. Self-propelled barges are far more common on the inland waterways of northern Europe than in the United States.

**bargee**   *n.* One who operates a barge (U.K. usage).

**bargemate**   *n.* An officer designated to steer a barge on ceremonial occasions.

**barge port**   *n.* Port equipped for handling barges, both loading and unloading operations, as distinct from cartage ports.

**barge yacht**   *n.* A shallow-draft sailing pleasure boat with a flat bottom and wall sides, and a sharp chine; leeboards reduce the leeway.

**bark (barque)**   *n.* A sailing vessel with three or more masts square-rigged on all but the mizzenmast, which is fore-and-aft-rigged. Traditionally used to carry freight, they are now chiefly built and sailed for sail training. See BARKENTINE; RIG; SHIP.

**bar keel**   *n.* A solid, external centerline keel.

**barkentine (barquentine)**   *n.* A vessel with three or more masts, square-rigged on the fore, with fore-and-aft sails on all others. See BARK; RIG; SHIP.

**barking**   *n.* The process of putting a protecting mixture of yellow ocher, tallow, cutch, and oak bark on sails and nets. The mixture was applied boiling hot with long brushes.

**barling spar**   *n.* A spar or timber with a length of about 30 feet and broad enough at the butt to make a heavy spar.

**barnacle**   *n.* Any of several small marine crustaceans of the order Cirripedia that form a hard shell in the adult stage. The immature animal swims free for two or three months until it attaches to a piling or a hull and then begins to secrete the material that makes the shell. Painting with toxic materials impedes their attaching to the objects in the water, but once attached, they must be removed physically. Freshwater will kill the animal after a few days, but the shell will stay on until scraped off.

**barometer**   *n.* Any instrument that measures and indicates the atmospheric pressure. A **mercury barometer** determines the atmospheric pressure by measuring the height of a column of mercury at the top of a graduated tube. An **aneroid barometer** works without mercury, such as a **barograph,** which is a barometer designed to record the changes in atmospheric pressure on the rotating drum of a **barogram.**

**barometric gradient**   *n.* The difference in pounds per square inch between isobars.

**barometric pressure**   *n.* The force of the air in pounds per square inch (psi) exerted at the Earth's surface, found to be 14.7 psi under standard conditions. Also *atmospheric pressure.*

**barometric tide**   *n.* The normal fluctuation of the barometric pressure during a 24-hour period.

**barothermograph**   *n.* An instrument that automatically records pressure and temperature.

**bar pilot**   *n.* A pilot who confines his or her activity to river and harbor entrances. See PILOT.

**barque**   See BARK.

**barquentine**   See BARKENTINE.

**barratry**   *n.* Any act committed by a master or crew, with criminal intent, in violation of their duty to the owners of the vessel and without the owners' consent. These offenses include willful casting away of a vessel to collect insurance, bottomry, and respondentia. Barratry is considered more heinous than mutiny, the penalty being a fine of up to $10,000.00 or 10 years in prison, while mutiny is punishable by fines of up to $2,000.00 and 10 years or both. One who commits barratry is a **barrator.**

**barrel**   *n.* (1) The rotating drum of a windlass, capstan, or winch. Also *cathead; gipsy;* or *wildcat.* (2) A measure of unrefined petroleum oil of 42 U.S. gallons.

**barrel bulk**   *n.* A unit of freight measurement of 5 cubic feet.

**barrel cargo**   *n.* General term for either liquid or solid goods stowed in barrels or similar containers.

**barrel sling**   *n.* A sling with a short length of rope and a cant hook at each end for grasping the staves or ends of a barrel.

**barricade**   *n.* (1) Rail near the stern of a man-o'-war from which protecting netting was hung to protect gun crews in that area. (2) A temporary barrier on an aircraft carrier used in emergencies when a returning aircraft is not stopped by the arresting gear, to prevent it from piling into the parked planes or going over the side.

**barrico**   *n.* (pron. bahreecoh) A cask or keg.

**barrier**   *n.* The edge of a large polar glacier that enters the sea but is attached to land.

**barrier combat air patrol (BAR-CAP)**   *n.* One or several divisions of fighter aircraft from a U.S. Navy carrier deployed in the direction from which an attack is most expected.

**barrier ice**   *n.* Ice that has broken off from the outer margin or barrier of an ice sheet.

**barrier island**   *n.* An offshore island separated from the mainland by a channel or lagoon.

**barrier patrol**   *n.* Detachment of ships or aircraft assigned to patrol, detect, and possibly take action against enemy aircraft, surface craft, and submarines entering or making passage through a particular area or across a designated **barrier line.**

**barrier reef**   *n.* A partially submerged coral outcrop separated from, but generally following the contours of, the mainland. A **fringing reef** is usually connected to the mainland.

**bar scale**   *n.* A graph at the bottom of a marine chart against which distances on the chart can be measured.

**bar stem**   *n.* The forward framing that forms the apex of the intersection of the sides of a vessel.

**bar weir**   *n.* A fish trap located near a bar to catch the fish as the tide leaves the bar. See WEIR.

**barycenter**   *n.* A theoretical point 810 miles beneath the surface of the Earth. It is the rotational center of the Earth and Moon. The gravitational attraction between Earth and Moon affects the oceans and their tides; centrifugal forces result from their revolutions around the barycenter.

**base course up**   *n.* One of the three orientations of a radarscope display, in which the target pips are at their indicated distances and in their displayed directions relative to a preset base course maintained as "up" in the display. See HEAD UP.

**base leg**   *n.* The final course taken by a racing boat prior to and in preparation for the approach to the starting line.

**base line**   *n.* (1) In radio navigation, the line perpendicular to the centerline between a master and a slave station. (2) The line along a state or nation's coast that separates its internal waters (including rivers, harbors, and bays) from the territorial sea. The various maritime zones are measured from the base line. The base line usually follows the low waterline except in highly indented coasts where it is straighter than the coast. The right of innocent passage in foreign waters terminates at the base line. The United Nations Conference on the Law of the Sea defined the base line for determining the limit of the territorial sea as the low waterline shown on large-scale charts of the coastal state (country). (3) A marine architect's term for the main line taken or representing a vessel's base.

**base speed**   *n.* Speed of a vessel along its intended course when zigzagging.

**basilisk**   *n.* Long brass cannon used from the 16th to the 19th century, ornamented with basilisks, fanciful reptiles hatched by a serpent from a cock's egg.

**basin**   *n.* (1) Round or oval depression in the ocean floor. (2) An enclosed area of water protected by quay walls. (3) An area of land that drains into a lake or sea through a river and its tributaries. (4) An almost landlocked area of water leading from an inlet, firth, or sound.

**basket**   *n.* An optional day shape for vessels under 20 meters engaged in fishing. The preferred is two cones with apexes together in a vertical line.

**basket boat**   *n.* A vessel with an outer hull made from basket work and coated with a heavy flexible material suitable for maintaining watertight integrity.

**bass rope**   *n.* A coarse-fiber rope made from rushes.

**bast**   *n.* The inner bark of lime or linden trees, shipped in bales and used for making coarse **bast rope** and street brooms.

**bateau**   *n.* A type of U.S. Army pontoon.

**bathyconductograph**   *n.* Device used to determine the heat conductivity of seawater at various depths while a vessel is underway.

**bathycurrent**   *n.* A deep-sea current that does not disturb the surface.

**bathymetric charts**   *n.* Maps of the ocean floor that give contour lines for the depths. Also *bottom contour chart.*

**bathymetric navigation**   *n.* The use of the fathometer or depth finder to assist in establishing a vessel's position by using ocean contours on the marine charts.

**bathymetry**  *n.* The branch of science that deals with the measurement of ocean depths to determine bottom topography.

**bathysphere**  *n.* A spherical chamber in which persons are lowered for deep-sea observation of ocean depths, topography, and flora and fauna.

**bathythermograph**  *n.* An instrument designed to give a continuous recording of ocean temperatures while underway or at anchor.

**batten**  *n.* (1) A thin strip of stiffening material fitted into a **batten pocket** in the leech of a sail to give it a better shape. See REEFING BATTEN. (2) Strips of wood, metal, or plastic used to secure hatches, hatchcovers, tarpaulins and other coverings. See CARGO BATTEN.

**batten**  *v.* (1) To secure a hatch with a thin strip of wood. (2) To secure a hatch. (3) To secure loose gear for rough weather.

**batten carvel-built**  *adj.* Hull-building technique with planking edges abutted lengthwise edge to edge, secured to interior battens attached to the framing. See CARVEL-BUILT.

**battery**  *n.* Guns of the same size or used for the same purpose; an antiaircraft battery might be guns of various calibers while the 5-inch battery would be all 5-inch guns.

**battery control**  *n.* Fire control of a given battery.

**battle bill**  See QUARTER; STATION BILL; WATCH.

**battle bridge**  *n.* The platform used by the commanding officer during engagements with an enemy.

**battle cruiser**  *n.* An early 20th-century class of warship of British origin. Heavily armed but lightly armored for high speed, they were designed for for-

ward reconnaissance work. See BATTLE LINE.

**battle dress**  *n.* Clothing worn by surface ship crews during battle as protection against flash and splinters.

**battle efficiency pennant**  *n.* A red pennant with a black ball flown by a U.S. Navy ship that has been awarded this distinction for efficient conduct in battle. The pennant is widely known by the slang name **meatball.**

**battle group**  *n.* An offensive unit in the U.S. Navy made up of a carrier, a battleship, one or more cruisers, a group of destroyers and frigates, and a support ship. Two or more battle groups make up a task force.

**battle honors**  *n.* A listing of battles in which a ship has taken part. On British ships, a ship will also list those battles fought by other ships that previously carried the same name.

**battle lantern**  *n.* A battery-powered lantern for emergency use, so devised that when the electric power goes out in an area, it is automatically turned on.

**battle lights**  *n.* Dim red bulbs used below decks during **darken ship,** red having a less detrimental effect on night vision than other colors.

**battle line**  *n.* A line of warships formed to engage an enemy in surface warfare. As the world advanced into powered vessels and wooden warships passed into history, the battle line became less practical. The heavily armored cruisers of the German Imperial Navy overpowered the lighter British battle cruisers at the Battle of Jutland and sounded the death knell for the time-honored battle line.

**battle port**  *n.* Hinged metal port fitted inside a porthole for additional protection from heavy seas and enemy gunfire.

**battleship**  *n.* Before the advent of the aircraft carrier, the heaviest warship built; the word derives from "line of battle ship," that is, a ship fit to sail in the line of battle.

**battle station**  See WATCH, QUARTER, AND STATION BILL.

**batture**  *n.* A riverbed or seabed that has been elevated to the surface.

**batwing sail**  *n.* A sail used on canoes and small pleasure boats whereby a greater effective area is achieved by extending the after edge with battens that run radially across the sail from the luff.

**baulk**  *n.* A heavy piece of timber.

**bawley**  *n.* An English shoal-draft, broad-beamed boat employed for fishing on the Thames and Medway estuaries.

**bay**  *n.* A body of water partially surrounded by land. For sailors, the body of water is usually saltwater. Under maritime law, a bay is closed on the sides and may have an established straight baseline at its mouth to enclose its "internal waters." An earlier definition under international law used a 10-mile limit. If the mouth of a bay was more than 10 miles wide, the maritime jurisdiction, then called the **seaward limit,** was placed at the most seaward point at which the bay narrowed to 10 miles.

**bayamo**  *n.* A violent squall on the southern coast of Cuba, especially near the Bight of Bayamo.

**bay craft**  *n.* Term for craft used on bays and canals for commercial work.

**bay ice**  *n.* New ice that first forms during autumn on the sea in such thickness as to prevent navigation. Also *gulf ice.*

**baymouth**  *n.* A bar that extends practically or entirely across the mouth of a bay.

**bayou**  *n.* An inlet from a bay or river, used especially in southern Louisiana. Also *slough.* See BAY.

**beach**  *n.* (1) A general term used by mariners for land especially when anchored or tied to a pier, as in "I'm going to hit the beach," meaning "I'm going ashore." (2) In oceanography, the land between the shoreline and a marked change in topography or where vegetation begins.

**beach**  *v.* To run a vessel ashore intentionally for whatever reason, to clean the bottom, to prevent sinking, and so on. See CAREEN.

**beach berm**  *n.* The nearly level portion of a beach that is formed by wave deposition of sand and has an abrupt drop. The seaward limit is called a **berm crest** or **berm edge.** See BERM.

**beachcomber**  *n.* Unemployed seaman, usually in a foreign port.

**beach gear**  *n.* Items of equipment used by the beachmaster during an amphibious operation, including heavy anchors, wire rope, and tackle, but not including supplies and equipment brought ashore for troops who have been landed.

**beachhead**  *n.* The objective of the initial assault of an amphibious landing. The beachmaster remains in charge of landing operations until a suitable port can be taken.

**beach party**  *n.* The naval personnel in a shore party.

**beacon**  *n.* A light or electronic fixed aid to navigation which emits a distinctive signal used to determine bearings, courses or location. See RADIO BEACON. Channel markers are frequently daybeacons consisting of a pile or cluster of piles (a piling) and one or several daymarks with identifying topmarks. See RADIO BEACON.

**beaconage**    *n.* A system of fixed aids to navigation comprising beacons and minor lights.

**beaconboat**    *n.* A small lightship without a keeper. Obsolete.

**beacon signal**    *n.* The characteristic radio signal given by a radio beacon.

**beacon tower**    *n.* A major structure with a supporting structure as distinctive as the topmark.

**beading**    *n.* Wooden half-round molding used along the joint between the decking and the sheer strake of a small boat.

**beak**    See RAM.

**beakhead**    *n.* The space above the ram (or beak) at the bow of a ship called the catheads, where the large anchors were "catted home." Beakheads often had a grating over them that was open to the sea below. These were used by sailors to relieve themselves; hence the word head for a ship's toilet.

**beam**    *n.* (1) A timber that extends from side to side on which a portion of the deck is laid. (2) Width of a vessel at its widest part. See ABEAM.

**beam bracket**    See BEAM KNEE.

**beam dividers**    *n.* Usually called **dividers,** a device used in navigation and having two legs, each with a point at the end and connected at the top by a bar from which each leg acts in a single plane independent of the other. If one of the legs has a pencil instead of a metal point, it is called a **beam compass.**

**beam-draft ratio**    *n.* A ratio directly related to the height and movement of

the transverse metacenter. See STABILITY.

**beam end**    *n.* The outermost part of a vessel's beam where it joins the side of the vessel. A ship is said to be on its **beam ends** when the beams are almost vertical, usually as a result of cargo shifting, heavy weather, or damage below the waterline. Only sailing vessels can survive such a condition.

**beam engine**    *n.* An early steam engine that used a pivoted wooden beam between the connecting rod from the piston and the pitman from the crank.

**beam filling**    *n.* Cargo suited for filling between the transverse structural members of a vessel's framing, such as bags of grain.

**beam knee**    *n.* An approximately right-angled, fitted support for a structural beam.

**beam mold**    *n.* The pattern used in construction to show length, camber, and position of each transverse structural member or beam.

**beam reach**    *n.* Point of sailing with the apparent wind at a right angle to the keel. See POINTS OF SAILING.

**beam rider**    *n.* Guided missile that uses a radar beam to find its target.

**beam sea**    *n.* A sea on the vessel's beam with the waves parallel to the vessel's course. A sea moving in a direction opposite to that of a vessel's heading is called a head sea. A sea from astern is called a following sea.

**beam tide**    *n.* A tidal current moving in a direction roughly 90° from the observing vessel's heading. See FAIR TIDE; HEAD TIDE.

**beam wind**    *n.* Apparent wind coming from an angle 90° from the head.

**beamy** *adj.* With relation to the length, an unusually wide vessel; with sailboats, beamy usually means a beam more than one-third the overall length.

**bear** *n.* A coconut fiber bag filled with sand used for scouring wooden decks.

**bear** *v.* To maintain a course or direction, said with respect either to an observed object or to the observing object.

**bear a hand** *v.* (1) To speed up. (2) To assist.

**bearding** *n.* (1) The forward part of a rudder. (2) The line of intersection of a vessel's keel, her deadwood, and her sternpost with the outer surface of the frame timbers.

**bearding angle** *n.* The angle the stem makes with the keel plates.

**bear down** *v.* (1) To approach from windward. (2) To apply pressure. (3) To move toward a vessel or other object quickly. (4) To put the helm down and turn toward the direction of the wind. Ordinarily "down" means downwind or to leeward. In this case it was the helm that was put downwind to head the vessel upwind; it was quite confusing and is no longer heard.

**bear in** *v.* To approach the shore, another vessel, or an object. See BEAR UP.

**bearing** *n.* (1) A device for limiting movement and wear between surfaces such as a propeller shaft and its journals or a compass needle and its support post. (2) The horizontal angle at a given point measured clockwise from a specific datum to a second point. **True bearings** are based on the geographic North Pole and South Pole for reference. **Magnetic bearings** are based on the magnetic north pole and have to be corrected to arrive at true bearing. **Relative bearings** are measured clockwise from the ship's bow, 000° to 360°. A vessel on the starboard beam is said to bear 90° relative; a ves-

sel abeam to port would be said to bear 270° relative. See AZIMUTH ANGLE.

**bearing circle** *n.* Ring fitted over a compass or gyro repeater with sights set up so that bearings can be taken on objects and other vessels and the bearings read off the compass. If they are fitted with mirrors for taking bearings on celestial bodies, they are called azimuth circles. See ALIDADE; PELORUS.

**bearing cursor** *n.* The radial line inscribed on a transparent disk of a radar scope that can be rotated about an axis that coincides with the center of the plan position indicator.

**bearing line** *n.* A position line established by getting a compass bearing on a known and charted landmark. With this information, that the ship is some place on the bearing line, a vessel can firmly establish position if a second bearing line can be established on a second known and charted landmark. Good practice calls for a third bearing line to be established when possible.

**bear off** *v.* (1) To steer more off the wind, more to leeward, a sailing usage. Also *bear away*. (2) To steer away from a shore, another vessel, or an object. (3) To sheer away from the established track. (4) To push away from a pier, small boat expression.

**bear up** *v.* (1) To put the helm up so the vessel will go more upwind. (2) To steer more to windward or toward shore or an object.

**beat** *v.* To sail as close to the wind as possible, usually to within 30° to 40°. Synonyms are to sail on the wind, to sail to windward, or to be close-hauled. Less frequently, beat is used to mean sail close to the wind by going back and forth from one tack to another. See POINTS OF SAILING.

**beat to quarters** *interj.* Royal Navy order announced by drummers with the specified rhythm of "heart of oak, heart of oak" calling the crew to battle stations.

**Beaufort scale**   *n.* A scale developed in 1805 by Admiral Sir Francis Beaufort (1774–1857) that has long been used to determine wind velocity by the appearance of the sea. Surprisingly, various authorities give different figures for the Beaufort scale.

**becalmed**   *adj.* Motionless for lack of wind.

**becket**   *n.* (1) A short piece of rope used to secure spars, awnings, oars, and so on, using a becket block and a running block. A becket is also the loop on a block that is used to make it fast to the standing part of the fall. See BLOCK. (2) The rope handle on a sea chest. (3) A rope with ends spliced together. (4) A short rope with loops spliced at the ends. (5) The eye of a block strap. (6) A short piece of rope with an eye spliced in one end and a button spliced in the other end, used to confine or secure spars and other objects.

**becket block**   *n.* A block with an eye or becket to which other ropes can be attached.

**becket bridle**   *n.* A short piece of rope knotted at one end with an eye spliced in the other end, or sometimes an eye at each end and no knot, used for temporarily confining lines.

**becket rowlock**   *n.* A rowlock that consists of a rope eye on a thole pin.

**becue**   *v.* (pron. beecue) To secure the anchor cable to the crown of an anchor and then seize the cable to the ring. If the anchor is in hard ground and won't let go, a sharp tug on the cable will break loose the seizing at the ring, and the anchor can be hauled up by the fluke or crown. Also *scowing.*

**bedeni**   *n.* A dhow with one or two masts, used for trading on the Gulf of Oman.

**bedplate**   *n.* The foundation for a marine engine consisting of longitudinal and transverse girders anchored to the engine keelsons. The engine frame and main bearings are bolted to the **bedframe.**

**bee**   *n.* A wooden piece fitted with an eye and fastened to the outer bowsprit through which a foretopmast stay is rove. When a block is used, it is called a **bee block.**

**before the beam**   *phr.* A term that describes the position of an object that is forward of the beam but not straight ahead.

**before the mast**   *phr.* Expression used to describe the accommodations for seamen, as distinct from those of officers who were berthed aft. Richard Henry Dana (1815–1882) wrote of his experiences sailing as a seaman in *Two Years Before the Mast.*

**before the wind**   *phr.* With the wind coming from astern or from the quarter. Sailing before the wind is a broad reach or a run. See DOWNWIND; POINTS OF SAILING.

**belat**   *n.* A strong wind from north or northwest encountered on the southern coast of Saudi Arabia during the winter months.

**belay**   *v.* (1) To secure to a pin or cleat, to make fast. (2) To cancel a command: "Belay my last order."

**belaying cleat**   *n.* Single-horned or double-horned device used for belaying a line.

**belaying pin**   *n.* A movable pin used to secure a line.

# BEAUFORT WIND SCALE

| Force | Description of wind | Mean wind speed in knots | Specification for use on land and at sea |
|---|---|---|---|
| Force 0 | Calm | Less than 1 | Calm, smoke rises vertically. Sea like a mirror. |
| Force 1 | Light air | 1–3 | Direction of wind shown by smoke drift, but not by wind vanes. Ripples with appearance of scales are formed, but without foam crests. |
| Force 2 | Light breeze | 4–6 | Wind felt on face; leaves rustle; ordinary vane moved by wind. Small wavelets, still short but more pronounced; crests have a glassy appearance and do not break. |
| Force 3 | Gentle breeze | 7–10 | Leaves and small twigs in constant motion; wind extends light flag. Large wavelets, crests begin to break; foam of glassy appearance; perhaps scattered white horses. |
| Force 4 | Moderate breeze | 11–16 | Raises dust and loose paper; small branches are moved. Small waves becoming longer; fairly frequent white horses. |
| Force 5 | Fresh breeze | 17–21 | Small trees in leaf begin to sway; crested wavelets form on inland waters. Moderate waves, taking a more pronounced long form; many white horses are formed (chance of some spray). |
| Force 6 | Strong breeze | 22–27 | Large branches in motion; whistling heard in telegraph wires; umbrellas used with difficulty. Large waves begin to form; the white foam crests are more extensive everywhere (probably some spray). |
| Force 7 | Moderate gale, Near gale | 28–33 | Whole trees in motion; inconvenience felt when walking against wind. Sea heaps up and white foam from breaking waves begins to be blown in streaks along the direction of the wind. |
| Force 8 | Fresh gale, Gale | 34–40 | Breaks twigs off trees; generally impedes progress. Moderately high waves of greater length; edges of crests begin to break into spindrift; foam is blown in well-marked streaks. |
| Force 9 | Strong gale | 41–47 | Slight structural damage occurs (chimney pots and slate removed). High waves; dense streaks of foam; crests of waves begin to topple, tumble, and roll over. |

## BEAUFORT WIND SCALE (*Continued*)

| Force | Description of wind | Mean wind speed in knots | Specification for use on land and at sea |
|-------|--------------------|--------------------------|------------------------------------------|
| Force 10 | Whole gale, Storm | 48–55 | Seldom experienced inland; trees uprooted; considerable structural damage occurs. Very high waves with long overhanging crests; the resulting foam, in great patches, is blown in dense white streaks; the sea takes a white appearance; the tumbling of the sea becomes heavy and shocklike; visibility affected. |
| Force 11 | Storm, Violent storm | 56–63 | Very rarely experienced; accompanied by widespread damage. Exceptionally high waves at sea (medium-sized ships might be lost to view behind the waves); the sea is completely covered with white patches of foam; visibility affected. |
| Force 12+ | Hurricane[1] | 64 and above | The air is filled with foam and spray; sea completely white with driving spray; visibility very seriously affected. |

1. Force 13: 72–80 knots; force 14: 81–89; force 15: 90–99; force 16: 100–108; force 17: 109–118. Sources: Smithsonian Institution, *Smithsonian Meteorological Tables* (1966); Hydrographer of the Navy (UK), *Ocean Passages for the World* (1977).

**belaying pin rack** *n.* Wooden or metal holder at the base of a mast for holding belaying pins. Also *fife rail, pin rail.*

**Belfast bow** *n.* A bow that rakes forward from the waterline to give more stowage room aboard. It was not unique to the Belfast shipbuilders, but it came to be called that over the years.

**Belfast rig** *n.* A three-masted full-rigged ship with double fore and main topgallant sails and a single topgallant on the mizzen. According to the *International Maritime Dictionary* by De Kerchove, these were built by Harland and Wolff at Belfast, and all three masts had an uncommonly sharp rake.

**belfry** *n.* An ornately decorated little house over the ship's bell in sailing ships.

**bell** *n.* A sounding device required by the *Navigation Rules* of all vessels 12 meters or more in length for use when anchored, aground, or in a fog. See BELLS.

**bell book** *n.* Log of engine room orders from the bridge maintained in the engine spaces.

**bell-bottom trousers** *n.* Sailor's uniform trousers that are wider at the bottom; the purpose for the flare was to make it more convenient for a sailor to roll up his trousers when swabbing decks and doing other wet chores.

**bell buoy** *n.* A buoy with a bell that is activated by the action of the water. It is a steel float with a short skeleton tower at the top in which a bell is fixed with four movable clappers inside. If the sea motion is apt to be negligible, the bell is activated mechanically or by compressed air.

**bellman** *n.* One who assists a diver, pearl fisherman, or sponger in putting on diving suit and helmet and who watches air and communications lines and supplies tools or other equipment needed by the diver before the diver enters the water.

**bellpull**   *n.* The brass handle on the engine room telegraph located on the bridge by which the engineer is signaled the desired speed.

**bell (or bell's) purchase**   *n.* A block and tackle made up of four single blocks, two fixed blocks, and two movable blocks; one bight of the fall is fixed to one of the movable blocks.

**bell rope**   *n.* The short piece of rope that is secured to the clapper of a bell, usually made with fancy rope work.

**bells**   *n.* A method of announcing the time of day and change of watch. The watch is changed at 0400, 0800, 1200, 1600, 2000, and 2400 (0000). Each of these times was established as eight bells. One bell is sounded one half-hour after the change of the watch, two bells at the hour, and so on. Two watches break the standard 4-hour watch period, these being the 2-hour dog watches from 1600 to 1800 and 1800 to 2000, which keep the same watch sections from standing the same watches day after day. The first dog watch is relieved at four bells, and the second watch at eight bells. See WATCH.

### Ship's Bells

| Bells | Hour of the Day (A.M. or P.M.) | | |
|---|---|---|---|
| 1 | 12:30 | 4:30 | 8:30 |
| 2 | 1:00 | 5:00 | 9:00 |
| 3 | 1:30 | 5:30 | 9:30 |
| 4 | 2:00 | 6:00 | 10:00 |
| 5 | 2:30 | 6:30 | 10:30 |
| 6 | 3:00 | 7:00 | 11:00 |
| 7 | 3:30 | 7:30 | 11:30 |
| 8 | 4:00 | 8:00 | 12:00 |

**bell whistle**   *n.* A vessel's whistle with either air or steam forced into the bell-shaped casting that is fitted on a spindle. It makes a very low note that can be heard over a great distance. Also *dome whistle.*

**belly**   *n.* (1) The bottom of a sail between the foot and the first set of reef points. (2) The part of the sail that bulges in the wind; that part of a sail between one-fourth and three-fourths of the sail from the mast on a fore-and-aft rig. (3) The concave side of a curved timber.

**belly band**   *n.* A strip of sailcloth sewn across the midpoint of a sail for extra support.

**belly robber**   *n.* Nickname for chief steward, who had the responsibility of keeping the crew fed for as little money as possible, and who was paid less than others at his level because he could keep what he saved.

**belly stay**   *n.* A stay above a half-mast, when a mast requires additional support. See BACKSTAY.

**belly strap**   *n.* A rope passed around a small boat when carrying the anchor out for kedging. The anchor hangs beneath the boat from the strap; this would only be used when the anchor is too large or heavy to be handled by the crew in the boat.

**below**   *adv.* On or to a lower deck. Below the upper deck.

**belt**   *n.* A large feature of pack ice longer than it is wide, from 1 kilometer to more than 100 kilometers in width.

**belt gripes**   *n.* The two pieces of sword matting that secure a lifeboat against the strongback. The upper ends of the matting are secured to the davit heads, and the lower ends are secured to lashings that set up the gripes.

**belting**   *n.* A protective band of soft material at or near the waterline. Strips for the same purpose higher up on the hull are called **rubbing strips.**

**bench**   *n.* (1) A fore-and-aft seat in a boat, as distinct from an athwartship seat, which is called a **thwart.**

**bench hook**   *n.* A hook and lanyard on a sailmaker's bench used to keep the fabric taut during hand sewing.

**bend**   *n.* (1) A knot that fastens one piece of line to another line. See HITCH. (2) The bowsprit chock.

**bend**   *v.* To fasten one piece of line to another line or object, or to fasten a sail to boom or yard. To bend on a sail is simply to secure it to the spar; to set sail includes hoisting and allowing the sail to fill with air.

**bending moment**   *n.* The measure of the tendency of a beam to bend as a result of external vertical shearing stresses on the beam.

**bending shackle**   *n.* The shackle that connects the chain cable to the anchor ring.

**bends**   *n.* (1) The ailment divers develop from too rapid ascent from deep water without taking time for proper decompression. When the ascent through the water is too fast, nitrogen bubbles form in the blood, producing severe pain, paralysis, vertigo, and possibly death. See WALE.

**bendy mast**   *n.* A mast that can be bent by using the standing rigging to change the shape of the sail.

**beneaped**   *adj.* Grounded by a neap tide so that the vessel must wait for the next spring tide. Also *neaped.*

**beneath**   *prep.* (1) To leeward. (2) Under.

**Benguela Current**   *n.* A slow-moving ocean current that flows northwesterly along the west coast of Africa and into the South Equatorial Current. See OCEAN CURRENT.

**bent frame**   *n.* A timber that has been bent by steam treatment. Bent frames are lighter for the required strength than a sawed frame.

**Bentinck**   *n.* Small triangular storm sail invented by Captain Bentinck of the Royal Navy in the early 19th century. These later gave way to storm trysails.

**bent timbers**   *n.* Ribs of the frame of a vessel that curve to fit the vessel's side.

**bergy bit**   *n.* Floating ice 1 to 5 meters above sea level and 100 to 300 square meters in area.

**Bering Current**   *n.* The northerly flowing current that flows through the eastern half of the Bering Sea, the Bering Strait, and the eastern Chukchi Sea.

**berm**   *n.* A narrow ledge, a raised embankment at a riverbank or at the seashore where it usually marks high water.

**Bermuda rig**   *n.* A fore-and-aft-rigged vessel first developed in the West Indies during the early 19th century. The sails used were the leg-of-mutton design, the triangular sails we know today that run on a mast track and are hoisted by a single halyard. Also *Bermudian rig; jib-headed rig; Marconi rig.*

**Berne List**   *n.* The complete list of international call signs and radio stations published by the International Telecommunications Union (ITU).

**berth**   *n.* (1) A place to sleep on a ship. (2) A job on a ship. (3) A vessel's assigned place at anchor or at a pier. (4) A wide margin. "To give something a wide berth" is to avoid a dangerous shoal, or to give a vessel that is having difficulties maneuvering a wide safety margin. (5) The ship's mess.

**berthage**   *n.* (1) An assigned space at a wharf for a vessel to receive cargo. (2) Fee paid for an assigned berth.

**berth cargo**   *n.* Goods that consist of commodities that line vessels carry to fill up surplus space when more profitable cargo is not available.

**berth charge**   *n.* The fee charged by the port authority for use of a wharf while a vessel loads or discharges. It is recognized as a port charge and not dues on cargo.

**berth charter**   *n.* A charter that allows a charterer to charter without a definite cargo; he or she is able to place the vessel "on the berth" and hold it in the loading port while soliciting shippers' bookings.

**berth clause**   *n.* Stipulation in a charter party that waives time spent while the vessel waits its turn for loading and unloading so that the time is not charged.

**berthing**   *n.* The outside planking above the sheer strake. Also *bulwark*.

**berthing master**   *n.* The person responsible under the harbor master for berthing, loading, and unloading vessels in a port.

**berthing signal**   *n.* The flag, shape, or light used by harbor authorities to indicate berth assignments to incoming vessels. This is now accomplished by radio.

**berthing space**   *n.* Sleeping quarters for the crew of a U.S. Navy vessel.

**berth rates**   *n.* Freight rates on partial cargo loads charged by shipping lines.

**berth terms**   *n.* An expression used in charters that indicates the vessel is to be loaded as fast as customarily possible at a particular loading port, and it is to be discharged as quickly as it can deliver at the port of discharge.

**beset**   *adj.* Said of a vessel that has become locked in ice with no control over the rudder. See NIPPED.

**best bower**   *n.* The heaviest anchor carried on a ship. Two bower anchors were carried at the bow, one on each side of the stem. The best bower was about 15% heavier than the two rigged for immediate use and was usually carried in the waist. See STORM ANCHOR.

**between decks**   *n.* Space between any two decks. See 'TWEEN DECKS.

**between the devil and the deep blue sea**   *phr.* Nautical equivalent of "between a rock and a hard place." The devil was the outermost deck seam that was paid with hot pitch while hanging over the side over the deep blue sea. The devil also referred to the seam between the garboard strake and the keel, which could be paid only when the ship was careened.

**between wind and water**   *phr.* The area of the hull that is alternately underwater and exposed to the air as the vessel heels and rolls. To receive a hit in this area of the hull is especially dangerous because it will allow water to enter and sink the ship. It is a term that is not heard as much anymore, but before torpedoes it was a constant concern.

**bevel**   *n.* The angle between the flanges of a frame or other member. An **open bevel** is one that forms an obtuse angle (greater than 90°); a **close** or **closed bevel** is one that forms an acute angle (less than 90°).

**bevel**   *v.* To cut a plate at an angle. You must bevel the edges of steel plate before attempting to butt weld it.

**beyond soundings**   See OFF SOUNDINGS.

**bhandary**   *n.* A cook with an Asiatic crew who specializes in rice-based and East Indian dishes.

**bias error**   *n.* A navigation term for a constant error such as the gyro bias error (or drift), an internal disturbance that causes a distortion of the output signal from the gyroscope.

**bibbs**　*n.* Additional supporting pieces fastened to the hounds of a mast at the point where the trestletrees are held.

**bible**　See HOLYSTONE.

**bifurcation buoy**　See MIDCHANNEL AIDS TO NAVIGATION.

**bight**　*n.* (1) A bend or loop in a line or cable. (2) A recess in a coastline or riverbank.

**bilge**　*n.* (1) The lowest part of a vessel's hull, where any water in the hull collects. (2) The widest part of a barrel.

**bilge**　*v.* To stave in a ship's bottom, to cause it to leak.

**bilge-and-ballast system**　*n.* The system of pipes that can be used to pump bilges dry or to pump seawater into the bilges for ballast.

**bilge and cantline**　*n.* A method of stowing barrels or casks so that the bilges of the higher tier fit into the cantline of the lower tier.

**bilge blocks**　*n.* Built-up blocks on which a vessel rests while in dry dock. Also *bilge cribbing.*

**bilge board**　*n.* On small boats, retractable keels on both sides of the boat at the bilges or the point where the vessel's hull becomes more vertical; the boards retract into trunks. The windward board is retracted when sailing close to the wind.

**bilge bracket**　*n.* A bracket that connects a ship's inner bottom to the frames at the bilges.

**bilge ceiling**　*n.* Inboard members fitted at the turn of the bilge of a vessel.

**bilge-free**　*adj.* Describes a method of stowing casks so that the **quarters** or butts are supported by chocks and the bilges do not rust on the deck or floor of the hold.

**bilge injection**　*n.* An emergency system that makes possible the pumping of the engine spaces through the circulating pumps and condenser and over the side in case of an emergency such as a collision or fire.

**bilge keels**　*n.* Longitudinal fins found at the turn of the bilge on both sides of the keel. Designed to reduce roll, they also give added structural support to the hull. Also *antirolling chocks.*

**bilge keelson**　*n.* A longitudinal member that connects the ribs.

**bilge pumps**　*n.* Pumps that remove water from the bilges; they are usually located above the bilge or in a sealed housing that prevents water from entering the motor.

**bilge rail**　*n.* A handrail above the waterline of a lifeboat.

**bilge strake**　*n.* A course of plates at the keel.

**bilge ways**　*n.* Paths across which bilge blocks are placed when a vessel is about to be put in the dock.

**bilge well**　*n.* A sump into which bilge water drains.

**bill**　*n.* (1) The pointed end of the arm of an anchor that first digs into the ground when the anchor is dropped. See ANCHOR. (2) An assignment of duties such as the watch, quarter, and station bill. (3) A narrow promontory (chiefly U.K.).

**billboard**　*n.* The vertical protective plate against which an anchor is housed; the billboard is continguous with the hawsepipe. See ANCHOR BED.

**billet**   *n.* (1) An assigned place in which to sleep. (2) An individual's assigned duties.

**billethead**   *n.* The ornamentation at the top of the stem. The scroll on the billethead turned aft or inward, as opposed to the fiddlehead, which turned outward.

**bill of entry**   *n.* Document given to a customs entry clerk by a merchant importing and exporting merchandise that gives an inventory of goods entered at the customhouse.

**bill of health**   *n.* Certification of the state of the health in the port from which a vessel has come. Also *certificate of pratique.*

**bill of lading (B/L)**   *n.* A negotiable instrument that is prima facie evidence of the shipment of goods on board a particular vessel. Its legal importance lies in the fact that it is a receipt for goods, a contract for transportation, and a title to the property. A clean bill of lading has no exceptions as to the condition of the merchandise. An unclean bill of lading with a letter of indemnity is illegal. A **straight bill of lading** is used when the consignee becomes the owner of the goods prior to the carrier and the goods are shipped directly to the consignee named in the B/L. The straight B/L is nonnegotiable, and is the usual document for shipment of munitions to a foreign power engaged at war. A **to order bill of lading** (previously called an ocean bill of lading) is a negotiable instrument and, because it permits full flexibility of negotiation, is more common. It is made "to order" or "order of" a person, bank, or firm, or to the order of the shipper so that the shipper retains title to the goods. A **uniform bill of lading** states that a carrier has received certain goods that the carrier agrees to transport and deliver to a designated person for such compensation as is agreed upon and such conditions as are indicated. A **through bill of lading** is one that covers a shipment through its final destination; such B/L's place the entire responsibility on the primary carrier, even after the carrier has passed the goods on to another carrier, such as a truck or railway. A **shipped bill of lading** is used only after the goods have actually been shipped on board the vessel. The **received for shipment bill of lading** is less specific and offers less security than the shipped B/L, the standard document. While both are negotiable, bankers are less inclined to accept the received for shipment B/L. An **export bill of lading** covers goods destined for foreign markets, as opposed to a **domestic bill of lading,** which covers only domestic traffic.

**bill of stores**   *n.* (1, U.S.) A customs license granted a merchant ship to carry stores and provisions for a voyage duty-free. (2, U.K.) A license permitting reimportation of goods that have been exported from the United Kingdom within five years.

**bill of sufferance**   *n.* Permission from customs to land and load dutiable goods at sufferance wharfs while engaged in coastal shipping.

**bimini**   *n.* Any awning over the cockpit and other open areas of powerboats and sailboats. See AWNING.

**binder**   *n.* A brief note from an insurance company that indicates the nature of the risk, the voyage, cargo, and so on, and initialed by the insurer. The policy is written from a copy of the binder, but the insured is covered per the terms of the binder even if he or she does not receive the policy by the time the binder takes effect.

**binding**   *n.* Steel support around deadeyes and blocks.

**binding strake**   *n.* (1) On wooden ships, a longitudinal timber running outboard a line of hatches and notched to accommodate the beams. (2) An especially heavy strake.

**binge**   *v.* To soak and rinse a wooden cask in which food or drink has been kept.

**binnacle**   *n.* The pedestal and case in which the gimbaled compass is kept on deck. The meaning has broadened to include the nonmagnetic stand on which the compass, compass light, the Flinders bar, and the compensating spheres or magnets, and, sometimes, the steering wheel are found.

**binnacle cover**   *n.* A canvas hood or metal cover, often stainless steel, that protects the compass from exposure when not in use.

**binnacle light**   *n.* Red light fitted over the compass to make the compass legible after dark. The light must be red so as not to temporarily destroy the night vision of anyone looking at the compass.

**binnacle list**   *n.* The list of men excused from regular duties by the medical officer and, originally, placed on the binnacle for the officer of the watch. Men on the list are referred to as **top yard men.**

**bioluminescence**   *n.* The scientific name for the phenomenon popularly known by the misnomer "phosphorescence" or "phosphorus" in seawater. It is frequently seen in warm waters of the southern latitudes at night when the movement of propellers, fish, or people swimming all light up the surrounding water. The light is emitted from living marine organisms in the sea.

**bird cage**   *n.* Slang term for the air control officer's island on a carrier.

**bird farm**   *n.* Slang term, especially among the black shoe Navy, for an aircraft carrier.

**bird's nest**   *n.* A foothold above the crows's nest where a lookout could climb for a better look.

**bisquine**   *n.* (pron. beess-keen) A French lug-rigged fishing boat with two or three masts, the foremast of which is placed in the eyes abaft the bowsprit. The tonnage varies between 30 and 40 tons.

**bite**   *n.* The short end of a rope sling; the long end is passed through the sling before it is hooked to the cargo whip.

**bite**   *v.* Said of an anchor when it grabs the seafloor.

**bitt**   *n.* (1) An assembly of short metal columns (usually two) mounted on a baseplate attached to the deck for the purpose of securing wire ropes, hawsers, and so on, that are used to tie a vessel to a pier or tug boat. (2) A frame composed of one or two upright pieces of timber, called pins, and a crosspiece, fastened horizontally near their heads; they are used to belay cable and rope. The **cable** or **riding bitts** are the largest and are those to which the cable is **bitted** when the vessel is at anchor. USCG terminology calls them a cruciform and a double cruciform.

**bitt**   *v.* To take a turn on a bitt to maintain control but not to stop it or cleat it.

**bitter end**   *n.* (1) The end of a rope, cable, or anchor chain. (2) The end that might be bent on a bitt, thus the term.

**bitt pin**   *n.* The crosspiece of a bitt that is used for preventing the cable from leaving the bitt while it is being veered.

**bitumastic enamel**   *n.* Bituminous covering used to protect structural steel from corrosion over long periods when such members are difficult to reach.

***Black Book of the Admiralty***   *n.* The earliest codification of admiralty law when the English Admiralty adopted the Laws of Oleron in 1336. Oleron was an island owned by Eleanor of Aquitane, Queen of Henry II and mother of Richard I; the island was populated largely

# Bitts and Cleats

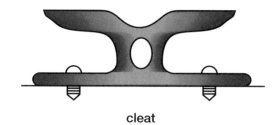

cleat

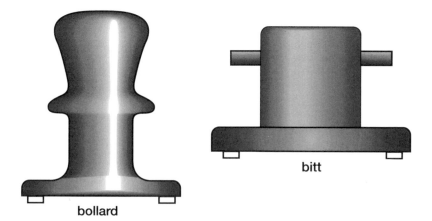

bollard

bitt

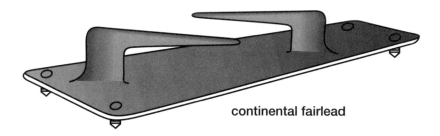

continental fairlead

by seafarers. The laws developed were similar to, and undoubtedly derived from, the Mediterranean Rhodian Law and were brought to Oleron in 1190.

**black can buoy**   *n.* Marker that resembles a large can, is painted black, and marks the left side of the channel entering from seaward and, in Region B countries, obstructions that should be kept to port. The opposing markers are red nun buoys. Black cans have been replaced by green buoys.

**black double-cone topmarks**   *n.* The most important of the cardinal marks indicating the best channel or best water by configuration of cones. A north mark has the points of both cones pointing up; this means to go north of the mark. A west mark has the points together, and looks like a wine glass. East, the cones point away from each other, and for south both points point down.

**black double-sphere topmark**   *n.* The most significant feature of an isolated danger mark by day, the cardinal marks. These are two large black spheres in an over-and-under configuration and clearly separated.

**black down**   *phr.* To rub a mixture of pine tar and coal into a hemp rope to preserve it against the elements.

**black flag**   *n.* (obsolete) A race committee flag indicating a boat had crossed the starting line prematurely and was disqualified; the flag was discontinued because it could not be seen at night.

**black gang**   *n.* Unlicensed or enlisted members of the engine room force. The still-prevalent term originated in the coaling days when they were quite literally black from coal dust.

**blacking**   *n.* The mixture of pine tar and coal used to black down hemp for preserving it against the weather and rot.

**black jack**   *n.* (1) Sailors' nickname for bubonic plague. (2) The apocryphal pirate flag; if it was ever flown, it is supposed to have had a black background and a scull and crossbones.

**black oil**   See NAVY STANDARD FUEL OIL.

**black shoe**   *n.* Slang for U.S. Naval officers on surface ships. Surface vessel officers did not wear khakis or brown shoes until World War II. To say an officer was "very black shoe" was to say that he was conservative, Old Navy, not sympathetic toward submariners and aviators who were allowed to wear brown shoes. See BROWN SHOE.

**black strake**   *n.* In old wooden ships, the boundary for topside painting at the upper edge of the wales. It was distinctive because it was covered with pitch.

**black stream**   *n.* Sailor's name for the Kuroshio.

**blackwall hitch**   *n.* A simple but effective way of attaching rope to a hook so that the heavier the load, the tighter the hitch.

**blade area**   *n.* The surface of the face or after side of a propeller.

**blanket**   *v.* (1) To take the wind out of the sails of another boat by moving to a windward position. The leeward boat is said to be "blanketed." (2) To cancel or obscure a weak radio signal by a stronger radio signal.

**blast**   *n.* A whistle signal used for navigation communication between vessels. A short blast is about one second's duration; a long blast lasts from 4 to 6 seconds. The danger signal is five or more short blasts and takes precedence over radio signals. (The whistle is the device that makes the sound and not the sound itself.)

**bleed**  *v.* To slowly draw off, via **bleeder valves,** liquids or gases either to reduce pressure or to remove gas or liquid that would prevent the system from functioning properly.

**bleeders**  *n.* Plugs placed in the bottom of a ship that may be removed to allow easy escape of water and other fluid material when the vessel is put in dry dock. Also *dry-docking plugs.*

**bleeding**  *n.* The breaking down of bags of grain or similar material into bulk cargo to allow more economical storage.

**blind buckler**  *n.* A plug for the hole in the deck through which the anchor cable leads to the anchor. The plug was necessary when the ship was underway to keep water from flushing the decks through the unplugged hole. Also *hawsepipe plug.*

**blind hatch**  *n.* An opening leading to a 'tween deck space with no opening to the next deck above.

**blind hole**  *n.* A hole in one of two pieces of plating to be riveted together with no hole in the second piece of plating. See FAIR.

**blind rollers**  *n.* Heavy and possibly dangerous swells caused by water motion reaching steeply shoaled water.

**blind sector**  *n.* An area on a radar scope in which echoes cannot be received because of an obstruction between the antenna and the object such as a stack or a tall building close aboard.

**blink**  *n.* Reflected sunlight over white sand, ice, or snow. It appears as a heavy haze in the distance.

**blinker, yardarm**  *n.* Signal lamp on a yardarm or spreader that is keyed from the signal bridge.

**blinker tube**  *n.* The tube that directs the signal light for transmission of code

from one vessel to another or between a vessel and a shore station.

**blip**  *n.* An echo that registers on sonar or radar. Also *pip.*

**blister**  *n.* (1) An additional outer skin or hull over the waist of a vessel to improve transverse stability. (2) Bulge or extra skin with tank capacity inside used on warships for added protection from mines and torpedoes. The resulting tank can be flooded or pumped as needed for stability or other requirements.

**blizzard**  *n.* A violent, cold wind defined by the National Weather Service as "a wind of 32 miles per hour or higher, low temperatures, and sufficient snow in the air to reduce visibility to less than 500 feet." A **severe blizzard** has wind speeds exceeding 45 miles per hour with temperatures near or below 10°F., and visibility reduced to near zero.

**block**  *n.* A device with a roller through which a rope or chain is rove for moving an object. The block is made up of the **shell** (or frame), one or more **sheaves** (pulleys), a **pin** that acts as the axis for the sheave(s), and a **strap** (or **strop**) that goes around the shell to hold the parts together. A **block and tackle** is two or more blocks with the necessary rope rove through them. The part of the rope that is stationary and extends to the first moving block from the fixed end is called the **standing part.** That part to which the initial stress is applied is the **hauling part.** The **running part** is the section of rope that runs in the blocks.

**blockade**  *n.* An attempt by one belligerent nation to obstruct a port of another nation to prevent seaborne shipping and communication with that nation by neutrals. International law has long held that a belligerent nation must be on the spot to enforce the blockade and that paper blockades or declarations of intent are not binding on neutrals. Furthermore, the belligerent nation cannot apprehend or detain a vessel later because it is known that vessel ran the blockade. There are four types of blockade: (a) **wartime blockades**—under the laws of war, a belligerent nation is entitled to establish a blockade off the enemy coast and thus attempt to isolate the enemy; (b) **pacific blockades**—under international customary law, a state was entitled to blockade the enemy's coast with a pacific blockade as a reprisal in keeping with the initial offense; (c) **blockades for self-defense**—under the rules of international customary law a nation foresee-ing the need to blockade another nation for its self-defense could do so. The blockade of Cuba during the Cuban missile crisis was put in place under this doctrine; (d) **UN blockades**—under the UN Charter, the Security Council may determine the existence of a threat to the peace, breach of the peace, or act of aggression and may then decide what measures are to be taken to ensure or restore international peace and security.

**block-and-block**   See TWO-BLOCK.

**block coefficient**   *n.* Ratio of the total immersed volume of a vessel to the product of waterline length, beam, and draft.

**block correction**   *n.* A corrected reproduction of a small area of a nautical chart intended to be pasted on the chart it corrects. Also *chartlet*.

**blocking**   *n.* General word for any system of shores and blocks placed under a vessel's keel and bilges on the building berth of a dry dock.

**block off**   *v.* To wedge cargo when there is not enough to fill a hold so that it will not shift during heavy weather.

**blockship**   *n.* A sunken ship, intentionally or unintentionally, that blocks a harbor.

**block span**   *n.* A wire stretched between the two lower purchase blocks of lifeboat falls; the block span prevents twisting while the falls are rounded up.

**blood money**   *n.* Money paid to a **crimp** for kidnapping or otherwise ensnaring men on the street and delivering them to a shipmaster for crew.

**blooper**   *n.* A lightweight overlapping headsail used when running or racing.

**blow down**   *v.* (1) To force water from a tank or boiler with compressed air. (2) To be driven by the wind.

## Block

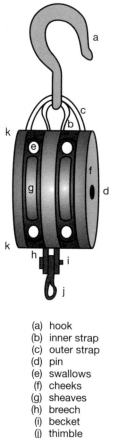

(a) hook
(b) inner strap
(c) outer strap
(d) pin
(e) swallows
(f) cheeks
(g) sheaves
(h) breech
(i) becket
(j) thimble
(k) shell

**blower** *n.* Fan used to ventilate living spaces, to force-feed air for boilers, and to ventilate engine spaces that may have explosive gases prior to starting engines.

**blow tubes** *phr.* To force steam through the fireside of the boilers to remove accumulated soot. Illegal in most ports, this is usually done by dark of night or when steaming alone. The expression "to blow your stack" comes from this operation.

**bluebacks** *n.* Privately published charts backed in blue used by coastal fishermen and yachtsmen in the United Kingdom.

**blue ensign** *n.* One of the national flags of United Kingdom; the blue ensign is flown by ships belonging to colonial services of state and vessels under government orders. Merchant ships whose masters are officers in the Naval Reserve and manned by a crew of at least 10 men of the Naval Reserve are allowed to fly the blue ensign.

**bluejacket** *n.* U.S. Navy sailor below chief petty officer. Also *swab jockey; white hat.* See TAR.

**Bluejacket's Manual** *n.* The basic training manual for enlisted personnel in the U.S. Navy. It was first prepared in 1902 by Lieutenant Ridley McLean, USN, and has been continually updated.

**blue light** *n.* A pyrotechnic light used by pilot boats to attract the attention of passing vessels entering port.

**blue magnetism** *n.* The magnetism displayed by the south-seeking pole (the **blue pole**) of a magnet; opposite of "red magnetism."

**bluenose** *n.* (1) A Nova Scotia native or seaman; from the name of a purplish potato peculiar to Nova Scotia. Many Nova Scotia ships and small boats have been named *Bluenose.* (2) Name given to anyone who has been north of the Arctic Circle.

**blue peter** *n.* International signal pennant that meant a ship was ready to sail; it is a blue flag with a white square center, now called Papa in the phonetic spelling system, but previously called Peter. British sailors called it the salt horse in anticipation of their meals at sea after departure.

**blue pigeon** *n.* Nickname for a hand lead.

**Blue Riband** *n.* A prize given to the ocean liner with the fastest transatlantic crossing. Begun in the 19th century when the development of larger, more powerful passenger ships was a matter of intense international rivalry and national pride, the Blue Riband was last won by the SS *United States,* which averaged 35.59 knots in 1952.

**blue-water** *adj.* Used to describe a sailor or boat that has offshore sailing experience; or an oceangoing navy.

**bluff** *n.* An almost perpendicular headland or cape.

**bluff-bowed** *adj.* Of a vessel with a full bow; opposite of fine or sharp-bowed. Also *bold-bowed.*

**board** *n.* (1) A windward tack or a leg when working to windward. Also *streth* (rare). (2) From its obsolete meaning, "side of a ship," comes a variety of expressions: **go by the board,** to go overboard, to escape from a ship by jumping over the side. To go or be **on board** or **aboard** is to enter a vessel or be in it. **Overboard** means simply "over the side."

**board** *v.* (1) To enter or go aboard a vessel whether invited or uninvited. (2) To hail and enter a vessel on official business to examine papers, cargo, and crew by health officers, customs, and other authorities.

**boardboat**  *n.* Any of a number of designs of small single-masted sailboats the hulls of which resemble surfboards. Also *sailboard.*

**board foot**  *n.* Lumberman's measure equivalent to a piece of timber 1 foot by 1 foot by 1 inch or 144 cubic inches. A thousand board feet is called a **mile** in the trade and is equal to $83\frac{1}{3}$ cubic feet.

**boarding book**  *n.* Notebook carried by a boarding officer to note details that he or she observes.

**boarding call**  *n.* A courtesy call between naval ships or other government ships either in domestic or foreign ports. The call is initiated by the ship with the highest ranking commanding officer, who sends a **boarding officer** junior to the commanding officer of the other ship. The purpose of the visit is to exchange information of mutual interest. Courtesy demands a return visit as quickly as possible.

**boarding clerk**  *n.* Company employee whose duty is to establish communication with company ships as they enter port.

**boarding inspector**  *n.* A government agent who boards a vessel as a representative of the Department of Agriculture, Customs, Immigration, or other agency.

**boarding netting**  *n.* (1) Netting rigged from the masts to the deck to prevent boarding. (2) Netting thrown over the side and rigged from the deck to the water to assist people climbing the sides.

**boarding officer**  *n.* Officer in charge of a boarding party when boarding another vessel in search for contraband or other material for war use.

**boarding party**  *n.* Group sent from one ship to another ship to inspect it for contraband or illegal activity.

**boarding pike**  *n.* A sharp-pointed weapon used to repel boarders from another ship.

**boarding station**  *n.* An anchorage where boarding inspectors are able to board. Vessels entering harbor "bring to" to allow inspectors to board.

**board the tack**  *phr.* To secure the tack-jigger to the weather clew of either the foresail or the mainsail and haul it down when sailing close-hauled.

**boat**  *n.* In general, a small craft that can be hoisted aboard a larger craft. However, boat is also used to refer to submarines, tugs and tow boats, steamboats, and a variety of vessels used on lakes and rivers as well as ferries and excursion vessels.

**boatage**  *n.* A line-handling charge; originally a charge for carrying lines ashore in a small boat.

**boat barn**  *n.* Submariner's slang for a submarine pen.

**boat boom**  *n.* A spar that can be swung out at right angles to a vessel to which small boats are secured by a **boat line** when a ship is at anchor or dead in the water. Also *swinging beam.*

**boat chock**  *n.* The wooden or steel deck support for a small boat that conforms to the hull shape of the boat, used when a boat is stowed on deck.

**boat cloak**  *n.* An officer's cloak.

**boat cloth**  *n.* Canvas spread over the stern sheets for officer passengers.

**boat crutch**  See ROWLOCKS.

**boat davit**  *n.* Small derrick used for hoisting a boat and for securing a boat when it is not expected to be needed. See DAVIT.

**boat deck** *n.* The deck on which lifeboats are kept. It is usually above the main deck and is often a partial deck. On passenger liners and most other ships, it is the deck above the one from which passengers and crew would climb into lifeboats in an emergency.

**boat drill** *n.* Practice for passengers and crew in using life jackets, finding abandon-ship stations, and lowering and entering lifeboats. With passenger ships, the passengers do not ordinarily practice entering lifeboats, but simply assemble at their lifeboat station and find out who their lifeboat officer is. Boat drills are also required aboard nonpassenger Merchant Marine, Coast Guard, and Navy ships.

**boat drill signal** *n.* Six or more short blasts and a long blast on the ship's whistle followed by the same combination on the general alarm. One blast on the whistle tells boat crews to launch boats. Three short blasts tell all participants they are dismissed from the drill.

**boat fall** *n.* A purchase of two blocks and a length of rope for hoisting a boat to its davits. Also *davit fall.*

**boat gong** *n.* A signal used to indicate the arrivals and departures of officers' boats.

**boat gripes** *n.* Lashings used to hold a boat in place in its davits against a longitudinal timber called a strongback. See GRIPE.

**boat group** *n.* The basic unit of landing craft in an amphibious operation.

**boat-handling signals** *n.* A ship's whistle signals used to control handling of lifeboats at sea.

**boat hook** *n.* An aluminum or wooden pole with a hook at the end to help fend off from piers and other obstacles, and to pull lines toward the boat. On western rivers the boat hook is called a **pike pole.**

**boat keg** *n.* A cask kept filled with water on a lifeboat. See BREAKER.

**boat lamp** *n.* A lifeboat lamp showing a 32-point white light with reservoir sufficient to sustain a flame for 8 hours. These are constructed of nonmagnetic metal.

**boat lashing** *n.* Any configuration of ropes used to secure a small boat in boat chocks. See BOAT CHOCK.

**boat plan** *n.* Drawing that shows frame lines and elevations. Different from "plan view" in marine architecture, which is the view "from the top."

**boat plug** *n.* Tapered plug placed in the drain hole of a small boat to keep water from entering.

**boat-propeller gear** *n.* A mechanism that went the full length of a lifeboat on both sides that enabled passengers unaccustomed to rowing to be able to assist in propelling the lifeboat. With a pair of levers at each thwart, passengers on both sides were able to help turn a propeller when no other power source was available.

**boat rations** *n.* Rations required to be kept on lifeboats at all times while a vessel is at sea.

**boat recall pennant** *n.* A prearranged signal flag that recalls small boats to a ship, usually accompanied by a sound signal.

**boats** *n.* Traditional nickname for a boatswain.

**boat skate** *n.* A fender fitted on a lifeboat that is designed to help slide a lifeboat down the side of a listing hull.

**boat skids** *n.* Deck device for securing a boat on deck.

**boat sling** *n.* A rope or chain loop used under the bow and stern of a small boat to raise or lower it to the water. At the bow, the sling attaches to a ringbolt, while the stern sling is fastened to a plate on the keel.

**boat stands**   *n.* Cast-iron columns that support boat chocks on a boat deck to allow easier passage inboard of the boats. These are not as elaborate as davits, since they only hold the chocks.

**boat station**   *n.* Assigned position at a lifeboat for a member of the crew or a passenger. This assignment is posted on a **boat stations bill.** The station usually goes with the berthing areas and is posted inside the door of each cabin.

**boatswain**   *n.* (pron. bosun) A warrant officer or petty officer in charge of the ship's deck crew and equipment. In the U.S. Navy, a boatswain is a chief warrant officer or warrant officer, and subordinate petty officers who supervise the deck force are **boatswain's mates.**

**boatswain's chair**   *n.* A board with appropriate tackle on which members of the crew are hoisted aloft or let over the side for work on the ship. It is also used to swing a man across open water to another ship.

**boatswain's chest** (or **locker**)   *n.* A locker used for stowing boatswain's stores such as marlinespikes, rigging screws, marline, and so on.

**boatswain's mate**   *n.* Petty officer who supervise the deck force aboard a naval vessel.

**boatswain's pipe** (or **call**)   *n.* A small shrill whistle used by boatswain's mates for signaling changes in watch, general quarters, taps, and various duties, and for piping ranking officers and dignitaries over the side.

**boat tackle**   *n.* A purchase consisting of two blocks doubled or tripled and a length of rope for handling lifeboats.

**boat team**   *n.* Personnel assigned to a single amphibious vessel or vehicle for ship-to-shore movement during an amphibious operation.

**boat winch**   *n.* An electric winch used for handling lifeboats. Also *boat hoist.*

**boatwright**   *n.* A person who builds or repairs boats.

**bob a light**   *phr.* To quickly raise and lower one's head and the height of eye to determine if the observer is at the geographic range of a light when first observed.

**bobbin shaft**   *n.* Shafting sometimes fitted near the after end of the drive tunnel to facilitate withdrawal of the propeller shaft for inspection.

**bobstay**   *n.* The chain, steel bar, or wire from stem to the bowsprit used to counteract the upward pull of the headstay. It is similar to a martingale, which is outside of the bobstay. See SQUARE-RIGGED VESSEL.

**bodkin**   *n.* A sailmaker's tool for piercing holes in a sail.

**body plan**   *n.* A drawing that shows transverse frame lines in elevation.

**boggin line**   *n.* A chain with a wire pendant shackled on both sides of the rudder horn to be used for steering in case of an accident to the steering mechanism.

**boiler**   *n.* A steam generator on a vessel that provides steam for propulsion and heat. The two principal types are the Scotch marine boiler, also known as a fire-tube boiler, and the cross-drum water-tube boiler.

**boiler capacity**   *n.* The maximum output in horsepower of which a boiler is capable. Maritime practice is to base the capacity on 10 square feet of heating surface per horsepower.

**boiler casing** *n.* The trunk that extends above the boiler and through decks and superstructure to allow removal and replacement of the boiler and space for stacks and ventilator ducts. See BOILER HATCH.

**boiler chock** *n.* A block of steel welded to the boiler foundation to keep the boiler firmly in place in the event the foundation bolts shear.

**boiler efficiency** *n.* Ratio of heat transmitted to the water in the boiler to the total heat produced in the firebox.

**boiler foundation** *n.* Boiler foundation welded to a vessel's structure.

**boiler hatch** *n.* A hatch over the boiler room fitted around the stacks and uptake from the boiler. It is usually made large enough for the removal and installation of boilers.

**boiler horsepower (HP)** *n.* One HP traditionally equals the power generated by the evaporation of 34.5 pounds of water per hour at 212°F.

**boilermaker** *n.* An unlicensed member of the crew on large ships who is assigned to boiler repair duties.

**boiler stool** *n.* One of several cradles consisting of vertical plating and angle iron used to support a cylindrical boiler.

**boiler technician (BT)** *n.* A petty officer who oversees the maintenance of necessary steam pressure in ships powered by steam and who supervises the engine room watch. Formerly **water tender.**

**boil-off** *n.* The vaporization of liquid natural gas (LNG) or other gases when high pressure is applied with severe cooling. This problem is encountered with specially built LNG carriers.

**bola line** *n.* A heaving line with two padded weights, or monkey's fists, thrown

from one ship to another or to a pier; a larger line is tied to the heaving line so that it can be pulled after the heaving line.

**bold hawse** *n.* A ship is said to have a bold hawse when the hawse is well above the waterline near the forecastle deck.

**bold shore** *n.* A steep coastline, one that can be approached closely without grounding. Such a coastline is said to be **bold-to.**

**boll** *n.* A half-decked Dutch fishing boat used on the Zuider Zee, gaff-rigged with fore-and-aft sails, a single mast, main topsail and jib foresail.

**bollard** *n.* A single iron or steel post or double vertical steel posts on a pier to which ships' mooring lines are secured. Double bollards are sometimes raked away from each other. See BITT.

**bollard cleat** *n.* A combination bollard and cleat for warping and mooring vessels at a pier.

**bolster** *n.* Any piece of soft wood or other soft material used between a piece of rope and the hull, mast, or other equipment to prevent chafing.

**bolster plate** *n.* A doubling plate around a hawse hole that protects the deck plating from the anchor cable.

**bolter** *n.* (1) A person who assembles parts with bolts in a shipyard. (2) An aircraft that misses the arresting gear when attempting to land on a carrier deck and takes off again for another try.

**bolter-up** *n.* A person who aligns rivet holes with bars, jacks, and drift pins and temporarily bolts the plates together. Also *plater.*

**boltrope** *n.* A rope to which the edges of a sail are sewn to strengthen them and prevent their splitting. That part of a boltrope that is on the sides of a square sail is called the **leech rope,** that at the top, the **headrope,** and that at the bottom, the **footrope.** On triangular sails, the boltropes are named after the leech, luff, and foot.

**boltrope needle**   *n.* A curved needle used for sewing boltropes on sails and awnings. See SAIL NEEDLE.

**bombard**   *n.* A name for the earliest cannon, from the 15th century.

**bombard**   *v.* To attack with bombs or to shell with artillery.

**bomb farm**   *n.* Stockpile of bombs used for rearming aircraft on a carrier.

**bombing range**   *n.* A mapped area of land or a charter area of water showing the limits of a range available for bombing practice along with the airspace above the area.

**Bonaventure mizzen**   *n.* The fourth mast and sail on four-masted ships from about the 15th to the 17th centuries. Both the third (mizzen) and fourth (Bonaventure mizzen) masts were lateen-rigged

**bond**   *v.* To protect vessels from electrical discharge and possible sparks; especially important for tankers and other vessels carrying flammable or explosive material, such as flour.

**bonded stores**   *n.* Ship's stores delivered under special license or bond from a bonded warehouse to a vessel without paying duty and which may not be consumed until the vessel is in international waters.

**bonded value**   *n.* A marine insurance term, the gross market value of goods sold "in bond" and not requiring duty.

**bonded value clause**   *n.* A maritime underwriter's policy clause in which the underwriter agrees to adjust claims for particular average of the gross value on arrival at destination, less duty, instead of including duty.

**bonded warehouses**   *n.* A privately owned or public storage facility licensed for storage of dutiable merchandise until such time as duty is paid and the merchandise is removed, or it is transferred under bond.

**bond note**   *n.* A form required by customs before dutiable goods can be transferred or transported from a bonded warehouse. Also *customs warrant.*

**bone**   *n.* Froth at the bow where it meets the sea. A ship going at great speed is said to have "a bone in her teeth."

**bonnet**   *n.* Additional sail laced to the foot of a square sail or a jib. A bonnet on a triangular sail is called a **studsail** (which should not be confused with a studding sail).

**booby hatch**   *n.* (1) A hood covering the aftermost hatch. The booby hatch covers a lazarette or aftermost locker. (2) An access hatch leading from a weather deck into the accommodations for passengers and crew. (3) A small hatchway used for going from one compartment to another without removing a main hatch.

**boom**   *n.* (1) A general-purpose word for a spar. Boats are secured to booms out over the water; a sail is secured at the foot on a boom as distinguished from a yard or a gaff from which quadrilateral sails are suspended. See GAFF; MARCONI RIG. (2) Any device used as a barrier to contain pollutants, logs, or other materials in one area.

**boom ballasting**   *n.* System of ballasting sailing vessels by securing ballast to booms out over the side of the vessel in port while loading and unloading. The boom is supported on the vessel by a chain or topping lift.

**boom band** *n.* Narrow sleeve at the outer end of a boom to which a sheet block can be attached.

**boom cleat** *n.* Cleat on a boom used for reefing.

**boom crutch** (or **crotch**) *n.* A frame on which a boom rests when not in use. Also *gallows*—a permanent structure.

**boomer** *n.* Slang term for a ballistic missile submarine.

**boom guy** *n.* A steadying rope or tackle used for steadying a spanker boom when running free.

**boom horse** *n.* Curved bar at the outer end of a boom on which the sheet block rides and that acts as a traveler for the sheet block.

**boom irons** *n.* Two flat steel rings formed into a single fitting used to connect studding sail booms to the yards. **Quarter-boom irons** are secured to the yard with a clamp.

**boom jack** or **boom vang** *n.* Any device used to hold the boom down or stationary when handling cargo or when sailing on a reach or a run; it also serves to prevent an accidental jibe on sailboats. Some authorities make a distinction between the boom jack and the boom vang, with the boom jack being used to exert a downward force on the boom, and the vang being used specifically to prevent the boom's lifting while a sailboat is reaching or running.

**boom jigger** *n.* The tackle used to get the studding sail booms out. Also *boom tackle.*

**boomkin** (or **bumpkin**) *n.* Spar projecting from the stern to which is secured a backstay, jigger, mizzen, or main brace.

**boom off** *v.* To hold a vessel away from a pier or mole by means of heavy logs or booms.

**booms** *n.* The space between the foremast and mainmast in which the boats and spare spars were stowed.

**boom saddle** *n.* The device on which the boom rests at the mast when there is no gooseneck.

**boom table** *n.* A heavy steel structure near the base of a mast that supports cargo booms and gives sufficient clearance when a number of booms are working from the same mast.

**boom vang** See BOOM JACK.

**boot** *n.* A U.S. Navy recruit, so called until he or she finishes boot camp. The usage came about during the Spanish-American War when sailors started wearing leggings especially at "boot camp."

**boot top** *n.* (1) A stripe of hard, slick paint just above the waterline that serves the purpose of indicating if the boat is riding lower than normal. (2) Hard black paint applied to hatch coamings where scuff marks would otherwise appear.

**boot topping** *n.* The surface of the outer plating between the light and load lines.

**bora** *n.* A violent, cold katabatic wind that spills suddenly out of a mountain and comes down on the sea on the Dalmatian coast of the Aegean during the winter season. See TRAMONTANA.

**borasco** *n.* A thunderstorm or violent squall, especially in the Mediterranean.

**borderland** *n.* A coastal area usually adjacent to a continent, normally associated with a shelf, but highly irregular with depths considerably greater than those of a shelf. Also *continental borderland.*

**bore**   *n.* The inside of a gun barrel from the after end of the rifling to the muzzle. See TIDAL BORE.

**bore**   *v.* To force a vessel through a field of light ice using either sail or power.

**borrow**   *v.* To move in closer to a shore.

**boss**   *n.* (1) The rounded hub of the propeller. (2) The rounded section of the stern of a vessel at the propeller shaft. (3) The center cap of a compass card that rests on the pivot.

**boss frame**   *n.* A side frame that is bent to clear the stern tube.

**bossing**   *n.* The thicker part of an anchor shank where the stock goes through the shank.

**boss plate**   *n.* The shell plate that covers the curved portion of the hull where the propeller shaft passes through the hull.

**bosun**   See BOATSWAIN.

**bottle rigging screw**   *n.* A turnbuckle with either a single screw at one end and a set eye or swivel at the opposite end, or with a screw at both ends.

**bottom**   *n.* (1) A vessel's hull from keel plates to turn of the bilge. (2) The entire bottom of a hull up to the waterline. To coat the bottom with red lead would be to paint red lead from the bottom of the keel to the boot top at the waterline. (3) The ground under a body of water, any ground covered by water.

**bottom**   *v.* Submarine term meaning to lie on the ocean floor.

**bottom boards**   *n.* Removable grating in the bottom of a small, open boat.

**bottom characteristics**   *n.* Designations used on surveys and marine charts to indicate the consistency, color, and classification such as rocky, mud, shale, and so on.

**bottom contour chart**   *n.* Charts published by the Defense Mapping Agency Hydrographic/Topographic Center that show depths in contour lines very much as topographic maps of land give heights.

**bottom log**   *n.* Early term for speed logs fixed to the bottom of a vessel when patent logs were still towed behind the ship to determine a vessel's speed.

**bottom pintle**   *n.* The lowest pintle on a rudder. Because it supports the rudder, it is a heavier fitting than other pintles.

**bottomry**   *n.* An emergency mortgage on a vessel and cargo that must be paid in an established number of days after the vessel reaches its destination. If the vessel is lost, the lender loses the money and the interest. The practice is almost unheard of today with radio communication: a captain simply notifies the owner and the owner arranges for repairs and financing. See RESPONDENTIA.

**bottomry bond**   *n.* The document the master of a vessel signs for a bottomry loan that establishes penalties, and so on.

**bottomry lien**   *n.* Lien against a vessel established by a bottomry bond. A bottomry lien is subordinate to liens for crew's wages, master's wages, freight, and so on.

**bottom shell**   *n.* The plating on the bottom of a ship.

**bottom strakes**   *n.* Planking on the bottom from garboard to bilge strakes.

**bouncer line**   *n.* The imaginary line off an enemy beach at which underwater demolition teams (UDTs) are launched in their rubber rafts.

**bound** *adj.* (1) Condition of a vessel such as fogbound, tidebound, or icebound. (2) A condition that keeps a vessel in port, such as **bound wind** or **bound tide,** an adverse wind (or tide) that prevents a vessel from sailing in an intended direction.

**boundary angle bar** *n.* Any bar that fastens a bulkhead to the hull, deck, or another bulkhead.

**boundary disclaimer** *n.* A declaration on a chart advising that an international boundary is not necessarily recognized by the state publishing the chart.

**boundary layer** *n.* A layer of water next to the hull that is carried along as a vessel goes through the water.

**boundary lines of inland water** *n.* The lines on a marine chart that divide the high seas from rivers, harbors, and inland waters and that indicate the area in which the Inland Rules apply and the area in which the International Rules apply. On U.S. charts, these are called COLREGS Demarcation Lines.

**boundary plank** *n.* Especially dense hardwood planking used around hatches, coaming, casings, and so on, where the wood comes into contact with metal; hardwoods resist rust and corrosion from metal better than less dense woods.

**boundary (or internal) waves** *n.* Subsurface waves between layers of water of different densities. While surface waves caused by wind action rarely reach more than 60 feet from trough to crest, boundary waves often reach 300 feet.

**bounty** *n.* A reward given by a government or a private individual or company for benefits received, especially a reward given by a government for reenlistment or for capturing an enemy ship.

**bouquet mine** *n.* A collection of several buoyant mines secured to the same anchor, so that if a minesweeper's equipment cuts one case loose, another rises to a predetermined depth.

**bow** *n.* The forward part of a vessel or aircraft. British usage is somewhat different and refers more to the sides and is often spoken of in the plural: "The bows of the ship." See RELATIVE BEARING; STEM.

**bow and beam bearings** *n.* A method of determining a vessel's position by observing a fixed object of known position when it lies 45° off the bow, then determining the distance from the vessel to the object when the object is abeam. The distance run between the two points of observation is the distance to the object from the second point of observation. See DOUBLING THE ANGLE ON THE BOW.

**bow breast mooring** *n.* A permanent mooring using a chain from the bow to an anchor.

**Bowditch** *n.* The common name for *The New Practical Navigator* by Nathaniel Bowditch (1773–1838). Originally published in 1799 and revised the following year, this was actually a corrected edition of the leading navigational text of the day, John Moore's *The Practical Navigator.* Bowditch then decided that a completely new work should be written and in 1802 the first edition of his *The New American Practical Navigator* was published. As well as including an improved method of determining longitude, the new book contained information on winds, currents, tides, a glossary of terms, marine insurance statistics, directions for surveying, instruction in mathematics, and the extensive tables of navigational data Bowditch had developed. Bowditch paved the way for American supremacy of the seas and was without question the father of modern navigational methods. His two-volume *American Practical Navigator* is continually updated. It is now published by the Defense Mapping Agency Hydrographic/

Topographic Center and is basic to any marine library at sea or ashore.

**bower**   *n.* One of the two anchors carried on the bow, one on each side of the stem. See BEST BOWER.

**bowgrace**   *n.* A frame of old rope laid around the bow, stern, and sides to prevent damage, as on tugboats. Also *pudding* or *puddening.*

**bow insignia**   *n.* Pennants, flags, stars, and so on, displayed at the bow of a gig or barge.

**bow lighthouse**   *n.* A steel housing for sidelights on each side of the forecastle. Also *sidelight castles.*

**bow line**   *n.* A mooring line led through a bow chock and led forward from the vessel to a cleat or bollard on a pier. See MOORING LINE.

**bowline**   *n.* Called the "king of knots" because it forms a loop that does not slip and also does not jam. See KNOT.

**bowline-bridle**   *n.* Ropes attached to the cringles on the leeches of square sails and to the bowlines.

**bowline-on-a-bight**   *n.* A bowline made using the doubled line when extra strength is needed or when the end of the line is not available. See KNOT.

**bowlines**   *n.* The ropes fastened to the bowline-bridles on the leech (or sides) of a square sail. Bowlines are used to extend the windward edges of the sails forward to prevent shivering when the wind is unfavorable. See SQUARE-RIGGED VESSEL.

**bowman**   *n.* The forwardmost oarsman and one who handles forward lines when approaching a boat or pier. Also *bow hook.*

**bow number**   *n.* The number painted on the bow of U.S. Navy ships.

**bow port**   *n.* An opening in the bow of sailing ships that carried lumber which allowed logs to be loaded into the hull lengthwise.

**bow roller**   *n.* A roller at the bow over which an anchor cable is led.

**bow rudder**   *n.* A rudder fitted at the bow of vessels such as ferries to make the reverse passage less awkward.

**bowse (or bouse)**   *v.* To hoist or pull with block and tackle.

**bowser boat**   *n.* A fuel craft used for refueling boats, aircraft, and vehicles.

**bowsing tackle**   *n.* Usually a twofold purchase (two sheaves in each block) equipped with a cleat adjacent to the floating block of each boat fall, used primarily in launching and recovering lifeboats.

**bows-on**   *adv.* Heading directly.

**bowsprit**   *n.* A spar projecting from the stem or bow to which are attached forestay(s), allowing better support for the forward mast and making it possible to set more sail. A **running bowsprit** is one that can be run out to set additional sails. See JIBBOOM; SQUARE-RIGGED VESSEL.

**bowsprit bed**   *n.* Wedges placed at both sides of the bowsprit to hold it in place.

**bowsprit bitt**   *n.* The step for a bowsprit that is braced and secured to beams below decks.

**bowsprit cap**   *n.* The fitting over the forward end of the bowsprit into which the jibboom is stepped. Also *cranse; cranse iron.*

**bowsprit horses**   *n.* Timbers or footropes on which the crew tending the bowsprit and headsails can stand. Also *manropes.*

**bowsprit shroud**   *n.* A supporting cable led from the bowsprit cap back to the **bowsprit shroud plating.**

**bow thruster**   *n.* Athwartships tunnel below the waterline close to the bow fitted with a propeller that pushes water one way or the other to move the bow laterally. It makes maneuvering in close quarters more practical, often even eliminating the necessity for a tug. Some vessels have stern thrusters.

**bow wave**   *n.* The wave formed as the bow moves through water; it is a determining factor in the displacement and the hull speed.

**box**   *n.* (1) A space between the sternpost and the backboard of a rowboat where the coxswain sits. (2) An area kept vacant for carrier operations in a convoy of naval vessels. Usually the box is to the rear of the fleet or convoy in the commodore's column with empty stations on both sides; this allows room for a carrier to maneuver and launch aircraft into the wind and at the same time give other ships in the convoy a fighting chance to get out of the way, which was not always true before the box became accepted procedure.

**box engines**   *phr.* To have one engine going ahead and one astern.

**box haul**   *v.* To change tack in a square-rigger when close-hauled by backwinding the headsails when a vessel refuses to tack and there is not room to jibe.

**box-hearted timber**   *n.* Lumber so cut that the heart is still completely enclosed inside the full length, especially desirable for keels and masts.

**box hook**   *n.* A longshoreman's hook with a short wooden handle used for handling crates and boxes.

**box mold**   *n.* Built-up mold of wood used to obtain correct shape of a plate or a curved surface.

**box off**   *v.* (1) To ease the bow off the wind when a stay has parted. (2) To fall away from the wind making sternway by backing the headyards. (3) To backwind the headsails when a sudden windshift has put the vessel too far to windward. See BOX HAULING.

**box the compass** (or **box ship**)   *phr.* To name the 32 points of the compass, each point being $11\frac{1}{4}°$ in their order from north clockwise.

**boys' town**   *n.* Slang for junior officers' quarters aboard ship.

**brace**   *n.* A rope used to turn a yard or sail horizontally around a mast. Heavier yards were controlled by blocks through which the braces were rove. The mainbrace is the brace used at the mainmast. See SQUARE-RIGGED VESSEL.

**brace block**   *n.* The block through which the controlling brace, the **brace pendant,** is rove, with the fixed end spliced to the yardarm.

**brace boomkin**   *n.* A projection outboard both quarters of a square-rigger used for shackles controlling the mainbrace, the main lower topsail brace, and main upper topsail brace.

**brace in**   *v.* To rotate a yard to a position more nearly athwartship to run before the wind, or to run free.

**brace sharp**   *v.* To haul in the brace or braces to have a minimum angle with the keel, to be close-hauled, opposite of "to brace in." Also *brace square.*

**bracket**   *v.* To fire two salvos at a target, one on either side. The next salvos are corrections on the first two that, it is hoped, produce a **straddle** or a hit.

**brackish**  *adj.* Briny, said of a mixture of saltwater and freshwater, technically defined as being water with a saline content of 0.50 to 17.00 parts per thousand.

**braid**  *n.* (1)The gold braid on an officer's uniform, more properly, but rarely, called **gold lace.** (2) Rope that has been braided instead of twisted.

**brails**  *n.* Ropes passed through blocks on a gaff and fastened to the leech of a fore-and-aft sail to truss or brail it up.

**brail up**  *v.* To haul in on the brails to reduce sail.

**brake beam**  *n.* A handle on a manual pump windlass.

**brake horsepower (BHP)**  *n.* The power at the crankshaft as can be determined by a brake. Also *shaft horsepower (SHP).* See HORSEPOWER; INDICATED HORSEPOWER (IHP).

**brash**  *adj.* (1) Describes timber that does not splinter when stressed, usually a sign of rot. (2) Used to describe brittle ice easily broken through by a ship.

**brass**  *n.* Alloy of copper and zinc with smaller amounts of other metals such as manganese, nickel, lead, and tin. Brass is used on ships for drain plugs, nameplates, and so on

**brassard**  *n.* Cloth armbands such as worn by shore patrol or beach guard.

**brass hat**  *n.* An officer authorized to wear a hat with gold braid.

**brave west wind**  *n.* The strong and usually stormy winds that blow from the northwest and west-northwest between 60°S and 40°S. See ROARING FORTIES.

**Bravo**  *n.* The phonetic word for the letter "B." When used as a single-letter hoist, it means "I am taking in, or discharging, or carrying dangerous goods."

Bravo is flown during a fueling operation.

**bravo pattern**  *n.* Scheme for finding bottom contours in an area of less than 100 fathoms by bathythermograph; bravo refers to bottom and not the instrument used.

**Brazil Current**  *n.* That branch of the South Equatorial Current that follows the coast of Brazil and curves southward as a warm, highly saline current. See OCEAN CURRENT.

**breach**  *n.* A sea breaking over the sides of a vessel. A "clear breach" describes seas breaking all the way across the weather deck.

**breaching**  *n.* A Y-shaped pipe or stack that connects two boilers with one funnel.

**bread-and-butter model**  *n.* A model built up in horizontal layers and glued together.

**breadth**  *n.* A vessel's greatest width. **Molded breadth** is the distance between the outer faces of the frames. **Registered breadth** is measured between the outer faces of the shell plating.

**break**  *n.* The point at which a deck stops and steps lead to the lower or higher level.

**break**  *v.* (1) To display a flag or pennant hoisted and unfolded. (2) A new commanding officer "breaks his pennant" when he relieves or assumes command of a vessel. (3) Said of a sea when the waves topple over on the surf. A Beaufort force 7 with wind speed 28 to 33 knots is described as "Sea heaps up; white foam from breaking waves begins to be blown in streaks." See BREAKER.

**breakage**  *n.* (1) Lost space when cargo is stowed. Actual cargo stowed is never quite as much as measurement would project. The difference is breakage. (2) Allowance made for loss of merchandise in transit. (3) In bills of lading, goods broken due to unavoidable circumstances such as acts of God, and not attributable to carelessness or negligence on the part of the owner or those working for the owner.

**break bulk**    *phr.* To destroy the integrity of a ship's cargo as a unit by opening the sealed hatches and beginning discharge operations.

**break-bulk cargo**    *n.* Bales, boxes, and loose cargo. Term used to distinguish such commodities from bulk, tanker, or unitized or containerized loads.

**breakdown clause**    *n.* A charter party clause that suspends the contract if the vessel is delayed more than 24 hours as a result of inadequate crew, need for stores and provisions, engine malfunction, or other causes that constitute a reasonable obstacle to the proper operation of the vessel.

**breakdown lights**    *n.* (obsolete) Under the Rules of the Road, certain lights used when a vessel was not under command.

**breaker**    *n.* A wave that has become unstable and begins to topple forward. The three general classes of breaker are (a) a **spilling breaker,** which breaks gradually over a considerable distance; (b) a **plunging breaker,** which tends to curl over and break with a considerable crash; and (c) a **surging breaker,** which peaks up, but surges up the beach without spilling or plunging. (2) A cask, usually filled with water; often applied to the small barrels of water kept in a lifeboat. From the Spanish *bareca,* barrel.

**breakers**    See SHIP-BREAKER.

**break ground**    *phr.* Said of an anchor when it has broken loose from the bottom. See ATRIP; AWEIGH.

**break off**    *v.* To stop or discontinue.

**break out**    *v.* (1) To open or release, to make available. (2) To move cargo from a hold to the square under the hatch, stevedore's term. Also *unstow.* (3) Turn out a detail of men. (4) To release an anchor from the bottom. Also *break ground.*

**breakup clause**    *n.* Marine underwriters' term for a total loss claim. It has to do with whether a vessel is a constructive total loss or an actual total loss. The insured value is the repaired value.

**break sheer**    *phr.* To change relationship with the anchor when the current changes. If a ship riding to an anchor tends to port, and the tide changes so that the vessel is going to ride to a starboard anchor, it may break sheer and foul the anchor; with a little helm, it will change direction and ride to the anchor tending to starboard; then it is said to keep its sheer.

**breakwater**    *n.* (1) An embankment or emplacement, usually artificial, used to protect anchorages, harbors, and marinas. (2) A forward bulkhead on a vessel to prevent seas coming through the hawse pipe or over the bow from going aft, by sending them out through the scuppers. Also *manger board.*

**bream**    *v.* (1) To clean the barnacles and seaweed from a vessel's bottom by use of a blowtorch. (2) To clean a wooden ship's hull of barnacles and seaweed by firing the bottom enough to partially melt the tar so the bottom can be more easily scraped clean.

**breastband**    *n.* A belt worn by man heaving the lead in the chains; the belt is secured to the ship to prevent his falling overboard.

**breastbeam**    *n.* A timber at the break of a deck, usually poop or foredeck.

**breasthook**    *n.* A triangular gusset plate extending horizontally immediately abaft the stem for stiffening the stringers and stem. See COLLISION BULKHEAD.

**breast off**  *v.* To moor a vessel far enough from a pier that lighters and tenders can work between the vessel and pier; the vessel is held off with **breast-off spars.**

**breastplate**  *n.* Small plate between the bow chocks of the stem for strength and for stiffening. Also *stemhead plate.*

**breastrope**  *n.* (1) The line attached to a breastband used to secure the leadsman in the chains while he heaves the lead. (2) A docking line or mooring line led from a vessel perpendicular to the fore-and-aft line of the vessel. Also *breastline.* See MOORING LINE.

**breast the sea**  *phr.* To head straight into the waves. Also used in the sense to "make a clean breast of it" or to head through a difficult sea condition.

**breastwork**  *n.* (1) The rails and stanchions on the foremost end of the quarterdeck and stern. (2) Athwartship railing found at the break of the poop or the forecastle in old wooden ships. Also *breast rail.*

**breech**  *n.* (1) Larger end of the bore of a gun where new rounds are placed, opposite end from the muzzle; the area in a rifle or cannon into which the powder and shell or cartridge were loaded. With bagged-powder weapons it was vital for the gun captain to see or hear **clear breech** because a spark from the preceding shot could have prematurely set off the powder. (2) The part of a block opposite the swallow and farthest from the hook or eye. See BLOCK.

**breech block**  *n.* Locking device that seals the firing chamber before a round of ammunition is fired.

**breeches buoy**  *n.* Combination of buoy and canvas fitted with leg holds or short trousers for transferring personnel from ship to ship or ship to shore by using a highline with block and tackle to support the person in the breeches buoy.

**breeze**  *n.* Light air current technically defined as between 3.5 and 30 knots.

**Breton red**  *n.* A brownish red, the traditional color for sails on fishing boats that work off the coast of Brittany. The color has been adopted for yachtsmen's cotton clothing, especially trousers.

**bridge**  *n.* (1) The area of a vessel running athwartships from which the vessel is navigated or conned and from which visual signals are transmitted. The term "bridge" arose from the practice of watch officers on paddle wheel steamers who conned their ships from the bridge or walkway between the two paddle wheels. Also *wheelhouse.* (2) In submarines, the open area at the top of the sail that is used for conning the ship when the boat is not submerged.

**bridge piece**  *n.* An arch or bridge between the stern frame and the rudder post.

**Bridge Record Card**  *n.* A card required to be posted in the wheelhouse or chart room of all ships in U.S. waters. When USCG inspectors come aboard, they note on the card any violations or deficiencies they find.

**bridge the seas**  *phr.* To ride the wave crests without going down into the troughs.

**bridge wings**  *n.* The open decks of the navigation bridge (also of the flag bridge if there is one) on either side of most ships.

**bridle**  *n.* A V-shaped device with the open ends of the V attached to spread the tension across a wider area.

**bridle port**  *n.* Gun port forward on the gun deck of a sailing warship.

**brig** *n.* (1) A two-masted vessel, square-rigged on both masts. See RIG. (2) Ship's area used for confining prisoners.

**brigantine** *n.* A two-masted vessel, square-rigged on the foremast and fore-and-aft rigged on the mainmast. Formerly, a brigantine carried a square topsail on the mainmast. Also *hermaphrodite brig*. See RIG.

**brightwork** *n.* (1) Brass, chrome, and stainless steel that are kept polished; this usage is heard most often on naval vessels. (2) Varnished wood trim, especially on pleasure boats. Brightwork is never used in connection with painted surfaces.

**bring about** *v.* (1) To bring a vessel to the wind or a new course. (2) To cause another vessel to heave to with a shot across her bow.

**bring up** *v.* (1) To anchor. (2) To stop suddenly as when an obstacle is hit.

**brisote** *n.* A stronger-than-usual northeast trade wind on the Cuban coast.

**Bristol-fashion** *adj.* Maintained in mint condition, usually in the expression "shipshape and Bristol-fashion." The reference is to Bristol, England, a large shipbuilding center where a great deal of the refurbishing of ships was done.

**British thermal unit (BTU)** *n.* Heat needed to raise one pound of water one degree Fahrenheit when at 39.2°F.

**broach** *v.* (1) To veer dangerously and unintentionally broadside to the wind and waves. (2) Of landing craft, to be turned sideways on a beach by surf and unable to retract. (3) Of submarines, to break the surface but not come fully to the surface steaming position. (4) To break into the ship's cargo for personal use, "to broach the cargo."

**broach to** *v.* Said of a sailing ship when the wind is on the quarter and the head suddenly comes up toward the wind as a result of the sea striking the stern or bad helmsmanship; this is a frequent cause of dismasting.

**broad before the wind** *phr.* To sail with booms out before the wind while sailing downwind.

**broad command pennant** *n.* A blue-and-white pennant flown by a fleet commodore below flag officer rank.

**broad on the beam** *phr.* Bearing 090° or 270° relative to the ship's heading, either port or starboard. A bearing of 090° would be broad on the starboard beam, while 270° would be broad on the port beam. If the bearing is approximate, "broad" is omitted from the expression. See RELATIVE BEARING.

**broad on the bow** *phr.* A bearing of 045° (broad on the starboard bow), or a bearing of 315° (broad on the port bow). If the bearing is approximate, the proper expression is "on the starboard (port) bow." See RELATIVE BEARING.

**broad on the quarter** *phr.* A bearing of 135° (broad on the starboard quarter), or 225° (broad on the port quarter). If the bearing is approximate, the appropriate expression is "on the starboard (port) quarter." See RELATIVE BEARING.

**broad pennant** *n.* An oblong swallow-tailed flag with the fly about double the length of the hoist.

**broad reach** See POINTS OF SAILING; REACH.

**broadside** *n.* (1) The side of a vessel above the waterline. (2) Showing the full length of one side, opposite of end on.

**broadside** *v.* (1) To position a vessel so that the enemy is in the line of fire for all the guns on one side of the ship. (2) To fire all guns on one side simultaneously. See SALVO.

**broadside on**   *adj.* or *adv.* Beam to the sea or waves.

**broken stowage**   *n.* Term used in the timber trade for lumber shorter than standard that can be used to fill up small spaces; such timber carries a lower freight rate.

**broken water**   *n.* (1) Ripples, eddies, or small waves on otherwise smooth seas. (2) A change in wave pattern possibly caused by a shoal.

**broker**   *n.* A person licensed to sell boats and ships and who represents one party to another.

**brokerage clause**   *n.* The clause in a charter party that states the amount the broker is to be paid.

**brow**   *n.* A portable ramp or bridge secured to the deck with a hinge at the **brow landing** and fitted with wheels, the truck, at the pier end to automatically adjust to tide differences. See GANGWAY.

**brown shoe**   *n.* Used to describe aviation and submarine officers. Prior to World War II when khakis were introduced for all officers, only aviation and submarine officers wore khakis or greens with the brown shoes. See BLACK SHOE.

**brown-water**   *adj* Of or pertaining to riverine operations carried out in small, shallow-draft boats, as distinct from **blue-water navy.**

**Brucker survival capsule**   *n.* A patented survival vessel lowered from an offshore drilling rig or a submersible in the event of fire or other emergency; it is self-contained, self-propelled, and equipped with first aid and life-support systems.

**bubble pulse**   *n.* Echo recorded on electronic equipment caused by the collapse of the large bubble that results from an underwater explosion.

**bubble sextant**   *n.* A sextant with a bubble to establish the horizontal plane instead of using the true horizon, designed specifically for and most often seen in aircraft. Occasionally used for land navigation, it is rarely seen at sea.

**buccaneer**   *n.* Pirate or freebooter, seafaring plunderer with no national identification such as a privateer enjoyed, therefore disreputable. The term came from the name given the West Indian cattle rustlers for the word they used for smoked meat, *boucan.*

**buck**   *n.* In larger ships with a mess made up of officers of similar rank, small object such as a napkin ring placed on the wardroom table to mark the place of the officer to be served first. In smaller ships, such as destroyers, in which all officers eat together from captain to the George ensign, there is no buck. The captain or presiding officer is served first, then the executive officer to his right; the third-ranking officer is seated at the captain's left, but the stewards serve counterclockwise from the captain.

**buckler**   *n.* A plate fitted in a port or, more often, a hawse pipe to prevent water from coming through the opening.

**bugeye** (or **buckeye**)   *n.* A flat-bottomed, centerboard schooner with a jib-headed headsail and mainsail, usually built with a cabin aft, used by oystermen on the Chesapeake Bay.

**builder's trials**   *n.* Tests conducted by shipbuilders to determine the ship's readiness before acceptance trials.

**built mast**   *n.* A mast constructed in several pieces and joined in a way to strengthen or reinforce each other in a completed mast.

**bulbous bow**   *n.* A type of bow in high-speed ships in which the entry expands in a bulbous shape so as to reduce the size of the bow wave.

**bulk cargo**   *n.* Homogeneous cargo, such as liquids, grain, coal, or ore, that is handled in bulk and not bagged or containerized. It usually occupies the entire cargo-carrying capacity of the vessel.

**bulkhead**   *n.* Transverse and longitudinal partitions separating portions of a vessel. Some bulkheads are watertight, and some are only partition bulkheads.

**bulkhead**   *v.* Slang for airing grievances within hearing of a senior officer without addressing the officer directly.

**bulkhead deck**   *n.* The uppermost deck on a ship to which watertight bulkheads and the watertight shell extend.

**bulk terminal**   *n.* A dedicated terminal equipped to handle specific types of bulk cargo, for example, coal, but no grain.

**bullchain**   *n.* The bitter end of a single-whip topping lift that is secured to the deck.

**bull ensign**   *n.* The senior ensign on board. See GEORGE ENSIGN.

**bull gear**   *n.* The first gear on the inboard end of the propeller shaft. The largest, slowest-turning gear in the gear train.

**bullhorn**   *n.* Electrically operated directional megaphone.

**bullnose**   *n.* A closed chock set in the stem of some vessels.

**bull rope**   *n.* An elastic cord or shock cord on a line leading from a vessel to mooring buoy used to ease the shock when tide or wind cause the ship to charge back and forth. See SQUARE-RIGGED VESSEL.

**bull's-eye**   *n.* (1) A thick convex glass device fitted into a weather door or skylight cover for the purpose of admitting light. (2) A round or oval piece of hard wood with a groove around the outer surface. It is fastened to a square sail, and leech lines or buntlines are led through it.

**bull the buoy**   *phr.* To bump a buoy with the side of a vessel.

**bulwark**   *n.* The extension of the ship's side above the weather deck. Also *berthing.*

**bumboat**   *n.* A small boat that comes alongside with articles for sale while a ship is in port.

**bumkin**   *n.* A short spar or timber that projects from each side of the bow to extend the clue or lower edge of the foresail to windward, and held in place by a **bumkin shroud.**

**bummock**   *n.* The subsurface of a hummock in an ice field. Bummocks have **ice keels** similar to the ridges in hummocks.

**bumper**   *n.* Antichafing material found on piers and pilings. See CAMEL; FENDER.

**bunk**   *n.* A small bed fitted into a vessel. See BERTH.

**bunk covers**   *n.* Flameproof covers thrown over bunks during general quarters.

**bunker**   *n.* (1) A fuel oil compartment. (2) Fuel oil. Also *bunkers.*

**bunker**   *v.* To fuel a ship with bunker fuel for the main propulsion boilers.

**bunker crude** (or **bunker C**)   *n.* Black, thick, and unrefined or only slightly refined crude oil burned on steam-powered vessels. Also *black oil.* See NAVY STANDARD FUEL OIL.

**bunkering facilities**   *n.* Ships and shoreside facilities in a port that can furnish fuel for ships.

**bunkering station** (or **port**)   *n.* A shore facility with the capability of loading fuel on a ship.

**bunt**   *n.* The middle section of a sail, especially a square sail.

**bunting**   *n.* (1) Cotton or woolen material of a weight suitable for making flags. (Synthetic materials used today are not usually called bunting.) (2) Streamers and decorative flags.

**bunt leech lines**   *n.* Lines used to furl square sails by bringing the leech and foot up to the yard.

**buntline**   *n.* A line used for dousing a square sail by hauling the foot up to the yard.

**buoy**   *n.* Any floating, heavily anchored object that conveys navigational information to mariners by its shape, color, number, light phase characteristic, and/or sound. The lateral system of buoys includes can buoys, nun buoys, lighted buoys, bell buoys, gong buoys, whistle buoys, and combination buoys. See LIGHTSHIP.

**buoyage**   *n.* A system of buoys. The International Association of Lighthouse Authorities (IALA) Maritime Buoyage System (combined Cardinal-Lateral System) designates virtually every maritime buoyage jurisdiction worldwide as either **Region A** buoyage (red to left returning to land) or **Region B** (red, right, returning). The major difference in the two buoyage regions is in the lateral marks. In Region A red will be to port; in Region B red will be to starboard. Shapes of lateral marks are the same in both regions, can to port and cone (nun) to starboard. Cardinal and other marks continue to follow current guidelines and may be found in both regions. A modified lateral mark, indicating the preferred channel where a channel divides, is to be introduced for use in both regions.

**buoyancy**   *n.* Upward pressure on the hull of a vessel exerted by the surrounding water equal to the hull's displacement.

**buoyancy, height of center of (KB)**   *n.* The vertical distance of an upright vessel's geometrical center above the top of keel or the lowest faying surface of floors. For a ship of normal shape, the KB is about 5.3 times the draft. For a barge with vertical sides and a flat bottom, the KB is around 0.50 times the draft. See STABILITY.

**buoy station**   *n.* The established and charted position for a buoy.

**buoy tender**   *n.* A vessel designed to service aids to navigation.

**burden** (or **burthen**)   *n.* The capacity of a ship.

**burdened vessel**   *n.* The vessel that does not have the right of way under the rules of the road. The term has been rendered obsolete by the current *Navigation Rules:* the burdened vessel is now called the **give way** vessel. See STAND ON.

**burgee**   *n.* Small flag displayed on yachts and yacht clubs for purposes of identification. In general, clubs use triangular burgees, and owners use swallow-tailed burgees for personal flags.

**burn bag**   *n.* On U.S. Navy ships, a container for classified material that is to be destroyed.

**burton**   *n.* A tackle with double or single blocks used for tightening rigging, shifting weights, or, in sailing ships, to set up and support the topmast shrouds.

**bushing**   *n.* (1) A guide for the sheave pin in a block. (2) Any device used for reducing friction, reducing the diameter of a hole, or increasing the diameter of a shaft, as a bearing.

**bust**   *v.* To reduce someone in rank.

**Buoys**

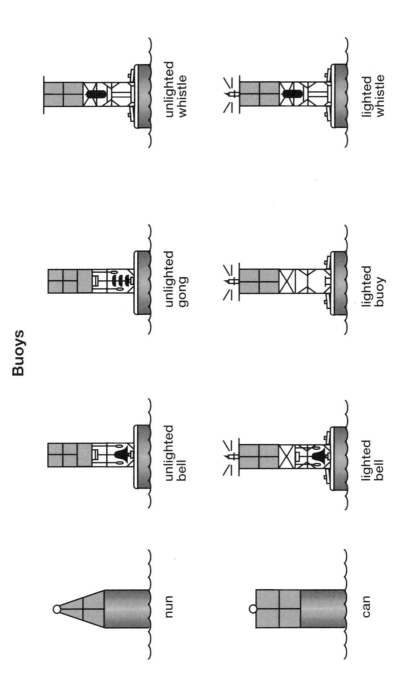

nun

can

unlighted
bell

unlighted
gong

unlighted
whistle

lighted
bell

lighted
buoy

lighted
whistle

**Butterworth**   *n.* A method of cleaning tanks with high-pressure steam and a spinning nozzle, used on tankers.

**butt-jointed**   See HERRINGBONE STITCH.

**buttock**   *n.* The line around a ship's hull where the hull begins to turn down towards the keel.

**buttock line**   *n.* A naval architecture term for a fore-and-aft section of a hull made by drawing an imaginary line around the hull parallel to the keel.

**button**   *n.* (1) A small piece of thick leather under the head of a nail that is driven through a rope. (2) A button is also a short mushroom-shaped device used for fairleading lines and wires.

**Buys Ballot's Law**   *n.* (Buys rhymes with puss) "Law" for determining the direction of the center of a storm. In the Northern Hemisphere it means that if an observer faces the wind, the center of low atmospheric pressure will be from 8 to 12 points on the observer's right hand. In the Southern Hemisphere, it will be the same on the observer's left hand. Named for the Dutch meteorologist C. H. D. Buys Ballot, who published his finding in *Comptes Rendus* in 1857.

**by and large**   *phr.* A point of sailing. Sailing by and large is sailing on a reach. See LARGE.

**by the head** (or **stern**)   *phr.* Said of a vessel drawing more water than normal at the bow (or stern).

**by the lee**   *phr.* Sailing on a run with the boom to windward.

**by the wind**   *phr.* Sailing close-hauled, sailing as close to the wind as possible and still keeping the sails filled. Also *on the wind.* See FULL AND BY; LARGE; POINTS OF SAILING.

**by your leave**   *interj.* Courtesy request for permission to pass when overtaking a senior officer while walking and is accompanied by a salute; the senior officer returns the salute and responds, "Permission granted."

# C

**C**   See CHARLIE.

**cabin**   *n.* (1) Living quarters for officers and passengers. (2) On Navy ships, embarked admirals and the captain have cabins, other officers have staterooms. Seamen have quarters. (3) Enclosed space above the hull on small boats.

**cabin passengers**   *n.* Obsolete term for passengers who are assigned cabins, as distinguished from "steerage passengers," who sleep in common areas. The British Board of Trade also specified the type of food and the **superficial area** that had to be allowed cabin passengers.

**cabin sole**   *n.* The floor of a cabin.

**cabin trunk**   *n.* In small craft, that part of a cabin that appears above the deck. Also *doghouse.*

**cable**   *n.* (1) Cordage 10 to 30 inches in diameter with three plain-laid or hawser-laid ropes twisted in a left-handed direction or "against the sun." See CABLE-LAID. (2) Heavy fiber or wire rope or often an anchor chain. (3) A unit of measurement at sea, which varies from country to country. German and British navies used one-tenth of a nautical mile, or 608 feet. In the past, the U.S. used 120 fathoms, or 720 feet, but today there is a growing consensus that a cable is equal to 100 fathoms or one-tenth of a nautical mile.

**cable buoy** *n.* A buoy used to mark one end of a cable being worked by a cable vessel.

**cable chock** *n.* Deck device made of bronze or other metal with horns projecting upward and inward to restrict ground tackle and to prevent chafing.

**cable flags** *n.* Numbered indicators used by anchor-handling detail to keep the bridge informed on the amount of ground tackle that is out.

**cable jack** *n.* Deck equipment used for lifting the anchor chain free of the deck to insert the slip hook.

**cable-laid** *adj.* Describes rope consisting of nine strands made by laying three plain ropes together left-handed. The fibers are first laid clockwise to make the yarns; the yarns are laid counterclockwise to make the strands; the strands are laid clockwise to make the finished rope. To make cable, one more operation is needed: three ropes are then laid counterclockwise. With lang lay wire rope, the wires in the strand and the strand in the rope are laid in the same direction. This can be either right lang lay (or just lang lay) or left lang lay.

**cable markings** *n.* Paint or turns of wire used on an anchor cable placed on each shot, or every 90 feet, to show how much has been let out or taken in. At the first shot the connecting link is painted red, and the first link above and below the red link is painted white, and the stud in the center of the link is wrapped with one turn of seizing wire. On the second shot, the two links above and below the connector are painted white, and the stud on each second link marked with two turns of seizing wire. The entire length of cable is marked this way. Therefore if the connector is out of the water or spillpipe

at all, you can tell how much is out either visually or by feel.

**cable molding** *n.* Carving in the form of rope, sometimes seen as fancy work around or near the vessel's name.

**cable ship** *n.* A ship fitted to lay and repair telecommunication cable under the water.

**cablet** *n.* Cable under 9 inches in circumference laid counterclockwise.

**caboose** *n.* (obsolete) A topside galley or cookhouse or the stove used for cooking on an open deck on coastal vessels.

**cadet** *n.* Student in a naval or military officers' training school. See MIDSHIPMAN.

**caduceus** *n.* In Greek mythology a herald's wing and staff with two serpents entwined around it and carried by Hermes. In the U.S. Navy. it is the insignia of the Hospital and Pharmacist Corps. (Medical staff officers wear a spread oak leaf embroidered in gold, surcharged with a silver acorn. Dental officers wear the same emblem with two acorns at the base instead of the single acorn in the center.)

**cage** *n.* The structure at the top of a buoy used as a daymark or as a support for a topmark.

**cage** *v.* To build a gyroscope or to lock one in place by means of a **caging mechanism.**

**caique** *n.* (pron. kah-eek) (1) A long narrow double-ended boat used for rowing on the Bosporus. (2) A sailing vessel of the eastern Mediterranean still seen today.

**caisson** *n.* (1) The floating or sliding gate that opens and closes a dry dock. Any gate that keeps out water such as locks, dams, and ship's caissons. Floating caissons are sunk by allowing water into the chambers; when the basin is to be opened, the caisson chambers are pumped out so they will float to be more easily handled. (2) A watertight chamber for repairing hulls and seawalls below the waterline or below sea level. See COFFERDAM.

**caisson disease**   See BENDS.

**calculated altitude method**   See MARCQ ST. HILAIRE METHOD.

**calendar day**   *n.* The period from midnight to midnight. The calendar day is 24 hours of mean solar time and coincides with the civil day unless a time change occurs during the day.

**calf**   *n.* (1) A young sea mammal such as a whale or manatee. (2) A small piece of a glacier or iceberg that has broken off. See CALVE.

**caliber**   *n.* The inside diameter of a gun's bore expressed in inches; the inside diameter of a .40 caliber bore is four-tenths of an inch.

**calibration radio beacon**   *n.* A radio beacon built and operated for the purpose of calibrating shipboard radio direction finders.

**California Current**   *n.* A broad stream formed by the combination of a part of the North Pacific Current and the southern branch of the Aleutian Current and which flows southeastward along the coastline of the Baja California; it then swings sharply westward to form the major portion of the North Equatorial Current. See DAVIDSON CURRENT; OCEAN CURRENT.

**call**   *n.* (1) Visits exchanged by naval officers between ships. See BOARDING CALL. (2) A series of musical notes played on a boatswain's pipe. (3) Formal social visit by a naval officer and his or her spouse on another naval officer and spouse.

**call away**   *v.* To pipe a boat crew to prepare their boat for a trip.

**call book**   See MORNING CALL BOOK.

**calling for orders**   *phr.* The practice of ships stopping in a port to pick up orders for their next destination before the days of radio.

**call sign** or **call letters**   *n.* (1) A federally assigned radio signal used to identify vessels with radio transmitters. (2) Any combination of letters and numbers or words used to identify a communicating station.

**calm**   *n.* Absence of appreciable wind, a force 0 (less than 1 knot) on the Beaufort scale.

**calm belt**   See DOLDRUMS.

**calve**   *v.* The process by which a piece of ice breaks off from an iceberg, a glacier, or an ice shelf to form a calf. See CALF.

**cam**   *n.* An eccentric wheel on a shaft for repetitive timing of an operation, for example, on an engine's valve train.

**camber**   *n.* (1) The slight athwartship arch of a deck that allows for quick drainage. Also *round of beam*. See SHEER. (2) A sail's draft; the belly of a sail. (3) British word for a small basin, particularly one with a narrow entrance inside a harbor.

**cam cleat**   *n.* A fitting with interlocking teeth on eccentric half-wheels with springs that tend to keep the teeth together, used instead of a cleat with horns for quick insertion and release.

**camel**   *n.* A float placed between a vessel and a pier, or another vessel, to protect both the pier and the vessel, or vessels. See BUMPER; FENDER.

**can**   *n.* (1) A cylindrical buoy with straight sides and flat top, odd-numbered, painted black or green, and found on the left-hand side of the channel when entering from the sea in **Region B.** See BUOY; BUOYAGE; NUN BUOY. (2) Slang term for destroyers or "tin cans," because of their small size, light construction, and instability relative to cruisers, battleships, and carriers.

**canal**    *n.* Waterway built for shipping, irrigation, or other purposes.

**Canary Current**    *n.* The Southeast Drift Current after it flows south past the Bay of Biscay and approaches the Canary Islands and the Cape Verde Islands between the Azores and Portugal. Also *Canaries Current.* See OCEAN CURRENT.

**cancel**    *v.* To call off or discontinue a race. When a race committee decides to cancel a race, the race is not sailed later.

**canceling date**    *n.* The contract date beyond which the charterer has the option to cancel the contract if the vessel is not ready to be loaded. The owner, however, is still liable for his or her obligation unless released by the charterer. The clause that stipulates the date is called the **cancellation clause.**

**candlepower**    *n.* Luminous intensity used in the *Light Lists,* measured in candelas, published by the Defense Mapping Service and equivalent agencies of other maritime nations.

**canister**    *n.* A can made to fit in the bore of a gun and filled with shot, used in the 17th and 18th, and early 19th centuries as an antipersonnel weapon.

**canning plate**    *n.* Steel plate used as a cover over a compartment with nuclear components, lined with lead or polyethylene and welded closed.

**cannon shot rule**    *n.* The "rule," based on the maximum range of early cannons, by which the 3-mile limit of the territorial sea was established.

**canoe**    *n.* Long, slender open boat used with paddles or sails chiefly on rivers and other inland waters.

**canopy**    *n.* (1) Covering over a boat, usually canvas or metal. (2) Cover over the stern sheets of a small boat.

**cant**    *adj.* (1) Used to describe a timber that does not stand square, a deviation from either a horizontal plane or a vertical plane.

**cant**    *v.* (1) To turn something over to expose the other side. (2) To turn a vessel in a channel or harbor. (3) To tilt or place in an inclined position. (4) To swing around from a position, as to cant a yard.

**cant body**    *n.* That part of a vessel near the bow and stern where the frames depart from the perpendicular.

**cant frame**    *n.* Frame that is not square with the keel line.

**cant spar**    *n.* Pole carried aboard for the purpose of making temporary masts or spars.

**cantilever**    *n.* A projecting beam or truss supported only at one end.

**cantilever tanks**    *n.* Freshwater tanks carried in the gunwales. Also *gunwale tanks; wing tanks.*

**cantline**    *n.* Stevedore's term for space between fore-and-aft laid casks. See CHINE; CONTLINE.

**cantling**    *n.* A support for a cask while lying on its staves.

**canvas**    *n.* (1) A heavy woven fabric of hemp, cotton, or flax used for sails, characterized by having a double warp and a single weft. Various countries used different weights for the designation numbers. A #4 canvas in the United States is not the same weight as #4 in Great Britain. (2) A general term for all sails on a vessel regardless of the material used.

**canvas boat**   *n.* Long, narrow boat with bone or wood ribs and canvas covering.

**canyon**   *n.* Relatively narrow and deep furrow with steep slopes in the ocean floor or on land; the bottom generally has a continuous slope.

**cap**   *n.* (1) The block that holds two masts together. Two holes are cut through the block, one round for the top of the lower mast, the other square for the bottom of the upper mast. (2) The top of a mast. See TRUCK. (3) The fitting secured to the outer end of the bowsprit into which the jibboom is fitted. Also *bowsprit cap.*

**cap**   *v.* To cover the end of a rope with a piece of canvas.

**capacity plan**   *n.* An outline of the spaces available for cargo, freshwater, fuel, water ballast, and so on, with a list of the spaces giving the capacity in either weight or volume.

**cape**   *n.* A point or headland that juts into the sea or other body of water; a promontory or headland. See BILL.

**Cape Breton Current**   *n.* A stream originating in the Gulf of St. Lawrence, flowing southeasterly in the southwestern half of Cabot Strait and merging with the Labrador Current Extension. It is sometimes influenced by the tide-influenced Gaspé Current to the northwest.

**Cape doctor**   *n.* A strong southeasterly that blows on the South African coast.

**Cape Horn**   *n.* The southern tip of South America, known for the severity of its storms and the difficulty of rounding the Horn, particularly from east to west. See CAPE STIFF (slang).

**Cape Horn Current**   *n.* The current formed by the West Wind Drift (a current that flows easterly around Antarctica) as it flows past Cape Horn and on toward the Falklands to become part of the Falklands Current. See OCEAN CURRENT.

**capel**   *n.* Metal cap at the end of a cable.

**Cape Stiff**   *n.* Slang for Cape Horn, used by sailors of the Cape Horn square-riggers.

**capital ship**   *n.* A vessel greater than 10,000 tons with guns larger than 8 inches, essentially battleships and cruisers but not aircraft carriers. The term is rarely used today.

**cap jib**   *n.* The headsail that is set on the bowsprit cap.

**cap log**   *n.* A timber fastened to a pier used as a fender to protect the pier and vessels lying alongside.

**cap shore**   *n.* A timber undergirding a mast cap to better support the topsail yard.

**capsize**   *v.* (1) To turn over. Most commonly it means the inadvertent turning over of a boat. To capsize an oil drum is to turn it over, usually to gain access to the bung. To capsize a lifeboat would be to turn it over with the bottom up to prevent rain from getting in it. (2) A knot that changes its structure under strain is said to capsize.

**capstan** (or **capstern**)   *n.* A machine with a rotating drum for heaving up anchors or for other jobs requiring heavy strain, and fitted with pawls to prevent reverse rotation under load. When a capstan is used for purposes other than heaving up the anchor, it is sometimes called a winch. See CATHEAD; GIPSEY CAPSTAN; WILDCAT; WINCH; WINDLASS.

# Capstan

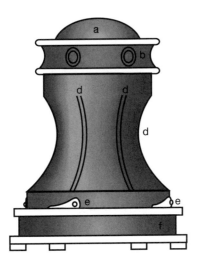

(a) drum head
(b) capstan bar hole
(c) drum
(d) whelp
(e) pawl
(f) base plate

**capstan bar**   *n.* A bar fitted to the capstan for manual operation. Several capstan bars would be fitted so that a number of men could work together to heave in the anchor. See CAPSTAN.

**capstay**   *n.* A rope running from one mast cap to the next for support. Also *triatic stay.*

**captain (Capt.)**   *n.* (1) A commissioned officer in the U.S. Navy or Coast Guard ranked below commodore or rear admiral and above commander. (2) The officer in command of a vessel. On some ships there are co-captains or staff captains, but there is always one ship's master who is ultimately in command of and responsible for the vessel's conduct and safe navigation. The exception to this is when the captain is relieved of navigational responsibility while his ship is in the hands of a compulsory pilot. But even

then, the captain is required to relieve the pilot if, in his opinion, the pilot exhibits manifest incompetence. (3) The proper address for anyone who is the master of a merchant ship or who has master's papers. (4) Proper address for the commanding officer of any U.S. Navy ship regardless of rank. (5) Courtesy title for person in command of and responsible for a yacht. See SKIPPER.

**captain of the port**   *n.* An officer of the U.S. Coast Guard designated by the commandant and who, under the district commander, gives immediate direction to Coast Guard law enforcement activities within his assigned area. The district commander acts as captain of the port with respect to areas in his district not assigned to officers designated by the commandant as captain of the port.

**captain's bridge**   *n.* A bridge off the captain's quarters below the navigation bridge on large merchant ships.

**captain's mast**   *n.* A public hearing on a ship in which the captain metes out punishment for minor offenses, listens to complaints, and awards commendations for work well done. To *see someone before the mast* is to put him on report.

**captain's walk**   *n.* A narrow gangway with railings built on the ridgepole of shipmasters' houses, especially in New England, from which the captains could watch the waterfront. Also *widow's walk.*

**capture**   *v.* To take a vessel and her cargo under control; such action is legal under admiralty law when accomplished by a belligerent in time of war in accordance with international law.

**car**   *n.* A device attached to the leech of a sail and fitted to a track on the mast. to raise and lower the sail.

**caravel**   *n.* A modest-sized trading vessel that evolved in and around Portugal starting from the 14th century. These three-masted vessels were either lateen-rigged on all masts (**caravela latina**) or square-rigged on the main- and foremasts with a lateen mizzen (**caravela rotunda** or **redonda**). One of the leading vessels in the age of discovery in the 15th century—Columbus's *Nina* and *Pinta* were both caravels—the largest were no more than 100 feet, and as the demands of trade and ocean voyaging increased, the caravel was superceded by the carrack.

**card**   See MERCHANT MARINER'S DOCUMENT; SEAMAN'S PASSPORT; Z-CARD.

**cardinal buoyage system**   *n.* Officially known as the Uniform Cardinal System, the IALA Maritime Buoyage System, using marks in conjunction with a compass—cardinal refers to the cardinal points of the compass—to indicate the direction of navigable water. See BUOYAGE; INTERNATIONAL ASSOCIATION OF LIGHTHOUSE AUTHORITIES.

**cardinal points**   *n.* The four points of the compass marking north, south, east, and west. Intercardinal points are those between. See POINT; THREE-LETTER POINT.

**careen**   *v.* (1) To put a vessel on its side, usually to work on the opposite side that is out of the water. (2) To list or to heel.

**careening tackle**   *n.* Rigging used to careen a vessel; this usually consists of tackle running from the masthead to a point on a pier or shore.

**cargo**   *n.* Freight carried in ships and aircraft. It is in containers, pallets, or bulk. Cargo is divided into general and bulk; general cargo includes such items as steel, fruit, lumber, and finished goods, while bulk cargo includes such items as phosphate, petroleum, and grain. See BREAK BULK.

**cargo batten**   *n.* Wooden strip or planking used to keep cargo away from the steel hull. See DUNNAGE.

**cargo boom**   *n.* Heavy boom used for handling freight. A large steel pulley used on the boom is called a **cargo block.**

**cargo chute**   *n.* A covered slide used to load or unload a vessel's cargo by gravity.

**cargo deadweight**   See NET CAPACITY.

**cargo documentation**   *n.* Papers required to enter or leave a port; these include the load manifest, crew list, bills of lading, tonnage certification, and so on.

**cargo gear**   *n.* Nonspecific term for all equipment used in loading and unloading cargo.

**cargo hatch**   *n.* An opening over a hold.

**cargo jack**   *n.* Screw press used to force baled goods into spaces smaller than the bulk of the bales.

**cargo mat**   *n.* Heavy mesh bag envelope filled with dunnage to protect the hull from cargo.

**cargo net**   *n.* Rope or chain mesh used for swinging cargo aboard a vessel or for off-loading cargo.

**cargo plan**   *n.* (1) Diagram showing each of a ship's holds and the capacity of each. (2) A stowage plan prepared by the pier superintendent and approved by the master; it shows where and how cargo is to be stowed and a copy goes with the ship for use by the stevedore in charge of unloading.

**cargo port**   *n.* Opening in the hull to allow loading and unloading of cargo in the 'tween decks spaces.

**cargo preference**   See FLAG DISCRIMINATION.

**cargo sharing**   *n.* The allocation of cargo to flags of a particular nation depending on the country of origin of the cargo being imported or exported.

**Cargo Ship Safety Construction Certificate**  *n.* A certificate issued by the American Shipping Bureau. It is used under the International Convention for the Safety of Life at Sea, 1974 (SOLAS) to certify that a vessel is constructed in accordance with international standards for subdivision and stability. Machinery and electrical installations, fire protection, detection, and extinguishing equipment are also covered under the certification. A supplement to the certificate is required for all tankers and cargo vessels engaged in carrying oil.

**Cargo Ship Safety Radiotelegraphy Certificate**  *n.* A certificate issued by the Federal Communications Commission under the provisions of the International Convention for the Safety of Life at Sea, 1974 (SOLAS). It certifies that the radio direction finder, the main and emergency transmitters, auto alarms, and the operator's watch hours comply with international regulations.

**cargo skid**  *n.* Bridge between ship and pier over which cargo is hauled. Skids are still used in Third World countries where labor is cheap and material-handling equipment relatively expensive.

**cargo spaces**  *n.* A general term for all spaces used for stowing cargo. Separate from engine spaces, living spaces, and so on.

**cargo ton**  *n.* A measure of volume equal to 100 cubic feet.

**cargo transshipment area**  *n.* An area usually outside the port limits that is designated for the transshipment of oil and other material from large ships to smaller ships and other carriers.

**cargo underwriter**  *n.* Specialist in insuring waterborne cargo.

**cargo whip**  *n.* A rope or chain with a derrick used for handling heavy cargo. One end of the rope or chain has a heavy **cargo hook,** and the other end is rove through the block on the derrick and led to the winch.

**Caribbean Current**  *n.* An ocean current that flows westward through the Caribbean Sea to the Yucatan Channel. It is formed by an extension of the Atlantic Equatorial Current and of the Guiana Current.

**carline** (or **carling**)  *n.* Short timber running fore and aft to connect and stiffen transverse deck supports, and also found around the inside edge of a hatch or a doghouse.

**carpenter**  *n.* A senior petty officer responsible for securing cargo hatches and ports, taking soundings of the fuel and water tanks, inspecting and repairing anchors and masts, and maintenance of wooden decks and other wooden equipment aboard. He is assisted by a **carpenter's mate.** Ships' carpenters are universally addressed as "Chips" by their peers and those senior to them.

**carpenter stopper**  *n.* Equipment for temporarily holding wire to prevent kinking or binding when not in use, but available for quick release.

**carrack**  *n.* An early square-rigged ship of two or, more commonly, three or four masts that evolved around the 14th century. Beamier, longer, and heavier than caravels, with which they were contemporary, they achieved great size—more than 1,000 tons—and dominated the global trade of Spain and Portugal until the 1600s. Carracks were characterized by especially high sterncastles and forecastles which made it possible for them to mount heavy guns, and carracks were the first big-gun sailing vessels. These heavy superstructures made them hard to work to windward, a problem largely resolved by removing the overbuilt forecastles—a development generally credited to the English seaman Sir John Hawkins, in 1570—which resulted essentially in the development of the galleon. Also *nao.*

**carriage**   *n.* That part of a gun mount that supports the bore.

**Carriage of Goods by Sea Act**   *n.* A 1936 act of Congress by which the shipper must show that damage of merchandise was due to unseaworthiness of the vessel in cargo claims litigation. The great bulk of maritime litigation is over cargo damage claims. Cargo is usually insured "warehouse to warehouse." Suits are generally brought by the underwriters against the ocean carriers in the name of the owners of the cargo to recover the amount of loss or damages. An explanation of this and the closely associated Harter Act is in *Merchant Marine Officer's Handbook* by Turpin and MacEwen.

**carrick bend**   *n.* A knot used for fastening cables or hawsers of different sizes.

**carrick bitt**   *n.* One of the supporting posts on a ship's anchor windlass. Also *carrick head.*

**carrier**   *n.* (1) An aircraft carrier. (2) Any organization that transports freight on land or sea. On land such an organization is known as a **common carrier.** The owner or charterer of a vessel who enters into a **contract of carriage** with a shipper is a carrier.

**carrier-controlled    approach**   *n.* Approach of an aircraft to a carrier when the pilot is guided in speed, heading, and altitude by a controller aboard ship.

**carrier's risks**   *n.* Shipowner's liability for loss or damage of goods while under his or her control unless otherwise stipulated by contract such as a bill of lading or charter party.

**carrier task force**   *n.* Aircraft carriers and their support auxiliaries, now called a **battle group.**

**carronade**   *n.* A short-barreled, long-bore, muzzle-loaded gun manufactured by the Carron Iron Founding and Shipping Company and introduced into the Royal Navy in 1779. These were mounted on slide, instead of wheeled, carriages. Their large, low-velocity ball produced greater destruction of wooden hulls at short range than previous high-velocity guns that made a cleaner hole.

**carry on**   *interj.* The command given to a crew by a senior person when he or she wants a detail to continue working and not stand at attention in recognition of the arrival of an officer. Also used by senior officers when a junior officer asks permission to pass while walking in the same direction. Another use is when a junior ship meets a senior ship at sea. The commanding officer of the junior ship will signal the senior ship, "Request permission to proceed as previously ordered." The captain (or admiral, if one is riding in the senior ship) can reply, "Carry on as previously directed."

**carry rudder**   *phr.* To be obliged to use either a weather helm or a lee helm. Usually this can be adjusted by trimming the sails, but some weather helm is preferred in case the helmsman should lose control, in which case the boat would head up into the wind instead of off the wind and thus jibe.

**cartel**   *n.* An agreement between governments. In maritime usage, it refers most often to an exchange of prisoners; a **cartel ship** is the ship that carries out the exchanges of prisoners or carries documents such as treaties. A cartel ship can usually be recognized by its flying the flags of both belligerent countries.

**cartometer**   *n.* A device with a small wheel calibrated to a map's distance scale that is used for measuring distances on charts and maps by running the wheel over the desired route.

**cartouche** (or **cartouch**) *n.* The panel on maps and charts, often decorated, that carries the chart or map name, distances, and scale.

**carvel-built** *adj.* Of or pertaining to a vessel built with flush planking as opposed to lap-strake- or clinker-built.

**casein** *n.* A milk and cheese protein used for making adhesives and plastics before the development of synthetic resins.

**cashier** *v.* To dismiss dishonorably an officer from military service.

**casing** *n.* (1) Bulkheads enclosing a portion of a vessel such as a boiler room. (2) Covering for machinery, boilers, and so on.

**cast** *v.* (1) To cause a vessel to head off to port or starboard or to gain sternway when getting underway by use of headsails, rudder, spring lines, or kedges. (2) To turn a ship in minimum space, the equivalent of a three-point turn in a land vehicle and accomplished in the same set of moves. (2) To veer to leeward. (3) To throw, as a line or sounding lead.

**cast anchor** *phr.* To let down the anchor.

**cast away** *v.* To intentionally cause a vessel to founder or to be abandoned.

**castaway** *n.* A shipwrecked person or object.

**cast off** *v.* Throw off (or take in) mooring lines to leave a slip. See TAKE IN.

**cast the lead** *phr.* To throw the lead line to take a sounding.

**casualty board** *n.* A computer display of a ship's compartments and systems that shows damage control needs used during emergencies such as battle damage, fire, or grounding.

**cat** *n.* (1) The tackle used to cat the anchor. (2) Slang for cat-o'-nine-tails.

**cat** *v.* To bring an anchor to the cathead by use of the catfall.

**catadioptric** *adj.* Used in describing a lighthouse using both **catoptric** (reflective) and **dioptric** (refractive) light.

**catamaran** *n.* (1) A platform secured to two or more floats used for work alongside a ship. (2) A twin-hulled powerboat or sailboat. Technically, catamaran can refer to two- or three-hulled vessels, although a trimaran is preferred for the latter. From the Tamil word *kattumaran,* a native sailing raft with pontoons used in the Indian Ocean.

**catapult** *n.* Deck device for launching aircraft from a carrier deck at flying speed.

**cat back** *n.* A rope bent on the cat hook to handle the anchor as necessary.

**catboat** *n.* A fore-and-aft-rigged sailboat with no headsail and the mast stepped well forward. Less common are two-masted ketches, cat yawls, and **cat schooners.** See RIG.

**catch a crab** *phr.* When rowing, to fail to make a stroke or to recover from a stroke.

**catch a turn** *phr.* To wrap a rope around something for temporary holding. Also *take a round turn (on a cleat).*

**cat davit** *n.* An especially designed davit installed on the bow that was used for swinging an anchor into its stowed position. It was also used for moving the anchor from the sea-stowage position to the cathead preparatory to letting go the anchor.

**catfall**   *n.* The tackle used for heaving up or catting the anchor from the water's edge to the cathead.

**cathead**   *n.* (1) A timber projecting from a ship's bow, used as a support for catting an anchor. The purpose of the catheads was to protect the bow from the anchor when it was let go or when it was heaved up or catted. The cathead was fitted with a block at the outer end and another at the inner end, the **cattail;** the anchor could be handled by these without hitting the bow of the vessel. The cathead was reinforced with a **cathead knee** beneath it. Cat's heads were traditionally carved into the forward ends. (2) The drum on a winch shaft around which cable is wound for hauling or hoisting.

**cathead stopper**   *n.* A chain that secures an anchor after it has been catted home.

**cathodic protection**   *n.* A method of preventing wastage of a vessel's hull plating, propeller, and so on, due to combined chemical and electrical reaction when a vessel is in saltwater. The most common method of protection is the mounting of zinc anodes on the hull, which waste away before the ship's plating and propeller.

**cat hole**   *n.* Same as a hawse pipe, but at the stern.

**cat hook**   *n.* The hook on the catfall to which the anchor is attached when it is catted in. The catfall is rove through a **cat block** at the cathead.

**cat-'o-nine-tails**   *n.* A short piece of rope made for flogging. The man to be punished made his own "cat" by unlaying the rope and tarring and braiding the parts into nine tails. Nails and other such objects could also be incorporated in the tarred tails. From this we have the expression "not enough room to swing the cat."

**catoptric**   *adj.* Pertaining to mirrors and reflected light that concentrate light into a parallel beam, used in connection with construction of aids to navigation. See DIOPTRIC LIGHT.

**cat's paw**   *n.* (1) A double loop formed by twisting two bights of line over the hook of a tackle. See KNOT (2) A ripple on the water caused by a light breeze.

**cat tackle**   *n.* The tackle involved in catting an anchor.

**catting chain**   *n.* Chain used for holding a stock anchor after it has been removed from its stowed position and is ready to be let go.

**cattle fittings**   *n.* Gear associated with care and maintenance of cattle on a vessel.

**catwalk**   *n.* Any narrow walkway, especially (a) the short piers that extend between slips for easier access to small boats; (b) the steel grating across the deck of a tanker or through the engine spaces.

**caught aback**   *phr.* Describes a vessel when the wind strikes the forward, rather than the after, face of a sail. This can be either from a sudden wind shift, perhaps while rounding a point of land, or helmsman error. See CHAPEL.

**caulk**   *v.* To fill or waterproof seams on a wooden vessel traditionally by the use of cotton or fiber rope dipped in tar. Modern **caulking compounds** are made of flexible polymers.

**caulking mat**   *n.* (1) The canvas mat used by sailors on men-of-war when sleeping on deck. (2) The mat used by sailors when lying on their backs caulking a vessel's bottom, hence the expression **caulking off** for someone who is loafing.

**cautionary signal**   *n.* A signal flag from the International Signal Book flown by a ship entering harbor to indicate her character, used before radios were universally mandatory.

**cavel**   See KEVEL.

**caver**   *n.* A gentle breeze in the Hebrides.

**cavitation**   *n.* The successive formation and collapse of air pockets in a liquid created by the rapid turning of a ship or submarine propeller as it goes through the water and which causes damage to propellers, motors, and bearings. As the bubbles escape from the area near the propeller to higher pressure areas, they collapse and cause noise. This can be controlled by the shape and size of the propeller blades; smaller blades are used more and more in modern submarines.

**cay**   *n.* A rock, a small low island, a sandbank, or a shoal.

**ceiling**   *n.* (1) In meteorology, the height at which the cloud base covers more than half the sky. (2) Inside planking or lining, **ceiling planking,** of a ship's bottom; this can continue up the inside of the hull as far as the lowest deck. See SPIRKETING.

**ceiling hatch**   *n.* An access opening through a ship's ceiling to the sides and bottom for cleaning when cargo has been discharged.

**celestial equator**   *n.* The equator of the celestial sphere that is an extension of the plane of the Earth's equator. Also *equinoctial.*

**celestial horizon**   *n.* The horizon parallel to the plane of the observer's visible horizon at sea and that passes through the center of the Earth. Also *rational horizon.*

**celestial meridian**   *n.* A great circle passing through the poles of the celestial sphere. Unlike an hour circle, which moves with the celestial sphere, the

celestial meridian is fixed in relation to the terrestrial meridians.

**celestial navigation**   *n.* The science of determining position by use of celestial bodies, as distinct from piloting or determining position by landmarks and buoys.

**celestial sphere**   *n.* An imaginary sphere with the Earth at its center, in which all celestial bodies are assumed to be at a fixed distance from the earth, to make it easier to visualize the concepts involved in spherical triangles.

**celestial triangle**   *n.* A triangle formed by arcs of great circles on the celestial sphere. See NAVIGATIONAL TRIANGLE.

**cellular container vessel**   *n.* A ship fitted with a cellular guide system to receive stack containers of cargo.

**cellular double bottom**   *n.* Multicompartmented space between the inner and outer hulls that is bonded longitudinally by flooring and transversely by **intercostal girders.**

**cement patch**   *n.* An emergency repair of shell plating using portland cement when a leak develops near or below the waterline.

**cement wash**   *n.* A portland cement finish used in water tanks to prevent rust. The process has been supplanted by various resins.

**centerboard**   *n.* A pivoted board or steel plate housed in a fore-and-aft **centerboard trunk** (or **centerboard well**) that can be lowered to prevent leeway in sailboats or that can be raised by means of a line, called a **centerboard pendant,** to reduce resistance when running downwind or in shoal water. See DAGGER BOARD; LEEBOARDS; MARCONI RIG.

**center cockpit**   *n.* A small boat layout with a cabin forward and one aft of the cockpit.

**centering chain**    *n.* A visual device used for centering a hull over a dry dock before the water is removed.

**center keelson**    *n.* A row of vertical plates extending along the center of a flat-plate keel. Also *vertical keel.*

**centerline (CL)**    *n.* A straight line running from bow to stern midway between the sides of a vessel from which all transverse horizontal dimensions are taken. See STABILITY.

**centerline bulkhead**    *n.* A fore-and-aft bulkhead running between hatches in holds of grain ships to act as a permanent shifting board.

**centerline controlling depth**    *n.* The charted depth that obtains only along the centerline of the channel. See CONTROLLING DEPTH; MIDCHANNEL CONTROLLING DEPTH.

**center of buoyancy (G)**    *n.* Center of gravity of the volume of a vessel's displacement; computations determining center of buoyancy are a part of the process for determining metacentric height. See STABILITY.

**center of effort (CE)**    *n.* (1) That point on a sail at which the wind pressure forward is equal to the pressure aft of the point. (2) The center of wind pressure in a sail plan.

**center of flotation**    *n.* Geometric center of the water plane in which a vessel floats. The pitch and roll are about this point.

**center of gravity (CG)**    *n.* The point at which the total weight of a ship and any other weight on board is taken to be concentrated. A vessel suspended in air at the CG would be perfectly balanced because the weight on all sides is counterbalanced equally. See STABILITY.

**center of lateral resistance (CLR)**    *n.* The center point of an immersed hull's resistance to lateral forces.

**center plank**    *n.* A fore-and-aft member on small, open sailboats secured to the tops of the thwarts and used to step the mast. Also *sailing thwart.*

**center plate rudder**    *n.* A rudder with a single plate aft of the rudderstock. See BALANCED RUDDER.

**centipede**    *n.* A line or wooden strip with stops running the length of a bowsprit and jibboom used for stowing headsails.

**central operating system (COS)**    *n.* The capability of a marine power plant's being controlled from a central station containing all the necessary devices to allow the engineer complete control.

**centrifugal pump**    *n.* An apparatus used for transferring liquids by sucking the liquid into the axis of a casing of spinning vanes that forces the liquid out an opening in the circumference of the casing. Used for either high pressure or high flow but not both.

**centum clause**    *n.* A clause in a charter party agreement on terms of war risk insurance premiums. Any difference above the figure established in the centum clause is paid by the time charterers.

**certificated**    *adj.* (1) Refers to tank vessels covered by USCG certificate of inspection. (2) When applied to men employed on tank vessels, it refers to a certificate of ability issued by the Coast Guard.

**certificate of classification**    *n.* One of two certificates issued by the American Bureau of Shipping. The Certificate for Hull certifies the vessel's seaworthiness. The Certificate of Classification for Machinery certifies the state of repair of the engines. These certificates have no expiration dates, but the vessel must be inspected periodically.

**certificate of discharge**  *n.* Document issued to a seaman upon completion of his shipping agreement.

**certificate of disinfection**  *n.* Document issued by port authority to the master of a vessel giving details of sanitation procedures used to disinfect the vessel for the information of authorities in subsequent ports of call.

**certificate of financial responsibility**  *n.* A certificate issued by the Federal Maritime Commission to a vessel operator to show that the operator has posted a bond or otherwise demonstrated to the commission's satisfaction that he or she is financially competent to meet future obligations that may result from pollution by his or her vessel. See CERTIFICATE OF INSURANCE OR OTHER FINANCIAL SECURITY.

**certificate of identification**  See MERCHANT MARINER'S DOCUMENT.

**certificate of insurance or other financial security in respect of civil liability for oil pollution**  *n.* A document showing that a tanker is covered by insurance or similar security and required of all ships carrying more than 2,000 tons of oil in bulk. Similar to the Federal Maritime Commission's certificate of financial responsibility, this certificate is issued under provisions of the International Convention of Civil Liability for Oil Production Damage.

**certificate of origin**  *n.* Document signed by a consular officer at the port of shipment of cargo that entitles the consignee to certain privileges at the port of discharge.

**cesser clause**  *n.* Charter party term relating to the termination of charterer's liability upon shipment of cargo. Also *off hire clause* or *breakdown clause.*

**chadburn**  *n.* Great Lakes term for an engine room telegraph, from the manufacturer's name, Chadburn and Company of England.

**chafe**  *v.* To wear a surface. A hull can be chafed by rubbing against a piling; lines chafe when allowed to rub against a cleat or chock for a long period.

**chafing batten**  *n.* Strips of wood or synthetic materials on standing rigging used to reduce wear on sails.

**chafing chain**  *n.* A chain led from the H-bitt on the stern of a tugboat to the towline; the purpose of the chafing chain is to prevent chafing of the hawser on the taffrail.

**chafing gear**  *n.* Any material used to prevent chafing.

**chafing mat**  *n.* A fabric bag or envelop containing dunnage or other loose material, used to reduce chafing on hawsers in hawse pipes, and so on.

**chafing piece**  *n.* Additional plating added on a hull at points subject to abnormal wear, such as cargo ports, hatches, and hawse pipes. Also *chafing plate.*

**chain boat**  See ANCHOR HOY.

**chain bolt**  *n.* A fastener used to secure the lower end of a shroud or backstay to the chain plate on a vessel's side or stern. The chain bolt passes through the **toe link** of the shroud and then through the chain plate or the side of the hull.

**chain cable**  *n.* Anchor chain made of links with bars at their centers to keep them from stretching; a shackle interrupts the links at the end of each shot. In the United States, a shot is 15 fathoms; in the United Kingdom a shot is $12\frac{1}{2}$ fathoms. See CABLE.

**chain fours**   *n.* Two lengths of chain each with a hook at one end and hooks at the opposite end for use as a cargo sling. Also *chain legs.*

**chain girth**   *n.* The maximum girth of a vessel measured from deck to deck and beneath the keel.

**chain hoist**   *n.* (1) A heavy-duty lifting device using a chain with a hook at the end and a motor to haul the chain. (2) A 1- to 5-ton hand-operated hoist used for raising and lowering oil drums, boilers, and other jobs in an engine room. Also *chain fall; planetary hoist.*

**chain hook**   *n.* Short device used to handle chain cable on deck or in the chain locker.

**chain locker**   *n.* The compartment in the bow in which the anchor chain is stowed.

**chain pipe**   *n.* Heavy steel trunk through which the anchor cable is led from the deck to the chain locker. Also *spurling gate* or *spillpipe.*

**chain plate**   *n.* The fittings on the hull that anchor the shrouds and stays.

**chain riveting**   *n.* Rows of rivets spaced so that the rivets in one row are opposite those in an adjacent row.

**chains**   *n.* The station for the leadsman on the side of a ship at the bow. To "put a leadsman in the chains" is to have a man taking soundings by means of a lead line. The term derives from the chains, or chainwales of sailing ships. Such a platform toward the bow was an ideal place for the leadsman to stand when observing depths by casting the lead.

**chain sheets**   *n.* Chains used to extend the foot of a square sail along the yard below.

**chainshot**   *n.* Two cannon balls connected by a chain and fired at an enemy ship and designed specifically to damage rigging and spars.

**chain slings**   *n.* The short chains used to lower and raise yardarms on square-rigged ships. See CHAIN FOURS.

**chain splice**   *n.* A bend for fastening chain and rope together.

**chain stopper**   *n.* A device such as a pelican hook that is designed to secure chain when it is under a load. A chain stopper is used on deck to secure the anchor chain after the anchor is let out.

**chain tiller**   *n.* A tiller controlled by a chain leading to the chain drum of the steering engine that is controlled in turn by the helmsman.

**chainwales**   *n.* (pron. channels) A platform outboard of the bulwarks to which the lower shrouds are led in larger sailing vessels. Also *chains.*

**challenge**   *n.* A demand for identification or authentication by one vessel of another. This demand can be in code or by use of the internationally recognized Morse code signal "AA." The challenged vessel is required to respond with name and destination unless it is a warship, which is only required to identify herself.

**chamfer**   *v.* To round off the sharp edge of a 90° corner or to trim to an acute angle.

**chandler**   *n.* A person or organization that deals in goods, equipment, and groceries, now applied only to those who supply ships and other vessels.

**chandlery**   *n.* The business or inventory of a chandler.

**change of trim**   *n.* The algebraic sum of the initial trim and the trim after a vessel's weight has been shifted, loaded, or discharged.

**channel**   *n.* (1) The navigable part of a waterway, usually deeper than the sides. (2) A waterway that connects two seas, such as the English Channel. (3) A band of radio frequencies within which transmitters of various forms of electronic communication must maintain their modulated carrier to avoid interference with stations with adjacent frequencies. (4) See CHAINWALES.

**channel bar**   *n.* Steel extrusion with a U-shaped cross section used for stiffeners and frames.

**channel buoy**   *n.* A buoy marking the side or center of a channel, an obstruction, or other navigational obstacle.

**channel fever**   *n.* The eager anticipation of returning home experienced by English sailors as they approached the English Channel.

**channel money**   *n.* A bonus or money withheld from a British seaman's pay and due him when he pays off at the end of his contract.

**chantey** (or **chanty**)   *n.* Sailors' songs sung to give rhythm to their work.

**chapel**   *v.* To wear a ship taken aback without bracing the yards, the result of bad helmsmanship during calm periods.

**chapels**   *n.* Grooves between the various pieces in a built-up mast, painted a different color from the mast for ornamentation.

**chaplain**   *n.* Minister, priest, or rabbi commissioned by a navy to conduct religious services and attend to other personnel-related needs. In sailor's slang the chaplain is known as the **sky pilot.**

**char**   *v.* To burn wood, especially a hull, to preserve it.

**character of the bottom**   *n.* The nature of the sea bottom, especially with regard to its anchor-holding capability.

**characteristic**   *n.* (1) The identifying rhythm and period of the light of a lighted aid to navigation; a light characteristic. (2) The identifying Morse code transmitted by a radio beacon (racon). (3) The number of blasts and period produced by a sound signal. (4) The Morse code transmitted by a racon.

**charge**   *v.* To install batteries in an unmanned aid to navigation.

**charges clause**   *n.* Charter party term stipulating which of the parties of the charter pays harbor tolls, wharfage, duties, and other fees.

**Charlie**   *n.* Phonetic word for the letter "C." (2) In radio communication, a single-letter signal meaning affirmative. (3) A sound signal used by a vessel to indicate it knows it is about to be overtaken. See AFFIRMATIVE; ROGER.

**Charlie Noble**   *n.* The smokestack for a galley stove, so named for a British merchant captain who insisted on the galley's copper funnel being kept polished at all times. **To shoot Charlie Noble** was to fire a blank cartridge down the funnel to shake loose the soot.

**chart**   *n.* A navigation map. Charts for U.S. waters are published by the National Oceanic and Atmospheric Administration; charts for other parts of the world are published by the Defense Mapping Agency Hydrographic/Topographic Center.

**chart, sonar**   *n.* Chart containing oceanographic information used in underwater echo ranging.

**chart block**   *n.* Term used in the *Notice to Mariners* referring to a chart reproduction.

**charted visibility**   *n.* The distance a light can be seen by an observer 15 feet above sea level on a clear night. This distance is based solely on the height of the light and has nothing to do with the strength of the light, although the stronger the light the more readily it will be seen.

**charter**   *v.* To let or hire a vessel. A **demise charter** or **bareboat charter** is a contract by which the shipowner leases the vessel to the charterer, who becomes completely responsible for the vessel as if it were his or her own; the charterer pays all expenses and accepts all responsibility. Some demise charters specify that the captain and chief engineer must be approved by the owner.

**charter commission**   *n.* The fee paid to a broker by a shipowner for the charter of a vessel.

**charterer**   *n.* A person to whom a vessel is leased by its owner.

**charter party**   *n.* The document of contract between shipowner and charterer, the person doing the hiring; it is a contract in which the shipowner agrees to lease and the charterer agrees to hire. That which is leased and hired may be a vessel, all the cargo space, or only part of it; the terms and conditions are set forth in the contract. A charter party with no fees or commissions to be deducted is said to be **clean.** The most frequently used charter parties are bareboat charter parties or demise charters (see CHARTER), **time charter parties,** and **voyage charter parties.** The term comes from the Latin *charta partita,* a document in which the contents were written in duplicate and then divided in two parts with each of the two parties getting half.

**chart room**   *n.* A small room adjacent to the pilothouse in which charts and navigation instruments are located. It usually has a chart table at which the navigator and quartermasters work.

**chart sounding datum**   *n.* The water level from which chart soundings and tide tables are calculated in the United States, either mean low water, or mean lower low water for charted depths. See TIDAL DATUM.

**chase**   *n.* The tapering of the outside of a gun from slide to muzzle.

**chaser**   *n.* A bow gun or a stern gun. The **bow chaser** was used for firing at vessels being chased while the **stern chaser** was used to target chasing vessels.

**check**   *n.* (1) To stop, slow down, or regulate a line that is being paid out too fast. (2) To anchor to stop a vessel, usually an emergency procedure. (3) To slow or stop a vessel by use of engines going contrary to the direction of the vessel.

**checkered plate**   *n.* Steel deck plating embossed with various patterns such as diamonds to reduce danger of slipping.

**checkline (or rope)**   *n.* A line made fast at one end with turns around a bitt or bollard at the other end to check the motion of a vessel.

**checkman**   See WATER TENDER.

**cheek**   *n.* (1) One of the two sides of the casing of a block. See BLOCK. (2) One of the two projecting timbers of a masthead that support the trestletrees. (3) A split in wood running with the grain, caused by improper seasoning.

**cheek block**   *n.* A block with one side encased in a mast or spar, which supports one end of the pin, the other end being attached to the side of the block.

**cheekpiece**   *n.* Stiffener fitted for the upper portion of a small boat rudder just below the pintle.

**chestrees.**   *n.* In a square-rigged vessel, a wood fitting bolted to the topsides abaft the fore channels with a sheave at the upper end. The clews of the mainsail were extended to windward by hauling home the main tack through the sheaves.

**chief clerk**   *n.* Lead clerk under the purser.

**chief engineer**   *n.* The senior engineering officer on any ship who is responsible for all mechanical and electrical equipment.

**chief officer**   *n.* Merchant service designation for the senior officer under the master of a ship. Also *first mate* or *chief mate.*

**chief of staff** (or **chief staff officer**) *n.* The senior officer on an admiral's staff, either a captain or a lower-ranking admiral in the U.S. Navy. The senior assistant to a commodore is a **chief staff officer.** The highest ranking officer in the U.S. Navy is the Chief of Naval Operations (CNO), the equivalent in the Marine Corps and the Coast Guard being the Commandant, and in the Army and the Air Force the Chief of Staff.

**chief of the boat**   *n.* The senior enlisted person on a submarine and the executive officer's liaison in matters pertaining to the crew.

**chief steward**   *n.* In cargo or passenger merchant ships, the head of the department in charge of food management and housekeeping duties for all crew and passengers.

**Chile Current**   See PERU OCEANIC CURRENT.

**chill box** (or **compartment**)   *n.* A refrigerated room on a ship where frozen food is thawed and fresh food is kept cold. Also *reefer; walk-in.*

**chime**   *n.* (1) The rim around a cask head formed by projecting staves. Also *chine.* (2) In wooden ships, the heavy part of a waterway next to the ship's side.

**chimney**   *n.* The chart term for a relatively small, upright structure that projects above a building. See STACK.

**chine**   *n.* (1) The line on a vessel's hull where the bottom and sides meet. If they come together at a sharp angle, the vessel is described as being **hard-chined;** if the angle is gentler, it is called **soft-chined.** A **nontrip chine** or a **multiple-chine** hull makes the transition in two or more longitudinal steps. (2) A water channel made in a thick projection extending above the deck of wooden ships. (3) The rim of a cask. Also *chime.* **Chine on chine** refers to the stowage of casks end to end. See CANTLINE; CONTLINE.

**chine hooks**   *n.* Hooks used to hoist casks by catching them under the chine.

**chine out**   *v.* To hollow out or to form a waterway in a deck.

**chine piece** (or **log**)   *n.* Longitudinal timber or girder that runs from stem to stern along the line where the side and bottom frames join in a V-bottom hull.

**Chinese jibe**   *n.* An accidental jibe in which the boom and bottom of a gaff sail or lugsail changes to the other side and the top stays on the same side, a common problem on Chinese junks.

**Chinese lug**   *n.* A balanced lugsail with battens as seen on Chinese junks and similar small craft.

**chinse**   *v.* To force caulking material into a seam by using a thin blade or **chinsing tool** when a caulking tool would be too thick.

**chip log**   *n.* A device used on sailing ships to determine speed. It consisted of a wood quadrant roughly 5 inches in radius with lead placed in the circular edge to cause it to float upright. The chip was fastened to the log line with a three-part bridle. The chip was streamed with the first 15 to 30 fathoms, called the **stray line,** and marked with bunting. The line after the stray line was marked with pieces of cord or marlin every knot (47 feet 3 inches). The log was allowed to run while the 28-second glass emptied. The result gave the rate of speed. The speed in knots was determined by the equation

$$\frac{28 \text{ seconds}}{3,600 \text{ seconds}} = \frac{X}{6,080 \text{ feet}}$$

**chipping hammer**  *n.* (1) Hand tool with a sharp projection or peen used for chipping paint, rust, and so on from metal surfaces. (2) Power-driven air hammer with a steel cutting chisel to remove excess metal, rust, and boiler scale.

**chips**  *n.* Traditional nickname for the ship's carpenter.

**chock**  *n.* (1) A deck fitting designed to guide an anchor line or deck line and to help reduce chafing. (2) Support blocks in a repair facility. (3) **Chocks of the rudder** are timbers used to stop the motion of the rudder beyond certain limits to prevent damage.

**chock**  *v.* To wedge V-shaped wooden pieces or chocks under loose gear or cargo to keep it from rolling. A **chock boat** is a cradle or support for a lifeboat.

**chock-a-block**  *adj.* When two blocks of a tackle are pulled firmly together, they are described as being chock-a-bloc. Also *two-block.*

**chock roller**  *n.* A metal deck device fitted with a sheave to prevent chafing.

**chocolate gale**  *n.* Local nickname for a brisk northwest wind in the West Indies.

**choke**  *v.* To foul a fall in a block, sometimes done intentionally to secure the fall temporarily.

**choke-a-luff**  *phr.* To place the hauling part (loose end) of a tackle between a sheave of one of two blocks along with

the line that runs through it to stop the movement of the blocks. This is a convenient system used on small sailboats.

**chop**  *n.* (1) Short, often irregular, waves, caused by conflicting tides and winds. (2) Change of command or change of authority, usually accompanied by time and date of transfer of authority. See CHOP LINE.

**chop line**  *n.* The boundary between two commands at which ships change from the control of one fleet, for example, to another.

**chopping**  *n.* The rapid and regular switching on and off of a transponder for recognition purposes.

**chord**  *n.* A line segment that cuts across a circle to form an arc on a circle. In sailmaking it is a line from the luff to the leech that is used for a mathematical description of the sail. For the camber, divide the chord depth by the chord length.

**chosen**  *adj.* British usage for "assumed," as in assumed longitude, assumed latitude, or assumed position.

**chronograph**  *n.* An instrument that produces a graphic record of time as shown by a clock; while the clock time is recorded, an external agent makes or keeps a simultaneous record. Boiler temperatures or atmospheric pressures are kept with the time of the changes.

**chronometer**  *n.* A highly consistent clock used for navigation; dictionaries frequently use the word "accurate," but consistency of error is more important than accuracy. Traditionally a chronometer is gimbaled and kept in a wooden box secured in chocks to minimize jarring. It is wound daily at noon, and the captain is so informed. When the ship goes to general quarters, it is the quartermaster's responsibility to place it between mattresses to reduce jarring when large guns are fired. These precision timepieces are rapidly being replaced by far less expensive and very accurate electronic timepieces. See QUARTZ CRYSTAL MARINE CHRONOMETER.

**chronometer correction** *n.* The amount of time that must be added algebraically to the chronometer time to obtain the correct time. Chronometer correction is numerically the same as chronometer error except they have opposite signs. When chronometer correction is used to correct chronometer time, the direction is indicated by plus or minus instead of fast or slow.

**chronometer error** *n.* The accumulated loss or gain in a chronometer as compared with Greenwich mean time (GMT) or Coordinated Universal Time (UTC). The error is rounded to the nearest second and is labeled either fast (F) or slow (S). The **chronometer correction** is the same as the chronometer error with the sign reversed; that is, if the error is 2 seconds fast, the correction must be minus 2 seconds.

**chubasco** *n.* A violent easterly wind of the western approach to Nicaragua.

**churada** *n.* A heavy rain squall in the Mariana Islands during the northeast monsoon.

**church pennant** *n.* A blue-and-white pennant flown during divine services at sea and the only pennant allowed to be flown above the national ensign.

**chute** See SPINNAKER.

**cigarette boat** *n.* Long, narrow, high-speed motor boat designed for racing.

**cigarette deck** *n.* Open deck abaft a submarine's bridge where the crew was allowed to smoke in the early days of submarines.

**Cinque Ports** *n.* Originally five ports of southeastern England on the Strait of Dover and the North Sea—Hastings,

Romney, Hythe, Dover, and Sandwich, and later including Rye and Winchelsea—that were granted special privileges by Edward the Confessor in return for their valiant defense of the coast. They enjoyed special privileges with the understanding they would furnish without charge a certain number of vessels to the crown. The Lord Warden of the Cinque Ports is the official who guards such privileges as still remain. From the French *cinq,* five.

**circle "C" formula** *n.* The calculation used by marine architects to determine the power and speed of a cargo vessel. The formula is as follows: $C = (427.1 \times \text{effective horsepower}) \div (\frac{2}{3} \text{displacement}) \times (\text{speed} \times 3)$.

**circle of altitude** *n.* A great circle on the celestial sphere that lies perpendicular to the observer's horizon and passes through the observer's zenith and nadir.

**circle of equal altitude** *n.* A circle on the surface of the Earth along which a given heavenly body has the same observed altitude at a given time.

**circle of illumination** *n.* The twilight area that separates the illuminated from the shaded hemisphere. Also *terminator.*

**circle of latitude** *n.* A great circle of the celestial sphere that is perpendicular to the ecliptic.

**circle of longitude** *n.* A circle of the celestial sphere that is parallel to the ecliptic.

**circle of right ascension** *n.* A great circle that passes through both poles of the celestial sphere and is measured east from the first point of Aries to the hour circle of the body.

**circle of uncertainty** *n.* A circle within which a craft is considered to be located, the radius of which is the maximum likely error of the position.

**circle of visibility**   *n.* The distance around a light that can be seen by an observer at a height of 15 feet.

**circular probable error (CPE** or **CEP)**   *n.* A circle within which there is a 50% probability of an object being located. The size of this circle is used in assessing the accuracy of a position: the larger the circle, the less accurate the position and the greater the probability of error. Also *sphere probability of error.*

**circumnavigate**   *v.* To sail around, usually with specific reference to the Earth, and also including other means of transport, such as flying.

**circumpolar**   *adj.* (1) Located or found near one of the poles. (2) Pertaining to a star that does not go below the horizon as seen from the observer's latitude, such as Polaris in the northern hemisphere. (3) A heavenly body that makes two meridian passages, one above and one below the pole of the observer's hemisphere, the **elevated pole.** The constellations of Ursa Major (the Great Bear or Big Dipper) and Cassiopeia are circumpolar for people in the United States and Canada who live north of 40°N latitude.

**cirripeda**   *n.* General term for barnacles and other parasitic marine animals.

**cirrocumulus clouds**   *n.* A principal cloud type that appears as a thin white patch without shadows. Cirrocumulus are easily confused with altocumulus. The consistent difference is the small patches and the lack of shadows of the cirrocumulus. See CLOUDS.

**cirrostratus clouds**   *n.* A principal cloud type that appears as a whitish veil, usually fibrous, but sometimes smooth and may cover the sky. See CLOUDS.

**cirrus (Ci)**   *n.* Wispy clouds composed of ice crystals that often announce an advancing warm front. See CLOUDS.

**civil salvage**   *n.* Compensation for salvage of a ship, its cargo, or its crew and passengers due salvors other than the owner and his company.

**clamp**   *n.* Ceiling timbers to which deck beams are fastened.

**clamp down**   *n.* A swabbing of the deck.

**clamp down**   *v.* To lightly clean an area by sprinkling the deck with water and then swabbing with a damp swab.

**clamshell bucket**   *n.* A large bucket consisting of two hinged scoops and used for removing coal, mud, or ore.

**clap on**   *v.* (1) To grab a line to haul on it. (2) To add a stopper or a tackle to a line. (3) To bend on more canvas.

**clapper**   *n.* (1) The tongue or pendulum inside a bell. (2) A fitting in the jaws of a gaff that prevents jamming.

**class**   *n.* (1) A group of boats of the same design to make racing a matter of technical skill rather than boat design. (2) A group of warships made to one design, as in the *Maryland*-class battleships. (3) Character of a commercial vessel determined by a professional classification society.

**class rates**   *n.* Insurance rates applying to a single type of cargo or freight.

**classification clause**   *n.* Marine underwriters' term for assigning base rates to various classes of vessels without a specific vessel having been surveyed.

**claw off**   *v.* To lay to windward off a shore against adverse winds, to work away from a lee shore against weather.

**claw ring**   *n.* Device to which the mainsheet is attached on booms with roller reefing. The claw ring stays in the same position while the boom is rotated.

**cleading**   *n.* A covering panel protecting ballast tanks in a lifeboat.

**clean air**   *n.* An airflow that is undisturbed by other boats or obstacles.

**clean ballast tanks (CBT)**   *n.* Cargo tanks reserved for ballast water.

**clean bill of health**   *n.* Certification that there were no infectious diseases in a port or on a ship at the time of its departure from that port.

**clean nonmilitary vessel**   *n.* In time of war, any merchant vessel of the United States, her allies, or a neutral nation whose movements for the previous six months give no cause for question and about which there is no question upon close examination.

**clean slate**   *n.* The slate on which courses were recorded during a watch to be transferred to the log at the end of the watch; when the courses were logged, the slate was wiped clean.

**clear**   *adj.* (1) Said of an anchor when it is not fouled. (2) Plain language text, not encoded. Also *clear text.*

**clear**   *v.* (1) To pass a point of land or a cape. (2) To depart. (3) To authorize.

**clear ahead**   See CLEAR ASTERN.

**clearance**   *n.* (1) The space between a vessel and what it is passing. (2) The height of an object above the surface of the water, or the width of an opening. Charts give horizontal and vertical bridge clearance. The vertical clearance is the clearance at mean high water. The same holds true for power lines above the water. (3) Permission from a regulatory authority such as the port director to enter or leave port. See PRATIQUE.

**Clearance Inward Certificate (or Note)**   *n.* Document issued by customs that lists dutiable goods remaining on a vessel after other cargo has been offloaded and before new cargo is loaded. A vessel is said to be cleared inward when such certification is granted.

**clearance outward**   *n.* Authorization by customs for a vessel to leave port and indicating the master of the vessel has met all regulations and paid all dues and charges.

**clear astern**   *adj.* Said of a yacht when the hull and equipment are abaft an imaginary line projected abeam from the aftermost point of another yacht's hull and equipment. The other yacht is **clear ahead.** The yachts are said to overlap if neither is clear astern, or if another yacht overlaps both of them.

**clear away**   *interj.* (1) The command to lay out a coil so that the rope will run freely, applied to downhauls, weather staysail sheets, and other running rigging. (2) Command to strike the tack-jigger.

**clear berth**   *n.* The unobstructed area surrounding a vessel at anchor. If a vessel has clear berth, she can swing with tide and wind and not touch an obstruction or another vessel.

**clear days**   *n.* Charter party term referring to the days when work can be done exclusive of the first and last days.

**clear for running**   *phr.* Said of a line that is free and will not foul while paying out. Also *free to run.*

**clear hawse**   *n.* Expression used when the anchor chain is clear, unobstructed, and not twisted so as to impede raising the anchor. If two bow anchors are out tending away from the bows on their respective sides, it usually means they have not become twisted around each other; you can assume you have clear hawses or open hawses. See OPEN HAWSE.

**clear hawse**   *v.* To untangle or untwist anchor cables.

**clear hawse pendant**   *n.* Short chain or heavy wire used for untangling anchor cable. Also *preventer hawser.*

**clear hawse slip**   *n.* Device used for reeving a cable through a hawse pipe.

**clearing marks** (or **ranges**) *n.* Marks or ranges positioned to take a vessel clear of danger or into open water.

**clear ship**   *phr.* To prepare for naval action by removing paint cans from the deck, the jack staff from its position, spars not needed for the navigation of the vessel, and to lay out such ammunition as is brought topside for use during general quarters.

**clear view screen**   *n.* A glass disk outboard of a bridge port; the disk is rotated during foul weather by an electric motor at a speed sufficient to throw the rainwater off and keep a clear view for the conning officer.

**clear visibility**   *n.* Meteorological visibility of 10 nautical miles. See VISUAL RANGE.

**cleat**   *n.* (1) A deck or pier fitting designed for securing a line without need for a hitch. See BITT. (2) Short strip of wood used to keep a gangway from slipping. (3) A clip on the frames of a vessel used to hold cargo battens. See BITT.

**cleat**   *v.* To secure a line to a cleat.

**clench**   *v.* (1) To secure a nail in place by bending the end of it, or to secure a bolt or rivet by capping. (2) To secure something permanently.

**clevis**   *n.* A U-shaped piece of metal with holes at the ends through which a pin is forced. The pin determines whether the shackle is a screw pin shackle, a clevis pin shackle, or a safety clevis shackle.

**clew**   *n.* (1) The after corner of a sail. The clew is the lower corner of a square sail or the aftermost corner of à staysail.

See TACK. (2) On a studdingsail, the clew is the outer lower corner. Also *clue.* See GAFF, MARCONI RIG.

**clew down** (or **up**)   *v.* To **clew down** is to haul on the clewlines, leaving the sheets fast and letting go the halyards, to pull a yard down. To **clew up** is to slack away the halyards and to let go the sheets and the clewlines are hauled tight.

**clew cringle**   *n.* The reinforced aperture at the clew. This hole used to be reinforced with rope, but today it is a steel ring, known as a **clew ring,** sewn into the boltrope and sail.

**clew garnet**   *n.* A line led from the bottom corner of the mainsail of a square-rigged ship to its spar at the top and used to haul the sail up to the spar. Only the mainsail has a clew garnet; other sails simply have clew lines.

**clew line**   *n.* The rope bent on a square sail at the clew and led to the yardarm and then down to the deck. Clew lines are used in striking sails.

**clew outhaul**   *n.* The line used to stretch the foot of a sail aft along a boom.

**clew patch**   *n.* The strengthening fabric piece sewn into the corner of a sail at the clew to resist wear.

**clew traveler**   *n.* A ring or other device attached to the clew of a sail so that it can be hauled out along the boom. Also *outhaul.*

**climate**   *n.* The meteorological conditions that include temperature, precipitation, and wind that characteristically prevail in a given region. This is in contrast to weather, which is the state of the atmosphere at any given time.

**clinch**   *n.* A half-hitch stopped to itself by seizing. Before chain cables and shackles were developed, for example, a line attached to the anchor ring by a half-hitch stopped with a clinch.

**clinch (or clench)** *v.* (1) To secure a rope to a ring by use of a clinch. (2) To create a burr on the end of a bolt or nail after it has been driven through the fabric or wood on which it is to be used; the burr prevents its pulling back out.

**clinker** *n.* The name given a system designed to sense heat from a submarine's wake.

**clinker-built** *adj.* Pertains to construction with overlapping planks or plates. Also *lap-strake*.

**clinometer** *n.* An instrument for determining degree of inclination of a roll, list, or heel.

**clip** *n.* Any device such as a spring-loaded snap used to secure the luff of a sail to the mast or a headstay. Also *hank*. (2) Angle iron used to fasten flooring or bracket plates to the vertical keel and longitudinal timbers. (3) The throat of a gaff.

**clip hooks** *n.* Two similar hooks used to form a single eye.

**clipper** *n.* Mid-19th century sailing ship characterized by a sharp concave bow or **clipper bow,** tall masts, square sails, and built for speed. Companies vied for captains able to get the most speed out of the ships as record after record was set.

**close** *v.* To get closer to another vessel or a place.

**close aboard** *adj.* Nearby in the water. Another vessel is said to be close aboard when it is within one boat length of the larger vessel.

**closed chock** *n.* A chock that is not open on the top and through which lines must be rove.

**closed-in spaces** *n.* A measurement term that refers to the spaces protected from the weather above the upper deck but having openings too small to be exempted by surveyors as open spaces.

**closed sea** *n.* (1) that part of an ocean enclosed by headlands within narrow straits. (2) That part of the ocean within the territorial jurisdiction of a country.

**closed stokehold** *n.* Fireroom with pressure maintained above the atmospheric pressure by blowers.

**close-hauled** *adj.* Describes a vessel with sails trimmed as close to the wind as possible in order to make maximum speed to windward. Vessels on this point of sail are said to be **beating, by the wind,** or **on the wind.** See POINTS OF SAILING.

**close pack ice** *n.* Ice of $\frac{6}{8}$ to less than $\frac{7}{8}$ concentration, composed mostly of floes in contact.

**close reach** *n.* A point of sail with the apparent wind forward of the beam, that is, with the wind coming from 90° relative to the ship's heading on either side, to about 45°, forward of the beam. See POINTS OF SAILING.

**close-reefed** *adj.* Said of topsails on a square-rigged vessel when all the reefs have been taken in to expose as little sail area as possible.

**close stowing anchor** *n.* An old-fashioned anchor or a stocked anchor with stocks and flukes so designed that when not in use, they can fold to lie in the same plane to be stowed.

**closest point of approach (CPA)** *n.* A collision avoidance term referring to the time or place a ship will come closest to another object or ship.

**close up** See TWO-BLOCK.

**close-winded** *adj.* Used to describe a vessel that is able to sail close to the wind.

**closing line**   *n.* The boundary at the mouth of a legal bay or river that forms part of the base line.

**closing strake**   *n.* The last bilge strake to be welded on the shell plating in a shipyard.

**cloth**   *n.* A width of material in a sail.

**cloud bank**   *n.* A fairly well defined mass of clouds observed at a distance covering an appreciable portion of the horizon sky, but not directly overhead.

**cloud base**   *n.* The lowest level in the atmosphere at which the air contains a perceptible quantity of cloud particles of a given cloud or cloud layer.

**cloudburst**   *n.* An exceptionally heavy brief rainfall, unofficially specified as being a rainfall rate equal to 100 millimeters, or about 4 inches, per hour.

**cloud cover**   *n.* The portion of the sky covered with clouds, usually measured in tenths of the visible sky, with 0 representing no clouds in the sky and 10 representing full cloud cover.

**cloud height**   *n.* The height of a cloud base above the local terrain.

**clouds**   *n.* Clouds are made up of numerous tiny drops of water or ice crystals that are formed by condensation of water vapor in the air and are, therefore, good indicators of meteorological conditions. Cloud names are composed of a number of Latin words used alone or in combination: *altus,* high; *cirrus,* curl; *cumulus,* pile; *fractus,* broken; *nimbus,* rain storm; *pallium,* curtain; and *stratus,* covering. Although several types can extend across more than one level, clouds are generally classified according to the altitude at which they occur.

Low clouds include **stratus** formations (about 2,000 feet), which resemble fog and from which fog itself descends; when broken by strong winds they are called **fractonimbus** or **scud. Nimbostratus** formations (about 3,000 feet) are dense, dark rain clouds. **Cumulus** (2,000–12,000 feet) are wooly, fair-weather clouds with flat bottoms and domed tops. **Stratocumulus** clouds (about 5,000 feet) are gray masses that usually precede clear weather. **Cumulonimbus** (5,000–30,000 feet) are massive, anvil-shaped thunderheads with masses extending into upper cloud levels.

Middle clouds include **altocumulus** (12,000 feet), sheeplike clouds that can become chaotic just before storms. **Altostratus** (15,000 feet) are gray or dark blue formations that frequently thicken to bring rain or snow; they make up what is popularly known as a **mackerel sky.**

Upper clouds include **cirrocumulus** (23,000 feet), a combination of cirrus and cumulus types with fair weather, but as they darken they may precede a storm. **Cirrostratus** (31,000 feet) are thin, mistlike formations that occasionally cover the entire sky. It is this veil that causes halos around the Sun and Moon. **Cirropallium** clouds make up a thin veil that slowly covers the sky in advance of a hurricane or typhoon. **Cirrus** clouds (20,000–40,000 feet) are generally associated with fair weather; when they form long streaks across the sky they are called **mare's tails.**

**clove hitch**   *n.* A double half-hitch, a good knot for securing mooring lines quickly or hitching ratlines to the shrouds. Hitches are used anywhere that jamming is no problem. See KNOT.

**club**   *n.* Originally a spar on a headsail or topsail; today a spar on the bottom edge of a sail, especially a headsail.

**club**   *v.* To intentionally drag an anchor while drifting with a current; the anchor is fitted with a trip line so that it can be put into service to bring the vessel broadside to the current. Rare. The maneuver is also used in docking in adverse conditions.

**club burgee**   *n.* Traditionally a single-pointed pennant (though some are swal-

# Clouds

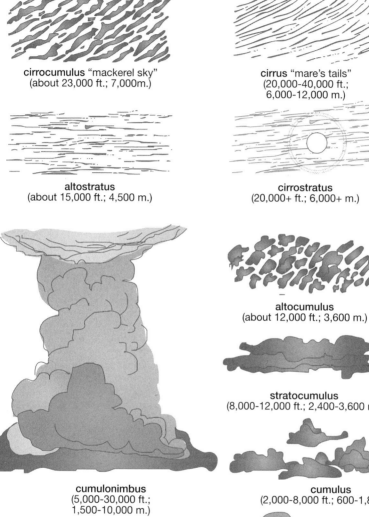

cirrocumulus "mackerel sky"
(about 23,000 ft.; 7,000m.)

cirrus "mare's tails"
(20,000-40,000 ft.;
6,000-12,000 m.)

altostratus
(about 15,000 ft.; 4,500 m.)

cirrostratus
(20,000+ ft.; 6,000+ m.)

altocumulus
(about 12,000 ft.; 3,600 m.)

stratocumulus
(8,000-12,000 ft.; 2,400-3,600 m.)

cumulonimbus
(5,000-30,000 ft.;
1,500-10,000 m.)

cumulus
(2,000-8,000 ft.; 600-1,800 m.)

stratus (about 2,000 ft.; 600 m.)
gray sheet

nimbostratus
(about 3,000 ft.;
900 m.)

low-tailed or rectangular) that bears a yacht club identification and is flown from the masthead of sailboats above the personal signal and on the bows of powerboats.

**club-footed jib**   *n.* A headsail laced along the foot to a boom that pivots at the headstay.

**club haul**   *v.* (1) An emergency method of tacking used by square-rigged vessels in heavy weather on a lee shore; the vessel is cast on the opposite tack by the use of a line from a kedge to the lee quarter. (2) To rig a wire from the quarter of a powered ship at anchor to the anchor or anchor cable to make sure the vessel swings in the desired direction when the tide changes.

**club topsail**   *n.* Three-cornered gaff topsail with upper part of its luff lashed to a spar or club extending above the truck.

**clump**   *n.* Heavy fitting welded to the stern of a minesweeper to which is attached a paravane chain.

**clump block**   *n.* A pulley with a solid, rounded shell, and wide sheaves. It is designed to accept a line half its circumference.

**clutch winch**   *n.* Winch with the drum and gear wheel keyed fast to the shaft instead of loosely fitted to the shaft as with a friction winch.

**clutter**   *n.* Radar interference of any kind, whether it be rain, snow, or other signals.

**coach**   *n.* The forward, and smaller, of the two cabins beneath the poop deck of early sailing ships. The after cabin was called the great cabin and was used by the senior officer aboard. The coach was used for the second-ranking officer.

**coach roof**   *n.* A cabin roof that is raised to give added room. Also *cabin top.*

**coachwhipping**   *n.* Ornamental ropework used to cover stanchions, tillers, handrails, and so on.

**coak**   *n.* Thames shipbuilding term for a tabular projection on a scarfed timber left to fit into a negative facing of the same design to prevent slipping when masts or timbers were joined. Called **tabling.** The joint between two timbers with pieces of hardwood placed in slots between the two timbers used to assist bolts and to prevent twisting or slipping is called a **coaked scarf.**

**coal bunker**   *n.* A storage area for coal used to fire the boilers.

**coal hoist**   *n.* Power-driven elevator for bunkering bagged coal.

**coaling port**   *n.* An opening in the side plating for use in handling coal on coal-fired vessels.

**coaling station**   *n.* A coal depot, often government-controlled, established for refueling coal-fired ships. The station at Dry Tortugas is an example.

**coaming**   *n.* (1) A raised rib around a hatch, skylight, or cockpit to keep out the water and that also prevents people walking along the deck from falling into the hold, and onto which a hatch cover is set.

**coaming bar**   *n.* Angle iron used to fasten coaming to a deck.

**coaming bulkhead**   *n.* Double plating reinforcing a bulkhead at the top and bottom.

**coastal boundary**   *n.* The intersection of the surface of the sea and land at a specified datum exclusive of one established by treaty or by Congress. Treaties and legislation frequently established separate coastal boundaries for political purposes.

**coastal confluence zone (CCZ)** *n.* The area of ocean that extends out from a nation's shore 50 nautical miles or to the 100-fathom curve, whichever is farther.

**coastal current** *n.* A stream running parallel to the shore and beyond the surfline, such as the Gulf Stream. See CURRENT, LONGSHORE CURRENT.

**coastal navigation** *n.* Navigation along a coast with landmarks in sight. See PILOTING.

**coastal pack** *n.* Pack ice attached to a shore.

**Coastal Warning Display System** *n.* A century-old system of flags and pennants used at coastal stations by the National Weather Service to warn of storms and hurricanes. It was phased out in 1989 when the system was superseded by NOAA Weather Radio Network, broadcast from its 380 sites across the country. Many marinas and other shore facilities continue to fly the flags and pennants as a matter of tradition and convenience for the many boats without radios.

**Coast and Geodetic Survey** *n.* Former name for the National Ocean Survey, now a component of the National Oceanic and Atmospheric Administration (NOAA).

**coaster** *n.* A vessel engaged in trade along a coast, but not, as a rule, equipped or certified for ocean passages. Also *coasting vessel.*

**Coast Guard** See UNITED STATES COAST GUARD.

**coasting lights** *n.* Land lights and lighted markers used for navigation along a coast. The term is rarely used today.

**coasting trade** *n.* Commercial exchange carried on among the ports of a country by way of vessels on the coastline.

**coastline** *n.* The general shape of a coastal area, usually distinguished from the more detailed shoreline. The coastline of Florida is a little over 1,300 miles from the state line north of Jacksonville to Key West and from Key West north along the west coast to the state line beyond Pensacola; the shoreline, however, is more than 8,000 miles.

**Coast Pilot** See RUTTER; UNITED STATES COAST PILOT.

**coastwise** *adj.* A term used to describe a route which is not more than 20 nautical miles offshore on any ocean, the Gulf of Mexico, the Caribbean Sea, the Gulf of Alaska, or other waters designated by the Coast Guard. See OCEAN.

**cobbing** *n.* A beating administered to sailors by use of a **cobbing board** or stick; often a cobbing was administered by fellow sailors for a breach of honor among themselves.

**cock** *n.* A valve that is opened and closed by giving a disc or tapered plug a half-turn.

**cockbill** See A-COCKBILL.

**cockboat** *n.* A ship's small rowboat, used as a tender. Also *cockleboat.*

**cocked hat** *n.* A triangle formed by the intersection of three navigational sights when they do not intersect exactly.

**cockpit** *n.* (1) The space on a boat abaft the cabin. (2) In a small boat, the space in which are found the compass and wheel, usually lower than the rest of the deck. (3) An exposed recess in the weather deck extending no more than one-half the length of the vessel measured over the weather deck.

**cockscomb** *n.* (1) Notched wooden device at the ends of a yardarm to facilitate extending the sail when the reef earings are hauled out. (2) Cordage around a ring, grommet, or becket that begins with a clove hitch followed with each end being fashioned around the object and secured with each turn by a half-hitch. Also *coxcomb*.

**cocurrent line** *n.* A line on a chart that connects points having the same current at the same time.

**cod** *n.* (obsolete). Recess of a bay or inland sea.

**cod line** *n.* An 18-thread line of un-tarred hemp or cotton used for hammock clews. Originally it was used for cod fishing. Also *hambroline*.

**code book** *n.* A compendium of international signals, with instructions for visual, sound, and radio communication between ships at sea and shore stations using alphabet flags, substitutes, numeral pennants, and the code pennant. Editions are available in many languages; the *International Code of Signals, United States Edition*, HO 102, is printed by the Defense Mapping Agency Hydrographic/ Topographic Center. See CODE PENNANT.

**code pennant** *n.* A red-and-white striped pennant used to introduce a signal to signify that the *International Code* is being used.

**coding delay** *n.* The time required between transmission by a master loran station and the slave station.

**codress** *n.* An addressee encrypted in a coded message.

**coffeegrinder** *n.* A sheet winch on a pedestal used on ocean-racing boats and usually fitted with two handles so that two or more people can operate it at the same time.

**cofferdam** *n.* (1) A chamber usually filled with cork or similar material found on old ships as protection from wear at wharfs at the waterline. (2) A watertight chamber on a ship's side to make possible repairs below the waterline. (3) A waterproof bulkhead constructed around a damaged area of a ship's hull when repairs to the hull are not feasible. (4) Double waterproof bulkheads.(5) A temporary watertight enclosure built in the water so that water can be pumped out to allow seawalls and other emplacements to be built.

**coffin plate** *n.* An inverted boss used on a propeller bossing of a multiscrew vessel. It looks like a coffin.

**coil** *n.* Rope wound in a series of concentric circles, one turn on top of the one before; rope is said to be coiled, or to be wound into a coil. Rope is often sold in coils of fixed lengths: variously 200 fathoms in length, 90 to 120 fathoms (hawser-laid), 106 fathoms (shroud-laid), and so on. Today 100 fathoms is most common for rope up to 8-inches in diameter.

**coin** *n.* A wedge placed under the breech of a gun to elevate or depress as needed. Also *quoin*.

**coir** *n.* (rhymes with lawyer) The fiber from the husk of a coconut used for making matting and low-grade rope. A **coir hawser** is a rope made from coconut husks, light enough to float.

**colatitude** *n.* The complement of a latitude on the celestial sphere. If the latitude is 40°, the colatitude is 50°.

**cold air mass** *n.* An air mass that is colder than the air around it or than the ground over which it is moving.

**cold front** *n.* A boundary between two air masses that moves so that the colder air replaces the warmer air of the relatively cold air mass.

**cold iron watch**   *n.* A security detail left aboard ship when the machinery is inoperative or when nothing can be done to get the vessel underway, such as when it is in dry dock.

**cold low**   *n.* A low-pressure system across which little or no gradient in temperature and moisture is found.

**cold ship**   *n.* Ship without any source of power for propulsion, heat, or communications. Also *dead ship.*

**Cold Wall**   *n.* The point off the Grand Banks where the Labrador Current meets the Gulf Stream. At that point, there is very little mixing of the two currents, but a sharp temperature change, the Cold Wall, is quickly detected. The Gulf Stream water passing along beneath the cold arctic air evaporates so rapidly that frost smoke rises above the water.

**cold wire**   *n.* An expression to describe a ship with the generators off and running on auxiliary power, usually in port.

**collada**   *n.* A 30–50 mph wind that blows from north or northwest in the northern Gulf of California and from the northeast in the southern part of the Gulf of California.

**collar**   *n.* (1) A flanged band or ring or a welded plate used to close a frame or beam penetration through plating. (2) A loop or eye at the end of a stay or shroud that goes around the masthead.

**collier**   *n.* A ship designed to carry coal for other than its own use.

**collier's patch**   *n.* A tar patch on a worn sail.

**collision**   *n.* The coming together of two vessels.

**collision bearing**   *n.* A constant bearing between two vessels while the distance between them is decreasing.

**collision bulkhead**   *n.* A transverse, waterproof bulkhead near the bow built to minimize damage from head-on collisions.

**collision clause**   *n.* Hull insurance clause usually included in addition to the ordinary marine risks in which the underwriters agree to pay their proportion of the cost of up to three-fourths damage inflicted on another vessel up to the value of the policy, but not exceeding such value.

**collision course**   *n.* A course that, if maintained, will cause a collision between two vessels.

**collision drill**   *n.* A damage control exercise in preparing for a collision by dogging watertight hatches and taking such measures in the engine room as securing the superheat.

**collision mat**   *n.* Heavy mat previously made from canvas and hemp, now more often made from synthetic materials, used for covering holes in the hull resulting from collisions and battle damage.

**colored light**   *n.* An aid to navigation lighted by a color other than white.

**colors**   *n.* (1) A national ensign. (2) The call that goes out at 0800 when the national ensign is raised. The colors are lowered at sunset in a ceremony referred to as "making colors."

**COLREGS**   See CONVENTION ON THE INTERNATIONAL REGULATIONS FOR PREVENTING COLLISIONS AT SEA.

**COLREGS Demarcation Lines**   *n.* Lines of demarcation between those waters upon which International Regulations for Preventing Collisions at Sea, 1972 (72 COLREGS) and the Inland Navigation Rules apply. The waters inside of the lines are known as **Inland Rules Waters,** and those outside the lines **COLREGS Waters.** The regulations establishing the COLREGS Demarcation Lines are spelled out in the U.S. Coast Guard's *Navigation Rules, Inland-International*.

**colt**    *n.* A short piece of rope with a knot in the end used for punishing sailors before the 19th century.

**column, open order**    *n.* Ships following a guide alternately a few degrees to port and to starboard with even-numbered vessels to port.

**colure**    *n.* Either of two great circles passing through the celestial poles dividing the ecliptic into four equal parts and marking the four seasons.

**COM**    Prefix indicating the commander of a military command. COMMINLANT refers to the Commander of Atlantic Minecraft, and MINLANT is a reference to the command itself.

**combatant ship**    *n.* A vessel with a primary mission to engage the enemy.

**combat chart**    *n.* A chart designed for naval operations, especially amphibious operations, that uses the characteristics of a map to represent the land area and the characteristics of a chart to represent the sea area, as well as special characteristics for the needs peculiar to such warfare.

**combat information center (CIC)**    *n.* The section of a ship manned and equipped to collect, collate, and distribute all tactical information during an engagement. A ship charged with the coordination of the CIC functions of the various ships in a task force is the **combat information ship**. Also *action information center*.

**combat loading**    *n.* Amphibious term for embarking troops and equipment for fast debarkation during an assault. Different from base loading, which is loading men and equipment for a base to be

further transferred for an assault or for training exercises.

**comb cleat**    *n.* A wooden half-circle bolted to a deck to receive a line.

**combers**    *n.* Waves at sea with foamy crests, as distinguished from breakers, which are breaking waves near shore that tumble over because their bases are on the ground.

**combination buoy**    *n.* A navigation aid that has two kinds of signals, such as a lighted gong buoy or a lighted whistler.

**combination framing**    *n.* Marine construction term referring to a design using longitudinal framing for decks and bottom and transverse framing for the sides.

**combination lantern**    *n.* A combination of sidelights and stern light allowed for sailing vessels of less than 20 meters and power-driven vessels of less than 12 meters.

**combined carrier**    *n.* A general-purpose commercial vessel designed to carry bulk cargo, either homogeneous or non-homogeneous, such as ore and petroleum oil.

**combined operations**    *n.* A military operation involving the forces of two or more allies.

**combustible liquid**    *n.* Any liquid with a flash point above 80°F. See FLAMMABLE LIQUID.

**combustion control**    *n.* The process of controlling steam pressure, superheat temperature, airflow, fuel flow, feedwater flow, and other procedures related to the production of steam for the power plant.

**come about**    *v.* To tack through the wind, to bring the vessel from one tack to the other while keeping the wind forward of the vessel. See JIBE.

**come-along**   *n.* A cable or chain fitted with a ratchet used for lifting or taking a strain when the ratchet is engaged.

**come home**   *phr.* An anchor is said to be coming home when it drags across the ground toward the ship as it is hauled in; if an anchor is properly set, the ship will go to the anchor before the anchor breaks loose of the bottom.

**come round**   *v.* To turn more toward the direction from which the wind is coming, to luff.

**come to**   *v.* An anchoring expression meaning the anchor has grabbed the ground and the vessel has stopped drifting and started to ride to the anchor and cable.

**come up**   *v.* (1) To continue on the same tack, but to come closer to the wind. (2) To ease off after hauling to belay the gear. (3) To slacken a line or ease a line. To come up the fall is to slacken the tackle.

**come up behind**   *interj.* Order to the crew member who is to belay the fall of a tackle being hauled upon so that all hands can release the fall while the crew member takes a turn on a belaying pin.

**come up on the capstan**   *phr.* To turn the capstan so as to allow some slack in a rope that has been hauled in.

**command and control**   *n.* A system that includes communication facilities and equipment, procedures, and personnel essential to a commander for planning, locating, directing, and controlling operations of assigned forces to assigned missions. Generally, locating capability, or position-fixing capability, exists in command and control systems.

**commandant**   *n.* The commanding officer of a U.S. Naval base. Formerly naval shipyards were under a commandant, but today they are under shipyard commanders.

**commander (Comdr. or Cdr.)**   *n.* (1) A commissioned officer in the U.S. Navy or U.S. Coast Guard who ranks below captain and above lieutenant commander. (2) Heavy mallet used by sailmakers when working on rigging.

**commanding officer (CO)**   *n.* The officer in command of a vessel, squadron of aircraft, or of a U.S. Naval activity with responsibilities outlined in *U.S. Navy Regulations.* The commanding officer of a hospital is a medical officer, and the commanding officer of a supply facility is usually a supply officer; otherwise most commanding officers are line officers.

**command master chief**   *n.* The top-ranking enlisted person on U.S. Navy ships and shore commands, the liaison between the captain and the crew; known as the captain's ears and the crew's voice. See MASTER CHIEF PETTY OFFICER OF THE NAVY.

**commendatory mast**   *n.* Ceremony at which the commanding officer commends or decorates a member of the ship's company. See MAST.

**commercial loading**   *n.* U.S. Navy term for loading of troops and equipment for maximum use of space rather than for combat readiness. The troops are usually in one place with the equipment in another, rather than each person sleeping with his or her equipment.

**commercial speed**   See SPEED, SERVICE.

**commissary store**   *n.* A grocery store for military personnel.

**commission**   *n.* (1) A period of duty during which a warship is assigned a particular duty. (2) See COMMISSIONED OFFICER. (3) A smaller vessel that has been taken out of the yard ready for use with rigging trimmed, sails aboard, and engine (if one is aboard) tuned is said to be "in commission." See COMMISSIONING YARD.

**commission** *v.* To place a ship in active service by placing it under the command of a commissioned officer who assumes command by breaking the commission pennant and setting the watch.

**commissioned officer** *n.* A member of the U.S. armed forces who has been commissioned under the authority of the president and confirmed by Congress as an officer. The phrase "an officer and a gentleman" has been dropped with the advent of female officers.

**commissioning yard** *n.* A boatyard term for the yard in which a boat is docked after it has been launched, to have mast, rigging, engines, and other gear installed.

**commission pennant** *n.* The pennant flown at the main truck on a U.S. naval vessel when under the command of a commissioned officer. It is red, white, and blue with seven stars. Also *narrow pennant.*

**committee boat** *n.* A boat used by a race committee to start and finish a race and to monitor it as it progresses.

**commodore (Commo.)** *n.* (1) A courtesy title for a U.S. Navy officer below the rank of rear admiral and above captain who commands a squadron, division, or other detachment of two or more naval vessels. From time to time, often during war, the rank has been made an active one, and an officer with the rank of commodore has been entitled to one star. (2) The senior captain of a merchant line, especially a cruise line. (3) The senior officer of a yacht club, other officers being styled vice commodores, rear commodores, and so on.

**common adventure** *n.* A maritime venture involving several persons with a common interest, such as shipowners, cargo owners, and underwriters.

**common carrier** *n.* A person or company in the business of transporting cargo or persons for a fee. A common carrier or **general ship** must serve all who apply in the order of application, without discrimination. See CARRIAGE OF GOODS BY SEA ACT; HARTER ACT.

**common establishment** See LUNITIDAL INTERVAL; VULGAR ESTABLISHMENT.

**common law lien** or **mechanic's lien** *n.* Liens existing by virtue of possession of a property. A common law lien exists against a vessel when repairs are made on that vessel. A lien is created against cargo when expenses are incurred by the master or owner for the protection and preservation of the cargo being transported.

**common link** *n.* The standard or normal size of the links of an anchor cable. A commercial link has been accepted by most nations as being one that is six times as long as its width.

**companion** *n.* Covering, usually wooden, over a ladder (stairway) to a cabin or to the cabin area.

**companionway (or companion ladder)** *n.* (1) A ladder leading from a companion hatchway to a cabin or saloon below. Traditionally, companions and companionways referred to the ladder leading to the commanding officer's cabin or to the admiral's cabin. (2) A hood over a small hatchway and ladder on a weather deck, fitted with weatherboards or other device to keep spray out of the spaces below.

**comparing watch** See HACK WATCH.

**comparison frequency** *n.* A Decca Navigator System term for the common frequency to which incoming signals are converted so that their phase relationships may be converted.

**compartment**   *n.* Any subdivision between bulkheads, for example, stateroom and engine room.

**compartmentation**   *n.* A damage control term for the establishment of transverse and longitudinal watertight bulkheads to enable a ship to remain afloat after its hull has been damaged below the waterline.

**compartment standard**   *n.* The designed number of watertight compartments in a vessel that may be flooded to the margin line without causing the vessel to sink.

**compass**   *n.* Any instrument that will give the heading of the ship based on magnetic north; this can have a digital or analog presentation. At sea, to prevent possible confusion or misunderstanding, the compass headings and bearings are given by the individual numbers. A course of 165° is spoken as "one six five" and not "one-sixty-five." A magnetic compass is sometimes known as a **standard compass** to distinguish it from a gyro-compass.

**compass adjustment**   *n.* The neutralizing of the magnetic effect that the metal in a vessel exerts on a magnetic

## Compass Card

Note: Every point (for example,
ENE to EbN) represents 11 1/4°.

compass. Permanent magnets and soft iron correctors are placed at carefully selected places near the binnacle to counteract the magnetic material on the vessel to reduce deviation. See COMPASS COMPENSATION.

**compass bearing**   n. (1) The points of the compass given in terms of points with each point representing $11\frac{1}{4}°$ ($11°15'$ or $\frac{1}{32}$ of $360°$). (2) The bearings used to describe the position of another ship or landmark from a ship; the bearing of a landmark or vessel will be said to be "one two zero, relative" meaning relative to the ship's heading, or "one two zero, true" if the helmsman is using a gyrocompass. See DIRECTION.

**compass card**   n. The indicating card that is calibrated for $360°$ of the compass.

**compass compensation**   n. The neutralizing of the effects of degaussing currents on a magnetic compass by placing **compensating coils** near the compass, but not the effects the craft itself exerts. See COMPASS ADJUSTMENT; COMPENSATE.

**compass course**   n. The vessel's heading according to the vessel's compass.

**compass error**   n. Variation and deviation combine to make the compass error, the difference between the heading indicated by the compass and the true heading.

**compass rose**   n. The points of the compass printed on coastal charts in a circle that usually includes annual variation. The difference between true north and magnetic north can be very little in some parts of the world, while in others it is quite significant.

**compass timber**   n. Lumber grown in the shape needed for curved and bent sections of framing, considered superior to sawn frames or timber that is bent through steaming.

**compensate**   v. (1) To correct a magnetic compass with the magnets and correctors so that the compass will point as close as possible to magnetic north. (2) To adjust water in the trim tanks of a submarine to attain buoyancy.

**compensating coils**   n. Coils placed near a magnetic compass to neutralize the effect of a vessel's degaussing system on the magnetic compass. See COMPASS COMPENSATION.

**complement (ship's)**   n. The authorized number and makeup of personnel for manning a ship for full operational effectiveness in combat.

**component**   n. (1) That part of a tidal current velocity that, by resolution into right-angle vectors, is found to act in a given direction. (2) One of the parts into which a vector quantity can be divided. The Earth's magnetic force can be divided at any time into horizontal and vertical components.

**composite-built**   adj. Built with mixed construction such as iron frame and wooden planking or Fiberglas on aluminum frames; a transitional design that was used when metals were just beginning to be a viable building material for ships.

**composite group flashing light**   n. A light similar to a group flashing light except that successive groups in a period have different numbers of flashes. See LIGHT PHASE CHARACTERISTICS.

**composite sailing**   n. Great circle sailing method used when avoiding a danger in high latitudes. The method involves great circle sailing and parallel sailing. When the navigator finds that the great circle track leads into ice or bad weather, he decides on one parallel of latitude as the highest he can sail safely. The shortest route is then a portion of that parallel and the arcs of two great circles that are tangential to it, one of which intersects the point of departure and the other the destination. An instance of such sailing is the course from the Cape of Good Hope to Australia, where the great circle route takes you too far south for safety. See GREAT CIRCLE.

**composite unit**  *n.* A pushing vessel that is rigidly connected by mechanical means (not including lines, hawsers, wires, or chains) to a vessel being pushed so they react to sea and swell as one vessel.

**compressor**  *n.* A device used in a hawse pipe to control the anchor cable.

**con**  see CONN.

**concluding line**  *n.* The line passing through the middle of the steps of a Jacob's ladder used to pull the ladder up on deck.

**condemnation**  *n.* In international law, the judgment or sentence of a prize court declaring that a captured vessel has lawfully been seized at sea and may be treated as a prize.

**condenser**  *n.* (1) A device that turns exhaust steam back to water to be recycled. (2) An electric circuit element that stores a charge temporarily.

**condition watch**  *n.* A watch stood under a given condition of readiness.

**cone**  *n.* A shape or visual aid hung in the rigging of a vessel between sunrise and sunset as prescribed in the *Navigation Rules* to indicate the vessel's navigational status. A cone has a base diameter of at least 0.6 meter and a height equal to the diameter.

**cone, speed**  *n.* One of the cone-shaped devices flown from the signal halyard of naval vessels in various combinations to indicate speed of the individual ship or of the formation.

**cone of silence**  *n.* An imaginary cone above a radio range station or below a sonar transmitter in which a signal being transmitted cannot be heard or in which the signal is very weak. The cone of silence beneath the sonar dome is ideal for an enemy submarine because it cannot be detected.

**conference**  *n.* A consortium or cartel of shipowners based on mutual interest in a particular trade to guarantee service rates and times.

**confluence**  *n.* The point at which two rivers join.

**confused sea**  *n.* Douglas scale reading of 9, indicating a state of maximum wave disturbance.

**confusion region**  *n.* The environment surrounding a target within which the radar echo cannot be resolved (distinguished) from echoes of other objects.

**conjunction**  *n.* The position of two heavenly bodies on the celestial sphere when they have the same celestial longitude.

**conn**  *n.* The responsibility for directing the steering of a ship.

**conn**  *v.* To direct the steering of a vessel by orders to a helmsman.

**connecting bridge**  *n.* A fore-and-aft structure between the bridge deck and the poop or the forecastle.

**conning tower**  *n.* The wheelhouse or control station on a warship, the captain's battle station. On a submerged submarine, it is the raised observation station above the hull from which the officer with the conn directs operations. On modern submarines the conning station is usually in the control room. The conning station at the top of the sail is called the bridge.

**consignee**    *n.* The person or other entity to whom goods are shipped as shown on a bill of lading by the shipper, or **consignor.**

**consol/consolan**    *n.* A long-range azimuthal radio navigation system of low accuracy operated primarily for air navigation, not sufficiently accurate for making a landfall, but useful to mariners for ocean navigation, the chief advantage being that it can be received on a standard communications receiver.

**consol chart**    *n.* A chart that is overprinted with radial lines originating at a consol station and used for converting a signal received from a consol station to a line of position.

**console**    *n.* (1) The housing of the main operating unit of electronic equipment, in which the indicators and controls are located. The term is usually limited to the large housings placed on deck that cannot be placed in smaller cabinets on tables or shelves. (2) The engine control and steering control station on small craft.

**constant helm plan**    *n.* A scheme for evasive action by a surface ship when enemy submarines are suspected of being nearby. While the ship changes course from time to time, the basic course and speed over the course are maintained.

**construction battalion**    *n.* Specially trained U.S. Navy personnel for military construction work, known as Seabees.

**constructive total loss (CTL)**    *n.* A vessel reasonably abandoned because its actual total loss is unavoidable or because it cannot be preserved from actual total loss without an expenditure in excess of its value at the time the expenditure would have taken place.

**consular invoice**    *n.* A statement of goods and values presented to a consul for certification and authorization for shipment to his or her country.

**consular shipping adviser**    *n.* A naval officer on a consular staff for control of shipping duties.

**contact**    *n.* Any echo detected on a radarscope and not evaluated as clutter or a false echo, but not necessarily identified as a specific target.

**container ship**    *n.* A vessel designed to take large standard metal boxes carrying different types of general cargo. The dimensions of standardized containers range from $8 \times 8 \times 20$ feet (1,065 cubic feet, or 40,000 pounds) to $8 \times 8 \times 45$ feet (3,035 cubic feet, or 64,300 pounds). See SHIP.

**container terminal**    *n.* A berth designed to accommodate container ships and to handle the transshipment of containers between ships and trains or trucks.

**contiguous zone**    *n.* A maritime zone lying to seaward of a territorial sea and extending to as much as 24 miles from the base line. The coastal state has limited powers in the zone with relation to customs, immigration, and fiscal and sanitation matters.

**continental fairlead**    *n.* A deck device used for directing a line with the horns angled so that it is easy to place the line in it, but the line is prevented from coming out when it is being used. See BITT; CLEAT.

**continental margin**    *n.* The zone that includes the shelf, the slope, and the rise that separates a continent from the ocean floor. The **continental shelf** is a zone of relatively shoal water extending from most continents from low-water line to a point where a marked increase in the slope becomes noticeable at a depth of between 130 and 200 meters. The **continental slope** is the zone of sharply increasing depth seaward from the continental shelf. The **continental rise** is the seaward zone of the continental margin that leads from the bottom of the slope to the ocean floor with a gradient of about 1:100.

**continuous display**    *n.* The presentation by any instrument that shows temperature, pressure level, position, speed, and so on, at all times.

**continuous floor**    *n.* An unbroken steel frame that extends from the keel to the turn of the bilge in a cellular double bottom.

**continuous quick flash**    *n.* A quick light in which a flash is repeated regularly. See LIGHT PHASE CHARACTERISTICS

**continuous voyage**    *n.* The doctrine invoked to justify capturing a vessel carrying contraband of war when the consigned port is neutral but the cargo is intended for a transshipment to a belligerent nation. Under this doctrine, the two voyages are considered as one, and the seizure of the cargo by a blockading vessel is justified.

**contline**    *n.* (1) The spiral intervals formed between strands of a rope. (2) The space between the bilges of two casks or two rows of casks. Also *cantline.* See CANT; SPACE SYSTEM.

**contour line**    *n.* On navigation charts lines that represent the same depth.

**contraband**    *n.* Under international law, goods such as arms and ammunition that may be seized by a belligerent power if shipped by another belligerent power by way of a neutral power.

**contract of affreightment**    *n.* A bill-of-lading term under which a vessel or a part of her cargo space is chartered while the vessel remains under control of the owner.

**contra solem**    See CORIOLIS FORCE.

**contrastes**    *n.* Two winds from opposite quadrants, frequently observed in spring and fall in the western Mediterra-

nean and in summer during the afternoon in central Florida. When the two winds meet, they come together almost explosively to cause confused, temporary winds as strong as 100 knots.

**controlled port**    *n.* A harbor or anchorage in which all traffic is controlled by military authority.

**controller**    *n.* A deck fitting through which an anchor chain passes, used to snub the chain by raising a block to hold a link. See CHAIN STOPPER.

**controlling depth**    *n.* The least depth in the approach or channel into an area, such as a port or anchorage, governing the maximum draft of vessels entering. (2) The least depth within the limits of a channel. The **centerline controlling depth** of a channel applies only to the channel centerline; lesser depths frequently obtain in the remainder of the channel. The **midchannel controlling depth** is the controlling depth of the *middle half* of the channel. The **federal project depth** is the depth of a channel as designed and constructed by the U.S. Army Corps of Engineers. The project depth is frequently greater than the anticipated goal of maintenance dredging once the channel has been completed. The Corps of Engineers may establish a federal project depth of 40 feet and initially dredge the channel to that depth, planning to maintain a depth of 38 feet. However, the depth that the Coast Guard and other surveying agency vessels find may be only 36 feet, in spite of the Corps of Engineers' best efforts to maintain 38 feet. Therefore, the controlling depth is 36 feet. This distinction between project depth and controlling depth applies equally to small craft operating in Corps-maintained waterways.

**control station**    *n.* The area in a small boat that contains the helm and the speed control system.

**control vessel**    *n.* The headquarters vessel in an amphibious operation.

**cont splice**   *n.* A splice in which the ends of two ropes are side-spliced with an eye between the two parts. Also *bight splice; cunt splice.* See CANTLINE; CONTLINE.

**convening authority**   *n.* A U.S. Naval command with authority to organize courts-martial, courts of inquiry, and boards of investigation.

**conventional direction of buoyage**   *n.* (1) The predictable direction taken by a mariner approaching a harbor, river, estuary, or other waterway from seaward. (2) The direction of buoyage must often be arbitrarily determined by appropriate authority in consultation with neighboring countries; in principle, the direction taken follows a clockwise pattern around landmasses.

**Convention on the International Regulations for Preventing Collisions at Sea, 1972**   *n.* A multilateral treaty developed by the Inter-Governmental Maritime Consultative Organization (IMCO), later named the International Maritime Organization (IMO), which codified and formalized the International Rules by which the world's ships navigate. See INLAND NAVIGATION RULES; INTERNATIONAL RULES.

**Convention on the Prevention of Marine Pollution by Dumping of Wastes and Other Matter (MARPOL)**   *n.* An international maritime convention (entered into force in 1975) that establishes what garbage can be disposed of at sea and where. Floating dunnage, lining, and packing materials cannot be disposed of within 25 miles of a country's baseline. Unground waste, paper bags, glass, metal containers, crockery, and similar refuse cannot be thrown out within 12 miles. Food waste, paper, rags, glass, and so on, ground up finely enough to pass through a 25-mm screen or finer can be thrown over beyond the 3-mile limit. No plastics, synthetic nets, and garbage bags are allowed to be thrown overboard anywhere.

**convoy**   *n.* A group of merchant ships and/or naval auxiliary vessels, usually escorted by one or more surface warships for protection.

**convoy, right of**   See RIGHT OF CONVOY.

**convoy commodore**   *n.* A U.S. Merchant Marine or Naval officer designated to command a convoy, but subordinate to an escort commander if one is designated.

**convoy escort**   *n.* One or more U.S. Navy ships sailing in company with one or more merchant ships or Naval auxiliary vessels such as supply ships and repair ships for their protection.

**coordinated universal time (UTC)**   *n.* The time scale available from most broadcast signals; it differs from International Atomic Time (TAI) by an integral number of seconds.

**coordinates**   *n.* A system of lines, planes, or angles established for determining an object's position on a plane, a sphere, or in space.

**copper**   *v.* To cover the bottom of a vessel with a thin sheet of copper for protection against teredos or ship's worms. The method was first used by the British Navy in 1761.

**copy**   *v.* (1) To monitor a radio continuously and to record all transmissions. Radio operators copy the fleet broadcast channel and other channels as required by the exigencies of the situation. (2) Among nonprofessional boaters, used to mean "say that" or to inquire whether a transmission has been received and understood, and as such is an invention of script writers.

**coral**   *n.* Any of a number of chiefly colonial marine coelenterates of the class Anthozoa, characteristically having calcareous skeletons that are massed in a wide variety of shapes, such as **coral**

**heads,** often forming **coral reefs** and islands.

**corange line**   *n.* (pron. co-range) A line that passes through two points of equal tidal range.

**corbel**   *n.* The protective buildup, generally of chrome ore, along the base of the walls of a boiler furnace. The movement of the slag erodes the bricks, but the corbel retards the damage.

**cord**   *n.* Several yarns hard-twisted together.

**cordage**   *n.* (1) Cords, ropes, lines, and fiber cables. (2) The general term for all the non-steel running rigging of a ship.

**cordanazo**   *n.* The name for a tropical cyclone on the west coast of Mexico and Central America.

**Corinthian**   *n.* An amateur sailor, usually a member of a racing crew.

**Coriolis force**   *n.* The name of the effect caused by the rotation of the Earth that diverts the air from a direct path between high- and low-pressure areas. The diversion of air is toward the right (counterclockwise) in the Northern Hemisphere and toward the left (clockwise) in the Southern Hemisphere, and each deflects the respective trade winds. Currents influenced by the Coriolis force are referred to as **contra solem.**

**cork light**   *adj.* Said of a vessel that is without cargo.

**corner reflector**   *n.* A radar-enhancing device used especially on small boats to increase their visibility to radar; these consist of planes at 90° to each other placed high in the rigging.

**coromell**   *n.* A light land breeze that occurs off the southern extremity of the Gulf of California from November until May.

**corposant**   See SAINT ELMO'S FIRE.

**corpsman**   *n.* An enlisted person in the U.S. Navy or Marine Corps trained in combat medical first aid procedures. The Army equivalent is a medic.

**correct**   *v.* To convert a magnetic compass reading to true compass. When you convert the true compass reading to magnetic, you uncorrect. One corrects the magnetic compass when doing chart work, but uncorrects the true compass course when giving a steering heading to a helmsman using a magnetic compass.

**corrected compass course**   *n.* A compass course with deviation calculated.

**corrected time**   *n.* (1) A racing boat's elapsed time minus its time allowance as determined by its measurement or rating. (2) Time corrected to a standard such as Greenwich Mean Time or Greenwich Civil TIme.

**corrugated bulkhead**   *n.* A bulkhead with a series of wrinkles or grooves that eliminate the need for welded stiffeners.

**corsair**   *n.* A Turkish or Saracen privateer, especially along the Barbary Coast, that engaged in piracy against Christians with its country's official sanction from the Middle Ages until the 18th century.

**corvette**   *n.* Formerly a small combat patrol sailing vessel, smaller than a sailing frigate. Also *sloop of war.* (2) A fast, lightly armed warship, lighter than a destroyer.

**cost, insurance, freight (CIF)**   *n.* A price quoted for goods that includes the cost of marine insurance in addition to the cost of the goods and freight. Under such a contract, it is the responsibility of the buyer to take delivery and pay the costs of discharge, lighterage, and landing, as stipulated in the bill of lading, as well as any duty, wharfage, or customs fees.

**coston signals**   *n.* Colored pyrotechnics with chemicals that produced red, white, and blue signals, invented by B. F. Coston in 1840. The colors could be managed in any sequence, and Coston's device offered a selection of 13 different coded message possibilities. These are no longer used. See PRIVATE SIGNAL.

**cot**   *n.* A bunk made of canvas on a frame suspended from the overhead. This is what officers slept on when ships' crews slept in hammocks.

**cotidal chart**   *n.* A chart showing **cotidal lines** along which the tide is the same and that connects the places where the tides arrive simultaneously.

**cotidal hour**   *n.* The average period between the Moon's transit over the Greenwich meridian and the time of the following high water at any place, expressed in either mean solar or lunar time units. If expressed in solar time, it is the same as Greenwich high-water interval. When expressed in lunar time, it is equal to the Greenwich high-water interval multiplied by 0.966.

**cotter key** (or **pin**)   *n.* A split pin that is forced through a hole in a turnbuckle or nut and then spread apart to keep the device in place. In Britain it is called a **split pin.**

**counter**   *n.* The underside of the overhang at the stern; the opposite is a **cruiser stern** that has no projecting overhang from the waterline.

**counterbrace**   *phr.* To brace the yards and sails on a square-rigged ship in a contrary direction to halt the ship. See ABOX.

**countercurrent**   *n.* A current that flows in the direction opposite to a tidal current or ocean stream outside the limits of the main current or stream. See EQUA-TORIAL CURRENTS AND COUNTERCURRENTS.

**counterflood**   *v.* To intentionally take on or let water into a vessel's tanks to counter a port or starboard list or an inclination toward the bow or stern.

**countermine**   *v.* To cause ammunition to discharge accidentally or deliberately by detonating a nearby explosive. Mines are placed at such a distance as to preclude countermining, the **countermining distance** being determined by the type of mine.

**countersink**   *v.* To taper or bevel the edge of a hole to allow the head of a rivet or bolt to go below the surface and not be left to make a rough spot above the plating.

**country**   *n.* An area adjacent to a compartment or quarters such as officers' country, flag country, or CPO country.

**couple moment**   *n.* The force created by two equal forces exerted in opposite directions and along parallel lines. In a stability diagram, these are the forces through the centers of gravity (G) and buoyancy (B). See STABILITY.

**course (C or Cn)**   *n.* (1) The horizontal direction to be steered or intended to be steered through the water by a vessel or an object, expressed as an angular distance from 000° at north, clockwise through 360°. A course is by definition a direction through the water and not the direction intended to be made good over the ground. To avoid confusion, an order for course 065° is given as "Come to course zero six five," spoken number by number. See COMPASS; DRIFT; TRACK. (2) A sail bent to the lower yard of a bark or full-rigged ship. The courses are identified by the names of their respective masts, as fore course, main course, or mizzen course.

**course angle** *n.* A course measured from 0° at a reference direction clockwise or counterclockwise through 90° or 180°. It must be labeled with the reference direction as a prefix and the direction of measurement as a suffix. A course angle S 45° E is 45° east of south or a course of 135°.

**course line** *n.* The graphic representation of a vessel's course with respect to true north.

**course made good (CMG)** *n.* The single resultant direction from a point of departure to a point of arrival at any given time. See TRACK MADE GOOD.

**course of advance** See TRACK.

**course over the ground** *n.* The direction of the path over the ground actually followed by a vessel. This is usually a somewhat irregular line.

**course protractor** *n.* Instrument used for determining the direction between two points on a chart. See PARALLEL RULES.

**courtesy flag** *n.* The flag of the nation in whose waters a vessel is moored. It is flown at the starboard yardarm or spreader. At the same time, the national ensign of the vessel's registry is flown from the stern.

**cove** *n.* (1) A small protected inlet. See GUNKHOLE. (2) The ornamental groove cut high on a vessel's side that runs most of the length of the topsides; the cove is usually painted or gold-leafed, called the **cove stripe**. (3) The arch molding sunk in the lower part of the taffrail.

**cover** *v.* (1) To place a boat between an opponent and the wind, or to place a boat between the next mark and an opponent. It is the maneuver of a winning boat to keep an advantage over a trailing boat. (2) To maintain a continuous radio watch with transmitter available.

**covering board** *n.* The most outboard deck plank that runs the full length of the vessel.

**covering note** *n.* Marine insurance note issued by the broker to the insured after the original note has been initialed for the total sum required. It does not have legal force until the policy is issued.

**covering strake** *n.* A narrow steel plate covering the butt joint of shell plating in a flush plating system.

**cowl** *n.* Air scoop projecting above the deck to allow air to spaces below.

**cowling** *n.* Removable cover such as on an inboard engine.

**cow's tail** *n.* Frayed end of a line. Also *fag*.

**coxswain** *n.* (pron. cocksin) (1) A U.S. Navy enlisted man in charge of a boat who usually assumes the steering duties. (2) Marine person in charge of steering a racing shell. Also *cox*.

**CQR** *n.* An anchor consisting of a single plow-shaped fluke and a pivoting shank. The CQR (a play on "secure") was developed by a Cambridge University professor, Sir. Geoffrey I. Taylor, and has enjoyed wide acceptance among yachtsmen, especially for use in mud and weed. Also *plow anchor*.

**crab** *v.* (1) To move sideways either to leeward or downcurrent. (2) Small portable capstan.

**crab winch** *n.* Small hand winch.

**cracker hash** *n.* A mixture of salt pork and hardtack mixed together and baked, not found on the first-class passengers' menu.

**cradle** *n.* The frame used to hold a boat upright whether it is in a boatyard or in the water in a place where tides leave boats high and dry; in the latter usage, the cradle is placed on a solid pad, called a **hard,** so that work can be done on the hull while the tide is out of the basin.

**craneline**   *n.*   (pron. cranlin)   An athwartships line on a square-rigger run between port and starboard shrouds used for crossing from side to side while aloft or for standing on while furling staysails.

**cranky**   *adj.* Tender, used to describe a boat that heels too easily; top heavy.

**cranse**  (or **crance, crans, cranze**) *n.* Metal band fitted near the outer end of a bowsprit to which the various lines and chains could be fitted for supporting the bowsprit and for attaching sails, stays, and so on. Also *bowsprit cap.*

**crayer**   *n.* (obsolete) A food supply vessel that followed a fleet of sailing warships.

**creeper**   *n.* A piece of equipment used to drag the bottom to recover something that may be there. See GRAPPLING IRON.

**creeping attack**   *n.* An antisubmarine warfare attack creating as little noise as possible with target information provided by an assisting ship. The attacking surface ship does not use sonar because it would alert the target submarine to the ship's presence.

**crest**   *n.* The top of a wave.

**crew**   *n.* (1) All personnel aboard a vessel other than the captain. (2) A detail of personnel assigned a station such as a gun crew or a liberty boat crew. (3) The sport of rowing in long, narrow boats called shells manned by two, four, or eight rowers.

**crew boat**   *n.* A boat, 40 to 120 feet long, designed to transport personnel and light cargo to offshore oil platforms.

**crew change**   *n.* U.S. Merchant Marine personnel change at the end of a voyage, usually between three weeks and two or three months. Everyone on the vessel, officers and crew alike, is replaced. The concept is difficult for Navy sailors to comprehend because they are accustomed to being attached to a ship for about two years, with leaves and liberty from time to time, and never a complete crew change at one time.

**crib**   *n.* (1) Any barrier such as heavy wire or concrete structure placed at the entrance to a harbor to prevent entry, to create a breakwater, or to support a bridge. (2) A locker in which spare parts are kept, especially engine-room parts.

**crimp**   *n.* A person who ensnared or kidnapped men ashore to serve aboard ship.

**cringle**   *n.* (1) Small loops in the boltrope of a sail, or a broad hem on modern Dacron sails, into which a thimble is sewn for extra strength. Sheets are fastened to the cringle for controlling the sail. (2) A hole in a sail through which a reef nettle is led.

**crinoline**   *n.* Heavy mesh fitted around a warship as an early defense against torpedoes.

**critique**   *n.* Conference review of a vessel's procedures, systems, performance, and so on.

**Cromwell Current**   *n.* A subsurface current in the central Pacific along the equator, named for Townsend Cromwell, who first identified it in 1952.

**cross**   *v.* To stand across another vessel's bow. A vessel is crossing another if it has the other between dead ahead and two points abaft the beam. The boat to starboard, in this situation, is the stand-on vessel. See GIVE WAY.

**crossband transponder**   *n.* A transponder that responds on a frequency different from that of the interrogator.

**crossbeam**   *n.* An athwartship supporting member between the hulls of catamarans and trimarans.

**cross bearings**   *n.* In both celestial navigation and piloting, two or more bearings taken from a vessel to determine its position.

**cross bollard**   *n.* Pier or wharf bollard with a cross for holding mooring lines of ships.

**cross bunker**   *n.* An athwartship bunker.

**cross chop**   *n.* The short steep waves of a confused sea.

**cross-cut sail**   *n.* A sail with seams running at right angles to the leech. Cross-cut sails are used for racing to reduce resistance to the flow of air, but they are not as durable as vertical-cut sails.

**cross-deck**   *v.* To send personnel from one ship to another ship for training.

**crossed**   *adj.* In square-riggers, said of yards in position ready for sea.

**cross gore**   *n.* Length of a gaffsail measured from the highest forward point to the clew.

**crossing situation**   *n.* A situation in which two power vessels are approaching each other so that there is apparently a risk of collision. In such instances, the vessel on the right has the right-of-way and the one on the left should keep out of the way and, if possible, avoid crossing in front of the vessel with the right-of-way. The main exception to this rule is that on the Great Lakes, western rivers, and other specified waters, a vessel crossing a river has to keep out of the way of a power vessel ascending or descending the river.

**crossing the T**   *phr.* Battle maneuver that called for a line of warships to cross ahead of the enemy's line of ships to concentrate fire on the lead vessels of the enemy.

**crossjack**   *n.* (pron. crojick) Lower yard of the mizzen mast. See SQUARE-RIGGED VESSEL.

**cross leech**   *n.* A line that runs diagonally across a main course from the head cringle to the middle of the foot to which the midship tack is shackled.

**crossover line**   *n.* Any one of several lines on a ship that go from one cargo system to the other for handling fuel, water, hydraulic oil, ballast, and so on.

**crosspiece**   *n.* A timber between two knightheads.

**cross planking**   *n.* Small-craft construction term referring to bottom planks at right angles to the centerline.

**cross-point**   *v.* To cut away the inner yarns of a rope and braid the remaining outer yarns to taper or point the end.

**cross sea**   *n.* A confused sea with waves going in different directions because of varying wind patterns.

**cross-seize**   *v.* To seize two lines at a right angle to each other; used for securing mast hoops.

**cross signal**   *n.* The response to a whistle signal with another of different meaning. If, for example, one vessel gives a second vessel one blast and the second responds with two blasts, it has responded with a cross signal. If there is reason to take exception to the first signal, the responding vessel answers with five short blasts. Also *cross whistle.*

**cross springs**   *n.* Collective term for forward and after spring lines.

**cross staff**   *n.* An early device used for determining altitudes. Also *Jacob's staff.*

**cross swell**    *n.* A deep, confused sea. See CROSS SEA.

**cross tackle**    *n.* Square-rigger term for a device set horizontally below the mast cap and used to bring the shrouds closer together.

**cross the line**    *phr.* To cross the equator.

**crosstree**    *n.* (1) A short flat piece of timber bolted athwartships on a trestle-tree to form a foundation for the top or a platform at the lower masthead. A crosstree also provides a means of spreading and securing the topmast shrouds. (2) In Britain, crosstree is used synonymously with spreader.

**cross wires** (or **hairs**)    *n.* Fine wires or lines at right angles to each other found on the object glass of telescopes.

**crotch**    *n.* Supports used for spare masts and spars on larger sailing vessels. Also *crutch, gallows, jacks, topping lifts.*

**crow**    *n.* Slang for the eagle worn on a petty officer's sleeve.

**crowd**    *v.* To carry excessive sail; to **drive.**

**crowd on**    *v.* To set all sail possible.

**crowfoot**    *n.* An assemblage of lines rove through a euphroe used to support an awning or hammock, or to keep the foot of the topsail from striking under the tops. The crowfoot is suspended from **crowfoot halyards.**

**crown**    *n.* (1) The point on an anchor at which the arms join the shank. Also *head.* (2) On a stockless anchor, the point on the shank where the arms pivot. See ANCHOR. (3) The top of a block. Also *throat.* (4) The curvature of a deck.

**crown knot**    *n.* (1) An end splice formed by back-splicing a rope end, used to prevent raveling. (2) The finishing knot

at the end of a rope that is woven from the strands used as a stopper.

**crow's nest**    *n.* A small platform encircling a mast and provided with wooden railing, to provide a lookout station below the masthead light or above the hounds. See TOP.

**cruciform**    *n.* A device on which to make a line fast; a post with arms or a double post with a crossbeam. Also **H bitt** or **double bitt.**

**cruise**    *n.* (1) A tour of duty at sea. (2) An enlistment period. (3) A sea voyage for pleasure.

**cruise**    *v.* To travel at an efficient speed. To say a ship cruises at 29 knots means that the vessel gets the most miles for the fuel consumed at that speed.

**cruiser**    *n.* (1) A warship that is lighter than a battleship, carries less armor, and is more lightly armed, but is faster. It is built for long-range steaming and carries several intermediate and secondary gun batteries. Today **guided-missile cruisers (CG)** are used primarily as antiaircraft escorts for aircraft carriers. (2) A powerboat or sailboat with living arrangements built for cruising more than for racing.

**cruiser stern**    *n.* A design in which the underwater surface toward the stern is broad and almost flat with a knuckle at the load waterline. The sides of the hull join at the centerline, and the widest part is close to the waterline. See ELLIPTICAL STERN.

**cruising radius** (or **range**)    *n.* (1) The distance a ship can travel without refueling. (2) A vessel's capacity to remain at sea expressed in days running at normal speed.

**crupper chain**    *n.* A short chain that connects the after end of the jibboom to the forward end of the bowsprit. (2) A chain used to support the heel of a topmast. It leads from the lower masthead, under the topmast, and up the other side to the lower masthead. Also *heel chain*.

**crutch**   *n.* (1) A support for a boom or yard. (2) A compass timber in the stern construction supporting transverse planking.

**cubic capacity**   *n.* Internal measurement in cubic feet that determines the amount of cargo that can be carried in a ship's compartments. See BALE CUBIC; GRAIN CUBIC.

**cubic measurement**   *n.* A reference to amount of cargo space available not considered on a deadweight basis. Cubic measurement as a rule is determined on a basis of 40 cubic feet per ton. See DEADWEIGHT CAPACITY.

**cuckold's neck**   *n.* A hitch used to secure a rope on a spar with the two parts of the rope crossing each other and seized together.

**cuddy**   *n.* (1) A small covered area over the forward part of an otherwise open boat. (2) (Obsolete.) A large room or cabin in which officers and passengers took their meals. (3) A deckhouse used for cooking. See CABOOSE.

**cuddy board**   *n.* Planking over the bow or stern of a whaleboat.

**culminate**   *v.* To reach the highest point of an observer's horizon, said of celestial bodies. The **culmination** is the highest and lowest (lower culmination) altitudes of a celestial body when crossing the meridian.

**culture**   *n.* In chart making man-made features shown on a chart such as cities, highways, submarine cables, and aids to navigation.

**cumshaw**   *n.* Originally a gift, gratuity, or tip. The beggars of Amoy, China, said *kam sia* or grateful thanks for any handouts they received on the streets. The term has come to have a variety of meanings, from bribes taken by officials, to equipment or supplies provided or work done with no personal gain involved. When a vessel such as a carrier gives a smaller vessel 10 gallons of ice cream while fueling at sea because the smaller vessel has no ice cream-making facilities, that is cumshaw.

**cumulative hours**   *n.* Coaling term referring to the several days' notice the owners of a vessel are required to give the charterers the day the fueling vessel will be in the loading port.

**cumulonimbus**   *n.* A heavy mass of clouds, a thunderstorm cloud, rising like a mountain. See CLOUDS.

**cumulus**   *n.* Thick, wooly clouds. See CLOUDS.

**cunningham**   *n.* A line on the luff or the foot of a sail used to flatten it or to make it fuller. The line is looped through a **cunningham eye** or a **cunningham hole.** It was developed by race car driver and 1958 *America*'s Cup defender *(Columbia)* Briggs Cunningham; it was first known as the **cunningham haul.**

**cunningham reef**   *n.* System of roller reefing used on square topsails by rolling the yard to furl the sail.

**cunting**   See CONTLINE.

**cunt splice**   See CONT SPLICE.

**cup**   *n.* The steel fitting in which the spindle of a capstan revolves.

**cupola**   *n.* A chart term that indicates a small dome-shaped tower or turret rising from a building.

**current**   *n.* A steady movement or flow of water in a horizontal direction. Currents can be tidal and nontidal. **Tidal currents** are caused by the gravitational interactions between the Sun, Moon, and Earth, and are part of the same general movement of the sea that is manifested in vertical rise and fall of water called tide. **Nontidal currents** include the permanent currents in the general circulatory systems of the sea as well as temporary currents caused by pronounced meteorological variability. The **set** or **current direction** is given with reference to the compass heading toward which the water flows (just the opposite is true of wind direction). See EQUATORIAL CURRENTS and COUNTERCURRENTS; TIDE.

**current chart**   *n.* A graphic presentation of tidal current data.

**current difference.**   *n.* The difference between the time of slack water (or minimum current) or strength of current in any locality and the time of the corresponding phase of the tidal current at a reference station. The predictions for these are given in the *Tidal Current Chart.* See TOTAL CURRENT.

**current ellipse**   *n.* A graphic representation of a rotary current in which the velocity of the current at different hours of the tidal cycle is represented by radius vectors and vectorial angles. A line joining the extremities of the radius vectors will form a curve roughly approximating an ellipse. The cycle is completed in one-half a tidal day or in a whole tidal day according to whether the tidal current is of the semidiurnal or diurnal type. A current of mixed type will generate a curve of two unequal loops each tidal day.

**current sailing**   *n.* The process of allowing for current when predicting the track to be made good or of determining the effect of a current on the movement of a vessel. See SAILING.

**Current Tables**   *n.* Published by the National Ocean Survey of the National Oceanic and Atmospheric Administration, they give data on tidal currents for the entire world.

**curtain plate**   *n.* Plate placed vertically over the edge of a deck or platform to protect it from excessive wear at gangways and cargo ports, for example.

**cusp**   *n.* (1) A small sand deposit caused by the action of the waves along a shoreline that appears as a long row of teeth. (2) The points of a crescent moon.

**customary average**   *n.* Charter party phrase that means that the franchise to be applied in the event of particular average shall be that which is customary to the insured party.

**customary deductions**   *n.* Allowances made by insurers when adjusting for a loss when old material and equipment must be replaced with new.

**customary dispatch**   *n.* A charter party term relating to loading and unloading with due diligence and speed within the law for a given port.

**customhouse**   *n.* A government building where customs fees are collected and vessels are cleared for entering and leaving port.

**customs authority**   *n.* Government officer entrusted with the collection of taxes, duties, tolls, and fees imposed by law on imported and exported merchandise.

**customs bond**   *n.* A deposit required by a customs authority for dutiable merchandise on which duty, the toll levied by the government, has not been collected; goods under customs bond are said to be **under bond.**

**customs broker**   *n.* A ship's agent licensed to attend to the entrance and clearance of vessels and goods through customs.

**customs duty**   *n.* Fees or taxes on imported and exported goods imposed by a government.

**customs warrant**   *n.* A bond note issued by customs authorizing the release of dutiable goods from a bonded warehouse.

**customs waters** *n.* The area beyond territorial boundaries over which customs authorities have jurisdiction enabling them to board, search, examine, and seize vessels and otherwise enforce the laws of the country.

**cut** *n.* A notch or depression produced by excavation (man-made) or erosion (natural). (2) The intersection of lines of position in a fix with particular reference to the angle of intersection.

**cut and run** *phr.* To get underway immediately by cutting the anchor cable rather than taking time to weigh anchor.

**cutaway forefoot** *n.* Said of a vessel's design when the intersection of the stem and keel form an obtuse angle. The angle itself is also so described.

**cutlass bearing** *n.* A propeller shaft bearing that is water-lubricated.

**cutter** *n.* (1) A double-banked, square-sterned ship's boat used for general duty. Similar to skiff. (2) A single-masted sailboat with the mast stepped farther aft than in a sloop to allow for a double headsail, the outer being the **jib topsail** and the inner being the **staysail**. See RIG. (3) Early revenue vessels used this design,

hence the name for the larger Coast Guard vessels today, even though these are powered by diesel.

**cutting iron** *n.* Tool used to remove threads of oakum so they cannot become caught and pull out a section of caulking.

**cutting out expedition** *n.* An operation with the objective of going into enemy waters and taking an enemy ship or similar objective, usually by surprise.

**cutwater** *n.* The leading edge of the bow. See STEM.

**cyclone** *n.* An intense revolving windstorm around a low-pressure area. An **anticyclone** consists of strong winds moving around a high-pressure area. See HURRICANE; TYPHOON; WATERSPOUT.

**cyclonic wind** *n.* A wind circulation in an area of low atmospheric pressure; in the Northern Hemisphere this wind moves counterclockwise, in the Southern Hemisphere, it moves clockwise.

**cylinder** *n.* A shape or visual aid hung in the rigging of a vessel between sunrise and sunset as prescribed in the *Navigation Rules* to indicate the vessel's navigational status. A cylinder has a diameter of at least 0.6 meter and a height of twice its diameter.

# D

**D** See DELTA.

**Dacron** *n.* Trade name for a polyester fiber that stretches very little and is used for sails and rope when little stretch is desired.

**dagger** *n.* Any structural timber or girder that is in a diagonal position. A

**dagger knee** is a structural knee placed diagonally, used chiefly in connection with lower deck beams to preserve as much stowage room as possible.

**dagger board** (or **dagger plate**) *n.* A board that is raised and lowered through a **daggerboard trunk** by hand without the mechanical advantage of a pivot or a hinge as with a centerboard. Dagger boards are found on small boats such as prams.

**daily aberration** *n.* The apparent displacement of a celestial body in the direction of motion of the Earth in its orbit caused by the rotation of the Earth on its axis. Also *diurnal aberration.*

**Daily Memorandum** *n.* A Defense Mapping Agency Hydrographic/Topographic Center daily publication of copies of "Hydrolants," "Hydropacs," and "Navarea" warnings from "Navareas" IV and XII. The broadcast warnings are restricted to the more important marine and navigation changes for which a delay could adversely affect navigational safety.

**daily rate** (or **chronometer rate**) *n.* The amount the chronometer error changes over a 24-hour period.

**daily supply tank** (or **day tank**) *n.* A tank in which the daily ration of water for cooking and drinking was kept, usually placed on top of machinery casing.

**damage certificate** *n.* A report signed by dock authorities certifying that damaged goods have been landed from a ship and giving the cause and extent of damage. Because cargo damage claims constitute the bulk of maritime litigation, such reports are of great importance. Cargo is usually insured from "warehouse to warehouse."

**damage control** *n.* Measures that are necessary aboard ship to preserve or restore watertight integrity, stability, and maneuverability; to control list and trim; to provide rapid repairs; to provide proper control of fire and chemical agents; to facilitate care of the wounded; and to restore offensive power to warships.

**damage control central** *n.* A compartment on warships that is located in as protected an area as possible from which damage control measures and preservation of the ship's offensive power can be directed.

**damage repair** *n.* Repair necessitated by heavy seas, collision, grounding, or perils of the sea rather than normal wear and tear. See VOYAGE REPAIR.

**damages for detention** *n.* A charter party term referring to monetary damages accruing from delays contrary to the terms of the charter. See DEMURRAGE.

**damages in admiralty** *n.* With both vessels at fault, the damages are divided between them. In common law, one guilty of contributory negligence is precluded from obtaining a judgment against the wrongdoer.

**damage stability** *n.* Stability of a vessel after flooding.

**damage survey** *n.* An inspection conducted by the owners or their representatives and underwriters to determine the extent of damage and the repairs necessary to put a vessel back in order. Owners' representatives and underwriters then submit a **damage report.**

**damp** *v.* (1) To reduce the movement of the compass card by filling the bowl with a viscous fluid. **Damping** is the reduction of oscillation and prevention of overcompensation of mechanical instruments such as compasses. (2) To retard or extinguish a fire by cutting off the air supply, perhaps by means of a damper.

**damper** *n.* (1) A device placed in intakes to control incoming airflow to fireboxes. (2) A device placed in flues and stacks to control the stack gases.

**damp haze** *n.* Small water droplets or moist particles in the air, smaller and more scattered than fog.

**dan buoy** (or **dan**) *n.* (1) A temporary marker used by minesweepers (or auxiliary vessels, called **dan layers**) to show the boundaries of the swept area.

They usually have a flag or a light. (2) A temporary float used for marking the location of fishing gear; with a radar reflector and strobe light, a dan buoy is called a **hiflyer** and is used by commercial fishermen.

**dandyfunk**   *n.* Sea biscuits pounded to a powder in a canvas bag, then mixed with water and molasses to form a thick paste; a sailor's dish not heard of since the days of tarred pigtails.

**Danforth anchor**   *n.* An anchor recognized for holding in most kinds of bottom. It was developed during World War II by William S. Danforth. See ANCHOR.

**danger angle**   *n.* A piloting term referring to a charter angle given to warn navigators of an obstruction within an angle between two landmarks, or when going beyond an angle with a single landmark. "Vessels are warned against going south of a bearing of 40° with the 'hotel cupola.' " This would tell the navigator that an obstruction exists somewhere south of a bearing of 40° with the hotel cupola. On the chart, the navigator should project the track using the danger angle that will keep the vessel off the obstruction. The line is marked NLT (not less than) or NMT (not more than) the danger angle.

**danger bearing**   *n.* Charted bearing of an obstruction such as a shoal with accompanying note telling vessels of the obstruction and the bearing from another mark to clear it. British usage is "clearing bearing."

**danger buoy**   *n.* A buoy marking an obstruction or danger to navigation such as a sandbar or a rock. If the top ring is red, leave the buoy to starboard when entering from seaward. If the top ring is black or green, leave it to port when approaching it from seaward.

**dangerous semicircle**   *n.* In the Northern Hemisphere, the right half of a circular storm (or the **right semicircle**) when facing in the direction the storm is moving. It is so called because as the storm advances the counterclockwise motion moves the wind on the right side faster than on the left side. In the Southern Hemisphere, the dangerous semicircle is on the left side of the storm which moves in a clockwise direction. See NAVIGABLE SEMICIRCLE.

**danger signal**   *n.* A signal of at least five short blasts on the whistle, which can be supplemented by five short, rapid light signals when vessels in sight of one another are approaching each other and from any cause either vessel fails to understand the intentions or actions of the other, or is in doubt whether sufficient action is being taken by the other to avoid collision. The regulations are spelled out in *Navigation Rules* 34 (d).

**danger zone or sector**   *n.* The red filtered sector of a light that indicates the presence of a hazard to navigation. The danger zone usually has rocks or shoals or other hazards to navigation. Charts show the area in which you will see only a red light when looking from the sea toward the lighthouse.

**darken ship**   *phr.* To extinguish all lights aboard a vessel that are visible from outside.

**dasher block**   *n.* The block of a small signal halyard secured at the end of the spanker gaff.

**date line**   See INTERNATIONAL DATE LINE.

**date-time group (DTG)**   *n.* A combination of digits and a letter that indicates the date, time, and zone of a communication. For example, 141830Z means the message was sent on the 14th day of the month at 6:30 P.M. in Zulu (Greenwich) time zone.

**datum**   See CHART SOUNDING DATUM.

**Davidson Current**  *n.*  A seasonal North Pacific Ocean countercurrent that flows northwest along the west coast of North America from just north of 32°N to about 48°N latitude; its path lies inshore of the southeasterly flowing California Current. See OCEAN CURRENT.

**davit**  *n.*  (1) Equipment used to hoist and retain small boats and anchors. A davit can be mounted on shore or on a vessel. See SQUARE-RIGGED VESSEL. (2) The piece of timber used as a crane to hoist an anchor into its berth.

**davit bollard**  *n.*  Small post used for checking boat falls when a boat is being lowered, to slow the rate of descent. Also *davit cleat*

**davit guy**  *n.*  A light line secured to an eye on a **davit head** to steady and swing a davit.

**davit lever**  *n.*  A metal lever used to lower and hoist the davit from its step or to lock it in place.

**Davy Jones's locker**  *n.*  The bottom of the sea. The term is often used with a sort of gallows humor to describe the destination of an object or a person lost over the side.

**daybeacon**  *n.*  A fixed, unlighted aid to navigation equipped with a **daymark** or **dayboard** for daytime identification. The dayboard is a square or triangle with a number and other identification. Daybeacons do not include buoys. See BEACON; LIGHT.

**daylight savings time**  *n.*  A variation in standard time that allows better use of daylight hours. The Congress of the United States adopted the Uniform Time Act of 1966 (P.L. 89–387) that established the annual advancement and retardation of standard time by one hour at 0200 on the first Sunday in April and the last Sunday in October, respectively, except in those states that have exempted themselves by law. In Europe this is called summer time. To avoid confusion, navigators base their calculations on Zulu time (Greenwich mean time).

**daymark** (or **daytime**)  *n.*  (1) The identifying characteristic (the *Light List* calls them **daytime identifiers**) of an aid to navigation visible by day. Daymarks refer to the shape (squares, triangles, and rectangles) and color (red, green, black, and white) of the distinctive sign, and not the pile or dolphin on which they are found. These are the equivalent in IALA B to topmarks in IALA A terminology. (2) An unlighted navigation mark.

**day of entry**  *n.*  The date a ship's master turns over papers to customs to obtain clearance to land cargo.

**day sailer**  *n.*  A small sailboat used for racing and cruising by day. The accommodations are limited, and the cabin, if there is one, is an open cuddy.

**day's duty**  *n.*  A tour of duty on a ship lasting 24 hours.

**days of grace**  *n.*  The period allowed for neutral vessels to clear a port before being blockaded.

**day shape**  *n.*  The term used in the *Navigation Rules* for the various shapes used by vessels by day such as baskets, cones, and balls; often simply called "shapes."

**day's run**  *n.*  The distance sailed by a vessel at sea during a 24-hour period, usually between 1200 and 1200.

**day's work**  *n.*  A navigator's reckoning for a 24-hour period from 1200 to 1200. A "day's work" is the daily routine of the navigation of a vessel at sea that includes evening and morning twilight observations, a morning Sun observation for a line of position, a Sun observation at or near noon for a running fix, an afternoon Sun observation for another line of position, morning and afternoon azimuths of the Sun for checking the compass, along with radio navigation using whatever such equipment may be installed.

**day work**  *n.* Work done by non-watch-standing crew. See DAY'S WORK.

**dazzle painting**  *n.* A method of painting a ship's hull and superstructure so that the characteristic form cannot be readily identified. During World War II, camouflage superseded dazzle painting.

**dead ahead**  *phr.* Directly ahead of a vessel's bow, 000° relative. If the bearing is only approximate, "ahead" should be used alone. See RELATIVE BEARING.

**dead astern**  *phr.* Directly behind a vessel, relative bearing 180°. "We had not changed course, our wake lay dead astern."

**deadbeat compass**  *n.* Magnetic compass invented by Messrs. Henry Hughes & Sons of London in 1920 with the card so constructed and the fluid such that the needle was minimally affected by the motion of the vessel. After being deflected, it returns by one direct movement to its proper reading without oscillation. Also *aperiodic compass.*

**dead before the wind**  *phr.* With the wind directly behind the boat. "We sailed dead before the wind most of the morning."

**dead downwind**  *adj.* Directly to leeward.

**dead-end**  *v.* To secure the end of a rope, usually to cleat it. "Dead-end the bow breastline on that forward piling."

**deadeye**  *n.* A wooden block with flat sides and three or four holes through which the lanyards are rove when setting up a shroud or stay. Because of the extreme strain placed on deadeyes, very dense, tough wood is used; lignum vitae, a tropical hardwood, when possible. Deadeyes have generally been super-seded by turnbuckles for setting up shrouds and stays with the improvement in alloys and depletion of lignun vitae forest around the turn of this century. See HEART.

**dead freight**  *n.* A claim for unoccupied cargo space or short shipment. If a bill of lading calls for 5,000 tons of grain shipped and only 4,800 tons are received, a dead freight claim for 200 tons of grain is filed.

**deadhead**  *n.* (1) A partially submerged log or pile. (2) A pile at a pier. (3) A block of wood used as an anchor buoy. (4) A bollard. (5) A nonpaying passenger such as one who is on a pass.

**deadhead**  *adj.* Pertains to the status of a commercial vessel sailing without cargo. "The ship took the grain from New Orleans to Zaire and returned deadhead."

**dead horse**  *n.* An advance in pay, usually a computer mistake today. "I'm working off a $1,000.00 dead horse over the next three months." When sailors were advanced pay before leaving port, they worked for several weeks at sea before they had worked off their "dead horses." When the day came that they had completed the work on their advance, an effigy of a horse was hoisted over the rail with much boisterous ceremony.

**dead in the water (DIW)**  *phr.* A vessel that is stopped and has no way on, but is not moored, anchored, or made fast to the ground or a wharf. The phrase can be used both of vessels that cannot move because of engine problems, and those that can but are not moving.

**deadlight**  *n.* (1) Hinged metal cover over a porthole or what in Great Britain is called a "sidelight." It can be constructed to allow air but can be baffled to sail under darken ship restrictions. (2) Heavy glass, a **bull's eye,** fixed in a door or deck to admit light within or below deck. (3) A heavy, hinged plate that can be bolted or dogged to protect a glass port during heavy weather. (4) The U.S. Navy uses the term **ventilating daylight,** which is an arrangement of baffles that permit air while preventing the passage of light.

**dead men**   *n.* (1) Loose ends of rope lying adrift that suggest bad housekeeping. Also *cow's tails* or *Irish pennants.* (2) Piles driven in the ground or ice securing a vessel's lines. (3) An improperly furled sail that has the appearance of a shroud.

**dead peg**   *v.* To work directly into the wind.

**dead reckoning (DR)**   *n.* or *adj.,* The determining of a position by course, speed, and time elapsed, but without a fix. A DR position is shown on the chart with a half-circle and a dot and the time the vessel was calculated to be in the position. With any other information included, such as wind and current, it is called an **estimated position.** The term "dead reckoning," comes from deduced reckoning or "ded reckoning," which later became "dead reckoning."

**dead-reckoning tracer (DRT)**   *n.* A plotting computer that automatically maintains a vessel's DR position from the compass and log.

**dead rise**   *n.* The slope of the line of the hull as it rises outward and up from the keel (expressed in inches per foot), or the angle between the hull and a line drawn horizontally out from the keel (expressed in degrees).

**dead rope**   *n.* A rope not led through a block or other fitting. "Secure any dead ropes before the captain's inspection."

**dead run**   *n.* A course with the wind directly behind the vessel.

**dead to windward**   *phr.* Directly upwind.

**dead water**   *n.* (1) The eddy under a vessel's stern. (2) The water pulled along by a vessel's hull as it goes through the water, especially toward the stern.

**deadweight**   *n.* The difference between a ship's light displacement (without cargo but with fuel and supplies) and the fully loaded displacement. See DEADWEIGHT CERTIFICATE.

**deadweight capacity (DWT)**   *n.* The weight of cargo, passengers, fuel, and provisions that brings a vessel from its light displacement to its summer load line mark. Measured in long tons (2,240 pounds), the deadweight capacity is the difference between the vessel's weight when empty (but including machinery) and when fully loaded. It is the usual unit of measure to describe the tonnage of bulk carriers and tankers. Also *deadweight tonnage.*

**deadweight cargo**   *n.* Any cargo with a stowage factor of 40 or less, which is to say it measures less than 40 cubic feet to the ton.

**deadweight cargo factor**   *n.* A loading constant used for determining the approximate deadweight cargo that a vessel can carry on its designed draft. Deadweight cargo factor multiplied by the registered tonnage yields the approximate deadweight cargo the vessel is allowed to carry.

**deadweight certificate**   *n.* A document, usually in the form of a letter from the marine architect at the time of the vessel's construction, that certifies the ship's full-load summer draft, the displacement at that draft, the light ship weight, and the resulting deadweight capacity.

**deadweight efficiency**   *n.* A deadweight capacity divided by designed displacement.

**deadweight ratio**   *n.* The ratio of useful load capacity to displacement at load draft in tons.

**deadweight tonnage (DWT)**   See DEADWEIGHT CAPACITY.

**deadwood**   *n.* (1) The planking forward and abaft the square frames of wooden ships on which the heels of the cant timbers are stepped. The deadwood is bolted to the keel and the sternpost aft and to the keel and stem forward. (2) The reinforcing planking between the keel line and the sternpost.

**deadworks**   *n.* A vessel's hull that is above water when the vessel is fully loaded. Also *upper works*.

**debacle**   *n.* The breaking up of ice in a river. From the Old French *debacler*, to unbar.

**debark**   *v.* To leave a ship, said of people and animals that walk off a vessel. Also *disembark*.

**debarkation**   *n.* The unloading of troops, equipment, or supplies from a vessel. Also *disembarkation*.

**debarkation station**   *n.* The place on a vessel where troops assemble to climb into boats.

**Decca chain**   *n.* A group of associated stations of the Decca Navigator System. These stations include one master and three slave stations with each of the latter called by the color of the associated pattern of hyperbolic lines printed on the chart.

**Decca Navigator System**   *n.* A short- to medium-range low-frequency (70–130 kHz) radio navigation system by which hyperbolic lines of position of high accuracy are obtained. The operation of the system depends on phase comparison of signals from transmitters brought to a common comparison frequency with the receiver.

**deck**   *n.* (1) A principal horizontal component of a vessel's construction that consists of planking or plating at the surface and extending to the sides: a deck rests on deck beams. Decks are the equivalent of floors on land; but see FLOOR; SOLE. (2) The highest complete deck is the **main deck.** The next complete deck down is the second deck, and below it is the third, and so on. (3) The officer of the deck, or deck officer, is said to "have the deck" when assigned the duty of being in charge of all deck functions. If the vessel is underway, the officer of the deck controls the ship's maneuvers or conns the ship unless relieved of that duty by another officer of the deck, the captain, or the executive officer.

**deck auxiliaries**   *n.* All upper deck machinery used in handling cargo and other deck jobs; these include capstans, winches, windlasses, and so on.

**deck beam**   *n.* Any transverse beam supporting a deck; deck beams act as ties connecting the vessel's sides.

**deck boy**   *n.* In merchant ships a member of the crew who ranks below an ordinary seaman. A deck boy qualifies as an ordinary seaman after completing six months' service as a deck boy.

**deck cargo**   *n.* Cargo carried on open decks and exposed to the weather.

**deck collar**   *n.* The deck fitting on a hawse pipe that secures the pipe in the deck.

**deck engineer**   *n.* A petty officer responsible for keeping deck equipment such as capstans, winches, steering systems, and the like in working condition along with plumbing below decks if no plumber is aboard.

**deck erections**   *n.* Those structures above the shell plating such as the bridge and poop.

**deck gang**   *n.* (1) Collective name for **deck hands;** all members of the crew assigned to the deck department as opposed to radio operators, electricians, quartermasters, and so on. In the merchant service, these are the able seamen, ordinary seamen, and the boatswain. (2) Longshoremen who work on deck during loading and unloading; these include boom riggers, winchmen, hatch tenders, sidemen, and slingmen. Also *deck crew.*

**deck gear**   *n.* General term for most equipment used on deck, such as cleats, winches, pad eyes, blocks, wires, cordage, and shackles.

**deck girder**   *n.* Longitudinal member running beneath the athwartship deck beams to distribute the weight of a row of stanchions.

**deck hand**   *n.* A member of the crew who works on deck. Also *deck ape,* used especially of one striking for boatswain's mate.

**deckhead**   *n.* The shipboard equivalent of a ceiling below decks.

**deck height**   *n.* The vertical distance between datum lines of two vertically consecutive decks.

**deck hook**   *n.* A triangular plate fitted at the bow to support the connection between side plating and stem.

**deck horse**   *n.* (1) The supporting structure on which a traveler rides from side to side when a sailing vessel is tacked. Most pleasure craft owners call the traveler and the deck horse together a traveler. (2) The extension from a hatch coaming that supports the hatch rails.

**deckhouse**   *n.* (1) A shelter built on deck. (2) On small boats, that part of the cabin that extends above the main deck is sometimes called a deckhouse, although more properly, it is called a coach roof.

**deckhouse forecastle**   *n.* A deckhouse forward, usually at the foremast, in which the crew of sailing ships are berthed. See FORECASTLE.

**decking**   *n.* Covering for decks to make them more durable and less slippery.

**deck ladder**   *n.* An outside, steel ladder used to go from one deck to another.

**deck light**   *n.* (1) Heavy glass prism fitted flush in a deck to allow light below. (2) A light placed above the deck for working at night. See WORKING LIGHTS.

**deck line**   *n.* A horizontal line of paint 12 inches long and 1 inch wide amidships on both sides of a vessel that is part of the Plimsoll mark; the upper edge marks the point where the continuation of the upper surface of the freeboard deck or deck stringer plate intersects the outer surface of the shell plating or planking. See PLIMSOLL MARK OR LINE.

**deck load**   See DECK CARGO.

**deck log**   *n.* The rough log kept during each watch that gives changes in course and speed, departures and arrivals, soundings, sea conditions, deaths, important landmarks and buoys passed— just about anything that the deck officer thinks about or cares about. If he changes his mind, he can draw a line through the error, but he can't erase anything. He must initial any corrections. The rough log is then transcribed; but in case of any inquiry, the rough deck log prevails over the smooth copy. The rough log is always saddle-stitched so that pages cannot be torn out readily. The deck officer completes his log at the end of his watch, using the quartermaster's log for such things as significant course and speed changes. He then signs the log before going off watch. See OFFICIAL LOG.

**deck longitudinal**   *n.* One of the closely positioned fore-and-aft members that reinforce deck plates on longitudinal framed vessels.

**deck officer**   *n.* (1) A U.S. Navy officer qualified to stand watch as officer of the deck (OOD) at sea, or an officer in training for that responsibility; deck officers are in line to succeed to command at sea. Another line officer is an engineering officer who may or may not have qualified to succeed to command except for shipyards and similar commands. See STAFF OFFICER. (2) An officer assigned to the deck department of a U.S. Navy ship. (3) An officer who is qualified to assist the master with navigation at sea, as opposed to an engineering or supply officer.

**deck passenger**   *n.* A class of passengers without berth assignment or accommodations. Overnight ferries frequently have accommodations for a number of deck passengers. In poorer countries, vessels often allow deck passengers who will be aboard for several days to bring along utensils to use for cooking their meals on deck.

**deck pipe (or still pipe)**   *n.* A trunk leading from the windlass to the chain locker through which the anchor cable runs. See CHAIN PIPE.

**deck plates**   *n.* (1) Removable decking over engine spaces. See DECK STRAKES; FLOOR PLATES. (2) The nameplate and fitting at the top of a shaft leading to the bottom of a tank used for taking soundings. The brass plate gives the name of the tank to which it leads.

**deck seamanship**   *n.* Care and use of all equipment topside including boats, anchors, rigging, booms and davits.

**deck steward**   *n.* (1) Member of the crew of a passenger liner who is in charge of the deck chairs, soup, and tea for passengers on the promenade and upper decks. (2) A union delegate representing the deck department.

**deck stopper**   *n.* (1) A line or cable with a toggle and a lanyard for lashing cable on deck. (2) A short line for stopping movement of another line. A mooring line is stopped-off when it is transferred from a capstan to a bitt, cleat, or kevel.

**deck stops**   *n.* Fittings that control the sweep of the rudder to prevent its going beyond 35°, as a rule, on each side. See RUDDER STOPS.

**deck strakes**   *n.* The rows of plating that make up the upper surface of a deck.

**deck stringer**   *n.* Outboard deck plating with its outer edge attached to the hull shell plating or to the inside of the vessel's framing by the **stringer plate.**

**deck tackle**   *n.* Heavy tackle associated with the ground tackle.

**deck transom**   *n.* The transverse member that supports the deck beams at the extremity of the stern.

**deck watch**   See HACK WATCH.

**declination**   *n.* The angular distance of a heavenly body (north or south) from the celestial equator, measured on a meridian passing through the body. This corresponds to a terrestrial latitude.

**declination compass**   *n.* A compass combined with a telescope that makes possible determining the magnetic declination when the astronomical meridian is known.

**declination of the zenith**   *n.* The angular distance between the equator and the observer's zenith, equal to latitude.

**declination reduction**   *n.* The processing of observed high and low waters or flood and ebb tidal currents to obtain quantities depending on changes in declination of the Moon, such as tropic ranges or speeds, height or speed inequalities, and topic intervals.

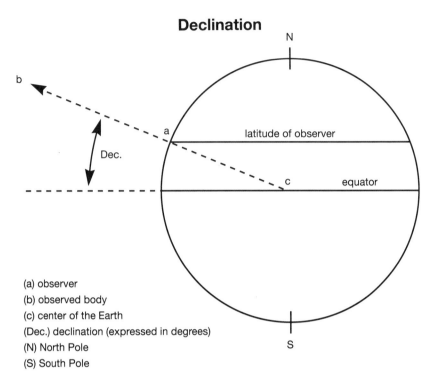

## Declination

N

b

a

Dec.

c    equator

latitude of observer

(a) observer
(b) observed body
(c) center of the Earth
(Dec.) declination (expressed in degrees)
(N) North Pole
(S) South Pole

S

**decoration**    *n.* A ribbon or medal given to a person, a ship, or a military unit for outstanding performance, courage, or skill.

**decoy ship**    *n.* A ship camouflaged as a noncombatant ship, with its armament and other fighting equipment hidden and with special provisions for unmasking its weapons quickly. Also *Q-ship.*

**deduced reckoning**    *n.* See DEAD RECKONING.

**deducted space**    *n.* Tonnage term denoting the enclosed spaces of a ship that are deducted from gross tonnage to arrive at net tonnage.

**deep**    *n.* (1) The length of line in fathoms between two successive marks on a lead line. If the man in the chains calls out, "By the deep, six," he means that the depth was greater than 6 fathoms but less than the next mark. (2) The deepest

level of a depression or trench in the sea bottom, usually with steep sides, usually found in depths over 3,000 fathoms. The greatest depths that have been recorded are in the Marianas Trench, over 6,000 fathoms. (3) Any deep place in a body of water deeper than 3,000 fathoms.

**deep creep attack**    *n.* Slow-speed surprise attack against a deeply submerged submarine.

**deepening**    *n.* Decrease in atmospheric pressure, especially within a low. See FILLING.

**deep floor**    *n.* The floors in the forward and after sections of a vessel that are deeper than those in the main body.

**deep scattering layer**    *n.* Ocean layers of organisms of uncertain composition that scatter or echo sound, about 150 to 200 fathoms during the day and much shallower at night.

**deep sea lead**   *n.* (pron. dipsy led) The heavy lead used for deep-sea soundings. The lead is usually 50 pounds, and the lead line is as much as 120 fathoms. Now replaced by echo sounders.

**deep six**   *n.* The expression for the place where something goes when it goes overboard, from the custom of burials at sea when the ceremony took place in not less than 6 fathoms of water. See DEEP. To give something the "deep six" is to throw it overboard.

**deep stowage**   *n.* The stowing of bulk cargo and bagged or drummed goods in holds not broken by 'tween deck spaces.

**deep-submergence rescue vehicle (DSRV)**   *n.* Small submarine that is easily transported by a larger submarine or aircraft to a submarine disaster where it can submerge and join a sunken submarine at the escape trunk.

**deep tank**   *n.* (1) A deep compartment usually extending from the plating of the double bottom to the lower deck. (2) Compartments designed with baffles and stiffeners to carry water or other liquids.

**deep-water**   *adj.* Offshore; a deep-water sailor is one who sails out of sight of land.

**deep-well pump**   *n.* Centrifugal pumps of a design used mainly on ships carrying a number of different refined products. The impeller is located at the end of a long vertical shaft that extends to the bottom of a tank.

**deflection**   *n.* A naval gunnery term relating to the lateral angle correction to a target bearing. See ELEVATION.

**deflector**   *n.* Compass adjuster's device for determining the *relative* directive force without reference to heavenly bodies or landmarks. The first deflector was invented by Sir William Thomson (Lord Kelvin), 1824–1907.

**degauss**   *v.* (rhymes with de-louse) To reduce the strength of a steel vessel's magnetic field to minimize the danger of magnetic mines and torpedoes. This is done with suitably arranged electromagnetic coils, permanent magnets, **degaussing cables,** or other means. The unit of measuring the strength of a magnetic field is a gauss, named for Karl. F. Gauss, 1777–1855, German mathematician, physicist, and astronomer. See COMPASS COMPENSATION.

**degaussing range**   *n.* An area for determining magnetic signatures of vessels; the signatures are used for determining required degaussing coil current settings and other corrective action.

**delivery clause**   *n.* The statement in all charter parties giving the time, date, and place the vessel is to be available to the charterer.

**Del Norte Trisponder System**   *n.* A short-range, line-of-sight, electric distance measuring system used for hydrographic surveys.

**Delta**   *n.* (1) Phonetic word for the letter "D." Used as a single-letter signal it means "Keep clear of me—I am maneuvering with difficulty." (2) A deposit of alluvial sand, usually triangular, at the mouth of a river or a tidal inlet.

**demise charter**   *n.* A charter party that allows the charter to take over the vessel without captain or crew. Also *bare boat charter.*

**demurrage**   *n.* (1) The act of holding a ship beyond the scheduled loading or unloading time. Demurrage days are the days beyond the lay days. (2) The amount paid for lost revenue time.

**demurrage lien**   *n.* The lien imposed against a charterer in favor of the ship owner for money owed for loading or unloading beyond the time provided by the charter party. High rates for loading and unloading make fast turnarounds imperative.

**dense fog**   *n.* In international meteorological understanding, fog limiting visibility to 25–50 feet.

**Department of Defense (DOD)**   *n.* A department of the executive branch of the U.S. government created by the Amendments of 1949 to the National Security Act. It includes the Army, Navy, and Air Force, and is under the Secretary of Defense. In time of war, the U.S. Coast Guard becomes a part of the Department of Defense, in peacetime it is under the Department of Transportation.

**Department of the Navy**   *n.* Executive head of the U.S. Navy and the U.S. Marine Corps. From 1798 to 1947, the Secretary of the Navy was a cabinet member in his own right, as was the separate Secretary of War. See NAVY DEPARTMENT.

**departure**   *n.* (1) The time and position when a ship begins a voyage and leaves an anchorage or harbor. The OOD might write in the ship's log "With Egmont Key Light bearing 083° at 8.9 miles, took departure from Tampa Bay for Key West on various courses and speeds." See TAKE DEPARTURE. (2) Distance made good east or west on course along a parallel of latitude expressed in nautical miles; it only relates to difference in longitude in degrees, minutes, and seconds, expressed in nautical miles, but does not include latitude change.

**deperm**   *v.* To reduce the permanent magnetism of a steel vessel by using energizing coils vertically around the hull. See DEGAUSS.

**deploy**   *v.* (1) To position ships and forces for battle or amphibious assault. (2) To send ships or squadrons to foreign waters for duty.

**deployment**   *n.* A vessel's tour of duty in foreign waters.

**depression**   *n.* A weather system identified by the presence of a low-density air mass that flows inward and counterclockwise in the northern hemisphere.

**depth**   *n.* (1) In marine construction, the height of a vessel from the base line at the bottom of the ship, the top of the floor, to the molded line of deck, the top of the upper deck beams. (2) The vertical distance from the plane of hydrographic datum to the bed of the sea, lake, or river. The charted depth is the vertical distance from the tidal datum to the bottom. See NET BOTTOM CLEARANCE.

**depth charge**   *n.* In anti-submarine warfare, an explosive device usually dropped off the stern of a warship that detonates at a predetermined depth, or in proximity to a submarine. Also *ashcan.* See HEDGEHOG.

**depth contour**   *n.* A line connecting points of equal depth below the hydrographic datum on a marine chart. Also *bathymetric contour* or *depth curve.*

**depth finder**   *n.* See ECHO SOUNDER.

**depth gauge**   *n.* Instrument designed to determine depth of water by means of the pressure exerted by the water.

**depth of floor**   *n.* The distance from the floor of the midships cargo hold to the upper deck beams.

**depth of water**   *n.* The charted depth plus the height of tide. The charted depth is a reference arbitrarily selected usually at one of the several low waters such as low or mean low, called the chart sounding datum, above which the tides usually rise and fall. The depth of water can be less than the charted depth when an exceptionally low water takes the water to a point below the reference level.

**depth recorder**   *n.* A depth sounder that records depths on a roll of paper.

**depth sounder**   *n.* An electronic device used for determining the depth of water under the vessel. Also *depth finder; echo sounder.* Fathometer is a trade name for a depth sounder and is capitalized.

**deratization**   *n.* The extermination of rats on a vessel with the object of obtaining a **deratization certificate** or **deratting certificate.** A phrase that was legitimized at the International Sanitary Convention in Paris in 1926 when it was required that virtually all vessels obtain such certificates, to be renewed every six months. Authorities in most foreign ports will want to see this document or a certificate of deratting exemption.

**derelict**   *n.* (1) An abandoned, floating vessel. To rescue a derelict is to salvage it. A **quasi-derelict** is a vessel that does not fully meet the definition of a derelict, such as a vessel the crew of which is physically or mentally incompetent to safely navigate it or a vessel that has been abandoned but is in good enough condition to be sailed. (2) Goods abandoned or reliquished by the owner. (3) Land that is left dry by the permanent recession of the waterline.

**derrick**   *n.* A large, movable crane with a stationary base, often mounted on a barge, used for hoisting heavy objects. Named for 17th-century hangman, Thomas Derick, who devised a portable gallows with which to perform his professional duties.

**descending node**   *n.* The point at which a planet, planetoid, or comet crosses the ecliptic from north to south, or a satellite crosses the plane of the equator of its primary from north to south.

**deserter**   *n.* A person who is absent from his or her command without authorization for a period of 30 days or more. Such absence is not complete legal proof of desertion, but the absentee is presumed to have deserted at that time, per the Universal Code of Military Jus-

tice. In the merchant service, the period differs with the various agreements. It also covers the failure of a member of the crew to join a ship in due time after "signing on."

**designator**   *n.* A U.S. Navy term for a four-digit code describing an officer's qualifications and specialties.

**designed displacement**   *n.* The displacement of a vessel floating at her designed draft. See FREEBOARD.

**destroyer (DD)**   *n.* A high-speed warship designed to operate offensively with strike forces and hunter-killer groups, and in support of amphibious operations. Destroyers also operate defensively to screen support forces and convoys. Guided-missile destroyers are designated DDG.

**destroyer escort (DE)**   *n.* Primarily an ocean convoy escort vessel developed during World War II. As its duty and mission changed, it was replaced by the frigate.

**detach**   *v.* A term only applicable to U.S. Navy officers and meaning to be ordered away from present duty; similarly, an officer is attached to a duty station or command. (Enlisted personnel are assigned and transferred.)

**detachable link**   *n.* A chain link that can be removed by taking it apart. A tapered forelock pin holds together two overlapping lugs. When the pin is removed, the link disassembles. The link when assembled or attached to connect two chains can go through the hawsepipe and around a wildcat, unlike a swivel. Also PATENT LINK.

**developed area**   *n.* The actual area of the blades of a propeller surface without regard for shape.

**deviation**   *n.* The error in a ship's compass caused by the vessel's own magnetic field set up by the iron hull and fixtures aboard. Deviation from magnetic north in an easterly direction is indicated as + or easterly; when the deviation is westerly from magnetic north, it is indicated as − or westerly. Compass error is the result of variation plus deviation.

**deviation clause**   *n.* Charter party reference to making allowance for the master's making the decision to call at ports other than the stated destination in the contract.

**deviation table**   *n.* A card or graph with the "deviation" of a magnetic compass recorded for each heading of the ship through 360°, usually recorded every 5°. A line drawn on the graph through the various changes in deviation makes it possible to interpolate deviation between recorded points. A deviation table is posted at each magnetic compass. With gyro compasses prevalent, the deviation card is rarely used, but must be available when the ship is inspected, or the navigator is gigged. See NAPIER DIAGRAM.

**devil**   *n.* (1) The seam in a wooden deck closest to the waterway. (2) The seam in the planking at or just below the waterline. (3) The seam nearest the keel. The devil is always a difficult seam to caulk. From this, the awkwardness of being "between the devil and the deep blue sea" is clear. (3) "The devil to pay" is a caulker's term for the difficult task of paying (caulking) one of the seams known as devils.

**devil's claw**   *n.* A stout hook used as a stopper for a chain, most often used on the anchor and anchor chain when stowing the ground tackle for sea. See COMPRESSOR.

**dew point**   *n.* The point of air saturation at which condensation begins to occur and fog forms.

**dew valve**   *n.* An automatic draining device for cylinders on deck machinery.

**dhow**   *n.* A long flat sailing vessel found especially in the Indian Ocean along the east coast of Africa, the Arabian peninsula, and Pakistan and India. The masts carry lateen sails and are usually raked forward.

**diagonal**   *adj.* In marine construction, it relates to the reference planes used in the line plans defining the longitudinal molded form of the hull through the turn of the bilge and above and below it. These reference planes are laid diagonally downward from the centerline plane.

**diagonal and longitudinal hull construction**   *n.* System of marine construction with double skin planking, in which the outer layer is laid running longitudinally similar to carvel design, and the inner layer is laid at an angle to the keel gunwale and stringers and lightly fastened. This dispenses with frames and ribs and is quite strong, but it is an expensive procedure.

**diagonally cut sails**   *n.* Any of several similar designs in which the cloths above the miter are sewn at right angles to the leech and perpendicular to the foot. The head and foot sections of cloths are joined at the miter and bisect the angle at the clew. See CROSS-CUT SAIL; MITER.

**diamond**   *n.* A shape or visual aid hung in the rigging of a vessel between sunrise and sunset as prescribed in the *Navigation Rules* to indicate the vessel's navigational status. A diamond consists of two cones having a common base.

**diamond beacon**   *n.* A topmark with a diamond shape found in the Region A buoyage system to mark the outer end of a middle ground.

**diamond shrouds**   *n.* Shrouds that start high on a mast, usually at the cap, and are led down across spreaders and then back to the mast to give extra strength to the mast. When viewed from forward or aft, they form a diamond shape. Also *jumper stays.*

**diaphone**  *n.* Stationary foghorn used as an aid to navigation in which a slotted piston moves back and forth by compressed air and usually emits two different tones.

**diaphragm horn**  *n.* A fixed aid to navigation that consists of a disc diaphragm that is vibrated by compressed air or electricity. Duplex and triplex units produce chimes.

**dicky**  *n.* British term for a small seat at the transom of a square-sterned rowboat; the dicky is used by the coxswain when the boat is being rowed.

**diesel fuel**  *n.* Petroleum fuel produced in the light gas-oil range and essentially the same product as furnace fuel. The **diesel engine,** an internal combustion engine, uses highly compressed air to ignite the spray of diesel fuel injected after the beginning of the compression stroke. The diesel engine was invented by Rudolph Diesel (1858–1913), a German mechanical engineer.

**diffraction**  *n.* The bending of rays around the edges of an obstacle or the bending of waves around an obstruction.

**dihedral reflector**  *n.* A radar reflector with two flat surfaces intersecting at right angles.

**dinghy**  *n.* In earlier days a ship's boat that was single-banked with four oars; today a dinghy is any small boat used for the convenience of passengers and crew especially on yachts. From the Hindi *dingi,* a small boat. Regional synonyms are **yawl boat** (western rivers), **pirogue** (Louisiana), **skiff** (various).

**diode**  *n.* An electric device that allows current to flow in only one direction and is highly resistant to current flow in the opposite direction. If the main switch is turned off before turning off the ignition switch with the engine going, the diode will blow.

**dioptric light**  *n.* A light concentrated into a parallel beam by means of refracting lenses or prisms. See CATOPTRIC.

**dip**  *n.* (1) In sextant observation, the correction for height of eye above the water, and always expressed as a negative. (2) A downward inclination of a compass's magnetic needle. (3) The vertical angle at the eye of an observer between the horizontal and the line of sight to the visible horizon. Altitudes of celestial bodies measured from the visible horizon of the sea are greater than the actual altitude by the amount of dip.

**dip**  *v.* (1) To salute by lowering and hoisting the ensign. The first ship to salute lowers the ensign partway until the responding ship lowers its ensign; the first ship then two-blocks the ensign, followed by the responding ship. A merchant ship lowers first and holds the flag "at the dip" until the warship returns the dip. Warships return passing honors but do not initiate them and do not dip to each other. (2) To cross the meridian, said of a heavenly body.

**dip circle**  *n.* An instrument for measuring magnetic dip.

**dip of the horizon**  *n.* The angle at the observer between the sensible horizon and the visible horizon.

**dipping line**  *n.* A line on the heel of a yard of a dipping lugsail used to swing the yard on the other side of the mast when tacking.

**dipping lugsail**  *n.* Fore-and-aft four-cornered sail with a gaff on the top edge. The forward part of the sail is carried forward of the mast so that to tack, the forward end of the gaff must be dipped.

**dip rope**  *n.* A length of chain or cable fitted with an eye and shackle and tailed with a length of rope; it is used with heavy mooring tackle.

**dipsey lead**  See DEEP SEA LEAD.

**dip the eye**   *phr.* To arrange the loops of two lines on a bollard or piling so that either line can be removed without removing the other. This can be done by passing the loop of the second one up through the loop of the first and then over the bollard or piling.

**direct acting pump**   *n.* A reciprocating pump with the plunger at the intake and driven directly by a rod from the steam power unit. Indirect action is usually through a crank driven by a turbine.

**direct drive**   *n.* A propulsion system used on reciprocating engines with the engine shaft connected directly to the propeller. Engine rpm's are the same as propeller rpm's.

**direction**   *n.* The position of one point relative to another without reference to the distance between. Direction is not an angle, but is often given with reference to a direction such as north (000°). See RELATIVE BEARING.

**directional light**   *n.* A light illuminating a sector or a very narrow angle and intended to mark a direction to be followed. These are identified in the U.S. Coast Guard *Light List.*

**directional stability**   *n.* A vessel's resistance to lateral forces such as wind and current that tend to throw it off the heading.

**direction of current**   *n.* The direction toward which a water current flows, called the set of the current. A northerly current is one that flows toward the north. (In contrast, a northerly wind is one that blows from the north.)

**direct steering gear**   *n.* Steering mechanism with no intermediate chains, rods, or shafting.

**dirty wind**   *n.* Confused or baffled wind on the leeward side of a sail caused as a rule by bad sail design.

**disabled**   *adj.* Describes an injured or impaired vessel that is unable to proceed; under the *Navigation Rules,* such a vessel is considered a "vessel not under command," as distinct from a "vessel restricted in her ability to maneuver."

**disbursement**   *n.* Payment by the master or ship's agents such as customs fees, bunkers, stores, repairs, and cargo-handling charges.

**disbursing officer**   *n.* An officer who maintains the pay records and pays salaries and claims.

**disc area**   *n.* The area of the circle described by the tips of propeller blades. The **disc area ratio** is the ratio of the developed area of a propeller to the disc area.

**discharge**   *v.* (1) To separate enlisted personnel from the service. (2) To remove cargo from a vessel.

**discharge**   *n.* The separation of an enlisted person from the service. "Jones received an honorable discharge."

**discharge current**   *n.* The current that flows away from a propeller, whether going forward or in reverse. See SUCTION SCREW CURRENT.

**discharging berth**   *n.* Space assigned a vessel for unloading cargo.

**disciplinary barracks**   *n.* A facility for confining prisoners so ordered by a court-martial. Popularly called the **brig.**

**discontinued**   *adj.* Describes an aid to navigation that has been removed from its position temporarily or permanently.

**discontinuous shroud**   *n.* A shroud made up of more than one section connected by turnbuckles to reduce stretch.

**discrepancy**   *n.* Used to describe an aid to navigation that has drifted from its proper position as described in the U.S.

## Directions and Courses

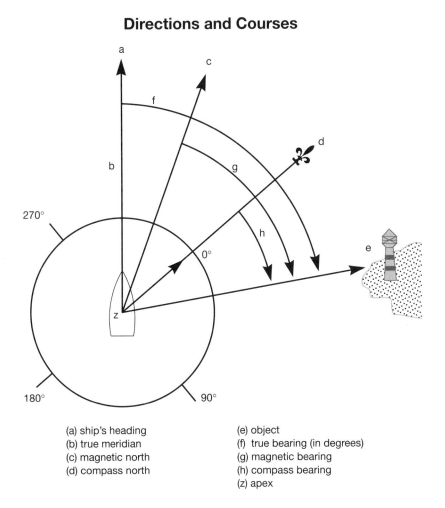

(a) ship's heading
(b) true meridian
(c) magnetic north
(d) compass north

(e) object
(f) true bearing (in degrees)
(g) magnetic bearing
(h) compass bearing
(z) apex

Coast Guard *Light List*. Such discrepancies are frequently described in Coast Guard bulletins on Channel 22A. If the problem cannot be rectified in a short time, the discrepancy will be published in *Notices to Mariners.*

**discrepancy buoy**   *n.* A buoy easily transported to temporarily replace an aid to navigation that is "not watching properly," as the *Light List* describes it.

**disembark** (or **debark**)   *v.* To land from a ship, usually by walking off of it. Cattle and people disembark from a vessel.

**disembogue**   *v.* To issue forth from a river or to leave a river or estuary. "We recognized the Amazon by the muddy water that disembogued into the Atlantic." "We were not able to disembogue the estuary until the following day when an easterly sprang up." From the Spanish *desembocar.* The word has been in dictionaries since the late 16th century, but has not gained in usage.

**dismantle**   *v.* To remove all of a ship's guns, stores, masts, spars, and rigging before being laid up in ordinary.

**dismast**   *v.* To remove a ship's mast accidentally, usually in a storm, collision, or stranding; it is also said of a vessel whose mast has been carried away in battle. If the mast is removed intentionally by owner or others responsible for the vessel, the mast is said to be unstepped.

**dismiss**   *v.* (1) To allow troops to leave. (2) To release a cadet, midshipman, or officer from a service without honor; such action is done by a court-martial or military commission.

**dispatch days**   *n.* Days saved on loading or unloading, less than the agreed time, within the lay days.

**dispatch money**   *n.* Charter party term, the opposite of demurrage. If a vessel is unloaded with dispatch or extra speed, the charterer is awarded dispatch money.

**displacement**   *n.* The weight of water displaced by a floating vessel, which is equal to the total weight of the vessel. The displacement can be expressed either in tons or cubic feet. A cubic foot of seawater weighs about 64 pounds, a cubic foot of freshwater 62.5 pounds. Therefore one long ton (2,240 pounds) of seawater is equal to 35 cubic feet, and one ton of freshwater is equal to 35.9 cubic feet.

**displacement hull**   *n.* A hull designed to remain in the water when underway and not to plane or hover.

**displacement tonnage**   *n.* The weight of water, measured in long tons (2,240 pounds) displaced by a vessel loaded to its summer loadline. It is the usual unit of measure used to describe the tonnage of warships.

**displacement/weight formula**   *n.* In determining a boat's racing class, a vessel's weight in long tons divided by $(0.01 \times$ the waterline length$)^3$.

**disposition**   *n.* (1) A prescribed arrangement of ships in a fleet. The oper-

ation order prescribes the arrangement of the stations to be maintained by the formations and single vessels of a fleet. (2) The distribution of the elements of command and duties assigned to each unit.

**distance**   *n.* A tactical term referring to the distance between foremasts of ships (or the cockpits of aircraft). Ships keeping station, say 500 yards apart, keep station with their foremasts 500 yards apart.

**distance line**   *n.* (1) Marked measuring line used to assist ships being fueled to keep proper distance from the fueling ship. (2) One of the upper lines used to hold a collision mat in place.

**distance made good**   *phr.* The distance over the ground along a course that has been traveled.

**distance signals**   *n.* Shapes, flags, and pennants larger than the usual code flags, used to signal over distances greater than usual when smaller standard flags would not be readable.

**distilling plant**   *n.* The equipment used to convert seawater to freshwater. Its primary components are an evaporator and a condenser.

**distinctive mark**   *n.* General term referring to flags and pennants flown from warships such as a personal starred flag of a flag officer, a Red Cross flag, a commission pennant, or a broad command pennant.

**distress cargo**   *n.* Denotes cargo forwarded at once at a higher rate than currently charged to satisfy the terms of a contract.

**distress frequency**   *n.* A communications channel—for radio telephones, channel 16 (156.80 MHz) on VHF or 2,182 kHz on the MF, and for radiotelegraphy, 500 kHz—used for international distress and for initiating calls. All ships at sea are required to monitor the distress frequencies 24 hours a day.

**distress signal**  *n.* Any of a number of devices used to draw attention to a vessel in distress, such as flares.

**district commander**  *n.* An officer of the U.S. Coast Guard designated by the commandant to command all Coast Guard activities within his district, including vessel inspections and law enforcement.

**ditty bag**  *n.* Small bag used by sailors to carry a sailmaker's palm, needles, twine, marlin, marlinespike, personal sewing necessities and other items.

**diurnal circle**  *n.* The circle on the celestial sphere through which a heavenly body appears to move daily as it moves across the sky from east to west.

**diurnal current**  *n.* A tidal current that cycles once a day with one ebb current and one flood current, separated by a slack water. See MIXED CURRENT; SEMIDIURNAL CURRENT.

**diurnal inequality**  *n.* The difference between two high waters or two low waters that occur in a single 24-hour period. The diurnal inequality changes with the declination of the Moon and, to a lesser extent, of the Sun.

**diurnal range**  *n.* The difference between high water and low water when there is only one tide. The **great diurnal range** is the average difference between all mean higher high waters and mean lower low waters over a 19-year period. See METONIC CYCLE.

**dive**  *v.* To submerge; said of submarines.

**dived tons**  *n.* A submarine construction term that refers to the difference between a submarine's displacement when running on the surface and when submerged.

**dividers**  *n.* A device used for measuring distances and coordinates on a chart. Compasses with two steel points instead of one or two pencils are called "dividers."

**diving planes**  *n.* Horizontal, finlike planes on submarines at the bow and stern (and less frequently on the sail) and used to control vertical motion of the boat under water.

**division officer**  *n.* A junior officer assigned by the commanding officer to take charge of a division, the basic administrative unit in which personnel are organized aboard a U.S. Navy ship.

**dobby**  *v.* To wash clothes.

**dock**  *n.* (1) The water next to a pier. Properly, a vessel is in its dock when it is tied to the pier, in its station in a basin, or (in earlier usage) at anchor in a creek. (2) A platform for loading or unloading cargo. The use of dock to mean the platform to which a boat is tied is of recent origin. Jetty, groin, wharf, pier, quay, or breakwater are more appropriate. (3) Basin, often artificial, providing suitable amenities for loading and unloading close to the sea.

**dock**  *v.* To put a vessel in a shore space at a platform or piling. It usually means to secure her in her position as well as to put her in the dock.

**dockage**  *n.* The charge to keep a boat at a dock. It also is used to mean docking facilities. "Dockage at Dry Tortugas is for day use only."

**dockage period**  *n.* The time during which tide and current will allow the watergates of a dock to be open for ingress and egress.

**docker**  *n.* One who works on the docks, a longshoreman. Also *dockhand; dockworker.*

**dock floor**   *n.* The floor of a drydock, usually with some inclination toward the center from the sides and toward the seaward end.

**docking**   *n.* The fee charged by a tugboat for assisting a vessel into dock.

**docking bridge**   *n.* Platform near the stern of a vessel on which the officer in charge of stern docking lines stands. Also *warping bridge.*

**docking keel**   *n.* A keel fitted at or near the turn of the bilge and used by the vessel in drydock. See BILGE KEELS.

**docking line**   See MOORING LINE.

**docking master**   *n.* A pilot who handles only docking maneuvers.

**docking plan**   *n.* Ship's plan giving all information on the hull below the waterline and which enables the dockmaster to set the blocking before the dry dock is filled or the vessel arrives.

**docking telegraph**   *n.* Communication device that advises the stern docking officer of the speed and direction of the engines and rudder. It consists of a set of telltale dials. Radios have replaced them almost completely, though they are still to be seen in older ships.

**dock landing ship (LSD)**   *n.* A naval ship designed to transport and launch loaded amphibious craft and vehicles with their crews and embarked personnel, and to render limited docking and repair service to small ships and craft, and one that is capable of operating as a control ship during an amphibious operation.

**dockmaster**   *n.* (1) An officer or civilian who supervises dry-docking. (2) Overseer of a marina or yacht harbor who helps customers or members with lines, fueling, and so on, and assigns visitors their slips. Developers, trying to add class to their new marinas, often prefer harbormaster.

**dock sill**   *n.* The foundation at the bottom of the entrance to a dry dock or a lock, against which the gates close.

**dock trials**   *n.* Tests of a vessel's equipment without leaving the dock.

**dockyard**   *n.* A yard on a body of water that offers facilities for building, repairing, and sometimes dry docking vessels. In Britain, a navy yard is frequently called a dockyard.

**doctrine of the last fair chance**   *n.* The doctrine recognized under admiralty law that provides that a master shall, when collision is imminent, do all in his power to avoid or lessen the disaster. The responsibilities of the master of the stand-on vessel are spelled out in the *Navigation Rules.*

**document**   *v.* To obtain U.S. papers to prove ownership and national registration of a vessel. This is a more sophisticated procedure than simply licensing a vessel and is important when planning a trip in foreign waters. It enables a vessel to enter and leave U.S. ports with a minimum of paperwork. See LICENSE.

**documentation**   *n.* Papers showing the type of occupation in which a vessel is allowed to engage.

**dodger**   *n.* A wind and water screen, usually of canvas, used to protect the watch and passengers on small boats, especially sailboats.

**dog**   *n.* An angled metal fitting used to secure watertight hatches, covers, ports, doors, and so on.

**dog**   *v.* To tightly secure a hatch or porthole. "Close and dog #6 hatch." Also *dog bolt.*

**dog-bitch thimble**   *n.* A device used to prevent the topsail sheet from making a half-turn in the clew.

**doghouse**   *n.* A shelter over a hatch.

**dograil**  See KNIGHTHEADS.

**dog's ear**  *n.* The bight of the leech of a reefed sail.

**dog-stopper**  *n.* A device used to make possible bitting a cable or to relieve the strain on a windlass. On smaller boats, a piece of rope with a stopper knot is used, while on larger vessels chain is used.

**dog-vane**  *n.* Bunting used on a sail or on the rigging to show the wind direction. Also *telltale vane; wind vane.*

**dog watch**  *n.* Either of the two 2-hour watches between 1600 and 2000. The purpose is to preclude the same watch section having the same hours day in and day out; the watch section changes, the next one comes on, and they are followed at 2000 by the third watch section. Dogging also makes it possible for the crew on both the watches to have the evening meal close to 1800.

**doldrums**  *n.* An equatorial trough of low atmospheric pressure that extends from approximately 5°N to 5°S; it is characterized by unsettled weather and light winds. See WIND.

**dollie**  *n.* Small dockside bollard less than a foot high.

**dollop**  *n.* A wave that breaks over the windward side and on the deck.

**dolphin**  *n.* (1) A group of piles driven into the earth slanted toward each other at the top and secured with steel cable. Also *cluster piling.* A single pile or a bollard on a wharf is also sometimes called a dolphin. (2) A rope lashed to the mast to support antichafing mats or puddening.

**dolphin striker**  *n.* A stout bar mounted downward from the bowsprit to spread the martingale stays. This rigging is similar to spreaders and crosstrees.

**dome**  *n.* (1) Indicated on navigation charts to identify a large rounded hemispherical structure rising above a building. (2) An elevation of the sea bottom rising steeply but with more than 100 fathoms of water over it.

**domestic registry**  *n.* Refers to merchant ships whose national flag and ownership are the same.

**donkey**  *n.* Small engine used for hoisting or for pulling. Ships are sometimes pulled through narrow canals by donkey engines. In the Panama Canal they are called **mules.**

**donkey boiler**  *n.* Auxiliary boiler that supplies heat to nonpropulsion units and to the heating system in port.

**donkey engine**  *n.* A steam engine that furnishes power for winches that hoist sail, weigh anchors, supply heat, and operate deck pumps.

**donkey's breakfast**  *n.* Sailor's term for a straw mattress.

**door**  *n.* An upright, hinged partition between compartments. If the door is through a nonwatertight bulkhead it is a **joiner door.** A watertight bulkhead would have a watertight door as thick as the bulkhead. See HATCH.

**doper**  *n.* Nickname used by U.S. Customs and Coast Guard for a vessel smuggling drugs.

**Doppler effect**  *n.* A change in frequency caused by relative motion between transmitter and receiver. The phenomenon is used in the Doppler sonar speed log to measure the speed of a vessel over the sea bottom. It is also used in antisubmarine warfare to identify sonar blips.

**Doppler radar**  *n.* Any form of radar that detects radial motion of distant objects relative to a radar antenna by means of change of radio frequency of echo signal due to motion.

**Doppler satellite navigation**  *n.* The use of a navigation system that determines positions based on the Doppler effect of signals received from artificial satellites.

**Dorade ventilator (or box)**  *n.* A ventilator that allows air to enter below decks but does not allow water to enter. It was first used on the yacht *Dorade*.

**dory**  *n.* A small flat-bottomed boat with high freeboard, designed to be especially seaworthy, usually fitted with an engine or a sail, of American origin.

**double**  *v.* (1) To run a line from a vessel around a bitt ashore and back aboard to allow better line husbandry. See DOUBLE UP. (2) To sail around a point of land. "We doubled Key West and headed into the Atlantic Ocean." (3) To overlap parts of two masts.

**double altitude**  *n.* (1) The use of a single heavenly body twice with an interval of time between when only one body can be seen. By including the distance the vessel runs between sightings, the navigator can obtain a rough position. (2) A method of determining longitude by taking the altitude of a body before and after meridian transit. By determining the difference between the two times that the body crosses the same altitude, the navigator can determine longitude. The accuracy of this method is low and should only be used from a fixed position.

**double awning**  *n.* The use of a second awning above the first awning with about a foot of airspace between to make the spaces below cooler than with a single awning.

**double-banked**  *adj.* (1) Describes a boat or galley with two men on a thwart on the same oar. (2) A naval frigate mounting broadside guns on two decks.

**double-bitt**  *v.* (1) To use two bitts instead of one for securing a line. "Double-bitt the forward bow spring." (2) To put more turns on a bitt than usual as an extra precaution.

**double block**  *n.* A block (pulley) with two sheaves.

**double bollard**  *n.* A bollard with two columns and a single base.

**double bottom**  *n.* A watertight subdivision or compartment next to the keel and between the outer bottom and the inner bottom; these are used for ballast, fuel storage, fresh water, or oil.

**double ebb**  *n.* An ebb tidal current during which, after ebb begins, the speed increases to a maximum called the **first ebb;** it then decreases, reaching a **minimum ebb** near the middle of the ebb period and may even run in a flood direction for a short period. It then again ebbs to a maximum speed called the **second ebb,** after which it decreases to slack water. See DOUBLE FLOOD.

**double ender**  *n.* A "double-bowed" vessel that can go backward as well as forward without turning around, such as ferryboats. The term is also applied to sailing vessels that are pointed at bow and stern.

**double flood**  *n.* A flood tidal current during which, after flood begins, the speed increases to a maximum called the **first flood;** it then decreases, reaching a minimum flood near the middle of the flood period, and may even run in an ebb direction for a short period. It then again floods to a maximum speed called the **second flood,** after which it decreases to slack water. See DOUBLE EBB.

**double-fluked anchor**  *n.* An anchor so designed that both flukes bite into the ground at the same time. The arms are hinged at the crown to make this possible.

**double futtock**  *n.* Planking in the cant members that extends from the deadwood to the run of the second futtock.

**double-grooved headstay**  *n.* A headstay with two grooves on the after side to allow one headsail to be bent on, ready to haul up before the first sail is hauled down. The luff is placed in the groove, and the halyard hauls it up without using hanks.

**double headsail**  *phr.* Describes a boat with a jib topsail set on the headstay and a staysail set on a forestay (inner headstay). See CUTTER; RIG.

**double luff**  *n.* A tackle with two sheaves for each block.

**double purchase**  *n.* Tackle with two single-sheaved blocks with the standing part of the tackle secured to one of the blocks.

**double-span mooring**  *n.* A permanent mooring that uses a ground chain between two spans with each span anchored at each end; a mooring buoy with mooring ring is secured to the ground chain by a separate chain. In this way, four anchors are used with the mooring riding the ground chain.

**double tide**  *n.* Two high tides or two low tides that are almost the same height and separated by very little change in tide height.

**double topsail**  *n.* A split topsail that replaced the single topsail for easier handling. The lower topsail had to have an additional yard called the **lower topsail yard.** The upper topsail has no clew lines; instead the clews are shackled to the lower topsail yard by a tackle called the **upper topsail downhaul.** See TOPSAIL.

**double up**  *v.* To double the docking lines. Larger ships always double up the lines when docking for more than a few hours. Small boats rarely double up the lines except when heavy weather is ex-

pected. You reverse the procedure by singling up when leaving a dock.

**double wharfage**  *n.* Double charge made for wharfage against a vessel that leaves without paying proper wharfage, recoverable in court.

**doubling**  *n.* The overlap of an upper mast and a lower mast.

**doubling plating** (or **doubler**)  *n.* The name of the plating that is either outside or inside another for reinforcement.

**doubling the angle on the bow**  *n.* A method of getting a piloting fix on a land object. The navigator takes a sight on an object when the angle is 35° relative to the ship's heading. The vessel proceeds along the course line until the object bears 70° relative to the ship's heading. The distance run will be the distance from the object. (Frequently navigators use 45° and 90°, which are not necessary, but precise bearings and distance run are mandatory for this to work at all.) See SEVEN-EIGHTHS RULE.

## Doubling the Angle on the Bow

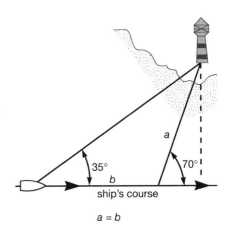

$a = b$

**doughnut** *n.* Antichafing gear on which a tow wire rides on a towing vessel's Dutch bar.

**Douglas scale** *n.* A system of expressing the condition of waves and swell used by navigators and oceanographers recommended by the International Meteorological Conference of Copenhagen, 1929. See BEAUFORT SCALE.

0    Calm. No wind; no swell.
1    Smooth sea; comparatively smooth water.
2    Slight sea; waves between $\frac{1}{2}$ foot and 2 feet.
3    Moderate sea, waves between 2 and 5 feet.
4    Rough sea; disturbed waves between 5 and 9 feet.
5    Very rough sea; wave heights running between 9 and 15 feet.
6    High sea; wave heights between 15 and 24 feet.
7    Very high sea; wave heights between 23 and 36 feet.
8    Precipitous sea; mountainous seas with wave heights over 36 feet.
9    Confused sea; state of maximum wave disturbance.

**douse** *v.* (1) To extinguish a lantern. (2) To lower or take in a sail.

**dousing chock** *n.* Part of a wooden ship's bow framing that supports the knightheads.

**down by the head** (or **stern**) *phr.* From unbalanced loading, a vessel is too low forward (or aft) in comparison with the stern (or bow).

**down-current** *adv.* In the direction toward which a current is flowing. "We sailed down-current."

**downflooding** *n.* The entry of seawater through any opening, especially one that cannot be rapidly closed watertight, into the hull or superstructure of an undamaged vessel due to heel, trim, or submergence of the vessel.

**downhaul** *n.* A line used to stretch or tighten the luff of a mainsail, the studding sails, or jibs to shorten sail. More often today the "downhaul" applies to the line that pulls a boom down at the mast.

**downhaul tackle** *n.* The gear used to haul down topsailyards in a severe blow to make possible reefing the sails when the violence of the storm prevents the yards' coming down by their own weight.

**downwind** *adj.* or *adv.* In the direction toward which the wind blows. "The downwind boat was at a disadvantage." "The channel lay downwind of us." See UPWIND.

**down with the sun** *phr.* (1) To lay down rope counterclockwise, "with the Sun." This is the correct way to lay right-hand-laid rope. (2) To coil a line clockwise or with the direction of the Sun—the recommended way to coil a line. Right-hand-laid rope is flaked down with the sun. See CABLE-LAID; ROPE.

**drabler** *n.* A small piece of sail laced to the bonnet to increase sail area.

**draft** (Brit., **draught**) *n.* (1) The depth of water required to float a vessel; the **navigational draft** is the distance from the actual waterline (not the designed waterline) to the bottom of the keel. If a transducer, sonar dome, propeller blades, or other projections are lower than the lowest part of the keel, that would be the point from which the draft is measured. The draft is indicated in arabic numerals on the hull of merchant ships. The **displacement draft** is used to compute the displacement and does not ordinarily include such items as indicated above because they do not add to the buoyancy. See NET BOTTOM CLEARANCE. (2) The parabolic curve in a fore-and-aft sail that improves its aerodynamic efficiency. (3) A single-sling cargo load. (4) A detail of personnel.

**draft gauge**   *n.* An inboard indicator of a vessel's draft that communicates with the water outside the hull by way of a seacock. The water or mercury in the calibrated column gives an accurate reading of the draft.

**draft marks**   *n.* The Arabic numerals on both sides of the bow and stern of a vessel to show the ship's draft. See PLIMSOLL MARK OR LINE.

**drag**   *n.* (1) The friction between the water and the hull, the force that resists forward motion. (2) The difference between the draft aft and the lesser draft forward. Ships are generally designed with a greater draft aft to make them handle more predictably. See TRIM. (3) One of the components that act on a rudder in a direction that is perpendicular to the vessel's travel. "The drag on the rudder is increased with the thickness of the rudder." See DROGUE.

**drag**   *v.* To draw an anchor along the ground. When done intentionally, it is called **dredging.**

**drag chains**   *n.* Coils of chain attached to a vessel's bottom by a wire welded to the shell plating used when launching a vessel into a narrow river and it is important that the ship not slide too fast. As the ship slides down the ways, the chain pays out and drags along the ground.

**drag circle**   *n.* The circle described between the anchor and the bow and dragged over by the anchor chain.

**drag surface**   *n.* The forward surface of a propeller blade. Same as the "back" of a propeller blade, even though it is toward the bow of the vessel.

**drain holes**   *n.* Holes drilled in floors and frames of vessels to lead water to bilges.

**draught**   See DRAFT.

**draw**   *v.* (1) Said of a sail when it fills with wind. "That new headsail is not drawing properly." (2) To require a certain depth to float. "The sloop draws 4 feet with the centerboard down." "We draw 40 feet." See DRAFT.

**dreadnought**   *n.* An "all big-gun battleship" combining a battery of guns of large and uniform caliber, heavy armor, and high speed. The name is taken from the first ship of this description, HMS *Dreadnought,* launched in 1906. With a main battery of 12-inch guns and a speed of 21 knots, *Dreadnought* revolutionized battleship construction. The primary rivals in the "dreadnought race" for naval superiority were Britain and Germany, until World War I, and thereafter Britain, the United States, and Japan. After World War II, the battleship was gradually superseded by the aircraft carrier as the core of the modern battle fleet.

**dredge**   *n.* (1) A vessel used to bring up oysters by use of scoops. (2) A vessel designed to deepen channels and to clear silt from waterways.

**dredge**   *v.* (1) To deepen a channel or waterway by scooping or suction. (2) To drag an anchor at the short stay (almost vertical) on the bottom to steady a vessel's head in a narrow channel. (3) To bring up oysters from the bottom with a scoop.

**dredged berth**   *n.* A place at a pier or wharf that has been dredged to accommodate vessels to keep them afloat at low water. Though the ebb may leave the channel dry, a dredged berth will still float the vessels for which it was designed.

**dress ship**   *phr.* To display national ensigns at each masthead along with the flagstaff. See FULL DRESS.

**drift**   *v.* To move with the tide, current, or wind without propulsion.

**drift**   *n.* (1) Sideways motion of a projectile caused by gyro action or wind. (2) A length of anchor chain on deck for working purposes. (3) Speed of a current (horizontal movement of water), usually given in knots, except for river currents, which are given in miles per hour. (4) The distance a craft is moved by current and wind. (5) Leeway, distance per hour of a vessel, "a 3-knot drift." (Set is the *direction* of flow of a current.) A boat's **drift angle** is the angle it must be steered different from the course to stay on its course line. If the course is 090° and the helmsman reports he has to steer 110° to stay on course, the drift angle is 20°. (6) Mathematical difference between a dead-reckoning position and a fix. (7) The distance shrouds are placed aft of the mast to give proper strength and balance. (8) Downwind or down-current motion of airborne or waterborne objects. (9) The horizontal component of real precession or apparent precession, or the algebraic sum of the two. When it is desirable to differentiate between the sum and its components, the sum is called the **total drift.**

**drift bottle**   *n.* A corked bottle thrown over the side to determine the drift of an ocean current. A "drift bottle" is also used to determine leeway if the vessel is underway.

**drift current**   *n.* A broad, shallow, slow-moving ocean current, especially any of the slow-moving currents on the western coast of Europe that complete the general circulation of the Gulf Stream.

**drifter**   *n.* A lightweight headsail used in light air.

**drift fishing**   *n.* Fishing while allowing the vessel to be carried where it may.

**drift ice**   *n.* Loose, open, pack ice in an area where water predominates over ice; such a situation is considered navigable.

**drift lead**   *n.* A lead line that is dropped over the side to determine if the vessel is moving, whether underway or at anchor.

**drift net**   *n.* A net used by fishermen that is allowed to drift with the current and is not moored.

**drilling rig**   *n.* A term used to indicate a mobile drilling structure, such as a semisubmersible rig or a drilling ship. Drilling rigs are only charted when they are converted to permanent production platforms.

**drilling tender**   *n.* A barge that acts as a supply vessel for small offshore drilling platforms.

**drill ship**   *n.* A self-propelled vessel equipped with a midship derrick for drilling deep-water wells. Such a vessel is self-contained and carries all the supplies, equipment, and personnel to drill a complete well. See SHIP.

**drive**   *v.* To hard-press a vessel with canvas, to carry as much sail as possible in heavy wind.

**driver**   *n.* The name for the fifth mast from the bow of a six-masted schooner.

**drogue**   *n.* A canvas cone streamed forward or astern of a vessel as a sea anchor to slow its sternway and to keep the bow into the wind. See PARA-ANCHOR.

**droits of admiralty**   *n.* (droits rhymes with quoits) Rights of the English Crown to property found upon the sea or stranded upon the sea or stranded on the shore, including fish, flotsam, wrecks, and enemy ships found in English ports. Admiralty droits are not recognized in U.S. courts.

**drop**   *n.* The depth of a square sail amidships from head to foot. The term is applied only to courses. See HOIST.

**drop** *v.* (1) To drop back is to slow a ship's speed to take a position farther back, perhaps in a column or in a screen, or to position a vessel behind another going in the same direction to allow an oncoming vessel to pass in a confined channel. (2) To go downstream.

**drop bolt** *n.* The bolt used on portholes and hatches with eyes at the end of a threaded bolt; the bolt is hinged or pivoted at the screw end, which is secured to the frame of the port; the bolt slides into a slot on the movable cover of the port or hatch and then can be tightened by use of the eye.

**drop keel** See CENTERBOARD.

**drop mooring** *n.* A method of anchoring with a bow and stern anchor when the anchor is dropped ahead of the spot where the vessel is to ride; the vessel is then allowed to drop aft with the current to a point astern of the proper place to anchor and the second anchor is let go. The bow anchor cable is then hauled in to the point chosen for the ultimate anchorage.

**drop rudder** *n.* In small sailboats, a rudder below the lowest point of the rest of the boat.

**drop strake** *n.* A strake that is discontinued near the bow or stern to abut in a stealer plate.

**droxtal** *n.* Very small particle ice 10–20 microns in diameter formed at temperatures below −30°C. Most of the restriction to visibility in fog ice is caused by droxtal.

**drumhead** *n.* The round portion of a capstan head with holes to take the capstan bars for manually rotating the capstan. See CAPSTAN.

**dry dock** *n.* An enclosed basin or vessel with watergates capable of holding the water on the outside. A vessel can be floated in, the gates closed, and the water pumped out. Work on the hull can then take place without careening the ship. See GRAVING DOCK.

**dry harbor** *n.* A harbor or basin that becomes dry or nearly dry at low tide. Vessels moored in a dry harbor must be shored up to stay upright or be allowed to lie on their sides. Flat-bottom vessels often use a pad, or a "hard" in Britain.

**dry rot** *n.* A type of decay often found in wooden structures, especially wooden boats. It is caused by fungi of the class Basidiomycetes (the mushroom group). The wood becomes lighter and weaker and less elastic as the fungus advances. In ships, the term is something of a misnomer because the wood is almost never dry.

**dry stores** *n.* Storage area aboard ship where non-refrigerated food is stored.

**dry suit** *n.* Waterproof body suit used for diving that seals at the neck, cuffs, and ankles to keep the body dry and warm. See WETSUIT.

**dry tank** *n.* The double bottom under boilers. This area does not carry water because of the problem that would be created by the interaction of the heat and the water on a steel hull.

**dry weir** *n.* (rhymes with pier) A fence placed in a tidal basin to catch fish as the tide ebbs; when the weir is dry, the fish are scooped up.

**dumb barge** See BARGE (2).

**dumb chalder** *n.* (1) A metal device bolted to the after side of a sternpost on which the pintle rests to relieve the weight of the rudder on the rudder braces. (2) A rudder brace. (3) A gudgeon.

**dumb compass** *n.* Name for pelorus, rarely heard today.

**dumb craft**   *n.* According to the *Navigation Rules,* any floating vessel that does not have propulsion or steering.

**dumb sheave**   *n.* (1) Groove at the end of a spar through which a line slides as through a block across a revolving sheave. (2) A block without a sheave through which a rope is rove.

**dummy funnel**   *n.* An extra funnel added to passenger vessels for aesthetic reasons.

**dummy gantline**   *n.* A whip purchase that uses old rope in combination with a working gantline. The dummy gantline is rove through the gantline block so that it can be used as a messenger when the working gantline is needed.

**dump**   *n.* Temporary storage of military supplies. A **floating dump** is a supply of materials ready for quick delivery ashore during amphibious operations.

**dumping ground**   *n.* An area in which dumping of dredged material and other nonbuoyant objects is either prohibited or where such dumping is allowed with permission and supervision of the U.S. Army Corps of Engineers.

**dump scow**   *n.* A vessel without self-propulsion with a hopper bottom that can be opened at the appropriate site to allow the material to flow out; used for dredged material, garbage, and so on.

**dunking sonar**   *n.* Sonar gear designed to be towed through the water by a helicopter for use in antisubmarine warfare.

**dunnage**   *n.* All materials used for securing and protecting cargo and supplies aboard a vessel, such as spars, matting, straps, and junk wood bought for the purpose.

**duration of flood (ebb)**   *n.* The time interval in which a tidal current is flooding (ebbing). These intervals are reckoned from the middle of the intervening slack waters or minimum currents. The average period for a semidiurnal tidal current is 12.42 (12 hours, 25 minutes and 12 seconds) hours, and for a diurnal current 24.84 hours.

**Dutch bar**   *n.* Structural member spanning the afterdeck of a towing vessel.

**dutchman**   *n.* A filler plate, usually small, used to connect two or more pieces, or a piece to fill in the gap between two construction members.

**Dutchman's log**   *n.* A method of determining a vessel's speed by dropping something off the bow and measuring the time it takes to go past the stern. With the length of the vessel known, the length divided by the elapsed time gives you the speed. According to Bowditch, it is the oldest speed-measuring device. Just why it is called a Dutchman's log is not clear.

**dutiable goods**   *n.* Cargo subject to import tariff.

**duty**   *adj.* Used to refer to a person who is on duty in a specific capacity such as the duty engineer, the duty pharmacist's mate, the duty master-at-arms, or a duty section.

**duty**   *n.* A tax on imported goods.

**duty officer**   *n.* The commissioned U.S. Navy officer who is on duty for a given period for a given assignment, such as the duty medical officer, the duty engineering officer, or the duty officer of the deck.

**dye marker**   *n.* Brightly colored dye that floats on the surface of the water or near the surface and spreads. Used for man overboard, or to mark a point where following ships are to execute a turn, and so on.

**dynamic stationing**   *n.* The system used for keeping a drill ship or a semisubmersible platform over a hole during drilling when the water is too deep for anchors. Computerized thrusters acti-

vated by underwater sensors keep the vessel on station.

# E

**E**   See ECHO.

**eagre (or eager)**   *n.* A tidal flood.

**earings**   *n.* (1) Small ropes used to fasten the cringles of sails and awnings. (2) Short lines used for securing a reefed sail to a boom.

**ease**   *v.* (1) To pay out or slacken a line. "Ease the starboard bow spring before you double up." (2) Order to reduce the amount of rudder or helm. (3) Order to allow the head to fall off a little after it has been close-hauled; to allow a vessel to run slightly to leeward of the most windward course. Also *ease the helm.* (4) To go slowly. "Ease into the berth." (5) To slacken a line slowly; to ease the sheet is to let out the line that controls a sail. Also *veer away.*

**easing-out line**   *n.* A line that is used to release an object or a line slowly, as opposed to a trip line. An easing-out line is used on a fuel hose as it is run to another ship when fueling while underway at sea.

**east about**   *adv.* Sailing ship term for leaving the China Sea by one of the so-called eastern passages instead of the more usual southern course through the Sunda Strait.

**East Africa Coastal Current**   *n.* An Indian Ocean Current that originates for the most part from the Indian South Equatorial Current that turns northward on the northeast coast of Africa in the

vicinity of latitude 10°S. In November at about latitude 4°N, a part of the current begins to reverse and expands northward and southward until February. Also *Somali Current.* See OCEAN CURRENT.

**easterly**   *n.* (1) A current flowing *toward* the east. (2) A wind blowing *from* the east. See WIND.

**East Greenland Current**   *n.* An ocean current that flows south along the east coast of Greenland carrying water of low salinity and low temperature. It is joined by most of the flow of the Irminger Current, and the greater part of the current continues through the Denmark Strait between Iceland and Greenland, with one branch turning to the east to form a portion of the counterclockwise circulation in the southern part of the Norwegian Sea. See OCEAN CURRENT.

**easting**   *n.* Distance toward the east in nautical miles. "Give me our easting for the past 24 hours."

**East Siberian Coastal Current**   *n.* The ocean current in the Chukchi Sea that joins the northerly flowing Bering Current north of East Cape. See OCEAN CURRENT.

**easy bilge**   *n.* A gentle curve of the bilge.

**easy sail**   *n.* Well-balanced main and headsail with not too much sail area so as to avoid straining the vessel and sails.

**ebb**   *n.* An outbound current. Ebb refers to a tidal current and bears little relation to the rise and fall of the tide. "We'll sail on the ebb at first light." The opposite of flood. For the vertical movement of water, "rising tide" and "falling tide" are used.

**ebb**   *v.* To fall back or recede, said of a receding current. "We sailed as the current ebbed and made open sea before the flood could begin."

**ebb current**   *n.* A seaward-bound horizontal movement of water. The movement of a tidal current away from shore or down a tidal river or estuary. In a mixed type of reversing tidal current, the terms **greater ebb** and **lesser ebb** are used.

**ebb strength**   *n.* The phase of the ebb tidal current at the time of maximum velocity.

**ebb tide gate**   *n.* The second or inner gate of a tidal dock or a lock chamber.

**eccentric error**   *n.* The error in sextant readings caused by the slight mechanical imprecision in centering the index arm pivot during manufacture, resulting in eccentric motion given to the index arm along the arc.

**Echo**   *n.* (1) The word for the letter "E" in the phonetic alphabet. Used as a single-letter signal, it means "I am directing my course to starboard." (2) A signal reflected by a target to a radar antenna. Also *return.*

**echogram**   *n.* A graphic record of depth measurements obtained by an echo sounder.

**echo ranging**   *n.* The determination of distance by underwater sound; today this is done electronically with sonar.

**echo sounder**   *n.* An instrument in which a pulse of energy is converted to sound energy and transmitted downward by means of a transducer on a vessel's hull. When the energy strikes the bottom or an object with density different from the ambient water, it returns as an echo to the transducer to be reconverted to electrical energy to indicate either the depth of the water or the depth of the object, such as a fish or a submarine. Also *depth finder.* Fathometer is a trade name and should not be used generically.

**eclipse**   *n.* (1) A phase of the characteristic of a flashing light during which the light is not visible. (2) The partial or complete obscuring of one celestial body by another as seen from a given position.

**ecliptic**   *n.* The path the Sun appears to take among the stars due to the annual revolution of the Earth in its orbit; it is considered a great circle of the celestial sphere and is inclined at an angle of about 23° 27′ to the celestial equator, but with continuous change. The **poles of the ecliptic** are the points everywhere 90° from the ecliptic north and south.

**economizer**   *n.* A device that takes the stack gas heat and uses it to heat the feedwater for the boilers.

**eddy**   *n.* A current (often circular) of water or air running counter to the main current. See COUNTERCURRENT.

**eddy wind**   *n.* An air current that is changed in direction by a sail, cliff, bluff, and so on.

**eductor**   *n.* A pump used for removing water from flooded spaces. Water is pumped past a constriction at a place where another line is attached. The water in the constriction creates a vacuum in the additional line so that the additional line can remove water to clean ballast or strip crude oil.

**effective horsepower (EHP)**   *n.* The power required to pull a bare hull through motionless water. EHP varies with displacement and speed.

**effluent**  *n.* A stream that flows out of a lake or other body of water. See AFFLUENT.

**eke**  *v.* Shipbuilder's term for joining a short timber to another to lengthen it by butt or scarph joints.

**elapsed time**  *n.* A racing term referring to the actual time a boat takes getting from one point to another without regard to its rating, size, or other time allowances.

**elbow in the hawse**  *n.* Expression used to describe the twist in the anchor cables that results when two bow anchors are down and the ship swings 360°.

**electric drive**  *n.* The system of propulsion whereby a vessel's power system is converted to electric power and the propeller is driven by an electric motor. Large passenger liners started using the system in 1927.

**electrician's mate**  *n.* A petty officer in the U.S. Navy responsible for repair and maintenance of power and lighting circuits. An electrician's mate does not look after electronic gear. **An electrician** is one who has been made a warrant officer.

**electric steering gear**  *n.* The system by which the movement of the steering wheel on the bridge and, on U.S. Navy ships, **after steering,** was transmitted to the rudder quadrants electrically instead of directly by means of cables and blocks.

**electric telegraph**  *n.* An electrically powered engine-order telegraph that replaced the direct telegraph that communicated between the bridge and engine room by means of cables and blocks. On the most ships today, the bridge has direct control of the engines.

**electric telemotor**  *n.* A small motor used to communicate steering wheel positions on the bridge to the steering engine at the rudder quadrants.

**electrodialysis**  *n.* The use of electricity to separate minerals, used in the production of freshwater from seawater.

**electrolysis**  *n.* Chemical change, such as decomposition, that takes place between two dissimilar metals in an electrolyte (such as saltwater) in the presence of an electric current. If a copper lightning arresting cable is lashed to a steel stay, the two dissimilar metals set up their own current. The salt spray supplies the electrolyte, and the cable begins to break down.

**electronic aid to navigation**  *n.* An aid to navigation that uses electronic equipment.

**electronic navigation**  *n.* Navigation by such electronic equipment as loran, shoran, radar, SATNAV, global positioning system, and so on.

**Elephanta**  *n.* A periodic heavy rain on the west coast of the Indian subcontinent.

**elevate**  *v.* To control the elevation of a gun or mount; to raise or lower a gun muzzle. See LAY; POINT; TRAIN.

**elevating fee**  *n.* The charge for use of an elevator while loading a vessel.

**elevation**  *n.* (1) Naval gunnery term referring to the vertical angle above the horizontal plane. (2) A geometric projection of an object on a vertical plane.

**elevator**  *n.* Electric equipment used to continuously convey grain from a vessel to storage silos or waiting vessels, called grain elevators.

**Elliot's eye**  *n.* A double eye-splice worked into the end of a cable with a smaller rope between and the three clapped together. Named for Adm. George Elliot.

**ellipse**   *n.* A plane curve that constitutes the locus of all points the sum of whose distances from two fixed points, **foci,** is constant; an elongated circle. The orbits of planets, satellites, planetoids, and comets are ellipses with the center of attraction at one focus.

**elliptical stern**   *n.* Stern with a short "counter" with the section above the knuckle elliptical in shape. This "round" stern is common in tugs on which the plating above the knuckle is vertical.

**El Niño**   *n.* A little-understood change in the temperature and circulation in the water in the Pacific off the west coast of South America that occurs every few years. It starts with the interruption of the Pacific trade winds, which causes changes in the ocean currents and ultimately causes changes in hurricane frequency and force in the Atlantic. The warmer Pacific water causes vigorous jet streams that carry heavy storms into the Gulf of Mexico. El Niño refers to the Christ Child because the pattern usually begins at Christmas. **La Niña** is the name given to the opposite condition. Cooler than normal conditions in the Pacific Ocean along the equator cause the jet stream currents to be weaker; this leads to fewer storms in the Gulf states. When this occurs, the Gulf states usually experience dry climates from October through April.

**embargo**   *n.* A government order suspending the movement of merchant ships in and out of a port.

**embark**   *v.* To go aboard a ship, most commonly said of passengers and troops with their equipment, but not of crew.

**embarkation deck**   *n.* A deck on which arrangements have been made for passengers and crew to embark in lifeboats, not necessarily the same deck as the boat deck.

**embarkation officer**   *n.* A landing force officer who advises naval unit commanders on combat loading and acts as liaison with troop officers.

**embay**   *v.* (1) To put a vessel or a force in a bay. (2) To force a vessel into a bay. (3) To hold a vessel in a bay. "We were embayed two extra days by the strong easterlies that prevented our sailing out of the narrow mouth."

**emergency astern test**   *n.* One of the tests conducted during sea trials. First the vessel is run ahead full and then suddenly full astern; then buoys are thrown over the side and watches are checked. The time and distance it takes the vessel to stop and reach full speed astern are carefully recorded.

**emergency boat**   See RESCUE BOAT.

**emergency drill**   *n.* An exercise performed by a vessel's crew to practice procedures for emergencies such as fire and rescue.

**emergency lighting system**   *n.* A self-contained electric generator capable of supplying electricity for lighting and other necessities in all parts of the ship. The generator is placed as high as practical so that it will continue to operate until the last possible moment on a sinking vessel.

**emergency position indicating radio beacon (EPIRB)**   *n.* A small portable radio beacon carried by vessels and aircraft that transmits on 2182 kHz, 121.5 MHz, and 243 MHz, to enable search and rescue vessels and aircraft to locate the transmitter and presumably the person or craft to which it is attached. (The frequencies 121.5 MHz and 243 MHz are aircraft frequencies operating with amplitude modulation and are used for homing purposes.)

**emergency tiller**   *n.* A tiller kept as a spare that can be fitted on the rudder post in an emergency to replace the steering wheel if there are breakdowns in the steering equipment short of the rudder post.

**employment clause**   *n.* Charter party clause by which the captain appointed by the owners is placed under the orders and directions of the charterers as far as loading and discharging.

**enclosed dock**   *n.* A protected area of water connected to port approaches by locks.

**enclosed space tonnage**   *n.* A term used in licensing and insuring vessels that refers to the measurement of the area of enclosed spaces used for cargo above the upper deck multiplied by the height of those spaces, with the product divided by 100. Spaces exempted from enclosed space tonnage include machinery spaces, wheelhouse, galley, lavatories, companion ways, and condenser spaces. See TONNAGE.

**end bulkhead**   *n.* A transverse bulkhead marking the end of a superstructure compartment such as the after end of the forecastle or the forward end of the poop.

**end coaming**   *n.* Transverse coaming of a hatchway.

**end-for-end**   *v.* To reverse an existing arrangement, as of the falls used to raise and lower boats. "End-for-end the boat falls to even the wear."

**end launching**   *n.* The launching of a vessel stern-first as opposed to side launching.

**end link**   *n.* An unstudded open link with parallel sides situated next after the bending shackle on an anchor cable.

**end tanks**   *n.* Buoyancy tanks at the bow and stern of a lifeboat.

**engineering duty officer (EDO)**   *n.* A restricted line officer who specializes in engineering afloat and ashore.

**engineering spaces**   See MACHINERY SPACES.

**engineer's bell book**   *n.* Official record of the engine orders received from a vessel's bridge. It is called a bell book because the orders are rung on the engine-order telegraph using bells. Most ships today have a direct linkage between the bridge and the propulsion equipment in the engine room.

**engineer-surveyor**   *n.* A marine surveyor, one who specializes in surveying marine engines and boilers.

**engine foundation**   *n.* The built-up plating and foundation structure for the main engines which distributes the weight to the framing and plating of the hull.

**engine hatch**   *n.* Large hinged hatch over the main engines of the engine rooms that provides access when the engines have to be removed for repairs. A skylight is often fitted into an engine hatch for lighting below.

**engine-order telegraph** (or **engine telegraph**)   *n.* The large brass device with handles on each side (on a twin-screw ship) located on a vessel's bridge and duplicated in the engine room. The orders to the engine room are given by means of the handles on each side (for port and starboard engines); these orders are rung down to the engine spaces on the duplicate device. To ring "starboard ahead one-third, port back two-thirds," the handle on the left side is pulled toward the operator, the lee helmsman, to the "back two-thirds" position while the right-hand handle is pushed forward to the "ahead one-third" position. U.S. Navy personnel refer to a crisis maneuver as "All engines ahead Bendix" (or Sperry or other contractor who supplied the telegraphs), meaning push the handles all the way forward to the manufacturer's nameplate at the bottom. In actual practice, the handles stop at the flank position and won't go straight down to the manufacturer's name. On most ships today, the bridge is linked directly with the propulsion equipment in the engine room with no "middleman" in the engine spaces carrying out the bridge orders. Also *annunciator.*

**engine room**   *n.* The space on a vessel provided for the operation of machinery and propelling engines. Also *machinery space(s).*

**engine room auxiliaries**   *n.* Machinery in the engine rooms that assists the propulsion plant such as feedwater pumps and heaters, evaporators, and so on.

**engine room bells**   *n.* A system of signals sent from the bridge to the engine room before the introduction of engine-order telegraphs. It consisted of a bell pull that sounded a gong and a jingle. If the ship was stopped, one bell meant ahead slow, and two bells meant astern slow. A jingle added to either of these meant full speed.

**engine room log**   *n.* The engineering officer's summary of the performance of engines and boilers that is kept over the life of all the equipment. Also *engineer's log book.*

**engine speed indicator**   *n.* A relay on the bridge from the engine room giving the engine revolutions per minute. See ENGINE-ORDER TELEGRAPH.

**enlisted personnel**   *n.* U.S. service personnel below the grade of warrant officer, a person who has voluntarily enrolled in a military service for a set time of enlistment. Such a person is an **enlistee,** as opposed to one who has been drafted, an **inductee.**

**ensign (Ens.)**   *n.* (1) The most junior **commissioned** officer in the U.S. Navy and U.S. Coast Guard, ranked below a lieutenant, junior grade, and above a warrant officer or petty officer. (2) A vessel's national flag, flown on warships from the gaff when underway and from the flagstaff when in port. See UNITED STATES ENSIGN; UNITED STATES YACHT ENSIGN.

**enter**   *v.* (1) To place a ship's papers in the custody of customs officers before landing goods. "Enter ship's papers with customs before landing cargo." (2) To declare goods bought in foreign ports. (3) To arrive in a port by sea.

**enter inward**   *v.* To clear customs on arrival at a port. The ship's report to customs is the **entry inward.**

**enter outward**   *v.* To clear customs before beginning to load cargo. The ship's report to customs is the **entry outward.**

**entrance**   See ENTRY.

**entrance lock**   *n.* A lock at the entrance to a tidewater basin or harbor that is located between the open water and the harbor or basin. The locks allow vessels to pass in and out at all periods of tide.

**entrepôt trade**   *n.* (pron. ahntre poe trade) Reexport trade.

**entry**   *n.* The act of conforming to customs regulations concerning an outward bound vessel or an arriving vessel. See PORT OF ENTRY. (2) That part of a vessel's bow lying below the waterline. Also *entrance.*

**entry craft**   *n.* A vessel hired by the master of a cargo ship to receive cargo when the consignee fails to take delivery according to the bill of lading.

**entry port**   *n.* A large opening on the side of a ship through which cargo is loaded and crew boarded.

**ephemeris**   *n.* (pl. ephemerides) A publication listing the computed positions of celestial bodies for each day of the year or other regular intervals usually published annually. See NAUTICAL ALMANAC.

**episodic wave**   *n.* A freak wave produced by a combination of waves and swells that are in opposition to a strong tidal current near the edge of a continental shelf.

**equal-angle bar**   *n.* Angle iron with both flanges of the same width.

**equal interval light**   *n.* A rhythmic light for which alternations of light and darkness are of equal duration; used on channel markers. Also *isophase light.*

**equal latitudes**   *n.* The method of finding the longitude by observing an altitude of the Sun by chronometer before noon and again when the body has dropped to the same altitude in the afternoon. The mean of these times is local apparent noon (LAN) at the place of observation, which, when changed to degrees, is the longitude. If these observations are taken while underway, a correction must be made for the distance covered between the two observations.

**equation of time (Eq. T.)**   *n.* The difference between solar time or mean time and apparent solar time, whether it is plus or minus; it never exceeds 16.4 minutes. Bowditch, in the *American Practical Navigator,* uses the convention for the equation of time as the time interval that must be added algebraically to the mean time to obtain apparent time.

**equator**   *n.* The great circle equidistant from the North and South Poles that separates the Southern Hemisphere from the Northern Hemisphere. See DECLINATION.

**equatorial currents and countercurrents**   *n.* The world's dominant ocean current systems work in such a way that currents north of the equator tend to flow in a clockwise direction, while those below the equator tend to flow in

a counterclockwise direction. Thus in the Atlantic, Indian, and Pacific Oceans there are currents north and south of the equator that flow from east to west. Between each of these north and south equatorial currents are weaker **equatorial countercurrents** that flow from west to east.

The **North Atlantic Equatorial Current** originates north of the Cape Verde Islands and flows west at about 0.7 knot, passing the Windward Islands of the Caribbean. The **South Atlantic Equatorial Current** is more extensive, flowing from the west coast of Africa toward the coast of South America at an average speed of 0.6 knot; the speed may reach 2.5 knots or more off the coast of South Africa. As the current approaches South America it forks, the southern part flowing along the coast of Brazil, and the northern flowing along the coast of the Guianas to unite with the North Atlantic Equatorial Current.

The **North Pacific Equatorial Current** flows westward in the general area of the northeast trade winds; near Japan, it flows into the Kuroshio Current. The **South Pacific Equatorial Current** flows westward in the area of the southeast trades.

The equatorial current patterns in the Indian Ocean are distinct from their counterparts in the Atlantic and Pacific Oceans because of the monsoon season. During the summer months, the **Monsoon Current** flows easterly and southeasterly across the Arabian Sea and Bay of Bengal to Sumatra where it augments the **South Equatorial Current** and sets up a clockwise circulation in the northern part of the Indian Ocean which causes an eastward flowing **South Indian Equatorial Current** below the equatorial countercurrent. See OCEAN CURRENT.

**equatorial tides**   *n.* Biweekly tides that occur when the Moon is over the equator.

**equiangular spiral**   See LOXODROME.

**equidistance principle** *n.* A maritime jurisdiction term for a median line drawn equidistant from two coasts of different and opposite states whose territorial seas overlap.

**equinoctial** *n.* Equator of the celestial sphere.

**equinoctial points** *n.* The two intersections of the celestial equator and the ecliptic. The equinoxes occur when the Sun reaches either of these two points.

**equinox** *n.* The term used for the two times of the year when the Sun crosses the celestial equator and when the lengths of day and night are approximately equal; the vernal equinox is on or about March 21, and the autumnal equinox is on or about September 21.

**equipage** *n.* The nonconsumable material determined to be necessary for a vessel to properly perform her mission. The word comes from the French word *équipage,* but the French nautical usage includes only personnel and crew and does not include gear, tackle, and so on. See KIPPAGE.

**erector** *n.* A person in an assembly yard who supervises hoisting parts and equipment into place.

**error** See RANDOM ERROR; SYSTEMATIC ERROR.

**escape hatch** *n.* A hatch installed to permit escape from a compartment when normal egress has been rendered impossible. See ESCAPE TRUNK.

**escape trunk** *n.* (1) An enclosed escape passage with ladders and lighting extending to the lowest level to allow quick escape in case of fire or flooding. (2) An escape compartment on modern submarines that is fitted to accept a rescue chamber or a deep-submergence rescue vehicle.

**escarpment** *n.* (1) An elongated, steep slope in the seafloor that separates flat or gently sloping areas. (2) A bank cut into the shore by tidal current. Also *scarp.*

**escort** *v.* To accompany for the purpose of protection, to convoy.

**escort vessel or escort** *n.* A destroyer escort that is now called a **frigate.** Today the term is used to identify any vessel escorting a single ship or a number of ships.

**escutcheon** *n.* An elaborate board on the stern of a vessel with the name and port of registry. It is also called an arch board when it is sunk at the lower part of the taffrail and frames the stern windows.

**establish** *v.* To install an authorized aid to navigation and place it in operation. "A new daybeacon 5A has been established at Osprey Point."

**establishment** See VULGAR ESTABLISHMENT.

**establishment of the port** See LUNITIDAL INTERVAL.

**estimated position** *n.* A position arrived at by advancing from a known position using tides, current, winds, course, speed, and elapsed time since the last known position. This is different from a dead-reckoning position, which takes into account only the course, speed, and elapsed time since the last known position. It also differs from a fix, which is based on landmarks or celestial observations.

**estuary** *n.* An arm of an ocean, sea, or bay that reaches inland to meet the mouth of a river, or the lower reaches of a river that are invaded by tidal water. Estuaries are tidal or saline. Estuaries are usually characterized by grass flats, savannas, and low-lying islands. A **tidal**

harbor is one that is formed in the lower reaches of a river in brackish water.

**etesian winds**  (rhymes with artesian) *n.* Annual summer winds out of the north found in the Mediterranean, especially the eastern Mediterranean. They are cool and can be a delight if not too strong.

**euphroe**  (pron. youfrow) *n.* A batten, usually wooden, with holes spaced along its length used to hold the crow's foot of an awning or the ends of a hammock to keep them from folding on themselves.

**evaporator**  *n.* A device used on ships to provide potable water and boiler feedwater from seawater by distillation. It is usually referred to as the "evap" by the engineers.

**evasion**  *n.* A course of action recommended to the commanding officer or the master to avoid a potentially dangerous weather system. The recommendation is usually made by a general direction without specifying the track.

**evening star**  *n.* The brightest body in the western sky following sunset. The evening star is not any particular star or planet; the stars pass it around.

**evening twilight**  *n.* The period of incomplete darkness following sunset. The darker limit of the nautical evening twilight. See TWILIGHT.

**even keel**  *n.* The trim of a vessel when the keel is either parallel to the surface of the water, or when the keel is in its designed position with relation to the surface. An even keel does not have anything to do with whether the vessel is heeled; it only relates to trim.

**even strain**  *n.* To evenly spread the force or strain on the supporting lines or timbers. "Put an even strain on all the docking lines."

**evolution**  *n.* (1) A tactical maneuver of vessels or aircraft such as a flank movement. (2) An exercise such as one vessel towing another. (3) A sequence of actions aboard a ship, as those involved in setting a sail or tacking.

**ex-**  *prefix* (1) In customs and shipping documents, ex-*John F. Drew* means that the goods or cargo have been brought in by the *John F. Drew*. (2) In naming vessels, used to denote a change in name such as *My Fair Lady* (ex-*Seductress*) or USS *Gherardi*, DMS 30 (ex-DD 643).

**excepted clause**  *n.* Marine underwriters' contract clause that makes specific that in case the claims under the collision clause cannot be recovered in full by the owner of the vessel because of the difference in the insured value and the sound value (that is, the original value of the vessel), the underwriters will accept liability in proportion to the excess as the sum insured bears to that difference.

**excepted days**  *n.* A charter party term for the days on which no work can be done because of a fault in the vessel, such as a breakdown in the machinery or boilers with consequent loss of power to the winches. The term also includes fires if they would cause an interruption of work. It is one of the several kinds of lay days.

**excepted perils**  *n.* Charter party term used to denote the perils that have been excluded by contract and include among others, acts of God, piracy, terrorism and barratry. The excepted perils clause is phrased so as to make clear that this means the perils could not have been avoided with reasonable care and diligence on the part of the shipowners and carriers. When these perils occur, the charter, shipowner, and carrier are not responsible.

**excessive speed**  *n.* Speed of a vessel to cause wash damage; passing another vessel or wharf, it is prudent to slow to such speed as to preclude damage to vessels, barges, wharfs, and so on. The logbook and the bell book should both show the time and the reason for the slow bell and the time for returning to speed, as these could be called for if action is later brought for damages.

**excluded ports**   *n.* In time charters, ports that a charter may not enter because of fever, hostilities, or other hazards at those ports.

**exclusive economic zone (EEZ)**   *n.* The 200-mile zone over which a coastal state has extensive but not exclusive resource and management rights under international law. In 1982 the United Nations Convention on the Law of the Sea formally established this concept. The United States is among the few nations that have not accepted the EEZ. See PA-TRIMONIAL SEA.

**exclusive fishing zone (EFZ)**   *n.* The zone out to 200 miles seaward from the base line in which a coastal state has been recognized since the 1960s as having extensive, but not exclusive, fishing rights.

**ex-dock**   *n.* A carrier's term meaning merchandise sold at dockside that does not include transportation or liability from that point. See EX-QUAY.

**executive officer (XO)**   *n.* Second in command of a U.S. Navy vessel, station, or aircraft squadron, informally referred to as "the exec." The executive officer is the captain's representative and carries out the ship's routine. If the commanding officer is incapacitated, the executive officer takes command.

**exempted space**   *n.* Open spaces in permanent structures on a vessel such as poops and bridges when they are not fitted with doors or other permanently attached means of closing them. They are not included in computing gross registered tonnage.

**exfoliation**   *n.* The gradual erosion of copper sheeting from the bottom of a copper-clad wooden vessel.

**exhaust ventilation**   *n.* The removal of air from compartments by exhaust fans with fresh air coming in through ports and hatches. This is done by means of **exhaust ventilators.**

**ex-meridian altitude**   *n.* An altitude taken slightly before or after meridian transit.

**expansion chamber**   *n.* An expandable bladder in a magnetic compass that makes possible the expansion and contraction of the liquid without the formation of bubbles.

**expansion hatch**   *n.* On tankers, a hatch with high coamings that allows for the expansion and contraction of the cargo as the temperature rises and falls.

**expansion joint**   *n.* A joint that expands and contracts to accommodate the demands of piping and decks.

**expansion trunk (or tank)**   *n.* A tank above a cargo tank that acts as a reservoir with fuel lines leading between the two tanks. The expansion tank keeps the main tank full when cold temperatures cause the fuel to contract, and is available to hold the extra fuel when the fuel expands, thus keeping the larger tank full at all times and relieving stress and motion problems.

**explosimeter**   *n.* Equipment used to detect the presence of explosive gases.

**export duty**   *n.* Tax required to be paid on certain goods when they are exported.

**exporter's invoice**   *n.* A list of all items being shipped with the quantities, weights, description, and selling prices. At the top of the list is the name of the vessel on which the goods are to be shipped along with the destination and consignee.

**exposed waters**   *n.* Waters more than 20 nautical miles from the mouth of a harbor of safe refuge and other waters that the Coast Guard determines to present special hazards due to weather or other circumstances.

**exposed ways** *n.* The portion of ground ways between the end of the sliding ways and the water's edge.

**express liner** *n.* High-speed passenger ship with three classes of passenger service, with capacity for mail and a small amount of high-rated cargo.

**ex-quay** *n.* Contractual agreement specifying the seller's financial responsibility for unloading cargo. See EX-DOCK.

**ex-ship** *adj.* A condition of sale of goods under which the purchaser or consignee is made responsible for taking delivery of the goods at the vessel's side when it leaves the vessel's slings. Also *free overside* or *free overboard.*

**extinguished** *adj.* Said of an aid to navigation that has failed to display a light signal and is not "watching properly."

**extrapolation** *n.* The process of estimating the value of a quantity beyond the known values by assuming the rate or system of change will continue. The process of determining intermediate values is **interpolation.**

**extra risks** *n.* Additional coverage added to a marine insurance policy to include war risk, pilferage, and so on. The additional coverage is usually typed onto the contract and initialed by all parties.

**extraterritoriality** *n.* Exemption from local laws and regulations such as is accorded diplomats. Merchant vessels were once accorded similar privileges in some ports, but for the most part that is no longer true. A vessel must abide by the laws of the country under whose flag it operates, but it also must adhere to local laws and regulations.

**extratropical cyclones and anticyclones** *n.* Migratory cyclones (lows) and anticyclones (highs) that form in the areas of prevailing westerlies of the temperate latitudes (outside the tropics).

**extreme breadth** *n.* Maximum beam possible outside plating, permanent fenders, beading, or other hull attachments. This is important in determining whether a vessel can transit a given canal, for example.

**extreme draft** *n.* The vertical distance from the designed waterline to the lowest point of the keel or any projection below the keel such as a transducer. Also *keel draft.*

**extreme length** *n.* The length of the vessel from the forward end of the bowsprit to the after end of any projection from the stern. In smaller vessels, this is called length overall.

**eye** *n.* (1) A loop in a rope that has been spliced, seized, or knotted. (2) The loop spliced in the end of a shroud or stay that goes over the masthead and slides down to the desired position. (3) The anchor eye to which the shackle is attached. (4) The center of a circular storm or hurricane at which the wind direction is vertical.

**eyebolt** *n.* A bolt with an eye formed at the head, used for securing lines and objects.

**eye brow** *n.* Metal lip just above a porthole that prevents rainwater and water from the deck from entering through the port.

**eyelet holes** *n.* Holes for lacing. (1) The holes in a sail used for reefing. (2) The holes in the luff to which robands are secured to the mast hoops. See CRINGLE; REEF POINTS.

**eyes** *n.* The forwardmost part of a ship on the weather deck. Fog lookouts are usually stationed in the eyes of the ship, as far forward as you can stand on the weather deck.

**eye seizing**    *n.* A seizing that shortens an eye in a rope.

**eye-splice**    *n.* A splice at the end of a line that leaves a loop for use on cleats, bollards, and so on.

# F

**F**    *See* FOXTROT.

**fabricated vessel**    *n.* A vessel built by preassembly with large sections assembled in fabricating shops and then brought to the ways by crane to be assembled with other sections

**face**    *n.* The **after** surface of a propeller blade; the forward surface is the **back.**

**face plate**    *n.* A narrow stiffening plate welded along the edge of any web or stiffener.

**facing**    *n.* The placing of one timber on another to add strength or finish.

**factory ship**    *n.* A mother vessel in a fleet of fishing boats or whaling craft fitted with equipment for canning, barreling, or otherwise preparing the catch with the object of obviating further processing. See FLOATING BASE.

**fag**    *n.* The frayed end of a rope. See IRISH PENNANT.

**fag**    *v.* To fray or untwist the end of a rope. A rope is said to be fagged out when it is worn and frayed.

**fag out**    *v.* To become knotted at the ends of yarns.

**fail-safe**    *n.* The design of an automatic system that precludes excessive damage in the event of failure of a part of the system. A fuel system controlled by a solenoid valve, for example, will shut down if the vessel's power fails.

**fair**    *v.* (1) To smooth a knot or splice. (2) To correct a ship's lines or structural members. (3) To bring rivet holes into alignment; when in alignment, holes are called **fair holes;** otherwise they are **unfair** or **blind holes.** The expression *to fair up* is heard in all three of the above. (4) Relates to relative wind direction as it moves aft on the sail to give it a lift. The wind fairs when it strikes the sail father aft. The opposite is to head, i.e., to move farther forward on the sail. These terms are different from veering (clocking) and backing in that they relate to the boat and not to the actual wind direction. The wind can veer (move clockwise) and give the boat a lift from fairing, or the same wind change can cause the boat to take a header, depending on which tack it's on.

**fair**    *adj.* (1) Said of a wind that blows in the direction that best maintains the desired heading, but not necessarily free of storm. "The wind was fair, but blew a mack'rel gale." John Dryden, "The Hind and the Panther." (2) Smooth, a fair plane.

**fair curve**    *n.* A curve without irregularities.

**fairing ribband**    *n.* A temporary timber or steel bar used to reduce buckling at the seams of decks and bulkheads during welding.

**fairlead**   *n.* A fitting (eyelet or pad eye) through which or over which a rope, line, or cable can be led so as to change its direction without excessive friction. A fairlead offers no mechanical advantage. A **fairlead board** is one with holes through which running rigging passes.

**fair line**   *n.* A smooth line. "The hull needs a fair line before we can paint."

**fair tide**   *n.* A tidal current favorable to the desired direction or course.

**fairwater**   *n.* The casting or formed plate used to preserve the streamline flow past a hull structure, a shaft coupling, or a propeller hub. A **fairwater sleeve** is a steel plate sleeve cut as a truncated cone and secured at the end of a strut bearing or stern-tube bearing to promote a better flow of water past it.

**fairway**   *n.* (1) The navigable portion of a body of water obstacle-free, but not necessarily straight, such as a channel, harbor, or a route between hazards available to larger vessels. (2) The usual course for entering a harbor. (3) The usual path of ships between ports. "We were standing down the fairway when the squall overtook us." Fairway must not be used when traffic separation scheme is meant. (4) A shipping lane established by the U.S. Coast Guard in offshore waters. Permanent oil platforms are prohibited in "fairways."

**fairway channel markers (or buoys)**   *n.* Midchannel markers with black-and-white vertical stripes in Region A countries of the IALA Maritime Buoyage System. The term has been superseded generally by the various cardinal and safewater marks.

**fair weather**   *n.* Favorable, clear, not stormy, but perhaps windy conditions.

**fake**   *n.* (1) A single turn of rope; several turns make a **tier.** (2) A coil of rope that is ready for running. See FLAKE.

**fake (down)**   *v.* To lay out rope in long flat fakes, each one overlapping the previous one, so that it is ready for running. See FLAKE; FLEMISH (DOWN).

**Falkland Current**   *n.* A current in the Atlantic Ocean and heading in a northeasterly direction from Cape Horn. Also *Malvinas Current.* See OCEAN CURRENT.

**fall**   *n.* (1) The length of line used in a tackle that includes the hauling part, the standing part, the leading part that is rove through the block, and the bitter end. (2) The hauling part of a tackle that is pulled on by manpower or by a winch or windlass. (3) The entire tackle including the blocks and ropes, as in a boat fall. See FALLS; MARRIED FALL; PURCHASE; SPLIT FALL. (4) Decrease in a value such as temperature or barometric pressure. See FALLING GLASS.

**fall astern**   *phr.* Said of a boat that is outdistanced by another vessel, whether intentionally or not. "We took our position in the convoy by falling astern and then increased our speed to move over two columns."

**fall block**   *n.* The block to which energy is first applied in a tackle.

**fall in**   *v.* To take a position relative to another ship. A ship can be ordered to fall in with a senior ship, for example, either ahead as in a screen position or 500 yards astern as in a plane guard position.

**falling glass**   *n.* A decreasing barometric pressure as indicated traditionally by a graduated glass tube with fluid that rises and falls with pressure. A falling glass means the weather is probably going to deteriorate, and suggests that the vessel should be secured for heavy seas.

**falling tide**   *n.* That portion of a tide cycle between high water and the following low water during which the depth of the water decreases. The opposite is a rising tide. Both of these terms refer to vertical movement and should not be confused with ebb and flood.

**fall off**   *v.* A sailing term meaning to head off the wind, to allow the head to go farther to leeward.

**falls**   *n.* The line in a tackle that is led through blocks for mechanical advantage. The term is most often associated with the boat falls of a lifeboat.

**fall tub**   *n.* A rack at a davit into which boat falls are allowed to drop while a boat is being hoisted.

**false colors**   *n.* Improper identification, flying improper colors intentionally. For a merchantman to identify herself wrongly to avoid capture by a belligerent is well recognized under international law, but it should only be resorted to when the master considers the situation grave, and should only be done for such period as is considered necessary.

**false keel**   *n.* A strip bolted to the outside of a vessel's keel to protect it. If a vessel were to go aground, the false keel would be damaged or carried away, leaving the true keel intact.

**false relative movement**   *n.* False indications of the movement of a target relative to a ship on a radar display that is not stabilized because of the continuous reorientation of the display as the ship's heading changes.

**false stem**   *n.* Scarfed timbers fayed to the leading edge of the stem extending from the gripe upward.

**false tack**   *n.* A pretended tack in racing, to luff as if to tack and then fall off on the same course again.

**fan**   *v.* To brace the upper yardarms slightly more aft to take advantage of the differences in wind speed at greater distance above the water.

**fancy line**   *n.* (1) A gaff downhaul. (2) A line used to cross-haul or overhaul a lee topping lift.

**fancy work**   *n.* Decorative knot work used on railings, awnings, and so on. See COCKSCOMB.

**fang**   *n.* A line fastened to a cringle near the foot of a wing sail, used both for securing a bonnet and for taking in the sail. Also *lee fang*.

**fanning**   *n.* The act of sailing slowly in light air.

**fantail**   *n.* (1) The after section of the main deck; the open section farthest aft. (2) Fan-shaped plating on centerline of a ship with an overhanging stern section; the plates forming the overhang on the stern.

**fantail grating**   *n.* Steel grating used on tugboats and fishing trawlers for stowing hawsers and other lines.

**fantail stern**   *n.* A pleasure boat stern in which the shell planking sweeps up to a point to join the deck planking to form an elongated counter and an exaggerated overhang. Vulnerable to excessive pounding in a seaway, the type is rarely seen today.

**fare**   *v.* To travel or wander. A **seafarer** is a sailor, a mariner, one who travels by sea for pay.

**farewell whistle**   *n.* Three prolonged blasts given on the ship's whistle as a farewell gesture when leaving port. Courtesy called for another ship to answer in kind, and the departing ship acknowledged this with a short blast. The farewell blast and the signal for vessels backing out of a slip and into a channel have been superseded in the *Navigation Rules:* rule 34(a) calls for three short blasts to mean "I am operating astern propulsion."

**farm**   *n.* Open storage area near a harbor or pier entrance. It usually has water tanks, fuel drums, and so on.

**fast**   *adj.* or *adv.* (1) Secure or securely. To make a line fast is to cleat it securely. See FAST CRUISE. (2) Speedy. "My boat is fast." (3) In the days of whaling ships a fast boat was a boat that was made fast to a whale by a harpoon.

**fast automatic shuttle transfer (FAST) System**   *n.* A method used to transfer materiél at sea from one ship to another, using specialized equipment on the supply ship.

**fast cruise**   *n.* Drills and trials carried out by a ship's officers and crew while still fast to the pier.

**fastening**   *n.* A screw or bolt that holds a plank to the frame. A fastening also applies to screws and bolts that hold cleats, chocks, and rails in place. Any device that secures, confines, or makes fast. See TREENAILS.

**fast ice**   *n.* Sea ice that forms along, and remains fast to, the shore along the coastline to an **ice wall,** an **ice front,** or between grounded icebergs. Vertical fluctuations may occur during changes in sea level.

**fata morgana**   *n.* A complex mirage observed when the Sun is near the horizon, with the result that objects are distorted vertically to appear towering and sometimes doubled.

**fathom**   *n.* A unit of measure equal to 6 feet, usually used to measure water depth. Ten fathoms is a water depth of 60 feet. Occasionally a "fathom" is used to describe horizontal distance, but this is usually in connection with a cable, which is defined as 120 fathoms. See FATHOMETER.

**Fathometer**   *n.* Registered trade name of an electronic device that measures depth in fathoms, manufactured by the Raytheon Co. The generic term is **depth finder** or **echo sounder.**

**favorable current**   *n.* A current that flows in a direction that increases the speed of a vessel over the ground.

**favorable wind**   *n.* A wind that aids a vessel in making progress through the water in the desired direction.

**favored end**   *n.* The tactically advantaged end of a starting line.

**fay**   *v.* To unite two surfaces usually by welding or riveting.

**faying surface**   *n.* The contact surface between two adjoining surfaces.

**feather**   *v.* (1) To luff a sail so that it catches less wind than is available. This is done when the wind is too strong; it is also done when entering a slip or approaching a mooring. (2) To turn an oar at the end of the stroke so that the blade is horizontal. (3) To make a thin edge. "Feather the rudder fairing strip flush to the rudder."

**feather merchant**   *n.* Derisive term for someone new to the U.S. Naval service, especially reservists.

**feaze**   *v.* To separate strands of old rope or the ragged end of a rope, called **feazings,** to form oakum.

**federal project depth**   *n.* The design dredging depth of a channel constructed by the U.S. Corps of Engineers. The actual minimum depth of a channel is called the controlling depth, which may be less than the dredged depth because of silting or other problems. Project depth and controlling depth should not be confused.

**feeder**   *n.* A loading trunk that carries grain from one deck to the next below and acts as a reservoir to hold extra grain to keep the hold full when the ship begins to roll.

**feeder currents** *n.* Those currents created by a rip and that form parallel to a beach and provide—or feed—seawater to the rip.

**feed heater** *n.* A heating device used to heat feed water for the boilers; an economizer.

**feedwater** *n.* Distilled water used for boilers, purer than potable water used by the ship's company, and quite tasteless.

**feeling the way** *phr.* To proceed into an unmarked channel cautiously with an eye on the depth by using either a depth finder or lead line.

**felloe** *n.* The part of a wooden wheel between the spokes. Also *felly*.

**fender** *n.* A bumper placed on the side of a vessel to prevent banging the hull against another boat, a pier, or a piling. A **fender board** is a board used as a fender, usually in conjunction with other cushioning devices. Also *fender bar; fender spar*. See CAMEL.

**fend off** *v.* To push off as from a pier or piling.

**ferrocement** *n.* Hull construction method of forming the frame with something like chicken wire reinforced with steel bars. The special mixture of cement is spread over the frame inside and out to give an exceptionally strong hull.

**ferry** *n.* Any vessel other than in coastwise or ocean service having provisions only for deck passengers and/or vehicles, operating on a frequently scheduled short run between two points over the most direct water route, and offering a public service comparable to that of a bridge or tunnel.

**ferry** *v.* To transport passengers and cargo short distances. This can be done by aircraft as well as waterborne vessels.

**ferrybridge** *n.* Any of several contrivances used to convey passengers, automobiles, and cargo from land to a ferry, and vice versa. They are usually hinged, floating devices capable of accommodating changes in the current.

**ferry rack** *n.* The combination of pilings used to guide a ferry into its slip.

**fetch** *n.* (1) The act of tacking, a 16th-century usage now obsolete. (2) The distance wind (and/or waves) travel without interference. "The long fetch between islands allowed a build-up of seas that became formidable." (3) The distance between a weather shore and the point where waves begin to make up.

**fetch** *v.* (1) To sight a piece of land or a landmark. "After a day's sail, we rounded Corfu and fetched Albania beyond Mt. Pantocratoras." (2) To fetch the point is to sail to and clear a point without having to tack. (3) To **fetch the mark** is to execute a tack so that a boat comes about to point directly toward the windward mark on her final tack of a board. Also *lay a mark*. (4) To stop, come to rest. "We were on Normandy Beach facing a determined enemy. . . . As soon as she fetched up, I headed amidships." Capt. Frank Farrar, *A Ship's Log Book*.

**fetch headway (or sternway)** *phr.* To gather headway (or sternway).

**fiber-clad rope** *n.* Rope with each strand enclosed in marline or hemp. Also *marline-clad rope*. See SPRING LAY ROPE.

**Fiberglas** *n.* Trademark owned by Owens/Corning Fiberglas Corp. to identify its product, made of glass fibers. The glass is drawn to extremely fine filaments, which have greater tensile strength than steel. A Fiberglas boat is usually constructed with the Fiberglas as the reinforcing material with a polyester resin, the glass making up about a third of the total. The great advantage of Fiberglas is that it is not susceptible to dry rot or teredos, and it has largely replaced wood as the primary material in the construction of pleasure boats.

**fiber rope**   *n.* Any rope made of nonsynthetic fibers such as hemp and manila. See ROPE.

**fid**   *n.* (1) A square bar inserted through a **fid hole** in the heel of the mast to support a housing topmast or topgallant mast. The ends of the fid that rest on the trestletrees take the weight of the mast and keep it in place. (2) A fid similar to (1) is used to keep a running bowsprit in place on small craft. (3) A round tapered pin made of steel or wood and used for splicing cordage. See MARLINESPIKE.

**fiddle block**   *n.* A pulley with an elongated shell and two sheaves with the larger one on the bottom and similar to a sister block. Also *long fiddle block.* See NINEPIN BLOCK.

**fiddle boards** (or **rack**)   *n.* Frames placed on shelves, dining saloon tables, and mess tables that help keep the china and glasses from falling to the deck in heavy seas.

**fiddlehead**   *n.* Ornamentation at a ship's bow similar to the scroll at the head of a violin. See TRAIL BOARDS.

**Fiddler's Green**   *n.* An imaginary place of sailors' dreams where all life is beautiful. When a sailor dies, he is said to have gone aloft to Fiddler's Green.

**fidley**   *n.* (1) Steel frame around a ladder or hatch leading to a lower deck. (2) A large opening for ventilators above a fireroom. See MACHINERY CASING. (3) Casing top over a boiler.

**fidley deck**   *n.* A platform around a stack.

**fidley gratings (hatches)**   *n.* Steel gratings that are fitted over boiler room hatches.

**field day**   *n.* A day or part of a day set aside for general housecleaning in a military ship, usually Friday before Saturday morning's inspection.

**fife rail**   *n.* A collar or rack surrounding a mast to hold belaying pins. Today, naval vessels use fife rails at the flag bag for holding flags ready to be hoisted. See SPIDER BAND.

**FIFO**   *n.* Acronym for first-in–first-out, a method of stowage with the first supplies stowed being the first to be used.

**fighting ship**   *n.* (1) A merchant vessel used to prevent a competitor from entering a market or one used to get another ship or shipping line out of a market. (2) Any government-owned or operated vessel that is capable of carrying out hostile acts against other nations' vessels, forces, or property.

**fighting top**   *n.* A top (platform) high up on the mast of a sailing warship from which sharpshooters could fire at an enemy at close range.

**figure-eight fake**   *n.* Method of laying rope over railing or lifelines in a figure eight with each turn overlapping the previous turn, for rapid paying out.

**figure-eight** (or **figure-of-eight**) **knot**   *n.* Knot placed at the end of a line to prevent its raveling or to prevent its being pulled through a block; it looks like a figure eight.

**figurehead**   *n.* A wood sculpture carried at the bow of old sailing vessels. Usually, but not always, these were carvings of women.

**filaments**   *n.* Oceanographer's term for sinuous or meandering branches of the eastern edge of ocean currents, for example, the Gulf Stream.

**fill**   *v.* To trim a sail to better catch the wind.

**fill away**   *v.* To allow a vessel's head to fall away from the wind so the sails belly out. After a vessel has been hove to and it is desired that it be allowed to continue on, the vessel will be allowed to fill away or it will **fill and stand on,** a phrase that means the same thing. See BACK AND FILL.

**filling**   *n.* (1) The increase in atmospheric pressure especially in a low. A decrease in pressure is a **deepening.** (2) A material used in worming a rope.

**filling frames** (or **timbers**)   *n.* Timbers placed between frames of larger wooden vessels for added strength where needed; they extend from the keel to the turn of the bilge.

**filling pieces**   *n.* Planks fitted athwartships between the keel and keelson.

**filling transom**   *n.* A transom built between two deck transoms.

**final diameter**   *n.* The diameter of a vessel's turning circle after it has completed 360° with the same speed and rudder angle. The "final diameter" is always a little less than the tactical diameter.

**final landing**   *n.* The date on which a bill of lading consignment arrives at its destination and is landed from the transporting vessel.

**final port**   *n.* The last port of a cruise; the final port may be beyond the port of discharge of cargo.

**find itself**   *phr.* A magnetist's phrase for a vessel after the chaos of launching and the subsequent settling of magnetic forces. "Let the ship find itself before we try to compensate the compass."

**fine**   *adj.* (1) Narrow, thin. A fine-ended vessel is one with a sharp V hull and a sharp or narrow entry. See FULL.

**fineness, coefficient of**   *n.* The index of displacement determined by comparing a vessel's volume to that of a box of the same length, breadth, and depth. If the volume of the vessel is 60% of that of the box, the coefficient of fineness is 0.60. See BLOCK COEFFICIENT.

**finger piers**   *n.* Long slender piers designed to give maximum wharfage on a limited shoreline to enable ports to use deeper water close inshore, such as can be seen in New York harbor.

**finish**   *v.* In racing, a vessel finishes when any part of hull, crew, or equipment in normal position, crosses the finish line from the direction of the preceding mark.

**finished with engines (FWE)**   *interj.* Order from bridge to engine room to notify the engine room that the vessel is tied up and propulsion will not be required. "I rang up 'Finished with Engines' and hurried below to the saloon." Capt. Frank Farrar, *A Ship's Log Book.*

**fin keel**   *n.* A deep but longitudinally narrow keel with added weight at the bottom. It provides lateral resistance with the added advantage of giving outside ballast as far as possible from the center of gravity. The fin keel also permits more responsive steering due to reduced directional stability without adding weight in the ends of the vessel as in a full keel.

**fire**   *n.* All fires fall into one of four classifications depending on the nature of the combustible material involved. **Class A** involve ordinary materials such as wood, paper or rags. **Class B** involve flammable and combustible liquids such as gasoline, diesel fuel or cooking oils. **Class C** involve live electrical equipment and wiring. **Class D** involve combustible metals such as magnesium or sodium.

**fire**   *v.* To light off a boiler.

**fire alarm signal**   *n.* A continuous rapid ringing of the ship's bell for not less than 10 seconds supplemented by a continuous ringing of the general alarm bells for not less than 10 seconds.

**fireboat**  *n.* A harbor vessel built for the purpose of carrying fire-fighting equipment to be used in fighting fires on ships and waterfront property.

**fire and rescue party**  *n.* U.S. Navy damage control team trained in fighting fires and rescuing personnel on other ships and shore facilities. Also *rescue and assistance party.*

**firebox**  *n.* That part of a boiler in which combustion takes place.

**fire bulkhead**  *n.* A bulkhead capable of resisting temperatures up to 1,500°F. for one hour. The mean distance between fire bulkheads in a superstructure cannot exceed 131 feet.

**fire control**  *n.* Direction of a vessel's offensive battery. **Shipboard fire control** encompasses both offensive and defensive weaponry.

**fire control technician (FT)**  *n.* A petty officer rating in the U.S. Navy for one who does major repair and maintenance of the fire control equipment.

**fire drill**  *n.* Exercise detailed in the fire stations bill and practiced by all officers, crew, and passengers aboard ship.

**fire main**  *n.* Saltwater system used throughout a ship for damage control and for flushing down decks and bulkheads.

**fireman (FN)**  *n.* Enlisted rating E-3 in the U.S. Navy for personnel in engineering spaces. See STOKER.

**fire party**  *n.* Duty team aboard U.S. Navy ships organized to fight fires under the direction of the damage control officer.

**fireroom**  *n.* The compartment in which boilers and their operating stations are found.

**fire ship**  *n.* In the days of the sailing navy, a ship filled with explosives, set on fire, and allowed to drift into an enemy formation or anchored fleet.

**firesides**  *adj.* Said of the heat imparted to boiler tubes in a water-tube boiler, or the fire tubes in a fire-tube boiler.

**fire station**  *n.* Assigned position for each member of a ship's company when the fire alarm is sounded.

**fire-tube boiler**  *n.* A type of boiler used extensively in merchant ship steam plants in which the exhaust gases are led through tubes that run through the water to be heated. Also *Scotch marine boiler.* See WATERTUBE BOILER.

**fire warp**  *n.* A cable led to a buoy or anchor from a vessel loading combustible material at a pier, and used to pull the vessel away from the pier quickly in case of an emergency.

**first assistant engineer**  *n.* Assistant to the chief engineer on U.S. merchant ships and equivalent to second engineer in British merchant ships.

**first differences**  *n.* The differences between successive entries in a latitude column of Bowditch, Table 2008. See SECOND DIFFERENCES.

**first futtock**  *n.* The curved timber of the first frame of a wooden ship counted from the bow.

**first lieutenant**  *n.* The officer charged with the upkeep and cleanliness of the vessel, its boats, and ground tackle. In the U.S. Navy, term has nothing to do with the officer's rank.

**first light**  *n.* The beginning of the morning nautical twilight, the darker limit, when the center of the Sun is 12° below the horizon, and before the horizon is visible.

**first mate (or officer)**   *n.* The second in command in the merchant service. Also *chief officer* or *mate.*

**first open water**   *n.* Charter party term meaning the earliest opportunity to enter port ready to load, when the port is sufficiently free of ice.

**first point of Aries**   *n.* A name often given to the vernal equinox because, when the name was given, the Sun entered the constellation of Aries about March 22.

**first watch**   *n.* The **evening watch** between 2000 and midnight. See WATCH.

**firth**   *n.* A narrow arm of the sea with high ground or mountains rising on both sides, such as the Firth of Clyde. See FJORD.

**fish**   *n.* (1) Any towed sensing device, such as a weight on the end of an aircraft's trailing antenna. (2 Nickname for a torpedo. (3) A tapered stiffener for a spar. (4) A heavy-duty purchase used to hoist the flukes of an old-fashioned anchor to the bow to stow the anchor after it has been catted.

**fish**   *v.* (1) To haul the flukes of an anchor toward the deck after it has been catted, to stow it. (2) To push or pull rope or wire through a conduit or through a channel. You may fish it with a long piece of stiff wire first. (3) To repair a mast or spars by bolting wooden pieces—fish—across the break and securing them with lashing. (4) To seize together two sections of rope as a temporary repair.

**fish block**   *n.* A double or triple sheave block with a heavy hook used for fishing an anchor.

**fisherman's bend**   *n.* A knot used to bend a line to a ring, used especially to secure an anchor warp to an anchor.

**fisherman's fender**   *n.* A fender made with several turns of hawser and served with smaller rope.

**fisherman's staysail**   *n.* A topsail used primarily on schooners above the main staysail.

**fishery, right of**   See RIGHT OF FISHERY.

**fish haven**   *n.* Piles of junk created for the benefit of sport fishermen. These are shown on the charts and should be avoided by navigators with deep-draft vessels. Fish havens are outlined in blue on the charts if they have an authorized depth of 11 fathoms or less or if the depth is unknown.

**fish hook**   *n.* (1) A broken strand of a wire rope caused by heavy use. (2) A large iron hook on a spar used to fish the anchor.

**fishing zone**   *n.* The offshore zone in which exclusive fishing rights and management are held by the coastal nation. The U.S. fishing zone is known as the "fishery conservation zone." Public Law 94–265 states: "The inner boundary of the fishery conservation zone is a line conterminous with the seaward boundary of each of the coastal states, and the outer boundary of such zone is a line drawn in such a manner that each point on it is 200 nautical miles from the baseline from which the territorial sea is measured."

**fish plate**   See FLOUNDER PLATE.

**fish trap areas**   *n.* An area established by the U.S. Corps of Engineers in which fish traps are allowed to be placed. These areas are shown on charts.

**fist**   *n.* A radio operator's sending hand. An operator is said to have a **good fist**

if he or she sends messages well but without personal characteristics, or a **glass fist** if he or she is incompetent. An especially fast operator is said to have a **copper fist.** It is important for radio technicians to resist including personal characteristics in their sending so that their identity is not apparent to an enemy.

**fitness report**  *n.* Periodic assessment of U.S. Navy officer's performance by the commanding officer that forms the basis for an officer's promotions or an officer's being passed over.

**fitting out**  *n.* (1) Precommissioning preparation of a ship for active duty by placing on board and installing all items on the allowance list, the list of items allowed by the owners or government building the vessel. (2) The completion of the construction of a vessel after it has been launched and is in the shipyard's **fitting out basin.** This includes stepping masts, installing engines, and so on.

**fittings**  *n.* (1) Small necessary parts or devices. (2) A marine insurance underwriter's term for the permanent devices as required for the activity in which it is to be engaged as well as the provisions for crew, fuel, and engines.

**fix**  *n.* An accurate position determined without the use of a former position. A small circle is used to indicate a fix on a chart. A dead-reckoning fix is indicated by a semicircle, while a square indicates an estimated position.

**fix**  *v.* To secure a cargo charter.

**fixed (F)**  *adj.* (1) Light phase description indicating a continuous, steady light. See LIGHT PHASE CHARACTERISTICS. (2) Said of a vessel (a) when definite arrangements regarding a charter have been completed, or (b) when a freight rate has been agreed upon.

**fixed and flashing (F FL)**  *adj.* Light phase description indicating a steady light varied at regular intervals by a light with a flash of greater intensity. See LIGHT PHASE CHARACTERISTICS.

**fixed mark**  *n.* A navigational mark with a fixed position.

**fixed star**  *n.* A star whose distance is so great that any movement it may have is not appreciable for navigation purposes except over a long period.

**fjord (or fiord)**  *n.* A long, deep, narrow arm of the sea between very high mountains. Fjords often have relatively shallow sills at their entrances. See FIRTH.

**flag**  *n.* Bunting or a similar material of various colors used to indicate nationality and to communicate. See SIGNAL FLAGS.

**flag bag**  *n.* The bin on a ship's bridge in which the signal flags are kept.

**flag bridge**  *n.* A separate bridge on larger ships designed for use by the flag officer and his staff; it is usually on a level different from the ship's navigating bridge.

**flag clause**  *n.* Charter party and bill of lading term used to indicate that the carrier's liability is determined by the laws of the country specified in the contract.

**flag discrimination**  *n.* Government policies that insure preferential treatment of the nation's merchant fleet to the exclusion of other flags. Also *cargo preference.*

**flag floozies**  *n.* Sailor's derisive term for the signalmen, usually used by the deck and engine gangs because the flag floozies don't get very dirty.

**flag hoist**  *n.* A signal to other ships within visual range made by signal flags run up on a signal halyard.

**flag lieutenant**  *n.* Personal aide to a flag officer afloat who acts as flag signal officer.

**flag of convenience (FOC)**   *n.* The practice of registering a vessel in a country other than the country of which the owner is a citizen, for the purpose of evading the stricter laws and higher taxes of the owner's country. The leading flag-of-convenience countries are Panama, Liberia, Cyprus, and Greece. Pleasure boats registered with Delaware corporations for tax reasons are not considered flag-of-convenience cases. See REFLAG.

**flag officer**   *n.* (1) A commissioned officer in the U.S. Navy or U.S. Coast Guard entitled to display a flag with stars that shows, by the number of stars, his rank. A fleet admiral has five stars, an admiral four stars, a vice admiral three stars, a rear admiral two stars, and a commodore one star. (2) An officer of a yacht club entitled to fly his designated flag on his boat.

**flags**   *n.* Nickname for a signalman.

**flag salute**   *n.* The courtesy extended by merchant ships to other passing vessels. The ensign is lowered one-third the height of the flagstaff and is kept there until the ship being saluted returns the salute, then it is two-blocked again.

**flagship**   *n.* (1) The vessel from which a unit commander (fleet commodore, commodore, or admiral) exercises command. (2) On passenger ship lines, the senior captain's ship is the flagship and the captain is usually given the honorary title of commodore.

**flagstaff**   *n.* The staff on which the ensign is hoisted at the stern when moored or in port. See JACK STAFF.

**flagstaff insignia**   *n.* A device fitted at the top of a flagstaff on officers' boats, and boats carrying civilian officials; the insignia include eagles, halberds, and stars.

**flag tower**   *n.* A chart label for a scaffold-like tower used for displaying flags.

**flake**   *n.* (1) A small scaffold put over the side of a vessel to support men working on the hull. (2) A single turn or several turns of rope in a coil, more properly called a **fake.** The term is controversial. In his standard work on knots, Clifford Ashley states that "The dictionary form *fake* is unknown at sea, . . . that a flake is a single turn in a coil, and that flaking is coiling in various ways." On the other hand, the highly respected U.S. Navy Captains John V. Noel and Edward L. Beach declare that "flake" is a mispronunciation of fake, as in **fake down.** Capt. John Smith's *An Accidence or the Pathway to Experience for All Young Sea-men* (1626) says "Coil your cable in small flakes." Capt. George Biddlecombe, in 1794, used the word "fake." Rear Admiral Austin M. Knight, in his 10th edition of *Modern Seamanship,* 1941, uses only "fake," which seems to be the choice of most 20th-century sailors.

**flake**   *v.* A variant of fake, to coil rope. In yachting circles, flaking (down), or faking, usually means coiling by forming a series of loose figure eights. See FLEMISH COIL.

**flame safety lamp**   *n.* A lamp devised so that it can be taken into oil and fuel tanks to test oxygen levels before sending personnel into the tanks.

**flammable liquid.**   *n.* Any liquid whose flashpoint is 80° F or below. See COMBUSTIBLE LIQUID.

**flange**   *n.* An angle turned in steel girders and beams to give added resistance to bending.

**flank speed**   See SPEED, STANDARD.

**flapper valve**   *n.* A valve with a swinging plate that seats firmly and can be closed remotely or automatically.

**flare**   *n.* (1) The upward and outward curvature of a hull above the waterline. The resulting concave shape of the bow reduces the depth to which the vessel plunges into the water. See TUMBLE HOME. (2) A pyrotechnic device used to attract attention when a vessel needs help.

**flareback**  *n.* (1) A sudden combustion of hot gases in the firebox of a boiler that causes a backfire into the fireroom. (2) The emission of flame and hot gases from a gun's breech.

**flash**  *n.* On a coastal beacon or lighthouse a relatively brief appearance of a light with a relatively long period of darkness. See LIGHT PHASE CHARACTERISTICS.

**flashing**  *n.* The process of reducing a hull's attraction to magnetic mines by placing a horizontal coil around the outside of a vessel and energizing the coil by a strong direct current at a predetermined level. When the correct magnitude and polarity of the vertical field of permanent magnetism is attained, the coil is removed. This process is not as effective as degaussing coils.

**flashing (Fl)**  *adj.* Light phase description indicating a light alternating between periods of darkness and light, with the total duration of light shorter than the total duration of darkness. Lights may be **single-flashing, group-flashing, composite-group-flashing,** or **long-flashing.** See LIGHT PHASE CHARACTERISTICS.

**flashing light**  *n.* In the *Navigation Rules,* a shipboard light flashing at regular intervals at a frequency of 120 flashes or more per minute.

**flash plate**  *n.* The steel plate on a forecastle on which the anchor chain rides. It is called a flash plate because of the sparks that are thrown out when the anchor is let go.

**flat**  *n.* A shipwright's term for a partial deck without curvature. See FLATS.

**flat**  *adj.* Refers to a sail that has been sheeted in as close as possible so that there is little or no belly.

**flat aback**  *adv.* Said of a square-rigged vessel with the wind bearing on the forward side of the sails. This can be done intentionally, as when stopping a ship or tacking, or accidentally.

**flat calm**  *n.* No wind.

**flat-cut sail**  *n.* A sail with flat draft used in heavy weather to permit sailing closer to the wind.

**flat keel**  *n.* The bottom shell strake on the centerline of a vessel. See KEEL.

**flats**  *n.* (1) A broad expanse of shallow water and marshes, larger than a bar. (2) Gratings or plating over bilges.

**flat seam**  *n.* A sailmaker's term for a seam that tables two overlapping pieces of cloth with the stitches running oblique to the seam, forming a zigzag to allow the cloth to stretch without tearing.

**flat seizing**  *n.* A seizing with only one layer of seizing stuff; a round seizing has two layers or turns.

**flat shoal**  *n.* A low shoal on which the waves break but that is always below the level of the water.

**flatten in**  *v.* To pull in the clew of a sail before tacking so that the vessel will come about more quickly.

**flattop**  *n.* Nickname for an aircraft carrier.

**flaw**  *n.* A gust of wind across the water, stronger than a cat's paw.

**flax**  *n.* Fibers from any of several small plants with blue flowers, usually the *Linum usitatissimum,* that can be made into fine linen, flax sail canvas, or flax rope. Flax makes stronger cordage and sails than do hemp (manila) fibers.

**fleet**   *n.* An organization of ships and aircraft under one commander, usually comprising several types of vessels and aircraft and their auxiliaries necessary for major operations. A **major fleet** is a principal, permanent subdivision of the operating forces of the U.S. Navy; these are the Atlantic Fleet and the Pacific Fleet, made up in turn of **numbered fleets:** the Third Fleet (Eastern Pacific), Seventh Fleet (Western Pacific and Indian Ocean), Second Fleet (Atlantic Ocean), and Sixth Fleet (Mediterranean Sea).

**fleet admiral (FAdm.)**   *n.* The highest-ranking commissioned officer in the U.S. Navy, ranked above admiral.

**fleet air wing**   *n.* An assortment of land-based and shore-based aircraft patrol squadrons that includes tenders and support squadrons.

***Fleet Guide***   *n.* One of a series of sailing directions for U.S. Naval bases for U.S. Navy use only.

**fleet the messenger**   *phr.* To prevent an override on a capstan by rearranging the turns.

**fleet train**   *n.* An organization of auxiliary vessels such as tankers, ammunition vessels, refrigeration ships (reefers), and repair ships, that follow warships to enable them to stay at sea for long periods.

**flemish (down)**   *v.* To coil rope flat starting with a tight fake at the center with each successive fake coiled tightly to the preceding one. Ropes are flemished either for appearance or to form a **flemish mat.** To cast a flemished line is to invite twists and snarls. See FAKE; FLAKE.

**flemish coil**   *n.* A coil of rope in which each fake rides the fake beneath it to insure the line's running clear. Also *French coil.* See FLAKE; SENNET.

**flemish eye**   *n.* An eye formed by taking one of the three strands of a rope and bringing the other two strands back on the rope to form an eye. The first strand is then laid around the eye in a contrary direction. The three strands are then seized at the crotch of the eye. It is quicker but not as secure as an eye-splice.

**flemish flake**   *n.* A flat coil of rope or line, either circular or elliptical, and used generally for decorative purposes. Also *French flake.*

**flemish horse**   *n.* An extra footrope at the end of a yard for the man who passes the earing at the yard arm.

**flexible rope**   *n.* Wire rope made up of a number of small-diameter wires and a hemp core. It can be used more easily for running rigging, towing, and mooring.

**flight**   *n.* A sharp rise in a part of a hull such as a counter.

**flight deck**   *n.* The top deck of an aircraft carrier that serves as a runway.

**Flinders bar**   *n.* A bar of soft iron placed in a vertical position at the side of a magnetic compass to neutralize the semicircular deviation due to induced magnetism, named for Capt. Matthew Flinders, RN (1774–1814). Today, ships' binnacles are provided with a tube into which the Flinders bar slides. After the proper adjustments are made, the Flinders bar is stabilized by packing the remainder of the space in the tube with nonmagnetic material. See QUADRANTAL SPHERES.

**flip**   *n.* A drink composed of beer, liquor, and sugar and heated with a red-hot iron, according to Graham Blackburn's *Overlook Illustrated Dictionary of Nautical Terms,* and introduced, it is said, by Admiral Sir Clowdisley Shovell (1650–1707).

**float**   See PADDLE WHEEL.

**float coat** *n.* A jacket with built-in buoyancy that usually has a hood.

**floater net** *n.* Lifesaving nets with floats, used to supplement rafts and lifeboats.

**floating aids** *n.* Buoys moored as aids to navigation. Floating aids are frequently moved by the action of wind, waves, and other forces, and their position should not be taken for granted, especially after rough weather.

**floating base** *n.* A factory ship that remains many months at sea to process (salt, can, freeze) fish from the daily catches coming from smaller vessels.

**floating dock** *n.* A wharf built on pontoons to create dockage.

**floating dry dock** *n.* A movable repair facility that can be submerged enough to allow a vessel to be floated into it; after the vessel is in place and shored, the water is pumped out so that repairs can be made on the hull below the waterline.

**floating dump** *n.* Critical supplies kept in reserve afloat for quick delivery as needed during an amphibious operation.

**floating harbor** *n.* A collection of timbers placed to seaward of a moored vessel to break the seas.

**floating policy** *n.* An underwriter's term for a policy that describes ship insurance in general terms and omits the name of the vessels and other details to be defined in subsequent documents.

**floating power** *n.* The utilized buoyancy, which is the buoyancy required to keep a vessel afloat with its correct total weight, plus the reserve buoyancy.

**flocculation** *n.* A biomass that forms in freshwater at the saltwater interface, as in the Mississippi River passes during low water; it is flushed out during high river stages. Flocculation can grow to be 10 to 15 feet thick and can pose a hazard to navigation because it can deflect or even stop low-powered ships.

**floe** See ICE FLOE.

**floe berg** *n.* A massive piece of sea ice made up of a hummock, or a group of hummocks frozen together and separated from any ice in the surrounding area. Floe bergs may be as much as 5 meters above sea level.

**flog** *v.* To beat severely with a whip or rod. Most navies, including the U.S. Navy, have outlawed flogging.

**flood** *n.* The period when the tidal current is flowing toward shore or up a tidal stream. The opposite of ebb. Flood and ebb refer only to horizontal movement of tidal current toward or away from land and should not be confused with fall or rise.

**flood** *v.* To admit seawater to a compartment below the waterline, especially to extinguish a fire.

**floodable length** *n.* The length of a vessel that can be flooded without danger to the vessel. The floodable length varies from one part of a ship to another; it is usually greatest forward and less amidships.

**flood axis** *n.* Average direction of tidal current at maximum strength of tide.

**flood current** *n.* The movement of tidal current toward the shore or up a tidal river or estuary.

**flooded ice** *n.* Sea ice that has been flooded by meltwater or river water and is heavily loaded with water and wet snow.

**floodgate** *n.* A gate that shuts out, admits, or releases a body of water. Also *sluice*.

**flood interval** *n.* The interval between the transit of the Moon over the meridian of a given place and the time of the following flood strength.

**flood strength** *n.* (1) The phase of flood current at the time of maximum speed. (2) The speed of the current at flood strength. Also *strength of flood.*

**flood tide** *n.* A tide that is in flood or flowing toward land.

**flood time** *n.* The period when the current or tide is flowing toward land.

**floor** *n.* (1) The lower portion of a transverse frame that extends from the centerline to the turn of the bilge and from inner to outer bottom. (2) Vertical transverse plating welded to bottom shell plating at each frame that goes from the turn of the bilge on one side to the turn of the bilge on the opposite side. (3) The essentially horizontal surface constituting the principal level of the ground beneath a body of water. Also *bottom.*

**floorboards** *n.* In small boats, wooden boards, usually removable, covering the bilge.

**floor ceiling** *n.* The portion of a hold ceiling, the planking fastened to the inner frames of a hold, that extends beyond the strakes to the keelson.

**floor clip** *n.* Angle device used to connect longitudinal members and brackets to the floor.

**floor heads** *n.* Outboard ends of flooring timbers.

**flooring off** *v.* Stevedore's term for stowing cargo in the lower tier of a hold.

**floor plate** *n.* A removable steel plate that forms part of the deck plating in the engine spaces.

**Florida Current** *n.* An Atlantic Ocean current that flows easterly through the Florida Straits northward between Florida and the Bahamas. It is the extension of the Atlantic South Equatorial Current that unites with the North Equatorial Current and flows east to west through the various passages of the Windward Islands toward the Yucatan peninsula. Part then flows into the Gulf of Mexico to form a **loop current** that flows clockwise from the Yucatan Peninsula around the Gulf of Mexico to the Florida Keys, while another branch flows north directly to the Florida Straits.

**flotation** *n.* Airspaces, tanks, and other devices that help to keep a swamped boat or a person from sinking.

**flotilla** *n.* (1) A small fleet. (2) In the U.S. Navy, an administrative or tactical organization of two or more squadrons of vessels along with a flagship and perhaps a tender.

**flotsam** *n.* Floating wreckage. See JETSAM; LAGEN.

**flounder (or fish) plate** *n.* A steel plate with reinforced holes at each of its three corners used for chain bridles during a towing operation. Also *fish plate.*

**flow** *n.* British usage, total current or the combination of tidal and nontidal currents. In British usage tidal current is called **tidal stream** and nontidal current is called **current.**

**flow** *v.* To ease sheets to spill the wind, as in "Flow the mainsheet."

**flower of the winds** *phr.* The device on charts to indicate the relative frequency, direction, and strength of winds in a given area. Also *windrose.*

**flue gas system** *n.* A safety device that replaces the air in a fuel tank or combustible cargo tank with carbon monoxide and carbon dioxide (from the engine exhaust) to blanket the cargo and reduce the possibility of fire or explosion. Also *inert gas system.*

**fluke**   *n.* The pointed or spade-shaped end of an anchor arm, including the bill, palm, and the end of an arm. See AN-CHOR. (2) An unpredictable wind shift.

**fluky**   *adj.* Constantly varying, such as a fluky wind, a wind without pattern.

**fluorescent chart**   *n.* A chart made using fluorescent ink to enable the user to study the chart under ultraviolet light.

**flush deck**   *n.* A continuous upper deck with no breaks, such as a raised poop or forecastle extending the breadth of the ship. A **flushdecker** is a ship, especially a destroyer such as the *Fletcher*-class destroyers of World War II, with a weather deck extending the full length of the vessel.

**flush plating**   *n.* Hull and deck plating with edges and butts joined edge to edge giving a smooth surface. Strips are added on the inside surface for additional strength. Also *flush system.*

**flux-gate compass**   *n.* An electrical compass oriented to the magnetic north pole. It does not have the weight or complexity of a gyroscope, but it also lacks the accuracy and dependability. It is used on small boats and aircraft.

**fly**   *n.* (1) The length of a flag from the hoist to the outer edge. (2) A pennant flown at the masthead to indicate wind direction on a sailboat.

**fly back:**   *n.* The upper block of a topsail tackle.

**fly block**   *n.* The large upper block of a topsail halyard.

**fly-by-night sail**   *n.* A small square sail or studding sail sometimes carried by schooners when running before the wind.

**flyer**   *n.* A course taken that is different from the rest of a racing fleet.

**flying**   *adj.* Used to describe a sail that is hauled aloft and set from the deck. Studding sails were set flying. It would be technically accurate to say that a jib is set flying when it is hoisted on its own luff, but the term is rarely used in this manner.

**flying boat**   *n.* A seaplane capable of floating on its hull and able to take off from or put down on water.

**flying bridge**   *n.* (1) The highest bridge on a ship, above the navigation bridge and above the flag bridge, and above the conning tower of a submarine (usually called the bridge). Frequently the flying bridge does not have a helm or engine-order telegraph, but only a voice tube or sound-powered telephone. (2) On pleasure craft, a high platform above a lower steering position. A flying bridge is usually exposed; it may have controls on small craft. If it's enclosed as on larger vessels, it becomes, more properly, an upper pilothouse or bridge. Also *flybridge.* (3) The deck on the top of the navigation bridge. At general quarters in destroyers and frigates, the air defense officer and the gunnery officer usually have their stations on the flying bridge.

**Flying Dutchman**   *n.* A mythical Dutch ship under Captain Vanderdecken (in the Dutch version, it is the seaman Van Straaten), who swore he would put into Table Bay, despite a storm, and for his blasphemy was condemned to haunt the waters of the Cape of Good Hope and never allowed to reach port. It was made into an opera by Richard Wagner as *Der fliegende Hol-länder.* To sight the "Flying Dutchman" was a bad omen.

**flying guy**   *n.* A sideways stay for a flying jibboom. See SQUARE-RIGGED VESSEL.

**flying jib**   *n.* (1) A light sail set on the foretopgallant royal stay. See SQUARE-RIGGED VESSEL. (2) The outermost jib when more than one headsail is carried.

**flying jibboom**   *n.* An extension of the jibboom. See SQUARE-RIGGED VESSEL.

**flying jibe**   *n.* A jibe that takes place when the headsail is not trimmed in close enough; an uncontrolled jibe that can carry away gear or personnel or create a **goosewing** (mainsail with top half on one side and the lower half on the other side). The goosewing jibe is also called a **Chinese jibe** because of the way a full-batten sail jibes. For many years, the only full-battened sails were on Chinese junks.

**flying kite**   *n.* A term applied to various sails carried above the skysails, as well as to the topgallant sail, the royal studding sails, spinnakers, balloon sails, and even bonnets.

**flying mooring**   *n.* A mooring accomplished by letting go the anchor while the vessel is still underway. Except in emergencies, this is a bad practice that endangers the ground tackle and the ship's personnel.

**flying nightingale**   *n.* Cable running from the flying jibboom down to the dolphin striker. This is similar to, but not the same as, a bobstay.

**flying sail**   *n.* Any sail that is set flying, that is, not bent to a yard or mast and set from the deck.

**flying start**   *n.* A racing start with the boat hitting the starting line going full speed just as the starting gun fires.

**flying studding sail**   *n.* Studding sail set between two masts of a schooner or similarly rigged vessel.

**foam line**   *n.* The front of a wave after it breaks.

**focsle**   See FORECASTLE.

**fog**   *n.* A visible assemblage of numerous tiny droplets of water or ice formed by the condensation of water vapor in air with the base of the assemblage near the ground. A **fogbank** or **patch** is an area of fog that can be seen at a distance through clear intervening air. See WEATHER.

**fog bell**   *n.* A bell sounded by a vessel at anchor or aground in or near an area of restricted visibility.

**fogbound**   *adj.* Immobilized, forced to lie at anchor because of fog. "We lay fogbound for most of the first day of the cruise."

**fogbow**   *n.* A white arc (similar to a rainbow) that is sometimes seen opposite the Sun.

**fog buoy**   *n.* A floating device towed in a fog so that a vessel astern and keeping station will be able to maintain an assigned distance.

**fog eye**   *n.* A spot of sunlight through a fog.

**fog gong**   *n.* Gong used by a vessel anchored or aground in fog. See FOG BELL.

**foghorn**   *n.* Any type of loud horn sounded by a ship to alert other ships of its presence when in a fog. Its specific use is detailed in the *Navigation Rules.*

**fog lookout**   *n.* A lookout stationed in the eyes of a ship when fog becomes heavy. Positioned lower than the bridge, the lookout can often see beneath the fog when bridge personnel can see nothing. Fog lookouts are also stationed on the flying bridge or other high points if the fog is low lying. The *Navigation Rules,* Rule 19(b), states: Every vessel shall proceed at a safe speed adapted to the prevailing circumstances of restricted visibility.

**fog signals**   *n.* (1) Different signals required of ships in a fog, depending on whether they are moored or underway, as dictated by the *Navigation Rules.* (2) Signals sounded by lightships in a fog.

**föhn (or foehn)**   *n.* A dry wind with a downward component that is warm for the season. Föhns occurs when a horizontally moving air mass hits a mountain and moves upward to be cooled below the dew point. With the loss of moisture, the air mass warms; when it clears the mountain and starts to descend, it becomes a föhn. See SANTA ANA.

**folding anchor**   *n.* An anchor, such as a Danforth, designed so that the flukes and shank can be folded against the stock for easy stowing.

**following edge**   *n.* The propeller's edge that does not cut through the water but follows the leading edge.

**following sea**   *n.* A sea running in the same direction as the vessel, thus making steering more difficult.

**foot**   *n.* The bottom edge of a sail, whether fore-and-aft or square sail. See GAFF; MARCONI RIG.

**foot**   *v.* To sail close-hauled with special emphasis on speed. "We were footing well until we rounded the cape."

**footband**   *n.* A strengthening piece of canvas on the after side along the foot of a square sail.

**footline**   *n.* A light line that adjusts the tension on the foot of a headsail or other loose-footed sail. See OUTHAUL.

**footlocks**   *n.* Strips of wood placed on the decks of vessels carrying cattle to help them keep their footing in heavy seas.

**foot outhaul**   *n.* A line leading from the clew cringle of a sail and rove through a block at the outer end of the boom to keep the foot of the sail taut.

**foot rope**   *n.* A served wire rope secured under a yard from the middle to the yardarm, supported by stirrups, to provide footing for sailors as they furled and unfurled square sails. Foot ropes were

also used under the bowsprit and jib-boom. (2) The boltrope on the foot of a sail.

**force**   *n.* (1) A number of ships operating together for a specific purpose. A force is a major division of a fleet, and is normally subdivided into groups. (2) A term used to describe wind and sea conditions. See BEAUFORT SCALE.

**forced draft**   *n.* Air supplied under pressure to the burners of a vessel's boilers.

**force log**   *n.* A speed indicator that measures the force of the water against a hinged plate. As the vessel goes through the water, the speed can be measured and transmitted to a remote gauge.

**force majeure**   *n.* (1) An overwhelming force of weather, such as a typhoon, that releases the owners from certain contractual obligations under charter parties and bills of lading. (2) A superior military force. (3) Compelling circumstances.

**fore**   *adj.* (1) Usually seen as a prefix denoting the forward part of a vessel, its machinery, its rig, and so on. For example, foredeck, forecastle, forefoot, or foremast. (2) Of or pertaining to the foremost, as in fore-topmast, fore royal, fore-topgallant stay.

**fore and aft**   *adv.* and *adj.* (1) From bow to stern. "We searched the ship fore and aft." (2) Longitudinal, parallel to the keel. A fore-and-aft rigged sailboat is one in which the luffs of the sails are attached to stays or masts, as distinct from square-rigged vessels in which the primary sails are set on yards crossing the masts. See RELATIVE BEARING.

**forebody**   *n.* Ship's hull forward of the beam.

**forecastle (or focsle)**   *n.* (pron. fokesl) (1) The forward section of a vessel reserved for the crew's quarters. (2) The name for the deckhands' berthing compartments wherever they are located.

**forecastle deck** *n.* The section of the deck forward of the mast.

**forecatharpings** *n.* Lines that brace the guys that brace the foremast.

**forecourse** See FORESAIL.

**foredeck** *n.* The deck covering the forward portion of a vessel between mast and bow or forward deckhouse and bow.

**foredeck man** *n.* A member of a racing crew who is responsible for raising, lowering, and changing headsails.

**forefoot** *n.* The part of the stem that joins the keel.

**foregirt** *n.* A short wooden boom used to extend the leading edge of a lugsail.

**foreguy** *n.* A line or wire that is led from the spinnaker pole to the deck to prevent the spinnaker pole from rising. British usage is *kicker.*

**foreign trade** *n.* Shipping term referring to transportation between countries other than the country of a vessel's registry.

**foreign voyage** *n.* In maritime law, a voyage within the jurisdiction of a foreign country.

**foreland** *n.* High point of land extending into a large body of water beyond the coastline. Also *headland; promontory.*

**foreman stevedore** *n.* U.S. term for a person in charge of a stevedoring gang. Also *dock boss.*

**foremast** *n.* (1) The forwardmost mast on vessels with three or more masts, and the forward mast on two-masted schooners. The forward mast on ketches and yawls is the mainmast. (2) On mod-

ern naval ships, the forwardmost mast from which flags are flown, the smaller, after mast from which the ensign is flown being called the mainmast. See SQUARE-RIGGED VESSEL.

**forepeak** *n.* (1) The compartment forward of the farthest forward bulkhead, the space between the collision bulkhead and the stem. This space is often used for a ballast tank. (2) The compartment farthest forward used for stowage. See PEAK.

**forereach** *v.* (1) To get ahead of another, said of sailboats only. (2) Said of a sailboat when she shoots ahead (to windward) while going about, luffing into the eye of the wind, or rounding a mark while luffing or changing a sail.

**fore rigging** *n.* All rigging related to the foremast.

**forerunners** *n.* Long, low swells that sometimes anticipate a storm.

**foresail** *n.* (pron. foresl): A triangular sail set on the forestay of a cutter or sloop; a jib or genoa. (2) On square riggers, the foresail is the lowest square sail set on the foremast.

**foresheets** *n.* A small platform or seat at the bow of a small boat. See STERN-SHEETS; SQUARE-RIGGED VESSEL.

**foreshore** *n.* The shoreline covered by water at high tide; the part of the shore between low water and the crest of the berm.

**forestay** *n.* The part of the standing rigging that runs from the bow and is designed to support the foremast on sailing vessels with two or more masts, or the single mast on sloops. Also *headstay.* See SQUARE-RIGGED VESSEL.

**forestaysail** *n.* A foresail bent on a forestay.

**fore steaming light** *n.* White navigation light on the foremast carried by powered vessels; the term is not recognized by the *Navigation Rules*.

**foretop** *n.* In square-rigged vessels, a platform at the fore lower masthead located several feet below the cap or upper end of the lower mast, and supported by trestletrees; they form spreaders for the topmast shrouds. See SQUARE-RIGGED VESSEL.

**foretriangle** *n.* The area described by the mast, the deck, and the headstay and used as a measure for the relative size of headsails. See HEADSAIL.

**foreturn** *n.* The twist in each strand of a rope. This differs from, and is opposite to the **afterturn,** which is the turn of the rope itself. See CABLE-LAID; ROPE.

**forge ahead** *v.* (1) To move ahead, usually by momentum or external force, as in a collision. (2) Said of a vessel when coming about or when approaching an anchor.

**forge over** *v.* To cross a bar by using the force of the wind and sea to carry you along while aground.

**forging** *n.* The term for any large steel structural piece such as the sternpost, the rudder, and the stem, the result of hammering, bending, or pressing hot metal into shape. Forgings have been replaced almost completely by castings.

**fork** *n.* The splice at the eye in a stay that surrounds a mast.

**forward** *adj.* Near, at, or in the bow.

**forward** *adv.* Toward the bow. See RELATIVE BEARING.

**forward brow** *n.* A gangway from the bow to a pier.

**forwarding agent** *n.* A freight agent who receives cargo for shipping and has

it delivered (forwarded) to the carrier. A forwarding agent is neither a consignor nor a carrier, but he can also perform other services for shippers. Many freight forwarders specialize in goods going to certain countries or in certain kinds of cargo.

**forward of the beam** *phr.* Any direction between broad on the beam and ahead. See ABAFT THE BEAM, RELATIVE BEARING.

**forward perpendicular** *n.* The vertical line through the intersection of the load waterline and the stem.

**forward quarter** *n.* Forward side of the ship aft of the bow.

**fother** *v.* To form a hairy mat by threading many lengths of yarn through a sail or other material; the mat so formed was used to cover a hole below the waterline on the outside of the hull. The water pressure kept the fothered sail pressed against the hole as long as it was held in place by ropes.

**foul** *v.* (1) To hit a boat with the right of way in a race. (2) To cause another boat to have to change course illegally.

**fouled** *adj.* Jammed, confused, tangled, or dirty. An anchor is fouled when the chain is twisted around it; a line is fouled when it is tangled or has a kink in it and cannot run free.

**fouled anchor** *n.* (1) Insignia showing an anchor encircled by its anchor chain used on yacht ensigns and in the U.S. Navy on chief petty officers' hats. (2) The British Admiralty's symbol and the official insignia of the First Sea Lord.

**fouled hawse** *n.* Tangled anchor chains leading to two anchors while moored.

**fouling** *n.* A general term for the seaweed and small animals that collect on a vessel's hull and slow it down.

**foul weather**   *n.* Stormy weather during which sailors on deck wear **foul-weather gear.**

**foul-weather parade**   *n.* A muster below decks or in a sheltered area usually during bad weather.

**foul wind**   *n.* A wind blowing contrary to the direction desired.

**found**   *adj.* Equipped. A well-found vessel is a well-equipped vessel.

**foundation**   *n.* The supporting structure for engines, boilers, and machinery.

**foundation plate**   *n.* A fore-and-aft member fitted atop floors for a foundation for the keelson.

**founder**   *v.* To sink due to loss of reserve buoyancy. When a boat is foundering, it is sinking but is still at least partially above the surface of the water.

**four bells and a jingle**   *phr.* (obsolete.) The signal from the bridge to the engine room for full speed astern. The bells indicated speed, and the jingle indicated astern. See ENGINE ROOM BELLS.

**fourfold block**   *n.* A block with four sheaves.

**fourfold purchase**   *n.* A tackle made up of two fourfold blocks.

**four-piper**   *n.* A vessel with four smokestacks. While some cruisers had four smokestacks, the U.S. Navy built a large number of flush-deck, four-stack destroyers. During World War II, 50 of these four-pipers were transferred to England before the U.S. entry into the war. In England they were called **four-stackers.**

**four-point bearing**   See DOUBLING THE ANGLE ON THE BOW.

**fox**   *n.* Twisted strands of several rope yarns used for seizings after being twisted against the lay and smoothed out.

**foxer gear (FXR)**   *n.* Noise-making apparatus towed astern to fox or foil acoustic torpedoes.

**Foxtrot**   *n.* Phonetic word for the letter "F." In a single-letter signal it means "I am disabled. Communicate with me."

**fractional rig**   *n.* A headsail rig with the headstay leading from the bow fitting to a point short of the top of the mast. Also *three-quarter rig.*

**fractonimbus**   *n.* Broken masses of driving nimbus clouds. Also *scud.*

**fracture**   *n.* A break or rupture through very close pack ice or consolidated ice. Fractures often contain brash ice or can be covered with nilas. A **large fracture** is more than 500 meters long; a **medium fracture** is 200–500 meters long; a **small fracture** is 50–200 meters long; a **very small fracture** is less than 50 meters long.

**fracture zone**   *n.* A long, major fault zone of irregular topography in the seafloor usually with seamounts, ridges, and troughs.

**FRAM**   *n.* Fleet rehabilitation and modernization program. The term applies especially to the rebuilding of destroyers, adding new capabilities not available when they were originally built, but without changing the basic designation or fundamental mission. See SLEP.

**frame**   *n.* (1) The skeleton of a vessel. (2) A transverse member that forms the rib of the hull; it is attached to the keel and stiffens and shapes the outside plating.

**frame line**   *n.* The fixed position or station of a frame.

**frame spacing**  *n.* The longitudinal spacing between frames.

**framing ribband**  *n.* A strip of timber or plating used during construction to hold frames in place temporarily.

**franchise**  *n.* A small percentage on hull and cargo insurance that the owners and underwriters agree will not be covered, similar to a deductible clause in liability insurance.

**Franklin life buoy**  *n.* A copper ring formerly carried on the sides of naval vessels. It was an emergency device equipped with an automatic release. When thrown into the water, a small canister of calcium carbide ignited to aid the man overboard in finding the life ring and to aid the vessel in finding the man.

**frap**  *v.* To lash with a number of crossing turns to tighten and secure. When at anchor, courteous sailboat skippers frap their halyards to prevent their flapping noisily.

**frapping lines**  *n.* Lines around the forward and after boat falls used when a boat is being lowered into rough seas; the frapping lines help keep the boat steady.

**fray**  *v.* To ravel a rope's end.

**frazil ice**  *n.* (pron. frayzle) The first small crystals of ice, called **spicules,** formed on the surface of seawater. From the French *fraisil,* coal dust or cinders.

**free**  *adv.* Used chiefly of square-rigged vessels, sailing with the wind from the quarter or from astern. A vessel is running free when it is not necessary to brace the yards to the fullest, or to sharp up.

**freeboard**  *n.* The vertical distance from the waterline to the freeboard deck; usually measured amidships.

**freeboard assignments**  *n.* A document issued by the American Bureau of Shipping when a ship is first surveyed to determine her allowable load lines and showing the required freeboard for each of the seasonal load lines. See LOAD LINE CERTIFICATE.

**freeboard deck**  *n.* The uppermost deck that is designed to be watertight. This is the deck from which the freeboard is measured and the deck at which the deck line is painted.

**freeboard length**  *n.* A measurement established by international convention in 1930 as being the length of the load waterline from the foreside of the stem to the after side of the rudder post.

**freeboard marks**  *n.* The lines and letters at a ship's waist that indicate the maximum permissible load line per design. See PLIMSOLL MARK OR LINE.

**freeboard zones**  *n.* Geographical areas of the world that were established at the 1930 International Convention on Load Lines. It was then that the summer and winter load lines, and so on, were established and the areas in which they applied. These were expanded and modified at the 1966 International Convention on Load Lines.

**free dispatch**  *n.* Charter party term that means no indemnity is owed for time gained in loading or unloading.

**freedom of the high seas**  *phr.* A doctrine that is now understood to include freedom of navigation, fishing, laying of pipelines, and overflight by aircraft. The doctrine is understood, but not necessarily accepted, by all coastal nations. The definition of a nation's territorial water—how far it extends from its coast—is unclear. The daily newspaper confirms the many disputes over this term, especially in places such as the Persian Gulf. When the subject of whaling comes up, there appear to be no high seas that are free. The same is quite properly true with many forms of pollution. In 1958, the

United Nations attempted to codify the law of the high seas, but failed.

**free gyroscope**  *n.* A gyroscope with three orthogonal axes about which the spin axis is free to rotate; the three **degrees of freedom** are (1) to spin on its axis, (2) to tilt on its horizontal axis, and (3) to rotate on its vertical axis.

**free in and out**  *phr.* A charter party phrase that leaves the responsibility of management of a vessel to the owner except for loading and unloading cargo and dry dock responsibility.

**freeing port**  *n.* One of a series of holes through a bulwark that provide ready drainage of water from the deck. See PIGSTY BULWARKS.

**free lighterage**  *n.* Gratuitous lighter and rail service that is included with the port fees in certain ports.

**free of turn**  *n.* A charter party term that establishes that loading and unloading will start as soon as a vessel arrives in a port regardless of delay in waiting for a berth.

**free on board (FOB)**  *adj. or adv.* Without a fee for delivery of goods on board a carrier or to a specified point. If coal is quoted FOB the carrier's pier in Jacksonville, it is understood that the person in Miami who buys the coal will have to pay freight from the pier in Jacksonville to the warehouse in Miami.

**free overboard**  *n.* A term that indicates the buyer of the cargo is to supply the craft to take delivery from the ship. The seller's responsibility closes when the goods leave the ship's sling.

**free overside**  See EX-SHIP.

**free pilotage**  *n.* A port term meaning that pilots are not required. Many ports are free for vessels of a certain class, while requiring pilots for vessels of other classes.

**free port (zone)**  *n.* (1) A port, or a zone in a port, in which imported cargo can be unloaded, held, and processed for reshipment without being charged a fee. (2) A port designated as a free trade zone in which goods may be exported without paying customs duty and are subject to minimum customs regulation.

**free surface**  *n.* Surface area of a liquid that is free to move from side to side as the ship rolls or pitches. The greater the free surface the more unstable, and thus dangerous, the freight. Baffles are used to reduce free surface.

**free time**  *n.* The time between the moment a charterer receives a chartering contract and the time the lay days begin.

**free wind**  See QUARTERING WIND.

**freight**  *n.* (1) Cargo carried by a vessel. (2) The charge for carrying cargo. Also *freightage; freight rate.*

**freightage**  *n.* (1) Commercial transportation of cargo. (2) The charge for carrying freight. (3) Cargo. (4) Total freight-carrying capacity of a vessel. In this context, it is expressed in tons as the quotient when the cubic capacity is divided by the cubic feet per ton of cargo.

**freighter**  *n.* A vessel designed primarily to carry cargo.

**freight forward**  *phr.* A phrase that means that under the transportation contract, freight is payable by the consignee at the destination port. See FREIGHT PREPAID.

**freight forwarder**  *n.* An agent of an exporter who handles the details of shipping, insuring, and documentation of cargo to be shipped.

**freight in full**  *n.* Charter party term that specifies that the shipowner pays all charges dealing with pilot fees, port fees, trimming, lighterage, and so on.

**freight pending**   *n.* Charter party term for the money owed by the charterer over and above the contract rate when the vessel has gone beyond the stipulated time.

**freight prepaid**   *n.* Charter party term for freight paid for by the consignee before it departed the loading port.

**freight release**   *n.* (1) A document issued to a dock superintendent by a shipping company or by a vessel's master or chief officer when the amount of cargo delivered is at variance with the bill of lading. (2) Document that gives authority to the master of a ship to deliver cargo to the holder of the document.

**freight ton**   *n.* 2,240 pounds or 1,016.06 kilograms and usually equated to 40 cubic feet. Also *stevedore ton.*

**French bowline**   *n.* A truss using a bowline, but with an additional loop to pass under a person's arm when lowered, for example, into a hold.

**French coil**   See FLEMISH COIL.

**French flake**   See FLEMISH FLAKE; SENNET.

**French reef**   *n.* A reef for square sails in which a jack rope and toggles fastened to the jackstay are used instead of reef points.

**French sennit (or sinnet)**   *n.* A braid similar to the flat sinnet except bulkier with an over-one-under-one weave. In France it is called *tresse Anglaise,* and in England it is called the French sinnet.

**fresh breeze**   *n.* Beaufort scale reading of 5, with winds of 17–21 miles per hour.

**freshen**   *v.* (1) To change the position of a rope to prevent chafing. Also *freshen the hawse; freshen the nip.* (2) To veer a cable slightly so as to put the chafe of a chock or hawsepipe in a different place.

**freshen**   *v.* With reference to wind to become stronger. "The wind freshened during the morning watch." A **freshening wind** is one that is increasing in strength.

**fresh gale**   *n.* Beaufort scale reading of 8, with winds of 62–74 miles per hour.

**freshwater**   *n.* For purposes of hull displacement, water having a density of 62.428 pounds per cubic foot. Slightly brackish water will meet this definition.

**freshwater king**   *n.* An enlisted person placed in charge of a vessel's evaporators and freshwater supply. Similar to the term "oil king."

**freshwater mark**   *n.* Load line mark for the maximum load allowable in freshwater. See PLIMSOLL MARK OR LINE.

**freshwater stay**   *n.* Schooner term for a wire rope between the foretopmast truck and the lower masthead of the mast next abaft.

**fret**   *v.* To chafe: "As the Sun came up, we discovered our dinghy painter had fretted on the transom."

**fretwork**   *n.* Ornamental three-dimensional handwork used for decorating handrails, and so on, made of small cordage.

**frictional wake**   *n.* The wake caused by the drag of a hull through water.

**friendly ice**   *n.* Primarily a submariner's term for an ice canopy containing large skylights that would permit a submarine to surface.

**friendship sloop**   *n.* Popular workboat used by oystermen along the Atlantic seaboard; it is sloop-rigged with centerboard, strong sheer, clipper bow, and high freeboard at the bow. Originally built in Friendship, Maine.

**frigate (FF)** *n.* (1) A warship designed to operate independently, or with strike, antisubmarine, or amphibious forces. Guided-missile frigates are designated FFG. (2) A high-speed man-of-war of the 17th, 18th, and 19th centuries.

**frigate bird** *n.* A great seabird seen in the tropics with wingspan of about 40 inches, often seen hundreds of miles from land gliding easily with the air currents. Also *man-of-war birds.*

**fringing reef** *n.* A reef attached directly to the shore of an island or landmass. The outer edge is submerged and often consists of algal limestone, coral rock, and living coral.

**frith** See FIRTH.

**frog knot** *n.* The flat, appliquéd knot used to decorate dress uniforms, usually at the buttons. Also *military frog.*

**frogman** *n.* Nickname for a member of an underwater demolition team (UDT) who uses underwater breathing equipment to perform clandestine operations, such as attaching mines to enemy ships.

**front** *n.* The leading edge between two air masses of different temperatures. The full term, rarely heard, is **frontal surface.**

**frost** *n.* The frozen moisture precipitated on surfaces when the surface is below the dew point of the surrounding air and the surface is at or below freezing. See WEATHER.

**frostbiting** *n.* Cold weather dinghy racing.

**frost smoke** *n.* Fog created by very cold air over open water that seems to rise from the water as smoke. Also *sea smoke.*

**Froude's law** *n.* A law and computation dealing with residuary resistance. The residuary resistance of hulls of similar design propelled at the same speed will vary with their displacements. First put forth by the British naval architect and engineer William Froude, 1810–1879. See PROPELLER HORSEPOWER; SPEED-LENGTH RATIO.

**frozen cargo** *n.* Goods frozen before shipment and kept frozen during shipment, such as bulk orange juice concentrate.

**fruit clipper** *n.* Nineteenth-century clipper ships used between Great Britain and Mediterranean ports to carry dried fruits such as figs, raisins, and dates.

**frustration of the adventure** *phr.* Charter party phrase regarding a delay with neither party at fault and not anticipated when the contract was signed. In such a circumstance the contract becomes voidable by either party.

**frustration clause** *n.* Marine underwriter's term that precludes the insured's claiming a total loss of cargo in case an outbreak of hostilities prevents the completion of a voyage.

**frustrum (or frustum)** *n.* Hexagonal navigation marker like a triangle with truncated ends.

**fuel oil** *n.* Heaviest grades of residual fuel burned on vessels at sea for propulsion. Fuel oils are measured by the gallon and by the 42-gallon (U.S.) barrel. The weight of a gallon of fuel oil can be determined by multiplying the weight of a gallon of water at 60°F by the specific gravity of the oil.

**fuel oil certificate** *n.* Authorization granted by the U.S. government to new ships to use fuel oil.

**fuel oil heater** *n.* Equipment used to bring fuel oil up to the optimal temperature for most efficient combustion.

**fuel trunk** *n.* Deck connection through which fuel is taken on.

**full**  *adj.* (1) Used of knots to mean double; a double carrick bend is a full carrick bend. (2) Well rounded, a full bow is a round bow as opposed to a fine or sharp bow.

**full and by**  *adv.* Describes the sailing of a vessel on a course as close to the wind as possible and still keeping the sails full.

**full and change**  See HIGH WATER FULL AND CHANGE.

**full and down**  *adj.* With all cargo spaces loaded and the ship loaded to her load line or down to her marks.

**full cargo**  *n.* Commodity loaded to exceed the registered net tonnage of a vessel. When a full cargo of bagged grain or raw sugar is carried, shifting boards are required as per the Board of Underwriters of New York.

**full depiction of detail**  *phr.* A term used on some large-scale charts to indicate that no details essential to navigation have been omitted.

**full dress**  *v.* A "full rainbow of flags" starting at the waterline and going over the masts and highest spars of a vessel. A ship is **dressed** when national colors are flown from all mastheads and the flagstaff. To "full dress" a ship, the flags from the International Code are arranged with flags starting at the waterline forward then up over the masts and spars and down over the stern to the waterline. On "full-dressed" ships, the national ensign is at the stern staff. On U.S. Naval ships, a flag officer's flag is displayed in the usual manner if aboard. Other signals, such as medical duty, are also displayed as usual. On pleasure vessels, the club burgee or squadron pennant is flown from the forward masthead, and a private signal can be flown from the mainmast. A ship is often "full dressed" on national holidays and other special events.

**full freight**  *n.* The total freight charges of a bill of lading.

**full-rigged**  *adj.* Said of a square-rigged ship carrying three or more masts square-rigged on each. See RIG.

**full rudder**  *n.* As far as the rudder can go, either port or starboard, short of hard rudder when it is in the stops. The maximum rudder angle is established for a class of ships by the designer. The command is "Right full rudder" or "Left full rudder." This is followed by something like "Come to a course of 130°," lest the ship wind up going around in circles.

**full sail**  *n.* All sail set and none reefed. Also *full spread.*

**fundamental frequency**  *n.* The radio frequency from which other frequencies in a chain are derived by harmonic multiplication in a Decca Navigator System.

**funnel**  *n.* A ship's smokestack.

**funnel marks**  *n.* Logos or color schemes painted on funnels to identify a vessel's ownership.

**funnel shroud**  *n.* A smokestack guy.

**furl**  *v.* To secure sails or awnings. Square sails are usually raised before being furled, while fore-and-aft sails are dropped before being furled.

**furling gear**  *n.* Any mechanical device that assists in furling sails.

**furling line**  *n.* A cord used for furling. Cords used on larger sails are usually called **gaskets.**

**furnace**  *n.* A heater or forge for heating plates or shapes for bending.

**furnaceman**  *n.* A person who reheats metal in a gas- or oil-fired furnace for fabrication, rolling, or shaping, who directs a work crew in the proper placing of the metal in the furnace, and who is in charge of maintaining proper temperature in the furnace.

**furniture**   *n.* A marine insurance term that denotes such items of equipment as are necessary for the safe navigation and loading and unloading of the vessel, even though not attached to the vessel, such as slings, hand trucks, and towmotors.

**furring**   *n.* (1) The act of using strips of wood to prepare a frame, beam, or brackets to bring them to an even level or to create airspace. (2) The strips of wood used for furring.

**furrow**   *n.* A closed, linear, narrow, shallow depression on the seafloor.

**futtock**   *n.* One of several pieces of timber that make up a vessel's frames.

**futtock shrouds**   *n.* Rods or served lines that lead either from the upper portion of the shrouds, or from a **futtock band** (or **futtock hoop**) around the lower mast, upward and outward to **futtock plates** inserted through the top to help brace the topmast.

**futtock staff**   *n.* A wooden or steel spar that is seized across the topmast rigging.

# G

**G**   See GOLF.

**gab rope**   *n.* A rope secured to the foot of a headsail to assist in furling. See HOGGING STRAP.

**gaff**   *n.* (1) A spar that extends the head of a four-sided fore-and-aft sail. See RIG. (2) On U.S. Navy vessels, the gaff is the spar on the mainmast (always shorter than the foremast) from which the national ensign is flown.

**gaff-headed**   *adj.* Describes a sail that has the head bent to a gaff; any sail used with a gaff. See RIG.

**gaff jaws**   See PARREL.

**gaff slide**   *n.* Metal device used to slide a gaff sail on the track of the mast.

**gaff topsail**   *n.* A fore-and-aft sail set over the gaff with the foot hanked to the gaff.

**gaff trysail**   *n.* A four-sided boomless storm sail.

**gaff vang**   *n.* A rope from the peak of the gaff to the boat's rail used for controlling the gaff.

**gain the wind**   *phr.* To get upwind of another sailing vessel.

**gale**   *n.* On the Beaufort scale, force 8 with 34–40 knots wind velocity. Also *fresh gale.*

**gall**   *v.* To chafe, used with reference to hawsers and anchor cables and, more common, to poorly lubricated bearings.

**galleass**   *n.* A large, fast galley originally used in 15th-century Venice. It carried three lateen sails and 30 to 40 oars, had raised fighting platforms at bow and stern, and a painted ram at the bow.

**galleon**   *n.* (1) Spanish name for a European ship of the 16th and 17th centuries used as both a merchantman and a warship. A development of the carrack, it had greatly reduced forecastles to improve its ability to sail to wind-

# Gaff Rig

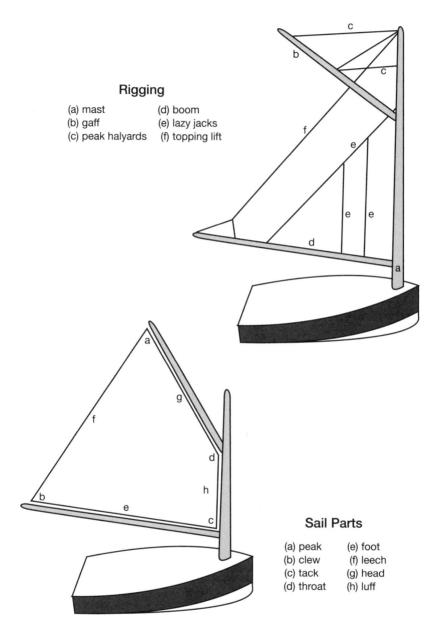

## Rigging

(a) mast      (d) boom
(b) gaff       (e) lazy jacks
(c) peak halyards    (f) topping lift

## Sail Parts

(a) peak     (e) foot
(b) clew     (f) leech
(c) tack     (g) head
(d) throat   (h) luff

ward. (2) A sardine fishing boat used by coastal fishermen off the coast of Spain.

**gallery**   *n.* (1) Balcony similar to a barbette at the stern of a vessel with access by way of stern windows. (2) A partial deck below the flight deck of an aircraft carrier.

**galley**   *n.* (1) A large oared warship or merchantman found in the Mediterranean until the 19th century. Sometimes fitted with auxiliary sails, the galley's primary propulsion was provided by oarsmen. Ships with two banks of oars were **biremes,** and three banks **triremes.** (2) A clinker-built open boat manned by a crew of about a dozen men and used by warships as harbor boats and for short runs by boarding parties. (3) A ship's kitchen. On U.S. Navy ships, it refers to the kitchen in which the crew's mess is prepared; the officers' mess is prepared and served from the wardroom pantry. If the captain has a separate mess, the food is prepared in the captain's pantry.

**galley dresser**   *n.* A cook's worktable.

**galley staysail**   *n.* A fabric wind scoop adjusted to pick up the wind and force it below for ventilation. Also *windsail.*

**galliot** (or **galiot**)   *n.* (1) A small galley, a low flat vessel propelled by both sails and oars, especially in the Mediterranean. (2) Powered coastal barge found in the Netherlands and Germany.

**gallows**   *n.* (1) The framework built on an upper deck for boat stowage and for stowage of spare parts. (2) A permanent support for the main boom of a small sailing vessel.

**gallows** (or **gallows frame**)   *n.* A frame on which the outer end of a boom rests when sails are lowered.

**galvanize**   *v.* To coat a metal with zinc for protection against rust.

**gam**   *n.* Any informal meeting or discussion.

**gam**   *v.* To stop at sea with another ship to get news. This was in the days when ships stayed at sea for months, and it was the only means of getting news. The custom was for the windward ship to back her main yards and the leeward ship to back her foreyards, called **gamming.**

**gammon**   *n.* To fasten the bowsprit to the bow of a vessel. The lashing is called **gammoning.**

**gammoning fish**   *n.* A wooden piece used on top of the bowsprit to which the gammoning is lashed.

**gammoning hole**   *n.* An aperture in the knee of the upper end of the bowsprit through which the gammoning is rove.

**gammon ring**   *n.* The ring that secures a bowsprit to the stem head.

**gangboard**   *n.* The longitudinal timber that runs amidships from the forward platform to the after thwart of an open boat. See GANGPLANK.

**gang cask**   *n.* A freshwater cask larger than a breaker, used for drinking water.

**gangplank**   *n.* A bridge from a ship to a wharf. A gangplank is less elaborate than an accommodation ladder. See BROW.

**gangway**   *n.* (1) The opening in the hull or the place on deck by which people enter and depart from a vessel. Also *gangway port.* (2) By extension, gangway also refers to an accommodation ladder, gangplank, or brow. (3) On sailing ships, bridges between the poop and forecastle were called gangways. (4) Old tankers have **crew's gangways** that go from poop to midship and midship to forecastle so that crews do not have to go on the lower decks when they are awash.

**gangway door**   n. A hinged section of the bulwark that swings away to allow for a gangway.

**gantline**   n. A line through a single block that is secured aloft and used for hoisting sails and rigging. Also *girtline.*

**gantry**   n. A bridgelike frame by which a crane is moved from place to place on ships and on land; the crane moves back and forth on the horizontal bridge while the gantry moves on tracks.

**garble**   v. To sort or cull refuse from usable merchandise, especially tobacco and spices. It is a term most often heard from customs people meaning to separate the unusable portions so that duty is paid only on the usable imported cargo.

**garboard strake**   n. The planking or plating next to the keel. Also *sand strake.*

**garland**   n. A line, piece of cloth, or gasket used to secure a spar while hoisting it.

**garnet**   n. (1) Lines secured to the clews of a course when hauling the courses up to the yards. (2) A purchase secured to the mainstay used for taking cargo in or out of merchant ships.

**gasket**   n. (1) Cordage used to furl a sail. In square-riggers, **arm gaskets** were those used at the extremities, **bunt gaskets** were used in the middle of the yards, and **quarter gaskets** were used between the middle and the ends. (2) An antileak collar or packing material placed between faying surfaces on pipe flanges or steam cylinders. (3) Watertight stripping on a watertight door or hatch cover.

**gas storage**   n. In refrigerated ships, or reefers, the process of storing perishable cargo under pressure in gastight spaces so that the temperature can be kept at 28° to 30° F.

**gat**   n. A natural or artificial channel that extends inland through shoals or banks. This is thought to be from the Dutch *gat,* opening.

**gate**   n. A movable structure at the mouth of a harbor or basin used to prevent the entrance or escape of water to keep boats out of the water in winter and to keep boats afloat at low tide.

**gate ship** (or **boat**)   n. A vessel used to open antisubmarine nets at the mouth of a harbor. A crane fitted with block and tackle is used by the ship to move the heavy net.

**gate valve**   n. A valve with a gate that moves in and out in linear motion to close and open the line on which it is placed.

**gatewood system**   n. A method of longitudinal framing.

**gathering lines**   n. Lines led from the top of a sail track to the sail boom that preclude a sail's falling on deck when it is released. Also *lazy jack.*

**gather way** (or **sternway**)   phr. To gain headway or to go astern.

**gatline**   n. An extra rope rigged aloft especially for hauling a member of the crew up the mast, usually in a boatswain's chair, instead of using a spare halyard.

**gauge**   n. The position of a vessel toward or away from the Sun or wind. With two vessels near each other, the one to weather is said to have the **weather gauge,** while the vessel to leeward has the **lee gauge.** Generally speaking, among fighting sailing ships, a ship with the weather gauge had the advantage because the ship to leeward would be heeled over so that its hull was exposed to gunfire while its own guns were pointed above the deck of the ship with the weather gauge.

**gauge glass**   *n.* Glass tube on a boiler or tank that indicates the level of liquids. Also *sight glass.*

**gaussin error**   *n.* (1) A temporary deviation of a magnetic compass caused by the Earth's magnetic field. (2) A temporary deviation of a magnetic compass caused by eddy currents due to changing lines of force when a ship changes course.

**gear**   *n.* A catchall word that can refer to ropes, blocks and tackles, sails, personal items, and so on.

**gear box**   *n.* The case that encloses a gear train of reduction gears.

**gear buster**   *n.* A race in heavy weather.

**geared bulkhead door**   *n.* A watertight door that can be operated from a station above the bulkhead deck or from a central location for emergency purposes.

**geared capstan**   *n.* Manually operated capstan with an increased mechanical advantage through gears.

**gear pump**   *n.* A type of rotary pump.

**gee radio system**   *n.* A hyperbolic navigation system in Great Britain, similar to loran, that operates in the 20–85 MHz range.

**gel coat**   *n.* The smooth nonporous outer coating of a Fiberglas hull

**general alarm**   *n.* A signal on warships to man battle stations and for other emergencies. The general alarm is by law always a bell alarm so as not to be mistaken for anything else.

**general arrangement plan**   *n.* Schematic diagram showing the basic layout of a ship deck by deck.

**general average**   *n.* A pool of money set up by all parties concerned in a joint venture in proportion to each contributor's cargo interest when a sacrifice has been made in time of peril to save the remainder of the goods. A **general average act** is an extraordinary sacrifice or expenditure intentionally and reasonably made or incurred for the purpose of preserving from peril the property involved in a common maritime adventure. See PROTEST.

**general average loss**   *n.* A loss that is caused by, or is the direct consequence of, a general average act and including a general average expenditure as well as a general average sacrifice. The property on whom the loss falls is entitled to a ratable (general average) contribution from the other interested parties. The matter of general average loss has a long history, dating at least as far as Rhodian law in 900 B.C. when "if in order to lighten a ship, merchandise is thrown overboard, that which has been given for all shall be replaced by the contribution of all."

**general bathymetric chart of the oceans (GEBCO)**   *n.* A detailed chart of the floors of the oceans. First published in 1903 and continually updated.

**general cargo**   *n.* Cargo composed of different and miscellaneous merchandise carried in nonspecialized container units that vary in size and shape, such as boxes, barrels, bales, and crates. **General cargo rates** apply to all items not specifically included in commodities rates lists.

**general mess**   *n.* On U.S. Navy ships, accommodations for feeding all hands except those with their own mess, such as wardroom, chief petty officers' mess, flag mess, and so on.

**general prudential rule**   *n.* The name commonly given to Rule 2(b) of the *Navigation Rules:* "In construing and complying with these Rules due regard shall be had to all dangers of navigation and collision and to any special circumstances, including the limitations of the vessels involved, which may make a departure from these Rules necessary to avoid immediate danger." The courts place great emphasis on the phrase "immediate danger."

**general quarters**  n.  Condition of readiness on U.S. Navy ships when action is imminent; all hands put on battle dress, all battle stations are fully manned, ammunition is put into position for immediate access, and all guns are loaded.

**generating area**  n.  The area in which ocean waves are generated by an air mass.

**genoa**  n.  A large headsail that goes to the top of the headstay and reaches aft beyond the mast to overlap the mainsail. The genoa occupies 130% of the foretriangle. It was developed by Swedish yachtsman Sven Salén in 1927 for a race at Genoa, Italy. Also *genny; jenny; reaching foresail.* See WORKING JIB.

**genset**  n.  An auxiliary generator used on yachts to accommodate microwaves, hair dryers, air-conditioning systems, and so on, ranging from 500 watts to 20 or more kilowatts, and run on gasoline, propane, or diesel fuel.

**gentle breeze**  n.  Beaufort scale reading of 3, with winds of 7–10 miles per hour.

**geo** (or **gio**)  n.  A narrow coastal inlet with high steep banks or cliffs.

**Geoceiver**  n.  The trade name for an antenna receiver capable of receiving signals from the U.S. Navy Satellite Navigation System and capable of computing a three-dimensional antenna location. The system is called NavStar or GPS for global positioning system. The earlier system was Transat. Generically the receivers are called SATNAV sets.

**geocentric latitude**  n.  The angle between the plane of the equator and a straight line to a point on the surface of the ellipsoid that represents the Earth.

**geocentric parallax**  n.  The difference between the apparent position of a celestial body as observed from the Earth's surface and the position if it were seen from the center of the Earth.

**Geochemical Ocean Sections Study (GEOSECS)**  n.  A study of the ocean currents, their general circulation, and their mixing process.

**geodesic line**  n.  The line that represents the shortest distance between two points on a mathematically defined surface. See GREAT CIRCLE; RHUMB LINE.

**geographical coordinate**  n.  Spherical coordinate defining a position on the Earth's surface, usually in terms of latitude and longitude. Also *terrestrial coordinate.*

**geographical plot**  n.  A plot of the movements of one or more vessels relative to the Earth's surface. Also *true plot.*

**geographic graticule**  n.  The system of coordinates using latitude and longitude to identify a position of the surface of the Earth with respect to the **reference ellipsoid.** The geographic graticule is the system most commonly used by aircraft and marine navigators.

**Geographic Long-Range Inclined ASDIC (GLORIA)**  n.  Sonar gear towed behind a survey ship and used for charting the floor of the ocean.

**geographic poles**  n.  Northern and southern ends of the Earth's axis, the **North Pole** and **South Pole,** located at 90° 00′N and 90° 00′S, respectively. See MAGNETIC POLES.

**geographic range of a light**  See VISUAL RANGE OF A LIGHT.

**geographic sign conventions**   *n.* An arbitrarily agreed upon system of signs used by mapmakers, chartmakers, and geodesists. These conventions are as follows: Longitude references are positive east from the Greenwich meridian to 180°, and negative west from Greenwich to 180°. Latitude is positive north of the equator and negative south of the equator. Bearings are measured clockwise, using north as the origin and continuing through 360°. Azimuths are measured clockwise beginning at south and continuing to 360°. Tabulated coordinates, or individual coordinates, are noted N, S, E, or W.

**geological oceanography**   *n.* The scientific study of the ocean floors and margins, which includes description of submarine relief features, chemical and physical compositions of bottom material, interaction of sediments, rocks, and seawater, and the action of various forms of waves in the submarine crust.

**geonavigation**   See PILOTING.

**GEOREF**   See WORLD GEOGRAPHIC REFERENCE SYSTEM.

**george ensign**   *n.* The informal term for the most junior ensign on board U.S. Navy ships. The most senior is called the **bull ensign.**

**geostationary satellite**   *n.* A satellite the orbit of which is fixed relative to the Earth so that it can be used to obtain electronic fixes for navigational purposes.

**geostrophic current**   *n.* An ocean current in which the horizontal flow is balanced by the Coriolis force. Geostrophic currents are calculated by careful measurement of salinity and temperature.

**ghanja**   *n.* A two- or three-masted lateen-rigged craft seen on the Persian Gulf and along the East African coast.

**ghost**   *n.* An unwanted image that appears on a radarscope due to echoes that go through multiple reflections before reaching the receiver.

**ghost**   *v.* To sail with scarcely any wind at all.

**ghoster**   *n.* A large light sail, usually a headsail, that can be used in light air.

**gib**   *n.* A plate or other fitting that holds a member in place or presses two members together, often a wedge or notched piece.

**gibbous Moon**   *n.* (pron. gibus) More than a half Moon but less than full, between first quarter and full quarter. "Gibbous" is also applied to other heavenly bodies when they present a similar appearance.

**Gibson girl**   *n.* A portable radio kept in life rafts. These have been replaced by EPIRBs.

**gig**   *n.* (1) A boat designated for use by the captain of a U.S. Navy ship. See ADMIRAL'S BARGE. (2) A spear used to catch fish. (3) Slang for informal reprimand in the U.S. Navy. "We received a gig from the fleet commodore when we failed to take our station expeditiously."

**gilhoist**   *n.* Vehicle used to transport small landing craft on land.

**gimballing error**   *n.* The error in a gyrocompass caused by the tilting of the gimbal mounting system of the compass that results from the vessel's motion such as rolling.

**gimbals**   *n.* A system of rings and pivots used for keeping horizontal such equipment as compasses, chronometers, and a yacht's galley stove despite the pitching and rolling of the vessel.

**gimlet**   *v.* To turn an anchor around after it has been hauled up to the hawsepipe.

**gin block**   *n.* A metal block with an open shell. It has an iron frame and a metal sheave, used for hoisting cargo or as a lead block.

**gin tackle**   *n.* A tackle made up of a double and triple block with the standing part being fast to the double block. This gives a mechanical advantage of 5.

**gipsey (gipsey head)**   *n.* A drum on a windlass for handling lines. Also *gypsey* or *gipsy.* See CAPSTAN.

**gipsey capstan**   *n.* A powered capstan without provision for hand operating. Also *warping capstan.*

**girder**   *n.* (1) A longitudinal member that supports deck beams, usually supported by pillars. (2) A heavy, main support beam.

**girt**   *v.* To moor with a short mooring line so that the vessel does not swing with the tide or the wind. Heavy ground tackle must be used when it is necessary to girt.

**girth**   *n.* (1) The measurement taken from gunwale to gunwale under the keel at any frame. (2) The measurement at any frame line from the intersection of the upper deck with the hull, around the body of the vessel to the same intersection on the opposite side.

**girtline**   See GANTLINE.

**give way**   *v.* (1) To make room or to stand clear. (2) To begin pulling on the oars of a boat.

**give-way vessel**   *n.* A vessel that in a right-of-way situation must keep out of the way of another vessel and that must, so far as possible, take early and substantial action to keep well clear of the stand-on vessel. The give-way vessel must change course and/or speed as necessary in a right-of-way situation. The term replaces the older expression, *burdened vessel,* which is no longer used in the

*Navigation Rules.* See GENERAL PRUDENTIAL RULE.

**glacier**   *n.* A mass of snow and ice that is continuously moving from higher to lower ground; if afloat, a glacier spreads continuously.

**glacier berg**   *n.* A floating iceberg carved from a glacier.

**glacier tongue**   *n.* An extension of a glacier projecting seaward, usually afloat.

**gland**   *n.* A seal that prevents the leakage of water, steam, or oil at a point along a shaft where it enters a housing and goes through the hull, such as a propeller shaft or a periscope.

**gland steam**   *n.* A gland on a shaft on which steam is used to maintain pressure to prevent air from getting into a turbine and to prevent the steam from escaping from the turbine.

**glass**   *n.* (1) A barometer. "The glass is falling" means the barometric pressure is falling. (2) A telescope (a long glass). To put the glass on a hoist means to use the long glass to read a flag signal. Binoculars are referred to as "glasses." On the quarterdeck, the token gesture for turning over the watch to the relief is for the relief to accept the long glass, the telescope. On the bridge, the same is true with the binoculars.

**global positioning system (GPS)**   *n.* A space-based navigation system developed by the Department of Defense under Air Force management and formerly called NAVSTAR. The GPS employs 18 satellites orbiting 10,900 miles above the Earth; these give three-dimensional coordinates—two horizontal coordinates accurate to within 5 meters and one vertical coordinate accurate to within 1 meter.

**globe lantern**   *n.* A ship's lantern with a 32-point globe-shaped lens used for a white anchor light or for the two red lights indicating the vessel is not under command. See NAVIGATION LIGHTS.

**glory hole** *n.* Facetious name for the lazarette, the stewards' sleeping quarters aft, or the firemen's quarters on steamers. On passenger liners, the steward who maintains the stewards' quarters is called the **glory hole steward.**

**gnomonic projection (or chart)** *n.* A chart used for great circle sailing on which great circles appear as straight lines. A light in the center of a transparent globe would cast a gnomonic projection on a sheet of paper held perpendicular to the plane of the equator. See MERCATOR PROJECTION.

**go about** *v.* To change to the opposite tack by going to windward so that the bow passes through the wind.

**go astern** *v.* Said of a ship, to make sternway or go backward.

**gob** *n.* (1) U.S. civilian slang for a Navy enlisted man, almost never heard in the Navy. (2) British slang for a member of the Coast Guard.

**gob line** See MARTINGALE GUYS.

**go by the board** *phr.* (1) To go over the side or to be carried away when decks are awash. (2) Something that has been forgotten is said to have "gone by the board."

**going free** See RUNNING FREE.

**go large** *v.* To sail with the wind on the quarter.

**gold lace** *n.* The gold stripes on a naval officer's uniform. The more popular expression is **gold braid.** Newly commissioned officers sometimes sprinkle saltwater on their gold lace before going aboard their first ship so that they will not look so brassy new themselves.

**golf** *n.* Phonetic alphabet word for the letter "G." When used as a single-flag hoist, it means "I require a pilot."

**gollywobbler (or golliwobbler)** *n.* A large jib hoisted on the main mast on a schooner, tacked on the foredeck, and sheeted to the end of the main boom.

**gong buoy** *n.* A floating aid to navigation equipped with gongs, usually four, each with its own clapper. Each gong has a different sound.

**goniometer** *n.* A pickup coil that eliminates having to rotate a radio direction finder antenna to determine position.

**goods** *n.* (1) Marine underwriter's term for merchandise that does not include personal effects and ship's provisions. (2) Charter party and bill of lading term that includes everything but deck cargo and live animals.

**good seamanship rule** *n.* Rule 2 (a) of the *Navigation Rules* and similar to the general prudential rule. It mandates that seamen take any precaution that may be required by ordinary practices of seamanship or by the special circumstances of the case. This includes observing the rules of the road; taking the most appropriate action to avoid collisions; taking the best action to lessen the effects of a collision; and proper radio use.

**gooseneck** *n.* A universal joint fitted at the forward end of a boom or cargo boom that secures the boom to the mast.

**gooseneck band** *n.* A fitting on the mast to which is fitted the gooseneck.

**goosewing** *v.* (1) To set only the leeward side of a square sail. When sailing with the wind abaft the beam, the mainsail might be "goosewinged" to prevent blanketing the foresail. (2) To set the main boom on a different side from the fore or mizzen. (3) To heave to a vessel with the bunt of a close-reefed topsail up and only a small triangular stormsail set at the yardarm.

**goosewinged sail**   *n.* (1) A sail that has caught on a spreader during a jibe. This is called a **Chinese jibe** because the full-batten junks frequently do this as a maneuver. (2) Describes the situation where the top of the mainsail on a bermuda-rigged boat is on the opposite side from the bottom of the sail, called such because of the double-jointed appearance of a goose's wing.

**gore**   *n.* A diagonally cut or triangular piece in a sail used to increase the width or give a desirable sweep to the leech, foot, or clew.

**gorge**   *n.* (1) The groove in a sheave of a block. (2) A deposit of solid matter that obstructs a channel or river.

**grab bucket**   *n.*  A double-hinged scoop for handling bulk cargoes and for dredging.

**grab dredge**   *n.* Dredge fitted with one or more cranes with grab buckets.

**grab rods**   *n.* Bent rods welded on a mast or a bulkhead to form a ladder.

**grab rope**   *n.* A line suspended from a boat boom used by occupants to steady themselves while standing in the boat.

**graduated meridians**   *n.* The vertical lines on a chart showing degrees, minutes, and seconds or tenths to assist in measuring latitude and distances. Because the distances between these vary from the top to the bottom on a Mercator projection, distances should be taken at the side of the chart at the parallel at which you are working.

**graduated parallels**   *n.*  Same as graduated meridians, but used for measuring longitude rather than distance.

**graft a rope**   *phr.* To taper the end of a rope and decorate it with a series of half hitches. Also *pointing*.

**grafting**   *n.* Yarns woven to cover a splice or ringbolt or to protect a rope from chafing.

**grain bulkhead**   *n.* A longitudinal grain-tight partition in a lower hold where grain is stored, and fitted to prevent the cargo from shifting.

**grain capacity**   *n.* The cubic-foot capacity of a grain-carrying vessel that includes the spaces between the frames, the top of the ceiling, and the tops of beams—spaces available for loading grain but not for other cargos such as lumber.

**grain certificate**   *n.* A document issued in U.S. ports by a surveyor appointed by the underwriters that certifies that the necessary precautions, such as bulkheads and **shifting boards** to prevent shifting from one side to the other, for the safety of a vessel have been taken.

**grain cubic**   *n.* The amount of grain or liquid such as oil or syrup that a compartment will contain in cubic feet. Grain cubic is always greater than bale cubic because grain and liquids can fit into spaces and between frames where bales cannot. Grain cubic is an entry in a vessel's trim and stability booklet.

**grain feeders**   *n.* Troughs, gutters, holes, or other such contrivances that allow a hold to be filled as completely as possible to reduce voids and prevent shifting; these also insure carrying the maximum cargo in the space available.

**grain-laden vessel**   *n.* Vessel carrying grain in an amount equal to more than one-third the registered tonnage. This is measured at the rate of 100 cubic feet to the **registered ton.** See GRAIN CAPACITY; GROSS REGISTERED TONNAGE.

**grape** *n.* Small cannon shot, primarily antipersonnel, used in the days of sailing warships.

**grapnel** See ANCHOR; GRAPPLING IRON.

**grapple** *v.* To secure a ship alongside another by means of a grappling iron for purposes of boarding.

**grappling iron (or hook)** *n.* A small four- or five-fluked anchor used for dragging the bottom to recover lost items. Also *grapnel anchor.* See ANCHOR.

**graticule** *n.* (1) The network of parallels and meridians created in any chart projection. (2) A scale at the focal point of an optical instrument to aid in the measurement of objects.

**grating** *n.* A wood, steel, or Fiberglas lattice hatch cover that allows light and air below. A **grafting cover** is a steel grating used over coal bunkers to allow ventilation.

**grating platform** *n.* Gratings used in engine spaces with ladders between levels.

**grave** *v.* To clean the bottom of a wooden vessel by using burning reeds and oil-soaked oakum **(breaming),** followed by scraping and tarring. Also *greave.* See GRAVING DOCK.

**graveyard watch** *n.* The watch from midnight to 0400. Also *midwatch.*

**graving dock** *n.* A dry dock in which ships are repaired and hulls cleaned and painted. A graving dock has watergates at the entrance that can be closed so that the dock can be pumped dry for hull work to be accomplished.

**gravity band** *n.* The ring fitted with a shackle on a stocked anchor near the center of gravity used for lifting and stowing.

**gravity tank** *n.* A tank well above the deck into which freshwater is hand-pumped from storage tanks and from which it can flow by gravity when needed.

**gravity wind** See KATABATIC WIND.

**grease ice** *n.* Ice formed when spicules on the surface coagulate to form a soupy layer on the sea surface.

**greaser** *n.* Unlicensed engine room hand who greases and oils bearings and other moving parts.

**great cabin** *n.* In sailing ships, a cabin in the stern for the exclusive use of the captain.

**great circle** *n.* The largest circle that can be drawn on a sphere; a line on the Earth's surface generated by a plane passing through the center of the Earth. A great circle course is the shortest route between two points. Meridian lines are great circles; a ship going north or south can follow the meridian for the most direct route. Latitudes, with the exception of the equator, are not great circles; the shortest course for a destination that lies, for example, southeast, must be calculated in accordance with a great circle formula to determine the shortest distance. Also *geodesic line.* See RHUMB LINE.

**great circle chart** *n.* A chart on which a great circle appears as a straight line or approximately so; a **gnomonic projection.**

**great circle direction** *n.* The horizontal direction of a great circle expressed as angular distance or heading from a reference direction.

**great circle distance** *n.* The length of the arc of a great circle joining two points, ordinarily expressed in nautical miles, which represents the shortest distance between the two points.

**great circle sailing** *n.* The course of a vessel along the arc of a great circle,

# Great Circle

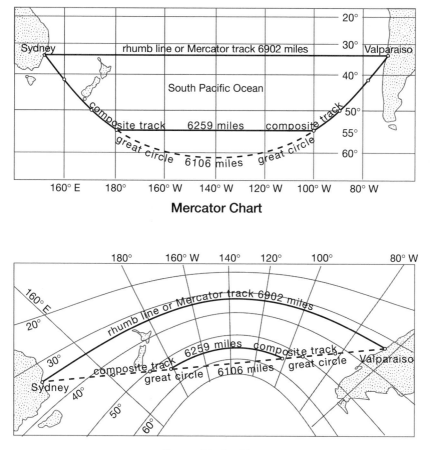

**Mercator Chart**

**Great Circle Chart**

Great circle, rhumb line, and composite
tracks from Sydney, Australia, to Valparaiso, Chile,
as shown on a Mercator projection (above) and
gnomonic projection (below).

the shortest distance between two points. To sail a perfect circle route would require continuous course changes, because a great circle intersects each meridian at a different angle (except when sailing straight along the equator). Since this is not practical, a series of points are established along the course, and the rhumb lines between them are sailed. See LOXODROME.

**Great Lakes**   n.   In the *Navigation Rules*, the Great Lakes refers to the waters of the five Great Lakes—Erie, Huron, Michigan, Ontario and Superior—and their connecting and tributary waters including parts of the Calumet River and Chicago River and the St. Lawrence River as far east as the St. Lambert Lock near Montreal.

**great tropic range**   n.   The difference between the height of tropic higher high water and tropic lower low water.

**greave**   See GRAVE.

**green flash**   n.   The last moment the Sun can be seen on the horizon when atmospheric conditions cause the last rays to bend in such a way that they appear green or blue or, on very rare occasions, violet.

**Greenland Current**   n.   A combination of the East Greenland and West Greenland Currents that comes from the Norway and Irminger Currents.

**green sea**   n.   An unbroken wave that comes aboard in such quantity that it appears green.

**Greenwich**   n.   Site of the Greenwich Royal Observatory established in 1675 by Charles II in England and through which passes the prime meridian.

**Greenwich apparent time (GAT)** n.   The hour angle of the apparent or real Sun with reference to the prime meridian.

**Greenwich civil time (GCT)**   n. Prior to 1952, the term for mean solar time calculated at the prime meridian at Greenwich; Greenwich mean time (GMT). See ZULU TIME.

**Greenwich hour angle (GHA)**   n. The angular distance from the Greenwich celestial meridian westward through 360°. It can be compared to longitude, but they are not the same.

**Greenwich mean time (GMT)**   n. The mean or average solar time measured from the prime meridian at Greenwich. See ZULU TIME.

**gregale**   n.   Name used by the Maltese for a strong northeasterly wind that blows out of the Ionian Sea during the winter.

**gribble**   n.   A shipworm *(Limnoria terebrans)* that is smaller than the teredo but goes back and forth in the wood and is therefore much easier to detect.

**grid**   n.   A series of lines, usually straight and parallel, superimposed on a chart, map, or plotting sheet that serves as a directional reference for navigation. See JAN GRID.

**grid bearing**   n.   A bearing relative to grid north.

**grid course**   n.   A course relative to grid north.

**grid equator**   n.   A line perpendicular to a prime grid meridian at the origin, usually the 90°W–90°E meridian.

**gridiron**   n.   A framework foundation with a cradle built just above the low-water mark. A ship can be floated over it at high tide so that work can be done on it at low tide.

**grid meridian**   n.   Any of the grid lines extending in a grid north-south direction.

**grid navigation**   *n.* A method of navigation using a grid overlay for direction reference.

**grid north**   *n.* An arbitrarily selected reference direction used with grid navigation. The direction of the 180th geographical meridian from north to south is almost universally recognized as the grid north.

**grinder**   See COFFEEGRINDER.

**gripe**   *n.* (1) The forefoot. (2) The ropes used to secure deck gear, especially boats and booms, to prevent their breaking adrift in heavy seas.

**gripe**   *v.* Said of a sailing vessel with excessive weather helm and a tendency to suddenly come into the wind. A crank vessel is thus said to gripe.

**gripe in**   *v.* To secure a lifeboat for sea by using gripes.

**grog**   *n.* Any alcoholic beverage. The original grog, a mixture of half water and half rum dating from about 1740, was named for the Royal Navy's Adm. Edward Vernon, called "Old Grog" because of his use of a grogram cloak. It is interesting to note that George Washington's brother, who built Mount Vernon, named it for the admiral, whom he served under in the West Indies.

**groins**   *n.* A series of jetties built out from a shoreline to protect the shore and to build up the shoreline. Usually a series of groins are constructed perpendicular to the shore.

**grommet**   *n.* (1) A ring of rope made by a single strand laid three times around. (2) Oakum built up with white lead and wrapped around a deck bolt or bulkhead pad eye to prevent leaking. More often called a gasket. (3) A metal ring in a sail or other fabric piece that reinforces the point to be used for heavy-duty work.

**grommet fender**   *n.* A portable protective device for ships' sides made up of fiber grommets covered with cordage.

**groove**   *n.* (1) The proper path to an aircraft carrier when making a perfect approach. The aircraft or pilot is said to be "in the groove." (2) The track of boats whose sails are trimmed so that the vessel is making maximum speed with little steering effort or a power vessel running at maximum efficiency and requiring little steering effort.

**grooved headstay (or mast)**   *n.* A headstay (or mast) with grooves to accept a sail's luff that can be inserted at the base and hauled up by the halyard.

**gross charter**   *n.* A charter party under which the owner retains responsibility for all expenses, including port charges for loading and discharging, stowing, and trimming cargo, as well as pilotage and towing.

**gross freight**   *n.* Freight total without allowance for navigation charges, cost of fuel, and other charges.

**gross registered tonnage (GRT)**   *n.* The volume, expressed in units of 100 cubic feet to the ton, of a vessel's total enclosed spaces below the weather deck and enclosed spaces above the deck including the bridge and accommodations. See TONNAGE.

**ground**   *v.* To run a vessel ashore onto a sandbar. A vessel can be grounded as an act of violence or through negligence, by accident or deliberate grounding. Amphibious craft are said to ground when they hit the beach. See STRAND.

**groundage**   *n.* Port charge for anchoring within the port jurisdiction.

**ground chain**   *n.* Heavy chain used when several anchors are used to secure a permanent mooring.

**ground fog**   *n.* Fog that obscures less than 60% of the sky and does not extend to the base of any clouds.

**grounding clause**   *n.* Marine underwriter's term to distinguish between a "touch-and-go" grounding that is not covered, and stranding, a long-term grounding (that may include destruction of the vessel) that is covered.

**ground log**   *n.* A log used in shallow water when the weight can go to the bottom; the speed over the ground is determined by the speed at which the line pays out. The direction in which the line lies on the top of the water tells the navigator the direction over the ground the vessel is taking. Different from a lead line or a patent log.

**grounds**   *n.* Transverse planking laid over the inner bottom at each frame to which ceiling planking is secured.

**ground swell**   *n.* A swell that passes over a shoal without breaking, but is affected in such a way as to diminish in speed and wavelength and to increase in height.

**ground tackle**   *n.* All of the gear used for anchoring and mooring, exclusive of the deck gear so used. See TACKLE.

**groundways**   *n.* Timbers and planking anchored to the ground and used for slides on either side of a keel for hauling and launching vessels.

**group**   *n.* (1) A number of ships operating together. Two or more groups make up a force. (2) A collection of ciphers.

**group control**   *n.* A system in which all the motor controls of the engine room are grouped into one large master cubicle to make possible repair, start, stop, indication information, and resetting of protective devices in one central location. The group control is usually close to the central operating system.

**group-rate marks**   *n.* Short marks worn on the left sleeve by nonrated U.S. Navy personnel. The marks are white for seamen, red for firemen, and green for airmen.

**growler**   *n.* Small floating piece of ice calved from an iceberg, less than 1 meter above the water. A growler is large enough to cause damage to a hull but smaller than a bergy bit.

**grub beam**   *n.* A laminated frame instead of several short pieces fastened together, forming the curved timber that forms the contour of a round stern.

**guaranteed freight**   *n.* Bill of lading term that guarantees to the shipowner that he or she will be paid even if the goods are not delivered according to contract, provided such failure is caused by forces beyond the shipowner's control.

**guarantee engineer**   *n.* An engine builder's appointed engineer who goes on new vessels. His duty is to verify on the owner's behalf the proper working of the entire plant over a stipulated period after the ship has left the builder's yard.

**guard**   *n.* (1) In U.S. Navy usage, a ship assigned the duty of maintaining a specific service. One ship will be assigned mail guard—that is will send a boat ashore and return to distribute mail to the various ships. Another will have the medical guard—that is a vessel with a doctor aboard, when possible, will be assigned medical guard. (2) A protective device around machinery. (3) A military term for a designated radio channel, "switch to guard."

**guard flag**   *n.* The flag flown by a U.S. Navy ship with a guard assignment that designates the ship's guard, such as medical, radio, mail, and so on.

**guard rail**   *n.* Uppermost rails around a ship's upper deck to help prevent man overboard, the minimum height is prescribed by the nation of registry.

**gudgeon** *n.* (1) A metal eye mounted on the stern of a vessel into which a rudder's pintle, or metal pin, slides to secure the rudder to the ship while enabling it to pivot from side to side. (2) A boss on a sternpost drilled for pins on which a rudder swings. See RUDDER BRACES.

**guest flag** *n.* Blue flag with a white stripe running diagonally from the top of the hoist, and flown only at the starboard spreader or yardarm during daylight hours when a guest is aboard but the owner is not.

**guest rope** *n.* (1) A secondary line used in conjunction with a towline as a backup or a preventer. (2) A grab line to assist small boats approaching a gangway. (3) A line used alongside or astern to secure small boats.

**guest warp** *n.* (1) A line led from the bow of a small boat through a thimble or bull's eye at the outer end of a boat boom used to secure the boat to the boom. The line is led back to the ship so that the boat can be allowed to drift back to the gangway when needed. (2) A secondary line used in conjunction with a towline as a backup or a preventer. (3) A line used alongside or astern to secure small boats. Also *geswarp* or *guesswarp.*

**Guiana Current** *n.* The ocean current that flows northward along the northeast coast of South America. The Guiana Current is an extension of the Atlantic South Equatorial Current that crosses the equator and approaches the coast of South America.

**guide** *n.* (1) Vessel that is designated in a group of U.S. Navy ships, such as a convoy or formation, as the one all others keep station on. (2) The fitting through which control lines lead. A leach line may run through guides to a more readily accessible position, or mechanical engine or steering control wires may run through guides.

**guided-missile vessel** *n.* A frigate (FFG), destroyer (DDG), or cruiser (CG), or submarine (SSG) designed and equipped to launch missiles whose trajectory or course can be altered by either internal or external mechanisms.

**guidon** *n.* (rhymes with ride on) A flag, such as a regimental standard, carried by a military unit or flown from a flagpole in a shore establishment. It represents the unit and is not the national ensign. In a marching unit, the person who carries the company's guidon is also called the guidon.

**guilder (or gulder)** *n.* A tidal phenomenon at certain points on the southern coast of Great Britain that is characterized by low low water. After the first low water there is a slight rise of a few inches and then another recedence to a double low water. These occur, among other places, at Portsmouth and Weymouth, about 4 hours apart.

**Guinea current** *n.* An eastward-flowing extension of the Atlantic Equatorial Countercurrent in the Gulf of Guinea off West Africa.

**gulf** *n.* A part of an ocean or sea that extends into the land, larger than a bay.

**Gulf Coast low-water datum (GCLWD)** *n.* The tide datum used as a chart datum from November 14, 1977, until November 28, 1980, for the coastal waters of the Gulf Coast of the United States. The GCLWD is defined as mean lower low water when the type of tide is mixed, and as mean low water when the type of tide is diurnal. The datum is still found on many, as yet unrevised, charts.

**Gulf Stream** *n.* A clockwise-flowing system of ocean currents that encircles most of the North Atlantic Ocean. The Gulf Stream generally follows the coast of the eastern seaboard of the United States from where the Florida Current and the Antilles Current join north of Grand Bahama Island, past Cape Hatteras where it becomes broader and slower. When the warm Gulf Stream meets the cold Labrador Current at the Grand Banks, a junction is formed, called the **cold wall.** Because the currents do not mix, the Stream continues on toward Europe and then southward. The Gulf Stream or the Florida Current flows at a speed up to 4 or 5 knots off Florida, but reduces speed as it passes Cape Hatteras. The color is a deep indigo and often contrasts sharply with the surrounding water. Vessels that take advantage of the stream as it heads northward can easily find it by checking water temperatures; salinity also changes sharply. At places the Gulf Stream is as much as 100 miles wide at the surface and a mile deep. By taking advantage of the Gulf Stream's flow, large tankers can save as much as $5,000 worth of fuel on a trip up the seaboard. See FLORIDA CURRENT; GYRE; OCEAN CURRENT.

**Gulf Stream system**   *n.* A system of ocean currents that consists of the Florida Current, the Gulf Stream, and the North Atlantic Current.

**gulfweed**   *n.* Any of several branching seaweeds of the genus *Sargassum,* with small air balloons resembling berries that keep it afloat, found in the Sargasso Sea and the Gulf Stream.

**guller**   *n.* A bit used in boatbuilding that makes a countersink for screws and bolts.

**gunar**   *n.* A U.S. Navy ship's electronic fire control system.

**gunboat**   *n.* (1) A light patrol vessel, armed but unarmored and unprotected, used in shallow water, of less than 2,000 tons. (2) The modern gunboat is a small, relatively heavily armed ship for patrol and escort duty.

**gun boss**   *n.* Informal name for the gunnery officer or weapons officer on board a U.S. Navy ship.

**gun captain**   *n.* A petty officer in charge of a gun crew on board a U.S. Navy ship.

**gundeck**   *n.* Covered deck with guns on a sailing warship under the main deck.

**gun director**   *n.* A computer on U.S. Navy ships that keeps information such as course and speed on friendly and enemy ships, as well as wind direction, air and water temperature and velocity, along with roller path and inclination. It passes the information directly to the guns in the form of elevation and bearing, and can fire the guns automatically when ready or on command from the gun boss.

**gunhouse**   *n.* The topside portion of a turret that is above the barbette. Today this is usually called an enclosed gun mount.

**gunkhole**   *n.* A shallow, protected sailing area, deep enough for sailing, protected enough for pleasant anchoring. The term dates from at least 1908, when G. S. Wasson used it in *Home from the Sea* to describe pejoratively a small fishing village.

**gunkhole**   *v.* To cruise and anchor in shallow, protected areas.

**gun layer**   *n.* One who points and trains guns.

**gun mount**   *n.* A structure with one to four guns of up to 5 inches with or without light armor. A gun mount is not as heavy as a turret, which is used for larger guns.

**gunner's mate (GM)**   *n.* U.S. Navy rating for a petty officer who maintains a ship's ordnance and is proficient in its operation. A gunner's mate should not be confused with a **gunner,** who is a warrant officer.

**gunnery officer**   *n.* The officer in charge of a U.S. Navy ship's gunnery department or all ordnance on a ship or in a squadron. On ships with a weapons officer, the gunnery officer is subordinate to the weapons officer. See WEAPONS OFFICER.

**gunning** *n.* Process of forcing caulking material with a putty gun between faying surfaces as a temporary expedient for a watertight compartment when welding or more permanent caulking is not practical.

**gunny** *n.* A coarse, woven fabric made from hemp or jute and used for bags.

**gunport** *n.* A hole in the side of a ship through which a gun projects. Formerly, gunports were closed by **gunport shutters,** which would be removed when guns were put into firing position.

**gun port door** *n.* An opening in side plating used for ventilation and various other purposes, such as a gangway.

**gunroom** *n.* The mess compartment on sailing ships in which the midshipmen ate. It was low in the ship next to the lowest gundeck.

**gunsling** *n.* A looped strap used for hoisting guns on a ship.

**gun tackle** *n.* A purchase that consists of two single blocks with the standing part secured to the fixed block and having a mechanical advantage of three. See TACKLE.

**gunter rig** *n.* A small boat category in which the **gunter,** a quadrilateral sail with a short luff and long leech, is extended above a short mast by a nearly vertical **gunter yard.** The gunter rig evolved from the big rig.

**guntub** *n.* A chest-high steel shield around an open gun mount.

**gunwale** *n.* (rhymes with funnel) (1) The top rail of the side of a boat or ship. (2) The intersection of the shell plating and the weather deck stringer plating. (3) The intersection of the plank sheer with topside planking on wooden ships. (4) The rail of a small boat at deck level.

**gunwale bar** *n.* Angle iron that connects the sheer strake to shell plates (the stringer plates on a weather deck.)

**gunwale rail** *n.* Handhold running along the gunwale of a lifeboat to facilitate climbing aboard from the water.

**gunwale tanks** *n.* Ballast tanks installed just below the weather deck to lower the metacentric height of a vessel when lightly loaded. Also *topside tank.*

**guppy** *n.* World War II submarine fitted with a snorkel, along with other refinements.

**gusset** *n.* A cloth added to a sail or a tarpaulin to increase size or to give additional characteristics.

**gusset plate** *n.* Any tie plate used for fastening frames, beams, and stanchions to other members.

**gust** *n.* (1) A sudden, temporary increase in wind strength. (2) The violent wind or rain squall that accompanies a thunderstorm.

**gut** *n.* A narrow channel connecting two bodies of water.

**gutter ledge** *n.* A bar on a hatchway that supports the hatchcover.

**gutterway** *n.* A sunken waterway on the outer edge of a shelter deck.

**guy** *n.* Wire or rope stays used to hold spars, booms, and so on, in place. See BRACE; PREVENTER; SHEET; SHROUD; STAY; VANG.

**guy span** *n.* A gun tackle with one block shackled to the head of a derrick and the hauling part leading along the derrick down to the deck to a cleat on a mast.

**guzzle**  *n.* A small channel leading into flats that are exposed at low water.

**gybe**  See JIBE.

**gyre**  *n.* (pron. jire) A circular or spiral motion, larger than a whirlpool or eddy. Various currents are described as having a gyre. The gyre of the Gulf Stream is its clockwise course north around the North Atlantic Ocean.

**gyro angle**  *n.* The relative angle measured between the firing ship's keel and the final track of a torpedo, measured clockwise from the bow of the firing ship.

**gyrocompass**  *n.* A north-seeking gyroscope fitted with a compass card, housing, and other pieces of equipment such as the stand, an azimuth ring, and so forth. The gyro compass is not affected by the Earth's magnetic field or the ship's own electromagnetic forces. For that reason corrections are not necessary for variation and deviation. A magnetic compass is still carried on all ships, however. PGC stands for per gyrocompass. See GYROSCOPE.

**gyrocompass repeater**  *n.* A device with a compass card driven remotely by a gyrocompass. The helmsman watches a gyrocompass repeater, the deck officers use repeaters on the bridge wings and elsewhere, and the captain's sea cabin and main cabin have repeaters, as do other remote installations on U.S. Navy ships.

**gyro error**  *n.* Error in the presentation of the gyrocompass, expressed in degrees east or west, indicating the direction in which the axis of the compass is offset from true north.

**gyropilot**  *n.* An automatic steering device connected to a repeater of the gyrocompass and designed to hold a ship's course without a helmsman. Also called an *autopilot,* especially on pleasure craft, although on pleasure boats the autopilot is usually operated from a magnetic compass.

**gyroscope**  *n.* An electrical motor with a rotor so adjusted that it will maintain its axis in the geographical meridian. The gyrocompass that is controlled by the gyro is oriented to true north and maintains that adjustment as long as the rotor continues to spin.

**gyroscope, pendulous**  *n.* Is one whose axis of rotation is weighted to remain horizontal. The pendulous gyroscope is the basis for nonelectronic gyrocompasses.

**gyroscopic inertia**  *n.* That property of a gyroscope that resists any force that tends to change the gyroscope's plane of rotation.

**gyroscopic stabilizer**  See STABILIZERS.

**gyrosextant**  *n.* A sextant equipped with a gyroscope to indicate the horizontal axis.

# H

**H** See HOTEL

**hachures** *n.* The short lines on a topographic map or nautical chart that represent relief and show the degree and direction of a slope. The inward-pointing **ticks** around the edge of a closed contour indicate a depression.

**hack watch** *n.* A good-quality watch with a sweep second hand that can be stopped, used by the navigator when taking sights to get the exact time and to compare it with the chronometer's time. Also *deck watch.*

**Hague Convention (1907)** *n.* A meeting of representatives of 44 countries that agreed on 13 protocols relating to the status of merchant ships at the outbreak of hostilities, conversion of merchant ships to warships, rights of capture in a naval war, and the creation of an international prize court. These were significant in their contribution to the body of maritime law.

**Hague Rules (1921)** *n.* Proposals for the codification of maritime law especially regarding steamships. The rules proposed at the 1921 conference related to the responsibilities, rights, and immunities of carriers under bills of lading as well as terms of charter parties. Out of this grew the International Conference on Maritime Law held at Brussels in 1922, that recommended to the represented governments the adoption of the Hague Rules of 1921. These were widely accepted among the maritime nations.

**hail** *v.* (1) To call a vessel. Either a small boat or a large ship coming alongside hails the other vessel. The navy coxswain of a gig hails the ship being approached by announcing *"Pinafore, Pinafore,"* which tells the deck officer of the ship that the captain of *Pinafore* is arriving. In this way, the captain of the ship being visited can be alerted, and proper honors can be rendered when the visiting captain comes aboard. (Honors begin when the visitor's hat reaches the level of the quarterdeck.) (2) To come from a port in which a vessel is registered. Today, when ships are often registered under a flag of convenience such as Panama, but actually sail out of, for example, San Francisco the hailing port becomes confusing.

**hailing station** *n.* The position at a harbor entrance where the harbormaster calls incoming traffic and outgoing traffic to discuss berthing arrangements and destination ports. This was formerly done by flag hoists or flashing lights using the Morse code, but today it is done by radio.

**hair bracket** *n.* An ornamental scroll at the upper end of the railing at the bow above the head and below the figurehead.

**half-beam** *n.* Deck beam interrupted by a hatch or other opening, as opposed to a through beam.

**half board** *n.* The maneuver to slow a sailboat when the helmsman luffs the sails by heading into the wind and then heads off without changing tack. This was also known as a **pilot's luff** because it was used to allow a pilot to step aboard the ship to be piloted or to leave the ship he had piloted.

**half-breadth plan** *n.* A plan or top view of half a ship divided longitudinally showing outlines of horizontal sections of the hull from main deck to keel. It also shows waterlines, bow and buttock lines, and diagonal lines of construction. Also *waterline plan.*

**half deck** *n.* (1) A partial deck located between decks. (2) A deckhouse located aft of the mainmast in which were quartered the carpenter, sailmaker, and their apprentices.

**half-decked** *adj.* A small-boat term meaning to have a boat partially decked and partially open.

**half gale** *n.* A force 7 on the Beaufort scale, a wind of 28 to 33 knots. More modern usage is **near gale.**

**half hitch** *n.* An underhand loop used to temporarily bend a line to a post or piling. See KNOT.

**half-mast** *n.* A sign of mourning when the national ensign is flown short of the top of the staff, usually about two-thirds of the distance to the top. The procedure in hoisting a flag to half-mast is to raise it to the top of the staff and then lower it to its half-mast position; in lowering the flag from its half-mast position, it is again raised before it is lowered.

**half model** *n.* A model of one side of a ship showing plate lines. Also *half-block model.*

**half port** *n.* The upper or lower part of a port that is divided in the middle.

**half sheave** *n.* A small-boat term for a groove at the point where a halyard rides on a mast that reduces the friction. A half sheave is often found at the masthead, but is also found near the gooseneck.

**half-siding** *n.* A shipbuilding term used with welded construction meaning the distance from centerline to the knuckle of the flat keel.

**half speed** *adv.* A merchant-vessel term meaning one-half standard speed. A similar order is used in the Royal Navy. In the U.S. Navy, the term is not used. See SPEED, STANDARD.

**half-tide basin** *n.* A harbor in which it is practical to keep the tidal gates open for a given length of time after high tide to accommodate late arrivals as long as they can clear the outer sill.

**half-tide level** *n.* The tidal datum that is halfway between mean high water and mean low water. Mean sea level only occasionally coincides with half-tide level, the variation being between 3 and 6 centimeters. Also *mean tide level.*

**halyard (or halliard)** *n.* A line used to hoist a yard, gaff, sail, or flags, as in jib halyard, main halyard, or signal halyard. The word is a corruption of haul yard.

**halyard rack** *n.* A frame for holding a halyard with the running part coiled in such a manner that it is ready for running without kinking.

**halyard tackle (or purchase)** *n.* A halyard fastened to a yard for hoisting or lowering.

**hambroline** *n.* Three-yarn, right-hand-laid, untarred hemp, tightly laid, used for lacing sails to yards on small craft. It is the same as "roundline" except that the latter is left-hand laid. Also *cod line.*

**hammerbox** *n.* A noisemaker used for sweeping acoustic mines.

**hammock** *n.* A sailor's canvas berth hung from deck beams from each end. **Hammock battens (or euphroes)** at each end keep the hammock from folding onto itself. The lines at each end are called **hammock clews.**

**hance** *n.* A curved rise. A step or curved rise, for example, at a poop deck or forecastle deck.

**hand** *n.* (1) A side of a vessel, as in lee hand or starboard hand. (2) A sailor, such as a deck hand or a member of the crew. "A good hand in the engine spaces." "All hands, fall in on the free-board."

**hand** *v.* (1) To bring in (a sheet or sail). (2) To furl (a sail). The ability to hand, reef, and steer was traditionally considered the A-B-C's of seamanship.

**hand-bearing compass** *n.* A small portable compass suitable for carrying about in the hand or pocket and so fitted as to be convenient for taking bearings.

**hand hole** *n.* An access opening in a bulkhead, deck, or boiler for inspection and cleaning and usually covered by a plate when not in use.

**handicap rule** See RATING RULE.

**hand lead** *n.* A small lead weight on a lead line used for determining depth. It can be armed with tallow or wax so that it will pick up a sample of the bottom to tell the character of the bottom. The ancient Greeks and Romans used lead lines with hand leads that were very similar to the ones found in chandleries today.

**hand rope** *n.* Any line on a lifeboat or raft or along a brow used for steadying purposes. Also *grab rope.*

**hand signals** *n.* Signals used on sailboats when shouting cannot be heard or is not desirable. To point forward means to ease the sheet; to point aft means to trim the sheet; to point aloft means to raise the sail; to point down means to lower a sail; to point upwind means to head up more; to point to leeward means to head down more; an open palm means avast, stop; hand up, heave in; hand

down, slack away; crossed wrists overhead, belay.

**handsomely** *adv.* Deliberately and carefully. "Coxswain, bring your boat alongside handsomely, and don't scuff our fresh paint."

**handy** *adj.* (1) Said of a commercial vessel that has considerable latitude in where it can trade because of the draft and also because of its ability to unload itself. (2) Description for sailboat that tacks easily, does not easily get in irons.

**handy billy** *n.* (1) A small portable force pump, usually manually operated. (2) A tackle comprising a single and a double block. Also *jigger; watch tackle.*

**hangar deck** *n.* The deck below the flight deck of an aircraft carrier where aircraft are parked and maintained.

**hanging compass** *n.* Compass designed to be suspended or fixed in the overhead and read from beneath.

**hanging locker** *n.* A small-boat term that describes a locker in which clothing can be hung, perhaps even to dry.

**hanging pendant** *n.* The pendant that holds the anchor to the belly strap when an anchor is being carried out in a boat.

**hanging stage** *n.* Platform hung on the side of a vessel for workers to use while working on the ship's sides.

**hank** *n.* (1) A coil of line or cordage. (2) A fitting to which the luff of a sail is fastened so that it can be hoisted and lowered on a stay or mast. In earlier days, hanks were wooden or iron rings that secured staysails to stays. In more modern times, hanks refer to the spring-loaded devices that are sewed to the sails to bend on the sail, especially a headsail to the headstay. The slides on the mast and boom track are not hanks, but **cars.**

**hank** *v.* (1) To fasten or bend on a sail using hanks. (2) To coil a line. "Hank the main halyard and put it on a cleat.

**Hannah Cook** *n.* A disparaging term used by seafaring people along the coast of New England and the Maritimes. To say that "something doesn't amount to a Hannah Cook" means it is worthless. The term is thought to have come from a "hand and a cook," the crew of a very small coasting vessel.

**harbor** *n.* A restricted body of water with some shelter and reasonably good holding ground.

**harbor chart** *n.* Charts with scale larger than 1:50,000 used for harbors and smaller waterways.

**harbor charter** *n.* A contract for the hire of a harbor craft such as a lighter or a harbor tug.

**harbor dues** *n.* Local charges against vessels entering a harbor or port that include tonnage dues, anchorage dues, buoyage dues, and so on. Harbor craft are usually exempted from harbor dues.

**harbor gasket** *n.* A French sennit used to lash a sail to a yard, to keep it furled in port.

**harbor line** *n.* A boundary along a waterway or on the shore surrounding a harbor landward of which the landowners have filling and developing privileges. See RIPARIAN.

**harbormaster** *n.* (1) An official who oversees harbor traffic and enforces regulations under a port director. Also *port captain*. See CAPTAIN OF THE PORT. (2) See DOCKMASTER.

**harbor pilot** *n.* A person whose knowledge of local channels and currents qualifies him to assist ships entering port. In the United States, Great Britain, and in other major international ports pilots are regulated by the government and

require extensive expertise. This is not true in countries where nepotism and political loyalty and patronage take precedence over other qualifications.

**harbor police** *n.* Representatives of the harbormaster in some ports, who board a ship on arrival or soon thereafter to obtain all pertinent information about the vessel and crew and to impart local information, rules, and regulation.

**harbor signals** *n.* The body of signals used locally in a port that are developed by the pilots, quarantine officials, and customs officials regarding their own duties and assignments, tide signals, and weather signals. With the extensive use of hand-held VHF radios, these are becoming obsolete.

**harbor tug** *n.* Tugs used in harbors, estuaries, and roadsteads as lighters, towing vessels, and mooring vessels, as opposed to ocean tugs that leave the harbor for open seas.

**hard** *n.* (1) A firm pad in a tidal harbor or basin where smaller vessels may tie up for cleaning and painting the bottom during low water. (2) A sloping jetty or road down to the water's edge for use in landing and putting in small craft. (3) A section of firm beach prepared for amphibious maneuvers.

**hard** *adv.* All the way over; one puts the tiller or rudder hard up or hard down (or over).

**hard alee** *(1) interj.* The command to put the helm over to leeward to come about. This is preceded by the command "Ready about." (2) *adj.* Describes the position of the tiller all the way over away from the wind, to leeward, all the way down. Same as hard down. The term refers to the position of the tiller, not the rudder or wheel (helm).

**hard and fast** *adj.* Describes a vessel that is hard aground on rocks or a firm shoal or beach.

**hard astarboard (or aport)**  *adj.* or *adv.* Position of wheel when it is turned as far as possible to the right (or the left).

**hard a-weather**  *adv.* The position of a tiller when thrown all the way over to weather (the windward side), or up, in order to go more downwind. In a vessel with a wheel the term would lead to confusion.

**hard down**  *adj.* The position of the tiller when it is as far to leeward as possible. See HARD OVER.

**harden (up)**  *v.* To pull in a sheet to make a sail harder to make it possible to get closer to the wind.

**hardening up**  *n.* A riveting term for the practice of getting a firmer set on the rivet point by giving the rivet a heavy blow after it has partially cooled.

**hard-lay**  *adj.* A cordage term denoting a sharper angle in the lay than the standard angle of twist. A hard-lay rope is not as strong nor as flexible as a standard-lay rope, but because it is more compact it does not easily absorb moisture.

**hard over**  *adj.* Said of a wheel or tiller when it is all the way to windward or to leeward. "The helm is hard over."

**hard patch**  *n.* A plate riveted to cover a hole or break.

**hardtack**  *n.* Hard biscuits baked without salt and dried in a hot oven or kiln. This was a staple provision for ships on long sea voyages before refrigeration.

**hard up**  *adj.* Said of a tiller as far to windward as possible to point the vessel downwind. "Put your helm hard up." When the tiller is hard up and the vessel still won't respond, you are in peril, thus the expression "hard up" meaning short of money.

**harmattan**  *n.* An easterly wind during the summer months of December, January, and February on the west coast of Africa between 30°S and the equator.

**harmonic constants**  *n.* Tidal constants composed of amplitudes and epochs of the **harmonic constituents,** the harmonic elements in the mathematical model for a single tide-producing force and in formulas for the tides. See NON-HARMONIC CONSTANTS.

**harness**  *n.* Chest and shoulder straps with a tether leading to a stanchion or a suitable spar, used for safety in heavy weather.

**harness cask**  *n.* A large cask filled with freshwater and divided into two parts, used on ships to leach the salt out of salt beef; the beef is put into one section for a few days and then in the other section to continue the process. The term was taken from the harness maker's tub of the same construction.

**harpings**  *n.* The forward parts of a vessel that encompass the bow and that are thickened to withstand the stresses on the bows caused by plunging in heavy seas and the strain on the headstays.

**harpins**  *n.* Temporary battens that are a continuation of the straight or almost straight ribbands forward and aft used during hull construction to hold cant frames in position until outside planking or plates can be worked.

**harpoon**  *n.* A missile for catching marine mammals and large fish; it consists of a barbed point and a shank with a long rope attached.

**Harpoon**  *n.* Surface-vessel-launched missile with conventional warhead used against surface targets. Modified versions can be fired from submerged submarines and aircraft. The range is 60 miles with 500 pounds.

**harpoon log**   *n.* The trade name for an early speed log; the entire mechanism, including rotator, gears, and indicator dial, was thrown into the water to be towed astern. The instrument was then hauled back aboard to be read. Because of the awkward procedure, the taffrail log with its continuous reading soon replaced the harpoon log.

**Harter Act**   *n.* An act passed by Congress in 1893, which, along with the Carriage of Goods by Sea Act of 1936, is the basis of litigation on bills of lading, loss of goods at sea, and so on. The Harter Act's chief points were that all clauses purporting to relieve the carrier of liability for negligence in care and custody of cargo are void, and that no clause is given effect that lessens the obligation of the carrier to stow and care for cargo properly. In order to collect damages, the cargo owners must prove negligence; if they cannot, the ship is excused.

**hasp**   *n.* A hinged, steel strap used to fasten the wedge holding the bowsprit in place.

**hatch**   *n.* (1) A watertight cover over an opening or hatchway that gives access to spaces below. (2) An opening in a deck that makes possible going from one level to the next. This usage is frequently heard, but the first definition is more common. The **wake** of a hatch is the area immediately below a hatch opening.

**hatch bar**   *n.* A bar by which wooden hatches are fastened.

**hatch battens**   *n.* Flat bars that are wedged against hatch coamings to secure tarpaulins or hatch hoods.

**hatch beam**   *n.* Portable support for a cargo hatch cover. Also *strongback*.

**hatch boom (or derrick)**   *n.* A cargo boom used with a yard boom. The hatch boom is used until the cargo is above deck level and then the yard boom takes the load to take it over the side. For loading operations, the procedure is reversed.

**hatch carling**   *n.* Longitudinal planking or bar at the side of a hatchway and beneath the coamings for hatch beam fastenings.

**hatch checker**   *n.* A clerk assigned to record cargo going into a hold.

**hatch coamings**   *n.* The two raised longitudinal pieces on a hatchway on which the watertight hatch cover fits. The two athwartship pieces are called head ledges.

**hatch cover**   *n.* A watertight cover that fits over a hatch.

**hatch davit**   *n.* A small, usually portable, davit used for working with lightweight cargo in a hold.

**hatch foreman**   *n.* A longshoreman responsible for a specific hatch and the efficient loading and stowage in that hold.

**hatch grating**   *n.* A wooden or steel grating used over a hatch to allow ventilation below; if used on a weather deck, it is fitted so that the watertight hatch cover can be lowered over the grating.

**hatch hood**   *n.* A water-resistant fabric cover placed over a hatch to keep out spray and rain.

**hatch-locking bar**   *n.* A bar run through two deck fittings on both sides of a hatch and padlocked to prevent unauthorized entrance. When bonded cargo is placed in a hold, the customs seal is placed on the bolt holding the hatch-locking bar.

**hatch mast**   *n.* A spar near a hatch used for cargo handling.

**hatch stanchion**   *n.* Portable stanchion for safety lines used at a hatch to keep personnel from accidentally falling into the hold.

**hatch tackle**   *n.* A whip over a hatch used for handling cargo. Also *sciatic stay.*

**hatchway**   *n.* (1) A deck opening for access below. See HATCH. (2) A large opening in a deck, usually square, through which cargo is lowered and hoisted.

**hatch whip**   *n.* Cargo-handling block and tackle on a spar used for handling cargo at a hatch.

**haul**   *v.* (1) To move a vessel from one part of a harbor to another; "to shift" is the more usual phrase. (2) To pull on a rope, line, or sheet, used with a preposition, such as "to haul in" on a line, "haul up" on a line, and so on. (3) Said of the wind when it changes in the clockwise direction. The wind is hauling, or the wind has hauled. Also to veer. To haul is not to be confused with backing, which means that the wind has gone counterclockwise without regard to the ship's heading.

**haul around**   *v.* To brace all yards at the same time when coming about.

**haul down**   *phr.* To lower a flag or sail.

**haul forward**   *phr.* Said of the wind when it changes direction nearer a vessel's head. Also *draw ahead.*

**hauling line**   *n.* (1) A small line thrown to another vessel or to a wharf attendant and used to pull a heavier line. More often called a **heaving line.** (2) A small line carried aloft by personnel working in the rigging; the line can be dropped to the deck to bring up additional items such as screwdrivers and wrenches. (3) Light line on the selvage of a net.

**hauling-off buoy**   *n.* A well-anchored buoy placed mid-stream for the purpose of assisting vessels departing a dock. When a vessel leaves a berth or anchor-

age, a line is led to the buoy to pull the bow or stern in the direction of the buoy.

**hauling part**   *n.* The free end of a tackle fall that is laid hold of when hauling in; that part of a tackle on which the pulling force is exerted. See STANDING PART.

**haul in with**   *phr.* To change course so as to head for a point of land or a point on a chart.

**haul off**   *v.* (1) To beat closer to windward to get away from a lee shore or another vessel. (2) To alter course to get farther away from a place or vessel. (3) The sailor's term "to haul off and knock him down" means to back off far enough to give room for a good healthy swing.

**haul out**   *v.* (1) To move out of a station in a formation. (2) To pull from the water whether personnel or cargo.

**haul to the wind (or to windward)**   *phr.* To bring the wind from aft to a point closer to the bow. In the same sense you will hear someone say to **haul your wind,** meaning to maneuver a sailing vessel so that the wind is more forward.

**haul up**   *v.* (1) To bring a vessel closer to the wind or to come closer to the wind. (2) To bring a vessel closer to the wind or to come closer to the wind when a vessel has been to leeward of the desired course.

**haven**   *n.* A harborage or anchorage, a port, a place of refuge accessible at all tides and weather.

**hawk**   *n.* A colloquial name for a wind indicator at the top of a mast.

**hawse**   *n.* (1) The section of the bow where the hawseholes and hawsepipes are found. (2) The arrangement of anchor cables when the anchors are secured. (3) The water between the ship and her anchor when the anchor is down.

**hawse** *v.* To caulk planking using tarred oakum; for this job, a large maul, called a **beetle,** and a wedge are used.

**hawse** *v.* To pitch and ride uneasily at anchor from being head to wind. "We hawsed badly through the night." Also *to horse.*

**hawse ahead** *v.* To move a vessel forward by hauling the cable.

**hawse bag** *n.* A bag of oakum that was kept near the hawsepipe to be placed in the hawsehole to prevent water from coming in during storms.

**hawse block (or plug)** *n.* A wooden plug used to close the hawsehole in rough weather.

**hawse bolster** *n.* A rounded piece on hawseholes to ease chafing of the anchor cable.

**hawse buckler** *n.* A steel cover used to prevent water from entering a ship by way of the hawsepipe.

**hawse-fallen** *adv.* To be anchored or moored to the sea so that the seawater comes up through the hawseholes. "We rode hawse-fallen with icy seas cascading across the forecastle head."

**hawsehole** *n.* An opening in the bow into which a hawsepipe is fitted.

**hawsepipe** *n.* The steel casting or fabricated steel through which the anchor cable runs at the bow. The actual hole created by the casting is called a hawsehole. In rough weather it was good seamanship to cover the hole because the hawsepipe became a nozzle; when the bow bit into a wave, a large volume of water would shoot up through the hole. The practice is less common today because the watch section is not out on the open deck as a rule.

**hawser** *n.* A cable or rope heavy enough for use in warping, towing, and mooring. Some authorities are more specific and say that a hawser is 5 inches or more in circumference, three-strand, plain-laid.

**hawser-laid rope** See PLAIN-LAID ROPE.

**hawser thimble** *n.* Steel or galvanized iron thimble large enough for a hawser to be spliced around it.

**head** *n.* (1) The toilet on a vessel. Today the term is often used to mean the space in which the toilet, basin, and other conveniences are found. The use of this definition comes from the days when the crew relieved themselves standing on the wooden grating near the water's edge at the bow or head of the ship. To go to the head was quite literally to go to the head of the ship. See BEAKHEAD. (2) The top edge of a gaff or square sail. (3) The top corner of a three-cornered sail, between the luff and the leech. (4) A vessel that draws more water forward than aft is said to be **by the head.**

**head** *v.* Said of the wind when it moves more toward the bow. This often means that you can no longer lay the mark. See HEADER.

**headache ball** See OVERHAULING WEIGHT; PICKLE.

**headboard** *n.* (1) A stiffener sewn into the head of a sail to reinforce the cringle. (2) The first bulkhead in the bow of a wooden ship.

**head cheek** *n.* A knee worked above and below a hawsehole in the angle formed between the stem and the planking.

**head cringle** *n.* The hole through which a halyard is rove in the peak of a quadrilateral sail, the upper corners of a square sail, and the head of a triangular sail.

**head down** *n.* To steer a boat away from the direction of the wind and more to leeward.

**head earing** *n.* A line used to secure one of the two upper cringles of a square sail to the yard.

**header** *n.* (1) A wind unfavorable to sailing in the desired direction when sailing close-hauled, a wind shift toward the bow. The opposite is a **lift.** (2) A pipe that serves as a connection for two or more smaller pipes. (3) A reserve water tank that serves as a terminal for boiler tubes. (4) A construction member added for local strength and not parallel to main strength members of a vessel. A header is used to distribute the load to other members when a main strength member has been cut or is going to be cut.

**heading** *n.* The direction in which a ship is pointing, usually expressed in degrees clockwise from north. Also *ship's head.* See COURSE.

**heading flasher** *n.* The line on an illuminated dial of a planned position indicator indicating the ship's heading on the bearing dial.

**headland** *n.* A point of land or promontory extending into a body of water.

**head ledges** *n.* The two athwartship pieces of a hatchway on which a hatch or hatch cover fits. The longitudinal pieces are called hatch coamings.

**headline** *n.* A mooring line secured forward of the vessel's pivot point.

**head off** *v.* To steer a vessel away from the wind. See HEAD DOWN.

**head on situation** *n.* A situation in which two vessels are meeting on a reciprocal or nearly reciprocal course so as to involve risk of collision.

**head outhaul** *n.* The halyard used to haul out the head of a gaff sail along the gaff.

**head rail** *n.* A curved rail that extends from the figurehead to the bow of a ship.

**head reach** *n.* The progress forward made by a vessel with greatly reduced canvas with no propulsion applied whether power or sail, coasting.

**headroom** *n.* The distance between decks. On yachts, **full headroom** is generally understood to mean a little more than 6 feet.

**head rope** *n.* The boltrope at the head of a sail.

**headsail** *n.* Any sail set forward of the mast and bent on the headstay and including any set on the bowsprit, stemhead plate, or jibboom. Headsails are classified according to the area of the foretriangle occupied by the sail. From smallest to largest, a spitfire occupies 35% of the triangle; a storm jib 60%; a working jib 100%; a lapper 100%; and a genoa 120%.

**head sea** *n.* A sea that is running in a direction approximately opposite to a ship's heading. The opposite is a following sea.

**headsheets** *n.* Lines or sheets used to control sails forward of the mast.

**headstay** *n.* The stay that is led from the masthead or near the masthead forward to the bow of a sailboat to support the mast and counter the backstay, and used for setting headsails. Also *forestay.*

**heads up** *interj.* A warning to watch out or clear a passage. Often the expression is used by a petty officer or junior officer to clear the way for a senior officer. The phrase is also used to alert personnel to overhead dangers such as cargo hooks, piping, swinging cargo.

**head tenon**   *n.* The square section at the masthead to which is fitted the masthead cap.

**head tide**   *n.* A tidal current that flows opposite to the heading of a vessel.

**head to wind**   *phr.* A vessel proceeding with its head directly into the wind.

**head up**   *v.* To luff or head toward the wind so as to luff, or to steer more toward the direction from which the wind is coming.

**headwaters** (or **headstreams**)   *n.* The waters from which a stream or river rises.

**headway**   *n.* Forward progress of a vessel over the ground. Some authorities simply define headway and its opposite, sternway, as movement through the water, but most authorities consider headway and sternway as meaning progress in a given direction. To say that you were making headway when you were actually going backward would be confusing. "Our log shows we are moving through the water at 3 knots, but because of the current we are making no headway; actually we are making sternway."

**head wind**   *n.* A wind coming from directly ahead of a vessel. Opposite of fair wind. Also *foul wind.*

**head yards**   *n.* Foremast yards on a full-rigged vessel.

**heart**   *n.* (1) A circular or heart-shaped wooden block with a single hole at the center, used with hemp rigging for extending shrouds and stays. When possible, hearts are made from *lignum vitae.* (2) A loosely twisted strand that forms the core of a shroud-laid rope in the center of a wire rope.

**heart shackle**   *n.* A three-way device used for making towing bridles. Also *fish plate.*

**heating coils**   *n.* Coils located on the bottoms of a ship's fuel oil tanks and in cargo fuel tanks to lower the viscosity for easier pumping.

**heave**   *v.* (1) To throw. "Heave that bucket over the side." "I hove (or heaved) it over last night. (2) To pull a rope by mechanical means, as opposed to hauling a rope manually. (3) To rise or fall, said of the vertical rise and fall of a vessel as it rides the waves, not to be confused with pitch, roll, yaw, sway, or surge.

**heave around**   *v.* (1) To put a capstan or windlass into operation as with a cable. (2) To start working hard. "Boats, I want to see the men heaving around when the new captain comes aboard this morning."

**heave away**   *interj.* Order to haul on the capstan.

**heave down**   *v.* (1) To careen a vessel. (2) To sail at an excessive heel, due to carrying too much sail for the wind.

**heave of the sea**   *phr.* The scend of the waves. The action of the sea that throws a vessel to leeward.

**heaver**   *n.* (1) A short stick used for tightening a rope or strap. (2) A rocker arm used in connection with a brake windlass to give leverage for turning the windlass barrel.

**heave short**   *v.* To bring in the anchor cable to a point that it is not straight up and down, but at the short stay. It is used when you want to be ready to weigh anchor when given the word, but when you need to hold your position until the command comes.

**heave taut**   *v.* To put a strain on a line or chain. To take a strain and hold it.

**heave the lead**   *phr.* (pron. led) To cast the lead to determine the depth of the water.

**heave the log**    *phr.* To throw a log chip over the side to determine a vessel's speed.

**heave to**    *v.* To hold a vessel in place or as nearly so as possible. On a sailing vessel this is done by bringing the head into the wind, securing the mainsail on or nearly on the centerline, and backing the headsail with the rudder over as if to come about, so as to keep the headsail backwinded; the vessel is then allowed to take its own course, which is usually a beam reach at about one knot. Vessels with power heave to with the use of wind, current, and engines. A power vessel or a sailing vessel may heave to to wait for a bridge to open. In heavy weather, heaving to in a sailing vessel offers remarkable relief from the action of the sea. Heaving to can also be accomplished by bringing the stern to the wind, but the action of heavy seas on the rudder can lead to emergency rudder problems. A large ship may heave to either by heading into the seas and just turning its engines enough to hold its steerageway or, in more severe conditions, by heading down sea and reducing power to a minimum level. If the shaft is not turning, this maneuver is called **lying ahull.** Past tense and past participle is **hove to:** "We hove to" or "We were hove to."

**heave up**    *v.* To hoist or raise an object such as an anchor.

**heaving line**    *n.* A light line bent to a heavier line and with a weight or monkey's fist at the end. The heaving line is thrown to a pier or another vessel, and the heavier line can be handed across. Also *messenger.*

**heavy cargo**    *n.* Cargo that causes a ship to be loaded to the load draft marks without filling all available spaces.

**heavy cruiser**    *n.* Cruisers of World War II with 8-inch guns, as opposed to light cruisers, which had only 6-inch guns.

**heavy floe**    *n.* Floe ice thicker than 2 feet.

**heavy ice**    *n.* An accumulation of ice heavy enough to make navigation difficult.

**heavy-lift ship**    *n.* A ship designed and fitted to carry heavy cargo such as locomotives or battle tanks. It has booms of sufficient capacity to accommodate a single lift of 100 tons.

**heavy weather bill**    *n.* Established procedure for readying a ship for riding out a storm. The bill lists such matters as rigging lifelines, securing loose gear, and setting optimum conditions for matériel and engineering readiness.

**hedgehog**    *n.* Antisubmarine weapon thrown ahead of the firing vessel. See DEPTH CHARGE; SQUID.

**heel**    *n.* (1) The base of a mast. (2) The after end of the keel. If a ship turns on its heel, it has a very short turning radius. (3) The convex section or elbow of a bar. (4) The inboard end of a bowsprit. (5) A temporary transverse angle of inclination of a vessel to one side or the other such as during a roll or caused by the wind. If the inclination is caused by an internal force, the vessel is said to list. (6) A small amount of liquid left in a tank or compartment.

**heel**    *v.* To lean to one side temporarily as a result of wind, waves or a turn. See LIST.

**heel and toe**    See WATCH AND WATCH.

**heeling adjuster**    *n.* An instrument that determines the approximate position at which the heeling magnet should be set in a magnetic compass. It consists of a small magnet balanced on a horizontal axis by means of an adjustable weight.

**heeling error**    *n.* The error introduced in a magnetic compass after it has been adjusted on an even keel, caused by displacement of the permanent and induced magnetic fields relative to the compass. When a sailing vessel is heeled for a number of days, the magnetic field changes and the compass can be adversely affected.

**heeling magnet** (or **corrector**)   *n.* The magnet placed below a compass to correct for heeling error caused by the deviation when a vessel is heeled.

**heeling moment**   *n.* the product of multiplying a vessel's displacement by the upsetting arm (GZ) in foot-tons, as opposed to righting moment. See STABILITY.

**heeling tanks**   *n.* Ballast tanks amidships in the sides of icebreakers used to produce rolling action to break loose the vessel from the ice.

**heel lashing**   *n.* The ropework that secures the inboard end of a boom when rigged out to a bulkhead, mast or spar.

**heel rope**   *n.* The cordage that is rove through a sheave hole at the heel of a topmast for lowering or heaving aloft.

**heel tenon**   *n.* The foot of a mast, usually square, that slips into the mortise of a mast step.

**height**   *n.* (1) On charts, the heights of lights, rocks, bridges, islets, wires over water, piers, and shoreline are measured from high water as defined by the agency and/or country that publishes the chart. (2) Vertical distance between any two decks. (3) In ship construction, height can mean the vertical distance between the base line and any waterline.

**height of eye**   *n.* The height in feet that an observer's eye is above the surface of the water.

**height of metacenter (KM)**   *n.* The vertical distance between the keel and the metacenter. Not the same as metacentric height. See STABILITY.

**height of tide**   *n.* The measurement of the tide above a given reference level or chart sounding datum, usually mean low water. The height of tide should not be confused with depth of water.

**height of wave**   *n.* The vertical distance from the trough to the crest of a wave.

**helm**   *n.* The steering mechanism of a vessel that includes the rudder, the tiller, the steering gear, and the wheel. Small boats often have only a rudder and tiller. Current usage often does not include the rudder but only that part of the total mechanism that is in the hands of the helmsman.

To put the helm to starboard (right) on a vessel with a wheel means to turn the wheel to starboard (clockwise), which will cause the rudder to go to starboard and the vessel to go to starboard. To put the helm to starboard on a vessel with only a tiller and no wheel, would cause the rudder to go to port and the head to go to port. Long after ships had wheels and a turn to the right was made by turning the wheel to the right, orders were given to the helmsman as tiller orders, just opposite to the way the wheel was to be turned.

Standardized **helm orders** for conning officers, pilots, and helmsmen were recommended at the International Conference on Shipping in London in 1928, and the time-honored use of "port" and "starboard" in helm orders was discontinued. The order given to the helmsman was to be "right" or "left," the direction in which the ship's head was to be turned. Whether dealing with a wheel or a tiller, the helmsman is told the direction the ship is to be turned. The Conference recommendations became law in Great Britain in 1931, in France in 1934, and in the United States in 1936.

**helm indicator**   *n.* Any device that continuously gives the angle of the helm, used for the benefit of the conning officer and helmsman. The helm indicator shows only the angle to which the helm has been turned, regardless of rudder response, and should not be confused with the rudder indicator that tells the angle of the rudder.

**helm port** *n.* The opening in the counter through which the rudderstock enters the hull; it is fitted with a stuffing gland to prevent water from coming aboard.

**helm's alee** *interj.* Information passed to indicate that the helmsman has begun tacking.

**helmsman** *n.* The person on the wheel or tiller. On U.S. Navy vessels, the **lee helmsman** is the man who operates the engine order (room) telegraph. During their watch, the helmsman and lee helmsman usually take half-hour tricks alternating the wheel and engine order (room) telegraph. Also *steersman.*

**hemp rope** *n.* (1) Cordage made from the fibers of the *Cannabis sativa,* native to Asia and the same plant from which hashish is derived. It is about 75% as strong as Manila. (2) **Sunn hemp** is made from *Crotalaria juncea,* a tropical Asian plant, from whose stems a tough fiber is made for use in cordage. Also *Bombay hemp, Madras hemp.*

**herald equipment** *n.* Harbor defense listening devices such as sonar.

**hermaphrodite brig** *n.* A two-masted sailing vessel, square-rigged on the foremast and fore-and-aft rigged on the mainmast. They were called brigantines by the British. Used during the mid-19th century. See BARK; BARKENTINE; BRIG.

**herringbone planking** *n.* A method of boatbuilding with the planking running aft at an angle from the keel.

**herringbone stitch** *n.* A sailmaker's stitch to repair a sail by a cross stitch that

allows the seam to be flat when repaired. Also *butt-jointed.*

**high** *adj.* Said of a headsail that is cut to be farther above the deck than is normal, a **high-cut jib.**

**high** *adv.* To windward. "We must sail high to skirt the shoal." *adj.* "You are high" means you are pinching or sailing too close to the wind. See WIND.

**high-and-dry** *adj.* (1) Above the high-water line. A vessel is high and dry when it is aground above that mark. (2) A high-and-dry marina is one that stores boats on several levels in a warehouse on land near the water.

**higher high water (HHW)** *n.* The higher of two high waters during a tidal day.

**higher low water (HLW)** *n.* The higher of two low waters during a tidal day.

**high focal plane buoy** *n.* A lighted buoy with the light mounted exceptionally high above the surface of the water.

**highline** *n.* A line between two ships underway used for transferring stores and personnel. The cargo bag or the personnel carrier is suspended from the highline, and a second line attached to both ships and to the goods or person being transferred controls the transfer. The exercise is called **highlining.**

**high-pressure cell** *n.* An air mass with atmospheric pressure higher than the surrounding air. Also anticyclone. See LOW-PRESSURE CELL.

**high sea** *n.* Douglas scale reading of 6, indicating wave heights between 15 and 24 feet with a short, heavy swell.

**high seas** *n.* (1) The open water of an ocean or sea beyond the territorial boundaries and maritime belts of any nearby country. Legally the high seas are the navigable waters of the oceans beyond the territorial boundaries. (2) The connecting seas and oceans lying to seaward of the 200-mile exclusive economic zone (EEZ). (3) Under international law, **freedom of the high seas** is the recognized right of all nations to navigate freely on the high seas.

**high water (HW)**   *n.* The maximum height reached by a rising tide. This height can be due solely to the periodic tidal forces, or it may be the result of prevailing meteorological conditions together with tidal forces. Also *high tide.*

**high-water datum**   *n.* The standard chart datum used for measuring the heights of land features. The standard used in the United States and its possessions is mean high water (MHW), the average height of all high water over a 19-year period.

**high-water full and change (HWF&C)**   *n.* The average high-water interval at the time of a spring tide when the Moon's transit occurs at noon or midnight. Also *mean high-water lunitidal interval.* See LUNITIDAL INTERVAL.

**high-water inequality**   *n.* The difference between two high waters during a tidal day.

**high-water mark**   *n.* The point on a shoreline reached by the mean high water.

**hike**   *v.* To put one's body out on the windward side of a sailboat to balance the force of the wind on the sails and trim the boat for more efficient sailing. Feet are sometimes placed under **hiking straps** and the helmsman may have an extension on the tiller called a **hiking stick.** Some boats are fitted with a **hiking seat,** or **hiking board,** which can be run out to the windward side to increase one's leverage.

**hill**   *n.* Small elevation above the seafloor, generally less than 200 meters.

**hinged watertight bulkhead doors** *n.* Rectangular doors in a bulkhead that are hinged, dogged from either side, and made watertight by a gasket running along the outer edge.

**hinterland**   *n.* (1) The land or countryside adjacent and inland from a coast. (2) That area from which a port receives and to which it dispatches cargo.

**hire and payment clause**   *n.* Charter party clause in which the amount to be paid for the hire of a vessel is stated and the method and time of payment given.

**hitch**   *n.* (1) Any knot that fastens a line to an object. See BEND. (2) Slang for a period of enlistment.

**hit the deck**   *phr.* Order to a ship's crew to get out of their bunks.

**hobbler**   *n.* In small ports, a pilot who has local knowledge of a port but does not have a license. Hobblers are not allowed to practice in U.S. ports.

**hobby horse**   *v.* To go up and down with the action of the sea when heading into the waves. The action is caused by too much weight at the ends of the vessel.

**hockle**   *n.* A kink in a cable, wire, or chain, or a kink in three-strand line where all strands take a reverse twist. Nylon line is especially susceptible to this because of its elasticity.

**hog**   *n.* Heavy scrubbing broom, brush, or mat used for scrubbing a vessel's bottom underwater.

**hog**   *v.* To support a vessel amidship without proper support at the bow and stern, which results in subjecting the main deck to excessive tensile stress. Hogging occurs when a vessel is riding the crest of a wave amidships, and the bow and stern are hanging over the troughs of two other waves. Many vessels, however, are normally hogged when light. See SAG.

**hog frame**   *n.* A longitudinal frame that forms a truss with the main frames to reduce hogging.

**hogging line**   *n.* (1) A line with an abrasive mat that is run under a ship's keel from one side to the other to clean the barnacles and weeds off the bottom. (2) A line attached to one of the corners of a collision mat.

**hogging strap**   *n.* A line used on towing vessels to hold a towing line close to the fantail. Also *gob rope.*

**hoist**   *n.* (1) The vertical edge of a flag or sail that is next to the flag staff or mast or stay. (2) The length of the luff of a headsail. (3) A signal flag display at a yardarm. (4) The amount of cargo that can be handled by a single sling. (5) The vertical distance from head to foot of all sails except the courses on a square-rigged ship. See DROP.

**hoist**   *v.* To lift, sometimes by means of a tackle, as in "hoist a sail," "hoist a cup after the race," or "hoist cargo aboard."

**hoisterman**   *n.* The operator of hoisting equipment on a buoy tender.

**hoisting eye**   *n.* A pad eye on a small vessel to which is attached one of the boat falls for hoisting. The pad eye is anchored to a backup plate called a **hoisting plate.**

**hoisting pole**   *n.* A spar used to extend the head of a club topsail above the top of the mast.

**hoisting rope**   *n.* A six-strand wire cable with 19 wires in each strand and a central core of fiber rope, used on derricks and dredges.

**hoist out**   *v.* To lower a small boat to the water on the boat falls.

**hold**   *n.* The below-deck cargo-holding spaces of a cargo vessel.

**hold**   *v.* Said of an anchor when it has caught in the sea bottom and it is holding the vessel and not dragging. "The anchor will hold in the heavy clay bottom."

**hold bunker**   *n.* A fuel compartment below the lowest deck.

**hold captain**   *n.* An enlisted person in charge of loading and unloading cargo from a hold during an amphibious operation.

**hold crew**   *n.* Longshoremen who work below deck.

**hold fast**   *n.* Any brace or dog that holds gear or cargo securely in place.

**holding ground**   *n.* A term used in describing the holding capacity of the bottom for an anchor in an anchorage. Clay offers the best holding ground, while sand is usually poor. An anchorage or gunkhole is described as having good holding or poor holding.

**holding tank**   *n.* A tank installed on a vessel to hold sewage to be pumped later into an authorized receptacle. See SLOP TANK.

**hold ladder**   *n.* A steel ladder leading from a hatch into a hold.

**hold stringer**   *n.* Longitudinal girders on a vessel's side above the turn of the bilge that increase longitudinal strength and prevent movement of frames.

**hole**   *n.* (1) A depression in the seafloor. (2) A small bay, New England term: Woods Hole.

**holiday**   *n.* A place that has been overlooked during scraping, scrubbing, painting, and so on.

**holiday routine**   *n.* U.S. Navy term for a day when no nonessential work or drills are carried on. The ship continues underway if at sea and the meals are not discontinued, but painting, scraping, drilling, and so forth, are not planned. See ROPE-YARN SUNDAY.

**hollow quoin**   *n.* A recess into which the heel of a pier or lock gate fits.

**holystone**   *n.* (pron. holly stone) A sandstone. Larger holystones were called **bibles,** and **prayer books.** The nomenclature came about because the crew used them on their hands and knees, as if in an attitude of prayer.

**holystone**   *v.* To scour a wooden deck with a sandstone and sand and water.

**home**   *v.* (1) To steer toward an electric or electronic beacon using a direction finder. "We homed on the radio beacon." (2) Said of a projectile or torpedo when its guidance system has sensed the target and heads for it. It is said to "home (in) on the target."

**home**   *adv.* Tight or tightly chock-a-block. "Hoist the sail home." An anchor comes home when it drags while kedging.

**home port**   *n.* (1) A naval base or naval air station at which a ship or aircraft unit is normally based. (2) The terminal port of a vessel, not necessarily the port of registry. (3) The port in which a seaman signs on.

**homeward bound**   *phr.* Said of a vessel returning to her terminal port.

**homeward-bound pennant**   *n.* A long streamer that was flown by homeward-bound naval vessels when they had been gone for more than a year. One foot represented each man on the ship. At the end of the cruise the pennant was cut up and passed out among the crew as souvenirs. The captain got the end at the fly with the star, the executive officer the next, and so on.

**honey boat**   *n.* Slang for sewage scow. Also *honey barge.*

**honors**   *n.* Traditional courtesies extended under various circumstances. "Be prepared to render the prescribed honors as we sail past the flagship."

**hood**   *n.* A cover for a companion hatch. See HATCH HOOD.

**hooding end**   *n.* The end plate of a strake where it fits into the stem or sternpost.

**hook**   *n.* (1) A curved or bent piece of metal used to hold or pull anything. See BLOCK. (2) A curved point of land with a spit, for example, Sandy Hook, New Jersey. (3) Slang for anchor. See STERN HOOK.

**hoop**   *n.* Circular bars of iron or wood used in various ways on ships. Clasp hooks are similar to others but are open and clasp the mast or spar. Buoy hoops hold buoys together. In some vessels wooden hoops are still used to bend sails onto the mast.

**hopper barge**   *n.* A barge used in conjunction with a dredge; the dredge fills the barge with sand, gravel, channel mud, or whatever its job happens to be. The barge is then taken to a convenient spot, and the bottom or hopper is opened and the material drops out of the vessel. A **hopper dredge** is simply a dredge and hopper barge combined in one unit.

**horizon**   *n.* The distant circle where the Earth or water meet the sky from the observer's position. The **visible** (or **apparent**) **horizon** is the line where the water and the sky appear to meet. The actual position of this line depends on the refraction of light and the height of eye above sea level. The **sensible** horizon is the circle on the heavens indicated by a plane at right angles to a line passing through the observer and the observer's zenith. This is the same as the visible horizon of an observer whose eye is at sea level. A plane passing through the center of the Earth and extending to the celestial sphere passes through the celestial sphere at the **rational horizon.**

**horizon glass** (or **mirror**) *n.* The glass of a sextant through which the horizon is observed. The other mirror is the index mirror.

**horizon system of coordinates** *n.* A set of celestial coordinates using the celestial horizon as the primary great circle.

**horizontal angle** *n.* The angle between two landmarks usually determined by using a sextant or pelorus to establish a position or a line of position.

**horizontal danger angle** *n.* An angle determined by a navigator in coastal piloting to keep a ship away from a given danger. As long as the angle between point A and point B is greater than (or less than) X, the vessel is beyond the danger.

**horizontal loading** *n.* Loading of items of like character in horizontal layers throughout the holds of a ship.

**horizontal sliding door** *n.* A door in a watertight bulkhead that slides horizontally and is usually operated from the navigation bridge.

**horn** *n.* A projection from the shell of a contact mine that, when broken off, causes the mine to detonate.

**horn** *v.* To set the frames of a vessel square to the keel after adjusting for proper inclination to the vertical with allowance for the declivity of the keel.

**hornpipe** *n.* A sailor's dance to music played on a hornpipe, a single-reed musical instrument of Celtic origin.

**horns** *n.* (1) The ends of booms and gaffs that slide against a mast. (2) Arms of chocks and cleats.

**horn timber** *n.* The longitudinal member at the bottom of a counter.

**horse** *n.* (1) A device used for winding rope around masts and yards tightly (woolding) to secure and confine them. (2) The steel bar or similar device secured to the deck on which the traveler rides. (3) A steel bar or rope used as a traveler. See BOWSPRIT HORSES.

**horse block** *n.* An elevated platform at the stern of a sailing vessel that was the station of the officer of the deck.

**horse latitudes** *n.* A region of weak pressure in either hemisphere, about 30° north and south, where light and variable winds prevail. Periods of stagnation are less persistent than in the doldrums. The origin of the name is grim. When sailing ships bringing horses from Europe and Asia became becalmed, the horses often died from heat and lack of water; when this happened they were thrown over the side. See WIND.

**horsepower (HP)** *n.* A unit of power in the U.S. Customary System, equal to 550 foot-pounds per second, or 745.7 watts. The **indicated horsepower** is the pressure on a cylinder developed by an engine during each stroke. The **shaft** or **brake horsepower** is the torque given a shaft and measured by a brake. The **effective horsepower** is the power expended to propel a vessel. In 1989, marine engine manufacturers began phasing in the international standard of kilowatts to replace horsepower. A kilowatt is equal to 1.34 horsepower. One horsepower is equal to 745.7 watts.

**horseshoe** *n.* A life preserver, or personal flotation device, shaped like a horseshoe.

**horseshoe plate**  *n.* A steel plate fitted on the counter where the rudderstock goes through the trunk.

**horseshoe rack**  *n.* A wooden rack at the base of a mast, used for blocks and fairleads for running rigging.

**horse up**  *v.* To harden the oakum in the seams of wooden planking by using a **horsing iron.**

**hose coaming**  *n.* The horizontal strakes at the top and bottom of a deckhouse.

**hospital ship**  *n.* A vessel designated AH, that is staffed and equipped to provide complete medical and surgical care, is unarmed, and is marked in accordance with the Geneva Convention.

**hostile ice**  *n.* An ice canopy on the ocean's surface that has no light areas through which a submarine might surface.

**hot bunk system**  *n.* Arrangement used when space for bunks is short and the same bunk is used by two or three different people, frequently necessary on earlier submarines.

**Hotel**  *n.* Phonetic word for the letter "H." The signal flag is white at the hoist and red at the fly and used alone means "Have pilot aboard."

**hot pursuit doctrine**  *n.* International maritime law doctrine that allows a government to seize a vessel of another country that has initiated an act of war on the government's territory and is pursued into international waters. The doctrine of hot pursuit allows the U.S. Coast Guard, for example, to closely and continuously pursue a criminal into waters or territory in which it does not otherwise have jurisdiction.

**hounding**  *n.* The lower portion of the mast between the deck and the hounds.

**hounds**  *n.* (1) Projections at the masthead that support the frame, trestletrees, topmast, and the rigging of the lower mast. Also *cheeks.* (2) The place on a mast where the jib halyard block is fitted. (3) Current usage applies to that point on the mast where the shrouds and stays come together; on a masthead rig, this is the masthead.

**hour angle (HA)**  *n.* A measure of the phase of the Earth's rotation used to calculate the angular distance of a celestial reference point west of the terrestrial reference meridian.

**hour circle**  *n.* A great circle of the celestial sphere that passes through the poles.

**house**  *n.* (1) On navigation charts, a complete structure as distinct from, for example, a spire. (2) A structure built on a vessel above the main deck, generally used as living quarters.

**house**  *v.* To stow an object or equipment such as ground tackle in the proper place.

**houseboat**  *n.* A vessel built more like a recreation vehicle on a hull with a motor or engine; they are usually built more for comfort on rivers and lakes than for safety on the high seas.

**house flag**  *n.* Company flag flown by a merchant vessel on the mainmast.

**houseline**  *n.* Tarred hemp cord laid right to left, stouter than marline.

**house of refuge**  *n.* One of a series of stations established and manned by the government along the Atlantic coast during the 19th century in which emergency supplies and equipment were maintained for the rescue of men and ships in distress.

**housing**  *n.* (1) The section of a mast from the top of the deck to the bottom of the step. (2) The inboard length of a bowsprit from the stem to the heel.

**housing line**   *n.* A line used to secure an awning. See LIFE LINES.

**housing stopper**   *n.* A short chain with a turnbuckle and hook at one end and a shackle at the other used for drawing the anchor close to the hawsepipe and to relieve the strain on the cable while at sea.

**hove**   See HEAVE.

**Hovercraft**   *n.* Trademark name for a vehicle that is propelled on a cushion of air over land or water.

**hovering vessel**   *n.* Customs term for a vessel that lurks off a coast and appears to be waiting for an opportunity to import cargo in violation of customs regulations.

**hoy**   *n.* A heavy harbor tender or barge used for carrying passengers and bulky or heavy gear short distances. Earlier usage was a sloop-rigged coastal vessel used for the same purpose.

**huddock**   *n.* A deckhouse on a collier.

**hug**   *v.* (1) To run as close to shore as possible, as in to "hug the land." (2) To sail as close to the wind as possible.

**hulk**   *n.* (1) The hull of an unseaworthy or wrecked ship, usually with all removable equipment and fittings gone. (2) Slang for a heavy ship, difficult to manage.

**hull**   *n.* The outer body or shell of a ship or a seaplane.

**hull**   *v.* To damage a vessel's hull, usually by shooting a hole in it, below the waterline, if possible.

**hull appendage ratio**   *n.* The ratio of the resistance of a naked hull to that with its underwater appendages such as shaft

bossings, bilge keel, rudder, propeller struts, and skeg. Also *hull factor.*

**hull auxiliaries**   *n.* General term for all auxiliary motors and machinery, exclusive of the propulsion machinery, such as refrigerating equipment, generators, deck auxiliaries, and pumps for handling liquid cargo and ballast.

**hull board**   *n.* A group of engineering officers convened to determine the condition of a vessel's hull.

**hull down**   *adj.* Said of a vessel when it is far enough away on the horizon that the hull cannot be seen by the observer, but the upper works such as masts and superstructure can be seen.

**hull efficiency**   *n.* A propeller designer's term for the ratio of net work (horsepower) required to pull a ship at a given speed when towed without a propeller, to the net work required to drive the hull through the water at the same speed by its propeller.

**hull girder**   *n.* Naval architect's term for the entire hull considered as a single box girder when analyzing its resistance to sagging and hogging.

**hull policy**   *n.* Marine insurance term that includes insurance of the hull, equipment, cabin fittings, provisions for officers and crew, boilers, fuel, propulsion equipment, deck equipment, and auxiliary equipment necessary for any special trade in which the vessel is expected to be engaged. It does not include cargo insurance, liability insurance, and so on. The person or organization who insures the hull under a hull policy is the **hull underwriter.**

**hull speed**   *n.* The theoretical maximum speed of a displacement-hull vessel.

**Humboldt Current**   *n.* Northward-flowing current along the west coast of South America. Also *Peru Current.*

Named for Friedrich Heinrich Alexander von Humboldt (1769–1859), German naturalist, author, and statesman. See OCEAN CURRENT.

**humidity, relative**  *n.* Dampness of the air relative to the maximum possible dampness at a given temperature. Cold air can hold less moisture than warm air, and as the temperature decreases, the relative humidity increases. When the air becomes saturated, or reaches the dew point, condensation takes place. The moisture squeezed out of the air and deposited on objects is called dew in temperatures above freezing, and frost in temperatures below freezing.

**hummock**  *n.* A mound field of pressure ice with the topography of numerous hillocks, called **hummocked ice.**

**hunter-killer force (HUK)**  *n.* A U.S. Navy force composed of an antisubmarine warfare carrier with aircraft and escort vessels.

**hurricane**  *n.* Beaufort scale reading of 12, with winds of 64 knots.

**hurricane deck**  *n.* A promenade deck above the bridge, poop, and forecastle.

**hydraulic current**  *n.* A current generated between two different tidal bodies in a strait. Because the tides are rarely in phase, they create a current of their own independent of other factors. The current in New York City's East River (which is not a river, but a tidal strait) between New York Harbor and Long Island Sound, is an example.

**hydraulic steering gear**  *n.* The steering mechanism used on ships to transmit helm movement to the rudder(s) by rams working in cylinders actuated by hydraulic (oil) transmission.

**hydrofoil**  *n.* (1) A surface vessel with underwater foils that enable it to rise above the water's surface, thus reducing hull drag and increasing speed. (2) The underwater blade or set of blades that enables a vessel to rise above the surface when the vessel moves forward.

**hydrographic chart**  *n.* A chart showing depths, nature of the bottom, contours of the bottom and coastline, tides and currents, in a given area of the sea.

**hydrographic datum**  *n.* A datum used as a reference for depths of water or heights of predicted tides.

**hydrographic survey**  *n.* The field work and assimilation of the material found in the study of hydrography.

**hydrographic surveyor**  *n.* A government officer in charge of a government hydrographic office.

**Hydrographic/Topographic Center** *n.* A division of the Defense Mapping Agency responsible for hydrographic, navigational, topographic, and geodetic data, charts, maps, and related products and services to the armed forces, federal agencies, the Merchant Marine, and mariners. Originating in the Depot of Charts and Instruments established in 1830, it later became the Hydrographic Office, from which comes the H.O. abbreviation used in older publications.

**hydrography**  *n.* The science of describing and analyzing physical characteristics of oceans, lakes, rivers, and other surface waters. It includes determining the contours of coastlines, harbors, river mouths, positions of coastline objects, rock shoals, the particulars of the sea bottom, and tides and current flow for the production of charts used for navigation.

**HYDROLANT**  *n.* A radio message broadcast by the Defense Mapping Agency's Hydrographic/Topographic Center to inform mariners of the more important incidents relating to navigation and that demand immediate release for navigational safety. HYDROLANTs are confined to those waters outside and eastward of NAVAREA IV in the Atlantic Ocean. See HYDROPAC.

**hydrometer**   *n.* Any instrument used to determine the specific gravity (S.G.) of liquids; in marine work, hydrometers are used to determine salinity of seawater.

**HYDROPAC**   *n.* The same as a HYDROLANT except that the HYDROPAC is broadcast to the area outside and westward of NAVAREA XII in the Pacific Ocean. See HYDROLANT.

**hydrophone**   *n.* An underwater sound-listening device.

**hydroplane**   *n.* (1) A racing motorboat designed with planing surfaces, **sponsons,** that provide lift for the hull. (2) A horizontal rudder on a submarine.

**hydroscope**   *n.* An optical instrument used for viewing objects below the surface of the water.

**hydrosphere**   *n.* The water of the Earth, as distinguished from atmosphere and lithosphere.

**hydrostatic pressure**   *n.* The pressure of an incompressible homogeneous fluid exerted on an object, measured in pounds per square inch (psi).

**hydrostatics**   *n.* The statics of incompressible fluids, a knowledge of which is especially important in the tanker business.

**hydrostatic test**   *n.* A test of a watertight compartment by filling it with water to verify the integrity.

**hygrometer**   *n.* An instrument used for obtaining the relative humidity and dew point. A **psychrometer** is the type of hygrometer most often used on shipboard and consists of a wet-bulb thermometer and a dry-bulb thermometer. The wet-bulb thermometer has its bulb in a small muslin tube that is kept wet by being in a small container of water. The difference between the two readings is compared with psychrometric tables to get dew point and relative humidity.

**hyperbolic navigation system**   *n.* A radio system of navigation in which hyperbolic position lines are determined by measuring phase differences between land-based transmitting stations.

# I

**I**  See INDIA.

**IALA Maritime Buoyage System** *n.* See INTERNATIONAL ASSOCIATION OF LIGHTHOUSE AUTHORITIES.

**I-beam**   *n.* A steel bar showing an "I" in cross section.

**ice anchor**   *n.* (1) An anchor designed for anchoring vessels in ice. (2) A timber buried in ice and used to secure a ship's mooring lines. Also *deadman.*

**ice atlas**   *n.* A publication that includes charts showing geographic locations of ice with the season or months. An ice atlas is similar to a pilot chart.

**ice beam**   *n.* One of several transverse beams placed at the load waterline below to give additional transverse strength for ships to be used in waters in which they can be expected to need protection against the pressure of ice.

**iceberg**   *n.* A massive floating body of ice showing more than 5 meters above the sea surface. A **large iceberg** rises more than 150 feet above sea level and is more than 400 feet long. A **medium iceberg** is 50 to 150 feet high and 210 to 400 feet long. A **small iceberg** is 4 to 50 feet high and 20 to 200 feet long.

**iceberg tongue**   *n.* A major accumulation of grounded icebergs projecting from the coast and joined by fast ice.

**ice blink**   *n.* The bright glare sometimes observed on the underside of clouds above an accumulation of distant ice.

**iceboat**   *n.* A vessel similar in design to a catamaran, with runners in place of pontoons to sail on ice.

**icebound**   *adj.* (1) Locked in by ice and unable to maneuver. (2) Covered by ice as in the case of a harbor, when ships cannot enter or leave.

**ice boundary**   *n.* The limit at a given time between fast ice and pack ice or areas of pack ice of different densities.

**ice breaker**   *n.* A U.S. Coast Guard vessel (designated ACB) designed with a spoon-shaped bow and rounded bow sections, protected propellers, and heavy engines for duty in heavy ice. The convex bow allows the vessel to ride up on top of packed ice and crush it with its weight. Some vessels are designed with a forward screw to pull the water out from under the ice and thus remove the support.

**ice bridge**   *n.* Surface ice that has become thick enough to impede or prevent navigation.

**ice buoy**   *n.* A heavy buoy, usually a metal spar, used to replace a lighter buoy when heavy ice is expected.

**ice cake**   *n.* A relatively flat section of ice not more than 20 meters across.

**ice canopy**   *n.* Pack ice and enclosed water areas, from the perspective of a submarine.

**ice cap**   *n.* A large area of ice formed on a flat plateau that stays through summer and winter. The ice cap on Greenland is as thick as 1 kilometer (km), and the one on Antarctica is 4.5 km thick.

**ice clause**   *n.* Charter party term that allows a vessel when precluded from entering an icebound port to deliver its cargo at the nearest accessible port after agreement with receivers.

**ice cliff**   *n.* (1) A cliff of old ice that has been covered by dirt and vegetation. These are found in Greenland. (2) The seaward end of a massive ice sheet 2 to 50 meters above sea level. Also *ice front.*

**ice cover**   *n.* The ratio of ice to the total area of sea surface in a geographic locale. The locale may be global, hemispheric, or a smaller area such as the Barents Sea. Also *ice concentration.*

**ice crystal**   *n.* Macroscopic crystalline form of ice. See DROXTAL; WEATHER.

**ice doubling**   *n.* Additional plating riveted on the bow at the waterline to protect a vessel against drifting ice.

**ice drag**   *n.* A large hook used as a kedge to pull a vessel through ice. The hook is walked out ahead of the vessel and then the vessel is pulled toward the ice drag by working the capstan.

**ice edge**   *n.* The boundary between heavy ice or pack ice and the open sea.

**icefield**   *n.* A mass of ice floes covering an area greater than 5.4 nautical miles across. A **large ice field** is 11 nautical miles across, a **medium ice field** is 8–11 nautical miles across, and a **small ice field** is 5.4–8 nautical miles across.

**ice floe**   *n.* Ice cakes and pancake ice frozen together and building a mass less than 10 kilometers across. Ice floe is considered redundant by most lexicographers.

**ice fog**   *n.* A dense fog of suspended particles of ice crystals 20 to 100 microns in diameter and chiefly droxtals 12–20 microns in diameter. It occurs at very low temperatures, usually clear, calm weather at high latitudes below −20°F.

**ice foot**   *n.* A narrow border of ice attached to a coast, unmoved by tides and remaining after the fast ice is gone.

**ice-free**   *adj.* Used to describe a harbor when the presence of ice is such that it will not impede navigation.

**ice island**   *n.* Large pieces of ice about 5 meters above the sea's surface that have broken away from an ice shelf 30–50 meters in thickness with an area of a few thousand square meters or considerably more.

**ice lane**   *n.* A stretch of ocean in which ice is frequently found.

**ice massif**   *n.* A heavy concentration of sea ice with an area of several hundred kilometers and found in the same area every summer.

**ice patch**   *n.* Pack ice less than 5.4 nautical miles across.

**ice port**   *n.* A bay where ships can moor alongside to unload onto the ice shelf.

**ice rind**   *n.* A brittle and shiny crust of low salinity with a thickness of about 5 centimeters formed from an accumulation of grease ice and shuga after it freezes.

**ice shelf**   *n.* A floating, flat ice sheet from 6 to 65 feet above sea level, very long, and usually attached to land. The seaward face is called an **ice front.**

**ice sky**   *n.* An ice blink or glare that extends from the horizon above snow and ice to the sky, usually on an exceptionally clear day with altostratus clouds.

**idler**   *n.* (1) A person who does not stand watches at sea and who generally works only during the day; idlers usually include the carpenter, sailmaker, boatswain, and others. (2) In a gear train, a gear that does not add anything; sometimes they are used to reverse the rotation within the train. Idlers are used in belt trains for tensioning purposes.

**ignis fatuus**   *n.* Phosphorescent light that hovers and flits over a low-lying swampy area. It is caused by the spontaneous combustion of gases, mostly methane, emitted from decaying organic matter.

**ignition point**   *n.* The minimum temperature at which a substance will burn without additional external heat being applied. Also *kindling point.*

**immatriculation**   *n.* The procedure by which a merchant ship acquires a nationality.

**immersion scale**   *n.* A graph showing the tons required to immerse a vessel to its various drafts.

**impeller log**   *n.* A speed-measuring device that uses propellers pulled through the water, either hull-mounted or towed, to determine the vessel's speed. A cable is led from the impeller to an indicator where it can be read.

**impressment**   *n.* The act of forcibly recruiting men for public service, formerly a common practice in increasing navy crews, especially in Britain.

**improved channel**   *n.* A channel maintained under the direction of the U.S. Army Corps of Engineers to provide an assigned controlling depth. Such channels are shown on National Ocean Survey charts by broken black lines on the lateral limits with the controlling depth and the date at which it was last dredged or observed at that depth.

**inactivate**   *v.* To place a vessel or military unit on inactive status, unmanned. Also *mothball.*

**in and out**   *n.* A method of construction used where of three strakes the two outer ones are riveted to the frames while the middle strake overlaps the other two and is riveted to them.

**in ballast**   *phr.* Said of a vessel when it is without cargo and it has been loaded with extra ballast, such as water in tanks or rocks, to give it stability.

**inboard**   *prep, adj.* or *adv.* (1) Toward the center of a ship or a group of ships. (2) Within the hull. (3) Inboard is also used more generally to mean inside. "Officers walking with ladies are expected to take the outboard position on the sidewalk."

**inboard engine**   *n.* A small-boat engine that is mostly inside the hull, with only the propeller and part of the shaft outside. An **inboard-outboard (I-0) engine** has the propeller and power train outboard, but the propulsion power unit is inboard with a crankshaft and gear unit connecting the two.

**inboard profile**   *n.* A drawing of the longitudinal section at the centerline of a vessel.

**inbound**   *adj.* Homeward bound, heading toward shore or up a channel. "Inbound traffic will keep to the north of the dredge in cut D." The opposite is outbound. See INWARD-BOUND.

**Inchmaree clause**   *n.* A clause in marine insurance policies that specifies that the underwriter agrees to cover loss or damage to hull or machinery resulting from the negligence of masters, charterers, mariners, engineers, or pilots, or through any latent defects in the ma-

chinery or hull. The name derives from a case brought before the House of Lords by the underwriters of the steamer *Inchmaree* in 1887. Damages were sustained by the vessel as a result of negligence on the part of the engineers. The decision was in favor of the underwriters on the grounds that the damage was not a result of a "peril of the seas" and therefore not covered in the hull policy.

**incineration area**   *n.* A government-designated offshore area for burning chemical waste by specially equipped ships. These areas are shown on charts so that passing vessels will not be led to believe the incineration vessel is on fire.

**inclination (or inclining) experiment**   *n.* An empirical study to measure a vessel's stability by computing the transverse metacentric height by use of weights to cause it to list.

**inclinometer**   *n.* (1) A device designed to measure the magnetic compass dip. Also *dip circle.* (2) It is also used incorrectly as a synonym for a clinometer, the device that records a ship's roll.

**increasing pitch**   *n.* In propeller design, the increase of pitch either radially or axially from the leading edge to the trailing edge.

**indemnity**   *n.* Underwriter's and admiralty term for security against loss or damage.

**indentures**   *n.* A contract binding a person in the service of another; an example would be the articles of agreement between shipowner and an apprentice in the British merchant service.

**independent surveillance**   *n.* The determination of a vessel's position requiring no cooperation from the vessel, such as by radar or sonar.

**index arm (or bar)**   *n.* The movable bar of a sextant that pivots about the center of curvature of the limb. The index arm carries the tangent screw and the vernier or micrometer drum.

**index correction** *n.* Sextant correction to allow for the index and horizon mirrors not being precisely aligned. Numerically the same as index error but with reversed sign.

**index error** *n.* The error that results when the index mirror and the horizon glass are not parallel.

**index glass** *n.* A mirror positioned perpendicular to the plane of a sextant at the top, or the pivot, of the instrument. To test the perpendicularity of the position of the mirror, place the index arm in the center of the arc, hold the instrument flat with the arc away from yourself, look closely at the inner edge of the index glass, and note if the direct and reflected images of the arc form a straight line. If so, the glass is perpendicular, if not, adjust the mirror by using the screws at the back.

**index mirror** *n.* The mirror mounted on the upper end of the index arm of a sextant.

**India** *n.* Phonetic word for the letter "I." The international code flag is a yellow flag with a black disk. When used as a single-letter signal, it means "I am directing my course to port."

**indicated horsepower (IHP)** *n.* The power delivered by an engine's pistons as calculated from its **indicator diagrams.** The power that is generated within the cylinder, which is greater than the power delivered to the drive shaft by the amount of mechanical friction that is overcome, is a calculated theoretical figure. See BRAKE HORSEPOWER; HORSEPOWER.

**indirect action pump** *n.* A pump powered by a separate reciprocating engine and linked by a bar connected to the piston rod of the separate engine.

**indirect connected steering gear** *n.* Steering mechanism powered by a steam engine that is controlled by valves connected to the helm.

**induced draft** *n.* A forced-draft system that draws the combustion gases out of a boiler uptake and into the funnel.

**induced magnetism** *n.* The magnetism acquired by soft iron while it is in a magnetic field. An iron ship that lies in one spot for several weeks, as it does in a shipyard, will acquire induced magnetism. Such magnetism in the ship will have a strong effect on the ship's compass. However, when the ship is moved, the induced magnetism dissipates and the compass will return to the normal position.

**inert gas system** *n.* The system of replacing flammable fumes in cargo tanks with inert gas from the ship's boiler flues to reduce chances of explosion.

**inertial guidance** *n.* A gyroscopic system of guiding missiles, aircraft, and ships by devices independent of outside influence or information. The system converts minute accelerations to distance in the direction of acceleration.

**inertial navigation** *n.* A self-contained navigation instrument for navigating a vehicle from one place to another with the aid of instruments that sense the vehicle's acceleration in a known direction using Newton's laws of motion. The system consists of accelerometers mounted on a stabilized platform and a computer that continuously determines direction and distance traveled from a known starting position. It is used mainly on civil and military aircraft and on U.S. Navy ships. The **Ship's Inertial Navigation System (SINS)** was developed by the U.S. Navy as an accurate, all-weather, dead-reckoning system. See INTEGRATED NAVIGATION SYSTEM.

**infection, theory of** *n.* A doctrine adopted by the United States, the United

Kingdom, and Japan according to which innocent goods seized on a vessel of a neutral nation when the vessel is found to be carrying contraband goods are considered to be contaminated and therefore of infectious nature and liable to confiscation.

**inferior mirage**    *n.* The phenomenon when refraction causes a ship or an island to appear to be floating above the shimmering horizon, possibly with an inverted image beneath it.

**inflammable**    *adj.* Easily ignited, subject to spontaneous combustion, or giving off vapors that are easily ignited. Inflammable liquids are those that give off vapors at temperatures at or below 80°F. Inflammable liquids carry a red label; inflammable solids and oxidizing materials carry a yellow label. See COMBUSTIBLE LIQUID.

**inflatable**    *n.* Life rafts and dinghies capable of being inflated either with air or a $CO_2$ cartridge.

**informing gun**    *n.* The discharge of a blank shell to alert a vessel that a government-authorized vessel intends to exercise its right of search. This procedure is not recognized by British and American authorities, and therefore not recognized in the waters under the control of those countries. This is the modern version of putting a shot across the bow.

**inhaul**    *n.* A line used to pull in an object or a clew. See BRAILS; OUTHAUL.

**inhauler**    *n.* A line used to pull in a headsail traveler.

**inherent vice**    *n.* The characteristic in some cargoes to change in a manner so that it may cause damage to itself and to other nearby commodities. Examples include cargo subject to spontaneous combustion and certain types of batteries that may deteriorate and leak. The shipper has a lawful duty to inform the carrier of any knowledge regarding in-

herent vice and the necessary treatment. See PERISHABLE CARGO.

**in irons**    *phr.* To lose headway at the point the wind is from dead ahead when coming about. With no headway, the vessel gains sternway and has difficulty bearing off in either direction. See IN STAYS.

**initial course**    *n.* The first course steered on a great circle routing.

**initial great circle route**    *n.* The direction, at the point of departure, of a great circle through that point and the destination, expressed as an angular distance from a reference direction, usually north in the Northern Hemisphere, to that part of the great circle extending toward the destination.

**initial stability**    *n.* A vessel's resistance to inclination from an upright position to as much as 15°, as computed from the metacentric height.

**in its gear**    *phr.* Said of a sail when it is properly stowed by its gear including buntlines, leechlines, and so on.

**in its lifts**    *phr.* Said of a yard when it has been eased down and is being supported by its lifts.

**inladen barge rig**    *n.* A drill rig installed on a barge for use in shallow water and swamps. These are not self-propelled, but are towed or pushed by tugs. Such barges have crew's quarters as well as the necessary drilling equipment.

**Inland Navigation Rules**    *n.* Usually referred to as the Inland Rules, the rules and regulations governing the proper conduct and navigation of vessels and specifying the lights, shapes, and sound signals that apply on inland waters. These were enacted in the Inland Navigation Rules Act of 1980. See INTERNATIONAL RULES; RULES OF THE ROAD.

**inland rules waters** See COLREGS DEMARCATION LINES.

**inland sea** *n.* A body of water nearly or completely surrounded by land, especially if large or saltwater. See CLOSED SEA.

**inland waters** *n.* The navigable waters of the United States shoreward of the COLREGS Demarcation Lines that divide the high seas from the harbors, rivers, and other inland waters of the United States and the waters of the Great Lakes on the United States side of the international boundary between the United States and Canada.

**inlet** *n.* (1) A narrow channel. (2) A stream running inland from the sea. (3) An estuary. (4) The water between two relatively close islands. (5) See PASS.

**inner bottom** *n.* Tank tops over double-bottom tanks that form an inner skin for a vessel.

**inner harbor** *n.* A harbor protected by piers, moles, or breakwaters and provided with cargo-handling facilities such as tidal quays for berthing and warehouses.

**inner jib** *n.* The first jib or headsail forward of the forestaysail.

**inner keel** *n.* A structural member fastened above and parallel to the keel for additional strength. Also *keelson.*

**inner post** *n.* The timber butted to the forward side of the main sternpost and on which the transom is seated.

**inner shell** *n.* A plated shell or surface inside the outer shell plating, used for additional protection in case of collision. The space between the shells is often available for ballast water or cargo.

**inner strake** *n.* Any strake in contact with frames or beams.

**innocent passage, right of** See RIGHT OF INNOCENT PASSAGE.

**inshore** *adj.* or *adv.* Close to shore or toward the shore. An **inshore current** is one that runs parallel or perpendicular to the shore.

**inshore traffic zone** *n.* A designation for the area between the landward boundary of a traffic separation scheme and the adjacent coast intended for local traffic.

**inside fastening** *n.* Construction term for a hull fastening made from the inside of a vessel.

**inside staging** *n.* Staging used on the inside of a ship during construction and repair.

**in soundings** *adj.* Said of a vessel in less than 100 fathoms of water. The opposite term, "off soundings," is more frequently heard. The term dates from the days of hand-held lead lines when the maximum line was 100 fathoms.

**inspection, certificate of** *n.* A document that certifies that a vessel has been inspected by the U.S. Coast Guard and that it is in conformance with the applicable vessel inspection laws and regulations. It also sets forth various conditions under which it can operate.

**inspection plate** *n.* A steel plate fitted with a gasket and bolted over an opening in a gearbox or crankcase. Removing the plate allows the gears or crankcase to be inspected and maintained.

**inspection port** *n.* An access panel in a watertight bulkhead.

**in stays** *adj.* The position of a vessel when in the wind while coming about. The term is often used synonymously with "in irons."

**insular borderland** *n.* The zone around an island beyond the limits of the insular shelf with depths well in excess of those of the typical insular shelf.

**insular shelf** *n.* The area surrounding an island that extends from the low tide level to the point that the land drops off rapidly.

**intact buoyancy** *n.* The intact space below the surface of a flooded area.

**integral Doppler navigation** *n.* Navigation by means of integrating the Doppler frequency shift that occurs during a specific interval of time as the distance between a navigational satellite and the navigation receiving station changes in order to determine the time. *See* DOPPLER EFFECT.

**Integrated Navigation System (INS)** *n.* A ship's inertial navigation system with the addition of an automatic star tracker, a multispeed repeater, and instrumentation to provide input on roll, pitch, and heading for radar stabilization.

**intended track** *n.* The path of intended travel with respect to the Earth as drawn on a chart.

**intercardinal points** *n.* The four compass points between the cardinal points: northeast, southeast, southwest, and northwest. *See* POINT; THREE-LETTER POINT.

**intercept method of sight reduction** *n.* A means of plotting one's position, developed in 1874 by the French naval officer Capt. Marcq St. Hilaire and used by merchant ships and the U.S. Navy until World War II. This method involved the cosine-haversine equations. The Marcq St. Hilaire method was superseded first by the Japanese Ogura method and later by the inspection tables that used H.O. 214, and most recently by hand computers and the various methods involved with each type.

**intercoastal** *adj.* Pertains to shipping trade between two separate sea coasts.

**intercostal** *n.* Shipwright's term for fore-and-aft members of a hull's structure that are used when continuous members are not possible because of obstructions. Longitudinal girders are **intercostals** in most ships. Floors are continuous and not considered intercostals.

**intercostal** *adj.* Shipwright's term for ship construction when the vessel is built in separate sections rather than continuous construction.

**intercostal plate** *n.* A fore-and-aft plate between two floors to prevent the floors from collapsing from vertical stress.

**Inter-Governmental Maritime Consultative Organization** *See* INTERNATIONAL MARITIME ORGANIZATION.

**intermediate frame** *n.* A frame in a double bottom with no floor plating where floor plates are fitted to alternate frames.

**intermediate link** *n.* A stud link on an anchor chain between the end link and the common link.

**intermediate port** *n.* A port of call between the port of departure and the port of destination.

**intermediate shaft** *n.* A length of the main drive shaft between the thrust bearing and the propeller shaft.

**intermediate vessel** *n.* One that takes both passengers and cargo, but more cargo and fewer passengers than ships in passenger service.

**intermittent light** *See* ISOPHASE.

**intermittent quick flashing light** *See* LIGHT PHASE CHARACTERISTICS.

**internal ballast** *n.* Ballast carried low inside the hull or in the keel. It is usually readily removable.

**internal line** *n.* Any line led inside mast or boom.

**internal waters** *n.* All waters lying landward from an established base line, including bays, rivers, and other inland waterways. There is no "right of innocent passage" on internal waters.

**internal waves** See BOUNDARY (or INTERNAL) WAVES.

## International Association of Lighthouse Authorities (IALA) *n.* An international conference established in 1957 to assemble maritime nations around the world to discuss technical matters such as leading lights, microwave aids to navigation, unification of buoyage systems, and buoy moorings. As recently as 1976, there were still 30 different buoyage systems in use around the world, many directly contradictory to others. In 1980, at an IALA conference in Tokyo, two regions were established for the world, Region A and Region B. The systems used in the two regions both combine lateral and cardinal systems, but in quite different ways. One significant difference is that buoyage Region B uses "red, right, returning" with green markers to the left when entering port, while A uses the opposite. North and South America and Japan use the Region B system, Europe and Asia (except Japan) use the Region A system. See BUOYAGE.

## International Code of Signals *n.* The 1931 International Code of Signals, effective January 1, 1934, was published in English, French, German, Italian, Japanese, Swedish, and Norwegian. The United States edition is H.O. 102. First issued in 1934, procedures applicable to all communications along with specific rules for signaling with flags, flashing lights, sound, radiotelegraphy, and radiotelephony, and signaling with hand flags with either Morse code or semaphore. In the United States, the *International Code of Signals* is published by the Defense Mapping Agency Hydrographic/Topographic Center. See CODE BOOK.

## International Convention for the Safety of Life at Sea (SOLAS) *n.* A group of marine experts who convene occasionally to discuss safety issues under the aegis of the International Maritime Organization (IMO) of the United Nations. The first such group met in 1914 to discuss the sinking of *Titanic* two years before. In 1960, the IMO established more than 600 codes, standards, and recommendations regarding maritime safety, pollution, and many other areas of concern to mariners the world over. Since then most maritime nations have made IMO's codes and standards into law. COLREGS '72 *(Navigation Rules)* and *Safety of Life at Sea* are two of its more important publications.

## International Date Line *n.* A line that follows the 180th meridian with modifications for inhabited territories. Ships traveling west to east advance their clocks to lengthen the days. When they reach the International Date Line, they set the date back one day. When ships are westbound, the clocks are continually set back until they reach the date line, when they are advanced one day.

## International Hydrographic Bureau (IHB) *n.* Established in 1921 for the purpose of reaching international understanding on methods of navigation and chart use. The IHB and the **International Hydrographic Organization (IHO),** also established in 1921, promote international uniformity in the preparation of and issuing of hydrographic studies and nautical publications.

## International Ice Patrol *n.* A U.S. Coast Guard patrol operated in accordance with international treaties and agreements to prevent collisions of vessels and ice. This was established in 1913 following the International Convention for the Safety of Life at Sea after the sinking of the SS *Titanic.*

**international maritime law** *n.* The code built up among maritime nations over the centuries that deals with affairs and business of the sea, the ships, the crews, and the conveyance of property and people. The division dealing with governments is the public international maritime law, and that which deals with settling litigation between subjects of different nations is the private division of international maritime law.

**International Maritime Organization (IMO)** *n.* Established in 1958 by the United Nations as the Inter-Governmental Maritime Consultation Organization (IMCO) to promote cooperation and communication between nations on such matters as international shipping, marine safety, and pollution. On May 22, 1982, the IMCO became the IMO, the specialized agency of the United Nations responsible for maritime safety and efficiency of navigation. The IMO is recognized as the only international organization responsible for establishing and recommending measures on an international level concerning ships' routing.

**international maritime satellite** *n.* A satellite that became operational in 1982, it provides exclusively maritime contact for distress, medical assistance, weather, navigational assistance, and so on, in all parts of the world.

**international measurement system (IMS)** *n.* One of the handicap rating systems used for sailboats in offshore racing, formerly known as the "measurement handicap system."

**international nautical mile** See NAUTICAL MILE.

**international number (of a navigational light)** *n.* The number assigned to navigation lights by the International Hydrographic Organization. These numbers are listed in the *Light List.*

**International Offshore Rule (IOR)** *n.* A handicap rating system used for sailboats in offshore racing.

**International Rules** *n.* The rules and regulations governing the conduct of vessels operating to seaward of COLREGS Demarcation Lines, and specifying the lights, shapes, and sound signals that apply on these waters. These were formalized in the Convention on the International Regulations for Preventing Collisions at Sea, 1972. Also *72 COLREGS.*

**International Yacht Racing Union (IYRU)** *n.* The governing authority for all recognized sailboat competition. The IYRU purview covers all aspects from racing rules to classes selected for the Olympics.

**interpolation** *n.* The proportionate selection of an intermediate quantity or point lying between two known or tabulated quantities or points. See EXTRAPOLATION.

**interrogatory** *interj.* In U.S. Naval messages, it means the message is unclear or the one receiving it does not understand.

**interrupted quick flashing light (I. Qk. Fl.)** *n.* An aid to navigation showing quick flashes for about 5 seconds followed by a dark period of about 5 seconds. See LIGHT PHASE CHARACTERISTICS.

**intertidal zone** *n.* The zone along a shoreline between the low-water line and the high-water line where a characteristic group of flora and fauna are to be found. Also *littoral zone.*

**intertropical convergence zone (ITCZ)** *n.* A zone near the equator where the trade winds of both hemispheres converge, characterized by low pressure and wet weather. See WIND.

**intertropical front** *n.* The boundary between the Northern Hemisphere trade winds and the Southern Hemisphere trade winds located in the area of low pressure called the doldrums at about 5°N.

**in the wind**   *phr.* In the direction from which the wind is blowing, windward.

**Intracoastal Waterway (ICW)**   *n.* A 2,500-mile-long system of protected and partially protected natural waterways and canals between New Jersey and Texas. The **Atlantic Intracoastal Waterway** begins at Manasquan Inlet (mile zero) in New Jersey and continues south to Key West, Florida. The Okeechobee section of the ICW crosses Florida from St. Lucie Inlet across Lake Okeechobee to Fort Myers. The **Gulf Intracoastal Waterway (GIWW)** starts at San Carlos Bay, Fort Myers (mile zero) and continues north and west around the Gulf of Mexico as far south as Brownsville, Texas, near the Mexican border. The lateral buoyage system is used along the whole ICW, with red marks kept to the right and green to the left, starting from New Jersey. ICW markers also carry a distinctive yellow marking to distinguish them from other navigational aids encountered in bays, inlets, and rivers along the waterway.

**inverse Mercator projection**   *n.* The projection used most often by mariners for charts, it is based on a cylinder tangent along a meridian. The more common Mercator projection used for world maps is based on a cylinder tangent to the equator. Named for the inventor Gerhardus Mercator, 1512–1594, a Flemish cartographer.

**inwale**   *n.* A wooden rib running longitudinally on the inside of a small boat. It may run the full length from stem to stern or only a short distance forward from the stern.

**inward-bound**   *adj.* Heading toward land or up a harbor away from the sea.

**inward charges**   *n.* Any charges for a vessel or her cargo such as port fees when entering a port.

**inward clearance certificate**   *n.* A document given to the master of a ship after it has been loaded and the customs officials have been satisfied, usually by inspection, that neither dutiable nor prohibited cargo or articles are aboard.

**inward manifest**   *n.* A list of stores and provisions that have to be declared that is handed by the master of an arriving ship to customs officials.

**Irish barrel**   *n.* A wooden, watertight container that holds 150 pounds of fish, 45 pounds of ice, and enough saltwater to float the fish to prevent undue bruising.

**Irish moss**   *n.* An edible seaweed, *Chondrus crispus*, found along the North Atlantic coasts of America and Ireland.

**Irish pennant**   *n.* Slang for a loose line that has no purpose. Also *Cow's tail.*

**Irminger Current**   *n.* A North Atlantic Ocean current that branches off the Gulf Stream System; it flows toward the west off the southwest coast of Iceland. A small part of it bends around the west coast of Iceland, but the bulk becomes mixed with the water of the East Greenland Current. See OCEAN CURRENT.

**ironbound**   *adj.* Said of a rocky coast without an anchorage or harbor.

**ironbound block**   *n.* A wooden pulley with wrought iron outside strap.

**iron mainsail**   *n.* Facetious name for an engine on a sailboat.

**iron-sick**   *adj.* Said of a wooden vessel when the fastenings have rusted and have become loose in rotting holes in the wood.

**isallobar**   *n.* (pron. eye-sal-o-bar.) Line on a weather chart connecting places of equal changes in air pressure during a given period of time. See ISOBAR.

**isallotherm**   *n.* Line on a weather chart connecting points in which an equal temperature variation has been observed over a 3-hour period.

**Isherwood system**   *n.* A system of building ships in which the main framing is longitudinal instead of transverse, as is more customary. The longitudinal timbers are fitted between transverse bulkheads, and the web frames are notched to accommodate them. Named for the British naval architect J. W. Isherwood, who first described the system in 1908.

**island**   *n.* (1) An area of land completely surrounded by water above the high-tide mark. See ATOLL. (2) The superstructure above the flight deck of an aircraft carrier where the command and flag bridges are located along with CIC, radars, and similar equipment.

**island shelf**   *n.* An area of shoal water surrounding an island similar to a continental shelf surrounding a continent.

**island slope**   *n.* The sharp increase in depth away from an island at the edge of an island shelf similar to a continental slope.

**isobar**   *n.* Line connecting points of equal atmospheric pressure shown on synoptic weather charts or **isobaric charts,** and oceanic subsurface analyses. See ISALLOBAR.

**isobath**   *n.* Line on a chart connecting points of equal depth on bathymetric charts.

**isobront**   *n.* Line on a chart along which the magnetic variation is the same.

**isoclinal chart**   *n.* A chart on which the points of the same magnetic dip or inclination are connected. The lines that connect the points are called **isoclinal lines** or **isoclinals.**

**isodynamic line**   *n.* Line on a chart connecting points of equal magnetic intensity on the Earth's surface.

**isogonic line**   *n.* Line on a chart connecting points of equal magnetic variation.

**isohaline line**   *n.* Line on an ocean chart connecting places with the same salinity.

**isomagnetic chart**   *n.* A presentation of equality of some magnetic element. The magnetic dates are compiled by the U.S. Geological Survey and the National Oceanographic and Atmospheric Administration in collaboration with the U.S. Naval Oceanographic Office. The seven elements shown on the seven different isomagnetic charts include (1) magnetic variation (the one most important to navigators) with lines connecting isogonic points, (2) magnetic inclination with isogonic lines, (3) horizontal intensity, (4) vertical intensity, (5) total intensity, (6) magnetic variation in north and south polar areas, and (7) magnetic grid variation.

**isophase (Iso)**   adj. Light phase description indicating a light alternating between equal periods of darkness and light. See LIGHT PHASE CHARACTERISTICS.

**isopleth line**   *n.* Line connecting areas of equal mean wave height on a **prognostic wave chart.**

**isopycnic line**   *n.* Line on a chart that connects similar seawater density at the same depth. Seawater density varies with pressure, salinity, and temperature. At a given depth, the density varies with temperature and salinity, and this can be charted.

**isothermal layer**   *n.* A stratum of water with the same temperature throughout.

**isotherm**   *n.* Lines drawn on a weather map or chart between all points having the same mean temperature over a given time period.

**isthmus**  *n.* A narrow strip of land connecting two larger landmasses.

# J

**J**  See JULIETT.

**J**  *n.* An admeasurer's symbol for the distance between the headstay and the mast when rating a boat for racing. See OUTREACH.

**jack**  *n.* (1) The flag flown at the bow "jack staff" of naval vessels when not underway but with crew aboard; a vessel in layup or mothballs doesn't fly the jack. (2) A device for moving heavy pieces of cargo. Also *jack screw.* See LAZY JACK.

**jack**  *v.* To turn the propeller shaft over to prevent sagging. To turn the shaft with a small auxiliary motor to prevent uneven heating of the turbine, used any time it's needed to rotate the shaft without putting way on and without engaging the main propulsion machinery. The auxiliary motor is called the **jacking screw.**

**jackass rig**  *n.* A term applied to any vessel that differs from the standard rig and lines of its class.

**jack clamp**  *n.* A device used for aligning adjacent structural members.

**jack crosstree**  *n.* (1) An iron rod crosstree at the head of a topgallant mast used for extending the shroud of a royal. (2) In fore-and-aft-rigged vessels, a hinged spreader that makes it possible to lower a topmast.

**jackknife**  *n.* A knife with a blade that folds into the handle, frequently carried by sailors for convenience and safety. The name comes from the Belgian cutler, Jacques de Liége, about 1590, the first man to make such a knife. On U.S. ships it is illegal to carry a sheath knife.

**jack ladder**  See JACOB'S LADDER.

**jack pin**  *n.* A belaying pin fitted across a shroud for the purpose of securing rigging.

**jack rope**  *n.* (1) In fore-and-aft vessels, the lacing that secures the foot of a sail to its boom. (2) In square-riggers, a line run through the grommets of a reef band used for reefing with a toggle on the jackstay.

**jack staff**  *n.* The staff at the bow on which the jack is flown. Merchant ships hoist the company flag on the jack staff, and warships hoist the union jack on the jack staff. The union jack is only flown in port.

**jackstay**  *n.* (1) The metal rod on the upper forward side of a yard to which the head of a square sail is bent and to which stirrups are seized to support the footropes. (2) A stiffening stay for a mizzen mast. (3) On a gaff-rigged vessel, a jackstay is a stay run from masthead over a strut at the height of the gaff jaws with sail hoisted and then down to the deck where it is fitted with a turnbuckle and fastened to the base of the mast.

**jack tar**  See TAR.

**jack yard**   *n.* A light spar secured to the head of a gaff topsail as a stiffener. Also *jenny yard.*

**Jacob's ladder**   *n.* A rope ladder with wooden steps used for going over the side or climbing a mast. A Jacob's ladder differs from a sea ladder in that a Jacob's ladder is portable and awkward to use. Also *jack ladder.*

**Jacob's staff**   See CROSS STAFF.

**jam**   *v.* (1) A rope is jammed when it cannot be hauled through a block. See PINCH; STARVE. (2) To sail so close to the wind that the upper section of the sail is backwinded; a ship is said to be **jammed in the wind** when this happens, but it is still making way and not in irons.

**jam cleat**   *n.* A cleat with horns of different lengths. The longer horn is closer to the deck or mast to which the cleat is fastened so that a line can be pulled under it and jammed.

**Jamie (or Jimmy) Green**   *n.* A clipper ship term for a fore-and-aft quadrilateral sail that is set on the bowsprit and jibboom under the headsails.

**JAN grid**   *n.* A grid system used by the Joint Army and Navy to afford a secure means for referring to geographical positions all over the world.

**Jansen clause**   *n.* A deductible clause in some marine insurance policies that leaves the owner liable for the first 3% of a claim in the event of a particular average on a ship although stranded, sunk, or burned.

**Japan Stream (Kuroshio)**   *n.* A North Pacific current that flows northeastward from Taiwan to the Ryaku Islands and along the coast of Japan, and meanders north and east. A part of it curves to the east around the Hawaiian Islands, but the larger part continues on to the Aleutians, this part being known as the North Pacific Current. The Japanese term *kuroshio* means "black stream."

**Jason clause**   *n.* Marine bill of lading clause that protects the owners of a vessel against the consequences of damage through unseaworthiness, latent defects, and so on, for which the shipowners are not responsible. The *Jason* clause provides that where the carrier has exercised due diligence to make the vessel seaworthy and properly manned, equipped and supplied, cargo and shipowner shall contribute in general average as if the loss had not occurred from negligent navigation. The name comes from a 1912 case regarding the steamer *Jason.* The Supreme Court upheld the clause as valid.

**jaw**   *n.* The distance between two points on a strand measured along the length of a rope. A hard-laid rope that brings the strands close together is said to have a **short jaw.** A soft-laid rope with strands loosely twisted is said to have a **long jaw.**

**jaw rope**   *n.* A rope between the jaws led forward of the mast to secure the jaws and their boom to the mast.

**jaws**   *n.* The semicircular extension of a spar or boom that forms the inner end of a boom, which partially surrounds the after side of a mast and holds the spar—usually a boom or gaff—in place.

**jeep carrier**   *n.* Small U.S. Navy aircraft carrier used extensively during World War II. It was named for a small animal in the comic strip *Popeye,* and has nothing to do with the land vehicle, the Jeep.

**jeers**   *n.* A heavy tackle with double or triple blocks (**jeer block**) used to hoist the lower yards up the mast to their proper position on the mast.

**jetsam**   *n.* Debris lost or thrown over the side to lighten ship and that washes ashore. See FLOTSAM; LAGEN.

**jettison**   *v.* To throw cargo or equipment over the side to lighten ship or improve stability. Marine underwriters consider the jettisoning of goods when carried out to save the ship as part of a general average loss. See JETSAM.

**jetty**   *n.* A wharf, pier, quay, or mole, built out from shore but connected to it, and used as a breakwater.

**jewel block**   *n.* (1) A small block on the outer end of a yard used for hoisting studding sails. (2) A small block on a signal yard used for hoisting signal flags.

**jewelry**   *n.* (1) Connecting devices used for holding sections of a pontoon causeway together. (2) Western rivers term for the same gear when used to raft barges.

**Jew's harp**   *n.* (1) The ring at the upper end of the shank of an anchor to which the shackle is secured. (2) Any U-shaped shackle.

**jib**   *n.* A triangular, fore-and-aft sail set on a stay forward of the mast: a headsail. The jib replaced the square spritsail in the early 18th century. A **flying jib** is set on a wire or headstay leading to a bowsprit and forward of the main jib. The jib was introduced in the Royal Navy in 1705, and may have originated in Holland as early as the mid-17th century. See MARCONI RIG.

**jib and jigger**   *n.* A sail combination using only a headsail and a jigger on a yawl.

**jib and mainsail**   *n.* A sloop rig when a topmast is not used. With the prevalence of such rigs, the term is rarely heard today.

**jibboom**   *n.* An extension of the bowsprit used on larger sailing vessels.

**jibboom saddle**   *n.* The wooden piece at the joint between the bowsprit and the jibboom that holds the heel of the jibboom in place.

**jibe (or gybe)**   (1) *v.* To turn a vessel to bring the wind around behind her and to the other side causing the boom to change from one side to the other. A fore-and-aft-rigged vessel is said to jibe or less frequently be jibed. (2) The maneuver that is executed either accidentally or on purpose when a sailing vessel is jibed. An accidental jibe can be injurious to the crew and rigging. A controlled jibe, however, is often necessary. See ABOUT; CHINESE JIBE; POINTS OF SAILING; TACK.

**jibe mark**   *n.* The mark at the end of a reaching leg of a race that requires a jibe.

**jibe-o (or jibe-ho)**   *interj.* The word from the helmsman when he turns the wheel to leeward and begins a jibe.

**jib guy**   *n.* The chain or cable that stays a jibboom laterally. See SQUARE-RIGGED VESSEL.

**jib halyard**   *n.* The line used for hoisting the jib. See MARCONI RIG.

**jib-headed**   *adj.* (1) used to describe a rig with only triangular sails and no square sails. (2) Any triangular sail such as staysails and Bermudian sails. A **jib-headed topsail,** for example, is a triangular fore-and-aft sail set above a spritsail.

**jib lead**   *n.* A deck device that leads the jib sheet to the cockpit. See FAIRLEAD.

**jib martingale**   *n.* A wire rope that leads from the jibboom to the dolphin striker to support the boom from beneath. See MARTINGALE.

**jib sheet**   *n.* The line attached to the clew of the jib that is used to control the angle at which the wind strikes the jib. See MARCONI RIG.

**jibstay**   *n.* The wire on which the jib is raised. See HALYARD; MARCONI RIG.

**jib topsail**  *n.* A triangular sail carried above and forward of the jib. On a cutter the inner jib is a jib staysail, and the outer jib is the jib topsail.

**jib traveler**  *n.* An athwartships guide aft of the jib along which a jib sheet block rides.

**jig**  *n.* A purchase on a loop or bight of a halyard.

**jig**  *v.* To take short hauls on the fall of a tackle.

**jigger**  *n.* (1) A tackle with a single and a double block; the standing part of the fall is secured to the single block to have a mechanical advantage of three or four, depending on which is the moving block. Also *handy billy; watch tackle.* (2) The mizzen on a yawl; the sail and the mast are both called jiggers. The term is not properly used on a ketch, which, by definition, has the aftermast forward of the rudder post. (3) The gaff sail on the fourth mast (the **jigger mast**) of a five-, six-, or seven-masted schooner. (4) The course on the aftermost mast (the **jigger mast**) of a four- or five-masted bark or ship.

**jigger boomkin**  *n.* A spar perpendicular to the stern of a yawl with a block on the outboard end through which is rove the jigger or mizzen sheet. See BOOMKIN.

**jigger yard**  *n.* The yard on which a jigger is extended.

**jimmy legs**  See MASTER-AT-ARMS.

**jingle (bell)**  *n.* A bell in the engine room used to transmit orders from the bridge for power astern. The jingle is used in conjunction with a gong to signal the engineer from the bridge for other movements. See ENGINE ROOM BELLS.

**jog along**  *v.* To sail slowly.

**jogged frame**  *n.* One of the notched frames of a lap-straked hull with each

strake fitted into a notch to give more support and a better connection between frame and planking.

**joggle**  *n.* An abrupt bend or offset in a plate, bar, or frame, to enable it to fit around a projection.

**joggled plating**  *n.* Plating that has been joggled at the edges to eliminate liners.

**joiner**  *n.* (1) A woodworker who does lighter, finished work than a carpenter, such as cabinets, deck covers, and wood railings. (2) An independent merchant ship sailed to join a convoy. Several **joiners** sailing together make up a **joiner convoy.**

**joiner bulkhead**  *n.* Light bulkhead used to build offices and cabins that is not designed for structural strength or watertight integrity.

**joiner door**  *n.* A conventional door on a ship, not waterproof.

**joiner shackle**  *n.* The shackle and pin used to join shots of an anchor cable.

**jolly boat**  *n.* (1) A work boat carried at the stern on merchant schooners. (2) A small racing centerboard sailboat that carries no ballast, larger than a pram or sailing dinghy but less than 18 feet in length. See RESCUE BOAT.

**jolly jumpers**  *n.* Clipper ship sails that were set above the moonrakers.

**Jolly Roger**  *n.* The traditional black pirate flag (probably never used by any pirate ship) with skull and crossbones, flown on naval ships during crossing-the-equator high jinks. "Roger" was the name for a rogue in 16th century England.

**Jones Act (1920)**  *n.* An act of Congress that became law in 1920. The law remains one of the most sweeping changes in maritime law as it pertains to a seaman's rights, especially in ending indentured servitude for seamen and enabling them to recover damages in the event of injury due to the negligence of the master or another seaman. The Jones Act also forbids the shipment of goods between two U.S. ports without an intermediary stop in a foreign port except by ships built in the United States. See LA FOLLETTE SEAMEN'S ACT.

**Juliett**   n. Phonetic word for the letter "J." As a single-letter hoist, it means "I am on fire; keep clear."

**jumbo**   n. A forestaysail set on a topsail schooner in place of a foresail with a **jumbo boom** laced to the after part of the foot; a jumbo appears upside down because the point is at the foremast and secured by a clew iron.

**jumper**   n. (1) A preventer that holds down a boom, spar, or yard. (2) A sailor's blouse.

**jumper guy**   n. A preventer used for holding down one of the ends of a bowsprit whisker.

**jumper stay**   n. (1) A stay that is led from a lower masthead to a tackle on the vessel's side. Also *preventer; spring stay*. (2) A stay set up in heavy weather to prevent a yard from jumping. (3) In fore-and-aft sailing vessels, a short stay that is led from the masthead over a short **jumper stay spreader** (or **jackstay strut**) to a point just below the head of the jibstay. It is rigged to increase the rigidity of the top part of the mast and counteracts the downward pull of the mainsail. Also *diamond shrouds*. See MARCONI RIG.

**jump of a sea**   n. A short, quick sea.

**jump ship**   phr. To leave a naval ship without permission and with no intention of returning; to desert.

**junction buoy** (or **mark**)   n. An aid to navigation placed at a channel junction or at an obstruction. See MIDCHANNEL AIDS TO NAVIGATION.

**junior officer**   n. In the U.S. Navy, commissioned officers with the rank of lieutenant commander and below, and the equivalent in other services. In practice, ensigns, lieutenants (j.g.), and lieutenants are considered junior officers.

**junior officer of the deck (JOOD)** n. A commissioned line officer in training to become qualified as an officer of the deck. An efficient and competent JOOD can relieve the awesome responsibilities of the OOD to a great extent, but the OOD can never be lulled into a false sense of security. In a general court-martial that has to do with navigation or the handling of the vessel by the bridge personnel, the proper conduct of the ship is taken to be the responsibility of the OOD and the captain.

**junk**   n. (1) A term applied in the western world to all Chinese luggers with high poops, overhanging bows, and full-battened square sails or gaff sails. The word comes from the Malay *jong,* a seagoing vessel. (2) Worn-out cordage that is ready to be teased apart and used for fenders, matting, caulking material, swabs, and so on. (3) Salted meat that became hard was called **salt junk.**

**jurisdiction**   n. Control and maintenance of law and order within a specified area. Federal jurisdiction over maritime affairs in the United States is maintained by a variety of agencies, the most important of which is the U.S. Coast Guard. Federal jurisdiction includes (1) coastal waters off beaches and all bodies of water open to the sea or connected to the sea by channels. "Open to the sea" in this context includes tributaries and bays off the Mississippi River as far away as Wisconsin. (2) Federal jurisdiction further includes bodies of water that lie in two or more states if vessels can use the body of water for interstate commerce. The construction of a dam on a river does not exclude it from federal jurisdiction even though the dam may preclude communication with the sea. (3) Any body of water that can be used for travel to a foreign country; lakes and inland rivers at the Canadian and Mexican borders would be examples. Federal law further preempts and takes precedence over control by the states on matters of safety standards, but allows states to go further in matters of safety to meet a local situation. States also are allowed control over licensing, trailering, and such matters.

**jury** *adj.* Makeshift or temporary, as in jury rig, a jury mast, or a jury rudder. An emergency arrangement made to enable a vessel to make port or a place where it can be repaired.

**Jutland Current** *n.* A narrow, local, nontidal current off the coast of Denmark. It originates partly from the counterclockwise flow in the tidal North Sea and is pushed by the prevailing winds from south to west to northwest over 50% of the year. The transverse current flows from the English coast towards the Skaggerak. The current, retaining its major nontidal characteristics, flows northeastward along the northwest coast of Denmark at 1.5 to 2 knots.

# K

**K** See KILO.

**Kamchatka Current** *n.* A branch of the Kuroshio Current that branches and passes by the Kamchatka Peninsula of northeastern Siberia and then toward the Aleutian Islands. See OCEAN CURRENT.

**kapok** *n.* A silky fiber from the tropical kapok tree fruit *(Ceiba pentandra)*, used for padding in life preservers.

**katabatic wind** *n.* A cold wind that blows down an incline; opposite of anabatic wind. The bora of the Adriatic is a dramatic example.

**kayak** *n.* Traditionally, an Inuit canoe made from bones (for the frame) and hides from seals and other animals for the covering, and used in the Arctic for hunting seals and whales. Modern materials have been applied to the design, which has been adapted to white-water competition.

**keckle** (or **kekle**) *v.* To wrap cordage, called **keckling,** around lines to prevent chafing. Keckling is usually used on bow cables and cables coming in contact with the vessel's bottom, and is also used simply to dress up docking lines.

**kedge** *n.* Any anchor used for pulling a boat or ship free after grounding.

**kedge** *v.* To pull a vessel by using an anchor, a kedge. The anchor is put in a small boat and taken ahead of the vessel to a place where it is dropped into the water; the anchor line is then hauled in to pull the vessel forward.

**keel** *n.* On large vessels, a structural member that is the backbone of the ship; it runs along the centerline of the bottom. On small craft, there are many external keel designs that do not run the length of the vessel, such as a **fin keel.** The purpose of the keel in small vessels, if it projects downward, is to resist leeway forces and to give additional stability. Framed vessels always have full-length keels. See FLAT KEEL.

**keel, vertical** *n.* A vertical plate used as reinforcement for the keel. Also *center keelson.* See STABILITY.

**keelage**   *n.* A fee levied against ships anchoring or mooring in a port or harbor.

**keel bender**   *n.* Heavy power press used in shipbuilding for flanging such members as a dished flat keel.

**keel blocks**   *n.* The blocks in a dry dock or ways on which the keel of a ship rests while being built or repaired.

**keelboat**   *n.* A shallow-draft covered barge usually propelled by sweeps or poles, and used for river transportation.

**keel bracket**   *n.* Usually a triangular plate that connects the vertical keel and flat keel plates found between the frames or floors of a vessel.

**keel condenser**   *n.* Tubing outside the keels of steam launches through which steam was pumped to be condensed before being recirculated to the boiler. The tubing was cooled by the surrounding seawater.

**keel cooler**   *n.* A set of tubes outside the hull through which coolant from the heat exchanger passes. Also *channel cooler.*

**keel depth**   *n.* (1) The vertical distance from the waterline to the bottom of the keel. (2) On submarines, it refers to the depth at which the boat is operating.

**keel docking**   *n.* The process of placing docking keels at the bilge blocks to help distribute the weight of a vessel when being built or repaired.

**keelhaul**   *v.* An ancient and extremely cruel form of punishment in which a man was pulled down one side of the ship and under the bottom, and up the other side; with heavy barnacle encrustation on the bottom, the victim would be badly cut and was highly likely to develop blood poisoning and die.

**keel rails**   *n.* Rails on the underside of lifeboats to provide handholds for struggling survivors if the lifeboat overturns.

**keel rider**   *n.* A plate that runs along the top of flooring to connect the flooring to the vertical keel.

**keelson**   *n.* (1) A large I-beam above the vertical keel on the rider used to reinforce the vertical keel. On vessels with double bottoms, the same member is called the **center girder.** (2) Fore-and-aft girders on the sides of the vertical keel or at the bilges.

**keelson lug**   *n.* A short piece of angle iron that connects the keelson to the floor plate.

**keel stop**   *n.* A small block on the keel of a ship's boat that prevents its sliding around in the deck chocks.

**keep her full**   *phr.* The order to stay off the wind enough to keep the sails filled. See JAM; PINCH.

**keep her off**   *phr.* Command to keep a vessel farther from the wind than she is at the time of the command.

**keeping ship**   *n.* Going through normal shipboard routine when the vessel is not exercising or operating.

**keeping station**   *n.* (1) Maintaining a position with relation to a given guidon; a vessel will be told to take a position, for example, in the van, 2,250 yards bearing 060° relative, from a given vessel that is usually one of the largest in the operation and easily seen on radar. (2) Said of an anchored vessel that is on station.

**keep the sea**   *phr.* Said of a commander with great admiration that he stays at sea and carries out his assigned mission under all reasonable conditions. "Captain Hawkins can be depended on to keep the sea as long as practical."

**keld** *n.* A smooth area of water in ruffled water.

**kellet** *n.* A weight placed on an anchor line to hold it down, thus steadying the anchor cable to help the anchor bite into the ground. See SENTINEL.

**kelpie** *n.* A sea sprite that haunts the northern British and Irish waters.

**kenter shackle** *n.* Formerly used as a connecting shackle for shots of anchor chain. These along with the U-shackle have been superseded by detachable links.

**kentledge** (or **kentlage**) *n.* Pig iron used either for weight to temporarily incline a vessel or for ballast and usually placed on keelson plates.

**kentledge goods** *n.* Cargo stowed in lower holds for additional ballast.

**ketch** *n.* A two-masted vessel with a shorter after mast (the mizzenmast) stepped forward of the rudder post. Some confusion arises when the after mast of a ketch is abaft the helm, but forward of the rudder post; when this is the case, the vessel is still a ketch. A yawl has the after mast, the **jigger mast,** stepped abaft the rudder post, although the distinction between yawl and ketch is sometimes based on the size of the mizzen or jigger, especially in Great Britain. A ketch differs from a two-masted schooner in that a ketch's mizzenmast, the second mast, is shorter than the mainmast. On a schooner, the two masts are the same height or the **foremast** is shorter; the mainmast being aft is the taller mast. See RIG.

**kevel** *n.* A heavy belaying cleat or pin for heavy cables See KEVEL HEAD; KEVELS.

**kevel head** *n.* The top of a frame when it rises above the level of a deck and can be used as a kevel.

**kevels** *n.* (1) A pair of timbers that are mounted in a step on deck or bolted to the side of a ship; at the top, they branch into horns to belay ropes. (2) A very large cleat. Also *cavil.* See BITT; BUTTON; CLEAT; CRUCIFORM.

**Kevlar** *n.* Trade name of a brown synthetic material manufactured by Du Pont and used to fabricate low-stretch sails and cordage.

**key** *n.* (1) Any tapered wooden or steel peg or wedge used to secure a steering wheel to its axle, a propeller to its shaft, a tiller to the rudder post, and so on. (2) A tapered shape used to wedge deck planking or to join wood tightly. (3) A low offshore island or reef such as any of the Florida Keys. From the Spanish *cayo,* with the same meaning. Also *cay.*

**keying ring** *n.* A lead ring driven around the forelock pin in an anchor shackle to key it in place.

**khamsin** *n.* (pron. cam-seen) A hot wind that blows across Egypt from late March through May. It carries heavy sandstorms far out into the eastern Mediterranean. The name is Arabic and means 50 (days).

**kick** *n.* (1) Sudden movement of the stern, used to describe the motion of the stern when the rudder is turned abruptly or when a wave pushes it to one side or the other. See KNUCKLE.

**kick** *v.* To throw the helm hard over abruptly, to throw the stern in order to avoid a man overboard or any other object in the water.

**kicker** *n.* (1) An outboard motor. (2) A lug mizzen sheeted on an outrigger (British). (3) British usage for "foreguy."

**kicking strap** *n.* (1) A general term that refers to a preventer that keeps a boom from rising, keeps a sail flatter, or holds a line in a chock (whaling term). (2) British usage for "hiking strap."

**kid**  *n.* (1) Variant of *kit,* such as mess kit. (2) British fisherman's term for an area in which the fish are kept and prevented from sliding into working areas by a **kid board.**

**killick (or killock)**  *n.* A stone used for an anchor on a small boat. To "up killick" is to weigh anchor. A killick is secured to the anchor rope by a **killick hitch,** a combination of timber hitch and a half hitch.

**Kilo**  *n.* Phonetic word for the letter "K." Used as a single-flag hoist, it means "You should stop immediately."

**king bridge**  *n.* A heavy timber or girder between two goalpost masts.

**king plank**  *n.* The center plank strip on a laid deck.

**king post**  *n.* (1) A heavy centerline pillar in a ship's hold. (2) A short mast that supports a cargo boom.

**king spoke**  *n.* The spoke of a wheel that is straight up when the rudder is amidship. The king spoke is usually wrapped or carved to make it easier to steer by feel and to know when the rudder is amidship when coming out of a turn, for example.

**Kingston valve**  *n.* Conical valve on a ship's bottom with the vortex inboard, designed to close on its seat from the pressure of the seawater. Used on ballast tanks.

**kink**  *n.* A twist in a line that keeps it from running free. See HOCKLE.

**kippage**  *n.* Mariners and seamen sailing aboard a ship. The word derives from the French *equipage,* which, when used in the nautical sense, includes personnel and crew but not equipment and accoutrement as does the military definition.

**kit**  See KID (1).

**kite**  *n.* (1) Nickname for spinnaker or a Genoa jib. (2) In square-riggers, the highest and lightest sails. (3) A device towed behind a ship for purposes of deceiving an enemy submarine.

**kiyi**  *n.* Small hand scrub brush made from coir fibers used by sailors to scrub clothes.

**knee**  *n.* An angular reinforcing structure used when two members come together at an angle.

**knee of the head**  *n.* A timber projected from the stem and designed to spread the upward strain on the bowsprit brought by the foremast rigging.

**knife edge**  *n.* Rim of a doorframe or a hatch that seats against a gasket to make a watertight fit.

**knighthead frame**  *n.* Frame used a short distance from the stem in steel sailing ships, connected to a small triangular bulkhead with an opening for the bowsprit.

**knightheads**  *n.* The first timbers on both sides of the stem that extend upward through the deck to support the bowsprit. Only seen on large sailing ships. Also *apostles; dograils.*

**knights**  *n.* Bitts on the after side of a mast through which the running rigging is rove.

**knittle**  See NETTLE.

**knockabout**  *n.* Sailing vessel of any size, sloop-rigged, with or without fixed keel, but always without a bowsprit. A similar boat with two masts was called a knockabout schooner. The knockabout was developed about 1900 with the headstay set on the stemhead plate.

**knock down**  *v.* To be pushed over by a sudden strong gust. See KNOCK-DOWN.

**knockdown** *n.* A sudden wind of sufficient strength to knock over a sailboat almost to the critical point or to the point it will not recover. Usually green water comes over the side during a knockdown.

**knoll** *n.* (1) An elevation of less than 1,000 meters above the seafloor and with limited plateau at the summit. (2) A small, more-or-less rounded hill.

**knot** *n.* (1) Any of almost innumerable configurations of rope or line either unintentional or for a specific function, as a bend or hitch. (2) The measure of a vessel or aircraft's speed, equivalent to one nautical mile per hour. To say "knots per hour" is redundant. "We averaged 16 knots for the day's run." A nautical mile is 6076.11549 feet (to which Bowditch adds "approximately").

**knotmeter** *n.* A word of recent coinage, it is a boat's speedometer with a display near the helmsman as well as other locations on some vessels. It usually shows speed through the water, but may indicate speed over the ground if driven by loran, SATNAV, or other derivatives.

**knuckle** *n.* (1) A sharp bend in a plate or a shape. (2) The angle formed at the intersection of the counter and the shell plating just below the deck at the stern. See KICK.

**knuckle line** *n.* The intersection of the upper and lower parts of the counter.

**knuckle molding** *n.* The line of quarter-round molding fitted at the knuckle line.

**knuckle plate** *n.* Any plate bent to form a knuckle.

**knuckling** *n.* Buckling of plating caused by the contraction of a weld across the top.

**Kona winds** *n.* Storms and southerly winds over the Hawaiian Islands.

**kort nozzle** *n.* A cylindrical casing built around a propeller of shoal-draft vessels to increase efficiency.

**Kuroshio** See JAPAN STREAM.

**kymatology** *n.* The study of waves and wave action.

# L

**L** See LIMA.

**L's of navigation** *n.* Traditional saying: lead, log, and lookout.

**labeled cargo** *n.* Goods labeled for special handling, such as explosives and corrosive chemicals.

**labor** *v.* Said of a vessel when it is driven against heavy seas.

**Labrador Current** *n.* The cold current that flows south from Baffin Bay to the Grand Banks carrying ice with it. At that point the current splits, with part going south inshore of the Gulf Stream while the rest flows eastward to become part of the North Atlantic Current. These two streams do not mix, but there is tremendous turbulence along the cold wall where they abut. See OCEAN CURRENT.

**lace** *v.* To secure a sail to a mast or spar by spirally wrapping a line, called **lacing,** through eyes on the sail. See LASH; LASKETS.

# Knots

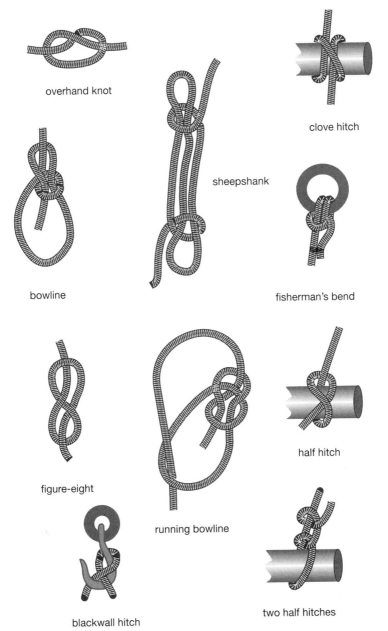

overhand knot

clove hitch

sheepshank

bowline

fisherman's bend

figure-eight

half hitch

running bowline

blackwall hitch

two half hitches

**lacing**   *n.* Cordage used to secure a sail to a boom or mast. See LACE.

**ladar**   *n.* (pron. laydar) A device that uses laser beams, instead of radio or microwaves as radar does, to detect a target and determine distance and velocity.

**ladder**   *n.* A stairway as well as what is commonly understood to be a ladder by landsmen. On a ship, any set of steps, whether inclined or vertical, that takes you from one deck to another is a "ladder." So there is the **mast ladder,** the **bridge ladder,** the **forecastle ladder,** and so on.

**ladder screen**   *n.* Sheeting fastened to the underside of a ladder to prevent loss of gear by people on the ladder.

**lade**   *v.* To load a ship with cargo or ballast.

**laden**   *adj.* Loaded; usually qualified to describe how a vessel is loaded, as **laden in ballast, laden in bulk, fully laden,** and so on.

**lading**   *n.* Cargo or freight put aboard a vessel. See BILL OF LADING.

**La Follette Seamen's Act (1915)** The basic act that improved working conditions and life in general for seamen on American ships. It was introduced by the Progressive Party senator from Wisconsin, Robert Marion La Follette, 1855–1925. The La Follette Seamen's Act and the Jones Act form the foundation for the rights of United States seamen. See JONES ACT.

**lagen**   *n.* (rhymes with wagon) A term used in maritime law for cargo that is thrown over in an emergency with a lanyard and buoy fastened to the cargo to make it easy to locate and recover later. This method of losing cargo for later recovery is widespread among drug smugglers. See FLOTSAM; JETSAM.

**lagging**   *n.* Insulation on steam and hot-water pipes to prevent dispersion of heat.

**lagging of the tide**   See PRIMING OF THE TIDE.

**lagoon**   *n.* A shallow body of water separated from the sea by sandbars or coral reefs.

**lagoon beach**   *n.* An elongated barrier of sediment separated from a coast by a lagoon.

**laid up**   *adj.* Said of a ship that is out of service, tied up at a pier, or in drydock, but not mothballed.

**lake**   *n.* (1) Any relatively permanent body of inland water. Occasionally, an especially large saltwater lake is called a sea. In Louisiana, some bodies of water that connect with the sea are also called lakes. (2) An expanded part of a river.

**land**   *n.* The shore above the surf. "No land in sight."

**land**   *v.* To come to land or to come ashore. A vessel lands when it comes to the shore or pier, but not when it anchors or simply loses way while underway. An aircraft lands when it puts down ashore or on a flight deck.

**land breeze**   *n.* A flow of air from the land toward the sea. The opposite of a sea breeze. Typically, a land breeze begins in late afternoon when the sea becomes warmer than the land.

**land, ho!**   *interj.* The hail given when anyone aboard first sights land.

**land ice**   *n.* Ice that has broken loose from a glacier and is floating in the sea.

**landfall**   *n.* The first sighting of land after being at sea for some time. Ships voyaging from New Zealand to England make landfalls at Cape Horn and Gran

Canaria, which is to say they set a course to sight land at these points.

**landfall buoy**   *n.* British term for "sea buoy."

**landfall light**   *n.* A primary seacoast light established to assist vessels in making a landfall.

**landfast ice**   *n.* Ice attached to land that has become beached or is held fast in shallow water. Also *land ice.*

**landing**   *n.* (1) The act of bringing a vessel to a pier or an aircraft to rest. See LAND. (2) A place where personnel or cargo are loaded or unloaded from a vessel. A **fleet landing** is a pier from which personnel and light cargo are loaded and unloaded to and from ship's boats that go between ships and the landing.

**landing craft**   *n.* Amphibious craft designed for carrying troops, equipment, and provisions for relatively short distances, with the ability to beach and be unloaded before putting to sea again. See LANDING SHIP.

**landing edge**   *n.* The edge of deck or hull plating that is inboard and not visible from the outside. See SIGHT EDGE.

**landing ship**   *n.* A vessel designed to make long sea voyages for the purpose of landing troops and supplies onto a beach and then removing itself from the beach. See DOCK LANDING SHIP; TANK LANDING TANK.

**landing ship, medium rocket (LSMR)**   *n.* Amphibious vessel used in shore bombardment operations and capable of firing 380 5-inch rockets per minute.

**landing stage**   *n.* A platform attached to the shore for the purpose of landing and embarking passengers and cargo.

**landing strake**   *n.* The strake just below the sheer strake and second below the gunwale.

**landlubber**   *n.* A derisive term for one who is not familiar with the ways of the sea and seamen.

**landmark**   *n.* Land objects such as flagpoles, stacks, hospital, or hotel cupola that are readily identified by vessels off a coast. These are shown by symbols on charts.

**land sky**   *n.* A dark pattern that is reflected on the underside of a cloud when it is over land but not over snow or ice.

**lang-lay rope**   *n.* A wire rope with the individual wires twisted the same way the strands are laid. Visually the strands run at a pronounced angle to the axis of the rope.

**langrage**   *n.* Case shot loaded with small shot and iron scraps to damage sails and rigging. Also *langrel; langridge.*

**lanyard**   *n.* A small line tied to an object. A boatswain's mate carries the boatswain's pipe on a lanyard around his neck. A lanyard on a port holds it open; a lanyard on a buoy makes it easier to pick up in the water. (2) In sailing vessels, lanyards are short lengths of rope rove through deadeyes for the purpose of making the shrouds taut.

**lap**   *n.* (1) The amount of overlay in a lap joint. (2) The amount a genoa jib overlaps the mainsail.

**lapper**   *n.* A headsail that barely overlaps the mast. It occupies 120% of the foretriangle, more than a working jib and less than a genoa.

**lapstrake**   *n.* Wooden hull planking in which the top strake overlaps the one next below it, and so on. Also *clinker-built.*

**larboard**   *n.* or *adj.* The port side.

**large** *adv.* To sail the wind abaft the beam and, in a fore-and-aft-rigged vessel, with sheets well eased out, as on a broad reach. To be sailing by and large is to be on a reach, while full and by denotes a close reach, and by the wind the same as close-hauled.

**large navigational buoy (LNB)** or **super buoy** *n.* Very large aid to navigation developed by the U.S. Coast Guard to replace lightships. These aids have light, sound signals, and often a radio beacon. These are about 40 feet in diameter and rise 30 feet above the surface of the water.

**lascar** *n.* An East Indian sailor employed on a British vessel. From the Hindi *lashkari*, soldier.

**LASH** *n.* Acronym for "lighter aboard ship," a system of shipping cargo in a lighter or barge on board a cargo ship. Cargo ships are designed to carry 70–90 barges that are unloaded at their destination and towed to unloading stations.

**lash** *v.* (1) To bind or secure with **lashing** (rope) or **wire lashing** by wrapping and tying with a **knot** (rope) or a **hitch** (wire). To tie together or to secure an object. "Lash the oil drums together to keep them from rolling around on deck." (2) To whip a member of the crew, now illegal in most countries. To "let the cat out of the bag and give him 40 lashes" was to take the cat-o'-nine-tails out of its bag and to whip the prisoner 40 times.

**lash and carry** *v.* To lash hammocks together and stow them in their netting.

**laskets** *n.* Small loops of cord used to secure the bonnet to the foot of the jib. The **latching key** was the final loop that was run through the laskets to prevent their unreeving. **Latchings** were the beckets in the bonnet through which the laskets were run to facilitate lacing the bonnet.

**latchings** See LASKETS.

**lateen** *adj.* A triangular sail set from a long spar at an angle to a short mast. It is the picturesque and ancient rig of Arabian dhows, feluccas; and other sailing vessels characteristic of the eastern Mediterranean Sea and Indian Ocean.

**lateral buoyage system** *n.* Officially known as the Uniform Lateral System, the system of aids to navigation in which the shape, number, and color of the aids indicate the navigable water. When used at the sides of channels they are assigned colors to indicate the side they mark and numbers to indicate their sequence along the channel. The lateral system is the primary system used in the United States. See CARDINAL BUOYAGE SYSTEM; INTERNATIONAL ASSOCIATION OF LIGHTHOUSE AUTHORITIES.

**lateral marks** *n.* The aids to navigation that mark the port and starboard sides of a channel.

**lateral resistance** *n.* A hull's resistance to being driven sideways. An external keel greatly increases lateral resistance.

**lateral sensitivity** *n.* The property of a range that tells a navigator when the vessel is moving laterally from the range line. The farther the ranges are apart, the greater the lateral sensitivity. See RANGE (8).

**latitude (L; lat.)** *n.* The angular distance north or south from the equator measured along a meridian beginning with 0° at the equator to 90° at the poles. **High latitudes** are those closest to the poles; **low latitudes** are closer to the equator. See DECLINATION; LONGITUDE.

**launch** *n.* A ship's boat; an open powerboat.

**launch** *v.* (1) To put a vessel in the water, whether a dinghy or a cruise ship. With larger ships today, launching is frequently accomplished by opening the gates of a dry dock to allow the water to come in around the ship to float it. (2) To put in flight, said of aircraft when "launched" from a carrier's flight deck.

**launch-ways**   n. The ground ways and sliding ways used when launching a vessel.

**lay**   n. The direction of the twist of the strands of a rope or wire cable. The strands of a **right-laid rope** spiral up to the right, while the strands of the much less common **left-laid rope** spiral up to the left. In **regular lay,** the yarns of the strands twist the opposite way from the lay of the strand, while with **lang lay,** the yarns are laid in the same way as the strands. Thus a rope or cable can be either right or left regular lay, or right or left lang lay. A fifth lay is the **reverse lay,** a right-lay rope with the lay of the individual yarns alternating between regular lay and lang lay.

**lay**   v. (1) To plan (a course). "We laid a course for Isla Majeures." (2) To aim

## Rope and Cable Lay

right lay, or hawser-laid rope, or Z-twist

left lay, or S-twist, rope

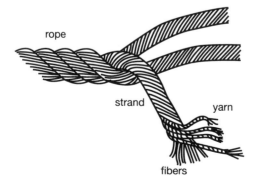

rope

strand        yarn

fibers

a gun or cannon in a vertical plane. The personnel who did this were **gunlayers.** In the sailing ship navy, gunlayers raised (elevated) and lowered the cannon while the captain turned the ship so that the guns would be pointed in the right direction, because the cannon had no freedom in a horizontal plane. On modern ships, gunlayer includes both pointers (the personnel who control elevation) and trainers (who control the horizontal "train"). (3) To place strands together to be twisted into rope. (4) To place a vessel in a specified position. "Lay USS *Missouri* alongside the wharf at the ammunition depot." (5) To go, with reference to an arbitrary position aboard ship. One could be ordered to lay below, to lay aloft (to go up a mast), or lay out on a yard (to furl a sail). To "lay up a vessel" is to tie it up and allow it to remain idle. (6) To stand by: "The ship is to lay at anchor for the night." (7) Used of wind velocity, to diminish in strength.

**lay barge**   *n.* A shoal draft barge used in constructing and laying underwater pipelines. Sections of the pipeline are welded and paid out over the stern as the barge is moved ahead. These barges are used in marshy areas and in offshore projects.

**lay-by**   *n.* Any place where it is possible to anchor out of the current and out of the traffic.

**lay day**   *n.* Free day at a dock before demurrage begins. Lay days are included in contracts for maintenance and repair downtime for both the ship and the shore facility. It is also used to mean a day between boat races to allow repairing gear and resting the crew. In contracting for lay days, **running days** are every day; otherwise Sundays and holidays are not lay days. Beware of charter parties that allow for holidays; some ports come up with a remarkable number of holidays.

**lay line**   *n.* A course that will take a close-hauled boat around a mark, close

aboard. A **starboard lay line** will take a close-hauled boat on a starboard tack around a mark. A **port lay line** does the same for a boat on a port tack.

**lay off**   *v.* (1) To chart or plot a course. "Lay off a course to the Cape of Good Hope." (2) To heave to in a general area and wait for further instructions. "Lay off the fantail until the Old Man is ready for the gig."

**lay up**   *v.* To put (a boat) in storage for a period, usually for the winter, when the tanks are drained, the waterlines flushed, and other tasks done. "We'll lay up *Nevasink* after Labor Day."

**lazarette**   *n.* (1) A small storage space at the stern of small craft or between decks on larger vessels. On larger ships, a paint locker in the 'tween decks is often called a lazarette. (2) An isolation hospital or a ship used as a quarantine station for people with contagious diseases. The name derives from the Biblical Lazarus, in the parable of the rich man and the beggar who was "laid at his gate full of sores" (Luke 16:19–31). Also *lazaretto.* See BOOBY HATCH.

**lazy guy**   *n.* One of two lines bent on the spinnaker pole to control the spinnaker. The lazy guy is the **slack guy,** while the controlling guy is called the **guy.** A guy that prevents the pole from rising is the **foreguy,** which is bent to the clew of the spinnaker. When the spinnaker is jibed, the lazy guy is slack and is secured in the new spinnaker pole; the pole is hoisted into position and set. Also *boom guy.*

**lazy jack** (or **line**)   *n.* A bridle system extending from the top of the mast to the sides of the boom on a sailboat that holds the sail as it is lowered. See GAFF. (2) A light line used for retrieving a hawser.

**lead**   *n.* A term for a narrow channel through pack ice.

**lead**   *v.* To run a rope or line through an object or several objects such as blocks or chocks to guide the rope.

**lead and lead line**   *n.* (pron. led) A cylindrical piece of lead with line attached used for determining depth of water. The lead weight is hollow at the bottom so that it can be armed with beeswax or tallow for picking up bottom mud to determine the nature of the bottom. The lead line is marked at regular intervals so that depth can be determined when the weight reaches the bottom. Also *sounding line.*

**leader cable**   *n.* A cable that carries electric current, the signals from which, or the magnetic influence of which, indicate the path to be followed by a vessel with suitable instruments.

**leading lights**   See RANGE LIGHT.

**leading marks**   *n.* Daybeacons that form a range. (British usage.)

**leading part**   *n.* The part of a tackle that is hauled on. Now more often called the hauling part. See FALLS; STANDING PART.

**leading wind**   *n.* A wind from abeam or from a quarter.

**leadsman**   *n.* (pron. leds-man) One who takes soundings using a hand lead in the chains.

**lead yard**   *n.* (pron. leed yard) The shipyard that produces the prototype of a design class of a vessel.

**league**   *n.* In the United States and Great Britain, a distance of 3 nautical miles (or 3,041 fathoms). In other countries a league measures from 2.4 statute miles to 4.6 statute miles.

**leave**   *n.* Permission to be absent from a ship or station for more than 48 hours. See LIBERTY.

**leaver**   *n.* An independent ship that leaves the main body of a convoy to go to a different port. Several ships sailing together make up a **leaver convoy.**

**leave rations**   *n.* A cash payment or advance given an enlisted person going on leave.

**ledge**   *n.* (1) A timber placed athwartships between beams. (2) A rocky projection or outcrop on the seafloor, commonly near shore.

**lee**   *n. or adj.* The side toward which the wind is blowing; the downwind side. You can refer to the lee side of the ship, meaning the side away from the wind, or you can sail in the lee of Gibraltar, the side that is protected from the wind. See LEEWARD.

**leeboards**   *n.* A pair of pivoted boards that are lowered through trunks in the bilges to improve lateral resistance on small sailboats. The leeward board is lowered, and the windward board is raised.

**lee bowing the tide**   *phr.* To choose a heading so that the tide is on the lee bow to counteract the lateral force of the wind.

**lee bow position**   *n.* In racing, the position of a boat abeam or forward of the beam and close to leeward of another boat.

**leech**   *n.* (1) The trailing edge of a triangular sail; the leading edge is the luff. (2) Either of the two vertical sides of a square sail.

**leech line (or leechline)**   *n.* A line used to truss leeches of the courses.

**leech rope (or line)**   See BOLTROPE.

**lee helm**   *n.* The tendency of a sailboat to fall off to leeward; this has to be corrected by turning the wheel to windward or the tiller to leeward. It is preferable to have the sails balanced so as to have a little weather helm so that if the helmsman leaves the helm (falls, or other crisis) the vessel will head upwind and luff. This has nothing to do with lee helmsman.

**lee helmsman**   *n.* The relief helmsman who operates the annunciator or engine order telegraph on U.S. Naval vessels. The weather helmsman (usually simply called the helmsman) and the lee helmsman alternate with half-hour tricks. The term comes from the days of sailing ships when the two helmsmen were required to handle the wheel in heavy weather; the weather wheelman was the senior and was responsible for the course steered, while the lee wheelman assisted him.

**lee ho**   *interj.* British equivalent of "Hard alee!"

**lee shore**   *n.* The shore off the lee side of a vessel.

**lee tide**   See LEEWARD TIDAL CURRENT.

**leeward**   *n. or adj.* (rhymes with steward) The side or direction opposite from which the wind is blowing. "When both [vessels] have the wind on the same side, the vessel which is to windward shall keep out of the way of the vessel which is to leeward." Rule 12a(ii) of the *Navigation Rules.* "The leeward islands in a chain can be unbearably hot during the warm months, while the more windward islands are kept comfortable by the trade winds."

**leeward tidal current**   *n.* A tidal current setting in the same direction as the wind is blowing. Also *leeward tide* or *lee tide.*

**leeway**   *n.* (1) The drift of a vessel to leeward as a result of wind or current. (2) The difference between a vessel's heading and the course made good over the ground. Also *set.*

**leeway angle**   *n.* The angular distance between the course through the water that is steered and the water track due to the wind's blowing a vessel to leeward.

**left bank**   *n.* The bank of a stream or river on the left-hand side of an observer facing downstream. The U.S. Coast Guard and the U.S. Army Corps of Engineers use the phrase **left descending bank** to avoid confusion.

**left-hand lay**   *n.* Strands of rope or cable laid from right to left. Also called s-twist as opposed to the more normal z-twist of a right-hand lay rope. See ROPE.

**left-hand propeller**   *n.* A propeller that turns from starboard to port, the direction in which the top of the hub turns. On single-screw vessels in the United States, most propellers are starboard-hand or right-hand screws. Also *left-hand screw.*

**left rudder**   *interj.* The command to turn the wheel to the left, which changes the heading to the left. The amount of rudder is part of the command: "Left ten degrees rudder" or "Left full rudder."

**left semicircle**   See DANGEROUS SEMICIRCLE; NAVIGABLE SEMICIRCLE; RIGHT SEMICIRCLE.

**leg**   *n.* (1) A brace to hold up a stranded boat or a boat in a boatyard. (2) The course of a sailing vessel between two buoys: "They made good time on the downwind leg." (3) A portion of a cruise. "The leg from Darwin to Freemantle was a nightmare."

**leg-o-mutton rig**   *n.* Traditional nickname for a Marconi rig or a jib-headed rig.

**legs**   *n.* Ropes branching from a knot or bend such as crowfoot legs.

**length**   *n.* The horizontal distance between fore and aft points on a vessel. **Length between perpendiculars (LBP)**

is the length measured between perpendiculars taken at the forwardmost and aftermost points on the waterline corresponding to the deepest operating draft. **Length on deck (LOD)** is the length between the forwardmost and aftermost points on a specified deck measured along the deck, excluding sheer. **Length on the waterline (LWL)** is the length between the forwardmost and aftermost points on a vessel's waterline. **Length overall (LOA)** is the length between the forwardmost and aftermost points on the hull of a vessel. **Sparred length** is the length between the extremities of any spars that overhang the bow or stern of a vessel, such as a bowsprit or a boomkin.

**leste**   n. A hot dry wind of the Madeira and Canary Islands.

**let fly**   v. Drop the sheets, let the sails go.

**let go**   interj. The command to drop the anchor.

**let go and haul**   interj. The command to brace the foremast yards to the opposite tack.

**let go by the wind**   interj. To cast lines off the pins or cleats and allow them to run out unimpeded.

**let her off**   interj. Order to head a vessel farther off the wind.

**let her up**   interj. Order to point closer to the wind.

**let out**   interj. The command to ease out a sheet, a tackle or a line.

**lettering**   n. Typographical style used to identify different types of features on charts. Perhaps the most significant difference is between vertical lettering and slanting lettering: Vertical letters indicate that an island, rock, or shoal is dry at high water. Slanting lettering is used for

water, underwater, and floating features with the single exception of soundings.

**letter of marque**   n. (pron. mark) A document issued by a government to an individual giving him or her permission to arm a ship to enable him or her to attack enemy shipping. The practice, in other words, of sending out privateers, which has been outlawed under international law. Also *letter of marque and reprisal.*

**levanter**   n. A strong northeasterly to easterly wind that blows across the Mediterranean, especially in the vicinity of Gibraltar, bringing cloudy, foggy, and sometimes rainy weather. Also *meltemi* or *euroclydon.*

**levanto**   n. A hot southeasterly wind that blows over the Canary Islands.

**leveche**   n. A hot, dusty wind in Spain or off the Spanish coast, either a föhn or a hot southerly wind before a low-pressure system from the Sahara Desert. The same wind is called a sirocco in other parts of the Mediterranean area.

**levee**   n. (1) An artificial embankment built to limit flooding at the side of a channel, such as the levees along the Mississippi River. (2) An embankment bordering a canyon, valley, or sea channel on the seafloor.

**level racing**   n. Ocean racing between two or more vessels of the same rating.

**liberty**   n. Authorized time off from duties for members of a naval ship's company or station to leave the ship or station for not more than 48 hours. Beyond 48 hours, it is called leave.

**Liberty ship**   n. A cargo vessel built by the U.S. Maritime Commission during World War II. They were designed to be built at minimum cost for simplicity of operation and construction at a time when the German wolf packs were ravaging the sea lanes of the North Atlantic. They were of welded construction with full scantlings, transverse frames, two continuous decks, five cargo holds, and eight watertight bulkheads. Machinery space was amidships with additional spaces in the number one hold. They measured 441.5 feet long with a beam of 27.5 feet, a draft of 37 feet, with a load displacement of 14,100 tons. The normal complement was 44 men. About 2,300 such ships were built. See VICTORY SHIP.

**license**   *n.* Certification required for all officers and members of the crew on merchant ships of United States registry and virtually all other maritime nations. The extensive requirements are detailed in the *Merchant Marine Officer's Handbook,* by Turpin and MacEwen.

**lie ahull**   *v.* Said of a vessel that is lying to when the force of the wind is such that it can carry no sail whatsoever. See LIE ATRY.

**lie atry**   *v.* To lie to winds of gale force or greater when it is still possible to carry some sail.

**lie to**   See HEAVE TO.

**lieutenant (Lt. or Lieut.)**   *n.* An officer in the U.S. Navy or Coast Guard ranked below lieutenant commander and above lieutenant, j.g.

**lieutenant, junior grade (Lt. j.g.)**   *n.* A commissioned officer in the U.S. Navy or Coast Guard, ranked below lieutenant and above ensign.

**lieutenant commander (Lt. Comdr. or LCDR)**   *n.* A commissioned officer in the U.S. Navy or Coast Guard, ranked below commander and above lieutenant.

**lifeboat**   *n.* A small boat available for emergency use on a ship. After the *Titanic* disaster, lifeboats sufficient for the number of crew and passengers on mer-

chant ships became mandatory under international law.

**lifeguard**   *n.* A vessel detailed to recover aircraft personnel in case a plane goes in the sea. Formerly called **plane guard.**

**life lines**   *n.* Lines on deck or on yards placed there for the protection of the crew. For the purist, the top line between the stanchions on the weather deck is the **life line,** the second is the **housing line,** and the third is the **foot line.**

**life preserver**   *n.* Any buoyant device held onto or worn by personnel to stay afloat, as a **life buoy, life ring,** or **life jacket.**

**life raft**   *n.* Any of a number of different boats, rigid or inflatable, that can be carried or towed, and can be used to carry personnel in case the larger vessel sinks.

**Lifesaving Service**   *n.* A string of lifesaving stations along the coast of the United States. In 1915 the service was combined with the Revenue-Cutter Service to form the United States Coast Guard. See LIGHTHOUSE SERVICE.

**lift**   *n.* A wind from a direction that will make it possible to sail closer to the course to the destination. The opposite of a header. (2) A rope from a yardarm to the masthead that supports and moves the yard. See SQUARE-RIGGED VESSEL. (3) A slight luff on square sails when the wind is at only a slight angle from the sail and strikes the leeches and causes them to shiver.

**lift**   *v.* To transfer marks and measurements from a drawing or model to a plate or other object by templates and measurements. To **lift a template** is to cut out the template for a given piece of plating or shape.

**light**   *n.* A construction term for a glassed opening in a hull, a window or a porthole. A **fixed light** is one that is not hinged.

**light air**   n. Beaufort scale reading of 1, with winds of 1–3 mph.

**light attendant station**   n. A shore facility for servicing minor aids to navigation within an assigned area.

**light bobbing**   n. To determine the distance of a light when first sighted by going one deck lower to see if it disappears. Then the navigator returns to the same deck to see it again. From this he knows that he is at the limit of visibility. By knowing his height of eye and the height of the light (according to the navigation chart), he is able to determine how far off the light is. Also *bobbing the light.*

**light breeze**   n. Beaufort scale reading of 2, with winds of 4–6 knots.

**light characteristics**   n. Light phases such as flashing, quick occulting, and so on. Sound, color, and shape are not included in the definition.

**light displacement**   n. The displacement tonnage, in long tons, of a ship when it is light, or unloaded, but including water in the boilers and permanent ballast if any.

**lighted beacon**   n. A beacon showing a light. Also *light beacon.*

**lighted buoy**   n. A buoy showing a light. See BUOY.

**lighten up**   v. To slack off a line.

**lightening hole**   n. A hole cut in plating to make it lighter without sacrificing strength; these are most often seen in steel highway bridges, but are used extensively in ship construction.

**lighter**   n. A self-propelled barge used to transport equipment, provisions, personnel, or passengers short distances,

usually within a harbor or port between a ship and shore. See LASH.

**lighter**   v. To load or unload a ship by means of a lighter. "We must lighter the cargo and not risk entering the shallow harbor."

**lighterage**   n. (1) The transportation of cargo over a short distance, usually in a harbor. (2) The fee charged for such transportation.

**light-float**   n. A buoy with a boat-shaped body showing a light. Light-floats are usually unmanned and are used instead of smaller lighted buoys in areas of strong currents.

**lighthouse**   n. Unofficial name for a primary seacoast light and of some secondary seacoast lights. They exhibit major lights and are placed on prominent headlands, at entrances, on isolated dangers, or other points where it is necessary to warn mariners. Lighthouses are simply called "lights" officially and in *Light Lists.* The first, and now the last, manned light in the United States was Boston Light, established in 1716 in Boston Harbor. Goat Island Light is also manned, but only part of the time. The Coast Guard has automated all the other lights. See LIGHT KEEPERS.

**Lighthouse Service**   n. An agency that had the duty of establishing and maintaining aids to navigation. It was combined with the Coast Guard in 1939. See LIFESAVING SERVICE.

**light keepers**   n. Name for the people who tend lighthouses maintained by the U.S. Coast Guard. See WICKIE.

**light list number**   n. The number used to identify a navigation light in the *Light Lists.* The **international number,** assigned by the International Hydrographic Organization, is shown in italic type, and is located under the **light list number.**

# Light Phase Characteristics

| International | National | Class of light | Illustration | Period shown |
|---|---|---|---|---|
| **Abbreviation** | | | | |
| F | F | fixed | | |
| Occulting (total duration of light longer than total duration of darkness) | | | | |
| Oc | Oc; Occ | single occulting | | |
| Oc(2) Example | Oc (2); Gp Occ | group occulting | | |
| Oc(2+3) Example | Oc(2+3) | composite group occulting | | |
| Isophase (duration of light and darkness equal) | | | | |
| Iso | Iso; E Int | isophase | | |
| Flashing (total duration of light shorter than total duration of darkness) | | | | |
| Fl | Fl | single flashing | | |
| Fl(3) Example | Fl(2); Gp Fl | group flashing | | |
| Fl(2+1) Example | Fl(2+1) | composite group flashing | | |
| LFl | L Fl | long flashing (flash 2s or longer) | | |
| Quick (repetition rate of 50 to 79 – usually either 50 or 60 – flashes per minute) | | | | |
| Q | Q; Qk Fl | continuous quick | | |
| Q(3) Example | Q(3) | group quick | | |
| IQ | IQ; Int Qk Fl; I Qk Fl | interrupted quick | | |
| Very quick (repetition rate of 80 to 159 – usually either 100 or 120 – flashes per minute) | | | | |
| VQ | VQ; V Qk Fl | continuous very quick | | |
| VQ(3) Example | VQ (3) | group very quick | | |
| IVQ | IVQ | interrupted very quick | | |
| Ultra quick (repetition rate of 160 or more – usually 240 to 300 – flashes per minute) | | | | |
| UQ | UQ | continuous ultra quick | | |
| IUQ | IUQ | interrupted ultra quick | | |
| Mo (A) Example | Mo (A) | Morse code | | |
| FFl | F Fl | fixed and flashing | | |
| Al.WR | Al; Alt | alternating | | |

**Light Lists** *n.* The U.S. Coast Guard *Light Lists* for the U.S. and its possessions, including the intracoastal waterway, the Great Lakes, and the Mississippi River and its navigable tributaries, and contiguous Canadian waters, describes aids to navigation, consisting of lights, fog signals, buoys, lightships, daybeacons, and electronic aids. (Aeronautical lights are not included.) *Light Lists* may be obtained from the Superintendent of Documents in Washington or local marine chart suppliers. This should not be confused with the *List of Lights.*

**light load line** *n.* The waterline of a vessel when all cargo has been discharged. See PLIMSOLL MARK OR LINE.

**light lock** *n.* A small compartment with doors at each side that close tightly so that light from the interior will not show through to the outside of the vessel.

**light off** *v.* (1) To fire a boiler. (2) To start an engine.

**light period** *n.* The time in seconds required for a lighted aid to navigation to complete its light cycle.

**light phase characteristics** *n.* The distinctive sequences of light and dark intervals or the distinctive combinations in variations of intensity of light on aids to navigation.

**lights** *n.* Under both Inland Rule #21 and International Rule #21 of the *Navigation Rules,* lights are required of all vessels operating at night, whether under way or at anchor. Among the most important and frequently encountered are the **masthead light, sidelights,** the **sternlight,** the **towing light,** the **all-around light,** and the **anchor light.**

**light sector** *n.* The arc over which a light is visible in degrees true as observed from a vessel approaching the light.

**lightship** *n.* Manned vessels of distinctive design and markings anchored in specific, charted locations as an aid to navigation. Equipped with lights, fog signals, and radio beacons, lightships are rare today, having been widely replaced by unmanned platforms.

**lightweight** *adj.* Describes a vessel with fixed ballast and with machinery liquids at operating levels but without any cargo, stores, consumable liquids, water ballast, people and their effects.

**lignum vitae** *n.* One of several tropical American trees (as *Guaiacum officinale* or *G. sanctum*), an evergreen with dense, durable, resinous wood used for propeller shaft bearings and deadeyes. Lignum vitae means "wood of life."

**Lima** *n.* (pron. leema) Phonetic word for the letter "L." The code flag is two black squares and two yellow squares. When used alone it means "Stop instantly, I have something to communicate."

**liman** *n.* (1) A shallow coastal lagoon or bay with a muddy bottom. (2) A region of mud or slime at the mouth of a stream. From the Russian, meaning "estuary."

**Liman Current** *n.* Part of the Tsushima Current and river discharge in the Tatar Strait; the coastal Liman Current flows southward in the western part of the Sea of Japan.

**limb** *n.* The edge of a graduated arc in a sextant.

**limber chains** *n.* A length of chain that is run through limber holes; the chain can be moved back and forth to clear any obstruction to the flow of bilge water through the holes.

**limber holes** *n.* Horizontal holes in transverse bulkheads in the bilge that allow water to drain to the lowest point where it can be pumped out.

**limey**    *n.* Nickname for a British sailor that has been broadened to include all Britons. The practice of issuing lemon juice (and later the less effective lime juice) to British sailors to prevent scurvy was introduced in 1795. As a result, British ships were also known as **lime juicers.**

**limited duty officer (LDO)**    *n.* An ex-enlisted person in the U.S. Navy who has been given a commission because of superior performance. The officer is limited to duties in the field in which he or she has had extensive experience.

**limpet mine**    *n.* Explosive mine that can be attached to the hull of a ship by frogmen.

**line**    *n.* The word applied to rope in many of its functional applications aboard ship. There are many exceptions, such as boltrope, footrope, and bell rope, or halyard, sheet, and cable.

**lineal number**    *n.* Order of precedence among U.S. Navy officers. Formerly called **signal number.**

**line drawing**    See PLAN.

**line of departure**    *n.* Amphibious operation term referring to the imaginary lines from which a wave of landing craft departs for the beach.

**line officer**    *n.* A U.S. Navy officer concerned with command and control of ships at sea, and eligible to succeed to command of a naval vessel. Only line officers can serve as deck officers at sea in charge of the navigation of the ship. Other officers such as officers of the Supply Corps, Medical Corps, and chaplains are staff officers. Line officers wear a gold star on their sleeves (dress blues) and shoulder boards. Staff officers wear the insignia of their specialty, a cross for Christian chaplains, an oak leaf and acorn for doctors, and so on.

**line of position (LOP)**    *n.* The position of a vessel established by using the vessel's course and speed with reference to the position of one known object calculated two or more times over a given length of time. In more general terms, a LOP is a single line of either range or bearing to an object, terrestrial or celestial.

**line of sight**    *n.* A straight line between two points. The line is in the direction of a great circle but does not follow the curvature of the Earth. Also *position line.*

**liner**    *n.* (1) A commercial ship, especially one that carries passengers on regular schedules between set destinations. (2) Obsolete expression for ship of the line. (3) Term for long-line fishing boats.

**lines of force of a magnetic field**    *n.* The representation of the direction of a magnetic field by lines on a chart.

**line squall**    *n.* A violent windstorm associated with a weather front.

**line-throwing gun**    See LYLE GUN.

**lipper**    See CAT'S PAW.

**liquefied natural gas carrier**    *n.* An ocean vessel designed to carry liquefied natural gas (LNG). See SHIP.

**list**    *n.* a transverse angle of inclination caused by internal forces.

**list**    *v.* Said of a vessel when it leans to one side due to internal forces such as water or cargo being out of balance. This is not the same as heeling, which is leaning caused by external pressure such as wind or grounding.

**Lists of Lights**    *n.* A series of publications promulgated by the Defense Mapping Agency Hydrographic/Topographic Center and listed as Publications 110 through 116. These cover essentially the same material for foreign waters that the *Light Lists* promulgated by the U.S. Coast Guard do for domestic waters.

littoral   n. The seashore or coastline.

littoral   adj. Pertaining to the seashore or the shoreline.

littoral zone   n. The area along a coastline that is between the low-tide limit and the high-tide limit, the habitat of a special group of flora (such as red mangroves) and fauna (such as sea roaches and coquinas).

lively   adv. Quickly. The term is often used alone to mean carry out the last command expeditiously.

Liverpool head   n. A device at the top of a galley smoke pipe (Charlie Noble) that consists of two drums, one inside the other, with staggered openings so that the seawater and rainwater do not enter.

lizard   n. (1) A short piece of cordage with an iron or wood thimble spliced into it. (2) An iron or wood thimble used for rigging a two-part purchase, as for boomless staysail sheets. (3) A short section of line that attaches to a safety harness worn by personnel and to a wire between two stanchions that enables a person to walk between the two points and continue to be tethered to the vessel. (4) A small line that travels on another; lifeboats used to have lizards to keep the boats from swinging while launching; they were used in addition to the frapping lines.

ljüngstrom rig   n. A single triangular sail attached along the vertical axis to a rotating unstayed mast. Also twin-wing rig.

Lloyd's   n. A London association of underwriters incorporated by an Act of Parliament in 1871. As a corporation, Lloyd's does not underwrite insurance business; its members individually or collectively conduct business on their own account, subject to the society's regulations. Lloyd's underwrites all types of insurance except life insurance. The name is from the coffee house in Tower Street, London, kept by Edward R. Lloyd where,

in about 1688, underwriters began gathering to transact business, primarily in the marine field. In 1696, Mr. Lloyd started publication of Lloyd's News, renamed Lloyd's List in 1726, which gives the latest information on shipping and the movement of the merchant ships of every nation.

Lloyd's Register of Shipping   n. The oldest of the classification societies, founded in 1760. Entirely independent of the underwriter's corporation, Lloyd's Register affords assistance to members of Lloyd's on matters relating to the insurance on a particular vessel. Its publication, Lloyd's Register of Shipping, lists virtually all British and foreign flag merchant vessels, with minor exceptions, giving for each the year of build, the name of builder, dimensions, power, tonnage, ownership, hull classification, machinery, and equipment.

load   n. Engineers' term referring to the proper performance of the ship's generator. When the lights grow dim and the chief engineer suddenly blanches and announces he has just "lost the load," he means that the generator has just failed.

load displacement   n. The weight of a vessel in long tons, including cargo, stores, and all else on board when floating at her summer load line. Load displacement is the usual unit of measure for warships.

load line certificate, international   n. A document issued by the American Bureau of Shipping on behalf of the U.S. Coast Guard under provisions of the International Convention on Load Lines (1966). The certificate shows the maximum draft in terms of minimum freeboard to which a vessel may load in each load line zone and season of the world. See FREEBOARD ASSIGNMENTS; PLIMSOLL MARK OR LINE.

load line disc   n. The disc on a ship's hull that is 12 inches in diameter and intersected by a horizontal line 18 inches long and 1 inch wide the upper edge of which passes through the center of the disc. The disc is placed amidships and below the deck line. See PLIMSOLL MARK OR LINE.

**load line marks** *n.* The marks on a ship's hull indicating draft limits. The load line marks are determined by the Classification Society with consideration given to length, breadth, depth, structural strength and design, superstructure, sheer, and so on as compared with those of a standard ship with an established summer freeboard. Load line marks show summer load line, winter North Atlantic load line, tropical load line, freshwater load line, and tropical freshwater load line. See PLIMSOLL MARK OR LINE.

**load line zones** *n.* Zones used for load lines depending on the season and the geographic area. For example, the load line for the tropical zone is different from the North Atlantic winter zone. Ships entering the various zones must have the appropriate minimum freeboard.

**load list** *n.* The inventory carried by a support force of a fleet underway.

**load on top (LOT)** *n.* A system of washing tankers. Oil is washed from the cargo tanks by steam lines into a slop tank; when the water has separated, it is allowed to drain into the sea while the oil remains on board for new oil to be loaded "on top."

**load waterline (LWL)** *n.* The waterline at which a ship will float when loaded to its designed draft.

**local apparent noon (LAN)** *n.* The moment the center of the Sun is over the upper branch of the observer's meridian, or when the apparent Sun is on the celestial meridian. It is the highest point to which the Sun will climb on that day. See ZONE NOON.

**local apparent time (LAT)** *n.* Time calculated using the apparent position of the Sun as the celestial reference and the local meridian for the terrestrial reference.

**local attraction** *n.* A magnetic anomaly strong enough to cause a noticeable deflection in a magnetic compass, usually noted on marine charts.

**local disturbances** *n.* Phrase used by navigators equivalent to what magneticians call **magnetic anomalies.** Also *local attraction.*

**local hour angle (LHA)** *n.* (1) Angular distance west of the local celestial meridian, measured either in time (up to 24 hours) or degrees (up to 360°). (2) The arc of the celestial equator between the upper branch of the local celestial meridian and the hour circle through a point on the celestial sphere, measured westward from the local celestial meridian 0° to 360°.

**local knowledge** *n.* Knowledge of local waters that goes well beyond that which is available on charts and in most publications and is gained through experience and familiarity. Local knowledge is the special province of the cruising guides found for most areas of the Western world.

**local mean noon** *n.* The instant the mean Sun is over the upper branch of the local meridian.

**local mean time (LMT)** *n.* The hour angle of the mean Sun measured westward from the lower branch of the local meridian.

***Local Notice to Mariners*** *n.* A written document providing information pertaining to the condition of aids to navigation and the waterways within each Coast Guard district on a weekly or "as required" basis. These should not be confused with the *Notice to Mariners* published by the Defense Mapping

Agency Hydrographic/Topographic Center.

**lock**   *n.* A section of a waterway fitted with a gate at both ends and by which ships can be raised and lowered from one level of the waterway to the next by pumping water either in or out as needed.

**locker**   *n.* A chest, closet, or small compartment used for stowage. A locker for stowing personal gear is usually called a **footlocker.** Other lockers are the paint locker, the vegetable locker, and the medicinal alcohol locker. Yachts have hanging lockers, which are closets in which clothing can be hung on hangers.

**lock on**   *v.* To continuously and automatically track a target in one or more coordinates such as range, elevation, or bearing.

**lodestar**   *n.* A guiding star, a point of reference, especially the North Star (Polaris). From Middle English *lode sterre,* a leading star.

**lodestone**   *n.* A magnet that occurs in nature and that is composed of black iron oxide called magnetite.

**lodgement area**   *n.* In amphibious operations, the consolidation of two or more beachheads for subsequent land operations.

**loft**   *n.* (1) A large room where a vessel's plans are laid out or rigging assembled. (2) A large room or area in a building where sails are cut and assembled.

**loft**   *v.* (1) To store in a loft. (2) To lay out drawings of the parts of a ship.

**loftsman**   *n.* A person who lays out a ship's lines and makes molds and templates from them in a mold loft.

**lofty**   *adj.* High aspect; a lofty ship has high masts with respect to the length of the hull. See ALOFT; LOFT.

**log**   *n.* Any device used to measure a vessel's speed through the water. See LOGBOOK.

**log**   *v.* (1) To make an entry in a vessel's log. "Quartermaster, log the time we weighed anchor." (2) To sustain a speed. "We logged 13 knots most of the day."

**logbook**   *n.* Usually shortened to "log," the logbook is the official record of all of a vessel's activities, especially navigational data, but including other special events that occur. Logbooks are kept by various departments: the quartermaster keeps a log on the bridge of a naval vessel, and from this log the officers of the deck write the rough copy of the ship's log that is transcribed to the smooth copy, the **deck log,** and signed by the various officers of the deck. The engineering department keeps a log of engine orders and other pertinent activities (maintained in the **logroom**) in that department; the radiomen keep another log; and the officer in charge of registered publications keeps another log, and so on. Merchant vessels have fewer logs, but logs abound on most ships. On yachts and smaller vessels, although there is no legal requirement to do so, a logbook should be kept routinely to be used in court, or for the Internal Revenue Service, or just to settle arguments on how long it took to get from point A to point C on a cruise three years ago.

**loggerhead**   *n.* (1) A heavy tool with a long handle that was heated to melt pitch. It was a tool that was readily available to settle disputes between members of the crew. Thus the saying, "They were at loggerheads." (2) A post on a whaleboat used for towing a harpooned whale.

**logroom**   *n.* The engineering record room on a ship.

**loll**   *v.* To wallow uneasily because of instability either because a vessel is top-heavy or has taken on too much water below decks.

**lolly**  *n.* An ice field in which the ice has broken into small pieces and is easily navigated.

**long board**  *n.* A long tack.

**longboat**  *n.* A large, general-purpose boat carried on sailing ships, used as the ship's boat and as a lifeboat.

**long flashing light**  *n.* Within the IALA system, a single-flashing light with a flash duration of 2 or more seconds. See LIGHT PHASE CHARACTERISTICS.

**long gasket**  *n.* A piece of rope used to keep a square sail secured to its yard at sea. A shorter gasket was used in port to make the furled sails neater in appearance.

**long glass**  *n.* A telescope usually of medium power (16× or less) used on ships for reading signal flags. It is referred to as the glass. The glass or binoculars are the traditional symbol of authority. In port, most U.S. Navy ships provide the officer of the deck with a long glass, usually covered with fancy cordage as a symbol of his office. This use of "glass" should not be confused with "glass" as used with barometer readings.

**longitude (Lo.; Long.)**  *n.* The angular distance east or west between the prime meridian that passes through Greenwich, England, and any point on Earth, up to 180°. See LATITUDE.

**longitude method**  *n.* The process of establishing a line of position from the observation of the latitude of a celestial body by assuming a latitude (or longitude) and calculating the longitude (or latitude) through which the line of position passes and the azimuth.

**longitudinal**  *adj.* Pertaining to any fore-and-aft member, as a **longitudinal frame** or action.

**longitudinal bulkhead**  *n.* A fore-and-aft bulkhead.

**longitudinal stability**  *n.* The tendency of a vessel to return to its original longitudinal position.

**long-legged**  *adj.* (1) A deep-draft boat or ship. (2) A fast ship.

**long-range active detection system (LORAD)**  *n.* A long-range sonar detection system used on U.S. Navy ships.

**long seas**  *n.* A condition of the sea in which the crests of the waves are far apart.

**longshore current**  *n.* A current that parallels the shoreline within the surf zone and that is generated by waves striking the shore at an angle.

**longshoreman**  *n.* A laborer who loads and unloads cargo from a ship. U.S. longshoremen are protected under the U.S. Longshoremen's and Harbor Workers Act (1927) in cases of injury in somewhat the same way seamen are protected under the Jones Act (1920). See STEVEDORE.

**long splice**  *n.* The splice of two pieces of cordage of the same diameter when the diameter of the splice cannot be larger than the original cordage (so that it can be rove through a block or thimble). A short splice is quicker to make, but it is also thicker. See SHORT SPLICE.

**long ton**  *n.* A unit of weight in the U.S. customary system of 2,240 pounds avoirdupois. Ship's tonnage can be given either in terms of long tons (weight), or displacement tons. See SHORT TON.

**long-waisted**  *adj.* Said of a ship with an unusually long waist (the distance between the forecastle and the poop deck).

**lookout**  *n.* Someone stationed on deck to observe and report objects that he sees.

**lookout station** *n.* A chart term for a tower with a small house on top in which a watch is maintained.

**loom** *n.* (1) Reflection or glow of a light that is below the horizon or on the horizon but distant. (2) The shaft of an oar.

**looming** *n.* The exaggerated appearance of a "mirage" when objects appear elevated and the visible horizon is farther away.

**loophole** *n.* A hole in the wall of the hull of a wooden ship (or a fortress) through which small arms and cannon could be fired.

**loose** *v.* To unfurl a reefed or fully furled sail.

**loose-footed sail** *n.* A fore-and-aft sail not secured to a boom along the foot.

**loosing the sails** *phr.* Unfurling sails before setting sail or to dry them when wet. See LOOSE.

**loran** *n.* A LOng RAnge radio Navigation position fixing system in which signals are transmitted from coastal stations and received and interpreted by vessels at sea to determine the vessels' positions. Loran was developed in 1940 in a joint effort by the U.S. Navy, Coast Guard, Army Air Forces, and the Office of Scientific Research and Development. The range is about 1,200 miles. The term loran does not apply to all long-range radio navigation systems but only to Loran-A, Loran-C, and Loran-D. It does not apply to Omega or to Decca, a later development that was first used in 1944 during the Normandy invasion.

**louver** *n.* An opening for light or air with overlapping, movable, or fixed slats. These were popular on passenger ships and yachts before air conditioning.

**low** *adv.* Said of a vessel sailing too far off the wind.

**low-cut sail** *n.* A sail, generally a headsail, that is cut so that its foot is on the deck.

**lower boom** *n.* An extension of a yard on which an additional studding sail could be set.

**lower deck** *n.* A deck between the main deck and the lowest or orlop deck. British ratings were berthed on the lower deck, and the term for the ratings as a group was "lower deck." "The lower deck is granted liberty until four bells in the dog watch."

**lower high water (LHW)** N. The lower of two high tides during a tidal day.

**lower limb** *n.* The half of the outer edge of a celestial body having the least altitude in contrast with the upper limb, that half having the greater altitude.

**lower low water (LLW)** *n.* The lower of two low tides during a tidal day.

**lower low-water datum** *n.* An approximation of mean lower low water that has been adopted as a standard reference for a limited area and is retained for an indefinite period. It is used primarily for river and harbor engineering purposes.

**lower mast** *n.* The lowest part of a compound mast with three parts. The lower mast rests on a step that is as low in the ship as possible, usually on the keelson.

**lower topsail** *n.* A square sail set above a course in a vessel with double (upper and lower) topsails.

**lowest low water** *n.* An extremely low tidal datum; the term refers to the lowest tide observed, or even a little lower.

**lowest normal low water** *n.* A datum that approximates the average of the monthly lowest low water exclusive of tides disturbed by storms.

**low-pressure cell (or low)**   *n.* An air mass with atmospheric pressure lower than the surrounding air. In many areas wind and rain can be expected as the front moves eastward.

**low water (LW)**   *n.* The minimum height reached by a falling tide. The term "low water" is preferred to **low tide.**

**low-water datum (LWD)**   *n.* An established datum of water level that remains the datum of reference for an indefinite period for a specific area.

**low-water equinoctial spring**   *n.* A low-water spring tide near the time of either of the equinoxes.

**low-water line**   *n.* The intersection of the land with the water surface at the elevation of low water.

**low-water spring**   *n.* Low water period of a tide during a full or new moon.

**low-water stand**   *n.* The period of time at low water during which the water level does not change. This is not related to slack water, which is a tidal current phenomenon, and they rarely coincide.

**loxodrome (or loxodromic curve)** *n.* Any rhumb line that spirals toward the pole. Meridians and parallels that maintain a constant true direction are considered special cases of a rhumb line and do not generate a loxodromic curve. See GREAT CIRCLE SAILING.

**lubber**   *n.* A clumsy seaman or unseaman-like person. Also *landlubber.*

**lubber's hole**   *n.* An easy access to a platform at the tops. It was considered both craven and lubberly for a sailor to use it instead of climbing up and out along the futtock shrouds and over the **barricade.**

**lubber's line**   *n.* A mark inside the bowl of a compass and adjacent to the compass card that shows the forward direction parallel to the keel. It is important when installing the compass to align it as precisely as possible because it is the index mark by which the ship is steered.

**lucky bag**   *n.* A locker in which lost articles are placed on U.S. Navy ships. Usually these are articles inadvertently left around the ship, and the unfortunate owners have to do a little extra duty to recover them.

**luff**   *n.* The leading edge of a fore-and-aft sail. See MARCONI RIG.

**luff**   *v.* To bring a sailboat into the wind so that the leading edge, the luff, of the mainsail begins to tremble.

**luff hollow**   *n.* Sailmaker's term for the concave section of a headsail built in to compensate for the slight sag of the headstay.

**luffing match**   *n.* In racing, the maneuver of a leeward boat that luffs and causes a windward boat also to luff to avoid a disqualifying collision and at the same time prevents the windward boat from passing to windward.

**luff rope**   *n.* The rope sewn into the luff of a sail for extra strength.

**luff round**   *n.* Sailmaker's term for the slight distortion built in the sail to compensate for a slight bend in the mast.

**luff tackle**   *n.* (1) The mechanism used to extend the luff of a jib-headed sail. (2) A tackle with a single-sheave block and a double-sheave block. See TACKLE.

**luff (up)**   *v.* To head into the wind to slow or stop a sailing vessel. "Luff up, if you please, so we can get a good fix on Cape May."

**lug (or lugsail)**   *n.* A fore-and-aft quadrilateral sail bent on a boom that is set oblique to the mast and about one-third the length of the mast from the top of the mast. With a **dipping lug,** the yard and sail must be lowered somewhat and brought about to leeward when tacking. A **standing lug** remains fixed on one side of the mast, though the sail may draw better when it is on the leeward side. A **balanced lug** is a dipping lug rig in which the sail is bent to a boom that also overlaps the mast but is not made fast to it.

**lugger** *n.* A sailing ship with two or three lugsails used frequently for privateering and coastal trade especially in England and France.

**lug pad** See PAD EYE.

**lull** *n.* A temporary attenuation of wind force; the brief period during which the eye of a hurricane moves through is an extreme example.

**luminous range of a light** See VISUAL RANGE OF A LIGHT.

**lunar day** *n.* (1) Used in analysis of tides, it is a 24-hour, 50-minute day in length, more or less, the time between two consecutive transits of the moon. Also *tidal day.* (2) The duration of one rotation of the Moon on its axis relative to the Sun.

**lunar distance** *n.* The angle at an observer on the Earth between the Moon and another celestial body. This was the basis of the method formerly used to determine longitude at sea.

**lunar month** *n.* The time required for the Moon to revolve around the Earth with respect to the Sun, which is $27\frac{1}{3}$ days. Also *synodical month.*

**lunar tide** *n.* That part of the tide that results solely from the effect of the Moon. The **solar tide** is that part of a tide that is attributable to the tide-generating force of the Sun.

**lunar time** *n.* Time based on the lunar day and the lunar month, which are the bases for tide predictions and analyses.

**lunicurrent interval** *n.* The interval of time between the Moon's transit (upper or lower) over the local or Greenwich meridian and a specified phase of the tidal current.

**lunitidal interval** *n.* The interval of time between the Moon's meridian transit over the local or Greenwich meridian and the following high or low water.

**lurch** *n.* A sudden roll to one side.

**lurch** *v.* To roll suddenly.

**Lyle gun** *n.* A .45-caliber line-throwing gun. One end of a light line, or messenger, is attached to the projectile while the other is made fast to the ship or to a heavier line that can then be pulled across either by another ship or by someone in the water.

# M

**M** See MIKE.

**macerator** *n.* The blenderlike device used in sanitary systems to finely chop

solid waste. See MARINE SANITATION DEVICE.

**macerator-chlorinator** *n.* A combination of a macerator and a device that takes the ground-up waste and treats it with a chlorine compound. See MARINE SANITATION DEVICE.

**machinery casing**   *n.* The steel casing that encloses the air shaft above the engine room. It provides light and air for the engine room. The casing is made large because it is part of the computation to obtain maximum machinery space allowance in working out tonnage. Also *engine room casing.* See FIDLEY.

**machinery chock**   *n.* Heavy platform over the full area of the bedplate beneath deck auxiliaries.

**machinery index**   *n.* The complete inventory of all machinery and equipment, exclusive of electronics, installed on a vessel.

**machinery spaces**   *n.* The spaces in a vessel where the propulsion equipment and auxiliary machinery are located; these spaces are under the supervision of the engineer officer. Also *engineering spaces.*

**machinery trials**   *n.* Tests usually carried out when machinery is installed or repaired, which test the main propulsion machinery.

**machinist**   *n.* A warrant officer in the U.S. Navy who has advanced from chief machinist's mate.

**machinist's mate (MM)**   *n.* A petty officer in the U.S. Navy who has been trained and has passed examinations to be able to operate a vessel's machinery.

**mackerel sky**   *n.* Nickname for cirrocumulus and altocumulus clouds, resembling fish scales, a harbinger of stormy weather.

**made block**   *n.* A wooden block (the pulley type) made from several pieces.

**made mast**   *n.* A wooden mast built in several sections. Also *built mast.*

**maelstrom**   *n.* A whirlpool; so called after an extremely dangerous whirlpool off the northwest coast of Norway in the Lofoten Islands between Mockenasa and Mockeno.

**maestro**   *n.* A northwesterly wind with good weather that blows especially in summer in the Adriatic and also on the coasts of Corsica and Sardinia.

**Mae West**   *n.* Life vest that fills with air, named for the entertainer with the famous silhouette.

**magenta line**   *n.* Nickname for a channel, after the color used on Intracoastal Waterway charts to indicate the channel. "We followed the long magenta line south to Florida."

**magnet chamber**   *n.* The part of a compass below the compass card that contains the compensating magnets that counteract iron and other distortions on a vessel.

**magnetic annual variation**   *n.* The small systematic temporal variation in the Earth's magnetic field that occurs after the trend for secular change has been removed from the average monthly values.

**magnetic anomalies**   *n.* The magnetician's word for natural magnetic irregularities that cover a wide area. Navigators usually call these deviations "local disturbances." They are produced by forces in the Earth's crust and deeper.

**magnetic bearing**   *n.* The horizontal direction from one point to another as determined by magnetic compass. See DIRECTION.

**magnetic compass**   *n.* A device using a magnetic needle or card that is attracted to the magnetic North Pole or points in the direction of the magnetic poles. A **mariner's magnetic compass** is a compass that consists of a compass card to which are attached several magnets that align the compass card with the Earth's magnetic field. This is placed in a gimbaled bowl of liquid to tell the direction in which a vessel is sailing.

**magnetic compass rose**   *n.* A device on marine charts the outer circle of which gives the true direction based on the true geographic poles while the inner circle gives magnetic direction based on the magnetic poles. By reading the appropriate circle, one can determine a direction between two points on a chart.

**magnetic components**   *n.* The five components—A, B, C, D, E—that affect a magnetic compass reading that make up deviation. A relates to the lubber's line's not being truly fore and aft. B is the fore-and-aft component of the semicircular deviation that relates to the subpermanent magnetism of the ship's hull. C is the athwartship component of B. D is the quadrantal deviation due to induction in horizontal soft iron. E relates to the unsymmetrical placing of vertical soft iron.

**magnetic course**   *n.* A vessel's course based on the magnetic compass and the magnetic North Pole, almost always different from the true course that is based on the gyro compass and the geographic North Pole.

**magnetic declination**   See MAGNETIC VARIATION.

**magnetic dip (I)**   *n.* The vertical angle generated by a compass needle or card caused by the Earth's magnetic field, measured as the angle between the horizontal and a line through the needle or compass card. The **magnetic latitude** of a given point on the Earth's surface is the angle having a tangent equal to one-half that of the magnetic dip. Also *inclination*. See INCLINOMETER.

**magnetic equator**   *n.* The line that connects points of zero magnetic dip. It almost coincides with the terrestrial equator. Also *aclinic line*.

**magnetic field**   *n.* (1) The field of influence that surrounds the Earth in which the magnetic forces of the North and South Poles operate. (2) A region of space near a magnet characterized by a detectable force at every point in the field.

**magnetic mine**   *n.* A mine detonated when a steel-hulled ship passes over it. Steel-hulled ships scheduled to be in areas that may be mined are degaussed to significantly reduce their magnetic fields.

**magnetic needle**   *n.* A magnetized needle or slender bar placed on a low-friction pivot and placed in a magnetic compass to indicate alignment of the local magnetic field.

**magnetic poles**   *n.* Poles to (North) and from (South) which the north end of a freely suspended compass needle points and over which the magnetic dip is 90° and where no horizontal East/West compass reading is possible. The exact location of the poles changes over time; in 1992, the **Magnetic North Pole** was located at about 78° 24′N, 104° 18′W, and the **Magnetic South Pole** about 64° 42′S, 138° 42′E. See MAGNETIC VARIATION.

(The magnetic poles are not the same as the **dipole positions**—sometimes known as the **geomagnetic poles**—which represent the north and south ends of a hypothetical bar magnet within the Earth, and which are also variable. These are located at about 79° 12′N, 71° 12′W, and 79° 02′S, 108° 42′E.)

**magnetic signature**   *n.* The strength of the magnetic field of a vessel as detected and recorded on a device designed for that purpose. Each vessel has its own distinctive magnetic signature that must be determined before a vessel can be degaussed.

**magnetic storm**   *n.* A worldwide upheaval in magnetic forces that lasts several hours or days and interferes with communications that depend on magnetic devices such as compasses. These storms are associated with abnormal solar activity.

**magnetic variation (V. or var.)**  *n.* (1) In navigation, the horizontal angle between true north and magnetic north measured in degrees east or west, according to whether magnetic north lies east or west of true north. Also *magnetic declination (D).* (2) In cartography, the annual change in direction of the horizontal component of the Earth's magnetic field.

**magnus hitch**  *n.* A turn around a spar jammed with a half hitch, to secure a line better than a half hitch.

**maiden voyage**  *n.* The first trip made by a vessel after it has been turned over to its owners by the builders.

**mail boat**  *n.* A vessel under contract to and subsidized by a government for the transportation of mail. Vessels so designated must comply with specific requirements for speed, equipment, and regularity of schedule. Vessels carrying mail under government contract fly the International Code "Y" flag at the starboard yardarm, the triatic stay, or below the house flag on the mast. Also *mail packet* or *mail ship.*

**mail declaration**  *n.* A statement by the master of a vessel signed before a customs officer declaring that all mail aboard has been delivered to the nearest post office. This statement must be signed before the vessel is permitted to break bulk or, in some ports, to discharge passengers. More often, the ship's agent makes arrangements with the collector to permit passengers to land and for work to begin. A vessel that carries mail flies a distinguishing **mail flag** or **mail pennant.** United States vessels that carry mail fly a flag with a spread eagle on a red background with blue stripes above and below.

**mail subsidy**  *n.* Contractual payments made to shipping lines to carry mail

for a government with the purpose of encouraging regular schedules and fast service.

**main**  *n.* Prefix indicating a mast, or a sail, or rigging fitted to that mast, on vessels with more than one mast, as main halyard, main sail, or main sheet. See SQUARE-RIGGED VESSEL.

**main beam**  *n.* The longitudinal beam running down the centerline of a ship and supported by king posts. On some vessels there are two main beams, one on each side of the centerline.

**main body**  *n.* The naked hull of a ship exclusive of all deck fixtures, spars, stacks, and so on.

**main brace**  *n.* A rope at the mainmast by which a square-rigged vessel's sails are trimmed to take advantage of the wind. The port and starboard braces of the main yards, the main braces or mainsail braces, were the heaviest and therefore the hardest to splice. See SPLICE THE MAIN BRACE.

**main breadth line**  *n.* The widest part of a ship amidships. If a ship's hull has a pronounced tumble home, the main breadth line will be below the bulwarks.

**main deck**  *n.* Depending on the source consulted, (a) the highest deck that extends from bow to stern; (b) the highest deck starting at either the bow or the stern; (c) the principal deck; (d) the deck below the shelter or awning deck; or (e) a deck forward of a quarterdeck.

**main floodplain**  *n.* The major flood current where branches of several tidal waterways come together in the same area.

**main hatch**  *n.* The primary hatch on the main deck of a ship, usually located amidships.

**main hold**  *n.* The hold below the main hatch.

**main injection valve** *n.* A large valve on the sea chest that controls the intake of seawater for the main circulating pump.

**mainland** *n.* The principal landmass of a country or continent.

**mainmast** *n.* On ships with two or more masts, the first mast is usually the foremast and the second is the mainmast in the tradition of schooners. U.S. Navy ships usually follow the same tradition even though the forward mast is usually the heavier one. Ketches and yawls have a heavy mainmast forward with a mizzen or jigger aft.

**mainsail haul** *interj.* The order to brace the yards of the mainmast over to the opposite tack.

**main tack** *n.* The part of the running rigging by which the lower weather corner of a square sail is controlled.

**main topsail schooner** *n.* A schooner setting square topsails on the foremast and mainmast. Also *two-topsail schooner.*

**main truck** *n.* (1) The top of the mainmast rigged with blocks and halyards for signal purposes. (2) The top of the uppermost mast of the mainmast.

**main trysail ketch** *n.* A ketch-rigged vessel with a triangular mainsail set without a boom. The clew is controlled by a wishbone.

**main yard** *n.* In a square-rigged ship, the lowest yard on the mainmast.

**main yard men** *n.* (1) The members of the crew who are stationed on the main yard. (2) Crew on the binnacle list are also so-called in U.S. Navy slang.

**major aid to navigation** *n.* An aid of considerable intensity, reliability, and range exhibited from a fixed structure or a marine site. Major aids are classified as primary and secondary and are either manned or remotely monitored. See MINOR AIDS TO NAVIGATION; PRIMARY LIGHT; SECONDARY LIGHT.

**major light** See MAJOR AID TO NAVIGATION.

**make** *v.* (1) To raise, as to "make sail" or to "make colors." (2) To make fast is to secure something in place. (3) To strike the hour. To "make eight bells" would be to strike four double strikes on the ship's bell. (4) To indicate engine RPMs. "Make turns for 15 knots" is an order to the engine room to turn the shaft or shafts at a speed that has been determined to propel the vessel at 15 knots.

**make a light** *phr.* To sight a light on the horizon. "Log entry: 0440, made Sombrero light."

**make and mend** *n.* A Royal Navy term for what the U.S. Navy calls rope yarn Sunday. It is a half-day when sailors are excused from their duties to do personal chores, such as, at one time, mending their clothes or making new clothes.

**make colors** *phr.* Hoisting the ensign in the morning, properly at 0800. This is an in-port procedure. See MAKE SUNSET.

**make fast** *v.* To secure a rope or an object. "Make the boat fast." "Make fast the topgallant."

**make land** *phr.* To sight and approach land from the sea.

**make sail** *phr.* (1) To spread the sails open to the wind, to get under way by sail and not power, to set sail. (2) To bend sails on bare poles to get ready to sail. If sails are already bent on and furled, they are said to be set and not made when they are raised.

**make sunset** *phr.* To lower the ensign at sunset. On a U.S. Navy regulation ship, sunset is established by the navigator or quartermaster, and the colors are lowered punctually. This is a procedure carried out in port but not at sea. See MAKE COLORS.

**make the course good**   *phr.* To maneuver a vessel so as to accomplish a desired course, taking into consideration compass deviation, drift, set, wind, and so on. A slight variation is to "make good a certain course" as "We intended to sail 140°, but were only able to make good a course of 120°."

**make up**   *v.* Build up, said of seas beginning to develop large waves.

**makeup feedwater**   *n.* The boiler feedwater with the boiler compound mixed at the proper dilution to replace the water lost between the boiler and the condenser.

**make way**   *v.* To move through the surrounding water. See WAY.

**making**   *adj.* Used to describe a tide that is between neap and spring and successive tide heights are increasing. Tides at that stage are said to be "making."

**Malvinas Current**   See FALKLAND CURRENT.

**man**   *n.* In the U.S. Navy enlisted men are referred to as men, and officers are referred to as officers. Captain to executive officer: "Have all officers and men not on watch report to the fantail."

**man**   *v.* To supply with sufficient men to operate. "Man the boat." "Man the forward gun mounts." Also used in the sense of ordering someone to work at a station: "Jones, man the pump." A vessel is **undermanned** when it does not have enough crew to properly execute its assigned duties. See MAN THE YARDS.

**management rate**   *n.* A British term for the charge made on cargo for landing, weighing, transporting, bulking, and displaying goods for sale.

**managing owner (partner)**   *n.* The owner appointed by the owners of a vessel or fleet to handle the day-to-day business affairs of that vessel or fleet.

**maneuvering board**   *n.* Graph paper available from the Defense Mapping Agency's Hydrographic/Topographic Center used by navigators and deck officers in solving relative movement problems. For example, a ship in a convoy heading north at 10 knots is told to abandon its position 2,000 yards northwest of the guide ship and to proceed to a position 2,000 yards northeast of the guide ship. The Officer of the Deck uses a maneuvering board to determine the course at the desired speed to use in going from the present station to the new one. It can also tell if, on that course and speed, the ship will run too close to any other ships in the convoy. The maneuvering board is also used for target plotting and many other vector problems. Related forms are the radar plotting sheet and radar transfer plotting sheet.

**maneuvering trials**   *n.* Tests conducted at sea to determine the steering characteristics of a vessel and to examine the steering gears and mechanism.

**manger**   *n.* A perforated false bottom or elevated bottom of a chain locker that prevents the chain from reaching the chain locker bottom and allows wet cable to drain.

**manger board**   *n.* An athwartship partition coaming abaft hawseholes designed to prevent water from coming through the hawsehole to wash over the decks. The coaming leads the water over the side by means of manger scuppers. Also *breakwater.*

**manger scuppers**   *n.* Waterways leading from the bottom of a chain locker.

**mangrove swamp**   *n.* A label seen on marine charts to indicate a common feature of tropical waters where flat, low-lying areas of mud and silt lie between high and low water and are covered with mangroves.

**manhelper**   *n.* A paintbrush lashed to a long pole to paint inaccessible places on the sides of a hull when staging is inconvenient.

**manhole**   *n.* An opening in a bulkhead or tank large enough to permit a man to go through it. A manhole is closed with a watertight (or steamtight) cover called a **manhole cover,** with seals called **manhole gaskets,** and secured in place with **manhole dogs.** The manhole is surrounded by a **manhole ring,** a ring plate that is welded or riveted in place to provide stiffening.

**manifest**   *n.* A document furnished to a carrier by the shipper and signed by the vessel's master that details goods received on board ("in ballast"), as required by customs authorities. This document calls for the name of the vessel, master, and port at which the cargo was loaded, the date of sailing, port of discharge, and other such particulars.

**manifold**   *n.* A metal cylinder or box containing valves and fittings for connections with pumps and water mains, fuel and gas lines, and so on. A manifold makes it possible for several pumps to draw from a point or to deliver to a connection with only one pipeline.

**Manila**   *n.* Fibers of a tropical plant, the abaca, used for making rope and, by extension,the rope itself.

**manned light**   *n.* A lighted aid to navigation that is operated and kept in service by a lighthouse keeper who is available to intervene at once if needed.

**manning level**   *n.* The percentage of personnel actually on board a navy ship at a given time.

**manning the rail**   *n.* An evolution in which the entire crew, except those on watch, line up along the ship's rail to honor a dignitary or on an occasion such as Independence Day.

**man-of-war**   *n.* A vessel equipped for warfare; a ship armed for war and a member of a recognized navy. In its current usage, not all commissioned U.S. Navy ships—for example, hospital ships—are men-of-war.

**man overboard maneuver**   *n.* Prescribed method of shiphandling in the event of a person's falling over the side of a ship. Common man overboard maneuvers include the Anderson turn, the racetrack turn, and the Williamson turn.

**manrope knot**   *n.* A round knot placed at the end of a manrope for safety.

**manropes**   *n.* (1) Ropes and ladders used for climbing the sides and masts of vessels, and also the bowsprit horses. (2) The side ropes of an accommodation ladder used as handrails. (3) Earliest usage was for the footropes under the jibboom.

**man the yards**   *phr.* To station the crew standing on each yard from the yardarm into the mast of a square-rigged ship on ceremonial occasions such as saluting a dignitary or in a parade of ships.

**Marconi rig**   *n.* A sailboat with triangular fore-and-aft sails, named for Guglielmo Marconi because of its resemblance, to the untutored eye, to the antennae used in Marconi's wireless telegraphy. See GAFF.

**Marconi topsail**   *n.* A triangular fore-and-aft sail set on the after side of a mast and flown above other sails.

**Marcq St. Hilaire method**   *n.* A method of determining a celestial line of position (LOP) based on the concept of circles of equal altitude, named for Commander Marcq St. Hilaire, a French Naval officer who explained the method in 1874. A line of position is established based on the observation of a celestial

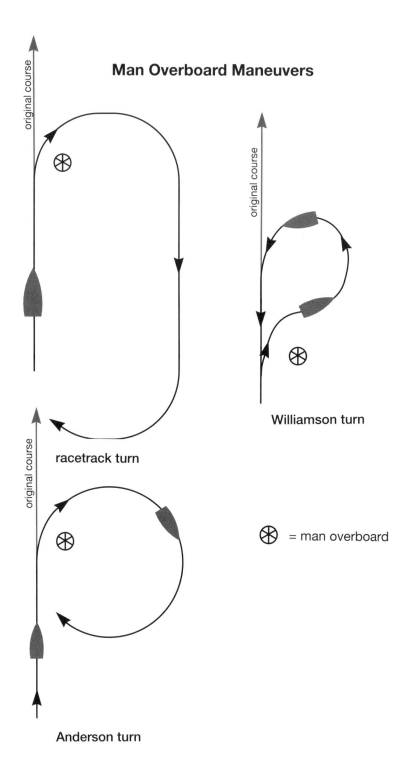

**Man Overboard Maneuvers**

original course

⊗

racetrack turn

original course

Williamson turn

original course

⊗

Anderson turn

⊗ = man overboard

# Marconi Rigging and Sail Parts

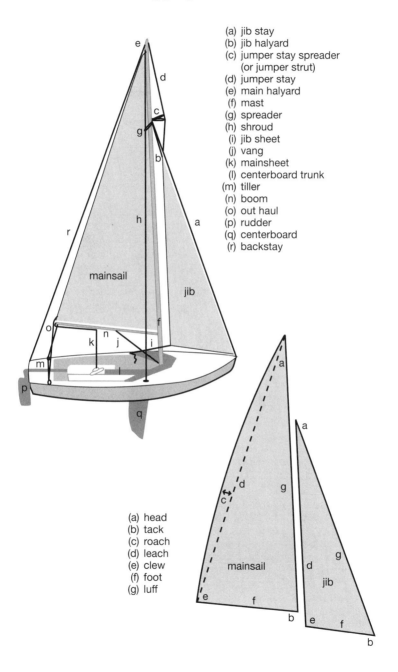

(a) jib stay
(b) jib halyard
(c) jumper stay spreader
(or jumper strut)
(d) jumper stay
(e) main halyard
(f) mast
(g) spreader
(h) shroud
(i) jib sheet
(j) vang
(k) mainsheet
(l) centerboard trunk
(m) tiller
(n) boom
(o) out haul
(p) rudder
(q) centerboard
(r) backstay

(a) head
(b) tack
(c) roach
(d) leach
(e) clew
(f) foot
(g) luff

body by the use of an assumed position, the difference between observed and computed altitudes, and the azimuth. The assumed position may be determined arbitrarily, by dead reckoning, or by estimating it. This is the basis for most of the sight reduction methods used today. Also *altitude intercept method*. See SUMNER LINE.

***mare clausum*** *n.* (Latin = "closed sea") A sea that is under one nation's jurisdiction and closed to vessels of all other nations.

***mare liberum*** *n.* (Latin = "free sea") A sea open to navigation by ships of all nations.

**mares' tails** *n.* Fluffy, tufted cirrus clouds that usually bring wind and often indicate the presence of the jet stream.

**marginal** *adj.* Running parallel to the shore, as in marginal quay.

**marginal sea** *n.* That part of the sea that lies within 3 nautical miles of a shoreline measured from the mean low-water line or from the seaward boundary of a bay or river mouth. (2) A sea that lies between an island arc and a continent, such as the Caribbean Sea or the South China Sea.

**margin clip** *n.* A lug that connects the bilge bracket to the margin plate.

**margin plank** *n.* (1) Planking at the outer margin or boundary of a deck. Also *waterway plank,* (2) Teak planking around a deckhouse or hatch against which deck planking is butted. Also *boundary planking; devil.*

**margin plate** *n.* The outboard row of plates of an inner bottom of a vessel's hull that connects the shell plating at the bilge. (2) A type of filler plate used where bulkheads, decks, and other structures are too short to make up adjoining members. (3) Longitudinal plating that closes off the ends of floors along the midship section.

**marigram** *n.* A graphic representation of a record of the rise and fall of the tide over a given period. The representation takes the form of waves.

**marimeter** *n.* Early name for a sonar instrument used to determine the depth of the water.

**marina** *n.* A harbor available to pleasure boats with dockage and supplies. High-and-dry boat storage warehouses are also called "marinas."

**marine** *adj.* (1) Pertaining to the sea— marine research, marine culture, marine chart, and so on. See MARITIME; NAUTICAL. (2) Pertaining to a nation's shipping interests such as the merchant marine.

**marine adventure** *n.* An admiralty and insurance underwriter's term for a voyage a vessel makes. A marine adventure exists (1) when a ship or cargo is exposed to the peril of the sea; (2) when the earning or acquisition of freight, passage money, commission money, profit, or other monetary advantage, or the security for advances, loans, or disbursements are endangered by exposure of insurable property to the peril of the sea; (3) when any liability to a third party may be incurred by the owner of the insurable property, by reason of exposure to the peril of the sea.

**marine belt** *n.* The margin or belt over which a nation establishes jurisdiction, traditionally from the shoreline out to 3 nautical miles. This is a protective belt for that nation, but international law does not of itself preclude ships of other nations from entering this zone, nor does it subject foreign ships passing through this zone to local laws.

**marine borer** *n.* General term for crustaceans and mollusks that attack wooden hulls and pilings. The most prevalent of the crustacean marine borers are the **wood lice;** the most common of the mollusks are the **teredos.**

**marine distance meter** *n.* British term for stadimeter.

**marine engineer** *n.* A licensed officer on a merchant ship in charge of the maintenance and operation of the ship's main propulsion equipment, auxiliaries, and boilers.

**marine engineering** *n.* The actions and activities that pertain to a ship's propulsion equipment and auxiliaries, including design, building, installation, operation, and repair of the machinery and equipment.

**marine inspection** *n.* The inspection by authorized U.S. Coast Guard personnel of a vessel's hull, machinery, and lifesaving, safety and other equipment, for the purpose of issuing the vessel a certificate of inspection. The certificate of inspection is carried out by a **marine inspector** or the **officer in charge, marine inspection** (OCMI), who is also responsible for issuing the certificate of inspection.

**marine insurance** *n.* The contract by which an insurance underwriter agrees to indemnify the insured in the manner and to the extent agreed to in the document against losses incident to the marine adventure. See MARINE POLICY.

**marine policy** *n.* The contract by which the underwriter agrees to insure the owner of a vessel against the perils, risks, and contingencies of the sea.

**mariner** *n.* An experienced sailor or seaman, rarely used to denote an amateur yachtsman.

**marine radio beacon** *n.* Radio beacon designed primarily for marine use (as opposed to aeronautical radio beacons that are intended primarily for air navigation). Radio beacons are of two kinds: **circular** and **directional.**

**marine railway** *n.* Tracks on an inclined plane going from dry land down into the water and used for hauling vessels up on the dry area of the railway for cleaning and repair.

**marine risk** *n.* A hazard due to the perils of the sea.

**mariner's lien** See MARITIME LIEN.

**mariner's splice** *n.* A splice in a cable-laid rope similar to a long splice but with the rope strands spliced instead of tucked.

**marine sanctuary** *n.* An area established under the provisions of the Marine Protection, Research, and Sanctuaries Act of 1972, for the preservation and restoration of the area's conservation, recreational, ecological, or aesthetic values.

**marine sanitation device (MSD)** *n.* General term for marine heads that includes macerator-chlorinators, recirculating toilets, and incinerators. On most inland and coastal waters, vessels are required to have a sanitation system aboard to prevent the discharge of untreated waste and to control pollution. The standards for these devices have been established by the Environmental Protection Agency for all ships in U.S. waters; regulations regarding their installation and operation have been promulgated by the U.S. Coast Guard.

**marine superintendent** See PORT CAPTAIN.

**marine surveyor** *n.* A person duly qualified by professional boards to examine vessels and their equipment to determine their seaworthiness and overall condition on behalf of the owners and underwriters.

**maritime** *adj.* (1) Pertaining to the sea. (2) In law, the term usually used to describe commercial sea traffic, laws, insurance, and so on, rather than nautical or marine.

**Maritime Administration (MARAD)**
*n.* An agency of the U.S. Department of Transportation that supervises the construction of U.S.-flag merchant ships for the federal government, promotes domestic shipping, and works to advance the work of the U.S. shipping and shipbuilding industries.

**maritime industrial development area (MIDAS)**   *n.* A large commercial zone close to port facilities at which industries dependent on maritime transportation for raw materials and manufactured goods become concentrated.

**maritime law**   *n.* A system of jurisprudence in the United States and Great Britain based upon merchant customs, statutory law, and precedents established by court decisions. In other European countries, maritime law is largely based on codes. Also *marine law.* See ADMIRALTY LAW.

**maritime lien**   *n.* One of the salient features of admiralty law, a lien against the vessel *in rem.* It can arise when a debt is owed or when the vessel has committed a tort. In the case of a debt, called **contract liens,** they arise over wages (a **mariner's lien**), towing fees, stevedoring, dockage, and so on. In the case of torts, maritime liens usually arise against the vessel found to be at fault in a collision. A lien follows the ship wherever it may go and can be enforced under admiralty law by any country that obtains jurisdiction over the ship. In the United States a ship is liable in an action at admiralty law and is taken into custody by the U.S. marshal.

**maritime peril**   *n.* An underwriter's term for perils that are a consequence of the navigation of the sea such as fire, war, barratry, and other perils that may be included in a marine policy.

**maritime radio navigation satellite service**   *n.* A radio navigation–satellite service in which mobile Earth stations are located on board ships.

**maritime territory**   *n.* A term in international law for an area or belt extending along a shore to the limit of a state's seaward jurisdiction, usually assumed to be the three-mile limit unless otherwise declared. Such an area is considered an ocean highway, such as a strait or large bay subject only to innocent passage through which hostile vessels may be forbidden to sail. Examples of maritime territories are the Dardanelles and the Strait of Messina.

**maritime tort**   *n.* Admiralty term for all unlawful or injurious acts committed on the sea or navigable waters connected with the sea. When used within admiralty jurisdiction, a tort has also been held to include wrongs suffered in consequence of the negligence or malfeasance of others, a broader application than in common law.

**mark**   *n.* (1) An indication on a lead line that shows the depth. See MARKS. (2) A buoy or other object, for example, the windward mark, specified in race instructions, that must be passed or rounded on the required side.

**mark**   *interj.* The call given by a helmsman, navigator, or other person when the compass passes a prearranged point or when an observation or azimuth is precisely as announced. Used when taking times of celestial observations. "Stand by . . . MARK . . . the altitude of Procyon is 15°22.3'." At "mark" the assistant reads the exact time and writes it down along with the body name and altitude. See MARKS.

**marker**   *n.* (1) A small radio beacon on a buoy, piling, or pierhead with a range of less than 10 miles. (2) A device used in shipyards for marking holes for rivets and other fastenings. (3) General word for all water signs, but applied to the buoys, beacons, and other signs of marine interest in the Uniform State Waterway Marking System. (4) Regulatory markers established by the states. These signs are white with an orange border. Going upstream, the state-regulated buoys are red to starboard and black or green to port.

**marker buoy**  *n.* A brightly painted, moored, temporary float that marks a location on the water while a buoy is being placed on station.

**marker radio beacon**  *n.* A radio beacon used to mark a specific location such as a jetty or channel entrance and usually used for homing by vessels at sea.

**markings**  *n.* Those marks on a vessel's hull that are required by law, such as the name of the vessel on both sides of the bow and on the stern, the port of registry, load line marks, and the bow and stern draft marks.

**marks**  *n.* The fathom marks on a lead line; for this purpose an established system of leather and cloth is used. The points between the marks are called **deeps**. See DEEP SEA LEAD; LEAD AND LEAD LINE.

**marl**  *v.* (1) To wrap or wind a rope with marline, twine, or other cordage and to secure each turn with a marline hitch. (2) To secure a sail or another line to a boom by using a series of marline hitches.

**marline**  *n.* Two-stranded, left-handed rope used for seizings, to fasten canvas around a rope, called parceling, and as braided rope yarns or sennit. Formerly it was tarred, but this is no longer necessarily true. **Common marlin** is 222 feet to the pound; **medium marlin** is 360 feet to the pound; **yacht marlin** is 520 feet to the pound. Also *marlin, marling.*

**marline hitch**  *n.* A hitch similar to the rolling hitch and used to marl ropes, to make up hammocks, and to bend sails to spars. The line is carried around the back of the spar through an eyelet, then hauled tight with an overhand hitch.

**marlinespike**  *n.* A straight, pointed steel spike used to separate strands of rope or wire for splicing.

**marlinespike hitch**  *n.* A hitch used to fasten seizing stuff before heaving.

**marlinespike seamanship**  n. The body of knowledge encompassing ropework, rigging, spiking, and other topside responsibilities.

**maroon**  *v.* To abandon someone on an island or a deserted coast with little hope of rescue.

**MARPOL**  See CONVENTION ON THE PREVENTION OF MARINE POLLUTION BY DUMPING OF WASTES AND OTHER MATTER.

**married falls**  *n.* A rig in which two cargo whips are connected to one cargo hook. See FALL.

**marry**  *v.* (1) To place two ropes side by side and seize them together for reinforcement. (2) To place the ends of two ropes together and worm them so that one can be pulled through a block behind the other. See FISH; SEIZE; SPLICE.

**marsh**  *n.* Area of soft wet land, usually flat land that is frequently flooded, either saltwater **(salt marsh)** or freshwater.

**martinet**  *n.* An early name for a leech line on a square sail.

**martingale**  *n.* A chain or spar that extends downward from the bowsprit or jibboom to the dolphin striker to counterbalance the strain of the headstays. The term comes from the part of harness used to prevent a horse from throwing his head back.

**martingale boom**  See  DOLPHIN STRIKER.

**martingale guys**  *n.* The ropes or chains led back from the lower end of a dolphin striker to each side of the bow. Also *gob lines; martingale backropes.*

**martingale stays** *n.* Stays leading from the jibboom to the martingale boom or from the dolphin striker to the stem of the ship. Also *jumpers.*

**maru** *n.* Part of the name of all Japanese ships. The word means circle or sphere in Japanese and implies perfection and completeness.

**mask** *n.* A device used to control the speed of a vessel as it slides down the ways toward the water.

**mast** *n.* (1) A vertical spar that supports gaffs, sails, and booms. See BUILT MAST; GAFF; MARCONI RIG. (2) When wooden masts are made up in sections, they are called, from the bottom up, **lower mast, topmast, topgallant mast, royal mast,** and **skysail mast.** (3) See CAPTAIN'S MAST.

**mast band** *n.* A steel band secured to the mast and used to anchor blocks.

**mast bed** *n.* The wood wedges or shims that secure a mast at the mast hole in the deck.

**mast boot** See MAST COAT.

**mast box** *n.* A cup in a deck into which a mast butt is stepped. See MAST STEP.

**mast butt** *n.* The bottom of a mast.

**mast cap** *n.* The fitting that holds two masts together, one on top of the other. The mast cap is made of wood with a square steel fitting that slides down over the square masthead of the lower mast and a round steel fitting into which the round base of the upper mast fits.

**mast coat** *n.* A boot at deck level on a mast that passes through the deck, to keep the water from going below. Also *mast boot.*

**master** *n.* The officer in command of a merchant ship. See MASTER MARINER.

**master-at-arms (MAA)** *n.* (1) A petty officer responsible for maintaining order. A vessel's police organization is headed by the chief master-at-arms. The masters-at-arms maintain law and order, keep the men in line on the mess decks, make sure orders are carried out. Known derisively as **jimmy legs.** (2) A member of the crew of a passenger vessel who is charged with police duties.

**master carpenter's certificate** *n.* A document signed by the shipyard's master carpenter that specifies for whom a vessel was built and where, the basic measurement, molded dimensions, gross tonnage, date built. Also *builder's certificate.*

**master chief petty officer (MCPO)** See PETTY OFFICER.

**Master Chief Petty Officer of the Navy (MCPON)** *n.* An office established March 1, 1967, to provide a direct unofficial channel of communications between enlisted personnel and the senior policy levels of the U.S. Department of the Navy. The MCPON is the senior enlisted adviser to the Chief of Naval Operations on matters pertaining to enlisted personnel.

**master mariner** *n.* An experienced seaman licensed as competent to command a merchant vessel.

**master station** *n.* A radio navigation term for the station in a chain of stations that provides a reference by which the emissions of other slave or secondary stations are controlled, especially for loran.

**master valve** *n.* A valve fitted in tanker piping at each point it passes through a bulkhead and enters the next tank. Master valves provide separation between tanks on the same line and make it possible to isolate a single tank.

**masthead (or mast head)** *n.* The top of a lower mast in which the foretop or maintop rests. Also *truck*. *See* MAST-HEAD LIGHT; MAST TRUCK.

**masthead light** *n.* A white light placed over the fore-and-aft centerline of a vessel and showing an unbroken light over an arc of the horizon of 225° and so fixed as to show the light from right ahead to 22.5° abaft the beam on either side of the vessel. The masthead light doesn't necessarily have to be at the top of the mast, and it often is not. On many sailboats, the masthead light is about three-quarters of the way up the mast, with the all-round light displayed while at anchor, at the very top.

**masthead rig** *n.* A sail plan in which the headsail is set on a headstay that goes to the masthead, as opposed to a three-quarter rig.

**mast hole** *n.* The hole in the deck through which the mast passes on vessels on which the mast is stepped on the keel. *See* MAST BED.

**mast hoops** *n.* Wooden hoops around a mast to which the luff of a fore-and-aft sail is bent. Found only on older boats or reproductions today.

**mast lining** *n.* Reinforcing material sewn on a sail at the point it will be chafed while rubbing against the mast.

**mast partner** *n.* (1) One of the deck beams that support a mast and distribute the weight. (2) The metal or wood reinforcing ring around the mast hole for the same purpose.

**mast pedestal** *See* TABERNACLE.

**mast rope** *n.* A line used to raise and lower a mast.

**mast step** *n.* The place where the bottom, foot, or butt of a mast is secured. This is usually on the keel, but on lighter boats it can be on the deck. It is

here that a penny was traditionally placed for good luck and fair winds, but watch out for the electrolytic action on an aluminum mast. The copper sulfate was a great rot preventative for wood masts as the penny corroded in the bilge water. When a mast is stepped on deck, it is said to be stepped into a mast box or tabernacle.

**mast table** *n.* The structure at the base of a mast that supports cargo boom pivots.

**mast truck** *n.* A circular wooden piece that caps the top of a mast, usually fitted with sheaves for halyards.

**mast wedges** *n.* Shims used to secure the mast in place within the mast partner in the deck. *See* MAST BED.

**master mariner** *n.* A person who holds a master's license and is hired as master of a merchant vessel. A U.S. Navy commanding officer is never referred to as a master because he does not (necessarily) have a master's license.

**mat** *n.* A fender woven from old yarns and ropes. *See* COLLISION MAT; FOTHER; MOORING MAT; PUDDENING. (2) A woven glass-fiber-reinforcing layer.

**match race** *n.* A race between two boats. The America's Cup race is the most famous match race in yachting.

**mate** *n.* (1) A merchant marine deck officer under the master. First, second, and third mates have different designated responsibilities. (2) In the U.S. Navy a petty officer who is an assistant to a warrant officer.

**material condition** *n.* A condition of damage control readiness on a ship. The three conditions are X-ray, Yankee, and Zulu, depending on the hatches and other closures that are called for to be closed under various conditions.

**Matthew Walker knot**   *n.* Any of several end knots that begin with a wall knot used for a stopper. The identity of Matthew Walker is a mystery to maritime historians, but he is one of the few men for whom a knot has been named.

**maxi boat**   *n.* An offshore racing sailboat with an overall length of about 80 feet with a maximum rating of 70 feet, the maximum allowed by the International Offshore Rule.

**mayday**   *n.* Along with "Pan" and "Sécurité," one of the three levels of urgency in radiotelephone communication. Mayday is the radio distress call that is closely monitored by the Federal Communications Commission and the U.S. Coast Guard. The word is the anglicized form of *M'aidez*, French meaning "Help me!" Maydays are broadcast on Channel 16.

**meal pennant**   *n.* A red-and-blue pennant (Echo) hoisted at the port yardarm of a U.S. Naval vessel when at anchor to indicate that the crew is at chow. Widely known as the **bean rag.**

**mean higher high water (MHHW)**   *n.* A tidal datum that is the average of the highest high-water height of each tidal day observed over a national tidal datum epoch.

**mean high water (MHW)**   *n.* The average high-water depth. Bridge heights and power line clearances are given on charts as the height above the surface of the water at MHW. See TIDAL DATUM.

**mean high-water lunitidal interval**   *n.* The average elapsed time from either the upper or lower meridian transit of the Moon until the next tide. Also *mean establishment.*

**mean high-water neaps (MHWN)**   *n.* The mean of high water heights occurring at the time of neap tides observed over a 19-year period. Rarely used. See METONIC CYCLE; TIDAL DATUM.

**mean high-water springs (MHWS)**   *n.* The mean of high water heights occurring at the time of spring tides observed over a 19-year period. See METONIC CYCLE; TIDAL DATUM.

**mean length**   *n.* The average of the length between perpendiculars and the length on deck.

**mean lower low water (MLLW)**   *n.* A tidal datum that is the average of the lowest low-water height of each tidal day observed over the national tidal datum epoch.

**mean low water (MLW)**   *n.* Average low-tide depth. Charted depths are at MLW. A shoal with a charted depth of 3 feet will be in deeper water at high water, depending on the tidal difference for the area. See TIDAL DATUM.

**mean low-water neaps (MLWN)**   *n.* The mean height of low water heights occurring at the time of neap tides observed over a 19-year period. See METONIC CYCLE; TIDAL DATUM.

**mean low-water springs (MLWS)**   *n.* The mean height of low water heights occurring at the time of spring tides observed over a 19-year period. This reference datum is used more often outside the United States; it is the level of reference for the Pacific approaches to the Panama Canal. See METONIC CYCLE; TIDAL DATUM.

**mean range**   *n.* The average range between mean high and mean low water. See TIDAL DATUM.

**mean range of tide**   *n.* The difference in height between mean high water and mean low water.

**mean rise of tide**   *n.* The height of mean high water above the reference or chart sounding datum.

**mean sea level (MSL)** *n.* Average height of the surface of the sea for all stages of a sea over a period of 19 years.

**mean tide level** See HALF-TIDE LEVEL.

**measurement** *n.* The calculation of the tonnage of part or all of a vessel according to specific rules.

**measurement rule** *n.* A system of measuring boats for racing so that boats with different designs can compete on an equal basis. A boat with a greater waterline length than another boat, for example, could have a greater handicap; on the other hand, the second boat may have greater sail area sufficient to have a similar handicap. See RATING RULE.

**measurement ton** *n.* A unit of measure equal to 40 cubic feet or 2,240 pounds, used to determine the gross tonnage of a vessel.

**Mediterranean mooring** *n.* A mooring with the vessel stern to the jetty, mole, or wharf. The anchor is dropped from the bow as the vessel is backed into the slip. The brow is put over the stern, and U.S. Navy ships establish the quarterdeck on the fantail. This is a popular practice in the Mediterranean where many harbors are short on wharf space.

**meet her** *interj.* The order to the helm to check the swing of a vessel in a turn, but not to stop it entirely.

**meltemi** See LEVANTER.

**mend** *v.* To refurl a sail that has been improperly furled or to rebend a sail on a boom. A closely furled sail is frequently called a **mended sail.**

**Mentor Current** *n.* A current that originates mainly from the easternmost extension of the South Pacific Current at about latitude 40°S, and longitude 90°W. The Mentor Current flows first northward and then northwestward. It extends about 900 miles westward from the

Peru Current to about 90°W at its widest section and tends to be easily influenced by winds. It joins the westward-flowing Pacific South Equatorial Current and forms the eastern part of the general counterclockwise oceanic circulation of the South Pacific. Also *Peru Ocean current.*

**Mercator projection** *n.* In concept a projection of a globe against a cylinder tangent to the globe at the equator. The relationship, however, of the latitude and longitude lines is actually derived from mathematical equations. See INVERSE MERCATOR PROJECTION.

**Mercator sailing** *n.* One of the five "sailings," or mathematical solutions to problems involving a single course and distance, that uses differences in latitude and meridian. See PLANE SAILING.

**merchant intelligence report (MERINT)** *n.* A report in plain language requested of merchant ships and fishing vessels when they sight anything that could relate to the national security.

**merchantman** *n.* A commercial ship.

**merchant marine** *n.* The private and government-owned commercial shipping of a country, exclusive of military and fishing craft and pleasure yachts. It is also used to refer to the personnel who man merchant ships.

**merchant mariner's document (MMD)** *n.* Commonly called a **Z-card,** this is the primary classification and identification for all personnel in the U.S. Merchant Marine. The MMD is issued by the U.S. Coast Guard to all personnel engaged in sailing U.S. merchant vessels, exclusive of vessels operating solely on the western rivers.

**merchant ship** *n.* A vessel that carries cargo for profit, not including riverine, estuarial, or harbor craft.

**merchant ship report (MEREP)** *n.*
A daily list of merchant ships arriving and departing from a particular port.

**meridian** *n.* Any great circle on the Earth's surface that passes through both poles. The **prime meridian** passes through Greenwich, England, at the original Royal Observatory. Meridians are used to measure longitude. The **standard meridian** is the meridian used for computing standard time in a given time zone. Most countries have adopted as the standard meridians those that are divisible by 15°. (The Earth revolves around the Sun once in 24 hours; 360° divided by 24 (hours) equals 15°.) The standard daylight saving meridian is usually 15° east of the standard meridian of the given zone.

**meridian altitude** *n.* The angle of elevation of a celestial body above an observer's horizon at the instant of the body's transit, as used in the determination of latitude. See ZENITH DISTANCE.

**meridian angle** *n.* The angular distance of a celestial body east or west of the celestial meridian.

**meridian angle difference** *n.* The difference between two meridian angles, especially between the meridian angle of a celestial body and the value used as an argument for entering a table.

**meridian day** *n.* The day gained at the 180° meridian (with variations for political entities), the International Date Line, when sailing eastward.

**meridian sailing** *n.* Following a true course of 0° or 180°, or sailing along a meridian. The dead-reckoning latitude then is assumed to change 1 minute for each mile run and the dead-reckoning longitude is assumed to remain unchanged.

**Merriman clip** *n.* Trade name for a device used to fasten the spinnaker to the spinnaker sheets.

**meshes** *n.* The holes between the cords of a net. Mesh is measured across the diagonal when the net is pulled diagonally. When a diagonal of a square thus pulled measures 12 inches, it is called a 12-inch mesh.

**mess** *n.* A group who eat together, as in the U.S. Navy the crew's mess, the officers' mess, the chiefs' mess. While the captain frequently dines alone on the bridge, his tray is referred to as the captain's mess. If a flag officer is aboard a ship, even though he frequently dines alone in solitary splendor in his quarters, his meal is referred to as the flag mess or the admiral's mess. The commissioned officers' mess is prepared and served by mess specialists, formerly called steward's mates, in the wardroom.

**messboy** *n.* (1) Obsolete term for a Navy wardroom waiter. (2) A member of the crew on a merchant ship who acts as the crew's waiter.

**messcook** *n.* Obsolete term for messman, one who serves meals to the crew.

**mess decks** *n.* The crew's dining area on a ship during the time the crew is eating.

**mess dress** *n.* Formal uniform for officers.

**messenger** *n.* (1) A small line with a weight that can be thrown across open water, perhaps from one ship to another, and that is bent on a larger, heavier line that needs to follow it. (2) A person who carries messages and runs errands for the commanding officer and officers on watch. (3) A small ring on a line used to get water samples; the ring slides down the line to close a bottle that has reached the desired depth. (4) A small line rove in advance to allow the correct size line to be pulled through later.

**messenger chain** *n.* An endless chain used to transmit energy from one machine, such as a capstan, to another, such as a windlass.

**mess gear** *n.* Eating utensils (knives, forks, spoons, cups, and so forth).

**messman** *n.* One who serves meals to the crew; now formally called a **mess management specialist.**

**messroom** *n.* Merchant term for a space where members of the crew have their meals. See GALLEY.

**metacenter (M)** *n.* The intersection of a vertical line drawn through the center of buoyancy of a heeling vessel with the centerline of the vessel (drawn perpendicular to the design waterline). The distance of the transverse metacenter above the center of gravity is a critical measure of stability. See HEIGHT OF METACENTER; STABILITY.

**metacentric height (GM)** *n.* The distance from the metacenter to the center of gravity of a vessel. If the metacenter is above the center of gravity, the vessel is stable. Not the same as height of metacenter (KM). See STABILITY.

**metalling clause** *n.* A term used by British underwriters to waive the underwriter's liability for loss arising from ordinary wear to which a vessel can be expected to be subject during the course of a voyage.

**meteorological equator** *n.* A belt of low pressure at the surface of the Earth located near the equator at about 5°N.

**meteorological tide** *n.* A change in water level caused by local meteorological conditions rather than by the attraction of the Sun and Moon. See TIDE.

**meteorological visibility** *n.* The greatest distance at which a black object of suitable dimension can be seen and recognized against the horizon by day; the information is necessary in determining the size and height of markers.

**metonic cycle** *n.* A period of 235 lunar months, or about 19 Julian years, when the phases of the moon recur in the same cycle and on the same days as in the preceding cycle. The Metonic cycle is used for determining average tide levels. It is named for Meton, the 5th century B.C. Athenian who determined the cycle.

**Mexico Current** *n.* A seasonal (late October through April) seasonal extension of the California Current that flows southeastward along the coast to about 95°W, where it usually turns west; it can extend southward as far as Honduras. Its speed ranges from 0.5 to 1 knot.

**micrometer** *n.* On a sextant, the screw and the graduated head that replaced the vernier carried by the index bar to move the index bar along the teeth of the limb.

**midchannel** *n.* (1) The line of greatest depth in a confined channel or waterway, represented on coastal charts by a magenta line. (2) When used in connection with midchannel controlling depth, the middle half of a channel.

**midchannel aids to navigation** *n.* Aids placed in the middle of a channel or fairway that can be passed on either side. These are black and white and have no numbers, but sometimes they have letters. If a preferred side is indicated, it will have red and green horizontal stripes with the top stripe showing the preferred side. Entering from seaward, such a **junction aid** will be either red or green at the top; red indicates that the preferred channel or side is to the left of the buoy as approached by the vessel ("red, right, returning"); another way of saying it is that the junction aid should be taken to starboard as if it were a red nun buoy. Also *bifurcation aids.*

**midchannel controlling depth** *n.* The point of least depth in the middle half of a navigable channel.

**middle**  v. To double a rope so that the two lengths are equal or to fold a sail in the middle.

**middle body**  n. The section of a vessel contiguous with the midship section. A **parallel middle body** has a uniform cross section along its full length and its waterline parallel to the centerline of the vessel.

**middle ground**  n. A shallow area with deeper channels on at least two sides. This is usually marked at both ends by **middle ground buoys.**

**middle jib**  n. A schooner man's term for the jib set next outboard the foretopmast staysail.

**middle latitude (Lm)**  n. The mean latitude between the point of departure and that of destination; when two places are on the same side of the equator, as a rule, the middle latitude is equal to half the sum of the two latitudes. Only rarely is middle latitude, or mid-latitude used when the two points are in different hemispheres; when so used, the mid-latitude is half the difference between the two latitudes.

**middle latitude sailing**  n. A quick and fairly accurate solution to a spherical-right-triangle problem (a) when the latitude and longitude of points of departure and destination are known and the course and distance are required; or (b) a solution to a spherical-right-triangle problem when the latitude and longitude of a point of departure are known, and the course and distance are known, and the latitude and longitude of the point of destination are required. It involves the use of the middle latitude to convert departure to difference in longitude when the course is not due east or west. The solution assumes that the course is steered at the middle latitude.

**middle mast**  n. (1) The middle mast on five-masted ships and barks. (2) A schooner term used occasionally for the third mast of a five-masted schooner, though this is more often called the mizzen mast.

**middle passage**  n. The name of the slave trade passage from Africa to the West Indies or America's southern colonies and later southern states. It was so called because it was the second of three legs in a triangular trade. The first was from New England to Africa with rum, the second was from Africa to the islands or southern colonies with slaves, and the third was from the islands or the south to New England with bulk cargoes such as molasses and cotton.

**middle seam**  n. A strengthening seam between regular seams in a sail. When used, usually each cloth will have a middle seam added in the middle of the cloth to prevent stretching between the seams.

**mid-ocean dynamics experiment (MODE)**  n. The study of the fluctuations in mid-ocean currents using the dynamics of eddies.

**midrats**  n. Short for midwatch rations, widely used in military vessels. Synonymous with **night lunch** in the merchant service.

**midship frame**  n. The frame at the midship section that is equidistant from the forward and after perpendiculars.

**midshipman**  n. A noncommissioned student officer enrolled either at the U.S. Naval Academy at Annapolis, Md., the U.S. Coast Guard Academy at Groton, Conn., the U.S. Merchant Marine Academy at Kings Point, N.Y., or in a U.S. Naval Reserve Officer Training Corps unit in a university. When a midshipman graduates from the Naval Academy or the Coast Guard Academy, he or she is commissioned as an officer (ensign) in the U.S. Navy or U.S. Marine Corps, or the U.S. Coast Guard, respectively. A graduate of the Merchant Marine Academy has the rank of third officer or third assistant engineer in the merchant marine and is a commissioned officer in the U.S. Naval Reserve. A midshipman wears a small gold braid stripe and ranks between a chief petty officer and a warrant officer.

The term "midshipman" comes from the custom in early U.S. Navy ships and in Royal Navy ships in the days of sail when the midshipmen were quartered amidships, the crew being forward in the forecastle, and the officers aft. In the services, midshipmen are known as **mids.**

**midships** *adj.* Short for amidships.

**midship section** *n.* The transverse section exactly halfway between the forward perpendicular and the after perpendicular. See PLAN.

**Mike** *n.* Phonetic word for the letter M. The signal is a white cross on a blue background. Used as a single-letter signal, it means "I have a doctor aboard." It is also flown by the vessel with medical guard duty in a fleet of U.S. Navy ships.

**mile** *n.* A unit of distance. There are two types of mile recognized in the U.S. The **statute mile** (which is used on land) is 5,280 feet, and is the legal unit of distance on the inland waters of the United States. The **international nautical mile,** adopted by the International Hydrographic Bureau in 1929, is equal to 1,852 meters, or roughly 6,076 feet. Because the nautical mile is based on the length of one minute of latitude at the equator, it is more convenient for navigation than any unit of length in the metric system. When short distances are involved, deck officers think in terms of 6,000 feet or 2,000 yards. A nautical mile is equal to about 1.2 statute miles and a statute mile is equal to about 0.9 nautical miles. See KNOT.

**mileage number** *n.* Numbers assigned to navigation aids that give the distance in statute miles along a river from a reference point to the aid, used on rivers such as the Mississippi and the Apa-

lachicola; they are more prevalent on western rivers of the United States.

**military salvage** *n.* The rescue of a ship and cargo from an enemy during war. Admiralty courts have jurisdiction over such cases and sit as a prize court.

**Military Sealift Command (MSC)** *n.* Formerly known as the **Military Sea Transport Service (MSTS),** it is the U.S. Navy-operated ocean freight and passenger service and is run for the Department of Defense.

**military standards** *n.* (1) General U.S. Navy qualifications that Navy personnel must have for discipline, ceremonies, regulations, and so on. (2) A document that establishes the standard of engineering and technical limitations to ensure uniformity in materials and products used by the armed services.

**millibar (mb)** *n.* A unit of atmospheric pressure. One millibar (1/1000 bar) is equal to 0.03 inches of mercury in a barometer.

**mimic** *n.* The display on a console that gives a graphic or diagrammatic representation of a particular process or arrangement. It may show status information on valves, the physical relationship of the main turbine, reduction gear, and propeller shaft bearings, or similar information needed by the duty operator.

**mind your rudder** *interj.* Order from the conning officer to the helm to be careful not to stray from the compass course. "Mind your left rudder" is the order to the helmsman to use left rudder to steady up the course. Also *mind your helm.*

**mine** *n.* An explosive device laid in the water with the intention of damaging or sinking ships or deterring shipping. They can be anchored, left on the bottom, or dropped from the air. Mines are detonated by various means, including direct contact or the influence of a ship's magnetic field, sound waves, or radio waves.

**mine countermeasure ship (MCS)** *n.* A ship designed to reduce or prevent damage to vessels from mines, including hunting for mines, sweeping mines, and other highly technical methods.

**minelayer** *n.* A ship designed to lay mines; in the U.S. Navy, it is usually an older destroyer converted for minelaying duties, but some are especially built of wood or, more recently, glass-reinforced plastic.

**minesweeper** *n.* A ship designed for clearing harbors and channels of mines. In the U.S. Navy, it is usually a converted destroyer, helicopter, or specially designed minesweeping boat (MSB).

**minor aid to navigation** *n.* Unmanned, unmonitored light on a fixed structure usually with low to moderate intensity; a minor aid is usually fitted with light characteristics and dayboards in accordance with its lateral position in a waterway.

**minor light** *n.* An automatic unmanned light on a fixed structure usually showing low to moderate intensity. Minor lights are established in harbors, along channels and rivers, and in isolated locations.

**minute** *n.* The 1/60th part of a degree. For practical purposes, the length of one minute of latitude (1′) is equal to one nautical mile.

**missed her point** *phr.* Describes a vessel making a turn either wider or closer than intended, usually in strong current.

**missile tube** *n.* Vertical tube on a submarine from which missiles are fired.

**missing** *adj.* (1) A term applied to a vessel that is overdue and presumed by its owners to have been lost at sea. When this occurs, application is made to the Committee of Lloyd's to "post" the vessel as missing to alert anyone who might have information regarding the vessel. After it is posted for a week, the vessel is considered lost and the underwriters become liable. See OVERDUE. (2) Said of a floating aid to navigation that is not on station with its whereabouts unknown.

**Mississippi River buoyage system** *n.* Significantly different from the intracoastal waterway system and should be understood before attempting to navigate the river. Buoys are not numbered; numbers on lights and markers are rough mileage figures and are numbered from downstream north; proceeding upstream, single green or single white flashes mark the left side, known as the right descending bank (RDB), while double red or white mark the right-hand side, known as the left descending bank (LDB); mileage figures on the flashing markers are exact to within one-tenth of a mile; crossing daymarks alert watch officers that the channel is crossing from one side to the other. A study of applicable charts and manuals is imperative.

**miss stays** *phr.* To fail to complete a tack because of wind or sea conditions when trying to come about. When this happens, a vessel is said to have "missed stays." See IN IRONS; MISSED HER POINT.

**mistral** *n.* A nor'wester along the coast of the northern Mediterranean from the Golfe du Lion (named for the storms that roar there) to the lower Adriatic Sea.

**miter** *n.* (1) A diagonal seam in a sail with the weave of the cloth on each side running in different directions. (2) Wood pieces precisely joined at an angle.

**mitered jib** *n.* Headsail cut with upper cloths at right angles to the leech, and the lower cloths perpendicular to the foot.

**mixed current** *n.* A tidal current that has two cycles part of the time and only one cycle, a low and a high, part of the time. Other places have either diurnal or semidiurnal tidal currents. See ROTARY TIDAL CURRENT.

**mixed layer (of seawater)** *n.* The first of the three layers of seawater, the one most influenced by air temperature. The lower two are the **thermocline layer** and the **deep-water layer.**

**mixed tide** *n.* Two high tides and two low tides in a 24-hour period with one high higher than the other and one low lower than the other. See MIXED CURRENT.

**mizzen (or mizzenmast)** *n.* (1) The shorter mast aft of the mainmast on a ketch or a yaw. (2) "The mizzen" is also short for "mizzensail"—or "mizzenmast." (3) The third mast on a ship, bark, or schooner with three or four masts, and the fourth mast on vessels with five masts. On the rare six- and seven-masted schooners, the mizzen was the third mast from the bow.

**mizzen** *adj.* Of or pertaining to sails, stays, masts, or fittings found on or attached to the mizzenmast, as mizzen staysail, mizzen top, or mizzen royal. The mizzen course is often called the **crossjack,** or **crojick.** See SQUARE-RIGGED VESSEL.

**model basin** n. A laboratory tank designed and used for testing models of vessels for speed, power, seaworthiness, and general behavior at sea. Waves, currents, and other natural phenomena are synthesized to make tests as nearly real as possible.

**moderate breeze** *n.* Beaufort scale reading of 4, with winds of 11–16 knots.

**moderate gale** *n.* Beaufort scale reading of 7, with winds of 28–33 knots.

**moderate sea** *n.* Douglas scale reading of 3, indicating waves between 2 and 5 feet with a short, moderate swell.

**mold (or mould)** *n.* Thin strip of easily bent wood, metal, or plastic used for shaping patterns or templates of a ship's frames.

**molded breadth** *n.* The greatest breadth of a vessel as measured from the heel to heel at its two largest frames.

**molded depth** *n.* The greatest height of a vessel measured from the top of its keel to the upper side of the upper deck beam.

**molded displacement** *n.* Displacement of a vessel computed to the outside of the frames exclusive of the submerged volume of planking.

**molded draft** *n.* The vertical distance from the designed waterline to the top of the keel.

**molded form** *n.* A vessel's structure or form over the frames before the plating or planking is put on.

**molded lines** *n.* The inside surface of the skin plating of a vessel. The molded surface is fair and smooth.

**molded-plywood construction** *n.* Hull construction utilizing successive layers of plywood glued together.

**molding** *n.* A half-round strip that goes the full length of a vessel at deck level outboard of the hull.

**molding edge** *n.* The edge of a vessel's frame where it comes in contact with its skin.

**mold loft** *n.* A shed or building with large smooth floors on which full-sized patterns, called molds or templates, for virtually all structural parts of a vessel, can be drawn to full size.

**mole** *n.* A large masonry structure, usually a breakwater, often used for wharfage, not necessarily connected to the shore. Mole is an international word, less common in the United States than elsewhere. By extension mole is often used to refer to the water within the structure.

**mollymawk**   *n.* Sailor's name for an albatross.

**monkey block**   *n.* A small single-block purchase with a swivel.

**monkey bridge**   *n.* (1) Narrow bridge between poop deck and forecastle. (2) A bridge above the pilothouse where the standard compass is mounted.

**monkey deck**   *n.* A small half round deck between the forward bulwark and the headrails.

**monkey face**   *n.* Triangular plate with holes at each of the three corners used to shackle the ends of three chains or ropes. See FISH PLATE; HEART.

**monkey forecastle**   *n.* Low shelter in the bow of a vessel in which the anchor and anchor gear are stowed.

**monkey gaff**   *n.* A spar extending from the aftermast for the halyard carrying the national ensign.

**monkey rail**   *n.* (1) A light rail above the quarter rail. (2) A rail on the forecastle that is used to belay headsail sheets.

**monkey's fist**   *n.* A knot created at the end of a line, sometimes enclosing a weight, to make heaving easier. A messenger almost always has a monkey's fist. See HEAVING LINE.

**monkey's tail**   *n.* (1) A length of rope added to running rigging or a bar to make it possible for more men to pull on it. (2) A curved bar fitted to the upper trailing edge of a rudder, used as an attachment for the rudder pendants.

**monohull**   *n.* A single-hulled vessel, as opposed to a multihulled vessel such as a catamaran or trimaran.

**monoplane**   *n.* A racing hull without a break in the wetted surface.

**monsoon**   *n.* A wind system found in the western North Pacific and Indian Ocean and in which the wind reverses itself from season to season. The summer monsoon, which blows from the southwest, is characterized by hot, moist air and heavy rains and lasts from April to September. The winter (northeast) monsoon lasts from October to March and is characterized by cool, dry air. The northwest monsoon, which also lasts from October to March, is found in the Indian and Western Pacific Oceans south of the equator. Monsoon winds generally blow at about Force 5 on the Beaufort scale.

**Monsoon Current**   *n.* A current that replaces the North Equatorial Current and the Equatorial Countercurrent during the winter of the Northern Hemisphere. The Monsoon Current flows eastward and southeastward across the Arabian Sea and the Bay of Bengal. See OCEAN CURRENT.

**Monsoon Drift**   *n.* A drift current of the northeast Indian Ocean located north of the Indian Equatorial Countercurrent and south of the Bay of Bengal.

**moonraker**   (1) See RAFFEE. (2) One who moves or changes aids to navigation to cause ships to founder in order to collect the salvage.

**Moon's age**   See AGE OF THE MOON.

**moor**   *v.* To make fast a vessel in its dock, to tie it to a mooring buoy, or to anchor using more than one anchor and cable.

**moorage**   *n.* The fee charged for mooring a vessel.

**mooring**   *n.* (1) A berth or anchorage in which a vessel is made fast. This is usually a charted berth for mooring a vessel, equipped with **mooring anchor, mooring buoy,** and **mooring link** on the buoy to which the vessel shackles an anchor cable or chain. (2) An authorized place in a river or harbor for mooring vessels. (3) A permanent anchor such as a concrete pad with a chain and float, called a **mooring anchor.**

**mooring, right of** See RIGHT OF MOORING.

**mooring bitts** *n.* Cast-iron pillars placed in pairs on a deck or wharf used for securing vessels. See BITT; BOLLARD; DOLPHIN.

**mooring bridle** *n.* Chains permanently attached to mooring anchors at one end and a buoy at the other, and taken aboard a vessel when using the mooring.

**mooring buoy** *n.* A permanent mooring with anchors and chain marked by a buoy with a heavy shackle to which a vessel can moor without using its own anchor. Also *moorings.*

**mooring chock** *n.* Deck fittings with inward-curving horns, used to control mooring lines and to prevent chafing.

**mooring lighter** *n.* A harbor tender or boat especially fitted to handle permanent mooring gear.

**mooring line** *n.* A line used to make fast a vessel to a wharf. Mooring lines, also called **docking lines,** are known by a variety of names depending on their particular function. **Breast lines** are led perpendicular to the keel; **spring lines** are led forward or aft from a given point on the vessel; **bow lines** are led forward from the bow and are forward of the **bow spring;** while **stern lines** are led aft from the stern aft of the **stern springs.** Mooring lines are further identified by the part of the vessel from which they are led. A **forward bow spring** leads forward from the bow; an **after quarter spring** leads aft from the stern quarter; a **waist breast line** is led perpendicular to the keel from the waist or beam.

**mooring mat** *n.* Heavy matting used on a ship to prevent chafing from the anchor chain. See MAT.

**mooring pipe** *n.* A heavy casting through which a mooring line is led as it goes over the side, used to prevent chafing of mooring line.

**mooring post** *n.* A heavy pile used for mooring vessels. See BOLLARD; DOLPHIN.

**moorings** See MOORING BUOY.

**mooring screw** *n.* A device used for permanent moorings in soft ground. The device is screwed into the ground to a depth necessary to securely anchor the mooring buoy. Also *screw anchor.*

**mooring staple** *n.* A large iron staple welded to a ship's side through which mooring chains and cables are led.

**Moorsom Rules** *n.* The basis for calculating the internal capacity of merchant ships by using the cubic footage and dividing by 100 to get the tonnage. (One hundred cubic feet equals one ton.) The rules were developed by George Moorsom, Surveyor General in Great Britain, in 1854. They were later adopted almost universally with some modifications. The United States adopted them in 1864. This is still the factor for determining gross registered tonnage and net registered tonnage.

**morning call book** *n.* A list of members of a ship's company who must be called before reveille; these include cooks, quartermasters, and navigators, and, when getting underway at an early hour, people in the engineering department.

**morning colors** *n.* The hoisting of the national ensign and the union jack at 0800 local time when not underway. When several U.S. Navy ships are in port, the senior ship makes morning colors first to be *immediately* followed by all other ships. This ceremony is usually preceded

# Mooring Lines

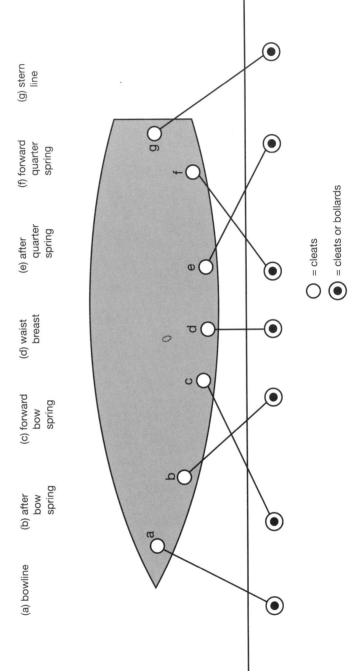

(a) bowline

(b) after bow spring

(c) forward bow spring

(d) waist breast

(e) after quarter spring

(f) forward quarter spring

(g) stern line

○ = cleats

◉ = cleats or bollards

by 5 minutes by the senior ship's hoisting the Papa signal flag (also known as **prep**) at the foremast yardarm.

**morning order book**   *n.* The book in which the executive officer of a U.S. Naval ship writes the orders for the ship's work scheduled for the morning. *See* NIGHT ORDER BOOK; PLAN OF THE DAY.

**morning star**   *n.* Popular name for the brightest planet in the eastern sky just before sunrise. It is not always the same star.

**morning watch**   *n.* The watch from 0400 to 0800.

**Morse Code (MO)**   *n.* Light phase description indicating a light in which flashes of different durations are grouped in such a way as to signal Morse Code characters. *See* LIGHT PHASE CHARACTERISTICS.

**mortised block**   *n.* A block carved from a single piece of wood with a chiseled space for the sheave and pin.

**mothball fleet**   *n.* Ships that have been taken out of commission but are maintained. *See* RESERVE FLEET.

**Mother Carey's chicken**   *n.* A small seabird *(Procellaria pelagica)* the presence of which near ships at sea is thought to signal that land is near or that a storm is coming. The name probably derives from the Latin, *Mater Cara,* Dear Mother, referring to the Virgin Mary, patron saint of sailors. The birds can appear to run lightly over the water, for which they are also called **stormy petrels,** after St. Peter.

**motorboat**   *n.* (1) In the U.S. Navy, a service launch built for heavy duty work. (2) A power-driven boat used for recreation. According to the Motorboat Act of 1940 (since superseded by the *Navigation Rules*), the maximum length was 65 feet.

**motor gunboat (MGB)**   *n.* A fast U.S. Navy patrol vessel, highly armed and armored.

**motor launch**   *n.* A heavy powerboat used on U.S. Navy vessels for transporting freight and for liberty parties.

**motorman**   *n.* A merchant term for an oiler who is in charge of lubricating machinery on a motorship. The term is rarely used today.

**motor-sailer**   *n.* A boat with both power and sail, but usually with more emphasis on engine than sail.

**motorship**   *n.* A diesel-powered vessel.

**motor torpedo boat (MTB)**   *n.* A high-speed boat armed with torpedoes, rapid-fire weapons, and missile armament. The most recent boats have hydrofoils.

**motor whaleboat**   *n.* A heavy double-ended open powerboat used by the U.S. Navy as liberty launch, lifeboat, and general-purpose small boat. *See* MOTOR LAUNCH.

**mould**   See MOLD.

**mounting area**   *n.* The assembling site where amphibious forces are trained and loaded.

**mouse a hook**   *phr.* To secure a hook with spun yarn or a small piece of line wrapped around the jaw of the hook to prevent an object on the hook from slipping out. *See* SEIZING.

**mousing**   *n.* Small stuff or wire seized on the opening of a hook to prevent a line held on the hook from jumping off.

**movables**   *n.* A marine underwriter's term for noncargo items such as money, securities, and documents.

**movement report system (MRS)** *n.* The U.S. Naval authority established to maintain current information on the status, location, and movement of flag commands, commissioned fleet units, and other ships under the operational control of the Navy. Among the subsidiary components of the MRS are the **movement report center (MRC)** and **movement report office (MRO).**

**Mozambique Current** *n.* The part of the Indian Equatorial Current that turns and flows along the African coast in the Mozambique channel. It becomes the Agulhas Current. See OCEAN CURRENT.

**mud berth** *n.* A berth in which a vessel rests on the bottom at low water.

**mud box** *n.* A steel case with a strum plate that is designed to keep sediment and foreign matter from entering the suction valve of the saltwater intake on a vessel. The mud box is similar to the rose box in the bottom of a hold or in a bilge.

**mud drum** *n.* A tank at the bottom of a boiler.

**mud pilot** *n.* A pilot who navigates by water color and other visual aids when aids to navigation are few or nonexistent.

**mud scow** *n.* Flat-bottomed boat used to haul mud from a dredge to a dump site.

**muffled oars** *n.* Oars silenced by wrapping canvas or other damping material around the oar at the point they work in the oarlocks; oars are muffled for surprise attacks and funerals.

**mule sail** *n.* A staysail hung with the point down and carried between the mainmast and the mizzen on ketches. The mizzen staysail is sometimes called a mule.

**multihull** *n.* Any vessel with more than one hull, as a catamaran or trimaran.

**Murmansk Current** *n.* A southeast-running current in the Barents Sea, the temperatures of which are responsible for keeping Russia's northwest seaport of Murmansk ice-free in winter.

**mushroom anchor** *n.* An anchor shaped like a mushroom and without flukes. It is most effective when used for anchoring small craft in soft mud. See ANCHOR.

**mushroom ventilator** *n.* A deck device used for ventilating cabin spaces. The airflow is regulated by adjusting the hood up or down.

**mustang** *n.* Slang for an officer who was formerly an enlisted person and did not graduate from the U.S. Naval Academy or under a Navy program in a college or university or from Officer Candidate School, but who "came up through the hawsepipe."

**muster** *v.* To assemble a specific group such as a ship's crew, the radio gang, the engine room watch. This is done for meetings, the day's orders, or to determine if everyone is on duty. In the last instance, the report, if true, is "All hands are present or [not 'and'] accounted for."

**muster out** *v.* To be discharged or released from active duty.

**mutiny** *n.* Refusal by a crew to obey a master's lawful orders. The refusal to obey orders by a single member of the crew is not mutiny. Mutiny is an attempt to take over command. A lesser offense is **inciting to mutiny,** which is the case when one of the crew incites another to disobey or resist the lawful orders of the master or other officer. Laying **violent hands** on the commander to hinder his fighting in defense of vessel or goods is punishable with life imprisonment.

**mutton**   See LEG-O'-MUTTON RIG.

**muzzle**   *v.* To tie an anchor cable to the throat of the shank or a fluke with light cordage in addition to fastening the cable to the ring. In this way, the anchor is prevented from catching unless it hits something heavy.

**muzzle bag**   *n.* A fabric cover placed over the muzzle of a gun to protect the bore from the elements; a temporary measure when a tampon is not practical.

**muzzler**   *n.* A strong wind coming from the direction in which a vessel should be headed.

**Mylar**   *n.* Trade name for stiff, low-stretch material used to make sails; the manufacturing process is owned by E.I. DuPont.

# N

**N**   See NOVEMBER.

**nadir**   *n.* That point on the celestial sphere that is directly beneath the observer and 180° from the observer's zenith, which is directly over his or her head.

**naked**   *adj.* Said of a wooden vessel with the copper sheathing removed from its hull.

**named policy**   *n.* Marine underwriter's term for a policy in which the vessel and particulars of the destination of goods are named, as distinguished from a floating policy.

**Nansen bottle**   *n.* One of a series of bottles dropped into the sea on a line to get samples of the seawater at various depths; named for its inventor Fridtjof Nansen, Norwegian Arctic explorer and scientist (1861–1930).

**Nantucket sleighride**   *n.* The run of a whaleboat attached to a harpooned whale that is swimming fast. It is so called because Nantucket was a center of whaling in the nineteenth century.

**nao**   See CARRACK.

**Napier diagram**   *n.* A graphic representation that conveniently plots compass deviation for various headings with the points connected by curves. It permits deviation problems to be converted quickly. Named for James Robert Napier (1821–1879). See RESIDUAL DEVIATION.

**narrow pennant**   See COMMISSION PENNANT.

**narrows**   *n.* The name sometimes applied to the narrowest part of the navigable waterway or harbor.

**national flag**   See ENSIGN.

**National Oceanic and Atmospheric Administration (NOAA)**   *n.* One of the two principal sources of marine charts in the United States; formerly known as the U.S. Coast and Geodetic Survey. The other agency responsible for charts is the Hydrographic/Topographic Center of the Defense Mapping Agency (formerly the U.S. Naval Oceanographic Office).

**National Ocean Service (NOS)**   *n.* A division of NOAA, the NOS provides charts and related publications for safe navigation for marine and air commerce. It also provides data for engineering and scientific purposes.

**National Tidal Datum Control Network** *n.* A network composed of the primary control tide stations of the National Ocean Survey. These stations, distributed along the coasts of the United States, provide the basic tidal datums for coastal boundaries and chart datums of the United States.

**National Tidal Datum Epoch** *n.* The 19-year cycle of periodic and apparent secular trends in sea level issued for all U.S. datums. It was adopted by the National Ocean Service and is reviewed for consideration at 25-year intervals.

**National Weather Service (NWS)** *n.* Provides marine weather forecasts and warnings for U.S. coastal waters, the Great Lakes, offshore waters, and the high seas.

**natural harbor** *n.* An area offering natural protection with sufficient depth for vessels of a given size; it may be a natural harbor that can accommodate yachts, or it may be a natural harbor that can accomodate aircraft carriers (such as Pensacola, Fla.).

**natural (fractional) scale** *n.* The **fractional scale** used on a chart such as 1:80,000, which means that one unit on the chart is equal to 80,000 of the same units on the Earth's surface. A legend such as "2 inches to a mile" is called a **numerical scale.**

**nautical** *adj.* Of or pertaining to ships, sailors, navigation, and the sea. It is a more general term than "marine," which refers to the sea (marine navigation), "maritime," to a relationship with or proximity to the sea (the Canadian Maritime Provinces), and naval, which refers to a nation's navy (the United States Navy). These distinctions are made in *The American Practical Navigator* by Bowditch; other authorities are less specific.

***Nautical Almanac*** *n.* A comprehensive listing of tides, tidal currents, stars used for navigation given by time period, sunrises and sunsets, and much more. It is published jointly by U.S. Naval Observatory and the Nautical Almanac Office, Royal Greenwich Observatory in the United Kingdom, and available from the Superintendent of Documents in Washington, D.C., and from the Royal Observatory at Greenwich, England.

**nautical astronomy** See NAVIGA-TIONAL ASTRONOMY.

**nautical chart** *n.* A representation of a portion of the navigable waters of the Earth and adjacent coastal areas on a specified projection to meet the needs of marine navigation. Most nautical charts include depths of water, characteristics of the bottom, elevations of selected topographic features, general configuration and characteristics of the coast, dangers and obstructions, aids to navigation, tidal data, and information on magnetic variation.

**nautical distance** *n.* The arc of a rhumb line intercepted between two points, expressed in nautical miles.

**nautical hydrography** *n.* The science of measuring and describing oceans, lakes, and rivers for navigation and commercial use.

**nautical instruments** *n.* Navigation instruments, including, but not limited to, azimuth circle, chronometer, compasses, depth finder, sonar, loran, dividers, and parallel rules. See NAVIGATIONAL AID.

**nautical mile (NM)** *n.* A unit of distance equal to one minute of arc on the Earth's surface. The United States has adopted the international nautical mile, which is equal to 1,852 meters, or 6,076.11549 feet. See KNOT.

**nautical surveyor** *n.* One who surveys tides, tidal currents, topography of the areas under study, and oceanography and meteorology as they affect navigation. A nautical surveyor is one who works in the field of nautical hydrography. See MARINE SURVEYOR.

**nautical twilight**  See TWILIGHT.

**nautophone**  n. A fog signal that works by an electrically operated oscillator.

**naval**  adj. Relating to the equipment, personnel, installations, and customs of a navy. See NAUTICAL.

**naval architect**  n. One trained in the science and art of designing boats and ships, not necessarily those used by navies.

**naval aviation**  n. An all-inclusive term for aircraft used by navies; these would include helicopters, dirigibles, carrier-based aircraft, and so on.

**naval base**  n. A shore command responsible for all naval shore activities in the area.

**naval campaign**  n. An operation or a series of operations conducted primarily by naval forces to gain control of the sea.

**naval control of shipping**  n. Control exercised by naval authorities of the movement, routing, convoy organization, and tactical diversion of allied merchant shipping during wartime.

**Naval district**  n. A geographically defined area with a single **commandant** under the Secretary of the Navy and the Chief of Naval Operations. The commandant is charged with responsibility for local naval defense, coordination of area naval activity, and security.

**Naval establishment**  n. Popular term for the entire U.S. Navy including the operating forces, the administrative Navy Department, and the shore facilities.

**naval law**  n. Rules and regulations for personnel in a naval service. In the United States, this body of law is found in Navy Regulations and the Uniform Code of Military Justice.

**Naval officer**  n. A person in the U.S. Navy who has been commissioned by the Congress of the United States as an "officer."

**Naval petroleum reserves**  n. Oil reserves in the United States set aside for national defense purposes by Congress (1923). These reserves, which are estimated to contain billions of barrels of crude, are in Elk Hill and Buena Vista, Calif., Teapot Dome, Wyo., and North Slope, Alaska.

**Naval station**  n. A U.S. Navy shore activity with fixed boundaries under the command of an officer.

**naval stores**  n. (1) Any articles or commodities used by a naval ship or station, such as equipment, consumable supplies, clothing, fuel, medical supplies, and ammunition. (2) In the sailing ship navy, products used in caulking, such as turpentine, pitch, resin, and oils.

**Naval Vessel Lights Act**  n. Congressional authorization for departure from the rules of the road for character and position of navigation lights for certain U.S. Naval ships. Such modifications are published in *Notice to Mariners*.

**NAVAREA warnings**  n. Broadcast information concerning the safety to navigation on the high seas. In cooperation with other nations, the Defense Mapping Agency's Hydrographic/Topographic Center is responsible for disseminating navigation information for the areas designated NAVAREA IV and NAVAREA XII of the World Wide Navigation Warning Service. Navarea IV broadcasts over the water bounded by the Atlantic Coast of the United States to the west to 35°W and between latitudes 7°N and 67°N. NAVAREA XII broadcasts cover the waters from the West

Coast of the United States to the International Date Line, and from 67°N to the equator east of 120°W, south to 3°,25'S, then east to the coast. The text for effective warnings of these two areas is printed in the weekly *Notice to Mariners.*

**navel futtock**   *n.* The lowest midship section of a wooden frame of a vessel.

**navel line**   *n.* A rope thrown over the yard of a square-rigged vessel to assist in hoisting or lowering it.

**navel pipe**   *n.* A deck fitting through which the anchor chain passes to the chain locker. Also *spillpipe.*

**navigable**   *adj.* (1) Deep enough and wide enough for a given type of vessel to pass through or pass over. "For our ship, the river was navigable only to the first settlement." (2) Said of a vessel or an aircraft that is capable of being steered, though not necessarily powered.

**navigable semicircle**   *n.* In the Northern Hemisphere, the left half of a circular storm (or the **left semicircle**) when facing in the direction the storm is moving. It is so called because as the storm advances, the counterclockwise motion moves wind on the left side slower than on the right side. In the Southern Hemisphere, the navigable semicircle is on the right side of the storm, which moves in a clockwise direction. See DANGEROUS SEMICIRCLE.

**navigable waters**   *n.* Rivers, streams, and other waters that are deep enough and wide enough for the passage of a vessel. In some specific instances, this only applies to water that is affected by the ebb and flow of the tides. The bed under the water belongs to the state in which it lies, but the right of passage and fishing belongs to the public unless the state or federal government has imposed specific restrictions.

**navigate**   *v.* To direct a craft's movements expeditiously and safely from one place to another.

**navigation**   *n.* The science of planning, recording, and steering the course of a vessel on water. Navigation is frequently distinguished from piloting as the science of conducting a vessel without landmarks, whereas piloting is confined to coastwise navigation. See COASTAL NAVIGATION; HYPERBOLIC NAVIGATION SYSTEM; INERTIAL NAVIGATION.

**navigation, right of**   See RIGHT OF NAVIGATION.

**navigational aid**   *n.* Any instrument, device, chart, method or similar aid intended to assist in the navigation of a craft. This term should not be confused with "aids to navigation," which refers only to devices external to the vessel such as buoys and lighthouses.

**navigational astronomy**   *n.* That branch of astronomy that is of direct use to the navigator and deals with celestial coordinates, time, and the apparent motions of selected heavenly bodies with reference to the Earth and to each other. Also *nautical astronomy.*

**navigational planets**   *n.* The four planets commonly used for navigation: Venus, Mars, Jupiter, and Saturn.

**navigational triangle**   *n.* A spherical triangle solved in computing altitude and azimuth and great circle sailing problems. The **celestial triangle** is solved on the celestial sphere by the great circles connecting the elevated pole, zenith of the assumed position of the observer, and a celestial body. A **terrestrial triangle** is formed on the Earth's surface by the great circles connecting the pole and two places on the Earth.

**navigation bridge**   *n.* The deck house, compartment, or enclosure in which the officer in charge directs a vessel's movements. Included on the navigation bridge is an area for the necessary charts and chart work. Usually referred to simply as the "bridge."

**navigation certificate (Navicert)** *n.* A document issued by the consular corps of a belligerent nation in a neutral country; it testifies to the inventory of a cargo ship and that the vessel is proceeding to a neutral port.

**navigation head**  *n.* A transshipment point on a waterway where cargoes are transferred between water and land carriers, similar to a railhead.

**navigation laws**  *n.* The body of law that deals with preference and exclusion by which maritime nations attempt to protect their merchant marine in foreign trade against foreign competition, and to exclude foreign competition from trading on equal terms with their own merchant marine. These laws are of maritime law, but separate from that branch that deals with the use of the seas.

**navigation lights**  *n.* A generic term for lights used by vessels under way. The term is not used in the *Navigation Rules.* See LIGHT.

*Navigation Rules* *n.* Statutory requirements enacted by the U.S. Congress to promote safety of navigation. These rules establish navigation lights, day shapes, steering and sailing rules, sound signals, and distress signals. The *Navigation Rules* include rules for international waters and rules for inland waters. The international rules were first established in 1889 and were only an agreement between some of the maritime nations. The *Navigation Rules* were adopted in 1972 and were called "72 COLREGS"; these became effective July 15, 1977. The international rules adopted as 72 COLREGS by the various participating maritime nations had the status of a treaty and became far more binding than the previous agreements. Rule 1(b) went a step further by stating that "Such special rules [established by appropriate

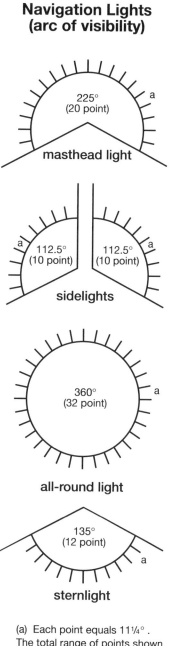

**Navigation Lights (arc of visibility)**

225°
(20 point)

a

**masthead light**

a

112.5°
(10 point)

112.5°
(10 point)

a

**sidelights**

360°
(32 point)

a

**all-round light**

135°
(12 point)

a

**sternlight**

(a) Each point equals 11¼°.
The total range of points shown
is the arc of visibility
(32 points = 360°).

government authority over its own internal waters] shall conform as closely as possible to these Rules.'' The *Navigation Rules* have been amended and additions have been made since their original promulgation.

**navigation satellite**   *n.* A man-made earth satellite that is used by vessels to determine their positions based on signals received from the satellite.

**navigator**   *n.* The officer charged with the responsibility of safely navigating a vessel.

**NAVSTAR**   *n.* An integral part of the global positioning system, the advanced worldwide navigation system that uses high-altitude satellites to transmit signals for continuous position fixes. Distances, for example, can be determined instantly instead of by the standard method employing celestial navigation. It will eventually provide all-weather, all-purpose position fixes. See NAVY NAVIGATION SATELLITE SYSTEM.

**nav station**   *n.* Yacht term for navigator's station.

**navy**   *n.* (1) All of a nation's warships. (2) All of a nation's military organization used for sea warfare. (3) A nation's navy also occasionally includes the merchant navy.

## Navy and Coast Guard ranks, U.S.

*Flag Officers*
  Fleet admiral
  Admiral
  Vice admiral
  Rear admiral
  Commodore (Navy only)

*Commissioned Officers*
  Captain
  Commander
  Lieutenant commander
  Lieutenant
  Lieutenant, junior grade
  Ensign

*Warrant Officers*
  Chief warrant officer
  Warrant officer

*Enlisted Personnel*
  Master chief petty officer
  Senior chief petty officer
  Chief petty officer
  Petty officer 1st class
  Petty officer 2nd class
  Petty officer 3rd class
  Seaman
  Seaman apprentice
  Seaman recruit

**Navy Cross**   *n.* U.S. Navy medal, first awarded in 1919, given to personnel who have displayed extraordinary heroism against the enemy. With the Air Force Cross and the Distinguished Service Cross, it is the nation's second highest award for bravery.

**Navy Department**   *n.* The administrative offices of the U.S. Navy located in Washington, D.C. See DEPARTMENT OF THE NAVY.

**Navy enlisted classification code (NEC)**   *n.* The system of four-digit codes that identify special skills and training for enlisted personnel. All enlisted personnel have a minimum of two NECs. Further details can be found in the *Manual of Navy Enlisted Classifications.*

**Navy exchange**   *n.* A store maintained for the benefit of U.S. Navy personnel and their dependents; it sells household and personal items at a small profit for the benefit of the Welfare and Recreation Fund.

**Navy League**   *n.* A national organization made up of civilians and retired service personnel interested in working for a strong Navy. The Navy League of the United States is headquartered in Washington, D.C., and is independent of the U.S. Navy or federal government.

**Navy Navigation Satellite System** *n.* An operational satellite navigation system that was conceived and developed at the Applied Physics Laboratory of the Johns Hopkins University for the U.S. Navy. The system is under the control of the Navy Aeronautics Group located at Point Mugu, Calif. It is an all-weather, worldwide, passive navigation system used primarily by surface vessels and submarines. See GLOBAL POSITIONING SYSTEM.

**Navy Oceanographic and Meteorological Automatic Device (NOMAD)** *n.* A small platform moored at sea to monitor and transmit data on weather and other oceanographic phenomena to shore stations.

**Navy Relief Society** *n.* A relief society operated for the benefit of U.S. Navy personnel and their dependents; it operates worldwide on a quasi-official basis.

**Navy standard fuel oil (NSFO)** A low grade of fuel oil, slightly more refined than Bunker C, used as fuel in ship's plants and large generating plants.

**Navy Unit Commendation (NUC)** *n.* An award given to a U.S. Naval unit for distinguished service in combat or other operations; the Presidential Unit Citation carries more prestige.

**Navy yard** *n.* Known as a Naval shipyard under the obsolete Naval Ships Systems Command, a U.S. Navy yard today is an industrial activity responsible for building, repairing, altering, and replenishing ships, as well as other services.

**neap** *v.* To ground a vessel at the height of a spring tide. A vessel is neaped, or one neaps a vessel.

**neap current** *n.* Tidal current produced by a neap tide.

**neap low water** *n.* Low water at the first and third quarters of the moon.

**neap range** *n.* Average tidal range between the full and the new moon. See TIDAL DATUM.

**neap rise** *n.* The height of a neap high water above the elevation of reference or datum chart. See TIDAL DATUM.

**neap tide** *n.* The tide with the smallest difference between the lowest high water and the highest low water that occurs during the lunar month; these occur at the first and third quarters of the Moon. One of the two semimonthly neap tides may have less difference than the other. See SPRING TIDE.

**nearest approach** *n.* The closest two ships will come if neither changes course or speed, a term used when plotting radar courses and speeds of ships that may appear to be coming close. This is now called closest point of approach (CPA).

**near gale** See BEAUFORT SCALE.

**nearshore current system** *n.* The current caused by wave action in or near the surf zone along a coastline. The current zone consists of four parts: (a) the shoreward mass transport of water; (b) longshore currents; (c) rip currents; and (d) the longshore movement of expanding heads of rip currents.

**neatline** *n.* The limit or boundary of a chart inside the margin of the chart.

**necessaries** *n.* A British Admiralty term referring to all the gear that a prudent owner would order for a ship for the service it is in. Admiralty law does not distinguish between the necessaries for the vessel and those for a voyage and the necessaries required for the adventure. Necessaries include anchors, cables, rigging, fuel, provisions, clothing and provisions for the crew, propellers, money for bills, customs fees, and so on.

**neck**  *n.* (1) A point of low-water resistance along a beach at which the **feeder currents** return to sea. (2) A narrow isthmus, cape, or promontory. (3) A body of water between two larger bodies, a strait.

**necking**  *n.* The molding on the taffrail.

**negative altitude**  *n.* Angular distance below the horizon.

**negative flag**  *n.* The "N" flag, which means "No" under some circumstances.

**negative stability**  *n.* A vessel with unstable equilibrium, lacking in statical stability needed to return it to an erect position when inclined. Negative stability exists when the center of gravity (G) coincides with the metacenter (M). See NEUTRAL EQUILIBRIUM; STABILITY.

**negligence clause**  *n.* A marine underwriter's clause that covers the shipowner against loss of freight when caused by accidents in loading, discharging, or handling cargo; negligence of masters, mariners, engineers, or pilots; explosions, bursting of boilers, breaking shafts, or latent defects in machinery or hull, as long as such loss has not resulted from want of due diligence by owners or the master of the ship. See INCHMAREE CLAUSE.

**Neptune**  *n.* The god of the sea in Roman mythology; he corresponds to Poseidon in Greek mythology.

**nest**  *n.* Two or more vessels moored side by side. (Also used as a verb.)

**net**  *n.* (1) A group of radio stations sharing the same frequencies and transmitting together. (2) A heavy mesh placed at the entrance to a harbor for protection against enemy surface vessels and submarines and torpedoes. Floating booms are often used to suspend the nets.

**net bottom clearance**  *n.* Depth between the bottom of a keel and the sea floor.

**net capacity**  *n.* The cargo tonnage a vessel can carry when loaded in saltwater to its summer load line. Also *cargo carrying capacity; useful deadweight.*

**net charter**  *n.* A charter party term that relieves the owner of expenses such as port charges for loading and unloading and stowing and trimming the cargo, pilotage dues, and towing. It differs from **gross charter** under which these charges are the responsibility of the owner.

**net layer**  *n.* A vessel designed for laying and tending antisubmarine and antitorpedo nets.

**net registered tonnage (NRT)**  *n.* The volume, expressed in units of 100 cubic feet to the ton, of the total enclosed spaces of a vessel (the gross tonnage) minus deductions for certified non-cargo spaces such as machinery, passenger quarters, crew's quarters, storerooms, and spaces used for navigation. The usual unit of measure to describe cargo and passenger ships, the net registered ton, is an indication of a vessel's earning capacity and is the normal basis for harbor dues and pilotage fees. See TONNAGE.

**netting**  *n.* Open weave rope net used for cargo and heavy work.

**netting knots**  *n.* Knots used for making nets, either reef knots for small mesh or single sheet bends for large mesh.

**nettle**  *n.* Small lines composed of two or three rope yarns plaited or twisted, used for fastening the service on cables, reefing sails by the bottom, grafting hammock clews, and tying the outer end of batten pockets. Also *house line; knittle.*

**net value clause**  *n.* Marine underwriter's term that allows underwriters, in the event of particular average, to adjust claims by comparing sound and damaged values of goods after deducting freight, duty, and ordinary charges payable at destination.

**net weight**   *n.* The weight of an object that results when the **tare,** the weight of the wrapper or shipping container, is deducted from the gross weight.

**neutral equilibrium**   *n.* The balance obtained when the center of gravity and the metacenter coincide and the metacentric height is zero. A vessel with neutral equilibrium does not tend to return to its upright position when inclined slightly. See NEGATIVE STABILITY; STABILITY.

**new danger**   *n.* A newly discovered hazard to navigation that has not been observed long enough to be on charts and *Notices to Mariners.* It is indicated by lateral and cardinal marks in the Region A Buoyage System.

**new sea ice**   *n.* Newly formed sea ice up to 10 centimeters in thickness and identified by needlelike crystals called spicules.

**new wind**   *n.* A racing term for a wind that comes from a new direction.

**nibbing plank**   *n.* A plank along hull margins that is notched to accommodate deck end planks and enables good joint caulking.

**nib strake**   *n.* Inner strake at the ends of waterways on wooden decks.

**Nicholson tube**   *n.* Early instrument used for measuring a ship's speed by having the lower end of a tube outboard in the water and measuring the pressure in that part of the tube that is inboard.

**night effect**   *n.* Inaccuracies in radio bearings at sunset and sunrise due to the changes in the level of the ionosphere.

**night glasses**   *n.* Binoculars with high light-gathering capability used for night work. The most common are 50mm objective lenses that have a net light-gathering ability of seven times that of the unaided eye.

**night order book**   *n.* The captain's orders aboard U.S. Navy ships addressed to the officers of the deck who stand watches during the night. They start with standing orders that are written in the front of the book. These include such matters as calling the captain when any vessel is sighted, advising the captain when any messages are received that require immediate attention, and so on. In addition, the captain writes specific orders for each night at sea, including courses to be set, speeds to be maintained, and lights to be expected; these are supplied to the captain by the navigator. Each night's orders are signed by the captain.

**night signal**   *n.* A signal transmitted from a shuttered lamp using Morse code.

**night vision**   *n.* The ability to see in dim light, as for watch personnel when their duty takes them outside the vessel or onto the bridge. To help preserve this vision, all necessary lights on the bridge are red; charts use colors other than red for that reason.

**nilas**   *n.* (rhymes with stylus) An elastic crust of ice of high salinity up to 10 centimeters thick with a matte surface.

**nimbostratus**   *n.* A low, amorphous rain cloud, dark and nearly uniform, about 50 to 2,000 feet. See CLOUDS.

**nimbus**   *n.* A heavy rain cloud that often has an edge lighted by the Sun or Moon.

**ninepin block**   *n.* A block used between bitt crosspieces; the block is shaped like a bowling pin with a single sheave at the top and at the bottom so that it can follow the motion of the line rove through it for which it serves as a guide. See FIDDLE BLOCK.

**nip**   *n.* (1) A sharp bend in a rope or cable. A hockle in a rope that causes it to jam is a nip. (2) The place or places in a line where you would expect chafing. Easing, or hauling a line to change the place being chafed is called "freshening the nip."

**nipped**   *adj.* Said of a vessel that is beset with the surrounding ice pressing against its hull.

**nipper**   *n.* (1) A small rope that connects a messenger to a heavier line. Similar to a sinnet or a selvagee. (2) A young boy on a sailing ship. They were so-called because when the anchor was weighed, the anchor cable was not actually brought to the capstan, but an endless messenger was led from forward round the capstan, and this ran alongside the cable. The messenger was secured to the cable by stoppers known as 'nippers.' The nippers were worked by the small boys on the ship who in turn became known as nippers themselves.

**nipper**   *v.* To stop ropes with several turns of rope yarn alternately wound around each and the ends made fast. The two ropes are said to be 'nippered.'

**nips**   *n.* The part of a rope around a thimble, the "nips of an eye-splice."

**no-bottom sounding**   *n.* A phrase indicating the lead found no bottom— the water is deeper than the lead line is long, traditionally 100 fathoms. See OFF SOUNDINGS.

**nock**   *n.* (1) The tip or extremity of a yardarm, lashed by earings (2) Forward side or luff of a staysail with a square tack. (3) The upper forward corner of a gaff sail.

**nodal point**   *n.* (1) A stopping or starting point; a point of land from which the current goes up the coast and down

the coast. (2) A place where there is little or no rise and fall of the tide but there are tidal currents.

**no higher**   *interj.* Order to the helmsman not to bring the vessel any closer to the wind.

**no-man's-land**   *n.* An area of a ship to which no one has been assigned to keep order.

**nominal range of a light**   See VISUAL RANGE OF A LIGHT.

**nonharmonic constants**   *n.* Tidal constants that include tidal ranges, inequalities, and intervals derived from observations of the high water and the low water regardless of the harmonic constituents of the tide.

**nonmagnetic vessel**   *n.* A vessel built with as little steel or iron as possible with a wood hull and copper fastenings. The vessel is designed for detecting the Earth's magnetism in different areas of the ocean.

**nonrated personnel**   *n.* In the U.S. Navy an enlisted person in the first three pay grades, below petty officer: a seaman, seaman apprentice, or seaman recruit.

**nonreturn valve**   *n.* A one-way valve that allows water to lift the valve only when the water is going in the desired direction. Discharge systems have such valves that allow the water to go overboard, but will not allow the seawater to come in.

**nonsaturable system**   *n.* A radio navigation system that can be used by any number of receiving stations simultaneously; loran is one such system.

**nonself-propelled vessel**   *n.* Any vessel that does not have installed either propulsive machinery or masts, spars, and sails.

**nonspinning rope** (or **cable**) *n.* A wire rope with the six inner strands laid in the direction opposite to the outer strands.

**nontidal current** *n.* Any current not caused by tide, such as those caused by the Earth's rotation and meteorological conditions.

**nontoppling block** *n.* Blocks designed to remain upright instead of dangling from the whip, such as cargo whip blocks and running blocks for boat falls.

**noon** *n.* The time of the Sun's transit of the upper branch of the meridian of a given point on Earth. See STANDARD NOON.

**noon interval** *n.* The period between a celestial observation (the morning sights) and local apparent noon when the Sun will be on the meridian and a meridian observation can be taken for latitude.

**noon position** *n.* The computed position of an observer as determined by a day's work at each noon from which the next 24 hours' course is plotted.

**nor'easter** *n.* A strong wind out of the northeast, used especially in New England and Canadian Maritime provinces.

**norman** *n.* (1) The pin that goes through the top of some bitts to aid in holding mooring lines. (2) Pin fitted through the rudder head. (3) Short bar shipped in a pigeon hole of a capstan head. (3) Staple-shaped bolt shipped on a windlass to keep the chain clear when running out. (4) Manually or hydraulically mounted bars on the stern of tugboats to selectively restrict the movement of the hawser.

**North Africa Coast Current** *n.* A nontidal current in the Mediterranean that flows eastward along the African coast from Gibraltar to the strait of Sicily. It is the most permanent current in the Mediterranean.

**North Atlantic Current** *n.* The current that flows from the vicinity of the Grand Banks northeast toward the British Isles. In the eastern Atlantic it branches to become the **Northeast Drift Current** and the Azores (or Southeast Drift) Current. It comprises part of the Gulf Stream. Also *North Atlantic Drift.* See GULF STREAM; OCEAN CURRENT.

**North Cape Current** *n.* An Arctic current that flows northeastward and eastward around northern Norway and curves northeastward into the Barents Sea.

**northeast monsoon** *n.* Prevailing wind from October to April in the Mozambique Channel, the North Indian Ocean, the China Sea, and part of the nearby Pacific. See MONSOON.

**Northeast Passage** *n.* Passage between the Atlantic Ocean and the Pacific Ocean along the northern coast of Europe and Asia. The Passage was pioneered by the Finnish-born Swedish explorer and geologist, Baron Nils Adolph Erik Nordenskjold (1832–1901), from 1878 to 1880 in the steam whaling ship *Vega* of 337 tons. Known as the **Northern Sea Route,** the icy passage represents the shortest sea route between ports in European Russia and Asian Russia.

**northeast trade winds** *n.* Surface winds caused by the rotation of the Earth from belts of high pressure to the low-pressure belt of the equator in the Northern Hemisphere; these blow in a southwesterly direction. See WIND.

**northerly** *n.* (1) A current that flows *toward* the north. (2) A wind that blows *from* the north.

**northern lights** *n.* The aurora borealis. The aurora australis is a similar phenomenon in the Southern Hemisphere.

**northill anchor** *n.* A light folding anchor with a stock set through the crown perpendicular to the plane of the arms thus causing one fluke at a time to bite into the seafloor.

**northing** *n.* The distance a vessel makes good in a northerly direction.

**North Pacific Current** *n.* A current that flows eastward from the eastern limit of the Kuroshio Extension to form the northern part of the generally clockwise circulation of the North Pacific Ocean. See OCEAN CURRENT.

**northwest monsoon** *n.* Light winds and frequent squalls that prevail from November until March in the Indian Ocean; these are found between the equator and 10°N southeast of the Seychelles Islands. See MONSOON.

**Northwest Passage** *n.* A polar passage from Davis Strait along the northern border of Canada to Alaska. It goes through Baffin Bay, Lancaster Sound, Barrow Strait, Melville Sound, McClure Strait to the Beaufort Sea. The Northwest Passage was first discovered by the Norwegian explorer Roald Amundsen (1872–1928) in his 47-ton sloop *Gjoa*. (Amundsen is better remembered as the first explorer to reach the South Pole.)

**Norway Current** *n.* That part of the Northeast Drift Current that continues in a northeasterly direction along the coast of Norway.

**nor'wester** *n.* A shifty wind out of the northwest, especially on the Pacific Coast.

**nose** *n.* (1) Dead ahead, a slang term used by racing sailors to indicate the wind was from the direction the boat would like to lay a course. "The wind was on our nose." Also *nose ender.* (2) A ship's cutwater is sometimes called the nose. (3) A fitting that protects the stemhead of a small boat.

**nosing** See MOLDING.

**nothing east of** *interj.* The command that the helmsman not err east (or other direction) of a given course. "Nothing north of the range markers" would mean that there are obstructions immediately north of the range markers.

**nothing off** *interj.* The command for the helmsman to watch the course to keep the vessel as close to the wind as possible or to not allow it to pay off farther from the wind.

**nothing to the right** (or **left**) **of** *interj.* Command to the helmsman not to steer to the right (or left) of a given course, range or bearing.

**notice of abandonment** *n.* The information by which an owner informs the underwriter of his or her decision to abandon and claim a total loss. This can only take place in the event of a "total constructive loss."

***Notice to Mariners*** *n.* Selected items from the *Local Notices to Mariners* and other reported marine information of importance to oceangoing traffic. They are published by the Defense Mapping Agency's Hydrographic/Topographic Center, and are prepared jointly with the National Ocean Survey (NOS) and the U.S. Coast Guard.

**noting a protest** *phr.* Action required of a master when the master has reason to think the vessel's cargo has been damaged during transit. See FORCE MAJEURE.

**November** *n.* Phonetic word for the letter "N." Used as a single-letter signal, it means "No."

**no wake zone** *n.* A stretch of channel or a harbor where vessels are allowed to proceed with only enough speed to maintain steerage and create a minimum wake.

**now hear this** *interj.* The usual preliminary phrase to get the attention of all hands on a vessel before making an announcement.

**nugger**   *n.* Small sailboat seen on the Nile in Egypt; it carries a square sail that is set obliquely; it appears to be a combination of a lateen rig and a single square rig.

**number**   *n.* A ship's four-letter identifying signal hoist, also used in radio communications. "*Tarawa* is 'making her number,'" means that it is hoisting its four-letter identification signal. U.S. Navy ship numbers all begin with "N," for example, NXTK.

**numbering**   *n.* The federally required licensing of boats in the United States. This is usually done by the states, except in New Hampshire and Alaska, where the U.S. Coast Guard administers the procedure.

**numeral pennant**   *n.* One of the number pennants of the International Code. All numeral pennants have the shape of a long, truncated triangle.

**numerical scale**   See NATURAL SCALE.

**nun buoy**   *n.* A cone-shaped, unlighted red buoy on the right-hand side of a channel when entering from seaward. Thus the catchy phrase, "Red, right, returning." This mnemonic, however, is only valid in Region B countries (those in North and South America and Japan). The opposite of nun buoy is the green or black vertical-sided can buoy. See BUOY.

**nut**   *n.* The ball at the end of an anchor stock that tends to bring the stock flat on the seafloor.

**nylon**   *n.* A synthetic fiber characterized by high strength and resilience. An 8-inch nylon towing hawser has the same tensile strength as a 12-inch manila hawser, with the added advantage of being lighter, easier to handle, less bulky. Nylon is also highly elastic and is therefore not a good material for sails because the sail shape is lost almost immediately.

# O

**O**   See OSCAR.

**oakum**   *n.* Untwisted fibers of rope treated with a combination of resin and pitch, used for caulking seams of wooden boats.

**oar**   *n.* Long shaft with a blade at one end and a handle fashioned at the opposite end, used for propelling a vessel either from the stern or from the sides.

**oarlock**   *n.* A fitting on a boat that holds the oars in place while the boat is being pulled. A **thole pin** is the most basic form of oarlock. Also *rowlock*.

**oath of arrival**   *n.* Master's oath to customs to the truth of the manifest upon arrival of a vessel in port.

**oath of departure**   *n.* Oath by master of a ship made before a customs official when handing over to him a copy of the manifest.

**oath of entry**   *n.* An oath by the importer of goods before a collector of customs attesting to the completeness of the merchandise import list.

**observation**   *n.* The act of determining the altitude of a celestial body by using a sextant to help find a vessel's position. The information obtained is also called an observation. If the azimuth, or bearing, of a celestial body is used, that information also forms part of the observation.

**observed altitude (Ho)**   *n.* The height of a heavenly body above the visible horizon after the corrections for index error and dip have been made.

**obstruction**   *n.* A racing term for any object, craft, or ship under way that is large enough to require a racing boat that is at least one overall length away from the obstruction, to make a substantial alteration in course to pass on one side or the other of the obstruction.

**obstruction buoy**   *n.* A buoy used alone to indicate a dangerous reef or shoal. The buoy can be passed on either side. See MIDCHANNEL AIDS TO NAVIGATION.

**obstruction mark**   *n.* A navigation mark that indicates a dangerous reef or shoal. The obstruction mark can be passed on either side.

**obstruction to navigation**   *n.* Any object or shoal that makes necessary a course alteration to pass to one side or the other.

**occluded front**   *n.* A meteorological term for the phenomenon that results at the surface when a faster-moving cold front overtakes a warm front or a stationary front.

**occultation**   *n.* The obscuring of a celestial body from an observer's sight by the intervention of another celestial body as happens when the Moon moves between Earth and Sun during a solar eclipse.

**occulting (Oc; Occ)**   *adj.* Light phase description indicating a light that alternates between periods of darkness and periods of light, with the total duration of light being longer than the total dura-

tion of darkness. Lights may be **single-occulting, group-occulting,** or **composite group-occulting.** See LIGHT PHASE CHARACTERISTICS.

**occupational standards**   *n.* The skills and training expected of a given rate or rating; formerly called "technical requirements."

**ocean**   *n.* (1) The vast expanse of saltwater that covers the greater part of the Earth's surface. (2) One of the major divisions of the vast expanse of saltwater of the Earth.

**ocean**   *adj.* A term used to describe a route which is more than 20 nautical miles offshore on any ocean, the Gulf of Mexico, the Caribbean Sea, the Gulf of Alaska, or other waters designated by the Coast Guard. See COASTWISE.

**ocean current**   *n.* Any well-defined horizontal movement of water extending over a considerable area of the ocean such as the Kuroshio or the Equatorial Current.

**oceangoing tug**   *n.* A vessel designed and built to tow or push barges or other vessels on the high seas.

**oceangoing vessel**   *n.* A legal term defined as any vessel that, under the usual course of employment, goes outside the line of demarcation between inland and international waters.

**oceanic circulation**   *n.* The collective term for ocean currents, both wind-driven currents and deep-water currents.

**oceanographer**   *n.* One who studies the physics, biology, chemistry, and so on, of oceans.

**oceanographic**   *adj.* Of or pertaining to oceanography and the knowledge of the oceans.

**oceanographic research vessel**   *n.* A vessel employed exclusively in ocean-

# Ocean Currents

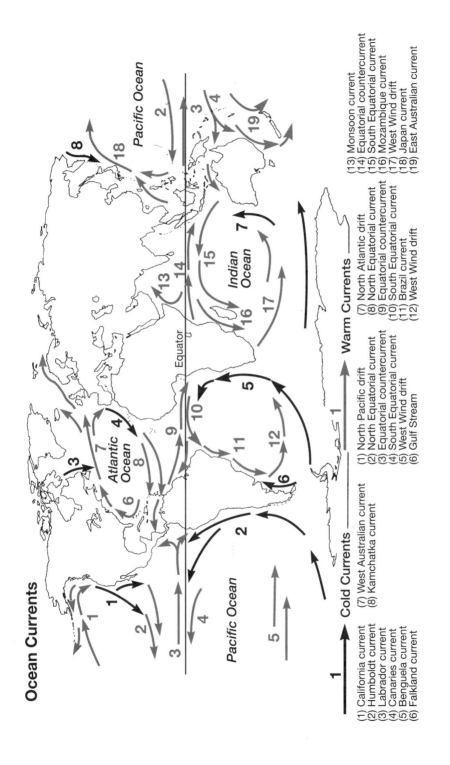

**Cold Currents**

(1) California current
(2) Humboldt current
(3) Labrador current
(4) Canaries current
(5) Benguela current
(6) Falkland current
(7) West Australian current
(8) Kamchatka current

**Warm Currents**

(1) North Pacific drift
(2) North Equatorial current
(3) Equatorial countercurrent
(4) South Equatorial current
(5) West Wind drift
(6) Gulf Stream

(7) North Atlantic drift
(8) Equatorial current
(9) Equatorial countercurrent
(10) South Equatorial current
(11) Brazil current
(12) West Wind drift

(13) Monsoon current
(14) Equatorial countercurrent
(15) South Equatorial current
(16) Mozambique current
(17) West Wind drift
(18) Japan current
(19) East Australian current

ographic or limnologic instruction or re-search.

**oceanographic survey**   *n.* The study of the sea that embraces and integrates all knowledge pertaining to the sea's physical boundaries, the chemistry and physics of seawater, and marine biology.

**oceanography**   *n.* The scientific exploration and study of the oceans and the phenomena associated with the oceans. See HYDROGRAPHY.

**oceanology**   *n.* The study of ocean technology and resources.

**ocean passage**   *n.* A nonstop offshore cruise over a long distance. Also *voyage.*

***Ocean Passages for the World***   *n.* A British publication relating to the planning and conduct of ocean passages. It is published by the Hydrographer of the Royal Navy, and it contains technical information on planning ocean passages, including information on meteorology, climate, fog, effects of wind, sea, and swell, ocean currents, ice, and electronic aids and position-fixing systems, as well as distances and routes between ports, and formulae for great circle sailing and rhumb line sailing.

**ocean ridge**   *n.* Among the largest features of the Earth's surface, a submarine volcanic mountain range that extends around the world more than 30,000 miles, characterized by much volcanic action.

**ocean rise**   *n.* A large area of the ocean basin that is elevated above the surrounding abyssal hills.

***Ocean Shipping Procedures***   *n.* The manual covering control of merchant shipping during periods of national emergency.

**ocean station ship**   *n.* A naval ship assigned to operate within a specific area of the ocean to provide services including search and rescue, meteorological information, navigational aid and communications facilities.

**ocean tug**   *n.* A type of tugboat or towing vessel designed for long-distance towing at sea with ample power, seaworthiness, and fuel capacity; also *ocean-going tug.*

**ocean waters**   n. As applied in the provisions of the Marine Protection, Research, Sanctuaries Act of 1972, the waters of the open seas lying seaward of the base line from which the territorial sea is measured.

**octant**   *n.* A navigational altitude-measuring device with an angular field (or limb) of 45° instead of the 60° angle of a sextant, of which it is a forerunner. Today, all altitude-measuring instruments are called sextants regardless of the angular field.

**odograph**   *n.* An instrument that records to scale a vessel's speeds, distances, and courses on a chart.

**off**   *adv.* (1) Away from, as in "sailing off the wind," not as close to the wind as possible, which would be "on the wind." Also *off course,* which means not on the anticipated course. (2) To seaward: "We were off the coast of Maine." *prep.* (3) To seaward of, "off soundings."

**off and on**   *adv.* (1) Upwind coastal sailing, tacking toward the land and then away from land. (2) A sailing ship waiting to enter a port after daybreak was said to lie "off and on," or hove to.

**officer**   *n.* (1) A member of a ship's staff certified to assist the master in navigation and operation of a vessel. Staff officers, such as supply officers, medical officers, and the like are commissioned officers without certification to navigate and operate a vessel. On merchant ships, officers certified to navigate and operate a vessel are called mates with the exception of the master. (2) In the armed forces, a person holding a commission signifying the position of command or authority. The certification required for naval officers is a commission. In the United States, Navy and Marine officers are appointed by the President and commissioned by the Congress, such commission being signed by the Secretary of Defense. U.S. Coast Guard commissions are signed by the Secretary of the Department of Transportation.

**officer candidate** *n.* A person in training at an officer candidate school to become an officer. While so enrolled, the person has enlisted status.

**officer of the deck (OOD)** *n.* A line officer taking his watch as the one in charge of the ship at sea or in port. He is the captain's representative and as such is senior to all other officers on the ship except the captain and executive officer. While the ship is at sea, he frequently has a junior officer of the deck (JOOD or JO) standing watch with him who is in training for qualification as officer of the deck. In the event of a collision, grounding, or other serious incident, the captain and the OOD bear full responsibility and only rarely is the JO considered culpable.

**officer of the watch (OOW** or **EOOW)** *n.* Engineering duty officer.

**officer's call** *n.* The bugle call on the PA system for all officers to take their stations. The officer's call precedes the call for all hands.

**official log** *n.* A document issued by the U.S. Coast Guard to vessels sailing under foreign articles, and required to be returned to the Coast Guard at the conclusion of the trip. See DECK LOG.

**official number** *n.* The number burned into a conspicuous beam on a vessel when it is "documented."

**offing** *n.* A seascape distant from shore but visible from land, usually a safe distance from shore for a vessel.

**off-load** *v.* To unload a cargo.

**offset** *n.* Naval architect's print that includes measurements and plans for a vessel's lines, including the horizontal distances from the centerline to the molded frame line on the waterlines, and the heights of the buttocks above the base line at each frame, and all dimensions of the hull plan. Offsets are arranged in tabular form on **offset sheets.**

**offshore** *adj.* (1) Relating to a sea area beyond a given boundary such as the 100-fathom curve. To be inside that boundary is to be inshore. (2) Coming from land toward the sea. "An offshore breeze held steady for several days as we headed south along the jagged coast." (3) Away from shore as "an offshore oil rig." "An offshore light station."

**offshore current** *n.* A nontidal ocean current that is not close to shore; it is independent of rivers and shoaling. If the current is along the coastline, it is called an inshore current.

**offshore fisheries** *n.* Japanese fisheries beyond the immediate coastal zone, but distinct from the far-seas fisheries.

**offshore light station** *n.* A permanent offshore navigation light station with a helicopter pad; offshore light stations have replaced lightships in the United States.

**offshore supply vessel** *n.* A vessel of between 15 and 500 gross tons that regularly carries goods, supplies, or equipment in support of exploration, exploitation, or production of offshore mineral or energy resources.

**offshore tower** *n.* Manned or monitored light station built on exposed marine sites to replace lightships.

**offshore wind** *n.* A wind from land blowing out over the sea.

**off soundings** *adj.* Beyond the 100-fathom curve.

**off station** *adj.* (1) A floating aid that is not on its assigned position, whether blown off station in a storm or taken out of service for repairs. (2) A ship is off station when it has strayed from its assigned station in a formation.

**off the wind** *phr.* Not close-hauled, the true wind is abaft the beam, downwind, or before the wind. "We sailed off the wind for a week after we found the trade winds east of the Bahamas." See FULL AND BY; REACH; RUN.

**oil** *n.* (1) An ancient remedy for troubled seas. "Why does pouring oil on the sea make it clear and calm? It is for that the winds, slipping the smooth oil, have no force, nor cause any waves." *Natural Questions,* Plutarch, (A.D. 46–120). (2) Oil for fuel is **fuel oil.**

**oil bag** *n.* A canvas or synthetic fabric bag with small holes filled with oil that can be floated on the water to calm rough seas. Vegetable oils and animal fat are better than mineral oils for this purpose.

**oil can** *v.* To snap in and out, said of a lightly constructed hull when being hit by crashing waves. Also *panting.*

**oiler** *n.* (1) A fuel tanker designed to replenish all types of ships while under way. Ships come alongside the tanker, which is equipped with booms and hoses with various fittings to accommodate all vessels. The U.S. Navy designation for an oiler is AO. (2) A seaman who works in the engine room and cleans and oils the main engine and auxiliaries.

**oil-fired** *adj.* Heated by fuel oil; refers to a boiler that is so heated to create steam for turbines as opposed to coal-, nuclear-, or electrically fired engines.

**oil hose** *n.* A hose used to transfer oil from ship to shore (or vice versa) or ship to ship.

**oiling** *v.* Steamers taking on oil were said to be oiling. As today, they flew the "B" flag by day and showed a red light at night. Today ships are said to be fueling, or taking on fuel, or bunkering.

**oil king** *n.* In the U.S. Navy a petty officer in the engineering department aboard ship charged with keeping the fuel oil records and preparing the reports on fuel oil consumption.

**oil lines** *n.* The piping that carries fuel oil to and from the various tanks and to the boilers.

**Oil Pollution Act** *n.* The act of Congress first passed in 1924 that made it unlawful to discharge oil in coastal waters of the United States from any vessel "using oil for the generation of propulsion power." The act has been updated several times.

**oil-separating equipment** *n.* Equipment used on board all ships today to separate oil from water by either centrifugal pumps or by gravity so that the water may be pumped over the side and the oil properly disposed of at an appropriate location.

**oilskins** *n.* Waterproof clothing or foul-weather gear made of waterproof cloth oiled with many coats of linseed oil; the term usually includes overalls, jacket, and hat. Adm. Edward Vernon (1684–1757) of the Royal Navy (for whom Mount Vernon was named) is said to have pioneered in the development of such apparel.

**oil stop** *n.* Any material soaked in shellac and red lead and used as a temporary measure to caulk a leaking oil line.

**oil tanker** *n.* A vessel designed and fitted with tanks and baffles for the transportation of liquids, especially fuel oil.

**oiltight** *adj.* Capable of holding oil. To make a tank oiltight, it must be more carefully riveted than a tank for water. Welded tanks are generally oiltight as well as watertight.

**oil wash** *n.* A light oil applied to tanks after being steam-cleaned.

**okta** *n.* An ice pack term that describes a one-eighth concentration of ice in an ice field.

**old-fashioned anchor** *n.* The name of a specific anchor fitted with a stock set at a right angle to the arms and to the shank. When the anchor chain pulls the stock along the bottom, the flukes stand upright to give maximum bite. The old-fashioned anchor was used throughout the world until about 1875 when it began to be replaced by the stockless patent anchors. It was still used by the U.S. Navy on older destroyers ("four-pipers") as recently as the beginning of World War II.

**old ice** *n.* Ice that has survived one summer's melt.

**Old Man** *n.* The popular but unofficial name for the commanding officer of any naval activity or ship or the master of any merchant ship. While he always knows he is called the Old Man, he is never referred to in that manner in his presence.

**Oleron, Laws of** *n.* Early maritime code adopted at the time of Richard I (king of England, 1189–1199). The laws embraced many facets of shipboard life, especially the responsibilities of ships' masters toward their crews, other merchants, pilots, and so on. We would consider them unduly harsh today. A pilot who through ignorance "cast a vessel away" was in danger of death; the master could have a pilot's head cut off without making any explanation.

**Omega Navigation System** *n.* Very low frequency (VLF; 10–14 kHz) radio navigation system, accurate only within 2 miles, that operates worldwide for both surface and subsurface craft. It uses phrase comparison of continuous-wave transmissions to get hyperbolic lines of position. The fully implemented system comprises only eight transmitting stations.

**omnidirectional light** *n.* A light showing the same intensity over the whole horizon. In the *Navigation Rules,* the simpler term "all-round light" is used instead.

**omnirange directional navigation** *n.* An aircraft navigation system with some application to marine use. The very high frequency (VHF) omnidirectional range, usually called "Omni," operates in the VHF band between 108 and 118 MHz and is limited to line-of-sight (plus a small percentage for bending over the horizon) use. For this reason its use for surface vessels is more limited than for aircraft.

**on board** *phr.* (1) Aboard a ship, anywhere on a vessel. (2) On the bridge or available. "The skipper remained on board until the pilot was dropped. . . . Then he went into the chart room and wrote up his night orders." Capt. Frank Farrar, *A Ship's Log Book.*

**on course** *phr.* Used as an adverb or adjective, on the desired route. "We were on course," or "we were sailing on course." The opposite is off course.

**on deck** *phr.* (1) On the weather deck. (2) Used as an expression that someone is awake, not in his bunk.

**one-design** *adj.* Refers to a racing boat that must adhere rigidly to hull design, shape, and construction to race with others of the same one-design class. With this constraint, all skippers and crews are racing against each other on the same bottoms.

**one leg beat**   *n.* A close-hauled race course that permits a close approach to the next mark without tacking.

**one-off**   *adj.* Refers to a custom-designed vessel. A vessel that is designed for a single customer's cruising or racing requirements.

**on**   *prep.* (1) In U.S. Navy usage one sails "in" rather than "on" a ship especially in formal communications. Until the 20th century, "on" was the accepted usage in the Navy as elsewhere. The merchant service and most writers still use "on" outside the Navy. (2) Close to, as "on the wind," as close to the wind as possible. Opposite of "off the wind."

**onshore winds**   *n.* Winds blowing toward land.

**on soundings**   *adj.* (1) A term that harkens back to the days of the deep-sea lead, which was usually 100 fathoms. When used today, it means that a vessel is near enough to shore to be within the 100-fathom curve. (2) Used to describe navigation using depth-sounding equipment.

**on station**   *phr.* (1) Said of a ship in a convoy or other group maneuver that is in its proper location relative to the other ships in the convoy maneuver. (2) Said of a ship that is patrolling an assigned area and is in the area performing its duty properly.

**on stream**   *phr.* Refers to a plant, pumping station, engine, or processing facility that is operating.

**on the beach**   *phr.* (1) Used to describe a seaman or officer who is out of work. (2) Used to describe a person who has left the ship temporarily with the intention to return, and has gone ashore. "The executive officer is on the beach this afternoon" means he has gone ashore.

**on the beam**   *phr.* At a right angle to a vessel's keel. "*Midway* was 1,000 yards on our beam when she suddenly headed in our direction to launch aircraft." See RELATIVE BEARING.

**on the berth**   *phr.* A charter party term to describe a ship that is available for loading; "loading on the berth" or "placed on the berth," available for loading general cargo.

**on the bow**   *phr.* Within the area from straight ahead of a vessel to 4 points from the bow to port or starboard. Said of another craft, landmark, or other object that is ahead of a vessel to one side or the other of dead ahead. (If it is ahead, it is said to be ahead or dead ahead.) It is usually said that the object is on the port or starboard bow. An object broad on the starboard (port) bow has a relative bearing of 45° (315°).

**on the line**   *phr.* (1) Said of operational aircraft that are ready for use. (2) Said of machinery and equipment that are operating. "Number one and number three boilers are on the line."

**on the putty**   *phr.* British slang for aground.

**on the quarter**   *phr.* In the direction of 45° or less from the stern, port, or starboard, said of another vessel, landmark, or object that is behind a vessel but not directly astern. If it is said to be broad on the starboard (port) quarter, it has a relative bearing of 135° (or 225°). See RELATIVE BEARING.

**on the wind**   *phr.* Close to the wind, or close-hauled.

**ooze**   *n.* A soft, slimy marine sediment made up of more than 30% shells and skeletons of microorganisms; the word is frequently found on charts. Going aground in ooze is usually not too much of a problem, but trying to anchor in ooze can present holding difficulties.

**open**    *adj.* (1) Used with reference to anchorages and boats. An open anchorage is one without protection. An open boat is one without decking. (2) An open circuit is one that is not working.

**open**    *v.* To move to a position farther away from an object or another vessel. A ship sailing in formation might be ordered by the flagship to "open to 5,000 yards from the guide." The opposite is to close.

**open basin**    *n.* (1) An open dock or basin in an area with a very small tidal range so that tidal gates are unnecessary. (2) The area of the ocean to seaward of the continental margin includes the deep-sea floor. See OPEN HARBOR.

**open berth**    *n.* A berth in an open roadstead.

**open boat**    *n.* A vessel not protected from the entry of water by a complete deck, or by a combination of a partial weather deck and superstructure that is seaworthy for the waters upon which the vessel operates.

**open bridge house**    *n.* Pilothouse with neither forward nor after bulkheads.

**open chock**    *n.* A fitting with an opening at the top to allow a line to be placed in it.

**open coast**    *n.* A coast with few places that offer shelter from the sea. A **hostile coast** is one that not only offers few refuges, but is also strewn with obstructions such as rocks and other threats to navigation.

**open gauging**    *n.* The process of measuring the contents of a tank without taking precautions to prevent the escape of vapor.

**open harbor**    *n.* An unsheltered harbor exposed to the open sea. See OPEN BASIN.

**open hawse**    *n.* To be anchored using two anchors but without a swivel; the two anchor chains lead from two hawsepipes without touching each other. The strain is evenly divided. Also CLEAR HAWSE.

**opening**    *n.* A break in a coastline or a passage between two shoals; an inlet.

**open-linked chain**    *n.* Chain with long links and no studs.

**open port**    *n.* (1) A port not closed by ice during the winter, such as Halifax, Nova Scotia. (2) A port with no regulations regarding the health and physical condition of ships' crews.

**open railing**    *n.* A life line on a weather deck that uses stanchions, rods, and handrails. Not a solid gunwale or bulwark.

**open roadstead**    *n.* An anchorage near open sea and some distance from the port or harbor. A quarantine anchorage is usually in an open roadstead.

**open sea**    *n.* (1) The main body of an ocean or sea not enclosed by headlands, sheltered by barrier islands, or by straits. (2) That part of the ocean outside the territorial jurisdiction of any country. See HIGH SEAS.

**open spaces**    *n.* In measuring a ship's tonnage, the spaces above the upper deck that are not fitted with doors or other permanent means of enclosing them.

**open stern frame**    *n.* A single-screw vessel's stern frame designed without a sternpost. The rudder area is unsupported between upper and lower bearings.

**open water**    *n.* An area of the sea or a bay in which total concentration of ice does not exceed one-eighth (or one "okta").

**operating area chart** *n.* A base chart with overprints of various operating areas necessary to control Navy fleet exercises. Submarine transit lanes, surface and subsurface operating areas, airspace warning areas, and other restricted areas are represented.

**operating differential subsidy** *n.* A government-paid subsidy given to the owner or charterer of a vessel to make it possible to compete with vessels of other nations that have fewer expenses.

**operating forces** *n.* U.S. Navy term that includes fleet, seagoing, sea frontier, and naval district forces as well as such activities and forces as the commander-in-chief or the Secretary of Defense may assign.

**operational control (OPCON)** *n.* Responsibility and authority in the U.S. Navy over combat, service, or training procedures.

**operations officer** *n.* In the U.S. Navy the officer designated to be responsible for the collection, evaluation, and dissemination of combat and operational information required for assigned missions of the ship.

**OPNAV** *n.* General title for the U.S. Naval staff at the Pentagon that is under the control of the Chief of Naval Operations (CNO). The CNO's personal staff is a part of OPNAV, but only a small part.

**opposed ram steering gear** *n.* An electrohydraulic steering system with athwartship cylinders 180° apart, attached to the tiller or rudder head.

**opposition** *n.* (1) The relative position of two celestial bodies when they are 180° apart with the Earth between them. The term is usually only used in relation to the position of a superior planet or the Moon with reference to the Sun. (2) The configuration of celestial bodies when the Earth lies on a straight line between the Sun and a planet.

**optimum routing** *n.* The best ship's route determined by the predicted weather conditions.

**Optimum Track Ship Routing** *n.* A U.S. Navy ship routing service that calculates shipping routes based on consideration of currents, weather, and wave conditions for maximum safety, crew comfort, minimum fuel consumption, and minimum time under way. Private organizations offer similar services for non-military shipping.

**optional cargo** *n.* Bill of lading term that allows the shipper or consignee the option of the port to which cargo is to be delivered. The port is made known about 24 hours before the arrival of the cargo.

**orderly** *n.* Messenger or personal attendant for senior officers.

**order port** *n.* A port that by prearrangement is established for a master of a chartered vessel with a number of ports of call to receive his orders concerning the next port of discharge or loading to which the vessel is to proceed.

**ordinary, in** *adj.* (obsolete) (1) Said of a naval ship that is not in commission but is maintained with a minimum of personnel. In contemporary usage, ships are now mothballed when decommissioned. (2) Officers of the Royal Navy were also said to be in ordinary when they were on the beach with no ship and on half pay.

**ordinary seaman (OD)** *n.* A member of the crew in the deck department who does not have the experience to advance to able seaman (AB) in the merchant marine.

**ordnance** *n.* A collective term for military weapons that includes ammunition and equipment to maintain the weaponry. From Middle English *ordinaunce,* same meaning.

**ore-bulk-oil carrier (OBO)** *n.* A vessel designed to carry either bulk ore or oil. See SHIP.

**ore carrier** *n.* A vessel constructed to carry large cargoes of ore in bulk. Ore is stowed in a central compartment with buoyancy spaces below and at the sides to lower the vessel's metacentric height and ease the roll.

**orient** *v.* To align an instrument with respect to a given reference. The engraved compass points of an alidade are oriented to the ship's heading.

**originator** *n.* Communications term for the command under whose authority a message is sent.

**O-ring** *n.* A circular gasket, usually rubber, neoprene, or Teflon used in flanges, valves, and other equipment to make joints pressure tight.

**orlop deck** *n.* The lowest deck of a ship, laid over the beams below the turn of the bilge. On sailing warships, the orlop was where ammunition and anchor cables were stored and it was used as the sick bay during battle because of the protection it had below the waterline.

**orthodrome** *n.* An arc of a great circle used for plotting long-distance courses.

**Oscar** *n.* Phonetic word for "O." Used alone in a flag hoist, it means "man overboard."

**oscillation, period of** *n.* (1) The time of a roll from port to starboard. (2) The swinging of a compass card before coming to rest.

**oscillator** *n.* An echo-sounding instrument used on submarines.

**otter** *n.* (1) A device near the end of a minesweeping wire to keep it extended laterally as far as possible. See PARAVANE. (2) A similar device used in keeping open the mouth of a fishing boat's trawl. Also *door.*

**outage** *n.* (1) The failure of an aid to navigation to function as described in the *Light Lists.* (2) The space available for use in loading liquids. More often called ullage.

**outboard** *adj.* (1) Beyond a vessel's hull; an "outboard motor." (2) Outward from the centerline toward the side. "The second message to the fleet was hoisted outboard of the first signal, which was still flying" means that of two signal halyards in use, the first was on the halyard closer to the mast and the second was "outboard," or farther from the mast than the first.

**outboard motor** *n.* A portable gasoline motor that mounts on the stern of a vessel, used for propelling the vessel. Also *kicker.*

**outboard profile** *n.* A plan that represents the longitudinal exterior of a vessel and shows the starboard side of the shell, the deck erections, masts, yards, rigging, and so on.

**outboard shot** *n.* A short length of anchor chain used between the anchor and the first length of chain to permit unshackling a stockless anchor while it is still in the hawsepipe.

**outboard freight** *n.* Freight carried on a vessel heading out to sea.

**outdrive** *n.* Combination of inboard and outboard motors in which the motor is mounted inside the hull while the propulsion unit (with propeller, water intake, and so on) is located outside the hull and able to act as a steering unit just as the lower unit of an outboard steers the boat.

**outer harbor** *n.* A protected harbor from which an inner harbor is entered.

**outer keel**   *n.* The outboard plate of a double-plate keel.

**outer strake**   *n.* A plating strake between two adjacent sunken strakes.

**outer waterway**   *n.* Waterway planking that fits against the frames of top timbers. See DEVIL.

**outfall**   *n.* The discharge end of a stream, sewer, or drain.

**outfall buoy**   *n.* A buoy marking the position of the outfall or discharge of a drain or sewer.

**outfit**   *n.* (1) The appurtenances and equipment used during the course of a voyage. (2) A sailing ship term that embraced supplies and equipment necessary for running the vessel, including sails, rigging, spare rope, and so on. For fishing boats, this includes fishing gear and other equipment.

**outfit**   *v.* To equip. A vessel is outfitted after it leaves the construction yard and is moved to the outfitting yard or area for masts, rigging, and so on.

**outfit insurance**   *n.* A policy separate from the hull and machinery policies that includes the outfit, but is only recoverable in case of a total loss.

**outfoot**   *v.* To move faster than another vessel; to outrun.

**outhaul**   *n.* A line used to haul the clew of a sail toward the end of a boom. Also a line used on the jib traveler to secure it in position when it is hauled out. Also *outhauler.* See INHAUL; MARCONI RIG.

**outlying**   *n.* Offshore; rocks and reefs offshore are often said to be outlying.

**out of trim**   *adj.* (1) Carrying a list or "down by the head" or "down by the stern." (2) Improperly loaded or ballasted, too much weight on one side or the other or forward or aft.

**out point**   *v.* To sail closer to the wind that a competitor.

**outreach**   *n.* The distance from the mast to the outer end of a boom. See J.

**outrigger**   *n.* (1) Heavy timbers used to reinforce rigging when a ship was careened. Ships were careened by being pulled over by forces acting on the mast or masts. The heavy strain on the mast was counterbalanced by outriggers with lines from the outriggers to the tops of the mast. (2) A pontoon that runs parallel to the keel of a small boat to give it extra stability on the leeward side. (3) Brackets that extend oarlocks. (4) An athwartships structure at the base of a mast that supports derrick spans and topping lift blocks.

**outsail**   *v.* To sail faster than another boat.

**outside cabin**   *n.* Passenger ship cabin with porthole that looks out on the sea.

**overall efficiency**   *n.* Ultimate efficiency of a marine engine installation; the ratio between actually developed power and the theoretical power available from the fuel.

**overboard**   *adv.* Over the side and into the surrounding water. To throw something overboard, jump overboard, or fall overboard are all within the meaning, whether done intentionally or not. See MAN OVERBOARD MANEUVER.

**overboard fall**   *n.* A tackle used with a stay tackle on a lower yard that is used as a derrick. This is a specific term that usually includes a heavy twofold purchase for work too heavy for a yard whip. Also *yard tackle.*

**overcanvassed**   *adj.* Said of a vessel setting too much sail, causing it to sail inefficiently or to heel excessively. To be overpowered. See OVERHATTED.

**overcarriage**   n. Cargo carried to a port beyond that to which it was consigned necessitated by poor stowage.

**overdue**   adj. Failure to arrive on schedule after allowing for unforeseen sea conditions. See MISSING.

**overfall**   n. A breaking sea due to a current over a shallow point.

**over freight**   n. Cargo shipped in excess of charter party terms.

**overhand knot**   n. A knot used as an end stopper to prevent raveling; it is tied with one end around its own standing part. See KNOT.

**overhang**   n. (1) The horizontal projection of the bow or stern beyond the waterline at stem or sternpost. Same as counter. (2) For measurement purposes, overhang essentially is the length overall less the waterline length; various systems refine this formula for their own special needs.

**overhatted**   adj. Overmasted or carrying too many spars.

**overhaul**   v. (1) To separate the several parts of a block and tackle along with ropes and deadeyes to lengthen the fall. See ROUND IN. (2) To repair an engine or vessel. (3) To overtake another vessel. (4) To clear or untangle a line by pulling a part of it through a block to slacken it.

**overhauling weight**   n. A weight placed on a crane or derrick hook so that when the light hook is empty it returns to the ready position. Also *headache ball*.

**overhead**   n. The nautical equivalent of anything that is called a ceiling on shore; the opposite of a deck.

**overhead compass**   n. An inverted compass used in remote locations such as over the captain's or navigator's berth. Also *telltale compass*.

**overland**   v. To remove more cargo in a port than is shown in the pertinent documents.

**overlap**   v. To overtake another vessel; when a line perpendicular to the centerline and tangent to the sternmost point of the overtaken vessel is crossed by the forwardmost point of the overtaking vessel, the overtaken vessel has been overlapped by the overlapping vessel. Various racing unions interpret overlap in different ways.

**overlay**   v. To place over a chart a transparent sheet with special information such as the positions of gunfire support units or navigational information.

**overpowered**   adj. Said of a sailing vessel when it has too much sail for current conditions. See OVERCANVASSED.

**overrake**   v. (1) To be continually covered by head-on waves while at anchor. (2) To incline a mast excessively. "Raking" is not the same as bending.

**overrigged**   adj. To carry heavier rigging than necessary, resulting in a heavier and slower boat. See OVERCANVASSED.

**overside delivery**   n. A delivery made from a side cargo port to a lighter.

**oversparred**   adj. Said of a vessel that is carrying too tall a mast or too long a boom. See OVERHATTED.

**overstand**   v. (1) To overshoot, to go beyond the objective, usually with the implication of a loss of time. "We overstood the downwind buoy while we got the spinnaker under control." (2) To go beyond a mooring buoy so that the vessel can drop back on it to pick up the hook.

**overstowage**   n. To stow cargo or provisions in such a way that the cargo for the second port of call is on top of the cargo for the first port, or to stow provisions so that those to be used later in the voyage are on top while those for the earlier part are lower down. Over-stowage does not mean too much stowage, but wrong stowage with the last out over the first out.

**overtake**   v. A vessel is said to overtake another when it comes up with that vessel from a direction more than 22.5° abaft its beam; that is, in such a position with reference to the vessel being overtaken that at night the overtaking vessel would be able to see only the sternlight of the other vessel but neither of its sidelights. See OVERHAUL.

**overtrim**   v. To trim the sails of a sailing vessel closer than the apparent wind warrants.

**over the hill (to go)**   phr. To desert.

**owner's pro hac vice**   phr. (Lat. "for this occasion") The legal transfer of liability from a vessel's legal owner to the charterer, under which the charterer must carry insurance to cover the financial exposure. This is especially common in bareboat chartering.

**owner's signal**   n. A boat owner's private burgee, usually of his own design and swallow-tailed. (Club burgees are generally triangular, not swallow-tailed.) Also owner's burgee; owner's flag.

**ox ball**   n. The ornamental ball at the head of a flagstaff.

**oxter plate**   n. The plate that fits in the curve where the sternpost meets the shell plating; the oxter plate is fastened to the sternpost. Also truck plate.

**Oyashio**   n. A counterclockwise current that flows southwestward from the Bering Sea along the coast of Kamchatka past the Kuril Islands to the point it meets the Kuroshio off the east coast of Honshu.

# P

**P**   See PAPA.

**pacific blockade**   n. A blockade exercised by a strong power for the purpose of bringing pressure on a weaker state without going to war. The pacific blockade was largely superseded by action of the Hague Convention of 1907. The term was first used by French writer Jean de Hautefeuille in his writings on maritime law.

**Pacific Equatorial Current**   See EQUATORIAL CURRENTS AND COUNTERCURRENTS.

**pacific iron**   n. A fitting at the end of a yard to which a Flemish horse, a short footrope at the end of the yard, is spliced; the stunsail boom iron is shipped over the pacific iron.

**packet**   n. A small, regularly scheduled boat that carries mail, passengers, and freight.

**pack ice**   n. Any area of sea ice whether it is a vast frozen sea as the Arctic Ocean during the winter or an isolated field of floating ice driven into a small mass.

**packing**   n. Longitudinal timbers in a launching cradle that fill the spaces between the bilge and the upper surface of the sliding ways beneath the flatter area of a wooden ship's bottom.

**packing gland**   n. A stuffing box or chamber that holds material firmly against a moving rod, shaft, or valve to prevent passage of gas or a liquid along the path of the rod, shaft, or valve.

**packing lashing**  n. Chains and wire passed under the keel and over poppet ribbands for launching. The packing lashing prevents the upper ends of the poppets from working out from under the weight of the vessel.

**pad**  n. A flat plate riveted or welded to a structural member to form a solid base for heavy equipment.

**padding**  n. (1) Superfluous words and phrases unrelated to text of coded messages. (2) A pattern of welding formed when parallel rows of beads are close enough together to form a solid mass. (3) The process of filling and maintaining cargo tanks and associated piping with an inert gas or liquid to separate the cargo from the air.

**paddleboard**  n. One of the paddles on the circumference of a paddle wheel.

**paddle box**  n. The wood structure that encloses the upper part of a paddle wheel. The athwartships supports consist of the **paddle beams** at either end; the box is supported longitudinally by the sponson beam on which the outer bearing of the shaft rests.

**pad eye (or pad)**  n. A metal eye with a metal backing welded on a surface, usually a deck, bulkhead, or hull.

**paint**  v. To brighten the plan position indicator screen through the echoes on the sweep. "We painted the target twice, then we lost it." **Paint** is also used for the part of the screen so highlighted.

**painted ports**  n. Gun ports painted on the hull of a ship that made it appear to have more guns than it really had, a stratagem that was practiced frequently on British merchant sailing ships in the 19th century.

**painter**  n. (1) A short piece of line attached to the bow of a small boat used for towing or making it fast to a pier or piling. A similar line from the stern is **stern fast.** See SEA PAINTER. (2) The name of a condition in Callao, Peru, when the water becomes discolored and takes on an unpleasant odor. It is caused by the change in ocean currents when the Equatorial Current displaces the cool Peruvian Current.

**paint line**  n. The upper limit of the boot topping.

**paint locker**  n. A small compartment, usually forward under the forecastle deck, where the ship's painting equipment is stored.

**pair masts**  n. Twin cargo masts abreast of each other, one on each side of the centerline. Also *goal post masts; king posts.*

**pale**  n. An interior shore used to steady the beams of a ship during construction.

**pallet**  n. A wooden- or steel-slatted platform used for handling freight and cargo with a forklift.

**palletize**  n. To stow cargo on pallets.

**palm**  n. (1) The flattened end of an anchor arm, or the fluke of an anchor. An anchor with a sharp-pointed palm is better for grassy bottoms, while the spade-shaped palm holds in mud more efficiently. See ANCHOR. (2) A leather device worn on the hand against which a sailmaker forces a needle to push it through the sail. (3) The flat coupling of a rudder stock. (4) The flat surface at the ends of struts and stanchions.

**pampero**  n. A storm that forms in the Argentine pampas and comes off the land with great suddenness.

**pan**  interj. A word, usually used in triplicate, to begin an urgent radiotelephone message concerning the safety of a vessel and/or its crew when neither is in immediate danger. Pan is the Greek for "all."

**Panama bow** (or **Panama lead**)  *n.* A special design of bow for more efficient towing at sharp angles through a canal.

**Panama chock**  *n.* A closed roller-chock required by the Panama Canal Authority for vessels transiting the canal. The plate across the top that holds a line in place is called a **Panama plate.**

**panamax**  *n.* A ship built to the maximum width and draft able to transit the locks and channels of the Panama Canal; approximately 950 feet long, with 105-foot beam and 38-foot draft.

**panel**  *n.* (1) One of the cloths that make up a sail. (2) A section of a mast. (3) The board on which is found a group of switches.

**panting**  *n.* (1) The puffing noise of a boiler when it has insufficient air for proper, continuous combustion. (2) The bulging and recession of hull plates in heavy seas. Also *oil canning.*

**panting beam**  *n.* An additional beam at the bow or stern of a propeller-driven vessel that supports panting stringers to alleviate or prevent panting.

**panting frame**  *n.* A forepeak frame of heavy scantlings constructed to withstand panting.

**panting strains**  *n.* The stress caused by the sea's resistance to a vessel pushing through the water.

**panting stringer**  *n.* A fore-and-aft girder fitted between side stringers at the bow and stern of propeller-driven vessels included in the vessel's design to counteract panting.

**pantry**  *n.* The compartment aboard U.S. Navy ships in which officers' food is prepared, smaller than the galley used for the crew's mess. Almost all but the smallest ships have a wardroom pantry. Larger ships have a separate captain's pantry when the captain is not a member of the wardroom mess. Still larger ships with admirals have a flag pantry.

**Papa**  *n.* Phonetic word for the letter "P." Used alone, if flown in harbor at the foremast head, the flag means "Return to the ship, we are about to depart." If flown at sea, it means "Your lights are out (or burning poorly)" or "Fishing, nets an obstruction." It is traditionally called "Blue Peter" because it is a white square on a blue background and Peter was the phonetic word before Papa.

**papagayo**  *n.* Sudden gale that blows off the northeast coast of Central America. Spanish word for "parrot," roughly the sound of the gale.

**paper jack**  *n.* Slang for a master who gets a command through influence and depends on his mate for professional ability.

**para-anchor**  *n.* A parachute-type sea anchor used in water too deep for an anchor when it is desirable to slow the boat. Also *drogue.* See SEA ANCHOR.

**parachute flare**  *n.* A flare with a parachute to keep it high in the sky while it is burning so that it can be seen from as far, and for as long, as possible.

**parachute spinnaker**  *n.* A popular term for a balloon spinnaker, generally called a chute. The triangular lightweight racing sail, the parachute spinnaker, was conceived by the Swedish yacht racer Sven Salen and first used on his 6-meter sailing yacht *Maybe* in 1927. Salen's part in the development of the spinnaker was to make both sides identical to facilitate jibing; he also cut the head wider to give it better lift. The word parachute is rarely heard today; chute has almost completely taken its place. See SPINNAKER.

**parade** *n.* The area on deck aboard U.S. Navy ships where the divisions muster for inspection or other purposes.

**parallactic angle** *n.* The angle formed by the intersection of the hour circle and the vertical circle at a celestial body. Also *position angle.*

**parallax** *n.* The difference in the apparent direction or position of an object when viewed from different points. **Geocentric parallax** is the difference in direction of a body in the Solar System as viewed by an observer on the Earth's surface as opposed to a theoretical observer at the center of the Earth. The tables are computed on the basis of the observer's being at the center of the Earth. The parallax correction is added to the sextant altitude to get the true observed altitude.

**parallax correction** *n.* A correction necessary for parallax especially for a sextant altitude due to the difference between the apparent direction from a point on the surface of the Earth to a celestial body and the apparent direction from the center of the Earth to the same body.

**parallel** *n.* A line of points of equal latitude going around the Earth parallel to the equator. The latitude equivalent of meridians in longitude.

**parallel, standard** *n.* (1) A parallel of latitude that is used as a control line when computing a map projection. (2) A parallel of latitude on a map or chart along which the scale is as stated in the legend.

**parallel of altitude** See ALMUCANTAR.

**parallel of declination** *n.* A circle of the celestial sphere that is parallel to the celestial equator.

**parallel rules** *n.* Two straight edges fastened so they stay parallel while being walked across a chart and used for transferring course lines and vectors.

**parallel sailing** *n.* An early method of navigation in which the courses were laid out only along meridians and parallels. One of the sailings.

**parallel sinkage** *n.* The increasing of a draft without a change of trim by increasing the draft forward and aft by the same amount.

**parameter** *n.* A constant or a variable in a mathematical expression with the value determined by the specific form of the expression. More specifically for shipboard usage, it often refers to the four components of a ship's permanent magnetic field or the nine components of induced magnetism.

**paravane** *n.* A device shaped somewhat like a torpedo towed from each side of a minesweeper and used for diverting, cutting loose, or detonating mines.

**parbuckle** *n. and v.* A rope sling made by the bights of two ropes used for rolling or lifting casks and similar cylindrical objects. To raise a barrel from a pier to a deck, for example, two ropes are secured to cleats or pad eyes on deck and passed under the barrel on the pier. The rope is then led back to the deck. When the standing part of the rope is hauled, the barrel acts as a movable pulley while it is raised or rolled. To handle an object in such a manner is to parbuckle it.

**parcel** *v.* To wrap a rope with heavy cloth to protect it from moisture or from chafing. See SERVE; WHIP; WORM.

**parcel tanker** *n.* A tanker designed to carry more than one petroleum product.

**parish-rigged** *adj.* Cheaply outfitted. In 18th-century England, the parishes established welfare systems to look after the less fortunate. These wards were looked after with hand-me-down clothes;

thus a ship that was outfitted as cheaply as possible was called "parish-rigged."

**par line**   n. The normal level of the barometric pressure at a given place.

**parrel** (or **parral**)   n. A sliding collar of wood, rope, or chain by which a yard or gaff is kept hard against the mast so that it can be raised or lowered.

**parrel ball**   n. A wooden ball with a hole through it through which a lanyard may be passed.

**parrel lashing**   n. Lashing used to secure the gaff of a fore-and-aft sail to the mast with freedom to slide up and down.

**parrel truck**   n. Wooden balls on the jaw rope of a gaff strung on it to reduce friction when the spar is being hoisted or lowered.

**part**   n. One of the several sections of a rope used in a block and tackle. Parts of rope in a tackle are **leading parts.** The **running part** is the section that runs in the blocks; the **standing part** is the section that extends from the fixed end to the first moving block.

**part**   v. To pull a line apart. "We lost control of the ship when the rudder cable parted."

**partially protected waters**   n. (1) Waters within 20 nautical miles of the mouth of a harbor or safe refuge. (2) Those portions of rivers, harbors, lakes and other bodies of water determined by Coast Guard authority not to be sheltered. See PROTECTED WATERS.

**particular average**   n. Damage or partial loss of ship, cargo, or freight; such loss is borne by the owners or the insurers of the property damaged or lost. It is a one-party loss as opposed to a general average loss.

**particular charges**   n. A marine underwriter's term for expenses incurred by or on behalf of the insured for the safety or preservation of the insured vessel, besides general average and salvage charges. None of the particular charges are a part of the definition of particular average.

**partition bulkhead**   n. A light partition used to subdivide a main compartment. It is a nonstructural bulkhead.

**partner**   n. A timber between two beams that forms a supporting base for masts, pumps, capstans, or other structures that pass through the deck.

**partner plate**   n. A heavy deck plate with significantly greater width than the base of the mast, through which the mast hole is made.

**pass**   n. (1) A navigable channel leading to a harbor or waterway from open sea. (2) A narrow opening through a reef.

**pass**   v. To reeve and secure a line or stopper. See PASS A LINE.

**passage**   n. (1) A navigable channel allowing access between two bodies of water. (2) A journey between two ports. To **work one's passage** is to work on board a vessel in exchange for being taken to a given destination, as opposed to paying one's way. (3) A part of a voyage, either outward passage or homeward passage.

**passage broker**   n. British institution, one who brokered steerage passages in any ship leaving the British Isles.

**passage money**   n. The charge made to passengers on a passenger ship for a voyage.

**passage sails**   n. Sails rigged wing-and-wing for long downwind passages, used frequently in the trade winds.

**passageway**   *n.* A hall or corridor aboard ship.

**passage wind**   *n.* A wind from the west or a westerly, including but not restricted to trade winds.

**pass a line**   *phr.* (1) To hand, throw, or project a line. A messenger is passed from an oiler to another ship so that the fuel line can be passed to the other ship. (2) To lead a line through a fairlead or block and secure it. "Pass the line through that pad eye" means to lead it through the pad eye.

**passaree** (or **pazaree**)   *n.* A line that extends the clew of a square foresail, especially in light winds. The passaree is lashed around a cathead and foretack to keep a tight leech.

**pass down the line**   *phr.* To repeat an order from a flagship to other vessels in a formation when all ships are not in visual contact with the flagship. It was popularly abbreviated PDL.

**passenger   accommodations**   *n.* Quarters provided for the use and convenience of passengers. See PASSENGER SPACES.

**passenger liner**   *n.* A vessel employed in carrying passengers, mail, and limited goods on stated schedules between established ports.

**passenger manifest**   *n.* A list of all passengers by name, sex, and nationality, their ports of embarkation and their destinations, signed by the master of the ship.

**passenger spaces**   *n.* Areas allotted for the accommodation, pleasure, safety, and convenience of passengers. The amount of space required for each allowable passenger is controlled by law and cannot be infringed upon for mail, cargo, or other goods.

**passenger vessel**   *n.* A vessel carrying more than 6 passengers. Under U.S. Coast Guard regulations, a vessel that carries passengers for hire. Vessels are certified according to their size and the number of passengers carried. A ship whose keel was laid on or after the 1960 International Convention for Safety at Sea rules came into effect is classified as a **new passenger vessel**. Others are classified as **existing passenger vessels.**

**passing honors**   *n.* Honors, exclusive of gun salutes, rendered by a junior ship to a passing senior ship or ranking officials. In the U.S. Navy a very senior ship would render passing honors when passing a junior ship with a high-ranking dignitary aboard, such as the Secretary of the Navy or a head of state. Otherwise a ship's seniority is determined by the seniority of the commanding officer.

**passing light**   See SUBSIDIARY LIGHT.

**passive navigation system**   *n.* A navigation system that does not require the user to transmit a signal. Daybeacons and lighthouses are passive, racons are active, meaning the user must transmit a signal.

**passive sonar**   *n.* Sound-sensing equipment that gathers information from the sounds made by the target and not from its own pinging.

**passport**   *n.* A document issued to a neutral ship in time of war that gives proof of the vessel's nationality, identity, the names of the master and crew, the owners, port of registry, the destination port, and so on.

**pass the word**   *phr.* To repeat an order or information to whomever the message is addressed. To pass the word before P.A. systems were developed was to pass the message by word of mouth throughout the ship. With P.A. systems and voice-powered telephones, word of mouth from person to person is no longer the system used.

**patch** *n.* A sailmaker's term for a reinforcing layer in a sail or awning at corners and other points of stress.

**patch** *v.* To put specific radio frequencies on line as directed by the communications officer or main radio. "For the coming operation, we'll patch in the usual NATO frequencies."

**patent anchor** *n.* Any of several stockless anchors such as the Danforth, Bruce, Dunn, Baldt, Norfolk, or Navy.

**patent block** *n.* A block with roller bearings. See SHEAVE.

**patent eye** *n.* A metallic device fitted on the end of a wire rope as a substitute for an eye-splice. Hot zinc is poured in among the strands after the fitting is in place. Also *socket.*

**patent link.** See DETACHABLE LINK.

**patent log** *n.* Any of a number of patented devices (the first dates from about 1683) for determining a vessel's speed, particularly a taffrail log.

**patrimonial sea** *n.* The term preferred among Caribbean states for what is more generally called the exclusive economic zone.

**patrol craft, fast (PCF)** *n.* A modified U.S. Navy patrol boat used for inshore and riverine operations in Vietnam. Also *swift; swift boat.*

**patrol vessel** *n.* A small war vessel used for escort duty and for patrols.

**paunch** *n.* (1) A heavy wooden shield used on the foreside of a mast to prevent chafing by the yards as they are raised and lowered. (2) Heavy interwoven mats used on ships to prevent chafing. Also *paunch mat; wrought mat.*

**pawl** *n.* A hinged or pivoted metal bar adapted to fit into the notched **pawl head** of a capstan or a ratchet, to allow the capstan or ratchet to turn in one direction but not in the other.

**pawl** *v.* To prevent backward motion of a capstan by use of a pawl that allows the pawls on the **pawl head** to drop into the **pawl rim**. See CAPSTAN.

**pay** *v.* To fill the seams of a wooden ship with pitch or oakum. "The devil to pay and no pitch hot" is an expression that refers to the longest and hardest seam to be caulked, the devil, when there is no pitch ready.

**pay grade** *n.* Level of pay for U.S. military personnel. In the Navy, E-1 to E-9 covers enlisted personnel from seaman recruit to master chief petty officer; W-1 to W-4 covers warrant officers; and O-1 to O-10 covers commissioned officers from ensign to admiral.

**paying shell** *n.* A container with a funnel spout used for pouring marine glue into the seams of wooden decks.

**paymaster** *n.* The name for the disbursing officer aboard a U.S. Navy ship, usually a member of the Supply Corps; often nicknamed **pay.**

**pay off** *v.* (1) To turn the bow to leeward usually to keep the sails full and to pick up more speed. It is heard on larger ships, but it is not used as a command. (2) To pay the members of the crew at the end of a voyage or to receive final pay. " 'If you can't work, pay off' [he said]. . . . So pay off I did." From Captain Frank Farrar's *A Ship's Log Book.* In this case, it means to quit and leave the ship. An officer or member of the crew is paid off when he is terminated. You also pay off when you quit, either amicably or otherwise.

**pay out** *v.* To let a line out slowly. "Pay out the painter until the dinghy is riding a wave."

**pea** *n.* The point of a palm of an anchor or of an anchor fluke.

**peacoat** or **pea jacket** *n.* A sailor's heavy, double-breasted, dark blue groin-length coat. Worn by U.S. Navy men below the grade of chief petty officer. Also *reefer.*

**peak** *n.* (1) The upper end of a gaff or the upper after corner of a gaffsail. See GAFF. (2) The narrowest point of a ship's bow or stern. See AFTERPEAK; FOREPEAK.

**peak boundary** *n.* The watertight bulkhead that forms a peak tank at the bow. In the stern, it is the last bulkhead aft and, if extended to the freeboard deck, it is a collision bulkhead.

**peak cleat** *n.* A small cleat fastened to the ceiling of a whaleboat for peaking the oars after the boat was made fast to the whale.

**peak downhaul** *n.* The line used to haul down the after end of a gaff.

**peak halyard** *n.* The line that raises and lowers the peak of a gaffsail or quadrilateral fore-and-aft sail. See GAFF.

**peak line** *n.* A flag halyard at the after end of a gaffsail.

**peak outhaul** *n.* The line used for stretching the peak of a gaffsail along the gaff.

**peak span** *n.* A piece of wire or rope that leads from the lower masthead to the peak of a standing gaff to support it in position.

**peak tank** *n.* A tank low in the bow or stern of a ship.

**pedestal steering** *n.* A small boat's steering mechanism with a wheel and pedestal in the cockpit.

**peggy** *n.* British term for a deck boy or cabin boy or ordinary seaman who does the most menial jobs.

**pelican hook** *n.* A quick-release hook used in various capacities ranging from minesweeping cable stoppers to boat falls. A bail shackle or a toggle is used as the holding device. It more or less resembles a pelican's beak, thus the name.

**pelorus** *n.* A graduated metal ring with sights, and fitted over a compass for taking bearings and azimuths. Peloruses are usually mounted on both bridge wings. The pelorus mounted on the gyro repeater is extremely useful in piloting and in maintaining position in a formation. When fitted with a mirror, a pelorus becomes an azimuth circle.

**pendant** *n.* A line secured to a spar or bulkhead with a fitting such as an eye or hook at the other end, used for holding various items in place such as life rings, fire axes, and so on. Pendants are used for specific purposes such as a **mooring pendant** for securing a vessel to the mooring.

**pendant tackle** *n.* A twofold tackle used for deck work, usually suspended from a lower mast pendant.

**peninsula** *n.* A section of land that is almost entirely surrounded by water, sometimes connected to a larger body by an isthmus. Examples are the southern part of the state of Florida and the Baja Peninsula.

**pennant** *n.* A flag or burgee that is longer in the fly than in the hoist; it usually tapers to a narrow end, either to a swallowtail (as personal burgees) or to a point (as club burgees and commission pennants). The numeral flags of the International Signal Code are called numeral pennants and the letters are called flags. See PRIVATE FLAG.

**pens** *n.* A series of parallel jetties for berthing small craft. Submarine pens are an example. In Britain, the term is used more generally for jetties and docks for small craft.

**perch** *n.* (1) A rod at the top of a buoy with a shape indicating a shoal, used in the cardinal buoyage system, but not in the Region B lateral system. (2) A British term for a small beacon marking a channel through mud flats, sometimes nothing more than a sapling stuck in the mud.

**performance boat** *n.* A high-performance cruising or racing vessel.

**Performance Handicap Racing Fleet (PHRF)** *n.* The system of rating rules for racing boats in which handicaps are assigned by a duly qualified committee.

**per gyro compass (pgc)** *n.* Phrase indicating the course, bearing, or heading is by gyrocompass and not by magnetic or standard compass or true.

**perigean (tidal) current** *n.* The increased strong tidal range that occurs monthly when the Moon is in perigee or nearest to the Earth. The **perigean range of tide** is the average semidiurnal range that occurs at the time of the perigean tides. The opposite current is the apogean current.

**perils of the sea** *n.* A marine underwriter's term for accidents and casualties covered under an ordinary marine policy but excluded under the terms of the bill of lading. The purpose of the policy is to indemnify against accidents that might occur but not against those that **should not** happen, such as loss through improper storage, inherent vice, or infestation. "Perils of the sea" as used in bills of lading includes marine casualties due to violent action of wind and waves, sweat when cowls cannot be uncovered because of weather, breakage and shifting because of heavy weather. "Perils of the sea" does not include loss or damage brought about by the owner's neglect or that of his employees.

**period** *n.* (1) The time required for completing a whole cycle of a lighted marker's light phase characteristic. (2) The time from crest to crest between waves—water, sound, or electromagnetic.

**periodic current** *n.* A current that changes speed or direction cyclically and at regular intervals. Tides are the typical example. See PERMANENT CURRENT, SEASONAL CURRENT.

**periodic error** *n.* In celestial navigation, a random error caused by the roll of the ship. The natural tendency is to mark the sight at either extreme of the roll, when the ship is steady.

**period of roll** *n.* The time it takes for a vessel to roll from one side to the other and back again. The longer it takes, the smaller is the righting arm and the less stable is the vessel. Also *period* of *oscilliation.*

**periplus** *n.* The first known sailing directions or cruising guide, written between the sixth and fourth centuries B.C. by Scylax, who may be credited as the first gunkholer. Pythias followed in the fourth century B.C. with his *Parts Around the World,* and Pliny in the first century B.C.

**periscope feather** *n.* The rooster tail formed on the surface of the water by a submarine's periscope while going through the water.

**perishable cargo** *n.* Any goods taken aboard that are subject to detrimental change during the period of the journey. See INHERENT VICE.

**permanent backstay** *n.* A backstay that is beyond the end of the boom so that the boom can move from one side to the other without moving the backstay. See RUNNING BACKSTAY.

**permanent ballast** *n.* Any ballast such as sand, concrete, or pig iron that is carried to improve stability or trim and is not removed to accommodate cargo.

**permanent bunker**  *n.* A compartment with structural bulkheads designed for the storage of bunker coal or oil.

**permanent current**  *n.* A current that exhibits little change in speed or direction either periodically or seasonally. The Gulf Stream and the Kuroshio are examples. See PERIODIC CURRENT; SEASONAL CURRENT.

**permanent light**  *n.* A lighted aid to navigation used in regular service.

**permeability**  *n.* (1) The percentage of hold space that would be taken up by water if the hold were completely filled with a given kind of good and the hold completely flooded. The permeability of tea in boxes is 80%, and the permeability of zinc in slabs is 15%. Permeability relates directly to a vessel's safety and buoyancy in the event certain cargo spaces are flooded. (2) The ability to transmit magnetism, magnetic conductivity.

**permissible factor**  *n.* A margin of safety allowed in spacing bulkheads in a vessel. The factor varies with the size of the vessel.

**permissible length**  *n.* Maximum length permitted between main and transverse bulkheads. This figure is found by multiplying the factor of subdivision by floodable length.

**permit to lade**  *n.* A permit issued by customs to the master of a vessel that gives him permission to load merchandise, passengers, and baggage.

**perpendicular**  *n.* A line that is at right angles to the water plane. An **after perpendicular** is a line drawn perpendicular to the water plane and tangent to the after contour of the stern. A **midship perpendicular** is such a line taken midway between the forward and after perpendiculars. A **forward perpendicular** is such a line that intersects the forward side of the stem at the designed load waterline.

The term is used in ship construction, damage control, admeasuring, and so on.

**personal flotation device (PFD)**  *n.* A Coast Guard term for various life preservers. U.S. Coast Guard regulations require that vessels carry sufficient USCG-approved PFDs for each person (passengers and crew) aboard.

**personnel diary**  *n.* The journal maintained for a given activity aboard a U.S. Navy ship in which are recorded the names of all personnel assigned to that activity.

**perspective chart presentation**  *n.* A representation produced by the direct projection of the points of an ellipsoid, which represents the Earth by straight lines drawn through them from a given spot. The projection is usually made on a plane tangent to the ellipsoid at the end of the diameter that joins the point of projection and the center of the ellipsoid.

**per standard compass (psc)**  *n.* Phrase or letters used to indicate that a course is set by magnetic compass. Confusion arises in the use of the letters "psc" because they are sometimes used to mean **per steering compass,** which is usually a different magnetic compass. The standard compass is usually kept near the bridge, but is the compass by which the error of the steering compass is determined. Properly, however, "psc" only means "per standard compass."

**Peru Current**  *n.* The current that flows northward from the southern tip of South America and along the west coast. Also *Humboldt Current; Peru Coastal Current.*

**Peru Oceanic Current**  See MENTOR CURRENT.

**petty officer (PO)**  *n.* A noncommissioned officer in the U.S. Navy and U.S. Coast Guard entitled to wear an eagle (facetiously called a **crow**) on his sleeve along with his specialty designation. Petty officers start with third class petty officer and ascend by examination and recommendation through second class, first class, chief petty officer (CPO), senior chief petty officer (SCPO), and master chief petty officer (MCPO), the latter two being by recommendation only. A petty officer, third class, ranks above a seaman, and an MCPO ranks below a warrant officer and ensign. See MASTER CHIEF PETTY OFFICER OF THE NAVY.

**petty officer of the watch**   *n.* The senior enlisted assistant to the officer of the deck.

**Phalanx**   *n.* A close-in weapons system providing automatic autonomous terminal defense against anti-ship cruise missiles. The system includes self-contained search and track radars, weapons control, and weapons systems.

**phantom**   *n.* That part of a gyrocompass that carries the compass card.

**phantom bottom**   *n.* A false bottom recorded on a depth indicator caused by a layer of soft mud, a school of fish, large quantities of small organisms, or by a second bounce of the transmitted signal.

**phantom target**   *n.* The indication of an object on a radarscope that does not correspond to an actual object at the point indicated. Also *ghost.*

**phase age**   *n.* The time interval between a governing Moon phase and the resulting tide.

**phase angle**   *n.* The angle of the Sun and Earth from a celestial body.

**phase characteristic of lights**   See LIGHT PHASE CHARACTERISTICS.

**phase inequality**   *n.* The variations in the tides and tidal currents caused by the changes in the phases of the Moon.

**phonetic   alphabet**   *n.*   Standard words used to represent the letters of the

alphabet when transmitting messages via radio or telephone.

| | | | |
|---|---|---|---|
| A | Alpha | N | November |
| B | Bravo | O | Oscar |
| C | Charlie | P | Papa |
| D | Delta | Q | Quebec |
| E | Echo | R | Romeo |
| F | Foxtrot | S | Sierra |
| G | Golf | T | Tango |
| H | Hotel | U | Uniform |
| I | India | V | Victor |
| J | Juliett | W | Whiskey |
| K | Kilo | X | X-ray |
| L | Lima | Y | Yankee |
| M | Mike | Z | Zulu |

**phonotelemetry**   *n.* The science of marine surveying using radio acoustic sound ranging.

**phosphorescence**   *n.* (1) The emission of light without sensible heat as a result of absorption of radiation from an external source, such as the continuing glow on the radar face that persists after the planned position indicator sweep has moved on. (2) Organically generated light; bioluminescence is a more accurate word.

**phosphorescent wheel**   *n.* A phenomenon of the Indian Ocean and the China Sea where a large rotating band of phosphorescence or bioluminescence in the sea is occasionally observed.

**picaroon**   *n.* A pirate ship. From the Spanish *picaro,* a pirate.

**picked ports**   *n.* A British chartering term for especially desirable ports for cargo vessels because of lower harbor dues and better working conditions.

**picket boat**   *n.* An armed small craft that is usually assigned sentry and patrol duty.

**picket duty**   *n.* A station or patrol area away from the main body of a naval formation; an example is air or submarine picket duty. A ship given such an assignment is called a **picket.**

**pickle** *n.* The weight on a cargo hook. Also *headache ball.*

**pickling** *n.* The process by which mill scale is removed from steel plates before use in a vessel's construction. This is done by placing the plates in a heated pickling bath of a dilute solution of buffered muriatic acid.

**pick-up buoy** *n.* A small buoy that marks a fixed anchor in an anchorage and is used for picking up the anchor or the chain that leads to the anchor.

**pier** *n.* A structure built over the water, supported by piles and used for security vessels of all sizes. As early as the 12th century, pier was used to mean the supports for bridges and other structures over water. Today, a pier is used to mean any structure to which vessels can be secured. Some authorities consider piers and wharves synonymous, while others maintain that a wharf is parallel to the shore and a pier is perpendicular to the shore.

**pier crew** *n.* Longshoremen stationed on a pier when cargo is handled between ship and shore.

**pierhead** *n.* The offshore end of a pier.

**pierhead leap** *n.* (1) A leap from a ship by a deserter as soon as the vessel is close enough to a pier to jump and run. (2) A last-minute embarkation as the ship leaves its berth. In their *Naval Terms Dictionary,* John Noel and Edward Beach note that this is "viewed with mixture of disdain, amusement, and admiration."

**piermen** *n.* Longshoremen who operate forklift trucks to bring cargo to a pier within reach of the vessel's cargo-handling gear. In Britain they are called **quaymen.** See PIER CREW.

**pig** *n.* Minesweeping term for a float at the end of a cable.

**pigboat** *n.* World War I slang for a submarine.

**pigeon hole** *n.* The holes in a capstan head into which the short bars, or normans, are placed to take a turn.

**pig steamer** *n.* Slang for a whale-back steamer.

**pigstick** *n.* The staff at the truck of the mainmast from which the commission pennant is flown.

**pigsty bulwarks** *n.* Bulwarks on wooden ships with every other section left out to allow water to flow freely from the decks in heavy seas. See FREEING PORT.

**pile and piling** *n.* A single heavy timber or spar driven into the bottom and extending above the surface of the water.

**piling** *n.* A cluster of piles.

**pile beacon** *n.* A beacon formed on a pile or a piling.

**pile driving** *n.* (1) The act of driving into waves when the vessel is not of sufficient length to bridge the seas. (2) The act of driving piles into the water's bottom.

**pilferage** *n.* In marine insurance policies, clandestine theft of a part of a thing, as opposed to theft, which means to take a whole package. The taking of the eyepiece of a sextant is pilferage; removal of the whole sextant is theft. Also *pillage.*

**pillar** *n.* (1) A support for a deck beam or other structural member of a vessel. (2) A support for a wharf or pier.

**pillar buoy** *n.* A tall cylindrical buoy on a broad base. Also *beacon buoy.*

**pillar ladder** *n.* A ladder made by fastening rungs between two pillars.

**pillow**  *n.* A wedge or block that supports the inboard end of a bowsprit.

**pillow block**  See PLUMMER BLOCK.

**pilot**  *n.* (1) One who is certified to take vessels through specific canals, channels, and harbors. A pilot licensed to take a ship through the Panama Canal is probably not licensed to pilot a ship into New York Harbor. When entering or departing a port or other designated waterway, a ship is boarded by a pilot who assumes the navigation of the vessel until the vessel is at its berth or clear of the port, at which point the pilot is said to be **dropped** (See PILOT BOAT). The ship's master does not relinquish his authority nor is he relieved of his responsibility for the vessel unless specifically advised by the ship's owner or the government. By law, however, in certain waters, the Panama Canal in particular, the pilot assigned to a vessel has complete control of movements and navigation of the vessel. In most circumstances, the master of the ship is required to interfere "in cases of the pilot's incapacity, in cases of danger which he does not foresee, and in all cases of great necessity. The master has the same power to displace the pilot that he has to remove any subordinate officer of the vessel." (2) A book of detailed sailing instructions, such as *The United States Coast Pilot.* (3) On western rivers, the executive officer of a vessel is given the title "pilot," while the chief boatswain is called the mate.

**pilot boat**  *n.* A seaworthy boat that takes pilots to meet incoming vessels and then meets the ship at the point the pilot is no longer needed to return the pilot to the pilot station. The opposite is true on the outbound run. In earlier days, pilot boats and pilots lay in wait for incoming ships. Today, using radio, the business of the pilot is arranged well before the ship is in sight.

**pilot books**  See SAILING DIRECTIONS; UNITED STATES COAST PILOT.

**pilot charts**  *n.* Charts published monthly by the Defense Mapping Agency's Hydrographic/Topographic Center that graphically present the averages obtained from data gathered over many years in meteorology and oceanography to aid navigators in determining the quickest and safest routes for the oceans of the world for each month.

**pilothouse**  *n.* That compartment on the bridge in which the controls and navigation instruments are found and the location of the personnel involved with the vessel's navigation. Also *wheelhouse.*

**piloting**  *n.* Coastwise and inland navigation by use of terrestrial landmarks, various aids to navigation, charts, and cruising guides. The other branch of surface navigation is celestial navigation. Also *inshore navigation.*

**pilot rudder**  *n.* A small rudder on the main rudder that directs the main rudder from side to side. Also *trim tabs.*

**Pilot Rules**  *n.* Regulations that supplement the Inland Rules portion of the *Navigation Rules.*

**pilot signals**  *n.* Visual signals established to hail a pilot and visual signals displayed on pilot vessels indicating a pilot is on board. These have been superseded in most ports by radio communications.

**pilot's luff**  *n.* To make the desired distance to windward by shooting the vessel into the wind until it loses way. This is done when picking up a mooring. "When we enter the anchorage, we will use a pilot's luff to ease up on the dolphin." See FOREREACH.

**pilot station**  *n.* Headquarters or office of pilots; a place where pilot services are obtained.

**pilot waters**   *n.* Waterways, channels, and harbors where it is necessary, and usually compulsory, to use a pilot.

**pin**   *n.* (1) Axle on which a sheave revolves. See BLOCK. (2) A device, such as a belaying pin, for securing lines.

**pinch**   *v.* To sail so close to the wind that the sails begin to luff. See *jam; starve.*

**ping**   (1) *n.* Signal emitted for echo-ranging equipment. (2) *v.* To emit such a signal.

**pink**   *n.* A narrow-sterned sailing vessel.

**pinnace**   *n.* (pron. pinis) A small sailing vessel used as a tender for merchant ships and warships.

**pinnacle**   *n.* A tall, pointed formation. A landmark that can be charted and used in piloting.

**pin rail**   *n.* A metal or wooden device with holes to hold belaying pins, usually found near the mast at main deck level. See FIFE RAIL; SPIDER BAND.

**pintle**   *n.* Pin or hook on a rudder that fits into the gudgeon fixed to the vessel to allow the rudder to swing back and forth. See RUDDER BRACES.

**pintle bearing**   *n.* A hemispherical steel disc fitted into a bottom gudgeon of a rudder to reduce friction.

**pinwheel**   *v.* (1) To turn a vessel in the smallest possible space by going ahead on one engine and backing the other engine. Also *boxing.* (2) Three or more lines of position that form a single point instead of a triangle. See COCKED HAT.

**pipe**   See BOATSWAIN'S PIPE.

**pipe berth**   *n.* A cheap, lightweight bunk made from tubing secured to the deck, overhead, and ceiling. These are frequently found on racing sailboats and

some naval vessels when reducing a vessel's weight is more important than providing comfort.

**pipe down**   *v.* To announce an activity, as "to pipe down chow."

**pipe the side**   *phr.* The ceremony of receiving an official on board a naval ship. The same ceremony is repeated when the official departs the ship. The boatswain's mate blows a special signal on the boatswain's pipe and side boys man the quarterdeck entrance—the higher the rank, the more side boys there are.

**pipe to**   *v.* To use the boatswain's pipe to call the crew to a given evolution; "pipe to chow," "pipe to colors," and so on.

**pipe tunnel**   *n.* Space forward of the engine and boiler rooms between the tank top and shell plating in the bilge at the centerline where much of the piping is laid.

**pipe up**   *v.* Said of the wind when the velocity picks up.

**piracy**   *n.* The act of robbing at sea or plundering from the sea by ship. It also includes murder and forcible depredation on the high seas. Piracy is done without the authority of any sovereign state so that no government can be held accountable.

**piragua**   *n.* A large Amazon Indian dugout constructed from a single tree trunk, similar to a Malaysian proa and the double dugout of the South Sea islands. See PIROGUE.

**pirate**   *n.* One who engages in piracy.

**pirogue**   *n.* (pron. peerow in southern Louisiana) An open, flat-bottomed, keelless boat used in the bayous of southern Louisiana, especially by the Cajuns. The size varies with the size of the owner's family, and some are quite large.

**pit** *v.* To corrode and form small cavities in metal through electrolytic or chemical action.

**pitch** *n.* (1) The angle of a propeller blade to the axis of rotation. (2) The distance a propeller would travel through a solid in one revolution if there were no slippage; the average value of the pitch is 1.2 to 1.4 times the propeller diameter. See PITCH RATIO. (3) The rise and fall of a ship's bow and stern especially in heavy seas; the motion of a vessel about its transverse axis. This is one of the six principal motions of a vessel. Others are rolling, yawing, heaving, swaying, and surging. (4) A resin from the sap of various coniferous trees, most especially pines, used to fill the seams of wooden ships.

**pitch mop** *n.* A brush or mop used for applying pitch to the outside of a hull. Flax mops are generally better than cotton or rayon because they are more resistant to heat.

**pitchpole** *v.* To capsize going end over end—an accident that is quite hard on the rigging and crew.

**pitchpot** *n.* The heavy iron pot used for heating pitch to pay the seams of wooden boats.

**pitch ratio** *n.* The ratio of a propeller's pitch to its diameter. As a rule, the pitch ratios lie between 1.1 and 1.6.

**pitometer log** *n.* An electrical device used for measuring the ship's speed through the water. Also *pit log; rodmeter.* See PITOT TUBE.

**pitot tube** *n.* (pron. peetoe) A device used to measure a vessel's speed. The tube extends 24 to 30 inches below the bottom of the ship and a pump inside the ship maintains a pressure in the tube to equal the pressure created by the water through which the ship is moving. Therefore, the speed of the pump is equal to the speed of the ship; a dial that mea-

sures the electrical input to the pump can be connected to the pump electrically to give the ship's speed in another location such as the bridge. See SWORD.

**pivot point** *n.* The point in a vessel's length about which it turns. On ships this is usually about one-third the vessel's length from the bow when making headway and one-fourth the length from the stern when making sternway.

**pivot port** *n.* A port chosen by a shipper for receiving and distributing containerized cargo that is being transshipped by feeder services.

**pivot ship** *n.* The axis position in a convoy formation when a wheel maneuver is called for.

**plain-laid rope** *n.* Rope with the yarns twisted from right to left. The strands are then left-hand laid and are twisted together right-handed, or plain-laid. This is the most common type of rope. Also *hawser-laid rope; Z-strand rope.* See LAY; ROPE.

**plait** *v.* To make a braid using small stuff.

**plan** *n.* A marine architect's drawing showing the outline of a ship's shape. The first working drawing, called the **sheer draught,** consists of the **elevation** or **profile** showing the ship from end-on view, half the ship being seen from the stern and half from the bow; the **half-breadth plan** showing the outline of half the vessel (both halves being assumed to be the same) from above; and the **sheer plan** showing an athwartship view. The construction plans include the **midship sections** showing the structural members of the ship and their dimensions, called **scantlings,** and the **elevation,** which shows the side view, usually with dimensions of the individual hull plates.

**plane** *n.* (1) A surface with no curvature. In navigation, you speak of the plane of the equator. (2) The angle at which a

plate 333

boat rides on the surface of the water to have minimum resistance from the water when it exceeds hull speed. "We were on a plane most of the way to the down-wind mark."

**plane** *v.* To ride on the surface of the water to have the least resistance to the water. Some small boat hulls are made to do this so that they can often outperform the theoretical hull speed. Small centerboard boats and, occasionally, small keel boats can accomplish this for short periods.

**plane guard** *n.* A fast U.S. Navy ship, destroyer or frigate, that accompanies an aircraft carrier to pick up personnel from downed aircraft. Usually one destroyer is assigned the position on the carrier's starboard quarter and another takes position on the port beam. Today such rescues as are necessary are frequently performed by helicopters.

**plane sailing** *n.* A method of solving navigation problems involving a single course and distance, difference of latitude, and departure, with the Earth's surface treated as a plane. This method is not intended to be used for long distances. See SAILING.

**planetary hoist** See CHAIN HOIST.

**planing hull** *n.* A hull designed to plane.

**planing speed** *n.* The speed a small boat must achieve before it can begin to plane.

**plankage** *n.* (1) Fee charged for use of stationary cargo-handling equipment. (2) The heavy platform over which cargo is rolled from ship to shore, and vice versa.

**planking** *n.* Broad planks used to form a wooden vessel's sides or to cover the deck beams.

**plankowner** *n.* A person who has been on a ship since its commissioning or at least for a very long time. See SHIPOWNER.

**planks** *n.* The lengths of wood spiked to the outside of a vessel's frames to form the outside skin and fastened to the beams to form the decks.

**plank sheers** *n.* The planking that covers the tops of the frames and sheer strakes.

**planning and overhaul yard** *n.* Formerly called a **home yard,** a shipyard that maintains design work, maintenance schedules, and records for ships regularly assigned to it.

**plan of the day** *n.* The schedule of a ship's work, training plans, recreation, meals, and other activities. It is prepared by the executive officer each night for the next day's activities. Also *morning orders.*

**plan position indicator (PPI)** *n.* The display unit of a radar that presents a picture of the area around the ship, showing all the objects on the surface of the sea relative to the ship, which is represented by the center of the PPI.

**plant** *n.* A ship's main propulsion engines. When the chief engineer passes the word to the department to "button up the plant," the main propulsion equipment should be secured, but certain auxiliary equipment (such as generators) will be kept on line.

**plat** *n.* (1) A sleeve parceled around a hemp anchor cable to prevent wear on the cable in the hawsepipe. When chain cables became practical, the plat was abandoned. (2) A French sinnet or a form of the French sinnet. Also *plait.*

**plate** *n.* A sheet of metal used to form a ship's hull. A completed hull consists of **plating** or **shell plating.**

**plate door** *n.* A semipermanent closure secured to a bulkhead by through bolts.

**plated mast** *n.* A hollow metal mast supported by interior angle bars.

**platform** *n.* A partial deck lower than the lowest complete deck; if there is more than one platform deck, they are numbered first, second, and third, from the top down.

**platform sling** *n.* A small, flat platform capable of being suspended from a tackle by bridles at the four corners. Platform slings are used for cargo handling.

**plating model** *n.* A half-block model prepared from a ship's sheer plan to scale.

**plebe** *n.* A first-year midshipman at the U.S. Naval Academy at Annapolis. From the Latin *plebs,* common people.

**pledget** *n.* Oakum used in rolls to caulk seams in wooden ships.

**Plimsoll mark (or line)** *n.* The figure on the side of a merchant ship that shows the various draft levels to which a ship may be loaded, depending on the region and season in which a vessel is scheduled to sail. The six loading levels are (from least to greatest freeboard, or most to least cargo): tropical freshwater (TF), freshwater (F), tropical, seawater (T), summer, seawater (S), winter, seawater (W), winter North Atlantic (WNA). Named for Samuel Plimsoll (1824–1898), member of Parliament, who caused it to be adopted in 1874–1876 in a hard-fought victory for the protection of seamen. Also *load line.*

**plot** *n.* (1) Planned course or courses drawn on a chart or graph for surface vessels, aircraft, or submarines. (2) The tactical operational control center of a U.S. Navy ship as related to the specific needs, such as air plot and flag plot. See COMBAT INFORMATION CENTER.

**plot** *v.* To draw a planned course or several courses on a chart or graph.

**plotting sheets** *n.* Forms designed for use at sea by navigators when no large-scale charts are available. These are Mercator charts showing only the graticule of meridians and parallels with a compass rose, but no other chart data. These sheets are especially useful in plotting celestial fixes and then transferring the fix to the working chart. Two types of sheets are available: those printed for a given band of latitude, and the universal plotting sheets (UPS), which can be used with any latitude. The Defense Mapping Agency's Hydrographic/Topographic Center publishes several series of plotting sheets at different scales with numbered parallels of latitude; the meridians of longitude are filled in by the navigator for the area of operation. Universal plotting sheets have unnumbered parallels of latitude, and a single meridian down the middle. They can be used any place a Mercator chart can be used, exclusive of the polar regions where the Mercator charts are not practical.

**plow anchor** *n.* A CQR anchor. See ANCHOR.

**plug** *n.* (1) A wedge fitted into a drain hole in the bottom of a boat. (2) Wooden dowl fitted over a steel bolt in a deck or side planking.

**plug hatch** *n.* A tapered hatch with insulated sides used on refrigeration compartments to keep the cold air from escaping.

**plumb** *v.* (1) To rig a block and tackle over a hatch. ''Plumb the main hatch so that the fresh provisions can be struck below.'' (2) To hoist frames into place during construction to give them the proper angle of inclination to bring them into plumb with the keel.

**plummer block** *n.* A bearing supporting the tunnel shafting. Also *pillow block; shaft block.*

# Plimsoll Marks

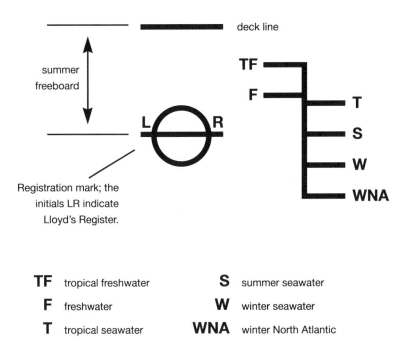

deck line

summer freeboard

TF

F

T

S

W

WNA

L        R

Registration mark; the initials LR indicate Lloyd's Register.

| | | | |
|---|---|---|---|
| **TF** | tropical freshwater | **S** | summer seawater |
| **F** | freshwater | **W** | winter seawater |
| **T** | tropical seawater | **WNA** | winter North Atlantic |

**ply**   *v.* (1) To traverse a regular route. "She plied between the islands on a monthly schedule." (2) To tack or beat to windward, usually tacking back and forth. Rarely heard today.

**pocket**   *n.* The space between a ship's side and the boiler casing that is usually utilized as a bunker.

**pocket battleship**   *n.* The name given to three German heavily armored cruisers of about 10,000 tons displacement built between 1930 and 1940.

**pocket piece**   *n.* One of the two lower longitudinals that form the base of a centerboard trunk.

**point**   *n.* (1) On a compass card, an interval of $11\frac{1}{4}°$. A point is $\frac{1}{32}$ of 360° and early compasses used 32 points for a complete circle before compasses started using 360°. See LIGHTS. (2) The working end of a line with knittles. (3) A reinforced hole in a sail through which nettles are rove for reefing. A sailmaker will put several reefing points in a sail to even the stress. (4) A narrow piece of land that extends into the sea.

**point**   *v.* (1) To sail close to the wind; one boat may point higher than, or outpoint, another of the same class. A boat that can point higher than another boat with the same waterline length and other characteristics that are similar has a decided advantage in a race. (2) To taper a piece of rope to a point for convenience in reeving it through a block. The rope is unlaid and the ends of the strands are thinned; by twisting the outside yarns into nettles, a mat is woven around the pointed portion. The purpose is to keep the finished product from **fagging out.**

(3) To control the direction of a gun in the vertical plane.

**pointer** *n.* (1) A person trained and assigned to control a gun's elevation or range. See GUN LAYER; TRAIN. (2) Name given to the two outer stars on the cup of the Big Dipper that point to the pole star, Polaris.

**point of departure** *n.* A fix on local bearings at the beginning of a voyage. See DEPARTURE.

**point of destination** *n.* The ship's position at that point when, for navigational purposes, the voyage has ended.

**point of intended movement (PIM)** *n.* The point or station assigned to all vessels in a widely dispersed fleet—over as much as several hundred square miles—with many vessels executing special maneuvers. The battle group center will have its own PIM on which all other ships take their positions.

**point of maximum separation** *n.* That point on a great circle track when the rhumb line and the great circle course are farthest apart, at which time they are also parallel.

**points of sailing** *n.* The principal directions a sailing vessel can sail relative to the wind direction. When a vessel's heading is 30° to 60° from the wind direction, it is said to be **beating.** When the heading is 60° to 135° from the wind direction, it is said to be **reaching.** When the heading is 135° to 180°, it is said to be **running.** When the vessel is being sailed as close to the wind as possible, the vessel is **close-hauled.** When the wind is on the quarter, the vessel is said to be **broad-reaching.**

**point up** *v.* To steer fairly close to the wind.

**polacca** *n.* A Mediterranean ship with two or three masts. The foremast is lateen-rigged, the mainmast is square-rigged, and the mizzen lateen has a square topsail. Also *polacre.*

**polar chart** *n.* A chart projection whose point of tangency is one of the poles.

**polar circle** *n.* The minimum north and south latitudes at which the Sun becomes circumpolar. These are 66°33'N and 66°33'S, respectively, and mark the limits of the North and South Frigid Zones.

**Polar Currents** *n.* In the North Atlantic, a current that enters the Arctic Ocean and flows easterly north of Siberia and across the North Pole and then down the Greenland Coast to form the East Greenland Current. In the Antarctic, the current is generally east, broad and slow-moving, and surrounds Antarctica and is called the West Wind Drift.

**polar distance** *n.* The angular distance from the celestial pole to a celestial body; the arc of an hour circle between the celestial pole and a point on the celestial sphere. The polar distance is found by subtracting the declination from 90° if the declination and latitude are the same name, both either North or South. If contrary, the declination is added to 90°. See ZENITH DISTANCE.

**Polaris** *n.* Astronomers' and navigators' name for the North Star, a second-magnitude star found at the end of the handle of the Little Dipper and almost at the north celestial pole. Also *polestar.*

**Polaris missile** *n.* A submarine-launched two-stage ballistic missile powered by solid-fuel rocket motors. It has been replaced by Poseidon and Trident.

**polar lights** See AURORA AUSTRALIS/ AURORA BOREALIS.

**polar projection** *n.* A chart projection on which either the North Pole or the South Pole is taken as the center of the projection.

# Points of Sailing

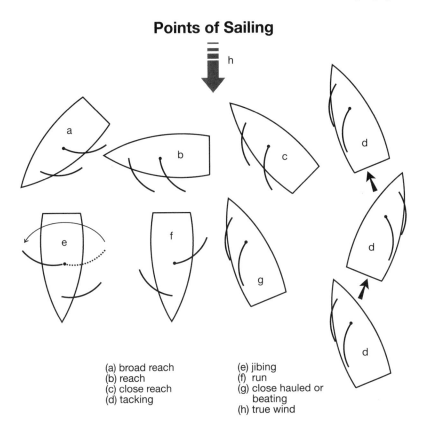

(a) broad reach
(b) reach
(c) close reach
(d) tacking

(e) jibing
(f) run
(g) close hauled or
    beating
(h) true wind

**pole**   *n.* The portion of the mast be-tween the truck and the highest rigging.

**pole**   *v.* To push a small boat by means of a pole. See PUNT.

**pole compass**   *n.* A magnetic com-pass high above a ship's magnetism, reached by a ladder. Found only in mu-seums today.

**pole mast**   *n.* A one-piece mast.

**polestar**   See POLARIS.

**police**   *v.* To clean up an area. The gallery is policed after chow is over and the dishes have been washed. It is usu-ally used to mean a light cleanup.

**policies**   *n.* Contracts between the owner or owners of a ship and the un-derwriters by which a ship or its cargo or both are insured against the various types of disasters that threaten the property. Types of marine policies differ from other types of liability policies. Among the var-ious marine policies are **yacht, fishing,** and **lighterage** policies, **freight** policies, policies on **port risk, open cargo** poli-cies, **transit floater** policies for coastwise trade, and **wager** policies that cover property when the insured cannot or does not give proof of ownership.

**polliwog**   *n.* Traditional name for someone who has not yet crossed the equator. See SHELLBACK.

**polynya**   *n.* (pron. poleeneeya) A large nonlinear patch of open water sur-rounded by ice. From the Russian *polyi,* open.

**pontoon**   n. (1) A boat in which buoyancy is established by a watertight subdivision in the hull. (2) A platform with two or more watertight tanks beneath it to keep it afloat.

**pontoon bridge**   n. A bridge that is kept afloat by means of large watertight tanks; frequently such a bridge is constructed to be easily opened for water traffic.

**pontoon hatch cover**   n. A steel, box-shaped member sometimes used in place of hatch beams to enclose a cargo hatch.

**poop**   n. A partial deck above the main deck located aft. The poop deck can also be the deck behind the helmsman when the helm is on the main deck. In deep-water sailing ships, the completely enclosed poop contained accommodations for the captain and officers. See FANTAIL; STERN.

**poop**   v. Said of breaking waves, to hit the stern. "Our cockpit filled with water when a following sea pooped us."

**poop rail**   n. A railing around the poop deck.

**poppet**   n. (1) A small wedge or block inboard of a boat's gunwale or washstrake that supports the oarlock. (2) A type of valve in an engine.

**poppet ribband**   n. A plate or channel that braces launching poppets.

**popping the whip**   phr. To sharply change the course of the towing vessel so that the towed vessel or barge suddenly swings wide. This maneuver usually is executed when the heading is changed 180°. Also *cracking the whip.*

**poptop cabin**   n. A cabin on a small boat that can be raised to provide more comfortable space below, and lowered to reduce windage when underway.

**porcupine**   n. A frayed wire rope.

**porcupine**   v. To fray a wire rope.

**porkchop**   n. Slang reference to the insignia worn by officers of the U.S. Navy Supply Corps. Supply officers are often referred to as **porkchoppers.**

**porpoise**   v. (1) Said of a vessel whose bow repeatedly plunges beneath the waves and breaks the surface, similar to the actions of a porpoise. (2) To ride with the bow up and out of the water. Rare.

**port**   n. (1) A coastal city usually with a protected harbor. A place where vessels enter or leave; a harbor. (2) An opening in a vessel's side such as a gun port. (3) The left-hand side of a vessel when facing forward "We shall pass a buoy on our port side," or "We will take the pile to port," or "We will leave Isla de Punta to port"—all mean that the vessel will proceed with the object on the vessel's left side. The left side was called the larboard side until the 17th century, when port was adopted to reduce the confusion caused by the similar-sounding larboard and starboard. The use of port and starboard have also begun to give way to left and right.

**portable deck**   n. Decking used on ships for carrying fruit when the ship will later be used for other cargo. The sections of such a deck are called hatches and are spaced so that cranes can pick them up and move them for stowing.

**portable lights**   n. (1) Temporary navigation lights for vessels used as backups when the principal lights fail. (2) Standby running lights that were kept ready in bad weather when the regular lights could not be kept burning. The portable lights were kept inside out of the weather and brought out when another ship was sighted.

**portage bill**   n. An invoice made up by the master of a ship billing the owners or the charterers. It includes the earnings of each member of the crew and overtime due along with any bonuses and gratuities that may be due under special circumstances, less any money advanced to the crew during the voyage.

**port authority**  *n.* (1) The duly authorized executive charged with the administration of a port. (2) A government officer or duly appointed official in charge of harbor operations. Also *captain of the port.*

**port capacity**  *n.* The estimated volume of cargo, usually expressed in tons, that can be cleared through a port or anchorage in 24 hours.

**port captain**  *n.* A company man who is in charge of the deck and engineering operations of all vessels in a company's fleet. Not the same as captain of the port. Also *marine superintendent; port superintendent.*

**port charges**  *n.* A catchall term for charges, dues, and fees of any nature (port dues, harbor dues, quarantine fees, towage, wharfage, customs fees) and any other similar charges against a vessel.

**port engineer**  *n.* A company official, similar to a port captain, stationed in a fleet's home port with the responsibility of hiring, controlling, discharging port and fleet engineering personnel, maintenance and repair of all the ships' machinery and the supervision of the ships' engineers' various reports.

**portfolio of charts**  *n.* A collection of all marine charts in a given series for a specific area.

**porthole**  *n.* Any opening or window on a ship, such as a gunport or cargoport, usually a circular window a foot in diameter or less. It may have a steel opaque covering, a deadlight, for protection from storms and enemy fire, and it may have a glass cover so that it can be closed, but will still let the light in; the latter is referred to as a **glazed port.** See PORT LIGHT.

**port holiday**  *n.* Days when seamen are not to be given unnecessary work: Sundays, New Year's Day, Independence Day, Labor Day, Thanksgiving, and Christmas.

**port lanyard**  *n.* A small line used to open a gunport. The lanyard was led up to the next deck from the outboard-hinged port.

**port light**  *n.* (1) The glass in a round porthole. (2) A small light on a pierhead or at the entrance to a port.

**port of adjudication**  *n.* A port designated by a belligerent nation where captured ships are held pending prize court proceedings.

**port of call**  *n.* A port at which a ship routinely stops to take on or discharge cargo, passengers, and fuel, which is not a destination port.

**port of delivery**  *n.* (1) The port designated in a charter party and where the owners will place a vessel to await the charterer. (2) A maritime law term denoting the delivery port as opposed to the intermediate ports of call.

**port of destination**  *n.* A term used in marine insurance policies that has been held to mean any port a ship may visit during the course of a voyage. Similar to port of call.

**port of discharge**  *n.* A port at which part of a ship's cargo is off-loaded. The **last port of discharge** is the port at which the last cargo is delivered; it may or may not be the **final port of destination.**

**port of entry**  *n.* A harbor or port at which a country's customs service provides facilities and personnel for the entry of vessels into that country from a foreign port.

**port of registry** *n.* The port at which a vessel is registered or documented and which is considered the vessel's home port. Bills of sale, assignments of mortgages, and other such documents are valid only after they have been recorded with the customs officials of the home port. Some home ports are notorious for laxness in regulations and are therefore used to skirt more stringent regulations in the country that would otherwise be the home port. See FLAG OF CONVENIENCE.

**port risk** *n.* An insurance term for the risk of a vessel lying in port before leaving for another voyage. A **port risk policy** establishes coverage that exists until the ship leaves its mooring to commence its voyage.

**port sanitary statement** *n.* A certificate issued by a port's sanitary authorities to the master of a ship that lists any cases of contagious diseases along with resulting deaths, if any, in the port during the two weeks period before a ship leaves. This is handed to the customs authorities at the next port.

**port service signals** *n.* Visual signals in a port indicating holidays, time, weather, mail delivery, fuel needed, tug service needed, police service needed, mutiny on board, and so on. With the universality of radio communications, such messages are now broadcast by voice, fax machine, or teletype from the agent.

**port sill** *n.* The heavy sill at the opening to a dry dock on which the caisson rests when the dry dock is closed.

**port speed** *n.* A term that refers to a vessel's efficiency in loading and unloading.

**Portugal Current** *n.* A slow-moving current that flows southward off the Atlantic coasts of Spain and Portugal. The current is easily influenced by wind and seas and is therefore quite unstable.

**port watch** *n.* The watch detail that is set in port; in the U.S. Navy the port watch may include officers and enlisted personnel who do not ordinarily stand bridge watches under way.

**Poseidon** *n.* Submarine-launched missile system capable of carrying up to 14 warheads that can be targeted separately, and each of which has a range of about 2,900 miles.

**position** *n.* The location of an object, vessel, or geographic area using recognized coordinates such as latitude and longitude.

**position angle** *n.* The angle of an object in the sky with the horizontal.

**position approximate (PA)** *n.* A chart term used when the position of a wreck, shoal or other obstacle has not been definitely determined or when the position of a marker is changed from time to time.

**position buoy** *n.* Before the advent of stadimeters, peloruses, sonar, radar, and other devices for keeping station, a buoy towed behind a ship for the benefit of a following ship when sailing in formation.

**position by observation** *n.* The method of determining a ship's position by taking the altitudes of celestial bodies.

**position doubtful (PD)** *n.* An expression used on marine charts when a wreck or shoal has been reported in the area with differing positions. See VIGIA.

**position line** See LINE OF POSITION.

**position signal** *n.* A flag hoist that gives a formation's position using the "P" flag to indicate "position follows": then follows the latitude and longitude.

**pound** *v.* To hit the waves so as to jar the boat. See PANTING.

**powder flag** *n.* A name sometimes given the "B" flag of the International Code that is used when gunpowder, ammunition, fuel, and other flammables and explosives are being handled. Also *fuel flag.*

**powder magazine** *n.* The compartment in which gunpowder is kept on a warship; formerly called the powder room. It is usually referred to simply as the magazine.

**powder monkey** *n.* A young boy used in sailing warships to run gunpowder from the powder keg to the guns. Because the space between decks was limited, small boys could move much more easily and quickly than men.

**power-driven vessel** *n.* According to the *Navigation Rules,* a vessel propelled by machinery. If a vessel is under sail but using its engine, that vessel is still power-driven according to the rule.

**power steering gear** *n.* Steering gear that is power-assisted. Non-power steering gear works with a direct linkage between helm and rudder with only the mechanical advantage of gear ratios.

**pram** *n.* A term of Dutch origin for various small craft used in the ports of the Baltic and North seas. Today it is generally used for a small sailboat of more or less rectangular shape. The Optimist's Pram, designed by Clark Mills of Clearwater, Florida, is widely used to help teach sailing and safety to young sailors. See PUNT.

**pratique** *n.* (pron. prateek) Permission or clearance to enter port after a vessel that has been outside the country has been examined by a port official who has established that the vessel has met health regulations and the crew and passengers can leave the ship. **Free pratique** is issued on white paper and indicates the vessel has met the requirements and no further delays are required. **Provisional pratique** is issued on

yellow paper and is conditioned upon additional specified procedures. **Radio pratique** may be granted 12 to 24 hours before a passenger liner arrives in port, provided an acceptable ship's doctor is aboard. From the French word of the same spelling meaning "practice."

**prayer book** *n.* Small holystone used for sanding confined spaces and lockers.

**preamble clause** *n.* The first part of a charter party, which describes the vessel and its principal cargo fittings.

**precautionary area** *n.* A ship routing area with well-defined limits where ships must navigate with particular caution and within which the direction of traffic flow may be recommended.

**precious cargo** *n.* Term in general use for precious metals and precious stones that are carried by special contract only.

**precipitous sea** *n.* Douglas scale reading of 8, indicating mountainous seas with wave heights over 36 feet with a long, heavy swell.

**precision graphic recorder (PGR)** *n.* A piece of equipment used with a standard hydrographic echo sounder for use in determining ocean depths where soundings cannot be recorded on the expanded scale of the standard recorder.

**preemptive right** *n.* The right of a belligerent to requisition neutral cargoes that are contraband of war or have been declared conditional contraband, on the high seas, provided the owners are justly compensated.

**pre-erect** *v.* To build portions of a steel hull such as bulkheads, bow, deckhouses, and so on, some distance from the ways, and to then transport them to the ways for assembling.

**prefabricate** *v.* To erect parts of a vessel's structure such as double bottoms, forepeak, and sternpeak at remote locations and then to take them to the ways for assembling. Prefabricate differs a little in usage from pre-erect in that the parts that are put together in prefabrication are as a rule larger than those in pre-erection, the bow and midbody, for example.

**preferred maritime lien**  *n.* A lien against a vessel and its owners arising out of torts for the crew's wages, general average, and salvage. Seaman's wages take first priority; salvage is next, and, in some circumstances, takes priority over the first; collision and other tort liens are third; liens for repairs, supplies, and other necessaries are fourth; bottomry liens are fifth; and nonmaritime liens are sixth. The more recent the lien, the higher is the priority in a given class. Liens are the most distinguishing feature of admiralty law. These are held to be against a vessel, *in rem.* Maritime liens follow a vessel wherever it goes and can be enforced in any admirality court throughout the world that obtains jurisdiction over that vessel.

**preformed rope**  *n.* Wire rope that uses preshaped wires and strands during fabrication instead of wires forced into the desired shape. Such rope eliminates the need for whipping; preformed rope also resists fatigue better than ordinary wire rope.

**preliminary entry**  *n.* Entry made by the master under oath to a customs officer before the formal entry is made at the customhouse; it is so made to obtain special license for passengers, their baggage, and express and perishable cargo.

**Presidential Unit Citation**  *n.* An award given to a Naval unit for distinguishing itself in combat or other operations. It is senior to the Navy Unit Commendation.

**press**  *v.* To use as much sail as possible, to crowd sail. A **press of sail** is all the sails a ship has the rigging to carry. See OVERCANVASSED.

**press gang**  *n.* A group of sailors whose job it was to round up men on shore to serve as sailors. This random and coerced conscription was called impressment, thus the name "press gang." The practice was widespread in merchant shipping until the latter part of the 19th century.

**press of sail.**  See PRESS; RUNNING BACKSTAY.

**pressure hull**  *n.* The pressure resistant cylinder of a submarine that encloses the operating spaces.

**presumed total loss**  *n.* Maritime insurance term that applies to a vessel that is so long overdue as to be posted as missing.

**prevailing wind**  *n.* A wind that can be expected to come from a given direction during a certain season in a particular area. See PASSAGE WIND; PILOT CHARTS.

**preventer**  *n.* (1) Any device used to limit the movement of a boom. (2) A rope used alongside another rope under heavy strain to ease the strain. See VANG.

**preventer backstay**  *n.* A temporary backstay set up to relieve the strain on the standing backstay under press of sail.

**preventer hawser**  See CLEAR-HAWSE PENDANT.

**preventer plate**  *n.* A backup plate at the lower end of the chain plate of a wooden ship to ease the stress on the lower rigging.

**preventer shroud**  *n.* An additional shroud used in heavy weather to ease the strain on the standing rigging.

**pricker**  *n.* (1) A sailmaker's tool used for making eyelet holes. (2) A small marlinespike; slang.

**primary light**   *n.* A major aid to navigation established for the purpose of making landfalls and coastwise passages from headland to headland, or for marking areas dangerous for mariners. Lighthouses and light towers are primary lights. Also *primary seacoast light.* See SECONDARY AID.

**primary shield tank**   *n.* Supporting structure and enclosure around the reactor core on a submarine.

**prime**   *v.* To displace the air in a pump with a liquid to prevent loss of suction.

**prime meridian**   *n.* The meridian of longitude 0°. All meridians are measured east or west of the prime meridian, which is almost universally accepted as the meridian that runs through the site of Britain's Royal Observatory (now part of the National Maritime Museum) at Greenwich, near London, England. A long brass marker at Greenwich identifies prime meridian.

**prime vertical circle**   *n.* The great circle through the observer's zenith and nadir and the east and west points of the horizon.

**priming of the tide**   *phr.* The effect of the Sun in causing a tidal bulge on the surface of the oceans. The tides are generally 50 minutes later each day due to the length of the lunar day; when because of the relative positions of the Moon and Sun the tide occurs earlier, it is called "priming." The opposite, when the tide is more than 50 minutes later, is called lagging.

**prismatic compass**   *n.* A hand-bearing compass that uses a prism to make possible simultaneous observations of the compass reading and the object being sighted.

**prismatic error**   *n.* An error in the mirrors and filters of a sextant that arises from a lack of parallelism in two opposing faces.

**private aids to navigation**   *n.* In U.S. waters, aids to navigation not maintained by the U.S. Coast Guard. Private aids include (a) aids established by other federal agencies with prior approval of the Coast Guard; (b) aids on marine structures or other works that the owners are legally obligated to establish, maintain, and operate as prescribed by the Coast Guard; and (c) aids that are merely desired by the individual corporation, state, or local government or other body that has established the aid with prior Coast Guard approval. Private aids are indicated on the marine charts as "'priv. maint.''

**private armed vessel**   *n.* A privately owned vessel that is armed for naval warfare for defensive purposes. The master of such a vessel is paid by the owners. Under admiralty law a private armed vessel of a belligerent state may carry armament and ammunition for defensive purposes without acquiring the legal onus of a warship or a privateer.

**privateer**   *n.* A privately owned vessel that is armed, controlled, and commissioned by a belligerent state to commit hostile acts against an enemy. The commission issued to a privateer by the belligerent state was called a letter of marque. The practice is no longer permitted under international law.

**private flag**   *n.* A yacht owner's personal burgee, conventionally swallow-tailed (as opposed to club burgees, which are triangular). In schooners and sloops, it is carried at the mainmast; in ketches and yawls, from the mizzen. A variety of customs govern the protocol of displaying private flags, their size, and shapes, and though these have eroded somewhat in recent years they are widely observed. See PRIVATE SIGNAL.

**private port**   *n.* A harbor or port that is owned and operated by a private concern such as a railway system or mining company. Charges, dues, and services are usually regulated under federal, state, and/or municipal statutes. See PUBLIC PORT.

**private signal**   *n.* A signal code used between ships belonging to the same owner when meeting on the high seas. This was done by Coston signals at night and flags and more discreet visual signals by day. This has been all but abandoned with the general adoption of radio communications. See PRIVATE FLAG.

**private vessel**   *n.* Any vessel not owned or chartered by a government.

**privileged vessel**   See STAND-ON VESSEL.

**prize**   *n.* A captured warship or merchant ship. Merchant ships are retained for prize proceedings while warships belonging to a belligerent are retained more often for political reasons.

**prize court**   *n.* A tribunal established upon the outbreak of hostilities to adjudicate cases of maritime capture under the rules of admiralty law. The purpose of the court is to determine (a) whether, according to international law, the ship and cargo in question were liable to capture, and if so (b) whether the capture was lawfully made.

**prize crew**   *n.* A detail of officers and men placed under the command of a **prize master** to board a prize ship and take her into port for adjudication.

**prize money**   *n.* (1) Money divided among officers and crew who bring a prize vessel into port. No longer paid by the United States or any other western government. (2) Bonus paid to enlisted personnel when their unit receives a battle efficiency pennant.

**proa**   *n.* A small boat used by the natives of Malaysia, having a single outrigger and a lateen sail.

**producer gas engine**   *n.* A reciprocating engine that operates on gas generated from coal, coke, peat, or wood. These were first developed around 1913 and operated in Russia (using wood) and Germany (using coal). German towboats used such engines and developed up to 350 horsepower.

**production boat**   *n.* A design from which several boats are made, as opposed to a one-of-a kind or custom-built boat.

**production platform**   *n.* A permanent offshore drilling structure equipped to control the flow of oil or gas. On charts, the term is extended to include all permanent platforms associated with oil or gas production, exclusive of submarine structures.

**profile**   *n.* A side elevation of a vessel's form.

**progressive trials**   *n.* Speed and power trials made over a measured distance for determining corresponding values of speed, revolutions, power developed, and fuel consumed.

**prohibited area**   *n.* A charted area in which navigation and anchoring are prohibited except as authorized by an appropriate authority.

**project depth**   *n.* The planned depth of a dredged channel as originally determined by the governing authority. The project depth is usually shown together with the date. See CONTROLLING DEPTH.

**projected area**   *n.* The plane of a propeller blade that is perpendicular to the axis.

**projected compass**   *n.* A magnetic compass with the capability of projecting a portion of the card through a lens for a display on a screen adjacent to the helmsman's position.

**projection**   *n.* Any systematic arrangement of meridians and parallels portraying the curved surface of the Earth on a flat surface.

**prolongation clause**  *n.* A charter party option that allows the charterer to continue the charter beyond the specified time provided he gives the owner notice in writing with the additional time specified.

**prolonged blast**  *n.* Sounding of the ship's whistle of from 4 to 6 seconds duration, as defined by both inland and international sections of *Navigation Rules.* See SHORT BLAST.

**promenade deck**  *n.* The uppermost deck on a passenger liner; it has railings but rarely a bulwark. Also *hurricane deck.*

**prompt**  *adj.* (1) A charter party term meaning that a ship is within about a week of the loading port. (2) Said of a ship that is ready to load.

**propeller**  *n.* A machine with blades radiating from a power-driven shaft, so arranged that it can propel a vessel through the water. The radial blades are carried on a hub called a **boss;** the after side of the propeller is called the **driving face.**

**propeller aperture**  *n.* The space between the propeller post and the sternpost.

**propeller efficiency**  *n.* The ratio of thrust horsepower at the propeller divided by the shaft horsepower delivered by the engine.

**propeller guard**  *n.* Protective framework around a propeller on a ship.

**propeller horsepower**  *n.* The shaft horsepower minus the losses caused by resistance at the thrust and line shaft and stern-tube bearings. See FROUDE'S LAW.

**propeller post**  *n.* The forward post of the stern frame through which the pro-

peller shaft passes in a single-screw vessel.

**propeller shaft**  *n.* The shafting that communicates engine power to the propeller.

**propelling power spaces**  *n.* A tonnage measurement term that includes engine and boiler room(s), shaft tunnel(s) with entrances and exits, and light and air casings above the upper deck.

**protected waters**  *n.* Sheltered waters such as rivers, harbors, or lakes presenting no special hazards from the weather.

**Protection and Indemnity Association**  *n.* A voluntary organization of shipowners formed to cover the various risks not ordinarily covered in marine policies, such as the deductible clause (3% of damages) and liability for loss of life and injury.

**protective deck**  *n.* On a warship, the deck fitted with the heaviest protective plating or armor. If there are two armored decks, the deck with lesser armor is called the **splinter** deck.

**protective location**  *n.* A tanker construction concept in which ballast tanks are strategically placed to minimize oil outflow in the event the oil tanks are reptured.

**protest**  *n.* (1) Sworn statement made by the master of a vessel before a notary public, consul, or other competent authority (a) when weather has precluded proper handling of perishable cargo, (b) when the condition of cargo at the time of loading was such that it was felt probable that further damage had occurred, or (c) when cargo may have been lost because of weather conditions. This sworn statement must be made within 24 hours of entering port. Then the hatches are surveyed and the cargo inventoried. The members of the crew who had knowledge of the event are then called to witness the **extension of protest.** (2) A sworn declaration made by a survivor of a shipwreck that gives the particulars as far as he knows them. See FORCE MAJEURE. (3) A complaint lodged by the skipper of a racing vessel against the skipper of another racing vessel when it is felt that the defending skipper has broken a racing rule.

**protest flag**   *n.* A flag flown by a racing boat that wishes to protest an action by another racing boat.

**protractor**   *n.* A brass or plastic semicircle marked from 0° to 180° used for determining bearings and courses.

**provision**   *v.* To provide the necessary food for a voyage.

**prow**   *n.* The bow above the waterline.

**proword**   *n.* (pron. prowerd) A short form for a phrase frequently used in voice-radio communications such as "wilco" or "over."

**public armed vessel**   *n.* A private yacht or commercial vessel converted for government use, commissioned and manned by armed services officers.

**public enemy**   *n.* A maritime law and underwriter's term for a wartime enemy of the country to which a public carrier vessel belongs. The term does not include pirates or belligerent mobs, but it does include rebellions that have become a national menace. In Britain, a public enemy is called the King's (Queen's) enemy.

**public port**   *n.* A port or harbor controlled and operated by a state, county, or municipality. Where the port is a combination of public and private facilities, it is considered a **semipublic port.** See PRIVATE PORT.

**public vessel**   *n.* A vessel owned or chartered by a government for public duties, including the transportation of troops, ammunition, stores, and so on. These include scientific expedition ships, naval tankers, and lighthouse tenders. They are considered a floating portion of their country when in a foreign port and may not, if neutral, be visited, searched, or detained by representatives and officers of a belligerent power.

**pucker**   *n.* A wrinkle in the seam of a sail.

**pucker string**   *n.* Line used to tighten the leech of a sail or to draw closed a sailbag or ditty bag.

**pudding** (or **puddening**)   *n.* An antichafing pad, often seen on the bows of tugs, made from rope yarns and similar material.

**pudding chain**   *n.* Small-link chain used for running rigging. Obsolete, replaced by flexible wire and rope.

**puff**   *n.* A light gust of wind, usually a little stronger and more sudden than a cat's-paw.

**pull**   *v.* To row. Nautical, and especially naval usage, prefers that a sailor be said to "pull an oar" than to help row the boat. See PULLING BOAT.

**pulling boat**   *n.* A large boat designed to be rowed by several men usually with a single oar for each. When such boats were used, the coxswain was in command and did the steering. Today in naval boats such as liberty boats, a coxswain is still in command, does the steering, and gives the orders to the engineer, the bow hook, and the stern hook.

**pulpit**   *n.* Originally a bow platform in a whaleboat for a harpooner; now, used more generally as the bow area that has a stout railing on two sides. The railings themselves are also called the pulpit. A similar railing at the stern is called a **stern pulpit** or, in British usage, a **pushpit.**

**pump** *n.* A machine powered by hand, steam, or electricity to move liquids or gases from one place to another. The six primary types of pump are centrifugal, eductor, gear, reciprocating, rotary, and screw.

**pump brake** *n.* The handle by which a pump is operated.

**pump dale** *n.* A sluice or channel (dale) that conveys waste water from discharge pumps through a vessel's side. In modern construction the pump dale is more often a pipe than an open channel.

**pumping** *n.* Fluctuations in atmospheric pressure that cause the barometer to rise and fall alternatively over a relatively short period.

**pumping-out station** *n.* A shore facility with the capability of accepting discharge from sewage-holding tanks on vessels.

**pumpman** *n.* A petty officer charged with the responsibility of maintaining pumps for liquid cargos such as sulfur, molasses, and bunkers being pumped aboard or unloaded from a ship. He monitors temperatures so that they are high enough to keep the flow moving, but below the flash point.

**punt** *n.* (1) A small dinghy with a flat bottom and usually with a square bow and stern, used for odd jobs on a vessel's hull near the waterline. Also *flat.* See PRAM. (2) Earlier usage included much larger craft such as ferries, barges, and lighters.

**punt** *v.* To pole a small boat, such as one might do with a friend.

**purchase** *n.* A tackle used to obtain mechanical advantage in moving cargo and objects against which great forces are at work, such as a boom or yard. The components of a purchase are the blocks and the rope, or fall, rove through the blocks. Mechanical advantage depends on two factors: the number of sheaves (in the blocks) through which the fall is rove, and whether the hauling part of the rope leads from the moving block or the standing block. Though other factors obtain, mechanical advantage is approximately equal to the number of times the line leads from the block attached to the object to be moved. See TACKLE.

**purge** *v.* To change the air in a marine boiler, forcing out old gases and fumes. Usually four changes of air are needed to clear a boiler. In an automated system, the purge is completed and proven before permission is sought for again lighting-off the boiler.

**purser** *n.* A clerk/officer on a passenger ship; his duties include keeping the ship's books, crew lists, passenger lists, all documents relating to cargo, and passenger's money and valuables when asked to do so. He also operates the ship's bank where checks can be cashed and money exchanged.

**purse seine** *n.* Fishing equipment used for catching shoal fin fish. Nets are streamed in circles to enclose the fish and then hauled in either by hand or by power.

**pursuit, right of** *n.* See RIGHT OF PURSUIT.

**put about** *v.* To change tack.

**put back** *v.* To return to port.

**put in** *v.* To go into a harbor or port; the usual usage implies an unscheduled stop. "We put in at Oslo to avoid a North Sea storm."

**put (out) to sea** *phr.* To leave port.

# Q

**Q**   See QUEBEC.

**Q-message**   *n.* A classified message, usually secret, relating to navigational hazards such as mines, aids to navigation, and channels swept for mines.

**Q-ship**   *n.* Disguised warship or merchant ship fitted for antisubmarine warfare first used during World War I. The use of Q-ships was highly controversial and ultimately prompted Germany's declaration of unrestricted submarine warfare. See DECOY SHIP

**quadrant**   *n.* (1) A metal fitting on a rudder head to which steering cables are attached. See RUDDER QUADRANT. (2) A navigation instrument similar to a sextant with a limb of one quarter of a circle. See OCTANT.

**quadrantal deviation**   *n.* Magnetic deviation that changes sign in each quadrant, being easterly in two quadrants and westerly in the opposite two. This is caused by induced magnetism in a vessel's horizontal soft iron; it is corrected by quadrantal correctors. See QUADRANTAL SPHERES.

**quadrantal spheres**   *n.* Two hollow balls of soft iron placed on either side of a magnetic compass to neutralize the effect of the ship's magnetic field and compensate for quadrantal deviation. Also *quadrantal correctors.* See FLINDERS BAR.

**quadrant tiller**   *n.* A tiller in the form of an arc of a circle, a half circle, or a circle built up in sections or **quadrants.**

**quadreme**   *n.* Oar-powered vessel of antiquity having four banks of oars.

**quadrilateral sail**   *n.* A four-sided sail such as used on square riggers and gaff-sail boats.

**quant**   *n.* Long pole used for propelling a punt. British usage.

**quarantinable diseases**   *n.* Infectious diseases that can cause a ship to be detained. These include anthrax, cholera, leprosy, bubonic plague, psittacosis, typhus, and yellow fever.

**quarantine**   *n.* The period of time a vessel is detained in isolation, "in quarantine," until free of infectious diseases among passengers and crew and granted free pratique.

**quarantine anchorage**   *n.* An anchorage at the entrance to a harbor or port, usually indicated by yellow buoys, in which vessels anchor for quarantine inspection and the exercise of regulations.

**quarantine boat**   *n.* Small craft that carries the health officer responsible for the enforcement of quarantine regulations.

**quarantine buoy**   *n.* Yellow buoys that mark a quarantine anchorage where quarantined ships may anchor while awaiting pratique.

**quarantine declaration**   *n.* A certificate declaring the state of the passengers' and crews' health. It is signed by the master and the ship's physician before the health officer of a port when a ship arrives at the quarantine station.

**quarantine dues**   *n.* A charge or fee against vessels arriving in a harbor to provide for the maintenance of quarantine service.

**quarantine flag** *n.* The "Q" flag, a yellow square displayed by vessels entering a port. "Q" means "My ship is healthy, and I request free pratique." "QQ" means "My ship is suspect," or "I have had infectious diseases more than five days ago," or "There has been unusual mortality among the rats on my ship." "QL" means "I have had infectious diseases less than five days ago."

**quarantine station** *n.* A medical control facility in an isolated area ashore where patients with infectious diseases from vessels can be taken.

**quarter** *n.* (1) A vessel's side usually from 45° abaft the beam to the stern. Although the term is usually understood to mean the after quarter, it is not uncommon to hear the term forward quarter, which means that part of a ship's side that is between the head and the beam. See QUARTERING SEA. (2) The direction from a vessel that is about 45° abaft the vessel's beam. "Our position was broad on the starboard quarter of the formation guide." That would place the vessel 135° relative to the guide's head. (3) The part of the yard between the slings and the yardarm. See QUARTERS; RELATIVE BEARING.

**quarter** *v.* To quarter waves; to head a vessel so as to meet the waves neither head on nor parallel. Quartering is a storm management maneuver resorted to by vessels in heavy seas.

**quarter badge** *n.* A rounded piece of hardwood fitted to the transom and plank endings in a square-sterned boat for protection.

**quarter bill** *n.* A document or schematic that outlines the living space for each member of the crew. This is usually combined with the watch stations of each member of the crew and is called "the watch station and quarter bill." On naval ships, it is the responsibility of the executive officer to keep the bill current. Sometimes called **quarters bill.**

**quarter block** *n.* (1) A lower block of the spanker sheet purchase. (2) A metal sheave fairlead through which wheel chains or ropes are rove to the tiller quadrant.

**quarter boats** *n.* Ship's boats mounted on davits at a ship's quarters.

**quarterdeck** *n.* (1) A part of the upper deck, usually extending from the mainmast to the stern or poop, reserved for use by officers. (2) The ceremonial area or section near the brow of the main deck in which the officer of the deck is stationed and for receiving visitors. The quarterdeck can be set up any place that the captain deems most accessible to boats arriving or for placing a brow or accommodation ladder; it can even be a cargo gangway below the main deck.

**quarter fender** *n.* Pudding used on the stern of a square-sterned open boat.

**quarter galleries** *n.* Ornamental projections from the quarters of square-sterned vessels.

**quartering sea** *n.* A sea that approaches from an angle of 45° abaft the beam on either side of the stern. Such a sea is said to strike the weather quarter. A sea from 180° from the ship's heading, or coming from astern, is a following sea. A head sea approaches from head on, and a beam sea approaches from either beam or from 90° from the ship's heading. See QUARTER.

**quartering wind** *n.* A wind from the weather quarter. See BROAD REACH.

**quarter iron** *n.* An inboard boom iron found on the topmast studding sail boom; it is located about two-thirds of the distance out on the yard and is fitted with hinges for clamping and unclamping around the boom.

**quarter lifts**   *n.* The topping lifts of a boom.

**quartermaster (QM)**   *n.* A petty officer in the U.S. Navy who assists the officer of the deck under way and who is qualified in bridge and deck routine, proficient in navigation, and assists the navigator. This is a different use from the Army and Marine quartermaster, who is responsible for food, clothing, and equipment. The Army Quartermaster Corps is similar to the Navy's Supply Corps.

**quartermaster's notebook**   *n.* A rough, pencil log kept by the quartermaster on watch that provides details of the watch for the deck log. It is an official document that may be used in the various courts. Any errors are crossed out and initialed, but never erased.

**quarter-point card**   *n.* Compass card that is divided into the 32 points of the compass, each point being $11\frac{1}{4}°$. It is further divided into quarter- and half-points. The quarter- and half-points, and three-quarter points are read away from the cardinals and intercardinals. NNE by E, and NNE by N are read "north northeast by east" and "north northeast by north," respectively. A thorough discussion and conversion table can be found in *Chapman Piloting Seamanship and Small Boat Handling.*

**quarters**   *n.* (1) An assembling of personnel for inspection or during shipboard fire drill (**fire quarters**). (2) An assembling at various stations. (3) Living spaces aboard ship.

**quarters, general**   *n.* Battle stations for all hands aboard U.S. Navy ships, or the call for all hands to go to battle stations.

**quarter stanchion**   *n.* Strong stanchions forming the extreme boundary in a square-sterned wooden vessel.

**quarter tackle**   *n.* A purchase secured to the quarter of a lower yard to hoist heavy equipment such as boats; the tackle is a double block and a single block with a hook and thimble. See QUARTER.

**quarter timber**   *n.* One of the timbers of a wooden vessel that is secured to the transom to become part of the transom.

**quartz crystal marine chronometer**   *n.* A quartz crystal clock used as a replacement or as a backup for the traditional spring-driven marine timepiece. The degree of accuracy and sophistication is such that it may track and correct itself so as to keep nearly perfect time (plus or minus 1 or 2 seconds a year) after being properly started and maintained. See CHRONOMETER.

**quay**   *n.* (pron. key, kay or kway) A cargo loading and unloading wharf, usually filled in with solid masonry.

**quayage**   *n.* (pron. keyij) (1) A charge for use of the quay. (2) The space available at a quay. "We are waiting for quayage." (3) Quays collectively. "Rotterdam has some of the best and dirtest quayage in Europe."

**Quebec**   *n.* Phonetic word for the letter "Q." See QUARANTINE; QUARANTINE FLAG.

**queenie**   *n.* A quadrilateral sail set on the triatic stay of the schooner.

**quenching**   *n.* A drop in underwater sound transmission and reception because of air bubbles trapped in the sonar dome, usually the result of rough seas.

**quick (Q; Qk)**   *adj.* Light phase description indicating a flashing light with a repetition rate of 50 to 79 (usually 50 to 60) flashes per minute. Lights may be **continuous quick, group quick,** or **interrupted quick.** See LIGHT PHASE CHARACTERISTICS.

**quick-closing gear** *n.* Equipment that makes it possible to close all bulkhead doors form the bridge.

**quicken** *v.* To lessen the radius of curvature to make a sharper bend in plates or bars. To quicken a waterline is to redesign it to make the curve more pronounced.

**quickwater** *n.* The wash from the propellers when the engines are going astern and the vessel is losing headway. If the quickwater is behind the vessel, the vessel is moving ahead more than 2 knots. As the vessel loses headway, the quickwater stays even with the stern at approximately 2 knots. If the quickwater moves up the hull to amidships, the ship is dead in the water or beginning to make sternway.

**quickwork** *n.* That part of a vessel's hull that is submerged when loaded.

**quilting** *n.* Matting used to cover and protect a vessel against ice in polar waters.

**quilting rivet** *n.* One of the fasteners placed in the center portion of a doubling plate to keep the faying surfaces together at all points.

**quincunx** *n.* A piling consisting of five piles, four in rectangular formation and one straight up the center.

**quintant** *n.* A double-reflecting device used for measuring altitudes of celestial bodies, an instrument similar to a sextant or a quadrant with limb of 72° or one-fifth of a circle. A quintant has a range of 144°.

**quoin** *n.* (pron. coin) (1) A chock used for supporting and wedging casks and similarly shaped cargo when stowed in a ship's hold. Also *cantick quoin.* (2) The wooden wedge on which the breech of a cannon rests.

# R

**R** See ROMEO.

**rabbet** *n.* The groove in a piece of wood into which another member fits.

**rabbet draft** *n.* The draft or distance from the designed waterline to the top of the keel. See MOLDED DRAFT.

**rabbet line** *n.* The intersection of outside planking or plating with the stem, the sternpost, or the side of the keel.

**race** *n.* A swift local current with conflicting motion; a strong, turbulent current of water usually found in a confined channel or near a coastline.

**race** *v.* To run an engine at high speed. An engine or propeller is said to race

when the propeller temporarily is lifted out of the water by wave action.

**racetrack turn** *n.* A man overboard maneuver. See MAN OVERBOARD MANEUVER.

**racing rules** *n.* Several different groups have set forth rules for yacht racing, the most frequently adopted being those of the North American Yacht Racing Union (NAYRU) and the International Yacht Racing Union (IYRU). By their definition , a yacht begins "racing" at the time of the preparatory signal and continues until it has either **finished**— clearing the finishing line or finishing marks—or retired, or until the race has been cancelled, postponed, or abandoned. In a match of team races, the sailing instructions may state that a yacht is racing from any given time before the preparatory signal.

**rack**   *n.* (1) A framework from which depth charges are dropped. (2) Sailor's slang for a bunk. To **rack out** is to take a nap. (3) A device for holding dishes on a table during meals in rough weather. Also *fiddle boards*. (4) On diesel engines the rack controls the engine speed.

**rack**   *v.* (1) To lash together two ropes with cross turns of spun yarn, which is then finished off as a round seizing. (2) To **rack a tackle** is to fasten together the fall of a tackle (or any two ropes) by passing two or more cross turns with light cordage around each part with an equal number of turns above them; the ends are made fast with a reef knot.

**rack block**   *n.* A set of blocks set in a single piece of wood, used for a fairlead.

**racking seizing**   *n.* Seizing made by passing small stuff around two lines in a series of figure eight turns.

**racking turns**   *n.* Figure eight turns used in seizing.

**rack stopper**   *n.* A stopper made of cordage used for binding the parts of a tackle together to cause them to jam.

**racon**   See RADAR BEACON.

**radar**   *n.* (From **RAdio Detection And Ranging**) An electronic system designed to transmit radio signals and receive reflected images of those signals from a target to determine the target's bearing and distance.

**radar beacon (racon)**   *n.* An active receiver-transmitter device that, when triggered by a surface search radar, automatically returns a distinctive signal that can appear on the display of the triggering radar providing range, bearing, and identification information.

**radar fix**   *n.* A position established by radar; the use of radar ranges and bearings to establish a fix.

**radar navigation**   *n.* The system by which radio waves, usually in the centimeter band, are used to determine the direction and distance to an object reflecting the waves to the sending transmitter. Radar navigation uses all the information that can be derived from a vessel's plan position indicator. All information that can be gathered beyond ranges and bearings is part of the navigation.

**radar picket**   *n.* Any naval ship stationed at a distance from the force it is protecting to increase the range of radar surveillance.

**radar picket frigate (FFR)**   *n.* A U.S. Navy escort vessel modified with expanded combat information center and electronic countermeasures and search equipment.

**radar range**   *n.* The distance to an object as determined by radar.

**radar reference line**   *n.* A midchannel line on a chart that corresponds with a line incorporated in a harbor radar display to provide a reference for informing vessels of their positions.

**radar reflector**   *n.* Any device installed on a vessel or an aid to navigation to increase radar reflection qualities. These are especially important on small craft at sea.

**radar reflector buoy (RaRef)**   *n.* A navigation buoy designed to enhance its radar-reflecting capability so that it can be seen more easily on the radarscope.

**radar scan**   *n.* The motion of a radar beam as it searches for an echo.

**radarscope**   *n.* The screen in a radar receiver that displays a received echo as a visual image.

**radar shadow** *n.* An area shielded from a radar by an intervening obstruction that absorbs the signal. The **shadow region** appears to be devoid of targets on the radar display.

**raddle** *v.* To interlace cordage to be used for such items as boat gripes; to plat.

**radial clew (or head)** *n.* Reinforcing panels that extend fingerlike from the clew or head toward the middle of the sail for reinforcement. This is seen in a **star-cut** headsail.

**radially increasing pitch** *n.* Propeller with greater pitch at the outer ends of the blades than closer to the hub.

**radiated noise** *n.* Underwater noise made by ships, submarines, and torpedoes.

**radiational tide** *n.* Periodic variation in sea level related to meteorological changes such as barometric pressure variations, sea and land breezes, and seasonal changes in temperature.

**radio aid to navigation** *n.* An aid to navigation that transmits navigation information by radio waves.

**radio alarm signal** *n.* A two-tone signal transmitted by a ship in distress for at least 30 seconds to enable automatic receivers on other ships to pick it up to alert ships that an emergency signal is to follow. This is followed by "Mayday" or "Pan" on 2182 MHz.

**radio and television aids to navigation (RATAN)** *n.* Aids to navigation with a central station transmitting a radar chart of a harbor, as an example, to ships with RATAN receivers, usually UHF television.

**radio beacon** *n.* A radio transmitter at a charted position used by vessels with appropriate radio direction finders to help establish a line of position.

**radio bearing** *n.* A bearing obtained by use of a radio direction finder. See OMNIRANGE DIRECTIONAL NAVIGATION.

**radio call signal** *n.* A series of letters and numbers assigned to a transmitting station in the U.S. by the Federal Communications Commission (FCC) to be used for identification when transmitting; e.g., WZN 4253.

**radio central** *n.* The main radio room (or **radio shack** as it is popularly called) aboard a vessel. Also *radio one; main radio.*

**radio compass** *n.* Early term for radio direction finder.

**radiodetermination** *n.* As defined by the International Telecommunication Union, the determination of position, or the obtaining of information relating to position, by means of the propagation properties of radio waves. See RADIO FIX.

**radio direction finder (RDF)** *n.* Radio with directional antenna that facilitates getting a fix by use of radio stations on land. The best fixes are on radio beacons the positions and frequencies of which are charted. If only one or two are within range, an alternate coordinate can be obtained by using a commercial station. But although these may be plotted on a chart, they are not calibrated for this use, and considerable error may result.

**radio distress frequencies** *n.* Frequencies established by international regulations to be used for emergency purposes. On double- and single-sideband transmission these are 500 kHz and 2182 kHz. On VHF, channel 16 (156.8 MHz) has been established as the calling and distress channel. See RADIO ALARM SIGNAL.

**radio electrician** *n.* A warrant officer in the U.S. Navy who has advanced from electronics technician (ET).

**radio fix**   *n.* A position established by radio bearings using two or more sending stations of known location. See RADIODETERMINATION.

**radio guard**   *n.* A ship or shore facility in the U.S. Navy that assumes responsibility for radio communications for itself and one or more nearby ships or facilities.

**radio horizon**   *n.* The distance radio waves will travel beyond the visible horizon as a result of refraction in the lower layer of the atmosphere.

**radio navigation**   *n.* More recently called **electronic navigation,** the use of radio waves to determine a position or line of position, course, and speed, or a combination of these. Radio navigation systems include Loran-C and Omega, which are operated by the Coast Guard; the systems operated by the Federal Aviation Administration, which include aeronautical radio beacons and Omni stations; and the global positioning system and TRANSIT operated by the Department of Defense. Some private systems exist, but they are rarely available to the boating public. Decca, however, has been available to anyone since World War II. It is privately owned and the shipboard equipment is leased by commercial vessels and yachts.

**radio pratique**   *n.* Permission granted to some arriving passenger vessels meeting certain health criteria to eliminate having to be held up by quarantine procedures. This is done by calling by radio 12 to 24 hours before arrival and giving all the particulars required by the health officers.

**radio room**   *n.* The compartment used by radio officers while on duty. It is usually soundproof and located in the upper part of the ship's superstructure near the bridge. See RADIO CENTRAL.

**radio sextant**   *n.* An electronic navigation device that receives radio waves from the sun and other heavenly bodies instead of light waves as does the traditional sextant.

**radio silence**   *n.* (1) A period of time when all radio traffic is required to cease to allow an emergency to be handled, for example, by the U.S. Coast Guard. (2) A period during which all radio equipment capable of emitting radio signals is kept inoperative to avoid detection by the enemy.

**radiotelephone (RT)**   *n.* A transmitter and receiver combination that links boats, ships, and shore stations. Primarily, this is by VHF/FM. Other systems are used as adjuncts. Cellular phones are now used extensively on coastal waters.

**radioteletype (RTTY)**   *n.* A radio system that activates a teletype machine to produce a printed message.

**radio tick**   See RADIO TIME SIGNAL.

**radio time signal**   *n.* Radio signal by which a navigator can get **time ticks** to determine the error in the ship's chronometers. The time is broadcast as coordinated universal time (UTC) and is transmitted automatically.

**radome**   *n.* A domed structure used to house radar equipment.

**raffee (or raffie)**   *n.* A triangular sail set over the highest yard. The foot lies along the yard and the head is hoisted in front of the mast to the truck. It is set in light winds to help increase the sail area to the maximum. Also *moonraker; skyraker.*

**raft**   *n.* A small flat-bottomed boat used for small jobs on the sides of larger boats and available for emergency service.

**raft**   *v.* To tie two or more boats together while at anchor, on a mooring, or at a dock.

**rafted ice** *n.* Cake ice that rides one piece on another.

**raghiens** *n.* Easterly gales that shift to westerly ones in the eastern Mediterranean off the coast of Syria, Lebanon, and Israel.

**rail** *n.* (1) The rounded cap or top of a bulwark. (2) A **bow rail** is tubing set on the bow for safety purposes to be used by someone standing on the bow pulpit. (3) A **grab rail** is the handrail along the cabin side. (4) **Pin rails** are the rails at the shrouds used for holding belaying pins. (5) **Fife rails** are the same as pin rails but are located on the mast. (6) The rails on ships, especially naval ships, are open fencelike structures made of rigid material as opposed to life lines. These usually enclose weather decks. Such railing is also used in the engine spaces. Other rails are ladder rails, handrails, and safety rails on ladders (shipboard staircases).

**rail cap** *n.* The top of the bulwark or rail at the outer edge of a deck. Also *cap rail.*

**rail loading** *n.* The practice of loading lifeboats when they have been lowered from their davits to an easily accessible weather deck rail; when loaded, they are lowered to the water.

**rail port** *n.* A port in which a larger portion of the cargo is off-loaded directly from ships to rail cars and vice versa.

**rail screen** *n.* Sheeting extended over open railing as a protection against spray or rain.

**rail stanchions** *n.* Vertical supports for railing, life lines, and so on.

**railway fashion** *n.* The sail-hoisting system using a track, cars, and gooseneck for the forward end of the boom to ride on instead of the jaws.

**raise** *v.* (1) To bring an object on the horizon closer and therefore into clearer view. "Have you raised the coast yet?" (2) To bring a station up on the radio: "See if you can raise *Ranger* on channel 16."

**raised foredeck** *n.* A break in the continuity of a weather deck forward created by a raised forward section of an upper deck located between pilothouse and forecastle.

**raised quarterdeck** *n.* An after portion of the weather deck built higher than the forward portion.

**raised tank top** *n.* A tank top that slopes from the centerline toward the bilges, usually to accommodate a high centerline girder.

**rake** *n.* (1) The angle of a mast, shore, or stack away from the vertical along the fore-and-aft line. "The mast was raked about three degrees aft in an attempt to correct a lee helm." To correct excessive weather helm, you can rake the mast forward, but only slightly. Thus, the term **rakish,** which means a smart, speedy appearance or jaunty. (2) The forward pitch of the stem and the backward slope of the stern or counter.

**rake** *v.* (1) To observe and call naval gunfire target practice—"Over 500 yards" or "Under 50 yards." Such observations are made by a **raking party** close to the target but out of the line of fire. (2) To aim heavy gunfire along the length of a deck or across the width of a deck.

**rake tank** *n.* A plumbed tank at the shaped portion of the bow or stern, the rake, of a barge, used as a ballast tank to hold any liquid.

**raking stem** *n.* A straight stem that has a forward rake or one that extends beyond the forward perpendicular. A raking stem, or **clipper bow,** promotes better flow of water past the bow and therefore makes the vessel faster.

**rally**   *n.* Crew united in driving wedges when launching a vessel.

**rally (in)**   *v.* To haul a line as fast as possible.

**ram**   *n.* (1) Heavy timber with reinforced steel ends used for exerting heavy blows against a ship's underpinning while on the ways. (2) A hydraulic cylinder and piston used for applying heavy force; among other applications "rams" are used in steering mechanisms. (3) An underwater extension of an iceberg or an ice cliff or ice front. The ram is one of the principal dangers of icebergs and ice cliffs. (4) Armored projections from the bow of a warship that were invisible to the enemy because they were below the waterline; used for ramming the enemy ships.

**ram**   *v.* To strike obstucting ice with full power, using an appropriately equipped ice breaker.

**ramark**   *n.* (From RAdar MARKer) A radar beacon that transmits continuously without being triggered by a ship's radar. The signal that is received appears as a radial line on the plan position indicator. Unlike racon, ramark does not provide the range to the beacon.

**ram bow**   *n.* A bow fitted with a projection below the waterline used on galleys and early steam-driven warships.

**ramp**   *n.* (1) The hinged bow section of an amphibious craft through which personnel and cargo are loaded and unloaded, especially when the craft is beached. (2) A concrete or steel structure designed to accommodate Ro/Ro ships.

**ramp**   *v.* To sail with as much sail as possible when on the wind. You are said to be **ramping** her when you do this.

**ram schooner**   *n.* A schooner that carries tall pole masts but no topmasts.

**ram tensioner**   *n.* A hydraulic system that maintains tension on the highline during refueling operations at sea.

**random error**   *n.* One that is not predictable and occurs by chance. If a number of observations of the altitude of a celestial body are made and there is no systematic error, but the observations appear to be too great, too small, or correct, the probability of a positive error is exactly equal to the probability of a negative error. In this instance, a graph is made to determine the normal distribution of random error.

**range**   *n.* (1) Distance to a target, expressed in yards. (2) A designated area for gunnery practice. (3) The extreme distance at which an object or light can be seen. See VISUAL RANGE OF A LIGHT (4) The difference between consecutive high tide and low tide. See RANGE OF TIDE. (5) A heavy two-armed cleat in the waist of a sailing ship for belaying tacks and bow lines. (6) A charter party term that is used when no destination port is given in the contract except that the master is to report to a given station for further orders. (7) A length of cable overhauled on deck. (8) Two or more objects in line. Such objects are said to be **in range;** the observer having the two objects in line is said to be **on range.** Beacons are frequently located to form a range to indicate a safe route or the centerline of a channel (called **leading marks** in Britain). (9) The distance a craft can travel at cruising speed without refueling, called **cruising range** or **cruising radius.** (10) A predetermined course along which a craft travels while certain data are recorded by instruments placed below the waterline, such as a **degaussing range.**

**range**   *v.* (1) To lay anchor cable along a deck or wharf. (2) To steer a course parallel to a shoreline or other feature. "We ranged the Adriatic coast for a week before finding a decent repair facility that could handle our ship." (3) Said of a vessel that sheers about while at anchor. "She ranged all night in the roadway because of an unfavorable wind and tide."

**range bearing** *n.* A bearing obtained by compass, or other similar direction-finding device when two objects are in line or **in transit.** The range so defined is called a **range line.**

**range daymark** *n.* One of a pair of unlighted structures used to mark a line of bearings, as for indicating the centerline of a channel. See RANGE LIGHT.

**range finder** *n.* An optical instrument that enables a watch officer to get the distance from his vessel to any object by sighting and matching up the mirrors without reference to height. A stadimeter is more accurate, but the height of the object, usually another ship, is required. Today radar and sonar provide better distance or range information than either stadimeters or range finders, but, being active, they are also easily detected. Also *telemeter.*

**range light** *n.* Two lights placed in such a way as to indicate the position of the centerline of a channel or the position of an obstruction. The back range light is higher than the front range light; the (higher) back range light tells a pilot negotiating the indicated channel if the vessel is to the right or left of the centerline of the channel. Occasionally a channel is marked by a single directed beam of light from a single range light so positioned that it cannot be seen from the vessel if the vessel is out of the channel. When a vessel is on range, the range is said to be **closed;** when it is off the range, the range is said to be **open.** See RANGE DAYMARK.

**range of stability** *n.* The amount of heel or roll a vessel can sustain and return to an even keel.

**range of tide** *n.* The difference between consecutive high and low waters. The **mean range** is the difference between mean high water and mean low

water. The **diurnal range** is the difference between the height of the mean higher high water and the mean lower low water. Where the tide is diurnal, the mean range is the same as the diurnal range.

**range the cable** *phr.* (1) To run out all of the chain or cable to overhaul it on deck, that is to clean and repair it, usually done either while at anchor or while in the yard. (2) The cable is ranged occasionally to allow the anchor to run more freely. That is, the cable is laid out on deck in long flakes to run freely from the deck instead of from the chain locker.

**rap full** *adj.* All sails filled on a close reach, but not close-hauled. "Our best speed will be attained when we are able to race with our sails rap full."

**Rapson's slide** *n.* A device for controlling a tiller by using a transverse slide along which the tiller is guided.

**ratchet block** *n.* A block with interfacing teeth or pawls that allow the sheave to go in only one direction.

**rate** *n.* (1) A level of advancement within a rating. Boatswain's mate is a rating, while boatswain's mate third class is a rate. (2) A system of rating sailing warships introduced by the British admiral George Lord Anson in 1752. The accompanying table shows the number of guns carried by vessels of different rates in 1754 and as revised in 1792.

**Number of Guns**

| Rate | 1754 | 1792 |
| --- | --- | --- |
| First | 100 | 100+ |
| Second | 90 | 98–98 |
| Third | 70–80 | 64–80 |
| Fourth | 50–60 | 50–60 |
| Fifth | 40 | 32 |
| Sixth | 20 | 20–30 |

**rater** *n.* British slang for a small boat.

**rat guard**   *n.* A large circular disc through which dock lines are run so that rats cannot board a vessel from the wharf. (The same rat guard also prevents their leaving.)

**rating**   *n.* (1) The general name for an enlisted sailor in Britain's Royal Navy. "Have the ratings muster on the quarterdeck." (2) A position or grade of a member of a ship's crew. See RATE. (3) A number that is given to a sailboat to be used for racing. The number is determined by an admeasurer who measures the various dimensions including sail area and applies them to one of the measurement rules or formulas. See RATING RULE.

**rating rule**   *n.* Handicapping system that makes it possible to race boats of different sizes and characteristics. This is customary especially among offshore racing boats. Two systems predominate: the **measurement rule,** such as the International Measurement System (IMS) and the International Offshore Rule (IOR), and the **handicap rule** such as the Performance Handicap Racing Fleet (PHRF). The first assigns ratings based on the vessel's dimensions, the second assigns ratings based on a committee's evaluation.

**rational horizon**   *n.* The celestial great circle with a plane parallel to the sensible horizon and that passes through the center of the Earth. Also *celestial horizon.*

**rations**   *n.* Food and special food provisions for an emergency, for a lifeboat, landing party, or other special duty away from a ship.

**ratio of tidal ranges**   *n.* A ratio between the high water and the low water at a reference station and the highs and lows at a subsidiary station.

**ratline**   *n.* (pron. ratlin) A rope step laid across the shrouds of a mast by which sailors go aloft on sailing ships. Eyes on either end of the ratline are seized to the foremast and aftermast shroud, and se-

cured to the inner shrouds with clove hitches.

**ratline stuff**   *n.* 12-, 15-, or 18-thread "stuff," tarred, right-hand laid, used for ratlines and heavy lashings.

**rattail**   *n.* (1) The tip of a boltrope that has been worked down to a point. (2) Tapered braid with palm-and-needle whipping at the end used for stoppers and in sailmaking. Sailmakers refer to a clumsy rattail as a **carrot.**

**rattail jigger**   *n.* A light purchase using a stopper shackled to a block.

**rattan rope**   *n.* Rope made from split and twisted rattan strips, used in the Far East for running rigging; replaced by hemp.

**rattle down**   *v.* To hitch and seize ratlines to the shrouds with clove hitches on the inner shrouds and eye-splices on the outer shrouds.

**rave hook**   *n.* A tool used for removing, reefing out, oakum from seams before caulking with fresh stock. Also *reef hook.*

**raze**   *n.* To cut in a ship's lines on a mold floor or on a service board using a pointed tool, a razing knife, or scriber.

**razee**   *n.* A ship that has been razeed. See RAZEE.

**razee**   *v.* To remove the upper deck or part of the upper works of a warship such as the poop deck or quarterdeck to lighten the vessel and thereby increase the freeboard and reduce the draft. From the French *raser,* meaning to cut down.

**reach**   *n.* (1) A straight course between bends in a river. (2) A sailing course with the apparent wind coming form the general direction of the beam. When a sailing vessel is on a **beam reach,** its course is 90° to the apparent wind. When a vessel is on a **broad** reach, the wind is from abaft the beam, but not from astern. When the vessel is on a **close reach,** the wind is from forward of the beam, but short of close-hauled. See POINTS OF SAILING. (3) A narrow body of water between an island and the mainland.

**reach ahead**   *n.* The distance traveled after a new speed is ordered until the new speed is made.

**reaching foresail**   *n.* A fore-and-aft triangular sail set on the forestay with a foot that overlaps the mainsail. Also *genoa.*

**reaching jib** (or **reacher**)   *n.* A large jib used in racing on a broad reach. It is cut with a high clew to reduce the chance of the foot of the sail scooping water when the vessel is sharply heeled.

**reaching strut**   *n.* A rigid bar or spar with one end hooked to the mast; it extends the spinnaker guy beyond the shrouds on a beam or close reach. The purpose is to decrease the stretch in the guy and the compression on the spinnaker pole. British sailors call it a **jockey pole.**

**readiness, condition of**   *n.* An all-inclusive naval term that refers to the particulars of a ship's state of preparation. It includes (a) engineering and the vessel's maximum speed immediately available; (b) material and what closures have been completed; and (c) armament and what weapons are manned and ready.

**readiness, notice of**   *n.* A document certifying a vessel is ready to load cargo. Also *notice of completion.*

**ready about**   *interj.* Command to a crew to stand by to come about, to bring the wind from one side, across the bow to the other side. When the crew reports "Ready to come about," the skipper or helmsman calls "hard alee" and tacks the vessel by putting the helm down or to

leeward and bringing the bow through the wind.

**ready for sea**   *adj.* Said of a ship that is outfitted, provisioned, and fully manned for a voyage when it is fully prepared to leave port. See SPENT.

**ready reserve**   *n.* All the U.S. Navy ships stationed around the world in a standby status. (2) The status of members of the Naval Reserve when called to serve under statutory military obligation or by written agreement.

**ready room**   *n.* A compartment on U.S. Navy aircraft carriers in which pilots gather to be briefed and where they remain while standing by.

**ready to jibe**   *interj.* Command for the crew to stand by to jibe. When the crew reports "Ready," the helmsman or skipper cries "Jibe-o" and puts the helm up to bring the wind under the stern on the opposite tack.

**ream**   *v.* (1) To enlarge an existing hole by inserting a conical tool with cutting edges. (2) (slang) To discuss a junior's infraction with the person with extreme vigor.

**rear admiral (RAdm.)**   *n.* A flag officer in the U.S. Navy or Coast Guard ranked below vice admiral and above commodore (USN) or captain (USCG).

**rebate**   *n.* (1) An allowance on a freight rate made by the carrier. (2) The recessing of a keel to make possible receiving a floor frame or futtock.

**receiver of wrecks**   *n.* A term used in Britain for a customs officer to whom an arriving master was required to report any derelicts, wrecks, icebergs, and collisions as soon after arriving as possible.

**receiving clerk**   *n.* A person responsible for receiving all cargo that arrives on a wharf.

**reciprocal bearings**   n. Bearings that are opposite to each other. A bearing *to* a given point is the reciprocal of the bearing *from* the same point, as 90° and 270°, or 192° and 12°. Reciprocal bearings are used to adjust a compass or to obtain a set of deviations. A **reciprocal course** is one that is opposite to a given course.

**reciprocating pump**   n. A pump with pistons moving axially in cylinders in the same plane as the drive shaft. Until World War II, these pumps served as the primary means of discharging cargo. The centrifugal pump has largely taken its place since then, especially when a large volume of liquids, such as pipeline fuels, is to be moved.

**recommended track**   n. The routing recommended for navigation after being carefully examined to ensure as far as possible that it is fuel-efficient with safe navigating conditions in mind.

**Red Cross flag**   n. The internationally recognized mark of an unarmed hospital ship and boats and shore activities in the medical service.

**redelivery clause**   n. Charter party term for the clause or section of the contract that specifies the time, date, and place the charter will terminate and the person or organization to whom the vessel will be delivered.

**Red Ensign**   n. The ensign flown on all British merchant ships and on many pleasure boats. Until 1864 it was the flag of the senior division of the Royal Navy when the fleet was divided into three squadrons, red, white, and blue. When these squadrons were abolished in 1864, the Red Ensign was given to the merchant marine. Naval auxiliary vessels and vessels belonging to certain yacht clubs were allowed to adopt the Blue Ensign, defaced, and the Navy kept the white ensign. The Red Ensign is widely known as the Red Duster.

**red lead**   n. An anticorrosive primer coating used on vessels' hulls.

**red sector**   n. Danger area, usually indicated on a chart with reference to a lighthouse. Such sectors are designated by their limiting bearings as observed from sea. If dangerous shoals lie off a cape between the bearings 045° and 005° from the light, those bearings will be shown on the chart as defining a red sector, and a red filter on the light will allow a mariner to see a red light only when he is within the defined sector.

**reduction**   n. (1) The conversion of arc (an angle measured in degrees, minutes, and seconds) into time. (2) The conversion from a solar interval of time to a sidereal interval. (3) The conversion of quantities given in the *Nautical Almanac* from Greenwich mean time to their equivalent values in local mean time. See SIGHT REDUCTION.

**reduction of latitude**   n. The correction necessitated in determining the true latitude by the Earth's being an oblate spheroid rather than a perfectly round sphere.

**reef**   n. (1) An offshore rock hazard with a depth of 16 fathoms or less. (2) That part of the sail that is between the foot and the eyelet holes or reef points; the part of a sail that can be reefed. A single reef is known as a **bag reef.**

**reef**   v. To take in sail to reduce its area when winds become strong enough to make it necessary. See OVERCANVASSED.

**reef band**   n. A reinforcing strip of canvas or other material sewn along the reef points.

**reef cringle**   n. A reinforcing device around a hole in the sail at the outboard end of a line of reef points, through which the earing is rove for the outhaul on a reefed sail.

**reef earing** *n.* A small rope with an eye-splice used to secure the reef cringle of a topsail to the yardarm to fasten the upper corner of a quardrilateral sail. See EARINGS.

**reefer** *n.* (1) A cold compartment on a ship where food is kept or one in which corpses are kept frozen until they can be properly embalmed. (2) A ship designed and insulated for keeping perishable commodities chilled during shipment. (3) A short, blue wool, double-breasted jacket worn by midshipmen, officer candidates, and enlisted personnel. Also *pea jacket.* (4) A heavy wool sweater worn by Royal Navy personnel.

**reef flat** *n.* A flat expanse of reef rock that is partly or entirely dry at low water.

**reefing batten** *n.* A vertical batten parallel to the mast in some small sailboats including sharpies, used for reefing sails by brailing them in close to the mast with brails.

**reefing becket** *n.* A sennet with an eye and toggle used when executing a French reef.

**reefing jackstay** *n.* A line run through the grommets of a reef band and secured to a jackstay set along the length of the mast with a toggle.

**reef knot** *n.* A square knot with one end returned to the knot so that it is possible to untie it by pulling the returned end. It was used for reefing square sails.

**reef pendant** (or **pennant**) *n.* (1) A short rope that is rove through cringles on the lower leech of a quadrilateral fore-and-aft sail, and then to a boom cleat to act as an outhaul when the sail is reefed. (2) A rope that secures a clew earing of a reefed sail.

**reef points** *n.* Short pieces of line sewn into a sail in a line parallel to the foot and tied around the boom or yard when shortening sail. The reef points are

rove through eyelets, which are usually reinforced with a reef band.

**reef rope** *n.* A line that passes from the deck through a block in the topmast rigging, then through a sheave in the topsail yardarm to control the topsail.

**reef tackle** *n.* A rope that is led from the deck through a block on the topmast and then through a sheave in the topsail yard and to a cringle below the lowest reef. It is used to draw the leech up to the yard to shorten sail. See SQUARE-RIGGED VESSEL.

**reem** *v.* To widen the space between planking with a **reeming iron** so that the seams can be caulked. See REAM.

**reeve** *v.* To pass a rope through something, as a hole or channel of a block, a pad eye, a ringbolt, a sail, and so on. **Rove** and **reeved** are the past tense and past participle, though rove is more commonly used. To remove a rope is to **unreeve** it.

**reeving line** *n.* (1) A small line spliced to a larger one to make it possible to pull the larger line through a block. (2) A line used on square sails in stormy weather for reefing or furling sails.

**reeving line bend** *n.* A method of connecting two lines together so that they can be rove through an opening without jamming.

**reference points** *n.* Lettered points of reference in a harbor plan that are used by naval ships as part of operations orders and so on.

**reference station** *n.* A geographical position given for tides and currents from which the tides and currents of other locations can be derived by adding or subtracting a given time period. In published tide tables, the times of high and low tides for the whole year are given for a reference station, such as St. Petersburg (municipal pier). The high or low tide at

Egmont Key can be determined by subtracting 24 hours and 27 minutes from the time shown for St. Petersburg. Reference stations were previously called **standard ports**. See SUBORDINATE CURRENT STATION.

**reflag**  *v.* To qualify a foreign merchant ship for protection from friendly naval forces. This is different from "flag of convenience."

**reflux**  *n.* An ebb tide. Rare today.

**refraction**  *n.* In the atmosphere, a light wave changes direction downward with changes in density, temperature, and humidity. Refraction is the correction applied to a celestial body's apparent altitude to allow the displacement of the celestial body.

**refrigerated cargo**  *n.* Any cargo on board that is maintained at low temperature for the purpose of preserving it while in transit; the three classifications, based on the temperature at which the cargo must be kept, are frozen, chilled, and air-cooled.

**refrigerated vessel**  *n.* A vessel designed and equipped for the transportation of foods such as orange juice, meat, fruit, butter, and eggs that must be kept refrigerated. Also *reefer; reefer ship.*

**regatta**  *n.* A boat race or a series of boat races. It was first used in the 17th century to describe boat races on the Grand Canal in Venice. From the Italian word *regata,* race.

**Regions A and B**  *n.* The two groups of countries that embrace one of the two separate buoyage schemes implemented by the International Association of Lighthouse Authorities (IALA) Maritime Buoyage System. The countries of North and South America and Japan make up Region B. All other coastal countries are Region A countries. See BUOYAGE.

**register**  *n.* A document issued by customs to a vessel to allow it to engage in foreign trade. It contains a description of the vessel, its measurements, and the master's name.

**registered breadth**  *n.* The width of a vessel measured at the widest point from the outside of the shell plating on one side to the outside of the shell plating on the opposite side.

**registered depth**  *n.* The depth of the hold measured amidships from the top of the double bottom (or from the top of the floor on vessels with no double bottom), or from a point not more than 3 inches above these points where ceiling planks are fitted to the tonnage deck beams at the centerline.

**registered length**  *n.* The length of a vessel from the forepart of the stem on the forecastle deck to the afterside of the sternpost or rudder stock in the absence of a sternpost. See LENGTH OVERALL.

**registered tonnage**  *n.* A vessel's certified tonnage, either gross or net, as determined by the legal method of measurement and shown on the ship's tonnage certificate. See TONNAGE.

**registry**  *n.* A ship's certifying papers issued by a customs officer of the port chosen by the owner and issued to the owner. The issuing government or the port of registration is placed on the stern of the vessel. The certificate of registry includes the name of the ship, the name(s) of the owner(s), tonnage, description of vessel, name of master, and the name of the person(s) or corporation entitled to custody of registration. Vessels engaged in foreign trade beyond the registering country's insular possessions (except Puerto Rico for the U.S.) are required to be registered.

**regulation lights**  *n.* Those lights required by the *Navigation Rules* under various circumstances such as when under way, at anchor, towing, and so on.

**reinforced concrete**  *n.* A material used in hull construction, first used in World War I and later in World War II.

**reinsurance**  *n.* The act by which a risk or contingent liability already covered by an existing contract is transferred in whole or part to a second underwriter, purpose being to relieve the original underwriter from a liability it cannot afford.

**relative bearing**  *n.* The direction of an object from a vessel relative to the vessel's head. Typically, the relative bearing is given as a horizontal angle measured clockwise from 000° (dead ahead) through 359°. It can also be given in points, an interval of $11\frac{1}{4}°$ as in "two points off the starboard bow."

**relative motion**  *n.* The movement of one vessel relative to another vessel or object. To be able to judge relative motion, that is, to be able to judge the changing distance and bearing between the moving vessel and a stationary object or another vessel is an important ability for the seaman to develop, and some are able to develop a **sailor's eye** much better than others. The opposite of relative motion is actual motion.

**relative plot**  *n.* A diagram usually presented on a maneuvering board or radar plot with the positions of ships or aircraft presented as relative to each other.

**relative position**  *n.* The position of an object or vessel relative to another vessel or object. Another way of expressing position is to give the **geographic position** with reference to geographic coordinates.

**relative wind**  See APPARENT WIND.

**relief**  *n.* The elevations of land surfaces represented on charts and maps by contours, hypersometric tints, shading, spot elevations, and hachures. Similar differences on the ocean floor are called **submarine relief.**

**relieve**  *v.* (1) To take over a watch or duty from someone else: "Sir, I am ready to relieve you." A command is relieved, a ship on station is relieved, or a person who must leave the duty station is relieved. When there were lightships, a lightship was said to be relieved for repairs; the substitute lightship would have the word RELIEF painted on the hull instead of the name of the station. See ASSUME; SECURE. (2) To release from duty or a station. See PAY OFF.

**relieved**  *adj.* Said of an aid to navigation that has been removed from a station and replaced by a temporary aid to navigation.

**relieving boards**  *n.* Planks placed on top of cargo in a hold to evenly distribute the weight of cargo placed on top of them.

**relieving tackle**  *n.* A tackle rove through multiple sheave blocks, one on either side of the rudder, used to ease the strain of shocks on the rudder and to the helm caused by the impact of the sea, especially during heavy weather. These are fitted when there are no spring buffers or a rudder brake. See RUDDER TACKLES.

**relighted**  *adj.* Used to describe an aid to navigation that has been extinguished and has been returned to its charted position.

**relocated**  *adj.* Describes the authorized movement of an aid to navigation from one position to another nearby position.

**remotely controlled light**  *n.* A lighted aid to navigation that is operated by personnel at a considerable distance from the light.

**rend**  *v.,* To split, said of wooden planking when it splits through exposure to the Sun or wind. Past tense is **rent.**

**render**  *v.* (1) To free a line so that it can pass freely through a block or dead-

# Relative Bearings

12 o'clock

0°

315°

045°

9 o'clock 270°

090° 3 o'clock

225°

135°

180°

6 o'clock

dead ahead

1 point on the port bow

1 point on the starboard bow

broad on the port bow

2 pts

2 pts

broad on the starboard bow

3 pts

3 pts

3 pts

3 pts

2 pts

2 pts

1 point forward of the port beam

1 point forward of the starboard beam

on the port beam

on the starboard beam

1 point abaft the port beam

1 point abaft the starboard beam

2 pts

2 pts

3 pts

3 pts

3 pts

3 pts

broad on the port quarter

2 pts

2 pts

broad on the starboard quarter

1 point on the port quarter

1 point on the starboard quarter

astern

# Shipboard Directions

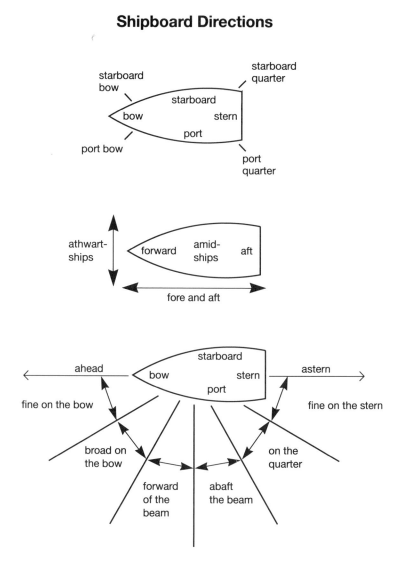

eye. "Be sure to render the main halyard before you drop the main." (2) To run a rope freely. Admiral William Henry Smyth's *Sailor's Work-book* (1867) illustrates the usage as follows: "Any rope, hawser, or cable is 'rendered' by easing it round the bitts." (3) To observe matters of nautical or traditional etiquette; to **render honors.**

**Rennell's Current**   *n.* A current in the English Channel that sets in a northwesterly direction at the southern entrance, caused by rising water in the Bay of Biscay during westerly gales. Named for the British geographer James Rennell (1742–1830).

**repeatability**   *n.* The measure of accuracy in a navigation system when the system allows the user to return to a given point as defined only in terms of the coordinates of that system

**repeater**   *n.* (1) A device that repeats at a distance the indications of a piece of equipment or instrument such as a compass repeater, gyro repeater, radar repeater, or steering repeater. (2) See SUBSTITUTE.

**repeater compass**   *n.* A compass that repeats a gyrocompass reading or a fluxgate compass reading at various parts of the ship such as the helm, the peloruses on the bridge wings, the captain's sea cabin, after steering, CIC, the director, and so on. Also *remote-indicating compass.*

**replaced**   *adj.* Used to describe an aid to navigation previously off station, adrift, or missing, replaced by an aid of the same type and characteristic. See RESET.

**replacement clause**   *n.* A clause in marine equipment insurance policies that restricts the insurer's liability to the cost of repairing or replacing the part lost or needing repair.

**replenishment group**   *n.* Fleet ships in the U.S. Navy with the duty of replenishing ships at sea; these include oilers, supply ships, ammunition ships, and repair ships, along with their escort screen. These ships supply food, stores, fuel, ammunition, and personnel to fleet combat units while at sea.

**report**   *n.* The recording of an enlisted person's infraction of a U.S. Naval rule or regulation under the *Uniform Code of Military Justice* and the notification that he is to appear before the commanding officer or executive officer at the next captain's mast. Such a person is said to have been placed on report.

**reprisal**   *n.* Act of force short of war. The action of one nation to suppress illegal actions by another.

**request note**   *n.* A permit to land goods such as perishable foods before clearing customs.

**rescue and assistance party**   *n.* The current name for what was known as the **fire and rescue party,** a detail of personnel sent from a ship or station with the necessary equipment to assist in rescue efforts, fire fighting, salvage, and so on. See DAMAGE CONTROL.

**rescue   basket**   *n.*   A   basketlike stretcher designed to lift injured or exhausted personnel from the water. Also *Stokes litter.*

**rescue boat**   *n.* A lifeboat, especially on passenger liners, rigged out ready to be lowered away at a moment's notice in the event of an emergency such as man overboard. Also *emergency boat.*

**rescue chamber**   *n.* A bell that can be lowered to a stricken submarine and attached to its escape hatch with a watertight seal, so that personnel from the submarine can be carried. It can be returned to the surface.

**reserve buoyancy**   *n.* The watertight volume of a vessel above the designed waterline, often expressed as a percentage of the vessel's total volume; it is the measure of the additional weight that could be loaded on a vessel before it would sink.

**reserve fleet** *n.* Inactive ships maintained as the U.S. Naval Ship Maintenance Facility, known more popularly as the **mothball fleet.**

**Reserve Officer Candidate program (ROC)** *n.* A program in selected colleges by which students may take summer courses to be commissioned as reserve ensigns in the U.S. Navy. See RESERVE OFFICER TRAINING CORPS.

**Reserve Officer Training Corps (ROTC)** *n.* U.S. Navy program for officer trainees (midshipmen) offered at selected colleges and universities under which the students take Naval training to be commissioned in the Navy or Marine Corps and ordered to active duty upon successful completion of their degree program. The training program is far more comprehensive than the ROC program, offers greater benefits, and requires longer obligated service.

**reset** *adj.* Used to describe a floating aid to navigation previously reported off station, adrift, or missing, returned to its assigned position. See REPLACED.

**residual errors** *n.* Those errors that remain in a magnetic compass on the various headings after it has been compensated.

**residual deviation** *n.* The deviation remaining after the compass adjustments have been made. Residual deviation is usually recorded at 15° intervals through the 360° of the compass on a deviation card. See NAPIER DIAGRAM.

**residuary resistance** *n.* In calculating speed and power, the residuary resistance is the towrope resistance minus the frictional resistance. It is considered to be made up of wave-making and eddy-

making resistance. Residuary resistance is significant in ship design in determining the size of engines needed to produce the required power for the anticipated occupation.

**residue cargo** *n.* Goods shown on a ship's manifest to be destined for a port other than the port at which the ship first arrives.

**resolution in bearing** *n.* The capability of a radar installation to separate the bearings of two echoes that are close together. The proximity to each other of two echoes that can be distinguished determines the resolution in bearing.

**resolving power** *n.* The degree to which an optical device can distinguish objects close together.

**respondentia** *n.* A loan obtained by the master of a vessel secured against the ship's cargo, to be repaid if the goods arrive; if the cargo is lost, the borrower is exonerated and does not have to repay. See BOTTOMRY.

**restraint of princes** *n.* An expression used in bills of lading to limit a shipowner's liability in case a ship is detained by government authority against the owner's will. It covers belligerent acts by countries other than that of the vessel's owners. The term dates from 1480 in English law.

**restrict** *v.* To restrain a person while on board a military or naval ship or station. A person may be restricted either for misconduct or for illness.

**restricted area** *n.* An ocean area with special restrictions to prevent interference by friendly forces; these include ammunition dumps, blind bombing ranges, submarine havens, and so on.

**restricted visibility** *n.* A term used in the *Navigation Rules* that means any condition in which visibility is reduced because of rain, fog, dust, sandstorm, snow, mist, or any other phenomenon.

**retard of the tide**   *n.* The time that elapses between the passage of the Moon and the tide that results from the Moon's passage. Also *age of the tide.*

**retract**   *v.* An amphibious operations term for backing off a beach.

**retreat**   *n.* A call by boatswain's pipe at evening colors or for personnel to fall out from a formation after inspection or other similar assembly.

**return**   *n.* (1) A signal that is reflected or returned by a target to a radar antenna. (2) An ambiguous object on the plan position indicator of the radar. "We have a return at 272°, 2,500 yards, but it's not solid."

**return trade winds**   *n.* The upper air currents that flow from the equatorial regions toward the poles. Also *antitrades.*

**revenue ton**   *n.* A unit of cargo in the United States that varies from port to port as well as company to company. All U.S. ships show it on their manifests and often show the weight of the cargo in long tons.

**reverse**   *adj.* Opposite to the normal configuration. A reverse transom slopes forward.

**reverse frame**   *n.* Angle iron or other stiffener riveted to the inner edge of a transverse frame.

**reverse tiller**   *n.* A tiller that extends aft of the rudder instead of forward of it. The reverse tiller is rarely found on small boats, but it is a routine engineering solution to space considerations on larger vessels, and designed so that the helmsman's tiller (or wheel) works in the same manner as it would with the tiller forward of the rudder post.

**reversible propeller**   *n.* A propeller with each of the blades mounted on a

pivot so that it can be rotated along its length sufficiently to change the direction of the propeller and thus the vessel. The pitch of the propeller is changed to reverse the direction of propulsion, instead of reversing the direction of the engine shaft. The use of reversible propellers allows a ship's engines to be run at greatest efficiency.

**reversible winch**   *n.* A winch that can be powered in both directions instead of using power to raise the cargo or anchor and gravity to lower the object.

**reversing current**   *n.* A tidal current usually in a restricted channel where the current floods in one direction and ebbs in the opposite direction.

**reversing falls**   *n.* The name of waterfalls that alternately flow in different directions with the ebb and flood of the tides. Such a phenomenon occurs in the St. Johns River, New Brunswick, Canada, where the high water of the Bay of Fundy floods up the narrow river channel and then reverses course with the slack water.

**revolution counter**   *n.* A device that counts shaft revolutions, especially propeller shaft revolutions. Also *shaft tachometer.*

**revolution table**   *n.* A list giving the various speeds that can be expected at various listed shaft revolution indications.

**revolution telegraph**   *n.* The mechanical signaling device between engine room and bridge for signaling the number of turns (revolutions) desired.

**revolving light**   *n.* A coastal light that appears and disappears at given intervals. The light is fixed and a screen revolves around it. The term was discontinued in 1930. They are also found at airfields where they are called **aerobeacons.** See ROTATING LIGHT.

**revolving storm**   *n.* A cyclone.

**rho-rho mode**   *n.* That method of electronic navigation in which the times for the signals to travel from each transmitting station to the receiver are measured. Each time (or range) measurement provides a circular line of position. Also *ranging mode.*

**rhumb**   *n.* (1) The line on a chart followed by a vessel proceeding on a single heading. (2) A wind blowing continuously in one direction. (3) Any one of the 32 principal points of the compass. (4) The angular distance between two successive points of the compass. (5) One of the 15° sectors of a compass printed on compass cards that are graduated into 360°.

**rhumb line**   *n.* A course with a constant true direction and that makes the same angle with all meridians. On a Mercator projection chart, a rhumb line is represented by a straight line. Unless a ship is traveling along the equator or a meridian, which are great circles, it would be going out of its way to follow the rhumb line instead of a great circle route if it were going a significant distance. **Rhumb line sailing** is sailing along a rhumb line.

**ria**   *n.* A flooded river valley or a bay into which several rivers flow; an especially favorable place to establish a port.

**rib**   *n.* Frame of a vessel.

**ribband**   *n.* A wooden batten running fore and aft used temporarily to align transverse frames or ribs while exterior plating or planking is put in place. **Ribband carvel planking** is a method of hull construction using carvel planking on the outer skin with the addition of permanent inside battens (ribbands) covering the seams. See BLUE RIBAND.

**ribband nail**   *n.* A nail with a ring at the head designed to be used without splitting the temporary ribband or from being pulled through it.

**ribbing**   *n.* The arrangement of ribs in a vessel.

**ride**   *v.* (1) To rest on the water; a ship is said to ride at anchor. (2) To be aboard a vessel at sea: "The fleet commodore is riding (in) *Mudfish.*" (3) To ride over, said of a rope when it overrides another, causing a jam.

**ride athwart**   *phr.* To ride at anchor broadside to the wind while a more dominant tidal current controls the vessel's heading.

**ride down the rigging**   *phr.* To tar the shrouds and stays working one's way down in a boatswain's chair.

**ride out**   *v.* To go through a storm reasonably well managed either at anchor or at sea. "We decided to ride out the storm under bare poles at sea rather than risk going into port."

**rider**   *n.* (1) A wooden ship construction term for a doubling timber bolted to the frame timbers. (2) A temporary support to a damaged ship, used between the keelson and the beams that support the orlop deck. (3) An extra weight lowered down an anchor chain to increase the anchor's holding power. See KELLET. (4) The upper tier of casks stowed in a ship's hold.

**rider frame**   *n.* A frame fastened to another as a stiffener.

**rider keelson**   *n.* A timber placed on the main keelson; such a member gives additional longitudinal strength and is used in large wood boats. Also *false keelson.*

**rider plates**   *n.* Bed plates at the top of the center keelson for the pillars to rest on.

**riders**   *n.* The top layer of barrels stowed in a ship's hold.

**ride to hawse**   *phr.* To ride with two bow anchors down.

**ridge**   *n.* (1) A wall of first-year ice piled randomly in the form of long walls or ridges, in a process called **ridging.** (2) A narrow extension of a high-pressure area. The opposite is called a trough.

**ridge rope**   *n.* (1) A rope above each side of a bowsprit that provides a handhold for men working the headsails. (2) The name sometimes applied to a safety line along the side of a small boat. (3) The center wire or rope of an awning, similar to the ridgepole of a roof. The **ridge tackle** is the tackle used to suspend an awning in the middle.

**riding anchor**   *n.* The anchor taking the main strain when two bow anchors are used.

**riding bitts**   *n.* Heavy bitts around which the anchor cable was given several turns to check the anchor.

**riding boom**   *n.* A hinged spar permanently fastened to the ship's hull. When the vessel is at anchor, the spar is lowered to a horizontal position and maintained with guys, used for the ship's boats to tie up. See BOAT BOOM.

**riding chain**   *n.* The chain to which a ship is secured at a permanent mooring.

**riding chock**   *n.* A deck chock at the bow or stern in which an anchor line rides.

**riding lights**   *n.* Name formerly used for lights required while riding at anchor (as opposed to running lights). Neither term is used in the *Navigation Rules,* anchor light having in general replaced **riding light.**

**riding sail**   *n.* A small sail carried on the mainmast while riding at anchor to keep the head into the wind and reduce roll. See TRYSAIL.

**riding stopper**   *n.* A mechanical device used to hold the anchor cable while a vessel is at anchor. These are used only on larger vessels to relieve the strain on the windlass; smaller boats are able to simply cleat the anchor line on a bow cleat.

**riding turn**   *n.* An accidental override of a rope or wire around a warping capstan.

**riffle**   *n.* The small rips caused by current or underlying obstructions.

**rig**   *n.* The arrangement of sails, spars, and masts that identify the type of sailing vessel regardless of hull design. Vessels can be either square-rigged—that is, with sails that are set perpendicular to the centerline of the vessel—or fore-and-aft rigged, that is with sails set parallel to and along the centerline. Square-rigged vessels dominated the world's ocean trade routes from about the 15th century to the 19th century, while the simpler and handier fore-and-aft rig prevailed in coastwise and river trade until the age of steam. The primary fore-and-aft rig vessels are the sloop, ketch, yawl, and schooner, all of Western origin, as well as various lateen rigs found in the Middle East and junk rigs in the Orient. The main square-rigged types are the brig, bark, and full-rigged ship. There are also many hybrid types, such as the brigantine and square-topsail schooner.

**rig**   *v.* (1) To devise or engineer shrouds, stays, braces, and various cargo-handling gear to fit them to their masts, booms, yards, or spars. (2) To prepare a vessel for a particular event such as heavy weather, visitors, or towing.

**rigged oar**   *n.* A steering or sculling oar in an oarlock or becket on the transom.

**riggers**   *n.* The shipyard crew who set in place the structural members such as

# Sailing Vessel Rigs

ketch (two masts)

cutter (one mast)

yawl (two masts)

catboat (one mast)

staysail schooner
(two to four masts)

Marconi rigged sloop (one mast)

gaff-rigged sloop (one mast)

gaff-topsail schooner
(two to seven masts)

barkentine (three or four masts)

square-topsail schooner
(two to five masts)

bark (three to five masts)

brig (two masts)

full-rigged ship (three to five masts)

brigantine (two masts)

masts, sternposts, and other heavy components that need special equipment for raising and lowering.

**rigging**  *n.* General term applied to all lines used to support masts, extend sails, or reduce sails. Shrouds and stays and even ratlines are generally considered rigging. See RUNNING RIGGING; STANDING RIGGING.

**rigging batten**  *n.* A rounded strip of wood seized in the running rigging along a stay or shroud to protect it from chafing against other gear.

**rigging loft**  *n.* A large shop where rigging is fitted and repaired.

**rigging luff**  *n.* A purchase used on lower rigging and stays; it consists of two double blocks and two single blocks. Sometimes called a **luff purchase.**

**rigging screw**  *n.* (1) A clamp designed to force the parts of a wire rope together to be spliced. (2) A turnbuckle, British usage.

**right**  *v.* To return a vessel to an upright position on an even keel. "The small boat righted herself quickly after nearly capsizing."

**right ascension**  *n.* The angular distance east of the vernal equinox; the arc of the celestial equator or angle at the celestial pole, between the hour circle of the vernal equinox and the hour circle of a point on the celestial sphere measured eastward from the hour circle of the vernal equinox through 24 hours. The angular distance measured west of the vernal equinox through 360° is the sidereal hour angle.

**right astern**  *adj.* In a place astern that is on a line with the vessel's centerline; dead astern.

**right bank**  *n.* The bank of a river that is on the right-hand side of an observer facing downstream. The U.S. Coast Guard and the U.S. Army Corps of Engineers use the phase **right descending bank** to avoid confusion.

**right-handed**  *adj.* Yarn, strands, or rope twisted from left to right or "with the Sun," so that the helical lines move upward from left to right. See LAY.

**right-hand lay**  *n.* Rope with the wire or fiber strands twisted to the right as you look at the rope or wire from the coil. See ROPE.

**right-hand propeller**  *n.* A propeller that propels the vessel forward with the blades going clockwise when observed by someone facing the propeller from behind the ship. Also *right-hand screw.*

**righting arm**  *n.* The distance between the line of force through the center of buoyancy (B), and the line of force through the center of gravity of a vessel (and its cargo) (G), assuming positive stability. See STABILITY.

**righting couple**  *n.* The combination of the opposing forces of gravity and buoyancy that tend to return a ship to an even keel when heeled to either side. See STABILITY.

**righting lever**  *n.* The product of the transverse metacentric height and the sine of the angle of the ship's inclination at a given time or position. Abbreviated GZ. See STABILITY.

**righting moment**  *n.* The force on a vessel that tends to move it back to the vertical position when heeled. See STABILITY.

**right of angary**  *n.* A government's right to seize, force into its service, or destroy the vessel or goods of a neutral as long as the owner is properly compensated. It is a right that is well established in international law. From Latin *angariare,* to force into service.

**right of approach**   *n.* The right of a warship to approach a merchant vessel closely enough to determine its nationality. Under such circumstances, the merchant vessel is not required by international law to heave to.

**right of convoy**   *n.* The right of neutral merchant ships led by a warship of their own nationality to be allowed by a ship of a belligerent to proceed without being inconvenienced, provided the warship commander asserts that none of the ships has contraband aboard. The right of convoy was never widely accepted and was flatly rejected by Great Britain.

**right of fishery**   *n.* The right to fish on the high seas was long accepted as a right of all nations, while the right of fishery within territorial waters was vested exclusively in the subjects of that country. Laws and regulations of a particular country, concerning fees, quotas, and seasons were the province of that country. These rights are being seriously challenged today by those who seek to protect certain species from overfishing or extinction, especially whales, sea turtles, and dolphins.

**right of innocent passage**   *n.* The right by which foreign ships may pass through another nation's territorial sea and not prejudice the peace, good order, or security of the coastal state. Submerged submarines are excluded from the right of innocent passage.

**right of mooring**   *n.* The right to anchor or moor in certain waters. This includes anchoring and the use of fixed moorings in the foreshore, and is considered incidental to the right of navigation. Lighters and tenders are considered under special rules.

**right of navigation**   *n.* The common right by which all vessels regardless of nationality may navigate on the high seas and, except during war, in territorial waters. This right extends only to navigation and does not include the right to land, embark, or disembark except at authorized places under local customs authorities and regulations. Local vessels such as lighters and tenders are generally excluded from the right of navigation and are considered under special rules.

**right of pursuit**   *n.* The right of any nation with a coastline to have its warships pursue and seize on the open sea any vessel that has violated the law of that country within its territorial limits. It is under this right that the U.S. Coast Guard is able to return vessels involved in drug smuggling to port for hearings and possible arrests.

**right of search**   *n.* Under admiralty law, the right of a commissioned vessel of a belligerent state to stop a neutral merchantman on the high seas and examine and search it, provided the examination of the ship's documents provide reasonable reason for suspicion of fraud. In practice, this right has eroded over the years, and many neutral ships have been searched by belligerent warships.

**right of seizure**   *n.* Under international law, the right of local and national government authorities to seize and take possession of a vessel in territorial waters for failure to observe local revenue laws, trade laws, and navigation rules.

**right of transit passage**   *n.* The right by which foreign ships may pass through straits for navigation between one part of the high seas or an exclusive economic zone (EEZ) and another. This right is similar to the right of navigation and includes submerged submarines, which are excluded in the right of innocent passage.

**right of visit and search**   *n.* In international law, the right of a nation's armed vessels in time of war to stop a merchant vessel to ascertain its nationality, cargo and employment.

**right of visitation**    *n.* The right of a belligerent vessel on the high seas to stop and visit a neutral merchant vessel to determine if that vessel is attempting to break a blockade, carrying contraband, carrying out an unneutral act, and so on. If the visited vessel is found to not be neutral, it can be seized by the belligerent. In time of peace, a warship only has the right of visitation when there exists reasonable suspicion of piracy. Also *right of visit, search, and seizure.*

**right of way**    *n.* (1) The order of precedence among meeting, overtaking, or crossing vessels on inland waters and in international waters. The proper order is set forth in the *Navigation Rules.* (2) The obligation of one vessel (the stand-on vessel) to proceed in front of another (the give-way vessel); such a vessel is said to have the right-of-way. The *Navigation Rules* now use the term stand-on vessel in place of privileged vessel, though the other earlier phrase is still heard along the waterfront.

**right rudder**    *n.* The command to turn the wheel (and hence the ship's heading) to the right. The amount of rudder is part of the command: "Right twenty degrees rudder."

**right semicircle**    See DANGEROUS SEMICIRCLE; NAVIGABLE SEMICIRCLE.

**rig in**    *phr.* To stow an item that has been rigged out, such as a boat boom.

**rigol**    *n.* (pron. rigohl) (1) A curved hood over a porthole to sluice water around the opening. Also *eyebrow; wriggle.* (2) A waterway or groove (obsolete).

**rig out**    *v.* To move something to its outboard position such as an accommodation ladder, a boat boom, or a cargo boom.

**rime**    *v.* To enlarge a grommet or a cringle by forcing or stretching it with fid or **rimer.** A hardwood, three-legged stool,

a **riming stool,** with holes of various sizes, is used by sailors engaged in riming. The fid or riming tool is forced through the grommet or cringle and through the hole of appropriate size in the stool.

**ring**    *n.* The ring on an anchor to which the cable is attached. See ANCHOR.

**ring bolt**    *n.* An eyebolt fitted with a ring through its eye and used on the bow and stern of a small boat for towing purposes.

**ring buoy**    *n.* A circular personal flotation device made from cork or unicellular plastic foam, often seen on sailboats.

**ring rope**    *n.* The rope bent on the ring of an anchor that is used to haul up the ring after the anchor has been catted.

**ringtail**    n. (1) Extra sail sewn on the luff of a fore-and-aft triangular sail, and extended by a **ringtail boom,** to catch more wind. (2) Also **ringsail.** The sail on self-steering gear.

**rip**    *n.* Short, steep waves found where two tidal currents meet.

**riparian**    *n.* or *adj.* The bank of a river, ocean, or other natural course of water. From the Latin *riparius,* a riverbank.

**riparian right**    *n.* The right of one who owns riparian land to control fishing, landing a boat, or other activities on his or her riparian.

**rip current**    *n.* A strong surface current flowing briefly out from shore. It results from agitated water piling up on shore and returning seaward. This is the proper term for the frequently heard rip tide.

**ripple**    *n.* Wavelets produced by a breeze of less than 2 knots.

**riprap**    *n.* Loose assemblage of stone and broken masonry that forms a base or protective shield for a seawall, lighthouse, or other structure that is occasionally buffeted by the sea.

**rip tide**   See RIP CURRENT.

**rise**   *v.* Of a celestial body, to cross the visible horizon while ascending.

**rise of tide**   *n.* The vertical distance from a chart sounding datum to a higher water datum. The mean rise of tide is the height of mean high water above the chart sounding datum. See RANGE OF TIDE.

**riser**   *n.* (1) A vertical pipe such as a fire main that rises from a larger pipe. (2) Longitudinal plank fastened to the gunwale of a small boat to support a thwart. (3) A heavy strake of bottom planking adjacent to the garboard *strake.* (4) A longitudinal bearing member that supports a deck.

**rising**   *n.* A side support for a thwart in a small boat.

**rising floors**   *n.* Floor frames that rise above the midship floors fore and aft.

**rising tide**   *n.* A tide in which the depth of water is increasing. The opposite is a falling tide. See EBB; FLOOD.

**risk of craft**   *n.* Marine underwriter's clause that waives or accepts risk incurred by goods during transportation by lighter to the side of a moored vessel.

**river buoy**   *n.* A light-weight nun or can buoy designed to withstand strong currents, sometimes fitted with skegs to prevent rotation.

**river estuary**   *n.* The lower reaches and mouth of a river emptying directly into the sea where tidal mixing takes place.

**river ice**   *n.* Ice formed in a river, regardless of where it is later found.

**rivet**   *n.* A short, round metal fastener used to connect two or more members together by clinching after being heated red hot or driven cold.

**roach**   *n.* (1) The inside curve of a sail, although the word is rarely applied to any but the mainsail. See ROUND. (2) More recently, roach has come to mean the extension of the leech of a mainsail that necessitates the use of battens in performance sails. The outside curve (or camber) is called the **draft.** See MARCONI RIG.

**roadstead** or **road**   *n.* An established anchorage that is more exposed than a harbor or marina. Frequently a roadstead is partially protected by shoals or rocks. Examples are Hampton Roads, Va., and Bolivar Roads, Tex.

**roadster**   *n.* A vessel lying at anchor in a roadstead.

**Roaring Forties**   *n.* The latitudes between 40°S and 50°S where the west wind blows strong and steady year-round. With little interference from landmasses, the winds blow strong enough to roar in the rigging, especially as vessels close 50°S latitude. **Brave west winds,** a term rarely heard since the days of commercial sail, was the equivalent of the Roaring Forties in the Northern Hemisphere. See WIND.

**roband**   *n.* (1) Small stuff, short bits of Manila or spun yarn, used for securing the luff of a fore-and-aft sail to the hanks. (2) Short bits of line used for fastening the head of a square sail to the jackstay. (3) Line used to secure the head of a gaffsail to the gaff when fitted with a jackstay. Also *nettles; rope-bands.*

**roband hitch**   *n.* A knot used for binding squared sails directly to the yard or backstay.

**rock awash**   *n.* A chart term for a rock that becomes exposed, or nearly so, between mean high water and chart sounding datum. On Great Lakes charts, the rock awash symbol is used for rocks that are awash, or nearly so, at low-water datum.

**rocket**   *n.* A self-propelled distress signal.

**rocket apparatus** *n.* Lifesaving equipment that fires a rocket carrying a **rocket line** to a person in the water or to another ship.

**rocket ship (LSMR)**   *n.* An amphibious landing ship in the U.S. Navy used for support of the assault waves during a landing and capable of rapid rocket firing.

**rocking shackle**   *n.* Shackle used on mooring buoys onto which a ship's cable is bent for rapid release, similar to a pelican hook.

**rocks and shoals**   *n.* Sailor's term for the excerpts from the *Uniform Code of Military Justice* that are periodically read to a ship's crew to keep them reminded of those parts of the *Code* that are especially pertinent to discipline and punishment.

**rode**   *n.* The line used on anchors on small boats. Early usage referred to the anchor cable for the coasting fishing schooners of New England. Also *roding.*

**rod fender**   *n.* A fender made from canes or rods once seen on piers and wharfs. Also *faggot fenders.*

**rodmeter**   See PITOMETER LOG.

**rod rigging**   *n.* Standing rigging that uses steel rods instead of flexible and more easily stretched wire rope.

**roger**   *interj.* The voice message word meaning "I have received your transmission, and it is understood." A holdover from the phonetic alphabet used in the 1940s and 1950s (the word for "R" is now Romeo), it is still used extensively. See WILCO.

**rogue's yarn**   *n.* A colored yarn twisted into rope to make it possible to identify its manufacturer or owner. Some navies and other large users of rope specify that the manufacturer twist a certain color in all their cordage. When a rogue steals a piece of the rope, there is evidence of where he got it.

**roll**   *v.* (1) Said of a vessel that oscillates from side to side along its centerline at sea. (2) The sea itself is also said to roll: "Roll on thou deep and dark blue ocean—roll!/Ten thousand fleets sweep over thee in vain." *Childe Harold's Pilgrimage,* Lord Byron.

**roll**   *n.* Motion of a vessel about its longitudinal axis. One of the six principal motions of a vessel.

**roller**   *n.* A long ocean swell that breaks or nearly breaks.

**roller chock**   *n.* (1) A chock fitted with one or more horizontal rollers to permit lines to ride in it with less chafing. (2) A chock with one or more vertical rollers used for mooring to prevent chafing. See ROLLING CHOCKS.

**roller furling**   *n.* A system of furling a sail by rolling it on a rotating head stay (jib) or into a mast (mainsail), when it is not needed. See ROLLER REEFING.

**roller reefing**   *n.* Mechanism found on many modern sailing vessels that makes it possible to roll the main boom at the gooseneck to shorten sail. See ROLLER FURLING.

**roller sheave**   *n.* Early name used for the sheave of a block when fitted with a metal bushing and rollers or ball bearings. It was also called a **patent** sheave.

**rolling caisson**   *n.* A caisson that moves on a track on rollers; the weight of the caisson is always kept greater than its displacement so that it can be used for work on hulls below the waterline.

**rolling chocks**  *n.* (1) A support for boilers and engine room equipment. (2) A wooden piece fastened to the middle of an upper yard and secured by a parrel to steady the yard. (3) A bilge keel. See ROLLER CHOCK.

**rolling hitch**  *n.* A hitch consisting of two round turns around a spar, piling, or line, with a half-hitch taken around the standing part; most often used for securing a rope to a spar when a knot that will not slip is needed.

**rolling swell**  *n.* Long, high waves with deep troughs.

**rolling tackle**  *n.* A purchase fastened to the windward part of a yard to steady the sail to leeward in heavy weather.

**roll on/roll off (ro/ro)**  *n.* A vessel designed to carry vehicles that can be driven aboard via loading ramps. (2) A system of loading cargo into land vehicles to be driven aboard ship at the port of origin and driven off at the destination. Automobiles themselves are so handled in ports equipped for ro/ro handling.

**Romeo**  *n.* The phonetic word for the letter "R." As a single-letter signal, it means "I have received your last signal." See ROGER.

**room to swing a cat**  *phr.* Old seafaring phrase, referring to the room to swing a cat-o'-nine-tails, a type of whip used in the days of sail. If there is not room to swing a cat, the space is very small.

**rooster tail**  *n.* High arch of water thrown up behind a fast-moving motorboat.

**rope**  *n.* Cordage over 1 inch in circumference. (When smaller than 1 inch, cordage is usually referred to as line, twine, or small stuff.) Rope is made of strands made up of yarns. Ropes on ships

generally have names according to their use, such as boltrope, buoy rope, breastrope, davit rope, wheel rope, bell rope, and so on. Some of the most specious and arbitrary writing has arisen over the use of the word "rope" on seagoing vessels. Some writers flatly declare that when cordage comes aboard a vessel it is line unless it is specifically named, as with boltrope; but this bit of mystique was unheard of a hundred years or so ago.

**rope**  *v.* To sew a boltrope into a sail or awning.

**rope clamp**  *n.* Clamps used to create a bight in wire rope.

**rope fender**  *n.* A fender fashioned from pieces of old rope usually plaited together, with the worst pieces being used as filler.

**rope ladder**  *n.* A ladder made with rigid rungs such as wood or steel but held together with rope; used for boarding ships from pilot boats and other such purposes. See JACOB'S LADDER.

**rope-yarn**  *n.* A single thread or yarn made from fibers loosely twisted together. Rope-yarns twisted together make up a strand, and strands twisted together make up rope.

**rope-yarn Sunday**  *n.* Time allowed at sea for the crew to work on personal matters such as repairs to clothing. Rope-yarn Sunday is usually Wednesday afternoon, if no work is scheduled. In port, rope-yarn Sunday is an afternoon when liberty is granted. Rope-yarn Sunday is always during the week and is not so called on Saturdays and Sundays. See MAKE AND MEND.

**ro/ro**  See RHO-RHO MODE; ROLL ON/ROLL OFF; SHIP.

**rose seizing (or lashing)**  *n.* A system for securing blocks or stays to a spar. Eye-splices are lashed with racking turns, and the ends are finished off by being alternately passed over and under each part.

**Rossel Current**  *n.* A weak northern branch of the South Equatorial Current that continues toward the west and northwest along both the southern and northeastern coasts of New Guinea and Australia during the Northern Hemisphere summer. Also *Australia Current.*

**rotary pump**  *n.* These include gear or screw pumps.

**rotary tidal current**  *n.* An offshore current in which the direction of flow under tidal influence is not restricted by landmasses. The flow is continuous, and the direction changes through all points of the compass. The rotation of directional change is clockwise in the Northern Hemisphere and counterclockwise in the Southern Hemisphere.

**rotating direction finder**  *n.* A radio direction finder fitted with a loop antenna that can be rotated to take bearings. See RADIO DIRECTION FINDER.

**rotating light**  *n.* A lighted aid to navigation with one or more electrically powered beams that rotate. Also *revolving light.*

**rotten clause**  *n.* Marine underwriting term that waives the underwriter's obligation if a vessel is found unseaworthy by reason of rot.

**rotten ice**  *n.* Ice that has had time for the brine to settle out and cause the ice to honeycomb. Such ice readily disintegrates as soon as it is exposed to warmer air and water.

**rotten stops**  *n.* Low-grade or rotten small stuff that is used to hold a sail together while it is hauled aloft in stops. One purpose of using such material is that the sail can easily be shaken free.

**rough sea**  *n.* Douglas scale reading of 4, indicating disturbed waves between 5 and 9 feet with a moderate swell.

**round**  *n.* The outward curve of the leech or foot of a sail. See ROACH.

**round**  *v.* To get around or simply to get past; to round Cape Hatteras means to have successfully passed it and changed heading appropriately.

**roundabout**  *n.* A routing measure used, for example, in crowded harbors, and consisting of a separation point or circular separation zone and a circular traffic lane within defined limits. Traffic within the roundabout proceeds in a counterclockwise direction around the separation point or zone.

**roundhouse**  *n.* (1) A square deckhouse at the after end of a quarterdeck, and of which the poop deck forms the overhead. (2) An enclosure for a privy at the forward end of the upper deck. (3) In sailing ships, deckhouse that accommodates petty officers and apprentices, and located near the stern.

**round in**  *v.* To haul in on a weather brace.

**rounding**  *n.* (1) Old ropes tightly wound around the part of an anchor cable that lies in the hawse or athwart the stem. (2) A rope that is wrapped around another rope or spar.

**rounding tack**  *n.* A tack that takes a racing boat around a mark.

**roundline**  *n.* Three-strand, right-hand small stuff used for seizing and in serving.

**roundly**  *adv.* Quickly and efficiently. "Haul in the lifeboats roundly so that we can get under way as soon as possible."

**round of sights (or bearings)**  *n.* Navigation sights taken over several minutes requiring adjustment for the advance of the vessel to obtain an accurate fix.

**round seizing**  *n.* A seizing either for two ropes or two parts of a rope held together to form an eye and thimble. See FLAT SEIZING.

**round splice**  See SAILMAKER'S SPLICE.

**round to**  *v.* To come up into the wind.

**round turn**  *n.* (1) The situation that exists when a ship has two anchor cables out and swings so as to twist them around each other. (2) A turn taken completely around an object such as a piling or spar to prevent a rope from slipping temporarily. A round turn and two half hitches are often used to secure a line to a spar or railing. (3) U.S. Navy slang for a reprimand. (4) To turn a vessel through 360°.

**round up**  *v.* (1) A sailing term that means to come up into the wind, intentionally or unintentionally. A little weather helm is preferable to a lee helm because, in case of an emergency at the tiller, the vessel will "round up" into the wind instead of falling off and jibing. One rounds up to slow a vessel that is going too fast or to pick up a mooring. (2) To pull in the slack of any line that passes through a block; usually applied to tackle as in to "round up the main tackle."

**rouse (or rowse)**  *v.* (1) To manhandle a cable or tackle without a capstan or windlass. "Rouse hearty, men." (2) To awaken the crew and get them on their duty stations. (3) To break out gear such as mooring lines.

**route chart**  *n.* A marine chart showing routes between various ports and usually the distances involved. See PILOT CHARTS.

**routing**  *n.* (1) Scheduled path for a message to be delivered and initialed. (2) A scheduled path for a vessel to follow for best sea conditions. (3) A plan of movement.

**rove**  See REEVE.

**rover**  *n.* A pirate or sea robber. From the Dutch *rover,* robber.

**roving**  *n.* The coarse glass cloth used in Fiberglas construction. It is not the same as mat, which is felt material, or cloth, which is a closely woven material.

**row**  *v.* To propel by oars.

**rowlocks**  *n.* The forked device in which oars are placed for rowing. Also *oarlock.* See THOLE PIN.

**rowser chock**  See CLOSED CHOCK.

**royal fish**  *n.* Sturgeons, whales, and porpoises cast on the shore of Great Britain or caught within the realm; so called because they are the property of the Crown.

**royal mast**  *n.* The fourth section of a wooden mast.

**royal sail**  *n.* A square sail set above a topgallant. See SQUARE-RIGGED VESSEL.

**rub back**  *n.* The interval between the tack of a mainsail and the sail track.

**rubber**  *n.* A device used by sailmakers to flatten the seams of a sail to protect them from being chafed or rubbed.

**rubbing bar**  *n.* A plate fastened to the bottom of a keel to give protection when docking and going aground. Also *shoe.*

**rubbing paunch.**  See PAUNCH.

**rubbing strake**  *n.* A protective stiffener running longitudinally a short distance above the waterline on ships' hulls, or a half-round molding on the outside of a gunwale on small boats, to protect them against damage from quays, piles, and other ships with which they may be moored. Also *rubber*.

**rubbing strip**   *n.* A piece of half-round molding that runs fore-and-aft just beneath the rail to protect the ship's sides.

**rubble**   *n.* (1) Loose, hard stones found on beaches; pebbles. (2) Fragments of hard sea ice roughly spherical and up to 5 feet in diameter, resulting from the disintegration of larger ice formations. When rubble is afloat, it is called brash ice.

**rub rail**   *n.* A protective outer rail on a vessel's hull. See RUBBING STRAKE.

**rucking**   *n.* The lowering of the peak and throat halyards to bring down a gaff topsail.

**rudder**   *n.* A device mounted near the stern of a vessel to control horizontal direction. The rudder is hung vertically on the after side of the sternpost with the pintles on the rudder slipped into gudgeons on the vessel's sternpost. The function of the rudder is to direct the water beneath the vessel to one side or the other to cause the vessel's stern to go in the direction opposite to the one in which the rudder is turned, thus turning the head in the direction the rudder is turned. A right rudder turns the bow toward the right, or to starboard. A **bow rudder** is a rudder installed at the base of the stern and controlled from a position in the forepeak. See MARCONI RIG.

**rudder angle indicator**   *n.* A device located near the helmsman that tells him the position of the rudder. Also *rudder telltale*. See HELM INDICATOR.

**rudder area**   *n.* The immersed surface area of a rudder. The rudder area is customarily expressed as a fraction of the lateral plane or underwater profile of the vessel. For high-speed liners, it is as little as 1/85, while for tugs it is about 1/30.

**rudder arm**   *n.* A horizontal member welded to the rudder post that supports and strengthens the rudder blade. Also *rudder band*.

**rudder blade**   *n.* The main flat part of the entire rudder that presents the resisting surface to the medium through which the vessel is traveling.

**rudder boot**   See RUDDER COAT.

**rudder braces**   *n.* Collective term for gudgeons and pintles. Also *rudder irons*.

**rudder bracket**   *n.* A device fitted within the vessel that prevents the rudder from going into the rudder stops.

**rudder bushing**   *n.* A metal sleeve in the gudgeon into which the pintle fits.

**rudder carrier bearing**   *n.* The fitting that supports the rudder and tiller either beneath the tiller or at the point where the rudder stock goes through the hull. It both absorbs the radial thrust and supports the weight of the rudder assembly.

**rudder chain**   *n.* One of the two chains led from a vessel's quarter to a rudder horn used for emergency auxiliary steering.

**rudder chock**   *n.* A device used to hold the rudder rigid while at anchor.

**rudder coat**   *n.* A piece of canvas wrapped securely around the rudder post at the point it goes through the counter to prevent seawater from sloshing through the hole. Also *rudder boot*.

**rudder eye**   *n.* (1) The eyebolt at the top of a rudder stock. (2) A hole on the trailing edge of a rudder used for relieving tackle in emergencies. See RUDDER HORN.

**rudder hanger**   *n.* Hollow steel fitting fastened to the sternpost for shipping the rudder. See GUDGEON.

**rudder hatch**   *n.* The opening above the rudder that is raised to accommodate the rudder stock prior to unshipping the rudder.

**rudderhead**   *n.* The upper part of the rudder stock onto which the tiller or quadrant is fitted.

**rudderhead bearing**   *n.* A bearing at the rudder head at deck level to support it against tiller stress.

**rudder horn**   *n.* A forked fitting at the trailing edge of the rudder to which rudder chains are fitted when normal control is lost. See RUDDER EYE; RUDDER TACKLES.

**rudder irons**   See RUDDER BRACES.

**rudder lock**   *n.* Any of several devices used to prevent the rudder pintles from slipping out of their gudgeons.

**rudder moment**   *n.* The stress brought to bear on the rudder stock as a result of the twisting force between the tiller and the rudder blade.

**rudder pit**   *n.* The depression in the bottom of a dry dock over which the ship's rudder is placed to allow unshipping the rudder for inspection.

**rudder port**   *n.* The access to the rudder well through the plating or planking of the hull.

**rudder post**   *n.* After post of the stern frame to which the rudder is hung. Also *back post; sternpost.* See RUDDER STOCK.

**rudder quadrant**   *n.* The fitting on the rudder stock to which the rudder cables are attached to control the rudder. As one cable is hauled out to turn the quadrant, the opposing cable is reeled in to keep tension on the side that is not being hauled. The cables are wound on the same reel but in opposite directions. As the helmsman turns the wheel to starboard, for example, the rudder blade

moves to starboard; as the rudder post moves to starboard with the quadrant, the starboard cable unrolls from the reel and the port cable winds on the reel. The so-called quadrant is often more than a quarter of a circle and may even be a complete circle, but it is still called a quadrant.

**rudder stock**   *n.* The shank of the rudder that extends up through the hull to the steering engine. See RUDDER POST.

**rudder stops**   *n.* Lugs on the sternpost that prevent the rudder from going beyond the maximum.

**rudder stuffing box**   *n.* The gland at the point where the rudder post enters the vessel, which prevents water from entering the vessel.

**rudder tackles**   *n.* Temporary tackles attached directly to the rudder during a rudder emergency. See RELIEVING TACKLE.

**rudder telltale**   See RUDDER ANGLE INDICATOR.

**rudder tiller**   *n.* The bar or lever connected to the rudder stock and controlled by the steering cables and quadrant.

**rudder trunk**   *n.* The casing or sleeve that surrounds the rudder post from the point at which it enters the hull to deck level.

**rudder well**   *n.* (1) The watertight fitting through which the rudderhead works. The rudder well is the through-hull opening for the rudder stock. (2) The pit in a dry dock into which the rudder can be dropped during repairs.

**rugged**   *adj.* Rock-bound, having irregular surfaces.

**rule of good seamanship**   *n.* The name commonly given to Rule 2(a) of the *Navigation Rules:* "Nothing in these Rules shall exonerate any vessel, or the owner, master or crew thereof, from the consequences of any neglect to comply with these Rules or of the neglect of any precaution which may be required by the ordinary practice of seamen, or by the special circumstances of the case."

**rule of sixty**   *n.* As stated in Bowditch, "the offset of the plotted bearing line from the observer's actual position is 1/60th of the distance to the object observed for each degree of error." For example, if an object 10 nautical miles (60,000 feet) distant is to be avoided, by altering course 1°, you will miss it by 1,000 feet, because 60,000 feet divided by 60 equals 1,000 feet.

**rules of the road**   *n.* Regulations for the proper handling of vessels, particularly as formalized in the Convention on the International Regulations for Preventing Collisions at Sea (72 COLREGS) and adopted in the United States under the International Navigation Rules Act of 1977 and the Inland Navigation Rules Act of 1980. The rules, including regulations for steering and sailing, lights and shapes, and sound and light signals, are published by the U.S. Coast Guard in *Navigation Rules, International—Inland.*

**rummage**   *n.* A thorough search that includes disarranging cargo, usually initiated for the purpose of uncovering contraband.

**run**   *n.* (1) A course with the wind from astern. (2) A channel for water caught by a coaming to lead the water overboard. (3) The distance traveled by a craft during any given time interval or since leaving a designated place.

**run**   *v.* To sail before the wind with the wind coming from astern and the sails set nearly at right angles to the keel, as opposed to reaching or beating. "We will run to Tortola before the trade winds." See POINTS OF SAILING.

**runabout**   *n.* Small powerboat used for day fishing, recreation, or water taxi service, but not fitted for overnight use.

**run aground**   *v.* (1) To accidentally touch the seabed or riverbed. (2) To become stranded on a reef or sandbar. See also STRAND.

**run down**   *v.* (1) To sail north or south to the latitude of the next port, then east or west until the port is reached. "We ran down Savannah from Ambrose light." See PARALLEL SAILING. (2) To collide with another vessel. Also *run into.*

**run in**   *v.* To haul or bring in a line or rope. "Run in the towing hawser." See RUN OUT.

**runner**   *n.* (1) A breast backstay runner or running backstay. (2) A line bent on an eyebolt or pad eye on the deck and then rove through a single block; an eye at the opposite end of the runner is available to clap on a tackle. See TACKLE. (3) A member of a **runner crew** hired to shift a vessel from one point to another after the regular crew has been paid off. Such persons are said to be **shipped by the run.**

**runner and tackle**   *n.* Same as a luff tackle as applied to a runner. The runner is rove through a single block. See RUNNER.

**runner tackles**   *n.* (1) Runners used to set up shrouds or to get the mastheads forward for staying the masts. (2) A luff tackle on a whip. See RUNNING BACKSTAY.

**running backstay**   *n.* One of a pair of stays at the stern that helps support the mast, the lee one of which must be slacked off for each change of tack to allow the boom to swing farther forward.

**running block**   *n.* A block that is attached to an object to be moved. Running blocks are found on objects that are occasionally raised, lowered, or moved.

A **fixed block** is similar, but does not move.

**running boat** *n.* A small craft that serves as a ferry service from a ship at anchor to a shore location.

**running bowline** *n.* A bowline with the standing part rove through the bight to form a slipknot or noose. See KNOT.

**running bowsprit** *n.* A bowsprit that can be run out to set additional headsails.

**running by the lee** *phr.* Sailing with the boom on the same quarter that the wind is coming from.

**running days** *n.* A term used in defining lay days and demurrage, meaning successive days without regard for holidays, a day being from midnight to midnight. In British shipping usage, Sunday is not considered a running day.

**running down clause** See COLLISION CLAUSE.

**running fix** *n.* A vessel's position established by two lines of position obtained by observations at two different times. By advancing the first observation along the course line for the distance traveled to the second observation, you obtain a two-line fix. Running fixes can be obtained from radar ranges, celestial observations, doubling the angle, satellite, the seven-eighths rule, the seventenths rule, and table 7 in Bowditch.

**running free** *v.* Sailing with the wind abaft the beam. Under previous Rules of the Road, a vessel under sail and closehauled had the right of way over a vessel running free. The rule harkened to square riggers when a vessel running free had more control than a vessel closehauled. In fore-and-aft-rigged vessels, this is not true. In the current *Navigation Rules,* the term "running free" is not used. See CLOSE REACH; FULL AND BY.

**running large** *v.* Sailing off the wind with sheets eased.

**running lights** *n.* Lights used between sunset and sunrise by vessels while under way. Though not used in the *Navigation Rules,* the term is in common parlance and refers to those lights a vessel is required by law to have lighted when running at night. The lights required depend on the size of the vessel and other circumstances covered in the *Navigation Rules.*

**running line** *n.* An unusually long rope running from a vessel to a wharf or buoy. See GUEST WARP.

**running part** *n.* The movable or hauling part of a fall in a tackle, as opposed to the standing part.

**running rigging** *n.* Ropes and lines used to adjust sails, raise and lower spars; all rigging that is rove through blocks: halyards and sheets but not shrouds and stays. See STANDING RIGGING.

**running survey** *n.* (1) A marine survey conducted while a vessel is under way without using the standard procedures of surveying vessels. (2) A survey of a coast. A vessel that runs a blockade during wartime would make a "running survey" if the coast were not familiar to the chart makers of the vessel's country.

**running tackle** *n.* Blocks and tackle used for heavy lifting on a ship.

**run out** *v.* To send out, usually applied to warps or hawsers used in mooring: "Run out the bow line."

**run the easting down** *phr.* An expression applied to the long easterly run from the Cape of Good Hope to Australia in the Roaring Forties, used by square riggers engaged in the Australian grain trade.

**rust bucket**   *n.* Derisive term for a vessel that has been allowed to rust or generally deteriorate.

**rutter**   *n.* The name given to sailing directions published in England during the 16th and 17th centuries. The word derives from the Portuguese *roteiro* (route) by way of the French word *routiers*.

# S

**S**   See SIERRA.

**sack**   *n.* Sailor's slang for a bunk. To **sack out** or to **hit the sack** is to go to bed whether for a nap or for the night.

**sacrificial anode**   *n.* A piece of metal such as zinc or aluminum that is installed on the interior surface of a cargo tank or the exterior surface of a hull to reduce deterioration, especially of propellers and shafts, by electrochemical reaction. The reaction takes place on the anode instead of the hull or tank. They are also called **zincs** if the metal used is zinc.

**saddle**   *n.* (1) A wooden device hollowed on the sides and fastened to the bowsprit to hold the jibboom. (2) A bracket for a boom to rest in. These are used to secure booms when the booms are not in use. See PREVENTER. (3) A diverting plate beneath a coal hatch used to shunt coal to side bunkers. Also *saddleback*.

**saddle strap**   *n.* Steel plate belly bands used at the bow of a vessel for support during launching.

**saddle hatch**   *n.* A coal bunker hatch over a boiler used to divert coal to the bunkers below.

**safe conduct**   *n.* (1) A written guarantee by a belligerent that a ship will be allowed to proceed in safety on a designated voyage. (2) An escort that ensures unmolested passage. A ship or person is granted or given a safe conduct.

**safe leeward position**   *n.* A sailboat racing term for the position of a vessel on the leeward bow of another when both are close-hauled. The leeward boat is able to direct the wind to the disadvantage of the close-hauled boat on its windward quarter.

**safety angle**   *n.* The critical point in a roll beyond which a vessel's righting power ceases.

**safety certificate**   *n.* U.S. Coast Guard certification issued to passenger ships after meeting requirements stipulated by the International Convention of Safety of Life at Sea (SOLAS), to watertight subdivisions, lifesaving and firefighting equipment, lifeboat drill procedures, and so on.

**safety factor**   *n.* The ratio of the breaking strength of a piece of equipment to the expected load, representing the reserve strength. A boat hoist designed for a load of 9,000 pounds, but only allowed to lift or lower a load of 3,000 pounds is said to have a safety factor of 3 or 3 to 1. See SAFE WORKING LOAD.

**safety hook**   *n.* A hook with a hinged catch that prevents its load from slipping off the hook. Also *drop lip hook; pelican hook*.

**safety lanes**   *n.* Specified sea-lanes designed for use in transit by submarines and surface ships to prevent attack by friendly forces.

**safety pin**   *n.* The pin inserted in an anchor stock to hold the shank chain in place.

**safety track**   *n.* A track on the upper hull of a submarine running longitudinally between the forward escape hatch and the after escape hatch. The track is rigged with a runner so that a person can attach a safety harness to it and be free to move about while the submarine is surfaced.

**safe-water marks**   *n.* Midchannel marks used to indicate navigable water for countries included in IALA Region A. The United States, a Region B nation, does not use safe-water marks as such, though midchannel marks are often seen and recognized in Region B countries.

**safe working load (SWL)**   *n.* The minimum breaking load of a device or material (such as cordage) divided by an appropriate safety factor. See SAFETY FACTOR.

**sag**   *n.* The longitudinal deformation that occurs under a stress that causes the waist of a vessel to drop below the bow and stern. See HOG.

**sag**   *v.* (1) To drop or tend to drop below the bow and stern structure under stress. A vessel is said to sag when the waist deforms under stress in this manner. (2) To make leeway. "We sagged from our rhumb line and this caused us to come dangerously close to the rocky shoal."

**sagging moment**   *n.* The effect of the product of the forces that cause a vessel to sag.

**sail**   *n.* (1) A piece of quadrilateral or triangular material set on a vessel to catch the wind and cause it to move. It is generally canvas or synthetic material, but thin alloy and plastic foils are being tried. Sails are set either from a mast (with or without a boom or other spar), a yard, or a stay. In general, sails take their identifying names from the mast, stay, or spar on which they are bent, for example, mainsail or mizzen topgallant staysail. The primary exceptions are the courses, jibs, and particular types of headsails such as a genoa or spinnaker. (2) A trip or cruise on a vessel. (3) That part of a submarine above the main deck or hull, which houses the periscope supports, retractable masts, and surface conning tower.

**sail**   *v.* (1) To cause a vessel to move by use of sails, or to move by means of "sails." (2) To get under way by either sail or power. "The *Queen Elizabeth 2* will sail at 0800." (3) To move on the sea either for a livelihood or for recreation. "I sailed in tankers for thirty years before I retired."

**sail area (SA)**   *n.* (1) The total surface of a sail, usually measured in square feet or square meters. This is a significant figure in determining ratings for racing purposes. (2) The area of the surfaces above the waterline of a vessel on which the wind acts, including the hull, masts, and stacks.

**sail bag**   *n.* The sailcloth bag used to stow a sail.

**sailboat**   *n.* A vessel propelled entirely or partly by sail. The term is applied only to smaller vessels. Under the *Navigation Rules*, a boat powered by both sails and machinery at the same time must abide by the rules governing power vessels and not sailing vessels, and if over 12 meters (39.37 feet) the vessel must show the appropriate day shape or light. See SAILING VESSEL.

**sail carrying power**   *n.* The result of the following formula:

$$\frac{D \times GM}{SA \times VD}$$

where   D = displacement in tons
GM = metacentric height in feet
SA = sail area in square feet
VD = vertical distance in feet
between the center of
lateral resistance and the
center of effort

In this formula, the wind pressure is assumed to act at right angles to the lateral plane with a pressure of one pound per square foot of sail area, or a force 6 on the Beaufort scale.

**sail cloth (or sailcloth)**   *n.* Any fabric used for making sails. This was cotton (in America) or flax (in Europe) traditionally; today the fabric is more apt to be nylon, dacron, Kevlar, Mylar or other synthetic material. (2) A British term for lifeboat sail canvas in 12-, 15-, and 18-inch widths. Also *yacht canvas.*

**sail cover**   *n.* A protective cover placed over a sail furled along a boom.

**sailer**   *n.* A vessel with sails, such as day sailer or motor-sailer.

**sail ho!**   *interj.* The cry heard from the lookout when the sail of another vessel is sighted on the horizon. The watch officer properly responds with "Where away?"

**sail hook**   *n.* A metal hook used by sailmakers to keep a sail taut while being fabricated or repaired.

**sailing**   *n.* (1) The departure of a commercial vessel from a port. Sailings are often listed in local newspapers. A busy port such as New Orleans lists dozens of sailings every day. (2) Any of the methods for solving the various problems involving course, distance, difference in latitude and longitude, and departure. They are known collectively as **sailings.** They are **plane sailing, traverse sailing, spherical sailing, middle-latitude sailing, parallel sail-**ing, **Mercator sailing, rhumb line sailing, great circle sailing** and **composite sailing. Current sailing** is sometimes included.

**sailing chart**   *n.* A small-scale (large-area) chart, usually 1:600,000 or smaller, used at sea for long voyages. The shorelines are usually very general with only principal lights and other landmarks shown. The charts are used for planning, fixing positions, and dead reckoning.

**Sailing Directions**   *n.* Books printed by the Defense Mapping Agency's Hydrographic/Topographic Center that supplement charts, describe foreign coasts and harbors, and give other information of interest to commercial, naval, and pleasure vessel owners and captains. The *Directions* are similar to the *U.S. Coast Pilot.* They differ from cruising guides published by private organizations and individuals. The United States publishes eight *Sailing Directions,* one for each of the world's ocean basins: Each of these is divided into five chapters covering the countries, ocean-basin environment, warning areas, ocean routes, and Navaid systems. They also contain applicable inland or special rules of the road or *Pilot Rules* and other information not shown on charts.

**sailing free**   *v.* Sailing with the wind from the quarter or from the stern. Also *running* or *running free.*

**sailing high**   *n.* Sailing closer to the wind than the course requires. This is sometimes done in anticipation of a header.

**sailing ice**   *n.* Ice loose enough for unreinforced vessels to get through. Also *very open ice.*

**sailing master**   *n.* The officer in charge of propulsion on large sailing vessels.

**sailing on a bowline**   *phr.* Said of square-rigged ships sailing close-hauled with the bowlines leading from the windward leeches hauled in taut.

**sailing on her own bottom** *phr.* (1) Said of a vessel that has paid for itself and the mortgagee has been paid off. (2) A racing rule that states that a participating vessel must arrive by sailing and cannot be brought in by truck or other overland means or by ship or aircraft. It was a stipulation in the Deed of Gift in the America's Cup in earlier days.

**sailing punt** *n.* A pleasure boat with square bow and stern found in British parks. They are built to the same specifications: 25 feet in length with 200 square feet of sail.

**sailing rules** *n.* Racing rules agreed on by any of several yacht racing unions.

**sailing school vessel** *n.* A vessel of less than 500 gross tons carrying six or more individuals who are sailing school students or instructors, principally equipped for propulsion by sail, and owned or demise chartered and operated by a qualified state or non-profit educational organization while the vessel is being used exclusively for the purpose of sailing instruction.

**sailing thwart** *n.* A longitudinal plank on a small workboat installed to support the masts.

**sailing trim** *n.* (1) The set of a boat's sails. It is used to mean the trim, good or bad, but it is also used to mean the most efficient set of the sails. To say, "She's in sailing trim" implies the vessel is trimmed for maximum speed. "Her sailing trim needed some work" has the more general meaning. (2) The angular deviation of a vessel's waterline from the water surface. A vessel loaded or ballasted to the extent necessary to make it seaworthy; the vessel is then said to be in sailing trim. See DRAFT.

**sailing vessel** *n.* (1) A vessel that can be propelled only by sails. (2) In the *Navigation Rules,* any vessel under sail provided that propelling machinery, if fitted, is not being used. See AUXILIARY SAILING VESSEL.

**sailing whaleboat** *n.* A double-ended, heavy-duty centerboard boat previously used by the U.S. Navy, which was fitted with a jib-headed ketch rig. This was called a whaleboat because it was similar to the heavy open boats used by whalers, who preferred double-enders.

**sail large** *v.* To sail off the wind, not close-hauled. See FULL AND BY.

**sail locker** *n.* A compartment, usually forward and close to a hatch, used for the stowage of sails, awnings, cots, and other similar gear.

**sail loft** *n.* Any building in which sails, awnings, tarpaulins, canvas covers, and so on are made.

**sailmaker** *n.* The person in a loft or on a ship who is in charge of designing, making, and repairing sails. On shipboard, the sailmaker is also in charge of fabrication and care of all other canvas pieces such as awnings and sail covers. He is assisted by a sailmaker's mate and traditionally does not stand watch.

**sailmaker's bench** *n.* A long narrow bench that a sailmaker straddles while working canvas.

**sailmaker's palm** See PALM.

**sailmaker's splice** *n.* A splice used on boltropes to decrease the circumference of the usual splice. Strands are usually tucked under, but with the sailmaker's splice they follow the rope line, or contline, with the lay of the rope. Also *round splice.*

**sailmaker's whipping** *n.* A method of reinforcing reef points, cringles, and similar gear exposed to continual chafing and frapping. Such whipping is accomplished by stitching the whipping twine through the rope with a needle. For this reason it is sometimes called **palm and needle whipping.**

**sailmaking** *n.* The art and science of making sails; this includes designing, cutting, sewing, roping, tabling, and putting in linings, grommets, reef points, cringles, and holes. While sailmaking is still very much an art, this industry with highly computerized models has become a high-tech science also.

**sail needle** *n.* A special needle used in sailmaking with a triangular cross section for half the length, beginning at the point, and round for the other half. Sail needles come in various sizes. The smaller the needle, the better the stitch will hold, but with heavier sailcloth, heavier needles must be used to pierce the material and to carry the heavier yarn needed.

**sailor** *n.* A person who has gone to sea and is knowledgeable in the ways of seas and ships. The term applies to officers as well as enlisted personnel. To say that the captain is a good sailor or a "real sailor" is considered a compliment. Also *mariner.*

**sailor-monger** *v.* To kidnap members of a crew by use of alcohol and violence and to sell them to outgoing ships for financial gain; a term used in U.S. courts. See PRESS GANG.

**sailor's whipping** *n.* The whipping most commonly seen, where the end of a rope is whipped by taking a number of turns around it after which it is hauled taut and laid out. The second end is laid back along the rope that is being whipped, and additional turns are made around the end using the loop that is formed. It is ultimately tightened by hauling taut the two ends.

**sails** *n.* Nickname for the ship's sailmaker.

**sail slide** *n.* A metal or plastic device sewn to the luff of a mainsail or mizzen; sail slides ride on a track or in a groove on the mast when the sail is raised or lowered. Also *hanks.*

**sail stop** *n.* Light spun yarn used to hold sail until it was ready to be hoisted when the yarn would easily part with a little yank. Today the term is used to mean more permanent cords. Also *sail tie.* See GROMMET.

**sail tackle** *n.* Gear used to hoist sail, usually a top-burton on gaff-rigged boats.

**sail track** *n.* Any track on which a sail is raised and lowered on the mast. Sometimes the track is external, as for a sail slide, and sometimes the track is a slot in the mast into which the boltrope of the luff is fed as the sail is raised.

**sail training** *n.* The practice of giving naval and merchant marine cadets experience in sailing ships as preparation for careers at sea. The practice originated in the sailing navy, but continued even after the advent of steam because it was seen to offer a multitude of benefits. It develops physical strength, a sense of the importance of teamwork and shared responsibility, and, at the same time, strength of individual character. In addition, because sailing vessels are so labor-intensive, a large number of cadets can be taught the rudiments of seamanship such as meteorology and navigation at one time. The sail-training movement has been responsible for the survival of square riggers; virtually all those sailing at the end of the 20th century were built specifically for sail training. Although governments are generally the only institutions that can afford to build and operate the largest sailing ships, sail training in smaller vessels, chiefly schooners, is increasingly employed to similar ends by a variety of special groups, including business professionals, juvenile delinquents, the learning disabled, and, in purpose-built vessels, the physically handicapped.

**Saint Elmo's fire** *n.* A visible brush-like discharge of induced electricity, often seen during a storm from a pointed object such as a mast spreader or an airplane wing. Also *corposant.*

**Saint Hilaire method** See MARCQ ST. HILAIRE METHOD.

**salinity** *n.* The total amount of dissolved salts in seawater. It is measured in parts per thousand (ppt) of seawater. Seawater runs, as a rule, between 33 and 37 ppt.

**salinity indicator** *n.* A device found on ships with boilers to warn the engineers of salt in the freshwater feed system. Also *salinometer.*

**sally** *v.* To rush from one position to another. When a vessel becomes icebound, the crew is ordered to sally from one side to the other to rock the ship and loosen it from the ice or from the ground. The same evolution is used to determine the roll of a ship.

**sally port** *n.* A large access hatch in the side of a ship.

**salmon tail** *n.* Extension on the trailing edge of a rudder used on vessels plying confined waters to decrease the turning circle.

**saloon** *n.* Officers lounge and mess area on a merchant ship. (2) A large social room on a passenger ship. The word comes from the French *salon*, a large hall or room.

**saloon deck** *n.* On ships with only one passenger deck, the deck with passengers' quarters.

**saloon stores** *n.* Supplies sold on board to passengers.

**salt** *n.* (1) One who has years of experience on and knowledge of the ways of the sea. (2) The various salts dissolved in seawater. See SALTY.

**salter** *n.* One who salts fish in the hold of a fishing vessel after the catch has been dressed—an unsavory, low-paying job.

**salt horse** *n.* Seaman's term for salt beef in the days when it was a shipboard staple along with hardtack. See LIMEY.

**salting** *n.* The process of filling all open spaces between frame timbers in wooden vessels from the light waterline to the plank sheer with coarse salt. The moisture attracted to the salt turns it to brine, which flows down to pickle the wood and act as a preservative. **Salt stops** are thin pieces of planking with small perforations that help hold the salt in place. Underwriters add one or two years to a salted vessel's life.

**salt marsh** *n.* A flat, poorly drained coastal swamp that is flooded by high tides.

**saltwater service systems** *n.* The various saltwater systems on shipboard that provide seawater for flushing decks, fire fighting, and so on.

**salty** *adj.* Used to describe an object that reflects a nautical tradition or a person who is wise in the ways of the sea. See SALT.

**saluting ship** *n.* A vessel designated by the Secretary of the Navy as being capable of rendering full honors, including the use of a band. This is usually a large warship.

**salvage** *n.* (1) Compensation for saving a ship or its cargo from destruction. (2) The saving or rescue of a ship and its cargo for reuse, refabrication or scrapping.

**salvage** *v.* To save a ship, to save lives aboard a ship, or to save the ship's cargo from destruction.

**salvage** *adj.* Used to describe any thing or person involved in salvage work, a salvage tug, salvage team or salvage group.

**salvage contract** or **agreement**  *n.* A contract between the owner or the owner's representative such as the master of a vessel in distress and a prospective salvor. This should be a written contract signed and witnessed by both parties. The standard form is available from the Committee of Lloyds in London.

**salvage clause**  *n.* The section of a marine insurance policy that deals with any salvage charges for which the underwriters would be liable.

**salvage lien**  *n.* A lien against a vessel or its cargo when either or both come into the possession of a salvor who has saved them from destruction at sea. All such services carry a well-established lien under international law.

**salvage loss**  *n.* A loss that is presumed to have been a total loss except for the salvage service rendered. **Salvage charges** are the charges for **salvage service.** The salvage losses are those that result from a shipwreck or the perils of the sea that preclude the vessel's proceeding on its voyage; the cargo from the salvaged vessel must be sold short of the destination. The insurance underwriters must be satisfied that the sale was to their benefit and that it would not have been to their benefit to forward the cargo to its destination. The underwriters then pay the difference between the price received and what would have been received at the final destination. The settlement is the salvage loss.

**salvage master**  See WRECK MASTER.

**salvage money**  *n.* Bonus divided by the crew of a vessel that has salvaged another and delivered it into the hands of authorities.

**salvaging**  *n.* The process of raising, refloating, and recovering shipwrecked vessels and their cargoes.

**salvo**  *n.* A pattern of shots fired simultaneously by the same battery at the same target.

**sampan**  *n.* Malay and Japanese word applied to various small, open workboats found in China and Southeast Asia.

**samson line**  *n.* Light line made from two- or three-strand hemp and manufactured in coils of 30 fathoms. When tarred, it is used for heavy seizings and service; untarred, it is used for lacings and signal halyards.

**samson post**  *n.* (1) A short mast or spar that supports auxiliary cargo booms; a king post. (2) In small boats and pleasure craft, a stout bitt near the bow for use with the ground tackle. (3) In wooden ships, a hold stanchion that rested on the keelson and supported the deck beams.

**sandspit**  *n.* A small island or small peninsula frequently covered or partially covered by tide with little or no vegetation.

**sand strake**  *n.* A garboard strake.

**sandsucker**  *n.* Nickname for a dredge that sucks sand and mud to deepen channels.

**sanitary passage**  *n.* A certificate issued by harbor authorities to passengers of a vessel that is suspected of carrying a contagious disease; the document enables local authorities at their final destination to keep the passengers under observation. "We were issued sanitary passage at Port Said when we left the ship for Cairo."

**sanitary pump**  *n.* A pump that supplies saltwater to washrooms for baths and toilets. These are not found on the better passenger liners.

**sanitary system**  *n.* The flushing system of a vessel's toilets.

**Santa Ana**  *n.* A "föhn" that blows down the Santa Ana (California) Valley and becomes strong enough to endanger small craft off the coast and in the Santa Barbara Channel at San Pedro.

**sargasso**  *n.* A mass of seaweed, especially **gulf weeds,** that are common in the warmer areas of the Atlantic Ocean.

**Sargasso Sea**  *n.* An area of the Atlantic Ocean that lies east of the Bahamas at roughly 25°N to 30°N, and 38°W to 60°W, where large quantities of seaweed float. This occurs because the clockwise current in the North Atlantic leaves this area without much current and the large accumulation of seaweed, mostly from the Gulf, drifts in and stays until it decays.

**sargassum**  *n.* A genus of brown algae characterized by a bushy form, a substantial holdfast when attached, and a yellowish brown, greenish yellow, or orange color. Two species, *S. fluitans* and *S. matans,* make up 99% of the vegetation of the Sargasso Sea. Also *gulfweed.*

**sastruga**  *n.* (pron. satrooga) Sharp irregular ridge formed on a snow surface by wind erosion and deposition. On mobile, floating ice, the ridges are parallel to the direction of the prevailing wind. From the Russian *zastruga,* groove.

**satellite navigation (SATNAV)**  *n.* Navigation by electronic means using the impulses generated by Earth satellites, known as **birds,** in polar orbits with known positions that are monitored by Earth tracking stations as they orbit the planet. These birds form a **birdcage** within which the Earth rotates. Vessels fitted with appropriate receiving equipment and computers can determine their positions from the orbital data and doppler on 150 and 400 MHz, the latter being the only one available for civilian use. This

system is being replaced by the global positioning system.

**saturable system**  *n.* A radio navigation system limited to a single user or to a limited number of users on a timeshare basis. See NONSATURABLE SYSTEM; RADAR BEACON.

**saucer**  *n.* (1) The concave socket in the step of a capstan in which the spindle revolves. (2) One of a number of metal steps fastened to the after side of a rudder post beneath a brace. The saucer keeps the pintle straps from coming in contact with the braces.

**save-all**  *n.* (1) Netting between vessel and pier rigged during cargo handling. (2) A pail or drum used to catch dripping oil or water. (3) A strip of sheet metal under a sidelight inside a vessel to catch water.

**sawed frame**  *n.* Wooden frames that are sawed instead of being bent. Sawed frames are not as strong, but because of the expense involved in bending frames, they are considered acceptable alternatives.

**scale**  *n.* Insoluble salts (calcium sulfate and magnesium sulfate) deposited on boiler tubes that reduce thermal exchange efficiency.

**scale effect**  *n.* Marine engineering and architectural term referring to the variations between the performance of a model in a tank or basin and the performance of the completed vessel under actual conditions.

**scaling hammer**  *n.* A chipping hammer used for removing scale, paint, and rust from plating.

**scallops**  *n.* (rhymes with wallops, not gallops) Slack sections along the luff of a fore-and-aft sail caused by improperly hauling on the sail halyard when setting the sail.

**scan** *v.* The continuous rotation of the radar or sonar through 360° of the range of search. One scans the horizon for targets or for enemy ships. The same usage obtains for sonar search.

**scandalize** *v.* (1) To reduce sail by lowering the peak and raising the tack. (2) To mishandle a sail in an unseaman-like manner, as to raise a headsail with several hanks missing or unused. (3) To allow a sail to shake by failing to trim the sheet as taut as would be most efficient. (4) To set the yards of a square rigger so they are not square to the mast when at anchor; usually as a sign of mourning for a death on board the ship.

**scanner** *n.* (1) A unit of a radar set that consists of the antenna and drive assembly for rotating the antenna. (2) The sensing hardware and signal of a power plant monitoring system. (3) A radio that sequentially monitors a number of frequencies.

**scanning antenna** *n.* Rotating radar antenna.

**scant** *v.* To sail as close to the wind as possible without luffing. The term comes from earlier usage when wind was said to scant when it moved ahead, which would cause the helmsman to have to steer more to leeward and perhaps farther from the goal.

**scantling** *n.* Dimensions of structural parts of a vessel. The word comes from the now obsolete verb, to scantline, to design or construct.

**scant wind** *n.* A wind that forces a vessel to sail as close to the wind as possible to make good the desired course. See HEADER; SCANT.

**scar** *n.* Exposed rocks or a cliff.

**scarf** *n.* An especially strong joint in a stem, bar keel, stern frame, or spar made by mortising tapered ends of the pieces to be joined.

**scarf** *v.* (1) To thin out or taper a corner or edge of a plate or shape to make a lap. (2) To lock together two construction members of like material either by mechanical or adhesive means. Wooden beams and spars are scarfed together with long diagonal joints to form a scarf with no sacrifice in strength.

**scarf nail (tack)** *n.* Small copper nail or tack not necessarily used for scarfing, but more often used for fastening small pieces of wood together and other such jobs.

**scarp** See ESCARPMENT.

**scend** *n.* The forward or vertical motion of the sea.

**scend** *v.* To heave upward on the sea.

**school ship** *n.* Any vessel used for seamanship training. A **nautical school ship** is any vessel operated by a state or political subdivision (but not the Coast Guard or Navy) and approved by the Coast Guard for the training of students to become able seamen or qualified members of the engine department. A **civilian nautical school ship** is one which offers instruction to students quartered on board for the primary purpose of training for service in the merchant marine.

**schooner** *n.* A sailing vessel with two or more (up to a maximum of seven) masts. If only two masts—the mainmast and the foremast—the mainmast must be as tall as or taller than the forward mast. Primarily gaff-rigged, schooners can carry square topsails in addition to gaffsails on the foremast, in which case they are known as **square topsail schooners.** A sailor with few belongings was said to be **schooner-rigged.** This came from the full-rigged sailor's disdain for the few sails on a schooner. See RIG.

**schooner barge** *n.* A seagoing barge used on the Atlantic coast of the United States; it was usually towed, but was fitted with short masts so that it was not helpless without the towing boat.

**schooner brig** *n.* A two-masted vessel with square-rigged foremast and fore-and-aft-rigged mainmast. In New England the same arrangement was called a **half-brig,** but most authorities called it a **hermaphrodite brig.** In England, the same rig is called a brigantine.

**schooner ketch** *n.* A term of questionable lineage used to describe a schooner with mizzenmast shorter than the mainmast.

**schooner stay** *n.* (1) A whip between two derrick heads topped for working cargo. (2) A midship guy or stay.

**schooner yawl** *n.* A two-masted schooner with a short main boom compensated for by a small jiggermast and sail.

**sciatic stay** *n.* (pron. sighattick) A wire rope that connects mastheads and supports a hatch tackle. The word was unknown among English seamen, but was used in early 19th-century America. See TRIATIC STAY.

**scooter** *n.* Early amphibious craft with runners and rigged with a jib and mainsail. It was capable of crossing patches of open water and was used for iceboating.

**scope** *n.* (1) The length of the anchor cable let out from hawsepipe to anchor. See SENTINEL. (2) The ratio of anchor cable let out to the depth of the water; under normal conditions a scope of 3:1 is usually sufficient, but during a blow as much as 7:1 to even 10:1 may be necessary.

**score** *n.* The groove in the shell or cheeks of a block that takes the strap.

**Scotch marine boiler** *n.* A boiler in which the gases from the firebox are led through tubes surrounded by circulating water that is being heated. Scotch boil-

ers have other uses, but the Scotch marine boiler has marine fittings and connections that make it different. Also *fire-tube boiler.*

**Scotchman** *n.* (1) Antichafing gear on a backstay. (2) Antichafing battens fastened to standing rigging. (3) A grommet in the luff of a topsail that can be used for a purchase for tightening the luff.

**Scottish cut** *n.* A diagonal cut on a triangular sail, in which the panels at the head are parallel to the leech while those at the foot are parallel to the foot. The cut is used for heavy weather sails and was used extensively on trading vessels.

**Scottish rig** *n.* A four-masted bark with double topgallant sails and a pole jiggermast.

**scour** *v.* (1) To dig sand from beneath a grounded vessel using high-pressure water hoses so that it can sink to its waterline and float off. (2) The natural movement of bottom matter by wave action and tidal currents. "The spring tidal current scoured the sandbar and increased the navigable depth over it by two feet."

**scouring basin** *n.* A basin or pond with gates that can be closed at high tide and opened at low tide to scour the entrance channel with the rush of water. Also *sluicing pond.*

**scow** *n.* An open flat-bottomed boat used for carrying sand, mud, gravel, garbage, or other bulk material short distances. Large scows are often called lighters or barges.

**scow** *v.* To bend a cable on the crown of an anchor instead of on the ring. The cable is then seized with small stuff at the ring. If the anchor is caught on rocks, a heavy pull on the line breaks the small stuff loose and the strain is then moved to the crown, and the flukes will usually come up with no further strain. While anchored in this manner, more scope must be allowed so that the strain on the anchor is along the shank.

**scow schooner**  *n.* A two-masted schooner with punt hull, centerboard, and a false cutwater. They were used on San Francisco Bay as market boats and tenders.

**scramble net**  *n.* Cargo nets rigged over the side of ships for people to climb up and down.

**scrape boat**  *n.* Small sailing boat used for crabbing on Chesapeake Bay. A **scrape** was a triangular iron frame with a base of from 2 to 5 feet. A mesh bag was attached to the side opposite the apex. The device was pulled along the bottom by a rope attached to the apex to catch the crabs.

**scraper**  *n.* A hand tool used for scraping paint, oxidized metal, and so on.

**scratch boat**  *n.* The boat with the highest rating in a handicap race.

**screen**  *n.* (1) A board used to limit the arc of visibility of a sidelight. (2) A group of naval ships stationed in such a way as to protect a main body or convoy against enemy attack.

**screen bulkhead**  *n.* A bulkhead placed between the engine room and boiler room, which is fireproof, dustproof, and air- and gastight.

**screened light**  *n.* Light in a box that is constructed so that the light can be seen only through a confined arc as with port and starboard lights and sternlights.

**screw**  *n.* A vessel's propeller.

**screw anchor**  *n.* A mooring buoy anchor with a shaft 3 to 10 feet long with broad flanges welded on the side. This is driven into ground that is considered too soft for more traditional anchors. Also *mooring screw.*

**screw current**  *n.* The stream caused by a vessel's propellers; the term is used for the stream ahead of the screw as well as aft of it.

**screw gammoning**  *n.* Plating or chain used to fasten the bowsprit to the stem piece and tightened by means of nuts and bolts.

**screw hoist**  *n.* A chain hoist in which the upper block is an endless screw turning against a worm gear.

**screw log**  *n.* A device used to determine the distance and speed of a vessel by registering the revolutions of a propeller trailed astern on a cable. As the vessel moves through the water, the rotator turns a cable attached to it that leads to the counter on the vessel. See TAFFRAIL LOG.

**screw mooring**  See SCREW ANCHOR.

**screw pump**  *n.* A type of rotary pump.

**screw shackle**  *n.* A U-shackle with a threaded pin.

**screw steamer**  *n.* A steamer with a propeller instead of a paddle wheel. The S.S. before the name of a merchant ship originally stood for screw steamer; today it signifies steamship.

**screw stopper**  *n.* A chain stopper on an anchor cable fitted with a turnbuckle.

**scribe**  *v.* To mark timber ends so that when cut to the lines scribed, they will butt smoothly.

**scrimshaw**  *n.* Handwork that uses bone for an etching medium for artistic endeavors. Long practiced by sailors and natives of the Arctic Circle.

**scrive board**  *n.* A portable platform made of soft, clear, planed lumber on which a full-sized body plan of a vessel can be drawn. The lines are cut (**scrived**) into the surface of the wood in grooves with a **scriving knife.**

**scroll**  *n.* Ornamental timber placed at the knee of the head under the bowsprit. They were usually finished off with a volute turning outward. See FIDDLEHEAD.

**scuba**  *n.* Acronym for self-contained underwater breathing apparatus. The device consists of a portable gas cylinder that permits its users to move underwater with ease, independent of the surface vessel.

**scud**  *n.* Low-lying mist clouds, or fractostratus.

**scud**  *n.* To sail before a gale with only enough exposed sail area to prevent pooping. A ship is said to be **scudding** when it is driving before a gale.

**scull**  *n.* A short oar light enough to be manipulated with one hand. (2) A one-person rowing boat, usually with a sliding seat and outriggers, propelled by sculls.

**scull**  *v.* (1) To move a boat by the use of an oar over the stern or one side only. (2) To move a boat by short oars, one on each side.

**scullery**  *n.* The area used for washing and stowing dishes, pots, and pans, as distinct from the galley, where the cooking is done.

**sculling notch**  *n.* A slot cut in the transom of a small boat that holds the **sculling oar.**

**scunner**  *n.* (1) A lookout in the foretop of a sealing vessel who watched for seals and ice and directed the movements of the vessel. (2) A lookout in the foretop of a sailing ship who directed the ship's movement through an ice field.

**scupper**  *n.* A small drain from a waterway or gutter on an open deck that leads to the sea, or a drain from an en-

closed space that leads to a drain system that carries the water over the side. Scuppers near or below the waterline are fitted with scupper shutters. See FREEING PORT.

**scupper hose**  *n.* A canvas or rubber hose connected to a scupper to take the water clear of the hull and down to the open water.

**scupper lip**  *n.* (1) A metal lip under the scupper that reaches out from the side of a vessel to keep the drainage clear of the hull. (2) A derogatory name for a shipmate.

**scupper shutter**  *n.* A valve on scuppers that opens from the pressure of water on deck but closes when pressure from seawater presses it against its seat.

**scurvy**  *n.* A disease once common on ships when the diet was lacking in vitamin C. It results in bleeding into the tissues, causes the flesh and gums to become spongy and the teeth to loosen, causes excessive langor and debility, and can be fatal. Resolution and prevention of the disease was achieved by a diet that included onions, citrus, black currants, or potatoes. See LIMEY.

**scuttle**  *n.* A trunk in a vessel's deck, a manhole, or a very small hatch, or the lid for any of these. In some areas, all small hatches are called scuttles.

**scuttle**  *v.* To intentionally sink a vessel, usually by opening the sea cocks or cutting holes in the bottom.

**scuttlebutt**  *n.* (1) A cask on deck used for the crew's drinking water; it was often kept over a scuttle for drainage. (2) More recently a scuttlebutt has become a drinking fountain. (3) Because much unauthenticated information finds its way through the crew by word of mouth at the drinking cask or fountain, rumors are called scuttlebutt. "Has anyone heard the scuttlebutt on our next liberty port?"

**scuttle hatch**  *n.* A steel hatch cover used on a scuttle. Also *scuttle hatch cover.*

**sea**  *n.* A large body of water. (1) An area of the ocean that has specific characteristics or boundaries that distinguish it from the wider ocean, such as the Sargasso Sea or the Norwegian Sea. (2) A large body of water that is almost entirely surrounded by land, such as the Mediterranean Sea. (3) A large body of freshwater, such as the Sea of Galilee. (4) A life aboard working ships as a mariner; one who **follows the sea:** "He went to sea at the age of 12 as a cabin boy." (5) A collective term for all the continuous saltwater bodies that cover most of the Earth. (6) The condition of the surface of a body of water with regard to its flow, swell, waves, or turbulence. "Heavy seas prevented our entering port on schedule."

**Sea-Air-Land Team (SEAL)**  *n.* The U.S. Navy equivalent of a commando team whose members are trained and equipped for covert paramilitary operations, including surveillance, reconnaissance, and infiltration in enemy territory by water, land, and air.

**sea anchor**  *n.* Any device thrown over the bow and dragged to keep the bow in the wind during a storm. A warp of line with tires, a drogue, or other similar item would act as a sea anchor.

**seabag**  *n.* A carryall of heavy fabric that seamen use to carry personal gear.

**sea bed**  *n.* The sea's bottom beyond the continental shelf.

**Seabee**  *n.* (1) U.S. Navy construction battalion (CB; hence seabee) established in 1941 to build Naval aviation bases and facilities. Amphibious construction battalion (ACB) and mobile construction battalion (MCB) are more specialized units. (2) A type of water barge developed by the U.S. Navy during World War II. (3) A mother ship with a number of independent barges that have access to canals and waterways otherwise inaccessible to the mother ship; LASH ship.

**sea biscuit**  *n.* Hardtack.

**seaboard**  *n.* (1) The seacoast. (2) The land near the sea, such as the eastern seaboard of the United States. Seaboard is a more general term than littoral, which applies specifically to the various parts of a region bordering the sea, including the coast, foreshore, backshore, beach, and so on. See SHORE.

**seaboat**  *n.* Used to describe a vessel's seaworthiness; a vessel capable of weathering a storm is considered a good seaboat. "As the wind reached gale force, we realized we had no worry because we had a good seaboat."

**seaborne**  *adj.* Carried by ship, carried on or over the sea.

**seaborne trade**  *n.* Commercial transportation by sea that includes passengers and cargo.

**sea breeze**  *n.* A wind that comes from the sea, as opposed to a land breeze that comes from the land. As the land heats up during the day, the sea breeze picks up; the opposite happens in the evening when the Sun goes down and the land cools faster than the sea.

**sea buoy**  *n.* The first buoy when returning from the sea that marks the entrance to a channel or harbor.

**sea cabin**  *n.* The quarters for the commanding officer of a naval vessel adjacent to or near the bridge, higher and smaller than the commanding officer's regular cabin.

**sea captain**  *n.* A master of a merchant ship, as distinguished from the naval rank of captain.

**sea card**  *n.* The card of a mariner's compass.

**sea chest** *n.* (1) A compartment through which seawater is admitted for freshwater and cooling water or discharged when dirty or heated. (2) A sailor's wooden trunk, usually decorated with a picture of his ship and ornamental beckets.

**sea clutter** *n.* Radar echoes from the surface of the ocean that interfere with radar reception. Also *sea return.*

**seacoast** *n.* and *adj.* Land bordering and near the sea.

**sea cock** *n.* A valve on a pipe opening to the sea. The usual purpose is to obtain seawater for various purposes, but it can also be used to scuttle the ship. Through-hull piping below the waterline usually has sea cocks installed. See SCUTTLE.

**sea conditions** *n.* Size of waves, state of the weather, and their predicted changes. See BEAUFORT SCALE; DOUGLAS SCALE.

**sea connection** *n.* A valve or sea cock fitted directly on a vessel's hull near or below the waterline.

**sea dog** *n.* One who has been at sea for many years; an old salt.

**seadog** See FOGBOW.

**sea duty** *n.* In the U.S. Navy, Marines, and Coast Guard, duty on ships and aircraft, and bases outside the continental limits of the United States.

**Sea Explorers** *n.* A co-educational division of the Boy Scouts of America that focuses on seamanship and other water-related activities.

**seafarer** *n.* (1) A sailor; a seaman. One who follows the sea as a livelihood. (2) A submarine extremely low frequency (SELF) radio communication system for use in communicating with deeply sub-

merged submarines. (3) An antisubmarine warfare blimp.

**seafaring** *n.* A life at sea; a sailor's calling.

**sea fog** *n.* A cloud or visible assemblage of tiny drops of water over water that are caused when warm damp air lies over a sea that is colder than the dew point of the air. When a vessel is sailing through a fog, a lookout can often be placed low enough to see under the fog or high enough to see over it.

**sea fret** *n.* A morning mist. See ADVECTION FOG.

**sea gasket** *n.* (1) A long line for furling a sail on a boom. (2) A short piece of line used to secure sails not in use.

**sea gates** *n.* Gates at the entrance to a basin that can be closed for protection against heavy seas.

**seagirt** *adj.* Surrounded by sea.

**seagoing tug** *n.* A towing vessel built for work at sea and longer and more commodious than harbor tugs. Also *ocean tug.*

**seagoing vessel** *n.* Under admiralty law, a craft that ordinarily is engaged in deep-sea navigation as well as inland and river navigation. In some instances, maritime law excludes such vessels as pleasure yachts, tugs, lighters, and barges even though they may indeed go to sea frequently.

**sea horses** *n.* Large breaking waves at sea, a little larger than white caps, that begin to occur at Beaufort force 5.

**sea ice** *n.* Ice formed from seawater.

***Sea Ice Nomenclature*** *n.* A publication of the World Meteorological Organization comprising sea-ice terminology and ice reporting codes.

**seakindliness** *n.* A vessel's reaction to sea conditions, including steering, pitching, yawing, rolling and so on, in heavy seas. Seakindliness is not to be confused with seaworthiness, which means a vessel's ability to survive heavy seas. A cork would be extremely seaworthy, but not seakindly.

**sea ladder** *n.* A fixed ladder on the side of a ship. See JACOB'S LADDER.

**sea-lane** *n.* Commonly used sea route. See TRAFFIC SEPARATION SCHEME.

**sea legs** *n.* Physical and physiological accommodation to the motion of the sea. After being on the beach for a few days, many seamen lose this accommodation and have to regain it when they go back to sea. The reverse process happens when they go ashore.

**sealer** *n.* A vessel designed and used for seal hunting.

**sea letter** *n.* A "passport" for a vessel; a document issued to a neutral vessel giving proof of its nationality and neutrality. The document includes a full description of the vessel, crew, names of the owners and the master, port of registry, and so on.

**sea level** *n.* The average height of the sea's surface midway between tides with no waves as determined over a 19-year period. Nineteen years is the time it takes for the Sun, Earth, and Moon to return to any given alignment. See METONIC CYCLE; TIDAL DATUM.

**seam** *n.* (1) A riveted or welded plate edge connection. A riveted seam overlaps; a welded seam may or may not overlap. (2) The line or junction formed when two pieces of fabric are joined along their margins. (3) The line of stitching between panels of a sail. (4) The space planking on a deck or a hull.

**seaman (SN)** *n.* (1) Any person serving on board a seagoing vessel who is not an officer under admiralty law, or an able seaman, an ordinary seaman, an oiler, a wiper. (2) A mariner or sailor. (3) In the U.S. Navy and U.S. Coast Guard an enlisted person ranked below a petty officer and above seaman apprentice.

**seaman apprentice (SA)** *n.* An enlisted person in the U.S. Navy and U.S. Coast Guard ranked below seaman and above seaman recruit.

**sea manners** *n.* Understood by good seamen to mean consideration for the other vessel and the exercise of good judgment under certain conditions when vessels meet.

**seaman recruit (SR)** *n.* Lowest rating in the U.S. Navy and U.S. Coast Guard below seaman apprentice. Slang: **boot,** because of the leggings (boots) they wear.

**seaman's head** See HEAD.

**seamanship** *n.* Skill in the art of managing a vessel in all kinds of weather and under all conditions. Seamanship does not necessarily include ability in the science of navigation.

**seaman's passport** *n.* A passport that is valid only for use in the line of a seaman's duties. A seaman cannot use his seaman's passport for a pleasure trip. See MERCHANT MARINER'S DOCUMENTS; Z-CARD.

**seamark** *n.* (1) A mark that can be seen from the sea and used for navigation. Included are buoys, lighthouses, beacons, and lightships, as well as church steeples, mountain peaks, or water towers, among others. (2) The line along a coastline marking the upper tidal limit.

**seamen's lien** *n.* Short for Liens of Master and Seamen, by which seamen have a lien for wages on their ship and on the freight. The master has a lien against freight, or the cargo, if the freight has not been paid, but unlike the seamen's lien, he does not have a lien against the ship.

**seamen's quarters**   *n.* Lodging place for deck hands. See FORECASTLE.

**seam lap**   *n.* A joint between overlapping plates along which rivets are received.

**seamount**   *n.* A mountain rising 1,000 meters or more from the sea floor with a limited area at the summit, the summit being at least 1,000 feet below sea level, usually conical. A broader summit would come under the definition of a plateau.

**sea mule**   *n.* A floating power plant and propulsion plant that can be attached to the hull of a barge or lighter to maneuver in a harbor or protected area.

**sea painter**   *n.* A heavy rope used for maneuvering a ship's boat away from the ship's sides when the boat is lowered while under way.

**sea pie**   *n.* A seaman's meal consisting of layers of fish or meat and vegetables between bread crusts or biscuits.

**seaplane**   *n.* Airplane fitted with floats so that it can land on or take off from water.

**seaport**   *n.* A port on or near the sea with facilities for handling seagoing ships. The important characteristic is that it has easy access to the sea. New Orleans, the largest seaport in the United States in 1990, is a seaport even though it is 116 statute miles upstream from the sea buoy at the mouth of the Mississippi River.

**sea power**   *n.* (1) A nation with a navy. (2) Naval strength that allows a country to keep open sea-lanes between itself and its allies for the purpose of conducting trade or military operations.

**search, right of**   See RIGHT OF SEARCH.

**search and rescue (SAR)**   *n.* A mission to search for a vessel presumed in distress, usually conducted by the U.S. Coast Guard or other government agency.

**searchlight**   *n.* Powerful light sometimes fitted with shutters for signaling other ships and shore stations. Also *spotlight*.

**sea return**   See SEA CLUTTER.

**sea ring**   *n.* An instrument used for getting the altitude of the Sun before the invention of the sextant.

**sea room**   *n.* (1) Space adequate for maneuvering a vessel. (2) A position far enough offshore to be clear of shoal water.

**seascape**   *n.* A view or picture of the sea.

**Sea Scouts**   See SEA EXPLORERS.

**seashore**   *n.* Legal term applied to the land between high water and low water.

**seasickness**   *n.* Nausea provoked by the motion of the sea.

**sea sled**   *n.* A bottom construction for small boats. Instead of a V-shaped hull, it is an inverted V to collect air under the bow to cushion the boat in seas.

**sea smoke**   *n.* A type of fog created when very cold air moves over cold open water to produce "steaming" on the surface. This can attain heights up to several hundred feet. It is usually observed in the Arctic and Antarctic Oceans and off the east coasts of Asia and North America in fall and winter.

**seasonal current**   *n.* A current that displays significant changes in speed and direction as a result of seasonal winds.

**sea stores**   *n.* Provisions, spare parts, and supplies carried aboard ship for maintenance of passengers and crew and the upkeep of the ship and her navigation equipment.

**seatrain**   *n.* A seagoing ferry capable of carrying complete railroad trains. It is used, for example, between the Hook-of-Holland, the Netherlands, and Harwich, England. Also *boat-train.*

**sea trials**   *n.* Trials conducted by builders with owners' representatives aboard after a ship has been built or repaired, but before it has been turned over to the owners.

**Seattle head**   *n.* A T-shaped fixture on a Charley Noble that prevents downdrafts to the galley stove. Origin unclear.

**sea turn**   *n.* A change of wind direction that brings a wind from the sea.

**sea valve**   *n.* A valve placed below the waterline to allow seawater to be brought aboard for fire pumps, discharging ballast tanks, and for blowing down boilers. Also *sea cock.*

**seawall**   *n.* An embankment that prevents erosion of the shoreline.

**seaward**   *adj. or adv.* At or toward the sea. One can refer to a "seaward buoy," one that is farther out to sea than another, or a vessel can be pointed "seaward."

**seawater**   *n.* Water from the sea. Seawater weighs 64 pounds per cubic foot, whereas freshwater weighs $64\frac{1}{2}$ pounds per cubic foot. See SALINITY.

**seaway**   *n.* (1) Waves or swells of the sea when not caused by a shoal. (2) A moderately heavy sea. "We had little time to secure the deck gear before we found ourselves in the seaway." (3) Headway for a vessel. (4) An inland waterway for shipping. (5) An established shipping lane. "The race course lay dangerously close to the seaway."

**seaweed**   *n.* General term for all marine algae including kelp and rockweed. Over 1,000 different species have been identified. Seaweed is widely used as fertilizer and primary food source, and it is a good source of iodine.

**seaworthiness**   *n.* The condition of readiness of a vessel for sea in construction, material, equipment, and crew, with relation to the trade for which the vessel is contracted. Breaches of warranty of seaworthiness are construed in overloading, any sort of disrepair of the ship that might cause damage to the ship or its cargo, improper stowage so as to make navigation difficult or dangerous. Seakindliness is a desirable aspect of seaworthiness, but it is not essential. Also *navigability.*

**seaworthiness, certificate of**   *n.* Document issued by a qualified surveyor after repairs have been made to a vessel following an accident. The certificate allows a vessel to proceed with a contract.

**seaworthy**   *adj.* Describes a vessel that is capable of going to sea. See SEAWORTHINESS.

**second**   *n.* (1) One-sixtieth of a minute and the smallest division of time ordinarily used in navigation. Some forms of electronic equipment, however, use the millisecond (one-thousandth of a second) and the nanosecond (one-billionth of a second). (2) One-sixtieth of a minute of longitude or latitude.

**secondary depression**   *n.* A small depression associated with a larger atmospheric depression; the isobars form a loop around which the wind may blow with significant force.

**secondary light**   *n.* Major lights other than primary seacoast lights; they are observed at harbor entrances and similar locations where high intensity and reliability are imperative.

**secondary shoreline**   n. A shoreline formed by marine and biological plants, animals, and forces, such as coral reefs, barrier shorelines, and estuarine marshes.

**second deck**   n. The first complete deck below the main deck.

**second differences**   n. (1) The term for the difference between comparisons of a chronometer on successive days. (2) The difference between quantities in a nautical almanac. The differences between the tabulated values are called the **first differences** and are refined for navigational purposes, but the differences between successive first differences are known as second differences.

**second-year ice**   n. Ice that has survived only one summer and that is thicker, less dense, and piled higher than first-year ice.

**Secretary of the Navy (SECNAV)** n. The head of the U.S. Department of the Navy within the Department of Defense with jurisdiction over the Navy and Marine Corps, and, in time of war, the Coast Guard.

**Secretary of Transportation**   n. The head of the U.S. Department of Transportation with jurisdiction over the Coast Guard in time of peace.

**secret block**   n. A block designed to prevent fouling by having a shell that covers the sheave with access only large enough for the rope on each side.

**section**   n. A tactical subdivision of naval ships or aircraft, or a subdivision of a division of enlisted personnel.

**sections**   n. Steel or iron rolled bars of the cross sections used in shipbuilding.

**sector**   n. As shown in the *Light List,* the area illuminated by a light that is either the danger area or the deep-water area. Charts and the *Light List* describe a light's characteristics in terms of sectors.

**sectored light**   n. A navigation light divided into sectors of different colors and described in the *Light List.*

**secure**   v. (1) To make fast, as "to secure the watertight hatch cover." (2) To fasten two or more things together; one secures piles to make a piling, or secures an emergency lantern to a bulkhead. (3) Cease or stop, as to "secure from general quarters," or "secure the watch," meaning write your log and leave, no one is to relieve you. (4) To turn off the main propulsion equipment, to "wrap up the plant," or to signal "finished with engines," marked FWE on the engine room telegraph.

**secure for sea**   interj. The order to lash movable objects down and prepare for the wave action at sea before getting under way.

**securité**   interj. Word used in radio communications to precede a safety message.

**seiche**   n. (pron. saysh) A wave in a lake, ocean, or other body of water caused either by a seismic or an atmospheric disturbance and that lasts from a few minutes to a few hours.

**seine**   n. (pron. sane) A large fishing net with floats at the top and weights at the bottom.

**seiner**   n. General term for any boat used in seining.

**seine roller**   n. A powered roller at the stern of a seiner used for pulling the seine aboard and to reduce friction on the warps as the net comes over the transom.

**seismic sea wave**   n. A sea wave of large amplitude, a long period, and usually of great force, and caused by an earthquake, a volcanic explosion, or an especially large submarine earth slide when one tectonic plate slides over or by the one next to it. The wave or waves so formed are often called by their Japanese name, *tsunami*. The expression **tidal wave** is a misnomer, because there is no tidal action involved. See TSUNAMI.

**seize** *v.* (1) To fasten two ropes together, or the end of a rope to its standing part to form an eye, by binding them with small stuff. (2) To secure a man to a shroud by his wrists preparatory to flogging. (3) To stop working for lack of lubricant, said of an engine or motor when it runs dry of lubricant, overheats, expands and stops functioning. (4) To arrive at, "to seize a shore," obsolete.

**seizing** *n.* (1) A lashing of small stuff, spun yarn, or marline. See WHIP. (2) A binding of two parts of a rope together. See FLAT SEIZING; RACKING SEIZING; THROAT SEIZING.

## Seizing

(a) seizing

**seizure** *n.* The act of taking possession of a vessel and its cargo for a violation of public law as with drug trafficking.

**seizure, right of** See RIGHT OF SEIZURE.

**selection board** *n.* U.S. Naval officers assembled to review the records and to recommend promotions for officers above lieutenant, junior grade. Also *promotion board.*

**self-bailing** *adj.* Describes a fitting that allows a cockpit to be drained automatically.

**self-closing door** *n.* Doors that can be closed from the bridge by means of hydraulic pressure.

**self-draining cockpit** *n.* A cockpit fitted with scuppers to provide discharge of water through the hull. See SELF-BAILING.

**self-reefing topsail** *n.* A square topsail fitted so that it can be taken in from on deck without sending men aloft.

**self-righting boat** *n.* A coastal lifeboat with high bow and stern air tanks and fitted with a heavy keel.

**self-steering** *adj.* Describes a device that allows a boat to steer itself. The term is more often used in connection with sailboats, and applies to a device that works without an electric motor but uses a sail and the wind to control the rudder. See AUTOMATIC PILOT.

**self-tacking jib** *n.* A club-footed jib with a boom similar to a mainsail and boom, to make control possible without changing sheets.

**self-tending sail** *n.* A sail that has the capability of changing tack with only minimum attention being paid to it. This is usually accomplished with a headsail with a boom that can go from one tack to another, such as a club-footed headsail, without striking the mast. It is still necessary to trim the sail for the appropriate wind slot.

**self-unloading vessel** *n.* Vessel designed to carry bulk cargo, such as coal, ore, cement, and aggregate, and fitted with the necessary unloading equipment to render it independent of shore-based unloading equipment and personnel.

**selsyn motor**  *n.* An acronym for self-synchronizing motor, a device for instantaneous transmission and reception from a generator to a motor. It is used in remote steering gear and engine room telegraphs.

**selvage**  *n.* (1) The edge of a piece of fabric, such as sail cloth that is woven so as not to ravel. (2) The side edges of a piece of net. Also *selvedge.*

**selvagee**  *n.* Several rope-yarns wound into a circular strop, then marled and often served as well. The resultant selvagee is stronger than a spliced strop and is used to attach the hook of a tackle to a rope or shroud. The selvagee is not as apt to slip as a rope. Two or more turns of the selvagee are taken around the shroud, and the hook is then fixed in place. It is also used for a chest becket.

**semaphore**  *n.* The use of hand-held flags, held in various positions to indicate letters and numerals. The flag hoist using "YZ-1" means "I am going to send a message by semaphore." The hoist is kept two-blocked until the semaphore message has been completed and acknowledged.

**semi-balanced rudder**  *n.* A rudder with part of the blade forward of the stock. This forward part is not as wide as the portion aft of the stock. While both the semibalanced and balanced rudders are actually balanced, the balanced rudder has a forward blade about 10% larger than that of the semibalanced rudder.

**semicircular corrector**  *n.* One of the several bar magnets placed symmetrically in holes running both athwartship and longitudinally with the binnacle. See COMPASS.

**semicircular deviation**  *n.* The compass deviation that changes sign as

the vessel swings around, giving a different deviation from easterly to westerly.

**semidiurnal**  *adj.* Pertaining to a period of approximately half a lunar day, or 12.42 hours.

**semidiurnal current**  *n.* A tidal current in which the tidal-day current cycle consists of two flow currents and two ebb currents, separated by slack water. A semidiurnal current in a rotary current is characterized by two changes in direction of 360°.

**semisubmersible**  *adj.* or *n.* A large, floating drilling platform attached to a buoyant structure that is partly beneath the surface of the sea. Except for propulsion, this operation is completely self-contained, with personnel and equipment located on lower decks to work on wells in deep water and miles from shore.

**senhouse slip**  *n.* British word for pelican hook.

**senior chief petty officer**  See PETTY OFFICER.

**senior officer present afloat (SOPA)**  *n.* The senior U.S. Navy line officer on active duty and eligible for command at sea, who is present and in command of any unit of the operating forces afloat in a given area.

**sennet** (or **sennit**)  *n.* Braided or plaited cordage using spun yarn or other small stuff. It is used for mats, stoppers, fenders, ropes, hot pads, and other purposes. There are many different patterns, such as chain sennet, eight-strand square sennet, and flat sennet. Clifford Ashley's *The Ashley Book of Knots* describes sennets in great detail. See FLAKE.

**sentinel**  *n.* An added weight used by smaller vessels to increase the holding power of light anchors. When the anchor is in place with the desired scope veered, the sentinel is attached to the anchor cable and, by means of a second

## Sentinel

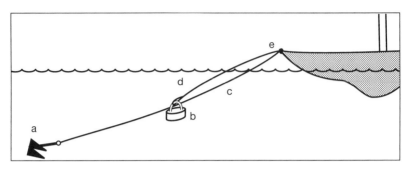

(a) anchor
(b) sentinel or kellet
(c) anchor cable

(d) light line to kellet
(e) bow chock
(f) a – e = scope

line attached to it, lowered to a point where the added weight rests on the bottom. The effect is to lower the anchor cable as it goes from the sentinel to the anchor, thus causing the anchor stock to be lowered and the anchor to dig in better. Also *kellet.*

**separation cloth**   *n.* Fabric sheeting placed between two different grades of grain or sugar when they are stowed.

**separation line**   *n.* A line separating the traffic lanes in which ships are proceeding in opposite or nearly opposite directions, or separates a traffic lane from the adjacent inshore traffic zone.

**separation zone**   *n.* A zone that separates the traffic lanes in which ships are proceeding in opposite or nearly opposite directions, or separates a traffic lane from the adjacent inshore traffic zone in a traffic separation scheme.

**separator tank**   *n.* A tank used to statically separate dissimilar liquid cargo.

**sequence of current**   *n.* The order of occurrence of the four tidal current strengths of a day, with special reference to whether the greater flood immediately precedes or follows the greater ebb. See EBB CURRENT; FLOOD CURRENT.

**sequence of tide**   *n.* The order in which the tides of a day occur, with special reference to whether the higher high water immediately precedes or follows the lower low water.

**serve**   *v.* To tightly bind a cable or standing rigging with continuous rounds of spun yarn or small stuff to protect the cable or rigging from chafing. A traditional sailor's phrase on the subject is "Worm and parcel with the lay [of the rope], turn and serve the other way." See PARCEL; SEIZING; WHIP; WORM.

**service**   *n.* The product of serving. Service is applied to wire rope to protect it in the chock. Tarred spun yarn or marline tightly bound outside of worming and parceling. See SERVE.

**service craft**   *n.* Small craft used in the U.S. Navy that are not large enough for commissioning, such as tenders and lighters.

**service force (SERVFOR)**   *n.* A U.S. Navy task organization engaged in logistic support for a fleet unit.

**service horsepower**   *n.* The level of power at which a ship's engines are run for maximum economy, normally about 80% of the engine's rated horsepower.

## Worming, Parceling, and Serving

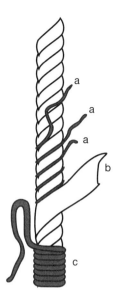

(a) worming
(b) parceling
(c) serving

"Worm and parcel with the lay
Turn and serve the other way."

—*Sailor's rhyme*

**service line**   *n.* A line of service ships ready to replenish a fleet unit.

**service medal**   *n.* A medal for service in a campaign or a theatre of operation, facetiously known as a **glory bar.**

**service stripes**   *n.* Sleeve markings on enlisted personnel's uniforms that show length of service. In the U.S. Navy, each red stripe represents four years service. After three such stripes with good conduct, the person is entitled to wear gold stripes. Service stripes are known to sailors as **hash marks.**

**service tanks**   *n.* Fuel tanks located near engine spaces or firerooms in ships

equipped with oil-fired boilers; frequently found in naval vessels.

**serving mallet**   *n.* A wooden cylinder with a handle, used for passing service around a rope. It has a groove along the surface opposite the handle to fit the size of the rope being served. The spun yarn is led from the rope being served and around the serving mallet so that when the serving mallet is turned around the rope, the service is taut and even.

**serving stuff**   See SPUN YARN.

**set**   *n.* (1) The direction toward which a vessel is carried by current, either to windward or to leeward. Set is often confused with drift, which is the amount that a current influences a ship. The difference between a dead-reckoning position and a vessel's actual position is entirely accounted for by the notation of the scalar values, set and drift together making a vector. See DRIFT. (2) The compass direction in which a current flows. (3) Several sails complementing each other and spread to the wind. Also *suit.* (4) The trim of the sails.

**set**   *v.* (1) To be moved in a given direction by the current. "We were being set north by the Gulf Stream." (2) To establish a course. "Mister, you may set the course for Cape Horn." (3) Of a visible celestial body, to cross the visible horizon while descending. See RISE. (4) To place a buoy on station.

**set a course**   *phr.* To give the course to the helmsman to steer.

**set flying**   *v.* To allow a sail to fly without its luff being attached to a mast or stay.

**set piling**   *n.* A piling (group of piles) driven deeply into the ground as a foundation for shipbuilding ways. A concrete slab is usually poured on top of it.

**set sail**   *phr.* (1) To begin a trip by water; the term is used routinely today even with ships propelled by machinery and without sails. (2) To loosen and extend sails, to spread the sails to the wind. The term does not include bending on the sail, or making sail. (3) To extend a sail on a boom or gaff. A spencer is carried on the foremast or the mainmast and is set on a standing gaff.

**set taut** or **set up**  *v.* To take the slack out of a line or out of the ground tackle. "Set the running gear taut before you commence heaving around."

**set the watch**  *phr.* To establish a new or a different watch. "Secure from general quarters and set the watch for special sea detail."

**settle**  *v.* To lower a yard into its position square by the lifts.

**settling tank**  *n.* A preliminary holding tank used to remove water from contaminated fuel by allowing the water to settle to the bottom and to be discharged into the bilge or a holding tank designed for the purpose. In earlier days, the water with its strong traces of oil was pumped over the side.

**set up**  *v.* (1) To balance standing rigging properly by bringing the shrouds and stays to proper tension to keep the mast straight and vertical, properly raked, and so on. Also *trimming.* See SET TAUT OR SET UP. (2) To tighten a nut on a bolt or stud. (3) Said of any fluid material allowed to harden or become firm whether through cooling (for example, sulfur), chemical action (concrete), freezing (water), or jelling (fuel oil).

**seven-eighths rule**  *n.* A method of determining a vessel's distance from an observation such as a point of land. By marking the time when the object lies 30° relative to the vessel's heading and again when it lies 60° relative to the vessel's heading, the distance run will be the distance from the vessel to the object at the time of the second observation (known as doubling the angle). By multiplying this

distance by $\frac{7}{8}$, you can determine the distance to the object when it is abeam.

**seven seas**  *n.* A figurative expression for all the major oceans of the world—Arctic, Antarctic, North Atlantic, South Atlantic, North Pacific, South Pacific, and Indian. Scientists today generally recognize only three major oceans—the Atlantic, Pacific, and Indian—as separate and distinct oceans, all contiguous saltwater bodies being regarded as marginal seas.

**72 COLREGS**  See CONVENTION ON THE INTERNATIONAL REGULATIONS FOR PREVENTING COLLISIONS AT SEA, 1972; INTERNATIONAL RULES.

**sew**  *n.* To fasten together two pieces of fabric, as panels in a sail.

**sewed**  *adj.* (pron. sued) To be aground; to be lacking in water by 2 feet is to be sewed (up) 2 feet.

**sextant**  *n.* An optical navigation instrument used for determining altitudes of heavenly bodies or for measuring the angular distance between two positions, for example, the vertical angle between the horizon and the pole star (Polaris or Stella Maris), or the horizontal angle between two landmarks when great precision is desired. For general navigation purposes, however, a pelorus is usually used because it is faster and accurate enough.

**shackle**  *n.* (1) A U-shaped fitting (with many variations on basic shape) with a pin across the open end of the U that slides through one side to screw into the opposite side. The threaded pin is held in place by a cotter. Shackles usually take their names from the type of pin used, for example, safety, towing, clevis, screw, chain, harp, bell, and heart. (2) A standard length of chain cable with each length connected to the next by a shackle, thus the name. In the U.S., the standard shackle is 15 fathoms; in Great Britain, it is $12\frac{1}{2}$ fathoms. Also *length of cable; shot.*

**shackle** *v.* (1) To encode a voice radio transmission. (2) To fasten two sections of chain or rope.

**shackle block** *n.* A block with a steel strap attached to a shackle and bolt.

**shackle pin** *n.* The threaded pin that goes through the open end of a shackle.

**shack locker** *n.* A compartment on a workboat, especially a fishing vessel, where food is kept available at all hours.

**shade-deck boat** *n.* A small open boat on which a light, full-length structure with roof and open sides has been built to shade the passengers and give minimum protection from the weather.

**shaded relief** *n.* The cartographic technique that provides an apparent three-dimensional configuration to terrain on maps and charts by showing shaded areas in the shadows of higher ground, as if the Sun were shining from the northwest (the upper left-hand corner of the chart or map).

**shade error** *n.* The error that results when the two faces of a sextant's shade glass are not parallel. See PRISMATIC ERROR.

**shadow** *n.* A four-sided spinnaker that is bent on a masthead gaff; the tack is bent on a spinnaker boom that controls the sail.

**shadow pin** *n.* The vertical pin at the center of a compass used for taking the Sun's azimuth. The shadow of the pin on the compass card gives the reciprocal of the Sun's azimuth. Also *gnomon.*

**shadow region** *n.* A region shaded from radar by intervening obstructions. Such a region appears devoid of targets on the radar.

**shaffle** *n.* The fitting on a mast through which the boom gooseneck pin passes to secure the boom to the mast.

**shaft alley** *n.* (1) The casing that surrounds a propeller shaft that extends from the engine room to the afterpeak and stern tube. Also *shaft tunnel.* (2) The area along which a propeller shaft runs.

**shaft block** See PLUMMER BLOCK.

**shaft direction indicator** *n.* A device located at the various steering stations that tells the helmsman the direction in which the propeller shaft is rotating, often incorporated in the shaft tachometer.

**shaft horsepower (shp)** *n.* The horsepower on the shaft as indicated by a torsion meter. This is somewhat more than indicated horsepower (ihp), while the maximum designed shaft horsepower is about 10% more than the actual shaft horsepower.

**shafting** *n.* The general term used to denote the components or sections of a propeller shaft. Engine power is transmitted to the propeller by means of shafting. Examples are **tail shaft, line shaft, crankshaft.**

**shaft liner** *n.* A brass sleeve that encases the propeller shaft to protect it against corrosion.

**shaft log** *n.* (1) Timber or other member connected to a keel and the after deadwood with a **shaft hole** through which the propeller shaft passes. (2) A revolution of the propeller shaft.

**shaft strut** *n.* A support close to the after end of the shaft used on vessels with propellers off the centerline, as in vessels with two or four propellers.

**shaft tube** *n.* The tube through which the propeller shaft passes to emerge from the hull.

**shake** *n.* A crack in a spar.

**shakedown** *n.* A period of training personnel and testing equipment after commissioning or overhauling a vessel. In the U.S. Navy, this also includes a **shakedown cruise,** which is usually to a foreign port.

**shake out**   *v.* To unreef a sail and hoist it to its full spread. "After the squall passed through, we shook out the reef and continued down the coast."

**shakings**   *n.* Waste rope, canvas, and small stuff.

**shallow-draft**   *adj.* Describing a vessel built for use in shallow water. See SHOAL-DRAFT.

**shallow floor**   *n.* Flooring of small depth, usually found in a single-bottom vessel.

**shallows**   *n.* An area of the sea in which the depth is relatively slight. Also *banks; flats; middle grounds; shores.*

**shanghai**   *v.* To kidnap a man to force him to be a member of a ship, now illegal. Often men were given whiskey to get them drunk, or were beaten into insensibility, and taken to a ship going to far-off ports such as Shanghai, China. See PRESS GANG.

**shank**   *n.* The main shaft of an anchor. See ANCHOR.

**shank painter**   *n.* A cable used to secure the flukes of an anchor to the tumbler arm.

**shanty**   See CHANTEY.

**shapes**   *n.* A visual aid hung in the rigging of a vessel between sunrise and sunset as prescribed in the *Navigation Rules* to indicate the vessel's navigational status. See BALL; CONE; CYLINDER; DAY SHAPE; DIAMOND.

**shape**   *v.* To give curvature to a plate or other member.

**shape a course**   *phr.* To take a course from a chart by parallel rules and give the heading to the helmsman.

**shark's mouth**   *n.* An opening in an awning for a mast or other upright member. See CROWFOOT.

**sharp bilge**   *n.* A sharply curved bilge. Also *hard bilge* or *hard chine.*

**sharpie**   *n.* Popular workboat for fishing and racing. It was originally a boat with two short masts that carried triangular leg-of-mutton sails extended with a sprit. The length-to-beam ratio was about 4:1. It has been modified, but it still is a long, flat-bottomed centerboard boat and usually has a loose-footed main.

**sharp-up**   *adj.* Yards braced as far as possible so as to sail as close to the wind as practicable. "The yards are sharp-up."

**shearing**   *n.* Pack ice when subjected to rotational forces such as an eddy. A shearing results from such forces.

**shearing punch**   *n.* A heavy tool used for driving a forelock pin out of an anchor shackle.

**shear line**   *n.* A line at which a shearing cut is to be made with a large machine tool to cut a large plate during the construction of a ship. See SHEER LINE.

**shear pin**   *n.* A soft metal safety device used to fasten a propeller to its shaft. When the propeller hits a snag, the pin shears, and further damage to the propeller, drive shaft, and other internal parts of the motor is minimized. The propeller is held on by a nut-and-bolt attachment but is free to turn on the shaft while disengaged.

**sheathing**   *n.* A metal skin, usually copper, that sometimes covers wood or glass hulls to prevent worms and the growth of marine grasses. The Chinese were the first to use metal sheathing to prevent worms and the growth of barnacles on the ships.

**sheathing paper**   *n.* A heavy, tarred or oiled paper placed between the sheathing and the wooden hull.

**sheath knife**   *n.* A sailor's knife with a fixed blade that fits into a sheath on a belt.

**sheave**   *n.* (pron. shiv) The grooved wheel in a block over which the rope or chain is led. The axis is called the **pin.** See BLOCK.

**sheave**   *v.* (1) To back a boat by pushing oars forward. (2) To fall astern. "With reduced sail we found we soon began to sheave and lose the other boats." Rare today.

**sheave ho**   *interj.* (pron. shiv) The call used when the blocks of a tackle have come together or have been two-blocked. See KNOT.

**sheepshank**   *n.* A knot made in a rope to shorten it. It consists of two long bights in the rope with a half hitch over the end of each bight.

**sheer**   *n.* (1) The curve of the deck upward from amidships to the bow and stern. (2) The fore-and-aft curvature of a vessel's main deck from bow to stern. (3) An abrupt change of course. (4) The position in which a vessel sometimes is kept riding in order to stay clear of its own anchor.

**sheer (off)**   *v.* To deviate from an established course either deliberately or carelessly.

**sheer clamp**   *n.* A longitudinal timber or stringer that forms the top of the hull below the deck inside the gunwale.

**sheer draught**   See PLAN.

**sheer hulk**   *n.* Any floating structure fitted with sheerlegs and used for harbor work.

**sheerlegs**   *n.* A temporary load-bearing frame made of two or three spars lashed together at the top with a **sheer head lashing** from which a **sheer head purchase** is suspended, and used for stepping and unstepping masts or for moving heavy weights. Also *sheers.* See SHEER.

**sheer line**   *n.* Drawings showing the freeboard throughout a vessel's length. See SHEAR LINE.

**sheer mast**   *n.* A mast made up of two spars, one on either side of the deck and brought together at the top in the form of a pair of shears.

**shear plan**   *n.* Drawings showing the longitudinal (broadside) profile of a vessel. Also *elevation, sheer draft.*

**sheer pole**   *n.* (1) A steel pin secured horizontally at the foot of a mast's standing rigging that prevents the shrouds from turning or twisting. (2) A steel or wooden batten seized across two shrouds above the upper deadeyes to serve as the lowest rung of a ratline. Also *sheer batten.*

**sheer ratline**   *n.* The name given to every fifth ratline, which extends to the after shroud and swifter.

**sheer strake**   *n.* In a wooden vessel, the uppermost plank which runs the full length of the vessel from stem to stern just below the main deck.

**sheet**   *n.* (1) A line used to control a sail's driving force whether it be bent on the sail's clew directly or on a boom that holds the sail. Sheets are named for the sails they control, such as jib sheet, mainsheet, and so on. To be "three sheets to (or in) the wind" is a square-rigger term meaning to be out of control, presumably drunk. See GAFF. (2) A piece of plating thinner than ⅛ inch.

**sheet anchor** *n.* The heaviest anchor on sailing ships that was used only in emergencies and was kept as far forward in the waist as practical, for which reason it was also called a **waist anchor.** Today sheet anchor is often used (incorrectly) as a synonym for bower, spare bower, or best bower.

**sheet bend** *n.* A knot used to join two ropes of different diameters; it is a double hitch formed by passing the end of one rope through the bight of the other. See KNOT.

**sheet home** *v.* (1) To haul in a sheet as taut as possible to leave scarcely any curvature in the sail. (2) To sheet in to correct trim.

**sheet ice** *n.* A thin, smooth sheet of new ice.

**sheet in** *v.* To pull in a sheet and its corresponding sail: "Sheet in the mainsail to the point that it stops luffing." See SHEET HOME.

**sheets** *n.* Seats in the forward end and after end of a small boat, but not those occupied by oarsmen, engineers, or boat handlers. A U.S. Naval Reserve pamphlet for Naval Reserve officers published in 1942 says "When a senior officer is present, [junior officers] do not sit in the stern sheets unless asked to do so." This advice to junior officers was to leave the drier, stern sheets for senior officers, a naval tradition of many centuries. Junior officers get into boats first to help hold the boat steady while the senior officers climb down the ladder and board last.

**sheet winch** *n.* A vertical winch used on sailboats for handling sheets; these can be powered or manually operated. They always have pawls, giving them the characteristics of a capstan rather than a gipsy or a windlass. Merchant sailing ships used winches with horizontal barrels for the same purpose.

**shelf** *n.* (1) A zone contiguous with a continent or an island; it extends from the low-water line to the line at which there is a marked increase in depth. (2) An inboard timber that follows the sheer of a vessel, bolted to the lower side of the beams to reinforce the frame and deck. (3) In shipyards, brackets riveted to the shell plating to form a bearing surface.

**shell** *n.* (1) A racing canoe, one such as is used in intercollegiate sports and propelled by one, two, four, or eight oarsmen. (2) The hull of a ship. (3) The outer casing of a block that houses a sheave. See BLOCK. (4) A projectile fired from a gun.

**shellback** *n.* (1) Anyone who has crossed the equator. (2) An old sailor.

**shell expansion** *n.* A plan showing details of a vessel's shell plating and shell longitudinals.

**shell landings** *n.* Points on the frames where the edges of shell plates are to be located.

**shell lugs** *n.* Pieces of angle iron that are riveted to the shell plating as support for stringer plates.

**shell plating** *n.* A general term for the outer plating of a vessel including bottom, bilge, and side plating.

**shell room** *n.* (1) Projectile storage area in a warship magazine. Also *projectile flat.* (2) Projectile stowage section at the base of a barbette.

**shelter deck** *n.* A continuous or partial superstructure deck above the freeboard or main deck. A **shelter deck vessel** is one with a shelter deck.

**shield** *n.* Heavy timbers used to check the sternway of a vessel as it slides down the ways. Also *mask.*

**shift**   *n.* (1) An accidental change in a vessel's cargo's position usually as a result of the action of the sea. Such shifting can often be significant enough to cause capsizing. (2) A change in the direction of wind or current. A wind that is not consistent is called **shifty.**

**shift**   *v.* To move a vessel from one place, usually a berth, to another.

**shift colors**   *phr.* To change the ensign and the jack from port to steaming positions, or vice versa.

**shifting backstays**   See RUNNING BACKSTAYS.

**shifting ballast**   *n.* Easily moved weights used as ballast on sailboats to trim the boat. The practice is illegal in most races, and most racing rules allow only the crew to be shifted for ballast.

**shifting beam**   *n.* A portable support used to hold hatches open, the ends of which are fitted in slots designed for that purpose.

**shifting boards**   *n.* Temporary or permanent longitudinal bulkheads used in holds required for vessels carrying bulk cargo such as grain to prevent the cargo from shifting. Shifting irons, or hooks, hold the temporary shifting boards in place.

**shift of butts**   *n.* Phrase applied to the arrangement of butt joints in plating.

**shift the rudder**   *interj.* The conning officer's command to the helmsman to change the rudder to the opposite side with the same angle of turn. If the helmsman has the wheel 30° to the right, the command means to shift to 30° to the left.

**shim**   *n.* (1) A piece of material such as metal, stone, or wood, usually tapered, used to level a frame or plate. (2) A piece of tapered metal inserted in bearings, shafts, or rudder posts to regulate clearance.

**shim**   *v.* To use a shim to adjust the alignment of a fixed or moving part. "We shimmed the propeller shaft to compensate for the wear and prevent excessive shaft noise."

**shingle**   *n.* (1) Sea gravel made up of large waterworn pebbles larger than gravel. (2) A beach covered with coarse gravel or shingle. A plural form is not used.

**ship**   *n.* (1) A vessel of significant size that is capable of deep-water navigation. (2) Any self-propelled vessel. (3) A three-, four-, or five-masted vessel with square sails on all masts. See BARK. (4) Under maritime law, any vessel intended for marine transportation regardless of form, rig, or means of propulsion.

**ship**   *v.* (1) To take on unwanted water, usually over the side. "We shipped water with every wave all through the night." (2) To set in place. A mast or oars are shipped when in place and ready for use. (3) To take on cargo, stores, fuel, and so on. "Ship the waist anchor before we sail." (4) To sign on; to enlist on a ship. In this context it is usually confined to the merchant marine. (5) To reenlist is to **ship over,** especially in the U.S. Navy, but not necessarily on a ship. You can ship over knowing that you will continue in a shore billet.

**ship alteration (SHIPALT)**   *n.* Shipyard term for authorized alterations to specified parts and machinery on a particular vessel.

**ship biscuit**   *n.* Hardtack, a biscuit that was made of flour, water, milk, and salt and would not deteriorate when stored for long periods. Weevils and roaches will attack them, however, and C. S. Forester mentions Hornblower's absentmindedly tapping his hardtack on the table to shake out the weevils before eating it.

# Ship Types

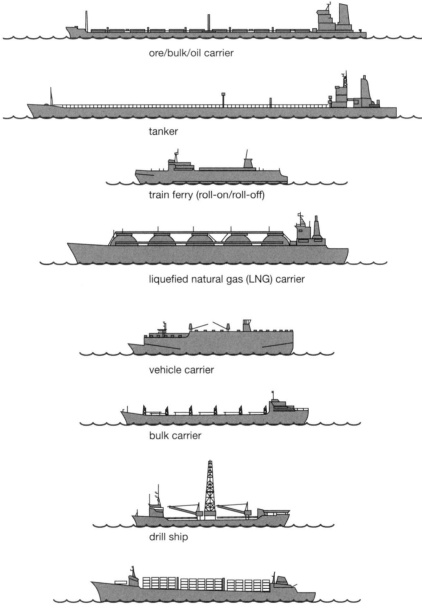

ore/bulk/oil carrier

tanker

train ferry (roll-on/roll-off)

liquefied natural gas (LNG) carrier

vehicle carrier

bulk carrier

drill ship

container ship

**ship-breaker**    *n.* A company that buys ships for their scrap value.

**shipbreaking**    *n.*    The    intentional scrapping of a ship when it has become obsolete or too old for service.

**ship broker**    *n.* (1) A person or firm engaged in transacting the business of chartering vessels and obtaining cargo space for shippers. (2) A person or firm that finds freight and passengers for a shipping company.

**shipbuilding**    *n.* The business of designing, constructing, and launching ships.

**shipbuilding lien**    *n.* The right of the shipbuilder to take or hold a vessel for sale when not paid as per contract for labor and materials furnished toward the vessel's original construction. A shipbuilding lien is not a part of admiralty law and is not enforceable in an admiralty court. Suits are brought in civil courts just as is the case with any similar contract.

**ship canal**    *n.* An artificial waterway deep enough for seagoing vessels. Canal dimensions vary considerably from one canal to another. The Panama Canal locks are 110 feet wide, and the canal has a minimum depth of 40 feet. The Suez Canal has a minimum width of 179 feet and a minimum depth of 33 feet at the banks and 40 feet in the channel.

**ship channel**    *n.* An established course for larger ships to follow entering and leaving a port or while navigating a river.

**ship characteristics**    *n.* The complete package that makes up a ship's ability to accomplish its mission: complement of men, battle stations, and material necessary for warfare.

**ship dunnage**    *n.* Any material used for dunnaging a ship, such as wooden wedges, batting, scantlings, and cordage.

**shipentine**    *n.* Same as a four-masted bark; rare.

**ship error**    *n.* The constant error introduced in radio direction finder bearings as a result of metal structures on a vessel.

**shipfitter (FP)**    *n.* (1) A person who performs the steel construction on a ship from the keel to the final superstructure. (2) An enlisted person in the U.S. Navy who effects metal and steel repairs, welding and riveting, on shipboard. Now called a **hull technician** (HT).

**ship foreman**    *n.* A stevedore superintendent who oversees loading and unloading a vessel. Not part of the ship's crew.

**ship handling**    *n.* The art and science required to direct the movements of a ship whether operating alone or in formation, docking, maneuvering, or mooring. Good **ship handlers** almost seem to be born with that innate ability to put the vessel where they want it when they want it, while others who are otherwise equally intelligent and diligent never pick it up as successfully.

**ship hour**    *n.* A unit of labor; the time a vessel is at a pier for loading and unloading.

**ship influence**    *n.* The magnetic, acoustic or pressure effects of a ship which are detectable by a mine or other sensing device.

**shipkeeper**    *n.* The person in charge of a vessel in port when there is no crew on board.

**shipletter**    *n.* Mail carried by a ship that is not classified as a mail vessel or mail boat.

**shipload**    *n.* The amount of cargo that will fill a vessel to its load line capacity. See FULL AND DOWN.

**shipmaster** *n.* The officer in command of a merchant vessel. One is licensed as a master, not as captain or commanding officer; but one is addressed as "Captain" and never "Master."

**shipmaster's declaration and warning notice** *n.* A document signed by the shipmaster of a commercial cargo vessel and a U.S. Department of Agriculture boarding officer that inventories meats, vegetables, and fruits of any kind purchased in foreign countries; it also addresses pollution control measures and other matters.

**shipmaster's lien** *n.* A master's claim under maritime law on the cargo of a vessel against the owners for the payment of a crew's wages and other disbursements. See SEAMAN'S LIEN.

**shipmate** *n.* Person with whom one is sailing or has sailed.

**shipmen** *n.* In British ports, longshoremen who work on ships, as distinct from those who work only on land.

**shipment** *n.* (1) The act of shipping goods. "The shipment was made on Friday the thirteenth." (2) Goods or cargo shipped. "The shipment was intact when it was delivered."

**ship of the line** *n.* A warship in the days of sail, with mounted guns, to fight in the line of battle when ships broadsided each other. In general, these were either first-, second-, or third-rate ships. Also *man of war.* See RATE.

**shipowner** *n.* One of the persons in whom title of a vessel is vested. See PLANKOWNER.

**shipper** *n.* A person or firm that consigns or receives freight for transportation; a shipping agent. The conditions for the transportation are spelled out in the bill of lading.

**shipper's export declaration** *n.* A customs form filed by the shipper of freight to foreign countries. Also *shipper's manifest.*

**shipper's protest** *n.* A notarized objection entered by a shipper against the master and owners of a vessel for refusal to properly sign bills of lading without qualifications or exceptions.

**shipping** *n.* (1) The business of transporting cargo. (2) All ships of a port or country, usually measured in terms of ships' combined tonnage or in absolute numbers of ships. In 1989, U.S. shipping included 39,209 vessels with a combined cargo capacity of 68,740,581 short tons.

**shipping agent** *n.* A person or firm engaged for the purpose of transacting all port business on behalf of shipowners and charterers. Contracts signed for by the agent are binding on the owner or charterer as in other agent and principal relationships. Also *ship's agent.*

**shipping articles** *n.* The written contract entered into and signed by officers and crew. The principal features of the voyage are enumerated, including wages, character of the voyage, and so on. The master is the only member of a ship's complement who does not sign shipping articles. See SIGN ON.

**shipping lane** *n.* A term used to indicate the general flow of merchant shipping between two ports.

**shipping ton** *n.* A unit of volume, and not of weight. In the United States it is equal to 40 cubic feet or 32.14 U.S. bushels. In Great Britain it is equal to 42 cubic feet or 32.72 Imperial bushels. See TONNAGE.

**ship rider** *n.* A member of a fleet training group assigned to assist in technical aspects of the ship's equipment on a shakedown cruise or a refresher training exercise.

**ship-rigged**   *adj.* Describes a vessel rigged with three or more masts, all square-rigged. See SHIP.

**ship's agent**   See SHIPPING AGENT.

**ship's bell**   *n.* A loud bell on a ship tolled every half-hour to announce the time or to be sounded as needed in a fog or conditions of reduced visibility. See BELLS; WATCH.

### Ship's Bells

| Bells | Hour of the Day (A.M. or P.M.) | | |
|---|---|---|---|
| 1 | 12:30 | 4:30 | 8:30 |
| 2 | 1:00 | 5:00 | 9:00 |
| 3 | 1:30 | 5:30 | 9:30 |
| 4 | 2:00 | 6:00 | 10:00 |
| 5 | 2:30 | 6:30 | 10:30 |
| 6 | 3:00 | 7:00 | 11:00 |
| 7 | 3:30 | 7:30 | 11:30 |
| 8 | 4:00 | 8:00 | 12:00 |

**ship's business**   *n.* The ship's paperwork including the preparation of all documents pertaining to stores and cargo, records of surveys, logs, and so on.

**ship's carpenter**   *n.* A petty officer whose duties include opening and securing hatches and cargo ports, the sounding of the bilges and tanks, the upkeep of wooden masts and booms, and the maintenance of wooden decks.

**ship's emergency transmitter**   *n.* As defined in the *International Telecommunication Union* (ITU), a ship's transmitter that is reserved to be used exclusively for distress, urgency, or safety purposes.

**shipshape**   *adj.* Tidy, neatly arranged. A vessel that is **shipshape and Bristol fashion** is one that is kept up well. In the heyday of the British merchant marine, Bristol, England, was an important shipbuilding and repair port, well recognized for its proficiency.

**ship's head**   *n.* A vessel's heading. See DIRECTION.

**ship's holiday**   *n.* A day off from labors not directly involved with keeping the ship going, in accordance with the laws of the nation whose flag the vessel carries. As a rule, the more remote the registry, the less apt the master is to respect the country's customs. A ship with a Monrovian registry and an American captain and crew probably would not worry about the Liberian New Year. See ROPE-YARN SUNDAY.

**ship's husband**   *n.* The owners' representative in managing the business affairs of a vessel who hires the officers and crew and is duly registered by the registering government. The limits of his responsibilities and authority are dictated by the registering country.

**ship's inertial navigation system (SINS)**   *n.* The self-contained dead-reckoning system that continuously tracks the vessel's position from :• e initial known position.

**ship's lantern**   *n.* A heavy, well-protected lantern placed in a ship's rigging as required by the *Rules of the Road.* Now replaced by sidelights and other lights in accordance with the *Navigation Rules.*

**ship's log**   *n.* The record of a vessel's activities from the time it is commissioned until it is decommissioned. It is usually called the **smooth log** to distinguish it from the **rough log** that is kept by the chief officer or the officer of the watch (Officer of the Deck). In the U.S. Navy while the rough log is frequently kept by the Junior Officer of the Watch or even the quartermaster, the OOD signs it and takes the necessary date from it to write the smooth log. The rough log usually has more detail on courses, speeds, weather, ships sighted, and so on, and it is kept as backup material in case of later questions regarding possible oversights in the smooth log. The rough log is bound with a saddle stitch so that pages cannot be cut out later. Changes must be initialed in red ink.

**ship's orders**   *n.* Aboard U.S. Navy ships, directives on single subjects signed by the commanding officer, addressed to members of the ship's company, and having the authority of law.

**ship's organization book**   *n.* The administrative and organizational compendium for a specific vessel in the U.S. Navy, based on a standard issued by a type commander. The complete term is the "ship's organization and regulation manual."

**ship's papers**   *n.* The documents required by international law to be carried by all ships and that must be available for inspection on demand by government authorities. They include certificate of registry, clearance certificate, load manifest, licenses, sea letter, passports, charter party, logs, ship's articles, bills of lading, and so on.

**ship's register**   *n.* Official document containing a description of the ship, her tonnage, and ownership, among other things. It is similar to a deed.

**Ship's Routing**   *n.* A publication of the Inter-Governmental Maritime Consultative Organization (IMCO) that describes the general provisions of ship's routing, traffic separation schemes, deepwater routes, and areas to be avoided, as adopted by IMCO. The details are promulgated through the *Notice to Mariners* along with their dates of implementation.

**ship's secretary**   *n.* A U.S. Naval officer who assists the executive officer with the ship's correspondence. On smaller ships, if there is no Chief Yeoman aboard, the ship's secretary is usually the equivalent of an office manager.

**ship's service store**   *n.* A compartment that serves as a small retail store for personal items from cigars to toothpaste, radios to perfume. See SLOP CHEST.

**ship's staff**   *n.* All officers belonging to the different departments of a merchantman, including deck officers, engineering officers, the ship's doctor, purser, and communications officer.

**ship's stores**   *n.* Any article or substance used on board a vessel for the upkeep and maintenance of the vessel, or for the safety or comfort of the vessel, its passengers, or crew, or for the operation or navigation of the vessel.

**ship timber**   *n.* Timber suitable for use as structural members, generally a tree with a trunk of 8 inches in diameter is considered ship timber.

**ship time**   *n.* Local apparent time. The ship's clocks are set every day at noon (1200) when the Sun crosses the meridian.

**shipway**   *n.* (1) The structure that supports a ship during construction. (2) A shipping canal.

**ship weather routing**   *n.* A service now provided by the U.S. Navy's Optimum Track Ship Routing (OTSR), the service determines optimum routing to various ports of the world with maximum safety, minimum fuel consumption, and other factors included. The service was first started by Benjamin Franklin when he was Deputy Postmaster General of the British Colonies. His work was carried further with the development of hydrographic charts by the very able U.S. Navy officer Lt. Matthew Fountaine Maury. Maury's interest in weather routing led him into the area of international cooperation and maritime law, and it was he who organized the first international maritime conference in Brussels in 1853. Commercial versions of the OTSR are also available.

**shipworm**   *n.* An elongated mollusk resembling a worm that bores into submerged wood and damages ships and wharf piles. The most common of these is the *Teredo navalis* as well as several species of the genus *Bankia*. The rudimentary shell is used for boring. Wood ships, especially those in the tropics and subtropics, use copper sheathing or copper paint to discourage these extremely destructive creatures.

**shipwreck** *n.* A ship that has been destroyed. "The Eastern seaboard of the United States is strewn with shipwrecks."

**shipwreck** *v.* To destroy a vessel, usually by collision, fire, storm, or grounding. "We were shipwrecked in the roaring forties."

**shipwright** *n.* The person responsible for seeing that all fabricated material is set in the vessel in conformity with the lines presented by the designers. A shipwright must be a skilled, many-talented worker who understands ship's carpentry, barge building, laying out, drawing, fastening, planking, and deck laying.

**shipyard** *n.* A place where ships are built and/or repaired. A Navy shipyard is one that is maintained by the U.S. Navy.

**shiver** *v.* To allow the sails to luff when coming up close to the wind. "The main shivered as the header hit us."

**shoal** *n.* An offshore hazard composed of sand, shell, and loose rock with a depth of 10 fathoms at most; a sandbank or sandbar. (2) A pod of whales.

**shoal** *v.* To reduce depth. Depths of water are said to shoal when they decrease.

**shoal** *adj.* Shallow.

**shoal-draft** *adj.* Said of a shallow-draft boat that is capable of going over shoals that are only inches deep. "Only a shoal-draft boat could be expected to negotiate Caxambas Pass."

**shoaling** *n.* The increase in wave height as a wave of the sea approaches the more shallow water of a shoal.

**shoal water** *n.* Shallow water or water over a shoal.

**shock cord** *n.* Elastic cord with hooks at each end and used for various jobs such as furling sails, lashing sails on deck, or securing bottles in the lazarette.

**shock line** *n.* Heavy rope pendant used between a chafing chain and the hawser.

**shod** *adj.* Said of an anchor that is caked with clay or mud so that it will not bite into the bottom. "The flukes of the anchor are too shod to grab."

**shoe** *n.* (1) A piece of wood placed over an anchor fluke to protect the ship's side. (2) A strut between the rudder post and the keel or sternpost. (3) Outboard piece of the cutwater. (4) A fitting at the bow of a ship used for antichafing when paravanes are being towed. See RUBBING BAR.

**shoe** *v.* To place a piece of wood over an anchor fluke to protect the ship's side. "Boats, shoe the anchor before we secure it for sea." See SHOD.

**shole** *n.* A fitting or plate that distributes the weight or force of a shore.

**shoot** *v.* (1) To allow the sails of a sailboat to luff while headway keeps the boat going, usually done while rounding a mark and preparing for a different tack or when coming up on a mooring buoy. "Hard alee; we'll shoot the mark from here and tack." See FOREREACH; HEAD REACH. (2) To observe the altitude, usually with a sextant, as in "to shoot the Sun."

**shore** *n.* (1) A temporary wooden member used in damage control and shipbuilding. See TOM. (2) Land or beach at the edge of the sea. When a sailor leaves his ship on liberty, he goes **ashore**. Shore is usually taken to mean a narrow strip of land in immediate contact with any body of water, as in the New Jersey shore, while coast is understood to mean a general region in proximity to the sea, as in the Gulf Coast. The **shoreline** is usually considered to include every indentation and projection of the land, in contrast to a **coastline,** which is more general and therefore a shorter measurement. The shoreline for the state of Florida is upwards of 8,000 miles, while the coastline is only about 1,200 nautical miles.

**shore (up)**    v. To brace with temporary construction. See TOM.

**shore boat**    n. A water taxi, a civilian-operated ship-to-shore passenger boat.

**shore establishment**    n. All activities of the Navy not included in the operating forces or in the U.S. Department of the Navy.

**shoreface**    n. The narrow zone to seaward from the water, over which the beach sands and shells actively move.

**shore fast**    n. Any mooring line that makes a vessel fast to the shore or a pier at the shore, as distinguished from a line to a buoy or dolphin.

**shore lead**    n. (rhymes with need) A path between pack ice and the shore or between pack ice and an ice front.

**shoreline**    n. See SHORE.

**shore patrol (SP or SHOPAT)**    n. A detail assigned to police duty ashore to maintain discipline and aid local police in handling U.S. naval personnel on liberty and on leave.

**shore ram**    n. A steel-headed battering ram used for knocking out temporary shoring.

**shore weir**    n. (rhymes with queer) A dam or fence that extends out from shore into the sea to catch fish, divert the flow of water, and so on.

**shore whaling**    n. The practice of catching whales and bringing them to shore rather than to a whaling vessel.

**shoring**    n. Temporary bracing in construction and damage control for horizontal support. See SHORE.

**short blast**    n. A whistle signal of about 1 second's duration. See PROLONGED BLAST.

**short board**    n. A short tack; a short distance on a single tack.

**shorten sail**    v. To reduce sail by reefing or furling.

**short-end link**    n. An open chain link that connects a shackle to a larger link.

**short-landed**    adj. Said of a delivery of cargo that is less than the amount shown on the manifest.

**short sea**    n. (1) A sea with waves close together, usually a warning that the bottom is getting closer. (2) A charter party term that refers to the Baltic and the White Sea (of the Barents Sea) trades.

**short-shipped**    adj. Cargo that is not loaded as anticipated because it did not arrive in time or there was not sufficient room on board.

**short splice**    n. A splice to join two rope ends using only a short piece of each rope for the splice. The short splice is bulky and should only be made on rope that does not have to be led through a block. See LONG SPLICE.

**short stay**    n. Said of an anchor chain when it has been hove in to the point that the scope is only slightly more than the water's depth, but before the anchor has broken ground. "The anchor detail reports the anchor's at the short stay."

**short tack**    See SHORT BOARD.

**short ton**   *n.* A measure of weight equal to 2,000 pounds.

**shot**   *n.* A length of chain or cable, usually 15 fathoms and marked by shackles at each end joining it to more cable or chain.

**shot line**   *n.* Three-strand, left-laid line used with a line-throwing gun.

**shoulder gun**   *n.* A line-throwing gun used on craft up to 300 tons.

**shoulder pipe**   *n.* Similar to a hawse-pipe, but used for back spring lines.

**shove off**   *v.* To leave. Literally, to push the bow of a small boat clear of a larger boat or a pier to be ready to leave.

**shower**   *n.* A brief precipitation as rain, sleet, or hail. Showers come from widely separated cumulus clouds. See WEATHER.

**shrimper**   *n.* A small vessel used for drag-netting shrimp. (2) One who catches shrimp for a living.

**shroud**   *n.* A wire or rope, part of the standing rigging, that leads from a mast to the side of a vessel to support the mast. See RATLINE; STAY. (2) A casing around propeller and turbine blades.

**shroud cap**   *n.* A protective covering at the upper end of a shroud.

**shrouded propeller**   *n.* (1) A propeller in a cylinder with little tolerance between cylinder and propeller blades. The shroud diverts the water flow and avoids loss due to rotary currents. (2) A propeller with a band of bronze at the edge of the blades. This forms more of a cone, with a thicker diameter on the forward edge. It strengthens the wheel, reduces vibration, and focuses the flow of water more directly astern. Also *Kurt nozzle*.

**shroud hoop**   *n.* A steel band on a mast to which shrouds are secured.

**shroud-laid rope**   *n.* Right-hand laid cable with or without a soft core, with four strands. It does not get as hard as hawser-laid lines.

**shroud plate**   See CHAIN PLATE.

**shroud ring**   *n.* A washer separating the propeller and the stern bearing.

**shuga**   *n.* An accumulation of spongy ice lumps a few centimeters across. The lumps are formed from grease ice or slush and sometimes from anchor ice that has floated to the surface.

**shut-out cargo**   *n.* Cargo that has failed to be loaded because of overbooking, lack of space, intervention of local or federal authorities, or some other cause.

**sick bay**   *n.* Infirmary or first aid station on naval vessels. The passenger liner equivalent is called a dispensary or clinic.

**sick seam**   *n.* Sailmaker's term for a worn seam.

**side bar keel**   *n.* A keel fitted with flanges inside the hull and that extended down through the hull. Today it is only seen on very old boats.

**side bench**   *n.* A longitudinal plank placed outboard to protect the air tanks in a lifeboat.

**side boy**   *n.* A sailor who mans the side of a naval vessel when rendering side honors to a visiting military officer or government official. The higher the visitor's rank, the more side boys are prescribed by tradition.

**side bunker**   *n.* A fuel compartment in the boiler room at the side of a boiler.

**side curtain**   *n.* Canvas or heavy synthetic material fitted in canopies of small boats to protect the passengers from spray.

**side dunnage**   *n.* Boards or spar ceiling on a ship's side fitted to prevent cargo from sliding into the frame spaces and obstructing ventilation.

**side echo**   *n.* The effect on a radar display produced by a side lobe of a radar antenna, a smearing of the plan position indicator. Ghosts, in contrast, appear as multiples of a target.

**side error**   *n.* A sextant error caused by lack of perpendicularity between the horizon and the frame of the instrument.

**side honors**   *n.* A ceremony accorded important military officers and government officials as they arrive and depart from a naval ship. The honors include side boys and piping by a boatswain's mate. It may include the appropriate march by a band if there is one aboard, and gun salutes if it is a **saluting ship.** The older term was **compliments.**

**side keelson**   *n.* A timber on the side of the keel between the keel and the chine to give extra strength and, in planing hulls, to add stability.

**side ladder**   *n.* A gangway ladder.

**side-launching ways**   *n.* A ways on shore from which a vessel is launched parallel to the water's edge, used when water is restricted and the shoreline is plentiful.

**sidelight**   *n.* (1) A green light on the starboard side and a red light on the port side each showing an unbroken light over an arc of 112.5° and so fixed as to show this light from right ahead to 22.5° abaft the beam on its respective side. (2) A British term for portholes.

**sidelight castles**   *n.* Small towers on either side of the forecastle with sidelights installed in them; most often found in non-U.S. flag vessels. Also *bow lighthouses.*

**sidelight frame**   *n.* The wooden or steel bracket that sidelights are carried in to ensure the proper angle of visibility. Also *sidelight screen.*

**sidelines**   *n.* Shipbuilder's term for straight vertical lines at the widest molded surface of the ship or amidship.

**side plating**   *n.* The material making up the shell from the turn of the bilge to the main deck. See SHELL PLATING.

**sidereal**   *adj.* (pron. sighdireeyul) Of or pertaining to the stars. While sidereal generally refers to the stars, and tropical refers to the vernal equinox, **sidereal time** and the **sidereal day** are based on the position of the vernal equinox relative to the meridian, and the **sidereal year** is based on the stars.

**sidereal day**   *n.* The time required for a complete rotation of the Earth measured between successive meridian transits of the vernal equinox. See GREENWICH HOUR ANGLE; LOCAL HOUR ANGLE; RIGHT ASCENSION.

**sidereal hour angle (SHA)**   *n.* The angular distance west of the vernal equinox, the arc of the celestial equator, or the angle at the celestial pole between the hour circle of the vernal equinox and the hour circle of the body, measured westward through 360°. Angular distance east of the vernal equinox is right ascension.

**sidereal time**   *n.* (1) The hour angle of the first point of Aries. (2) A solar day of 24 hours is 24 hours, 3 minutes, 56.6 seconds in sidereal time.

**side steps**   *n.* Narrow steps located near the gangway outside the hull and leading to the water.

**side stringer**   *n.* An internal longitudinal member running along the side of a vessel above the bilge.

**side tank**   *n.* A ballast tank in a double bottom that continues up the sides. Also *Macglashan tank.*

**side-wheeler**   *n.* A paddle wheel steamer with paddles on the sides instead of the stern.

**siding**   *n.* The width of a frame, a keel, a stem, or a sternpost.

**Sierra**   *n.* Phonetic word for the letter "S." When used alone, the signal flag means "My engines are going full astern."

**sight**   *n.* An accurately timed observation of the altitude of a heavenly body by an instrument to assist in establishing the geographical position of a vessel, as in sun sight or star sight.

**sight**   *v.* (1) To **sight an anchor** is to bring an anchor up to a visible level in the water to make sure it is clear before letting go again. (2) To see something with one's eyes or to "see" something on a radar screen. A marker can be sighted on radar (**electronically in sight**), or it can actually be seen by someone on deck or on the bridge (**visually in sight**).

**sight edge**   *n.* The visible edge of plating in a clinker-built hull.

**sight reduction**   *n.* The method of deriving from a sight the information needed for establishing a line of position. See MARCQ ST. HILAIRE METHOD.

**sight vane**   *n.* A sighting aperture on an azimuth ring or bearing circle.

**signal**   *n.* (1) A short message using letters, characters, flags, sounds, or other visual displays. (2) In electronics, any transmitted electrical impulse.

**signal book**   *n.* The *International Code of Signals,* a publication of the Defense Mapping Agency Hydrographic/Topographic Center intended primarily for communication at sea in situations involving life and death, safety at sea, and navigational safety, especially when language differences arise. The code is suitable for transmission by radiotelephone, radiotelegraph, sound, alphabetical and numeral flags, and so on. The system embodies the principle that each flag or combination of flags has a complete meaning. For example, "O" means "man overboard" and "AL" means "I have a doctor aboard."

**signal bridge**   *n.* The section of the navigating bridge on a U.S. Navy ship assigned for use by the signalmen with the flag bag and signal halyards. It is not to be confused with the flag bridge, which is reserved for flag officers and their staffs.

**signal flags**   *n.* An internationally recognized system of flags and pennants representing the letters of the alphabet, numbers, and repeat pennants by means of which ships can communicate in most instances by using not more than four flags. See SIGNAL BOOK.

**signal halyard**   *n.* A light line used to hoist signal flags in a vertical display.

**signal letters**   *n.* A four-flag system used by most maritime nations for designating their ships, both merchant and naval. The first letter (or two) identifies the nationality of the vessel. All United States ship's signals begin with "N." The signal is flown when entering port, when joining a formation, and on other occasions when identification is important. Beginning in 1943, the same code letters were used in radio communications.

**signalmen**   *n.* In the U.S. Navy the enlisted personnel who operate the signal halyards, read flags on other ships, and so on. They are derisively known as flag floozies.

**signal pistol**   *n.* A hand gun for distress signals on small boats.

**signal record book**   *n.* A log of all general signals received or transmitted by a vessel.

**signal rocket**   *n.* A cylinder containing pyrotechnic ingredients used for making a brilliant light in the sky, primarily used for distress.

**signal station**   *n.* A coastal station, usually manned by the U.S. Coast Guard or its equivalent in other nations, from which signals can be sent to passing ships. With the universal adoption of radios, signal stations have all but disappeared.

**signal yard**   *n.* A spar on the foremast with blocks for the signal halyards and signal flags.

**signature**   *n.* The graphic record of the magnetic properties of a vessel automatically traced as the vessel passes over the sensitive element of a recording instrument.

**sign off**   *v.* To discharge and make final payment of wages to seamen after returning to port and the completion of their contracts. "Upon our return after the first voyage, the first and second mates signed off and the Old Man offered me the mate's berth." From *A Ship's Log Book,* by Captain Frank Farrar.

**sign on**   *v.* To sign shipping articles before beginning a voyage. In U.S. ports, the articles are signed in the presence of the master. In a foreign port, the U.S. consul supervises the shipment and discharging of seamen.

**sikussak**   *n.* Very old ice trapped in a fiord; it resembles glacier ice since it is formed partly from snow.

**silent running**   *n.* Submarine condition of quiet operation of machinery to avoid detection.

**silk room**   *n.* A steel bulkhead compartment on vessels engaged in the silk trade in the Far East. They were usually built 'tween decks and lined with soft paneling and gratings and all possible precautions were taken to protect the valuable cargo from the hull's sweating.

**sill**   *n.* (1) A fitting placed under a scupper hole outside the hull to prevent water trickling down the ship's side and causing a streak. (2) A structure at the mouth of a basin built to keep the water from leaving boats high and dry in places where large tidal changes occur. (3) A beam at the entrance to a dry dock over which vessels pass when entering and leaving.

**silt**   *n.* Soft mud or sediment carried by water and deposited along the course of the water flow.

**siltation**   *n.* The depositing of sediments in estuaries, channels, harbor entrances, and similar places.

**simoon**   *n.* A strong, hot, sandy wind on the Sahara and Arabian deserts that blows across the Red Sea.

**simplex pump**   *n.* A reciprocating pump with a single cylinder as distinguished from a duplex pump with two steam cylinders in a single block. See PUMP.

**simultaneous altitudes**   *n.* A method for determining a ship's position by using the altitudes of two or more heavenly bodies. It had many shortcomings and the method was superseded.

**single-arm tiller**   *n.* A single direct tiller with no quadrant and no yoke.

**single-banked**   *adj.* Describing a small boat such as a whaleboat or dinghy in which one oarsman mans each thwart and oar; one man, one oar. A double-banked boat has two men on each oar.

**single block**   *n.* A pulley with only one sheave.

**single bottom**   adj. A vessel with only an outer hull and no inner bottom or tank.

**single-buoy mooring (SBM)**   n. A very large mooring buoy in open water used for tankers to moor while discharging their fuel to smaller vessels or at an offshore discharge station.

**single burton**   See SPANISH BURTON.

**single-leg propeller strut**   n. A propeller shaft support with only one brace attaching it to the hull.

**single-point mooring (SPM)**   n. A mooring that allows a vessel such as an oil tanker to swing on the mooring while loading or unloading.

**single-station range light**   n. A directional light bounded by two other lights of different colors. A vessel following the range on a channel has erred from the centerline when the color changes from white to red or from white to green. See RANGE LIGHT.

**single-tree mast**   n. A lower mast made from a single piece of timber.

**single up**   v. (1) To throw off the second mooring lines leaving only single lines to hold a vessel in its dock. When a vessel is secured to a wharf or quay, the lines are doubled up for extra security. When it is ready to sail again, the lines are singled up before they are thrown off (or brought aboard). (2) To unreeve the running part of a purchase.

**single-way launching**   n. A method of end launching in which the single sliding way is under the keel; two additional bilge ways prevent the vessel from swaying from side to side.

**single whip**   n. A tackle with a single block and no mechanical advantage. See TACKLE.

**sing out**   v. To call or announce with a loud voice.

**sinnet**   See SENNET.

**sinuate**   v. To steer a vessel in a series of curves from the base course as an evasive tactic. See EVASION; WEAVE; ZIG-ZAG.

**siren**   n. (1) A warning device designed to put out a wailing sound, used when an emergency appears imminent such as grounding or collision.

**sirocco**   n. A hot, humid south or southeast wind in the Mediterranean especially around Italy, Sicily, and Malta. It rises in the Libyan desert as hot and dry, but picks up moisture as it passes over the sea to become quite unpleasant; it occurs most often in July and August.

**sisal**   n. A fleshy Mexican plant with large leaves that yield stiff fiber used for manufacturing a rope that is similar to Manila, but with less tensile strength.

**sister**   v. To double up, often said of frames that abut each other.

**sister block**   n. A block with two sheaves set end to end rather than side by side with falls reeving in opposite directions.

**sister hook**   n. (1) A pair of hooks on a common eye. (2) Hooks that can be placed together to form a ring.

**sister keelsons**   n. Fore-and-aft members on both sides of the center keelson and fastened to it horizontally for greater stability.

**sister ship clause**   n. A marine insurance clause that specifies that the underwriters will be responsible in case of a collision between ships owned by the same company.

**sister ships**   *n.* (1) Vessels built to the same or similar design. (2) Ships under the same ownership.

**skag**   *n.* A heavy chain carried on barges to be thrown over the stern as a drag if necessary to steady a towed barge.

**skeg**   *n.* (1) The after part of a keel that braces the sternpost. (2) A small keel at the stern of small boats, surfboards, and sailboards. (3) A support for the rudder extending aft from the keel. (4) The support for the rudder post and sternpost on a single-screw vessel. (5) A fixed underwater fin used to promote directional stability of an object such as a river buoy. (6) A rudderlike projection from the stern of a barge for the purpose of reducing yaw; it may be movable, but limited to an arc of 10° to 15°. From the Old Norse *skegg,* a beard or projection.

**skerry**   *n.* A rocky ledge, often partially covered by water, British usage.

**skew**   *adj.* Describes a type of propeller with the blades raked slightly aft instead of at right angles to the hub to prevent eddies at the upper levels and to give better results in rough seas when the tops of the blades emerge from the water.

**skids**   *n.* (1) Timbers fitted over decks for stowing heavy boats. (2) A frame fitted over hatches while cargo is being loaded and unloaded to prevent injury to the ship's sides.

**skiff**   *n.* A general term applied to a number of shallow-draft small open boats. Usually they have pointed bows, flat bottoms, and flat sterns. They are propelled by poles, oars, motors, or sails. Earlier usage applied more to workboats than current usage does.

**skillygalee**   *n.* A mixture of oatmeal, sugar, and water drunk by firemen working in engine spaces aboard ship to prevent cramps.

**skimmer**   *n.* An oil-spill cleanup device that is propelled over the water as it sucks the water into a tank.

**skin**   *n.* (1) The inside and outside plating of a vessel's hull. The inside plating is sometimes called the ceiling, while the outside plating is called the casing or shell. (2) That part of a sail that covers the entire sail when furled.

**skin girth**   *n.* The measurement of a hull at the outside skin from gunwale to gunwale.

**skin resistance**   *n.* The resistance of the hull to the water based on the area below the waterline and the condition of the hull, but not the design.

**skipjack**   *n.* A derivative of the flat-bottomed sharpie, but with a modified V-shaped bottom, used along the Atlantic Coast especially by Chesapeake Bay oystermen and in Provincetown, Mass., where it is called a **corner boat** because of its sharp chines. The sail plan is generally a leg-o'-mutton mainsail and a stay foresail on a raked mast.

**skipper**   *n.* (1) The captain of any non-naval vessel large or small. Small boat captains are often addressed as "Skipper," though the usage is considered informal in the United States. (2) In Great Britain, "skipper" enjoys more status and is officially applied to a duly licensed person in charge of a fishing vessel.

**skivvy**   *n.* Sailor's word for underwear.

**sky diagram**   *n.* A representation of the heavens showing the apparent positions of the various celestial bodies with reference to the horizon. See STAR FINDER.

**sky-grazer**   *n.* A lightweight triangular sail set above the royal used on clipper ships. Also *skysail.*

**skylark**   *v.* To engage in horseplay, fun, or noisy, friendly chatter. Sailors who climbed the rigging and slid down the backstays were so called.

**skylight** *n.* (1) Thin places in ice (less than 1 meter thick) that are translucent from below; a large skylight is one large enough for a submarine to try to push through. See POLYNYA. (2) A hatch cover, either permanent or removable, fitted with glass and protected by grating or rods, that allows light and fresh air below.

**skylight cover** *n.* (1) The glass-paneled top of a skylight, usually hinged. (2) A tarpaulin cut to the desired dimensions to cover a skylight in bad weather.

**skylight grating** *n.* A steel grating built to be placed over the glass panes of a skylight for protection.

**sky map** *n.* The reflection of the refracted light of pack ice on distant cloud.

**sky pilot** *n.* Informal name for a ship's chaplain.

**skysail** *n.* A small square sail above a royal on square-rigged ships.

**skysail pole** *n.* The upper extremities of the mast above the skysail.

**skyscraper** *n.* A triangular sail used on clipper ships and set between the truck and skysail yard.

**slab** *n.* The slack part of a sail that hangs down when the leech lines are pulled up. The lines used to raise the mainsail of square riggers are the slab lines and bunt lines.

**slab hatch** *n.* A particularly heavy hatch cover made of several hatch covers bolted together, often used to prevent pilferage.

**slab keel** *n.* An extra plate fastened outboard the plate keel to give greater local rigidity.

**slab line** *n.* Similar to a buntline, a line used to furl the slack canvas of a squaresail after it has been taken in. Slab lines are run up on the afterside of the sail and rove through **slab line blocks** lashed to the jackstay. Also *slaplines.*

**slab reef** *n.* The upper reef in a topsail.

**slack** *n.* A length of line or rope that is not under strain. To give someone some slack is to ease up on the line.

**slack** *v.* To ease off a sheet or other rope. Also *slack away; slack off.*

**slack cloths** *n.* baggy sails.

**slack in stays** *adj.* Slow to come about, but not in irons. A boat is said to be slack in stays if it is difficult to bring about smartly. Also *balky; cranky.*

**slackness** *n.* The tendency of a sailboat to fall off from the wind and to require lee helm to keep it on a straight course.

**slack tank** *n.* A partially filled compartment. See FREE SURFACE.

**slack water** *n.* The moment when a reversing current changes direction and its speed is zero. The relation of the time of slack water to the tidal phases varies in different locales.

**slam** *v.* To hit the waves or swells in such a way as to significantly jar the vessel. Also *pound.*

**slant** *adj.* (1) A brief wind, usually before or during a change in direction, a cat's paw. (2) A favorable wind.

**slant (of wind)** *n.* A change in wind direction.

**slatting** *adj.* Said of sails that flap as a boat rolls when becalmed or nearly so.

**slaver**  *n.* A ship engaged in the slave trade. Also *blackbird(er)*.

**slave station**  *n.* A radio navigation term for a station of a chain whose emissions are made with reference to the emissions of a master station.

**sleeper**  *n.* A partially submerged log.

**sleepers**  *n.* The first tier of casks stowed in a hold.

**sleet**  *n.* Precipitation that is partially or entirely frozen rain drops—usually quite mushy. See WEATHER.

**SLEP**  *n.* A U.S. Navy acronym for Service Life Extension Program, an extensive rehabilitation that adds 10 or 15 years to the working life of the vessel. It is also used as a verb, as in "The *Kitty Hawk* is being SLEP-ed." See FRAM.

**slew**  *n.* See SLOUGH.

**slew**  *v.* (1) To yaw, especially when being towed. Also *advance; slide; transfer*. (2) To turn rapidly; a gun director slews the guns to get on the next target. (2) In ice navigation, to force a ship through ice by pushing apart adjoining ice floes. One speaks of "slewing" a ship through the ice.

**slewline**  *n.* A rope used essentially in clearing a foul hawse when a line is used to position one anchor when clearing the chain of another anchor.

**slick**  *n.* (1) An oily surface on the water. (2) Flat calm. (3) A relatively flat place on the sea's surface that is left to windward when a vessel is drifting to leeward. (4) A relatively flat piece of water in the lee of a wake caused by a ship's passing.

**slide**  *n.* (1) One of the metal lugs on a sail that slide in the sail track. (2) That part of a mount that supports the gun directly.

**sliding bulkhead door**  *n.* A watertight steel door that can be operated from an upper deck such as the bridge. Also *automatic door*.

**sliding ways**  *n.* The heavy planking that forms the lower part of the cradle that slides down the ways when a vessel is launched.

**slight sea**  *n.* Douglas scale reading of 2, indicating waves between $\frac{1}{2}$ foot and 2 feet with a long, low swell.

**slime**  *n.* Soft, fine, ooze often found on the bottom of a channel.

**sling**  *n.* (1) A length of wire, rope, or webbing with eyes or hooks in each end used for hoisting and lowering something, whether a yard along a mast or a load of cargo. (2) A single load of cargo being loaded or off-loaded by use of a sling.

**sling band**  *n.* A hoop around the middle of a lower yard to which slings are fastened.

**slinger**  *n.* A longshoreman who places the slings on the cargo and releases the cargo from the sling when it is put back on shore.

**slinging and lifting**  *n.* The charge made for securing cargo with chain, cable, or rope in a boat preparatory to lifting it to a ship.

**slings**  *n.* That part of a yard to which a sling is secured.

**slip**  *n.* (1) The difference between the theoretical and actual distance that a propeller advances through the water when turning under load, spoken of in percentage. Also *slip of the wheel*. (2) The space or berth for a vessel between two piers, jetties; a dock. (3) A sloping hard used for sliding vessels into and out of the water.

**slip**  *v.* (1) To let go the anchor quickly by unshackling the cable instead of hauling the anchor. "We slipped our cable as the enemy force appeared on the horizon rather than risk capture." Any captain who does this needs a good explanation of why he lost his anchor. (2) **To slip one's cable** is to die. (3) To haul a vessel out of the water.

**slip angle**  *n.* The angle between a propeller face and its line of advance.

**slip clutch**  *n.* A clutch used on larger engines on small craft that disengages the engine when the propeller hits a snag, used to prevent damage to the engine. On small outboard motors the same protection is afforded by a shear pin.

**slip fitting**  *n.* A nipple or similar fitting that slips over a length of pipe to repair a leak that results from corrosion.

**slip knot**  *n.* Any knot that can be adjusted or undone easily. Knots commonly tied so as to be easily slipped include the **slippery hitch** (a variation of the clove hitch), the **slippery reef knot,** and the **slippery bowline.**

**slipper**  *n.* The shoe that rides on a guide and controls the crosshead or joint between the piston rod and the connecting rod in a reciprocating engine.

**slippery**  *adj.* Used to describe certain knots so tied that they can be instantly released by pulling the free end of the line. See SLIP KNOT.

**slip stopper**  *n.* A device that holds an anchor cable to relieve the strain on the windlass when the anchor is down.

**slipway**  *n.* A sloping space in a shipyard with launching ways and keelblocks where ships are built and launched. See WAYS.

**slob ice**  *n.* A field of ice so broken up that it moves with the waves and swells. It usually contains flotsam.

**sloop**  *n.* A one-masted, fore-and-aft rigged vessel, almost always Bermuda-rigged, and able to set a mainsail and one headsail together with a spinnaker. Much debate is carried on over the subtle distinctions between this rig and a cutter. See RIG.

**sloop of war**  *n.* A full-rigged light cruiser of the sailing ship navies. It mounted 18 to 32 guns on one deck and was faster than a frigate. Also *corvette.*

**slop chest**  *n.* A chest or small compartment, from which members of the crew of a merchant ship can buy such personal items as tobacco, foul weather gear, boots, and so on. The purser keeps the slop chest and sells these **small stores** to sailors. From the Middle English *sloppe,* baggy trousers.

**slop chute**  *n.* A chute placed over the side to cast garbage and trash into the sea free of the ship's sides.

**slope oar**  *n.* A laggard oarsman.

**slops**  *n.* Clothing and other personal items sold to seamen on merchant ships.

**slop tank**  *n.* A tank designated to store oily waste for later disposal at an approved site.

**slot**  *n.* The space between two sails such as mainsail and jib or two headsails. The slot should be adjusted for optimal airflow for maximum driving power.

**slot effect**  *n.* The wind speed differential on a sailboat, especially when close-hauled, that can be observed as a rush of redirected air between the mainsail and the jib.

**slough**  *n.* (pron. sloo) A side channel, bayou, or marsh. Also *slew; slue.*

**sludge**  *n.* Sediment in fuel tanks.

**sludge vessel** *n.* A ship designed to carry sewage discharge out to sea for pumping over the side. Also *honey boat.*

**slue** *v.* To twist a spar or mast around on its axis.

**slug** See SAIL SLIDE.

**sluice** *n.* (1) An opening between two compartments, with a gate or sluice valve operated usually by a **reach rod** extending to a higher deck to allow the passage of liquids from one compartment to the other. (2) A floodgate.

**sluice gate** *n.* A large-capacity valve.

**sluicing pond** See SCOURING BASIN.

**slush** *n.* (1) Any lubricant used to make a mast greasy so that the rope parrals can slide up and down more easily. (2) Snow that falls into saltwater that is below 32°F and lies on top to be blown by the wind. (3) Early stage of freezing saltwater when it is viscous but not frozen solid. Also *slush ice.* (4) The unusable skimmings from the galley that are accumulated in a **slush bucket.**

**slush fund** *n.* Money raised through the sale of soft drinks and slush from the galley and used for recreational equipment.

**smack** *n.* A small fishing vessel with either cutter or sloop rig. In Britain, fishermen make a distinction between "smacks" and "boats," smacks being considerably larger and always used for trawling.

**small-area plotting sheet** *n.* A good approximation of a Mercator position plotting sheet, constructed by the navigator and based on a graphical solution of the secant of latitude.

**small boys** *n.* General name for smaller U.S. Navy ships in a fleet or convoy, such as destroyers, frigates, and auxiliary mine sweepers.

**small-craft advisory** *n.* A single red pennant displayed by day, or a red light over a white light displayed at night, indicating that winds up to 33 knots and/ or sea conditions dangerous to small craft (defined by the Weather Service as "small boats, yachts, tugs, barges with little freeboard or any other low-powered craft") are forecast for the area.

**small diurnal range** *n.* The difference in the height of water between mean lower high water and mean higher low water. The term is applicable only to semidiurnal or mixed tides.

**small ice cake** *n.* An ice cake less than 2 meters across.

**small stores** See SLOP CHEST.

**small stowage** *n.* Cargo that is of such size and shape that it can be placed in spaces between beams and other areas that would otherwise be wasted.

**small stuff** *n.* Cordage under 1 inch in circumference used for whipping and serving and other light jobs that would not require heavier rope. See SEIZING; WHIP.

**small tropic range** *n.* The difference in water height between tropic lower high water and tropic higher low water, applicable only when the tide is semidiurnal or mixed.

**smelling the bottom** *phr.* A phrase meaning a vessel is in shallow water with the results that the steering is awkward and the vessel's speed is reduced.

**smithwork** *n.* The installation and fitting of masts, derrick mountings, chain plates, davits, and so on, traditionally the work of a smith.

**smiting line** *n.* (rhymes with fighting) A rope that controls the stops on a furled sail that is kept aloft. The smiting line is so rigged that a quick jerk from on deck will release the sail so that hands do not have to be sent aloft. Admiral William Smyth described it in 1867 as "the mark of a seaman if well executed."

**smoke cover**  *n.* A sail cover used to protect sails that are downwind from the smoke pipe.

**smoke head**  *n.* A chimney for a stove. See CHARLIE NOBLE.

**smoke pipe**  *n.* A smokestack on a ship.

**smoke pipe lines**  *n.* Pipes leading from each compartment to a glass-fronted cabinet in the wheelhouse. Smoke rising in any compartment could quickly be detected by the smoke in the glass cabinet.

**smoke sail**  *n.* (1) A tarpaulin hoisted forward of the Charlie Noble on sailboats to allow the smoke from the galley to go up instead of into the sails. (2) A canvas protection for a forge being used topside.

**smokescreen**  *n.* A cloud of smoke generated on destroyers to screen the movement of ships in a fleet or convoy.

**smoke signal**  *n.* A pyrotechnic device that produces colored smoke to be used as a daylight distress signal.

**smoking lamp**  *n.* Originally, a shipboard lamp from which pipes were lighted. When smoking had to be stopped for a while, the smoking lamp was extinguished. Today, the phrase is used to determine whether smoking is allowed on a ship. When fuel is being transferred or ammunition is being brought aboard, for example, the word is passed that the "smoking lamp is out," which means that no one is allowed to smoke on the vessel until the order is canceled.

**smooth**  *n.* An area of relative calm that begins to appear after several stormy days.

**smoothbore gunner**  *n.* A commissioned officer who specializes in gunnery duties.

**smooth sea**  *n.* Douglas scale reading of 1, indicating comparatively smooth water with a short, low swell.

**smothering line**  *n.* A line carrying chemicals or steam led to a compartment for smothering fires.

**snake**  *v.* To wrap a smaller line about a larger one, similar to worming, to confine the ends of seizing.

**snaking**  *n.* Netting rigged to prevent objects on deck from going over the side.

**snaking the stays**  *phr.* To brace parallel stays with a rope going from one stay to the next down the length of the two stays so that if a part of the stay is shot away, the rope will transfer the pressure to the opposing stay.

**snatch block**  *n.* A block with a hinged opening above the sheave that makes it possible to lead a line through the block without having to feed the end through first.

**snib**  *n.* A handle on a watertight door that can be operated from either side. Also *dog.*

**snipe**  *n.* U.S. Naval slang for a member of the engineering department.

**snipe**  *v.* To cut a sharp bevel on a beam end or stiffener to give continuity of strength.

**snorkel**  *n.* Retractable tube on a submarine that allows the boat to breathe while submerged. From the German *Schnorkel,* snout.

**snotter**  *n.* (1) A rope with eye-splices at both ends, used as a sling when rove through the grommets of bags. (2) A short rope spliced into a circle and seized with spun yarn or rawhide, and seized to the mast with a bight to fit the lower end of the sprit which it secures to the mast. (3) A loop of small stuff used to prevent slipping used, for example, at the small end of a sprit to prevent the sprit from shipping down the mast. (4) The bell-shaped device at the end of a spinnaker pole to which the spinnaker tack is secured.

**snow**   *n.* A two-masted vessel similar in appearance to a brig, except that what appears to be a mizzen is actually a try-sail set on a short **snow mast** immediately abaft the mainmast.

**snow blink**   *n.* A bright glare on the underside of extensive cloud cover and brighter than the yellowish glare of ice blink.

**snub**   *v.* (1) To let out only enough anchor chain to allow the anchor to dig in and bring the ship up to an abrupt stop. (2) To let go an anchor and to bring a vessel to a quick stop on a short range of cable. (3) To slow a running rope, usually by putting a half-turn around a cleat so that control is maintained while it is eased out further.

**snug down**   *v.* To reduce sail in anticipation of a storm; to prepare for heavy weather.

**snug harbor**   *n.* A well-protected harbor.

**sny**   *n.* A small toggle on a pennant.

**socket signal**   *n.* A signaling flare fired from a railing-mounted brass socket.

**SOFAR**   *n.* An acronym for sounding, fixing, and ranging, an underwater distress signal that enables two or more shore stations to locate a vessel by tri-angulation.

**soft eye**   *n.* An eye-splice without a thimble.

**soft lay rope**   *n.* Rope made with the amount of twist less than regular lay when great flexibility is needed. Also *long lay.*

**soft patch**   *n.* A temporary plate on piping or plating secured with tap bolts. The soft patch is made watertight with a gasket, usually canvas soaked in red lead.

**solar day**   *n.* One rotation of the Earth with reference to the Sun. See SIDEREAL DAY.

**solar noon**   *n.* The instant the sun is over the upper branch of the reference meridian, 12 o'clock solar noon.

**solar tide**   *n.* (1) The part of the tide that is due to the tide-producing force of the Sun. (2) The observed tide in areas where the solar tide is dominant. See LUNAR TIDE.

**solar time**   *n.* Time as measured by the Sun as the reference point. Solar time may be **mean** if the mean Sun is used as reference, or it may be **apparent** if the apparent Sun is used as reference.

**solar winds**   *n.* Winds coming from land and sea alternately, depending on the position of the Sun, observed in coastal regions.

**SOLAS**   See INTERNATIONAL CONVENTION FOR THE SAFETY OF LIFE AT SEA.

**soldier**   *v.* Seaman's slang for shirking a task. "Jones will soldier on the job if he is not supervised." British sailors held very low opinions of soldiers.

**soldier's wind**   *n.* A wind from either side that makes possible sailing in both directions, so that "even a soldier could sail," no seamanship needed.

**sole**   *n.* Planking fastened to the foot of a rudder to carry it down to the level of the false keel. See CABIN SOLE.

**solid floor**   *n.* A continuous floor extending from the centerline to bilges, with holes usually cut to make it lighter.

**solid frame**   *n.* Continuous frame such as an angle bar, as opposed to a built-up frame.

**solid pintle**   *n.* A pintle cast solid with the rudder arm.

**solid spar**   *n.* A mast, yard, or other spar made from a single log with the heart at the center of the finished product.

**solstices**   *n.* (1) The two times of the year when the Sun reaches its maximum declinations. The maximum northern declination is about June 22 at 23.5°N; this is called the **summer solstice.** On or about December 22 it reaches the maximum southern declination of 23.5°S; this is called the **winter solstice.** These maximum declinations are called **solstitial points.** (2) One of the two points of the ecliptic farthest from the celestial equator; one of the two points on the celestial sphere occupied by the Sun at maximum declination. The midway points between the solstices are the equinoxes.

**solstitial tides**   *n.* The tides that occur near the times of the solstices. The tropic range may be expected to be especially large at these times.

**soma**   *n.* A Japanese trading junk.

**Somali Current**   See EAST AFRICA COASTAL CURRENT.

**sonar**   *n.* From sound navigation and ranging, a device that radiates a high-frequency sound signal to locate underwater objects. Accurate distances and bearings on objects can be obtained from the sonar. An earlier British name for such equipment was **ASDIC** (AntiSubmarine Detection Investigation Committee). See ECHO SOUNDER.

**sonarman**   *n.* An enlisted man who has proven through examination that he is qualified to operate sonar.

**sonobuoy**   *n.* A sonar device used to detect submerged submarines which when activated relays information by radio. It may be active or passive, or directional or non-directional.

**son of a gun**   *n.* A child born on a Royal Navy ship when women were allowed to sail with their husbands. In instances when the paternity was in doubt, the child was entered into the log as "son of a gun" because birth frequently took place on the gun deck.

**sound**   *n.* (1) A long, wide body of water, generally larger than a strait or channel, that connects two larger bodies of water. (2) A narrow body of water connecting two larger bodies, or a narrow channel between two pieces of land.

**sound**   *v.* (1) To measure the depth of the water. "We must sound the depth as we cross the bar." (2) To dive, a whale is said "to sound" when it plunges beneath the surface.

**sound buoy**   *n.* A buoy equipped with a gong, whistle, or bell.

**sounding(s)**   *n.* (1) Depth of water as shown on a depth indicator or chart. "When the soundings reach 100 fathoms, we can take a more direct course." (2) Traditionally a term that referred to the depth of the water. If a vessel was **on soundings,** it was in water that could be sounded with the deep-sea lead; a vessel that was off soundings was in water beyond the 100-fathom curve and the bottom could no longer be reached by the deep-sea lead. Today the terms still have the same meaning with relation to the 100-fathom curve, even though depth sounders can measure depths greater than 100 fathoms. "After an hour's sail, we were off soundings." See TIDAL DATUM. (3) The recording of bilge depths. "Soundings of all bilges should be taken on a regular basis to determine if any leaks have developed." See SOUNDING ROD; SOUNDING TUBE. (4) The determining of the depth of the sea by either (a) a lead line or (b) an electronic measurement of the time it takes for a sound to leave the ship and return (an echo sounding).

**sounding lead**  See LEAD AND LEAD LINE.

**sounding pole**  *n.* A graduated pole used to sound shallow areas.

**sounding rod**  *n.* A long rod used to sound tanks to determine the depth of fuel and water. Because the rod is now steel, it is coated with **thieving paste** so that the liquid remains visible when the rod is removed from the tank. See ULLAGE.

**sounding tube** (or **pipe**)  *n.* A tube through which a sounding rod is lowered to determine water depths in the bilge or fuel depths.

**sound-powered telephone**  *n.* A shipboard telephone that derives its electrical power from a voice-activated diaphragm with iron core and permanent magnet. The receiver is the same device in reverse. This is a highly effective means of shipboard communications that has proved to be virtually trouble free due to its simplicity. When a ship is at general quarters, most officers have an enlisted "talker" with a sound-powered telephone to talk to all parts of the ship.

**sound signal**  *n.* A blast emitted by a ship's whistle.

**South Atlantic Current**  *n.* The current that results from the confluence of the warm, highly saline Brazil Current and the cold, less saline Falkland Current off Uruguay and flows eastward to the Cape of Good Hope.

**Southeast Drift Current**  See AZORES CURRENT.

**Southern Cross**  *n.* A readily identifiable group of six stars near the South Pole. Four of the stars form a cross that serves as a point of reference for mariners in the southern latitudes. Also *Crux*.

**Southern Ocean Current**  See EQUATORIAL CURRENTS AND COUNTERCURRENTS.

**South Indian Current**  *n.* An easterly flowing current in the Indian Ocean that is continuous with the northern edge of the West Wind Drift.

**southing**  *n.* The distance a vessel makes good to the south. The opposite is northing. See EASTING; WESTING.

**South Pacific Current**  *n.* An easterly current in the South Pacific that is continuous with the northern edge of the West Wind Drift.

**southwest monsoon**  *n.* Wind found in the northern Indian Ocean and the southern China Sea.

**sou'wester**  *n.* (1) An oilskin hat (the term does not include an oilskin coat) with a broad brim for heavy weather. The term is said to come from England, where wind from the southwest brings dirty weather. (2) A strong wind from the southwest.

**space system**  *n.* A tunnel created by spacing bags of cargo in such a way as to create a fore-and-aft ventilating duct.

**spales**  *n.* Temporary beams for erected frames of a vessel under construction.

**span**  *n.* (1) Short rope with blocks, thimbles, or eyes spliced in both ends. The bight is hitched around a mast or spar, and ropes are rove through the ends for hoisting yards, and so on. (2) A rope with ends secured far apart with a **span block** in the bight, and used for cargo handling and other deck jobs. (3) The length of a bridge between supports. A quartermaster may give the navigator the bearing on the "middle of the center span" of a charted bridge.

**span** *v.* To confine by means of a span. Booms were spanned to the mast, for example.

**Spanish bowline** *n.* A knot that forms two loops, neither of which will slip, and used for swaying a man up the mast or from ship to ship; one leg is placed in each loop.

**Spanish burton** *n.* A tackle with two single blocks in series giving a 3:1 mechanical advantage. Spanish burtons were used by Gloucestermen when handling dories and baskets of fish and are a good tackle for raising heavy loads a short distance. Also *dory tackle; single burton.* See TACKLE.

**Spanish cedar** *n.* Neither Spanish nor cedar, it is a light, soft wood from Belize used for racing hulls. It is any of several trees of the genus *Cedrela.*

**Spanish fox** *n.* A single left-laid yarn used for seizing. See LAY.

**Spanish reef** *n.* An overhand knot in the head of a jib used in emergencies to shorten sail.

**Spanish windlass** *n.* (1) A wooden device turned by a marlinespike and used to bring two ropes together. (2) Two parts of a wire cable rove through a pad eye welded to the deck. "The on-deck stuff was secured with 'Spanish Windlasses'." From *A Ship's Log Book* by Captain Frank Farrar.

**spank** *n.* The heavy fall or slap of a vessel as it comes off a large wave.

**spanker** *n.* (1) The after mast and its sail on a schooner or square-rigged vessel with more than three masts. (2) A quadrilateral fore-and-aft sail set on the mizzenmast of a square-rigged ship. See SQUARE-RIGGED VESSEL.

**spanking** *adj.* (1) Fresh, brisk wind. (2) A quartering wind that keeps the spanker filled.

**spanner stay** *n.* A wire support that goes between two king posts.

**span shackle** *n.* Triangular shackle used to secure deck gear.

**spar** *n.* (1) A wood or metal pole such as a mast, yard, boom, or sprit. (2) See SPAR VARNISH.

**spar buoy** *n.* A long metal or wooden pole that projects above the water and is anchored at its lower end. They are most common in areas that become iced over because they are not swept away as easily as regular buoys.

**spar ceiling** *n.* An arrangement of spars starting at the bilges that keep the cargo from coming into contact with the shell of the vessel. See DUNNAGE.

**spar deck** *n.* A light upper deck above the main deck of wooden sailing ships where the spars, rigging, boats, anchors, and other heavy gear were stowed.

**spar down** *v.* To lash battens to the shrouds for the crew to use while rattling down.

**spare bunker** *n.* Collier term for a spare compartment that could be used for fuel or cargo.

**spar fender** *n.* A spar on a short rope used as a fender on the side of a vessel.

**sparks** *n.* Nickname for the radio operator.

**sparmaker** *n.* A ship's carpenter who specializes in making spars.

**spar varnish** *n.* A varnish made from **spar,** any of various nonmetallic minerals with vitreous luster such as feldspar. A fast-drying, water-resistant varnish results. It has an elastic finish that is especially suitable for ships and small boats where resistance to exposure rather than high gloss are required. From the Old English *spaer,* gypsum.

**spaul** *n.* A support fitted to the inside of the hull at specific frames. The arrangement of spauls effectively forms a cradle to support the bottom shell until the internal structure is secure and can be supported by shores and bilge cribbing.

**speak** *v.* To talk to a vessel that is in sight. First one hails a vessel, then one speaks (to) the vessel.

**speaking tube** *n.* A tube, usually made of brass, through which the human voice is carried without electrical or electronic boosters. It offers an efficient means for such applications as communication between the bridge and the captain's sea cabin.

**special anchorage areas** *n.* Areas established by the U.S. federal government for anchoring in which vessels of less than 20 meters in length are not required to exhibit the anchor lights and shapes normally required by the *Navigation Rules.*

**special cargo** *n.* Cargo that requires special handling and stowage because of its readily pilferable nature, such as liquor, perfume, cigars, jewelry, and other small valuables. See SPECIE ROOM.

**special devices** *n.* A general U.S. Navy term for training aids, tactical evaluations, and training methods.

**special duty officer** *n.* A commissioned officer in the U.S. Navy who has specialized in a particular field such as journalism, usually one who is not qualified for command at sea.

**special interest vessel (SIV)** *n.* Any ship identified by U.S. authorities as a potential threat to the national security while in U.S. waters.

**special flashing light** *n.* A yellow light flashing at regular intervals at a frequency of 50 to 70 flashes per minute; placed as far forward and as nearly as practicable on the fore and aft centerline of a tow, showing an unbroken light over an arc of the horizon of not less than 180° nor more than 225°, and so fixed as to show the light from right ahead to abeam and no more than 22.5° abaft the beam on either side of the vessel.

***Special Notice to Mariners*** *n.* A notice containing important information of great interest to all mariners such as caution on the use of foreign charts, warning on use of floating aids, use of the Automated Mutual-Assistance Vessel Rescue (AMVER) system, rules, regulations, proclamations issued by foreign governments, and so on. These are published annually in *Notice to Mariners No. 1* by the Defense Mapping Agency's Hydrographic/Topographic Center.

**special-purpose buoy** *n.* A buoy used to indicate a special condition that can be deduced from government-published lists.

**specials** *n.* Hazardous or undesirable cargo that generally gets a higher transportation charge, and special handling instructions are issued for it.

**special sea detail** *n.* A team aboard a U.S. Navy ship that has assigned duties when a ship is getting underway, mooring, anchoring, or maneuvering in tight quarters when the commanding officer wants to be sure the best crew are in the key positions. They take over the duties of the regular watch section and are relieved by the regular watch section when the evolution has been completed.

**special services** *n.* The welfare and recreation activities of U.S. Navy personnel, administered by a **special services officer.**

**special survey vessel** *n.* A survey ship built with material and equipment which, from the keel up, has been under the close scrutiny of surveyors certified by appropriate authority.

**specialty rank**   *n.* That insignia on a petty officer's sleeve badge that indicates his rating such as crossed anchors for boatswain's mate.

**special warnings**   *n.* Broadcast messages primarily intended to announce official U.S. government proclamations affecting shipping. These are broadcast by U.S. Navy and U.S. Coast Guard radio stations and are published in all editions of the *Daily Memorandum* and in the weekly *Notice to Mariners.*

**specie room**   *n.* A secure compartment designed and built to hold valuable or "precious" cargo such as gold and silver specie, precious stones, and mail, which are carried by special agreement. It is similar to a bonded warehouse and associated contracts on shore.

**specified command**   *n.* A military command assigned broad and continuing duties.

**spectacle clew**   *n.* A fitting with three rings in the same plane used as a base for three blocks with ropes rove in different directions.

**spectacle eye**   *n.* A metal piece fitted over the head of a davit and having two eyes, one for the guy and the other for the span. It is so named because it looks like a pair of eyeglasses or spectacles.

**spectacle frame**   *n.* A single casting support for two propeller shafts, bearings, and tubes.

**speed**   *n.* Rate of motion. The rate of motion in a straight line is **linear speed**. A ship's **speed** is measured in knots and means speed through the water unless speed over the ground is specified.

**speed, operational**   *n.* The highest speed that will be called for during a given operation. An operation order will state, for example, that the operational speed during Operation Icethaw will be 25 knots.

**speed, service**   *n.* (1) The speed of a vessel under optimum conditions—clean bottom, loaded to designed draft, engines exerting average power, and normal weather and sea conditions. (2) The mean speed over several similar voyages. Also *commercial speed.*

**speed, signaled**   *n.* In naval usage, the speed at which the designated guide ship in a formation has been ordered to steam at a given time. "The signaled speed for fueling will be nine knots."

**speed, standard**   *n.* The speed that has been established for a given type of ship, usually 15 knots. **Full speed** is about one-eighth faster than standard, and **flank speed** (top speed) is usually ordered by the knots or engine revolutions desired. Engine speeds are ordered by the conning officer in a command such as "All engines ahead two-thirds, make turns for 12 knots." Or, if executing a tight turn, the officer can order "Port engine ahead one-third, starboard back one-third." The crew member on the engine room telegraph repeats the order, rings it up, and when the engine room responds on the telegraph, he reports, "Port engine answers ahead one-third, starboard engine answers back one-third."

**speed, stationing**   *n.* An economical speed used for taking station or changing station in a formation.

**speed cone**   *n.* A yellow cone hoisted to the yardarms to indicate engine speeds to other ships in company. These are now obsolete in U.S. Navy.

**speed-course-latitude   error**   *n.* Gyrocompass error that results from other than east-west direction of movement. The error is westerly if any component of the vessel's course is north, and the error is easterly if any component is south.

The magnitude of the error is relative to the course, speed, and latitude of the vessel.

**speed curve**   *n.* A graph that relates engine speeds to speed through the water and used by watch officers while under way.

**speed key**   *n.* A device that makes it possible to send code at a much faster rate than with the familiar flat black key, and usually operated in a horizontal rather than a vertical plane. Radio operators call it a **bug.**

**speed-length ratio**   *n.* A ratio of speed in knots to the waterline length in feet. A displacement hull will usually have a maximum hull speed of somewhere near 1.34 times the square root of the waterline length. If a vessel's waterline length is 36 feet, the hull speed of the vessel may approach 9 knots. See HULL SPEED.

**speed light**   *n.* Combination of white and red lights at the after truck of a warship used to indicate speed changes to be followed by other members of a formation. Speed lights have been discontinued by the U.S. Navy.

**speed made good (SMG)**   *n.* In naval usage, the speed of a vessel along its track. Also *speed over the ground.*

**speed of advance (SOA)**   *n.* Speed intended to be made along a track; The average speed in knots that must be maintained during a passage to arrive at a destination at a scheduled time.

**speed of relative movement (SRM)** *n.* The speed of a vessel relative to another object in motion.

**speed over the ground (SOG)**   *n.* In naval usage, the speed along the actual path of travel over the ground. Also *speed made good.*

**speed table**   *n.* (1) A table used by conning officers to determine how many revolutions per minute (RPMs) need to be ordered to give a certain speed. If the formation speed is to be 10 knots, the officer looks at this speed table and finds that he will need 94 RPMs, for example. He then adjusts his speed to factor in the effect of wind and current, the condition of his own ship's bottom, and so on. (2) A table that gives the time required at various speeds to make good a specific distance.

**spencer**   *n.* A loose-footed gaffsail set on a standing gaff carried on the foremast or mainmast of a ship such as barks and full-rigged ships.

**spent**   *adj.* Said of a vessel at the end of a voyage with fuel and water used up, cargo discharged, and ballast tanks filled. See READY FOR SEA.

**sphere**   *n.* A curved surface all points of which are equidistant from a fixed point within, which is called the **center.** Although the Earth is not a perfect sphere, it is treated as one for most navigational purposes.

**spherical angle**   *n.* The angle between two great circles.

**spherical buoy**   *n.* A marker with a half-round top. These are often anchored at the edge of middle grounds, shallow areas in a channel surrounded by deeper water.

**spherical coordinates**   *n.* A system of coordinates that defines a point on a sphere or spheroid by its angular distances from a primary great circle and from a reference secondary great circle, such as latitude and longitude.

**spherical sailing**   *n.* A method of solving navigation problems using the principles of spherical trigonometry as opposed to plane sailing, which is based on the principles of plane trigonometry. Spherical sailing is used in long-distance sailing in computing great circle routes. See SAILING.

**spherical triangle**   *n.* A closed figure having arcs of three great circles as sides.

**spheroid**   *n.* An ellipsoid; a figure resembling a sphere. An **oblate spheroid** is one in which the shorter axis is the axis of revolution. The Earth is an oblate spheroid. A **prolate spheroid** is one in which the longer axis is the axis of revolution.

**spider**   *n.* (1) A lighted magnifying glass on a compass. The light is usually red to preserve the helmsman's night vision. (2) A strut or triangular outrigger used to keep a block clear of the mast or the ship's side.

**spider band**   *n.* A fitting at or near the base of the mast used for stowing belaying pins. Also *spider iron.* See FIFE RAIL; PIN RAIL.

**spike**   *v.* To force a spike into the vent of a muzzle-loading gun so that it cannot be used until the vent is cleared, usually by drilling. A spike is usually large and roseheaded with a square cross section.

**spike iron**   *n.* Caulking iron used for working material into tight places.

**spile**   *n.* (1) A long measuring rod or rule notched to hold a pencil and used by shipwrights. (2) A wooden replacement for a spike that has been removed from a hull. See TREENAIL.

**spile**   *v.* To mark off with a spile.

**spiling**   *n.* Set of figures showing distances along a curved beam or a surface from the edge of a template or curve.

**spill**   *v.* (1) To intentionally or unintentionally reduce wind pressure on a sail by easing it to a slight luff. (2) To accidentally discharge liquid cargo or fuel.

**spilling breaker**   *n.* A wave that breaks over a long distance, as opposed to a plunging breaker that crashes all at once.

**spilling line**   *n.* A buntline used for spilling wind from a square sail to assist in securing the sail.

**spin axis**   *n.* The axis of rotation of a gyroscope.

**spindle**   *n.* (1) The core of a made mast. (2) A beacon that appears to be a spar, but is fast to the bottom; these are not found in U.S. waters.

**spindrift**   *n.* Windblown sea foam; it begins to appear when the wind achieves Beaufort Force 5. Also *spoondrift.*

**spinnaker**   *n.* A triangular sail carried forward of the headstay on a **spinnaker boom** or **pole** opposite the main boom. It was first used on the British cutter *Sphinx* in 1866 and was jokingly referred to as "*Sphinx*'s acre," which later became "spinnaker." It is used for downwind sailing on Bermuda-rigged boats.

**spirit compass**   *n.* A magnetic compass in which the card floats in a solution of 45% ethyl alcohol. Various combinations of oils are used today, instead, because they damp the action better and do not freeze or discolor. Also *wet compass.*

**spirit flag**   *n.* A red flag with a white disc center flown on British tankers in port when carrying gasoline or spirits (alcoholic beverages). Bravo is used in U.S.

**spirketing**   *n.* Vertical siding; the thick strakes of ceiling inside a hull at the beam ends or just above the waterways of the 'tween deck.

**spit**   *n.* A narrow point of land extending into a body of water.

**spitfire**   *n.* A storm headsail, small and made from heavy material. A spitfire occupies about 35% of the vessel's foretriangle. See HEADSAIL.

**Spitzbergen Atlantic Current**   *n.* An ocean current that flows northward and westward from just south of Spitzbergen Island and gradually merges with the East Greenland Current in the Greenland Sea.

**splashboards**   *n.* Planking that can be slid vertically into grooves in a companionway to prevent water from entering below, used on smaller boats when doors are not practical.

**splashline**   *n.* The point off an enemy beach at night at which an underwater demolition team enters the water from rubber boats.

**splashnik**   *n.* A telemetric buoy that measures wave motion and relays the information to a ship or shore station.

**splice**   *v.* To join one rope or wire to another by interweaving the ends, or to unite the end of a rope with another part of itself as when making an eye-splice. See CONT SPLICE; EYE-SPLICE; LONG SPLICE; SHORT SPLICE.

**splice the main brace**   *phr.* (1) To add extra rope or an eye in the heavy braces or tackles used for trimming the main course. (2) To have an alcoholic drink. The term is said to have come from the extra tot issued to the men who carried out the arduous task of splicing the mainbrace. Extra tots were unusual, and the origin of the term is apocryphal. An extra tot was reserved for such occasions as Armistice Day, November 11, 1918, at 6:00 P.M., when the mainbrace was spliced by order of the Commander-in-Chief of the Royal Navy.

**splicing shackle**   *n.* A shackle on a chain on which a rope is spliced.

**spline**   *v.* To pay a wooden deck with wedge-shaped strips (splines) of teak or mahogany after the deck has been caulked for the purpose of holding the caulking and for appearances.

**splines**   *n.* Longitudinal strips, usually of teak or mahogany, used to separate and make planking more waterproof. The seams between the planking are caulked and glued after which the thin wedge-shaped splines are pressed into the seams.

**splinter deck**   *n.* Deck fitted with light protective plating to prevent splintering. See PROTECTIVE DECK.

**splinter screen (or shield)**   *n.* Light steel shield protecting the bridge and gun stations, designed for protection against shell fragments.

**split fall**   *n.* A stevedore's term for a cargo fall when both falls have cargo hooks, as opposed to a **married fall,** which has both falls attached to a single hook.

**split fix**   *n.* A fix using horizontal sextant angles obtained by measuring two angles between four objects or suitable charted features with no common center feature observed. The navigator generates two circles based on the two sets of observations. The vessel's position is at one of the two points at which the two circles intersect.

**split jigger**   *n.* A sail used on four-masted barks and full-rigged ships. The gaffsail on the jiggermast was rigged with upper and lower gaffs because of its awkward size.

**split link chain**   *n.* Chain made by riveting the two halves of each link together.

**split pin**   *n.* British term for a cotter key.

**split plant operation**   *n.* The division of a ship's engineering plant into two complete units for damage control purposes.

**spoil** *n.* Dredged material from a channel.

**spoil bank** *n.* An area, usually close to a channel, that has been approved for dumping the material or spoil dredged from the channel. Also *spoil area, spoil ground.*

**sponge dinghy** *n.* Small open boat used off Key West, Florida, for sponge fishing in shallow water.

**sponge hook** *n.* Metal hook with three prongs and inserted into a socket on a long pole, used for gathering sponges in shallow water without diving.

**sponson** *n.* (1) Any projection from the side of a ship such as a gun platform. (2) An air-filled projection or pontoon on the hull of a seaplane. (3) A bulge on the side of a canoe or other small craft that is designed to give added breadth when the boat is inclined. Origin uncertain.

**sponson beam** *n.* A fore-and-aft timber that supports the outer bearing of the paddle shaft and paddle box structure on a sidewheel steamer.

**sponson deck** *n.* The platform aft of the paddle wheel box on a paddle wheel boat.

**sponsor** *n.* The person, usually a woman, who christens a ship during the launching ceremony. Traditionally, it was considered bad luck to have a ship christened by a man.

**spoon bow** *n.* A bow made from full round sections and shaped somewhat like a bowl or spoon. It was seen on sternwheel steamers used in shallow water. Also *shovel bow.*

**spoondrift** *n.* See SPINDRIFT.

**spot** *v.* (1) To position cargo and handling gear, or to place cargo in a hold. "Spot this under the #3 hatch." (2) To position a ship at a wharf. (3) A charter-

ing term meaning to arrive at a destination: "The MV *Osiris* has been spotted" or "We spotted the *Osiris* at pier 63."

**spot charter rate** *n.* The per-ton cost of moving a cargo, usually crude oil, from one port to another on a one-time basis, as opposed to long-term charter party rates. Spot charter rates fluctuate with supply and demand of tonnage.

**spot elevation** *n.* A point on a chart or map, the height of which is noted as being above the datum usually by a dot or small sawbuck and elevation value.

**spotlight** See SEARCHLIGHT.

**spot ship** *n.* (1) A ship that is laid up with only a skeleton crew. (2) A charter party term meaning a ship that has arrived in port for loading and is ready to receive cargo.

**spray hood** *n.* A shield made of canvas or similar material used on small boats to protect the passengers from spray.

**spreader** *n.* (1) A horizontal spar fitted on a mast to spread the shrouds and stays. British usage is **crosstree**. See MARCONI RIG. (2) One of two timbers on each bow of a square rigger that extend the weather foresail clew. (3) A length of pipe or iron used to hold cargo hooks apart to facilitate cargo handling.

**spring** *v.* To bend a spar or to split it severely so that it is not safe to carry normal sail load.

**spring** *v.* To open a seam between planks in a hull and begin to take on water. When this happens the vessel is said to have **sprung a leak.**

**spring a luff** *v.* To steer a vessel close to the wind.

**spring buffer** *n.* A heavy coil spring set in the wheel chains to absorb the shock of heavy seas against the rudder.

**spring lay rope** *n.* Six-strand rope made up with alternate fiber and wire strands around a fiber core. Each wire strand is made up of three 19-plow steel wire strands and three fiber strands laid around a fiber core. Spring lay ropes are used primarily as mooring lines.

**spring line** *n.* (1) Docking line led at an angle from the fore-and-aft lines of a vessel. Spring lines are used to keep a vessel from going either forward or aft, depending on the lead of the spring lines. They can also be used to move a vessel forward or aft while using a breastline to keep a more or less fixed distance from the pier. Spring lines take their name from the direction in which they are led; e.g., **bow spring, stern spring, quarter spring,** and so on. See MOORING LINE. (2) A spring line off the quarter that can be led to an anchor cable to keep the vessel broadside to the anchor.

**spring log** *n.* A spring balance on which a chip log was dragged through the water to register resistance and thus the speed of the vessel.

**spring rise** *n.* The height of mean high water at syzygy. See TIDAL DATUM.

**spring stay** *n.* (1) A wire rope between mastheads of a schooner. (2) A preventer that reinforces a stay. (3) A horizontal stay between lower mastheads. A stay that runs between the mainmast and the mizzenmast on racing boats and controlled on deck. (4) Backup stay parallel to a principal stay on which staysails are set. (5) A stay between two masts or from mast to stack. See TRIATIC STAY.

**spring tide** *n.* A greater than average tide that occurs twice each lunar month, immediately after either a new Moon or full Moon, when the Earth, Sun, and Moon are in line (syzygy) and the lunar-solar tractive forces work together to cause tides that are higher and lower than normal. Spring tides have nothing to do with the time of the year. The maximum range between low and high tides is called the **spring range.** See NEAP TIDES.

**sprit** *n.* A spar used to hoist the peak of a quadrilateral sail with neither gaff nor boom. The sprit goes diagonally from the mast to the peak of the spritsail. The upper corner of the sprit fits in a grommet or a becket in the spritsail. Also *snorter; snotter.* See BOWSPRIT.

**spritsail** *n.* (1) A quadrilateral sail held in position by a sprit that extends diagonally from the base of the mast to the peak of the sail. The economy and simplicity of a spritsail rig made it a favorite for fisherman in areas with strong winds. (2) When ships carried extremely high bowsprits, a square spritsail was sometimes set on a yard under the bowsprit. This was eventually replaced by fore-and-aft headsails.

**spritsail topsail** *n.* A jib-headed gaff topsail the luff of which is extended beyond the mast truck by use of a sprit.

**spritsail yard** *n.* A spar that was carried athwartship on the bowsprit.

**spuds** *n.* Vertical piers on a dredge to hold it in place. You **spud down** the dredge.

**spun yarn** *n.* Cordage made of two, three, or four yarns tarred and laid up without being twisted.

**spur** *n.* The prong on a stockless anchor that helps position the anchor to dig in.

**spur beam** *n.* A plank faired into the side of a side-wheel steamer at the ends of the sponson beams.

**spur gear** *n.* A gear with teeth radially arrayed on the rim and parallel to the hub or shaft. Spur-geared winches are used with steam power, but are slower and much noisier than worm gears that are used on electric winches.

**spurling gate**   *n.* The cast-iron piece set in a deck through which the anchor chain passes.

**spurling line**   *n.* (1) A line between two forward shrouds that serves as a fairlead for running rigging. (2) A cable on a steering drum that controls a telltale to show the position of the rudder. Today electrical indicators are used instead.

**spurs**   *n.* Curved planks similar to half-beams.

**spur shore**   *n.* A heavy timber used to hold a vessel off from a quay to accommodate tenders and lighters between the quay and the vessel. The end held against the ship is made fast by one or more lanyards with a **spur shore shoe** used to protect the hull. A thrum mat is placed between the shoe and the ship. The spur rides on a truck at the shore end that rises and falls with the tide, but it is secured with cleats or dogs to prevent the vessel's surging against the quay or against the lighters and tenders.

**spur yarn**   *n.* Rough yarn laid up loosely left-handed and used for seizing.

**spyglass**   *n.* Hand-held telescope, usually called a **long glass.** The officer of the deck on a U.S. Navy ship in port frequently carries one that has been fancily wrapped in white line as his symbol of authority, similar to the OOD's binoculars at sea.

**squadron**   *n.* Two or more divisions of ships. If a commodore is not assigned, the senior captain becomes the commodore.

**squall**   *n.* A severe local storm with gusty winds, rain or snow, thunder, and lightning. The line along which they occur is called a squall line. A **white squall** is one characterized by a sudden burst of strong wind and no accompanying rain.

**squall line**   *n.* Any nonfrontal line or narrow band of active thunderstorms

(with or without accompanying squalls). See SQUALL.

**squamish**   *n.* A strong and often violent wind that occurs in many fjords of British Columbia.

**square**   *v.* To brace the yards at right angles to the keel and simultaneously bring them to a horizontal position with **lifts.**

**square**   *n.* The upper part of the anchor shank where the stock passes through.

**square**   *adj.* A term applied to the yards when they are at right angles to the keel. They are said to be **square by the braces** when they are at right angles to the keel. When they are horizontal, they are said to be **square by the lifts.**

**square away**   *v.* (1) Nautical slang for getting straight or settled in a new situation; you get squared away in a new duty assignment or a new ship. (2) To admonish abruptly. "The Old Man just got me squared away for using a toothpick in the wardroom."

**square cloths**   *n.* A sailmaker's term for sail panels cut square to the width of the fabric.

**square knot**   *n.* Same as a reef knot, considered the most useful knot. It consists of two overhand knots tied "right over left and left over right." A **granny knot** is two overhand knots but they are both right over left.

**square mark**   *n.* Tape or yarn placed on running rigging to show where a line should be cleated to have the sail in the right position.

**square-rigged vessel**   *n.* Any sailing vessel with quadrilateral sails extended by yards set perpendicular to the centerline on two or more masts. Also *square rigger.*

# Square Rig

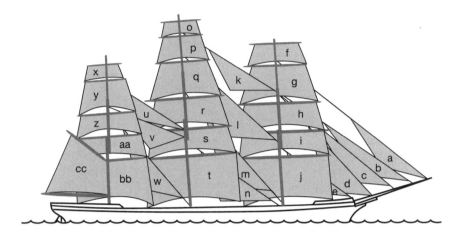

**Sails of a full-rigged ship**

| | | | |
|---|---|---|---|
| (a) | flying jib | (p) | main royal |
| (b) | outer jib | (q) | main topgallant |
| (c) | nner jib | (r) | main upper topsail |
| (d) | fore topmast staysail | (s) | main lower topsail |
| (e) | fore staysail | (t) | mainsail or main course |
| (f) | fore royal | (u) | mizzen topgallant staysail |
| (g) | fore topgallant | (v) | mizzen middle staysail |
| (h) | fore upper topsail | (w) | mizzen topmast staysail |
| (i) | fore lower topsail | (x) | mizzen royal |
| (j) | fore sail or fore course | (y) | mizzen topgallant |
| (k) | main royal staysail | (z) | mizzen upper topsail |
| (l) | main topgallant staysail | (aa) | mizzen lower topsail |
| (m) | main topmast staysail | (bb) | mizzen or crossjack |
| (m) | main staysail | (cc) | spanker or driver |
| (o) | main skysail | | |

**square sail** *n.* Quadrilateral sail set from a yard that pivots at the middle around the mast. The upper edge is the head, the sides are leeches, and the bottom edge is the foot; the lower corners are clews, and the upper corners are head cringles.

**square topsail** *n.* A quadrilateral sail set above the lowest course and carried on a topsail yard. The term is used especially to distinguish the sail from a fore-and-aft topsail set above a gaff in **square topsail schooners.**

**square up** *v.* To arrange all equipment in an orderly fashion. See SQUARE AWAY.

**squid** *n.* British-developed bow-launched antisubmarine warfare weapon.

See HEDGEHOG. (2) A derogatory term for a member of the U.S. Navy used by members of the other branches of the armed services, including the U.S. Marines.

**stability** *n.* The state or property of resisting change or tending to return to the original position after being disturbed or inclined. To maintain an upright position, stability conditions require that the ship's center of gravity lie vertically below the center of buoyancy. When these points are greatly separated, a vessel is comparatively stiff; when they are closer together, the vessel is considered tender or crank and liable to capsize.

**stability board** *n.* A visual presentation of the location of flooding, and the effect on list and trim, used for damage control.

**stability letter** *n.* The U.S. Coast Guard's endorsement of a ship's trim and stability booklet. It must be kept under glass in the pilothouse of all cargo ships at all times. See TRIM.

**stability of radarscope display** *n.* A radarscope display that is stabilized in azimuth and oriented to a fixed reference, usually north, called **north up.** The scope is said to be **unstabilized in azimuth** when the orientation of the display

# Stability and Trim

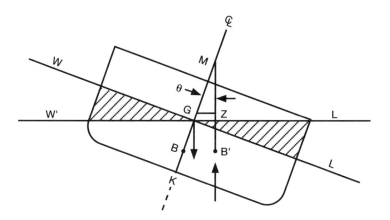

G  center of gravity of vessel and its cargo, location of downward force of gravity
B  center of buoyancy, the geometric center of the immersed portion of vessel, location of upward buoyant force
M  metacenter, intersection of upward buoyant force and the centerline when vessel is inclined
θ  angle of inclination
BM  metacentric radius
GM  metacentric height
Z  point on BM horizontal from G
GZ  righting arm, horizontal distance between downward force of gravity and upward buoyant force, small angles: GZ = GM sin θ
KB  height of center of buoyancy above keel with no list on vessel
KG  height of center of gravity above keel with no list on vessel
KM  height of metacenter above keel = KB + BM = KG + GM
₵  centerline
WL  waterline

play changes when the ship's heading changes. Radar and gyro manufacturers use azimuth in this sense even when they mean bearing.

**stabilizers** *n.* Mechanical fins used to damp the roll of cruise ships to keep them as stable as possible.

**stable equilibrium** *n.* The condition that exists when metacenter (M) is above the center of gravity (G). When stable equilibrium exists, a vessel tends to return to its original upright position after it has been inclined far enough for the edge of the deck to be underwater. See STABILITY.

**stack** *n.* (1) The smoke pipe that leads from the fireboxes under the boilers to a point above the top deck. (2) A chart term for a tall smokestack on land that may be surrounded by less prominent buildings.

**stack cover** *n.* A plate used to cover the smokestack while in port to keep rain and snow out of the boiler.

**stacked** *adj.* The yards of a square-rigged vessel are said to be stacked when each is parallel to the one below it.

**stack gas** *n.* The gases from a vessel's smokestack.

**stack wash** *n.* Gases from the smokestack above the wake of a ship.

**stadimeter** *n.* An instrument used on ships to determine ranges (distances) to objects of known height, good for distances from 200 to 10,000 yards. In the U.S. Navy an officer of the deck told to keep station 1,000 yards astern a guide ship could look up the height of the guide, adjust his stadimeter accordingly, and determine the variations in distance. Also *telemeter.*

**staff** *n.* A spar on which a flag is hoisted. Also *flagpole; flagstaff.*

**staff officers** *n.* Officers who perform staff functions in the U.S. Navy—supply officers, medical officers, chaplains, and so on—but who are not eligible (nor qualified) to succeed to command at sea.

**stage** *n.* A platform on the side of a ship used by personnel working on the hull above the waterline.

**staging** *n.* A worker's scaffolding whether supported from the ground or suspended over the side by ropes.

**staging area** *n.* (1) A place established for processing troops in transit. (2) Area for final training of an amphibious unit.

**staging standard** *n.* A wood or steel structure used for supporting outside staging during a vessel's construction.

**stake boat** *n.* A boat anchored to act as a racecourse marker.

**stanchion** *n.* (1) An upright pillar or post used for supporting awnings, lifelines, and so on. (2) A vertical structural member between decks on a steel vessel.

**stand** *n.* To sail, to steer, to direct a vessel's course A vessel can stand upstream or stand out to sea, or stand into a harbor or a shore.

**stand, to let all** *phr.* To leave a ship fully rigged.

**standard** *n.* A flag or banner, especially the ensign of a chief of state or a battle standard.

**standard compass** See COMPASS.

**standard noon** *n.* Twelve o'clock (1200) standard time, or the instant the mean Sun is over the upper branch of the standard meridian. **Daylight standard noon,** or **summer noon,** usually occurs one hour later than standard noon.

**standard parallel**   *n.* The parallel of latitude along which there is no distortion that is adopted as a control line in the transferring of points from the Earth's surface to a conic projection.

**standard port**   *n.* Obsolete term for reference station.

**standard rudder**   *n.* Rudder angle that will give a tactical diameter of 750 yards at 12 knots. **Full rudder** is maximum rudder angle less a few degrees to preclude jamming. Some services use **hard rudder** in place of full rudder.

**standard tactical diameter**   *n.* A prescribed tactical diameter for different classes of U.S. Navy ships of the same formation for maneuvers.

**standard time**   *n.* By law, the United States and its possessions are divided into eight time zones; the limits of each zone (which are roughly 15° wide) are defined by the Secretary of Transportation. The standard time within each time zone is the local mean time at the standard meridian that passes approximately through the center of the zone. See DAYLIGHT SAVINGS TIME.

**stand by**   *interj.* (1) A preparatory order meaning "be ready." "Stand by your oars" for example, means prepare to get your oars up or out. (2) An order to stand by can also mean to stay where you are, wait, take no action until another order is given. "Have the coxswain stand by until the captain is ready to leave the ship." (3) To substitute for someone else who has the duty. "Jones is standing by as messenger while Smith is in the mess."

**stand clear**   *interj.* An order for a person to get away or keep away from a given object. "Stand clear of the forward hold hatch while coal is being loaded." See STAND OFF.

**standing**   *adj.* Fixed in place; not easily moved, usually used to distinguish something from its "running" counterpart, as standing backstay, standing rigging, or standing bowsprit.

**standing block**   *n.* A block that is secured to a permanent position in a purchase with one or more running blocks.

**standing floe**   *n.* A separate (ice) floe standing vertically or inclined and enclosed in smooth ice.

**standing lights**   *n.* Dim red lights used in the interior of a ship, so that the eye does not have to adjust to the dark on deck as it would in going from a standard white light.

**standing officers**   *n.* Royal Navy term of the 17th and 18th centuries when ships were generally laid up and the crews paid off during the winter. Only the standing officers were retained with pay; these included the boatswain, carpenter, gunner, and cook.

**standing order**   *n.* A permanent order or directive issued by a commander, such as standing night orders.

**standing part**   *n.* (1) That part of a rope around which the end is worked in tying knots and other ropework. See SQUARE-RIGGED VESSEL. (2) The end of a tackle fall that is secured to a block.

**standing rigging**   *n.* Rigging set up in a fixed position to support the masts and sails, such as shrouds and stays. See RUNNING RIGGING.

**standoff**   *n.* A fitting that supports pipes and wires away from a surface.

**stand off**   *v.* (1) To remain at a distance from something, as a vessel or a shore. See HEAVE TO. (2) To sail away from the shore. (3) To **stand on and off** is to remain underway near a position, usually by sailing in a series of figure eights. This is sometimes done on naval patrols for extended periods.

**stand of the tide**   *n.* The period at high tide and at low tide when there is no discernible vertical movement. "Have the longboats ready to leave the beach at the stand of the tide."

**stand on**   *v.* To hold a course, continue with the same course and speed. See STAND.

**stand-on vessel**   *n.* The vessel with the right of way under the *Navigation Rules.* This term has superseded "privileged vessel" used in the older Rules of the Road. See GIVE-WAY VESSEL.

**standpipe**   *n.* Defined on navigation charts as "a tall cylindrical structure in a waterworks system, the height of which is several times the diameter."

**stand up**   *v.* To sail without heeling.

**stand watch**   *phr.* To take one's turn at a duty station, for the length of a watch.

**stapling**   *n.* Shipwright's term for angle bar collars that are fitted around longitudinals at the point where they pass through a bulkhead.

**star**   *n.* A large celestial body in true size, as contrasted with the much smaller but closer and apparently larger planets, satellites and comets. With the exception of the Sun, for practical navigation purposes the declination of stars is considered constant. There are 52 navigation stars.

**starboard**   *adj.* The right-hand side of a vessel as seen from the stern. The opposite is port, the left-hand side of a vessel. Only vessels have a starboard side; other things, such as piers and pilings, do not. "Take the piling to starboard" means pass the piling on the vessel's right-hand side. See RELATIVE BEARING.

**star finder**   *n.* A chart or other device used to determine in advance the azimuth of a celestial body. The current *Star Finder and Identifier* (No. 2102-D) is a circular star finder and identifier published by the U.S. Navy Oceanographic Office. It is popularly called the "Rude Star Finder" after the device of the same name patented by Captain G. T. Rude.

**star shell**   *n.* A projectile that releases an illuminating parachute on detonation during night action.

**start**   *v.* To slack a hawser, sheet, or other line. One starts a sheet to allow the sail to catch more wind.

**starting ram**   *n.* A hydraulic jack used to start a vessel down the ways when it does not do so by gravity.

**starting signal**   *n.* A signal used to start a race; which signals will be used and at what intervals are discussed at the pre-race skippers' meeting. Usually a system of flags raised and lowered along with a cannon is used.

**star tracker**   *n.* An automatic sextant that detects and maintains a line of sight to a star. It is mounted and gimballed and electronically controlled.

**starve**   *v.* To sail a vessel so high or close to the wind that the sails do not fill properly. Also *jam; pinch.*

**stateroom**   *n.* An officer's living quarters on a U.S. Navy ship. The captain, the commodore if one is aboard, and an embarked admiral have cabins. What was the executive officer's stateroom last week becomes the captain's cabin this week when the captain's cabin becomes the commodore's cabin.

**station**   *n.* (1) An assigned position in a naval formation or cruising disposition. (2) The place to which a person on a ship is assigned in time of special exercises or emergencies, as in battle stations. See STATION BILL. (3) Any naval activity at a fixed land location, such as a naval air station. (4) Any place of duty or a post or position in the field to which an individual or a unit may be assigned.

(5) The authorized location of an aid to navigation. Such an aid is said to be **on station** or **off station**. (6) One or more transmitters or receivers at one location for carrying on a radio communication service.

**station**  *v.* To assign or be assigned to a naval duty post or a battle station.

**stationary front**  *n.* A weather front that is stationary or nearly so, moving at a speed of less than 5 knots.

**station bill**  *n.* The posted list giving the duty station of each member of the crew of a U.S. Navy ship during maneuvers and emergencies. Usually called the watch, quarter, and station bill.

**station buoy**  *n.* An unlighted buoy set near a lightship or other important buoy as a reference point in case the primary aid is moved from its assigned position.

**station keeping**  *n.* The art and science of keeping a naval ship in its assigned station in a formation.

**station pointer**  *n.* A three-arm protractor used for plotting an observer's position by means of two observed horizontal sextant angles between three objects.

**station for stays**  *interj.* The order for the crew to take their stations for tacking ship.

**statute mile**  *n.* A measurement of distance over land of 5,280 feet used in navigation on U.S. rivers and lakes, most notably the Great Lakes. Except as noted, the nautical mile is universally used for air, surface, and submarine navigation. See MILE.

**staunch**  *adj.* Sturdy, watertight, as in staunch construction or a staunch vessel. Also *stanch.*

**stave**  *v.* To push in or crush. See STOVE IN.

**stay**  *n.* Rope of hemp or wire or stainless steel rods led from the deck to the mast or between two masts and used to support a mast along its fore-and-aft axis or from which to set a staysail. Shrouds, which also support masts and spars, are led to the sides of the vessel. See BACK-STAY; HEADSTAY; SHROUD; SQUARE-RIGGED VESSEL; TRIATIC STAY.

**stay**  *v.* (1) To incline a spar or mast forward, aft, or sideways by means of stays. (2) To come about; to go from one tack to the other by bringing the vessel's head through the wind.

**staysail**  *n.* A triangular or quadrilateral fore-and-aft sail set up on a stay. It is a more general term than jib, which is, by definition, triangular and set up only on the bow. A staysail can be set up any place, such as a mizzen staysail, a fisherman's staysail, and so on. See SQUARE-RIGGED VESSEL.

**staysail rig**  *n.* Once a popular racing and cruising combination for ketches and schooners, it was a fore-and-aft sail plan in which the gaff or Bermuda foresail was replaced by two staysails between each mast. The result was greater sail area and increased efficiency when sailing on the wind.

**staysail schooner**  *n.* A rig with at least two masts in which the gaff or Bermuda foresail was replaced by smaller staysails that filled the rectangle between the masts and the main topmast stay.

**staysail stay**  *n.* A stay used for the support of a staysail but not to support a mast.

**stay tackles**  *n.* Tackles secured to a stay to hoist weights to a midship position and lower them into a hold.

**steady**  *interj.* Order to a helmsman to keep a ship on the heading it has at the moment he is given the order. "Right ten degrees rudder . . . right standard rudder . . . rudder amidship . . . **steady**

as you go." The helmsman responds with "Mark. The course is one-eight-zero, Sir."

**steady bearing**   *n.* A steady relative bearing between two ships means they are on parallel courses, divergent courses, or a collision course.

**steady wind**   *n.* A popular expression for sailors, it means a wind of constant force and direction, such as trade winds.

**stealer**   *n.* A section of plating or a strake that does not extend completely to the bow or stern.

**steamboat**   *n.* A river or coastwise vessel propelled by steam power, as distinct from an oceangoing steamship.

**steam capstan**   *n.* A nonreversing vertical drum capstan; power is transmitted from the steam plant to the capstan spindle by a worm gear. See GIPSEY.

**steam engine**   *n.* An engine that uses steam as its working substance. Steam engine types vary widely, though the most successful marine engine type was the direct-action reciprocating, compound engine, these being further classified as double-, triple-, or quadruple-expansion engines.

**steam fog**   *n.* Fog formed when water vapor is added to air that is much colder than the source of the vapor. It is often formed when very cold air drifts across warm water. At temperatures below −20°F, ice particles or droxtals are often formed in the air to produce **ice fog** or **frost smoke.**

**steam generator**   *n.* A boiler in a nuclear plant with pressurized water in the primary loop on what corresponds to the fireside of an ordinary boiler. Heat from the primary loop is exchanged with the feedwater to generate steam.

**steaming light**   *n.* Obsolete term for masthead light.

**steamship**   *n.* A vessel using steam as the principal means of propulsion, as opposed to a sailing vessel or a motor vessel. Also *steamer.*

**steam steering gear**   *n.* Considered a marvelous step forward when invented; this was the first power steering for ships. Instead of the helmsman having to move the rudder manually with limited mechanical advantage from blocks and tackle, the rudder was moved by steam. It was very inefficient, but a great help in any blow at all. It did not maintain course as a marine automatic pilot does, but only assisted the helmsman in directing the rudder.

**steerage**   *n.* (1) Steering control; a ship loses steerage when its rudder is badly damaged. (2) The steering equipment on a vessel. (3) The slowest speed at which a vessel can go and still keep its head on the desired heading; "We approached the bridge, only maintaining steerage until the bridgetender seemed to be beginning to perform his duties." This is important in law, because to maintain steerage downstream can mean maintaining an otherwise dangerous and undesirable speed. By the same token, to maintain steerage in a "no wake zone" with a current can mean making only sternway as you try to make your destination which is ahead or appearing to be making excessive speed toward a destination. (4) The 'tween decks space where the lowest-paying passengers on immigrant ships travel. (5) The practice of steering; rare. (6) The junior officer's quarters; obsolete.

**steerageway**   *n.* A rate of speed sufficient to maintain steering control of a vessel without resorting to other means such as are used in docking maneuvers.

**steering column (or stand)**   *n.* The nonmagnetic post that supports the steering wheel. On most ships, an indicator showing the actual rudder angle and the angle being transmitted by the wheel is mounted on the column. On small boats, this is sometimes called the binnacle because the binnacle and steering column are frequently combined: but the difference between the two is important. See BINNACLE.

**steering compass** *n.* Technically, a magnetic compass before the helmsman that is used for steering; the term is often applied to the gyro repeater used by the helmsman.

**steering crutch** *n.* A metal swivel usually seen on a lifeboat transom to be used to support the steering oar.

**steering engine** *n.* The machinery that turns the rudder, usually a combination of hydraulic and electric devices.

**steering gear** *n.* All steering equipment, including the wheel, wheel ropes, steering engine, helm, and rudder.

**steering light** *n.* A small light carried abaft the funnel on a towing vessel for the vessel being towed to steer by.

**steering oar** *n.* A long oar used for steering when seas were too rough for the rudder to guide the boat.

**steering pole** *n.* A lighted jackstaff that was hinged at the base. On ships that were conned from well aft, the lighted pole projected forward from the bow and aided the helmsman and watch officer. See STEERING LIGHT.

**steering repeater** *n.* A gyrocompass repeater by which the helmsman steers a vessel. See STEERING COMPASS.

**steering sails** See STUDDING SAIL.

**steering telegraph** *n.* A device similar to an engine room telegraph and used to communicate between the navigation bridge and the steering engine room.

**steer small** *phr.* Order to steer with as little movement of the wheel as possible.

**steersman** *n.* Helmsman.

**steeve** *n.* The angle of the bowsprit above a horizontal plane; the greater the angle or steeve, the easier it is to work headsails on boats with little freeboard.

**steeve** *v.* To elevate a spar, bowsprit, or mast that has been placed on the deck. "After we are through the last fixed bridge, we will steeve the mast and trim it in its step."

**Steinke hood** *n.* Headgear worn to make possible escape from a sunken submarine at moderate depths.

**Stella Maris** See POLARIS.

**stem** *n.* (1) The upright timber of the bow; in fiber-reinforced plastic (FRP) boats with no timber, the stem is the heavy reinforced structure that makes up the stemhead and extends below the waterline. (2) A contract regarding cargo and loading schedule. (3) A forging, plating, or casting forming the extreme bow of a vessel extending from keel to forecastle deck.

**stem** *v.* To hold or make progress against a phenomenon such as current or wind. See STEM THE TIDE. (2) To agree to load cargo, especially coal, on a specific date and within a given time. "We are stemmed to begin loading on Christmas morning." See STEMMING LIST.

**stem dinghy** *n.* Dinghy with a pointed bow.

**stem fender** *n.* Name for a hemp mat carried at the stem of a tugboat that prevents damage to the tug's hull or to the hull of the vessel being pushed.

**stem foot** *n.* The forward end of a keel into which the stem is stepped on a full-keel vessel.

**stemhead** *n.* The top of the stem.

**stem(head) plate** *n.* The plate on the stemhead on which the headstay is set.

**stemlight** *n.* A light carried on the stem in inland waters. See STERNLIGHT.

**stemming list** *n.* Order of precedence determined by harbor authority that sets the berthage schedule. A **free stem** exists when a vessel is free to enter the docks without the restriction of a list. British usage.

**stemson** *n.* An inner stem for extra support.

**stem the tide** *phr.* To sail against the tide and hold position or make headway.

**stem-winder** *n.* Coast sailors' term for lake steamers with engines and accommodations aft.

**step** *n.* A block or reinforced plate on which the mast is stepped. Typically the mast is stepped on a block on the keelson, but on smaller boats it may be stepped on deck with reinforcing timbers, compression struts, or other material beneath that extend to the keelson.

**step** *v.* To place a vertical member, such as a mast, in its proper position. See MAST STEP.

**step off** *v.* To measure a distance on a chart by "walking" the dividers from point to point.

**stepped bottom** *n.* A construction used on high-speed powerboats with one or two steps in the bottom to reduce wetted surface and increase speed.

**stereographic projection** *n.* A perspective, conformal azimuthal chart projection in which points on the surface of the Earth are conceived as projected by radial lines from any point on the surface to a plane tangent to the antipode of the point of projection. Great circles project as straight lines. Stereographic projections are used for charts of polar regions.

**stern** *n.* After end of a vessel. See RELATIVE BEARING.

**stern all** *interj.* An order for all oars to backwater so as to either stop or gain sternway.

**stern anchor** *n.* Any anchor carried at the stern of a vessel. It is usually lighter than the bow anchor and is used when the room to swing on a single bow anchor is limited.

**sternboard** *n.* The condition of being in irons and sailing sternward. "Our unsuccessful attempt to come about put us in sternboard, and we began losing ground." See HEADWAY.

**sternboss** *n.* A reinforced propeller tube and shaft support in the hull of a single-screw vessel.

**stern bushing** *n.* The fitting in which the shaft rides at the after end of the stern tube made of such material as to withstand the wear of the shaft.

**sterncastle** *n.* A tower at the stern of a ship; a counterpart to the forecastle. The tower was used by a ship's archers in the era before effective long-range cannon were developed, and grappling and boarding were the preferred tactic of naval engagement.

**stern chaser** *n.* A cannon at the stern of a ship for firing at pursuing vessels.

**stern chock** *n.* An open brass or bronze fitting on the transom through which docking lines and towing lines are led.

**stern drive** *n.* An inboard-outboard engine on small boats; the propulsion unit is inboard, the gears and propeller are outboard, and steering is done by moving the outboard unit.

**stern fast**   See STERN ROPE.

**stern frame**   *n.* A large forging or fabrication attached to the after end of a hull to form the ship's stern. It includes rudder post, propeller post, and the throughhull for the stern tube.

**stern gland**   *n.* The cylinder that contains and compresses the packing material in the stern tube stuffing box.

**stern hook**   *n.* A strengthening timber, usually curved, fitted longitudinally across the forward side of the sternpost and extending to several frames on both sides for added support.

**stern ladder**   *n.* A ladder placed over the stern to accommodate the ship's crew.

**sternlight**   *n.* A white light placed as nearly as practicable at the stern and showing an unbroken light over an arc of the horizon of 135° and so fixed as to show the light 67.5° from right aft on each side of the vessel.

**stern line**   *n.* A line that is led aft from a vessel's transom to a piling, cleat, or bollard. See MOORING LINE.

**sternpost**   *n.* The aftermost vertical structural member stepped in the keel, usually serving to support the rudder.

**stern rope**   *n.* A docking line that leads aft at an angle of less than 45° from the fore-and-aft line. Also *stern fast*.

**stern sheets**   *n.* Seats in a small boat aft of the afterthwart. See SHEETS.

**sternson**   *n.* A metal bar between the keelson and the sternpost to strengthen the joint. The word is contraction of stern and keelson.

**stern tube**   *n.* A long bushing or bearing through the stern that supports the propeller shaft's exit through the hull.

**sternway**   *n.* Motion through the water backward: "As we gather sternway, release the breastline."

**stern-wheeler**   *n.* A paddle-wheel-driven vessel with the paddle wheel(s) at the stern.

**stevedore**   *n.* A person (or firm) who supervises stowage or unloading of cargo. Although not a member of the ship's crew, the stevedore is under the command of the master of the ship.

**stevedore's knot**   *n.* A knot placed at the end of a line to prevent its coming out of a block. The knot is a figure-eight with an additional turn.

**stevedoring**   *n.* The unloading and loading of material to and from a ship.

**steward**   *n.* (1) On U.S. Navy and cargo vessels, a member of the crew who handles food preparation and domestic chores for the ship's officers. (2) On passenger ships, the stewards wait tables and do housekeeping chores in the passengers' cabins. The dining saloon stewards are under the chief steward, while the cabin stewards are usually under the purser. **Stewardesses** are female stewards who do the same work as cabin stewards.

**stiff**   *adj.* Said of a vessel with a low center of gravity and a high metacentric height and that resists heeling relative to a more tender boat. See STABILITY; TENDER.

**stiffener**   *n.* An angle bar, T-bar, or channel used to strengthen stress points.

**stiffening**   *n.* Ballast maintained in a ship's hold or bilges to help maintain stability when the vessel is completely unloaded.

**stiff-leg derrick**   *n.* A derrick with the mast stayed by two timbers or steel beams that lead from the masthead down to the outer end of two ground timbers; the mast is stepped on the inner ends of the ground timbers.

**stile**    *n.* The vertical pin in the center of a compass that casts a shadow to indicate the reciprocal of the Sun's azimuth.

**still-water level**    *n.* The level the sea surface would assume at a given tide level in the absence of wind and waves.

**stirrups**    *n.* Short ropes that are seized to the jackstays to support the footropes.

**stock**    *n.* The crossbar of an old-fashioned anchor that positions the flukes to dig into the bottom. See ANCHOR.

**stock and bill**    *n.* A purchase used to handle a stock-type anchor.

**Stockholm tar**    *n.* A low-grade distillate from pine stumps left after the pine oil has been drawn off. It was used in wooden shipbuilding and to preserve cordage, especially standing rigging. It is a good disinfectant to prevent mold, but has a strong smell.

**stockless anchor**    *n.* Any of several types of anchor that have no stock to make possible easier stowage. See ANCHOR.

**stocks**    *n.* (1) An elevated shipway. (2) The blocks that form the foundation for laying a keel in a shipyard.

**stokehold**    *n.* The space on a steamship where the boiler fires are fed. Also *fireroom; stock-hole.*

**stoker**    *n.* A member of the crew in the engine spaces whose duties include firing the furnace and attending the boilers. In coal-burning ships, stokers shovel coal into the furnace. Collectively, stokers are known as the **black gang.**

**Stokes litter**    See RESCUE BASKET.

**stomach piece**    *n.* A reinforcing piece set in the after side of the stem. Also *apron.*

**stool**    *n.* (1) A support for the main shaft bearing in the shaft alley; a foundation. (2) Channel to which a backstay is sometimes set up, abaft the shroud channels.

**stopper**    *n.* A chain or rope used to firmly hold a cable or chain while it is being secured on deck. Biddlecombe's *The Art of Rigging* distinguishes in particular the **anchor stopper,** used to suspend anchors when catted; **bitt stoppers,** used to check cable; **deck stoppers,** used to retain cable when the ship is riding at anchor; and **shroud stoppers,** used to repair shrouds damaged by shot. Today anchor stoppers or chain stoppers are used when a ship is at anchor to relieve the capstan and anchor engine for other purposes.

**stops**    *n.* (1) Projections on a mast that support a yard, gaff, or other spar. (2) Small stuff used for furling sails.

**stopwater**    *n.* Canvas and red lead or similar material fitted between two metal parts to make a watertight joint.

**storage**    *n.* A fee charged by a port authority for warehousing goods in transit beyond the time considered in the wharfage.

**storekeeper (SK)**    *n.* A petty officer in the U.S. Navy charged with the clerical and manual work in the supply department such as issuing stores as needed.

**stores**    *n.* Any and all supplies.

**storm**    *n.* Beaufort scale reading of 11, with winds of 56–63 knots.

**storm anchor**    *n.* An especially heavy anchor that can be broken out for use in heavy weather. See BEST BOWER.

**storm canvas**  *n.* The sail inventory that includes specially cut storm trysails, storm staysails, storm mizzen, and so on. When storm sails were made from canvas, it was usually #1.

**storm jib**  *n.* A small, strong headsail for use in storms. A storm jib occupies about 60% of the vessel's foretriangle. See HEADSAIL.

**storm mizzen**  *n.* A triangular fore-and-aft sail used during storms in place of a quadrilateral gaff mizzen.

**storm oil**  *n.* Oil used during a storm to reduce the problem of breaking waves and, at least in effect, increasing surface tension. Oil carried in a bag on the windward bow or oil slowly dripped through a head on the windward side and forward can have a good effect. At one time it was required on all merchant vessels. Any oil will work, be it animal, vegetable, or mineral. Some ships carry storm oil in a **storm oil tank** near the stem under the forecastle.

**storm sail**  *n.* Any sail made for use in storms using extra heavy material such as #1 canvas or a synthetic equivalent.

**storm signal**  *n.* Visual signal hoisted at coastal stations to warn ships at sea of approaching storms. Now obsolete in the U.S.

**storm staysail**  *n.* A small staysail used for stormy weather but on the main or mizzen.

**storm surge**  *n.* High water produced by a tropical cyclone as it moves toward a coast; it is inevitably accompanied by a fall in barometric pressure. See SEICHE; TSUNAMI.

**storm tide**  *n.* A tide that results from continual blowing during a tropical cyclone and that can produce an increased water level of 3 to 10 feet.

**storm track**  *n.* The path of a storm, generally, but by no means exclusively, clockwise in the Northern Hemisphere. See PILOT CHARTS.

**storm trysail**  *n.* A gaff-headed or tri-angular loose-footed sail made from heavy-duty material with a comparatively short luff and set on the mast during heavy weather, usually when a vessel is hove to.

**storm valve**  *n.* A valve on freeing port outlets in a ship's hull that prevents water from coming aboard.

**storm wave**  *n.* (1) The forward edge of a storm; a front. (2) A wave generated by winds of gale force or greater.

**stormy petrel**  See MOTHER CAREY'S CHICKEN.

**stove in**  *adj.* The condition of being pushed in or broken in, especially the hull of a boat or ship. See STAVE.

**stow**  *v.* (rhymes with toe) (1) To furl a sail. (2) To put away goods or cargo neatly and efficiently. (3) To put gear in its place.

**stowage**  *n.* The science of efficiently placing cargo and materiel in a ship so that it will not endanger the vessel or its crew during a voyage.

**stowage certificate**  *n.* A document certifying proper stowage of cargo; it is given to the master of a vessel after stowage has been completed.

**stowage factor**  *n.* The number that expresses the space, in cubic feet, that one long ton of a particular cargo will occupy when properly stowed and dunnaged. The stowage factor varies depending on the packaging or the cargo. For example, apples in barrels have a stowage factor of 104, while apples in boxes have a stowage factor of 72. Cement in barrels has a stowage factor of 36, while cement in bags has a stowage factor of 35. Those with a stowage factor of less than 40 are considered **dead-weight cargo,** while those above 40 are termed **measurement cargo.**

**stowaway** *n.* A person who hides on a ship before its departure, for the purpose of getting free passage or passage from or to a country without authorization.

**straddle** *v.* To fire a salvo with some projectiles observed to be over and some to be short, and some on target or very near.

**straight oar** *n.* Oar with straight blade as opposed to spoon-shaped oar.

**strain** *n.* (1) Structural distortion of a vessel's hull, as caused by some severe storms. (2) To **take an even strain** is to put the same tension on all docking lines. A boatswain will order the deck crew to "Take an even strain on all lines," by which he means that they should adjust each of the docking lines to take the same strain in holding the ship. "To take a strain" is to tauten or stress a line in tension. (3) The lengthening or distortion of a member due to stress.

**strait** *n.* A narrow waterway that connects two larger bodies of water. Right of passage through a strait is determined in part by the status of the waters at either end—that is, whether they are exclusive economic zones (EEZ), territorial seas, or high seas. As a rule the right of innocent passage exists, and in some instances the right of transit passage exists.

**strake** *n.* A continuous row of plates that extend the entire length of the vessel. These are lettered from bottom ("A") to top. See RUBBING STRAKE.

**strake book** *n.* A list of longitudinal planks and plates in a vessel, used for stowage and damage control.

**strand** *n.* (1) Land bordering a body of water; beach. (2) A component part

of rope, strands are made up of yarns or wires laid opposite to the lay of the strand. See ROPE.

**strand** *v.* (1) To go aground; to run a ship on a strand, either by accident or by design—in the latter case, usually to save a vessel that has been holed below the waterline. Stranding is more serious than grounding and as interpreted in marine underwriters' policies it does not include a "touch and go," nor does it include the "taking of the ground in a tidal harbor" even if damage occurs as a result. To constitute stranding, a ship must be stationary for a stipulated length of time. See RUN AGROUND. (2) To part a strand in a rope or wire; the rope or wire is said to have been stranded.

**strap** *n.* (1) A metal or rope band used on a block or deadeye to hold its parts together. (2) A circle of rope made by splicing the ends, used for slings. (3) An iron ring used to fasten rigging or a block to a master spar. Also used as a verb, to strap a block or a rope. Also *strop.*

**strategic weather routine** *n.* Routing of shipping based on analyses of prevailing weather. See SHIP WEATHER ROUTING.

**stratiform** *adj.* Pertaining to or describing clouds that are of extensive horizontal development, contrasted with cumuliform or cirroform. See CLOUDS.

**stratocumulus** *n.* Dark globular clouds with a horizontal base and blue skies usually visible beyond. See CLOUDS.

**stratus** *n.* Low clouds forming a solid sheet with mean upper level of 6,500 feet. These resemble fog but do not rest on the Earth's surface. See CLOUDS.

**stream** *n.* (1) A current in the sea that tends to keep to the same path, such as the Gulf Stream. See OCEAN CURRENT. (2) A river or tidal stream when the usage is to place a ship at anchor instead of its being moored at the dock. "We have been assigned a buoy **in the stream** for tonight; plan to man the liberty boats.'' (3) That part of a fairway with the maximum current, **out in the stream.**

**stream**   *v.* (1) To drop over the side and to tow; a patent log is streamed and in mine clearing paravanes are streamed. (2) To move a ship out of its dock and into the channel, a towboat term.

**stream anchor**   *n.* A stockless stern anchor used with a bow anchor **(bower)** when the anchorage does not have enough room for the vessel to swing. It is usually somewhat lighter than a bower anchor and heavier than a kedge.

**stream chain**   *n.* A close-linked chain with no studs used with a stream anchor on small vessels.

**streaming**   *n.* A tugboat charge for assisting a vessel away from its berth. The opposite is a docking charge.

**strength deck**   *n.* The highest complete deck that resists longitudinal stress.

**strength of current**   *n.* The phase of a tidal current during which the speed is at the maximum.

**stress**   *n.* A force or combination of forces that tend to strain or deform an object by compression, twisting, pulling, or shearing, measured in units of weight such as pounds or tons. See FORCE MAJEURE; STRAIN.

**stress of weather** *n.* Continued weather upheaval; a sustained storm. ''The stress of weather (or press of weather) constrained us to stay in port beyond our schedule.''

**stretchers**   *n.* Athwartship members against which oarsmen brace their feet in a rowboat.

**strike**   *v.* (1) To lower the ensign as an act of submission. A ship is said to **strike its colors** when it surrenders. (2) To

come inshore close enough to reach bottom with the lead, as in to **strike soundings.** (3) To lower a mast and remove the fittings. A topmast is struck after it has been swayed, to lower it to the deck. (4) To remove from the deck to stow. ''Strike the cargo below in the number four hatch.''

**strike clause**   *n.* A caveat in charter parties and bills of lading stating just where the responsibilities lie in the event of a strike.

**striker**   *n.* A seaman working toward a specific petty officer rating.

**stringer**   *n.* An internal fore-and-aft member used to give longitudinal strength. Stringers are called after their location in the vessel, such as hold stringers, bilge stringers, side stringers, and so on.

**stringer plate**   *n.* A deck plate at the outboard edge of a deck connected to the shell of a ship with an angle or welded joint.

**string piece**   *n.* The timber that forms the edge of a wharf or pier.

**strip**   *n.* A long narrow area of pack ice about 1 kilometer or less in width.

**strip**   *v.* (1) To remove all rigging. (2) To remove the last liquid from a tank.

**stripping lines**   *n.* The piping of a tanker used for clearing the tanks. The stripping lines carry the steam and water to remove the residual oil after the main suction ceases to be effective.

**strip ship**   *v.* To remove as much unnecessary flammable and explosive material as possible from a ship when war is threatened; such items would include inflammable curtains, carpeting, and wooden framing for nonessential items such as awnings.

**stroke**   *n.* (1) The sweep of an oar, as in a **short stroke** or a **long stroke.** (2) The oarsman seated farthest aft who pulls the starboard oar and **sets the stroke.** Also *stroke oar.* (3) The distance a piston moves from full up to full down.

**strongback**   *n.* (1) A padded member against which a lifeboat is griped when swung in. (2) A bar or other rig used for straightening bent plates. (3) A temporary bar tack welded at the edge across a butt or seam to hold it in place while it is being permanently welded. (4) A bar or timber placed across a hatch cover to hold it in place.

**strong breeze**   *n.* Beaufort scale reading of 6, with winds of 22–27 knots.

**strong gale**   *n.* Beaufort scale reading of 9, with winds of 41–47 knots.

**strong room**   *n.* A remote compartment on passenger liners where spices, bullion, silk, and other valuables are kept. See SPECIE ROOM.

**structural bulkhead**   *n.* Any bulkhead that contributes to the strength of the hull and usually extends through several decks. As a general rule, a structural bulkhead is watertight or oiltight.

**strum plate**   *n.* A strainer placed at the intake of a pumping system to allow water to enter while keeping foreign matter out. Also *strum box.*

**strut**   *n.* A support for a propeller shaft outside the hull.

**strut of a shore**   *n.* In shipbuilding, the inclination of a shore from a vertical line.

**stud**   *n.* (1) A strengthening bar across the middle of a chain link. A **stud-linked chain** is one with a stud in each link. The studs keep the chain from kinking. (2) A bolt with no head.

**studding sail**   *n.* A light sail set on a studding boom that is fixed in place as an extension of a yardarm. Also *steering sail* or, more often, *stunsail.*

**studsail**   *n.* Strip of sail cloth fastened to the foot of a fore-and-aft sail to increase the area. Also *bonnet* (British usage).

**stuff**   *n.* A preservative made of tallow and turpentine for wooden spars and planking. Turpentine and resin are used on lower masts and tallow on topmasts.

**stuffing box**   *n.* (1) A device through which a shaft (such as a propeller shaft) passes to prevent leakage. Also *gland.* (2) A box used to surround a moving part to contain steam, oil, or water.

**stuffing tube**   *n.* A packing gland to ensure a watertight fitting or connection through a bulkhead for cables, shafts, or pipes.

**stunsail**   See STUDDING SAIL.

**S-twist**   *adj.* Rope with the strands twisted left or counterclockwise, left-hand lay; the opposite of Z-twist rope. See ROPE.

**subassembly**   *n.* The construction of parts of a ship's structure on platens before they are brought into the ship.

**subcharter**   *n.* An agreement by a charterer to sublet the vessel in part or in whole to a third party. A subcharter does not relate to a charter party except as the original document permits or forbids subchartering; no relationship is established between owner and subcharterer.

**subdivision**   *n.* Dividing a ship's spaces with watertight bulkheads for damage control purposes. Following the sinking of the *Titanic* in 1912, new regulations requiring such subdivision of passenger liners were agreed on at an international conference. Naval ships use much greater compartmentalization than merchant ships to contain flooding in case of attack or accident.

**submarine (SS or SSN)**   *n.* A warship designed for subsurface operations with the primary mission of locating and destroying ships, including other submarines. Nuclear-powered submarines are designated SSN. A guided missile submarine (SSG or SSGN) is designed to have an additional capability to launch guided-missile attacks. A fleet ballistic missile submarine (SSBN) is a nuclear-powered submarine designed to deliver ballistic missile attacks from either a submerged or surfaced position; popularly known as a **boomer.**

**submarine bell**   *n.* A fog signal used on lightships and buoys. The bell and clapper are in a watertight container placed below the surface of the water, and the sound produced can be heard many miles further than a bell can be heard through the air. See SUBMARINE SIGNAL.

**submarine cable**   *n.* An insulated waterproof wire or bundle of wires that carries electric current under water. Such a cable is placed on or near the bottom.

**submarine chaser (PC) or (SC)**   *n.* A 100- to 200-foot patrol vessel tasked specifically to detect and destroy submarines.

**submarine current**   *n.* A current that flows beneath the surface of the water, often in a different direction from the surface current.

**submarine emergency buoyancy (SEBS)**   *n.* A system that allows a submarine to surface rapidly using a gas generator for emergency deballasting.

**submarine escape lung**   *n.* Emergency escape device. See STEINKE HOOD.

**submarine locator acoustic beacon**   *n.* An electronic device for emitting a repetitive sonic pulse underwater and used by submarines in distress.

**submarine marker buoy**   *n.* Two yellow spheres with a transmitter that can be released from a sunken submarine to aid salvage and rescue vessels and aircraft in locating the boat. Also *submarine radio rescue buoy.*

**submarine patrol area**   *n.* A geographically defined area assigned to a submarine for its area of action usually associated with an enemy's high-traffic area; more permanent than a submarine patrol zone.

**submarine patrol zone**   *n.* A restricted operating area established in the ocean to allow unrestricted submarine warfare without danger of attack by friendly forces.

**submariner**   *n.* A person assigned to duty on a submarine; in the U.S. Navy, it is pronounced submaREENer, and in the Royal Navy, subMAriner (as in ancient mariner).

**submarine relief**   *n.* Variations in elevation of the seabed or their representation by depth contours or soundings.

**submarine rescue chamber**   *n.* A bell-like device that can be lowered and fitted to a submarine escape hatch so that several persons can escape to the surface at one time.

**submarine sentry**   *n.* An early type of mechanical depth finder, this device was towed behind a vessel at a depth below that of the ship's keel. When the sentry struck bottom, it rose to the surface and sounded a gong. Submarine sentries were soon replaced by electronic depth-finding devices.

**submarine signal**   *n.* An underwater speaker the signals from which can be picked up by a ship's underwater receiver many miles away. See SUBMARINE BELL.

**submarine site**   *n.* The location of an underwater structure.

**submerged**   *adj.* Beneath the surface of the water, as a submerged piling.

**submerged lands**   *n.* Lands covered by water at any stage of the tide, as distinguished from tidelands, which are attached to the mainland or an island and covered and uncovered with the tide.

**submerged rock**   *n.* A rock submerged on the chart datum but shallow enough to be dangerous to navigation.

**submerged screw log**   *n.* A small propeller in a cylinder attached to the hull below the waterline that measures the speed of the hull through the water by the speed of the propeller in the cylinder; an electric charge is generated and is shown on an indicator on the bridge.

**submersible pump**   *n.* (1) A watertight pump used to pump bilges and able to operate under water. (2) A small watertight pump that can be submerged in a flooded compartment to remove water.

**subordinate current station**   *n.* (1) A current station from which a relatively short series of observations are conducted to be compared with simultaneous observations from a reference station. (2) A station listed in the *Tidal Current Tables* for which tidal predictions are obtained by means of differences and ratios applied to the predictions at a reference station.

**subpermanent magnetism**   *n.* The permanent magnetism that comes about during ship construction while iron lies in the same position for a long period and is subject to the same influence of the Earth's field day after day.

**subrogation clause**   *n.* Marine cargo policy clause that prevents the underwriter from suing the carrier in the name of the insured to seek reimbursement when a loss can be proven to be the result of the carrier's negligence.

**subsidiary light**   *n.* A light placed on a main light and having a special navigation purpose. A **passing light** structure for instance, enables the mariner to keep the light in sight when he has gone beyond the beam of the main light.

**subsidy**   *n.* A grant by a nation to its merchant marine vessels engaged in competitive bidding against other nations for trade, to give them a competitive edge.

**subsistence allowance**   *n.* Extra shore pay allowed in place of food being furnished. This is usually for officers only unless there is no general mess.

**subsolar point**   *n.* The geographical position of the Sun; the point on the Earth's surface at which the Sun is in zenith at a given time.

**substellar point**   *n.* The geographical position of a star; the point on the Earth at which the star is in zenith at a given time.

**substitute**   *n.* One of three single-pointed pennants used in spelling words in a signal hoist. The first substitute is used to repeat the preceding letter; the second is used to repeat the second letter before it; and the third is used to repeat the third letter preceding it. For example, "apple" is spelled as A-P-first substitute-L-E.

**substitution clause**   *n.* A clause in a bill of lading that enables the shipping company to carry the cargo by the ship named in the bill of lading or by any other vessel.

**subsurface current**   *n.* A current below the surface of the sea only. See SURFACE CURRENT.

**subtropical anticyclones**   *n.* High-pressure belts that prevail on the poleward sides of the trade winds and are characterized by calm air and dryness.

**suction box** *n.* The intake compartment for seawater in the hull of a vessel. A strum plate at the seaward opening prevents debris from entering. Also *sea chest.*

**suction dredge** *n.* A vessel with a centrifugal pump fitted to large pipes on either side of the pump. The piping on the pulling side is lowered to the mud to be dredged, and the piping on the other side is led to the barge or spoil bank that is to receive the dredged material. This method of dredging is highly effective and economical in areas where few rocks can be expected.

**suction screw current** *n.* The stream of water that flows into a propeller, whether it is going forward or in reverse. The opposite is the discharge current.

**sudd** *n.* Floating vegetation that obstructs navigation in or near the mouth of a river.

**sue, labor, and travel clause** *n.* Marine underwriting term that induces the insured to make every possible effort for the protection or recovery of the cargo or vessel insured. The insurer agrees to pay his percentage of any expense incurred in such efforts.

**suegee** *n.* (pron. soogee) Soap and water built with caustic soda or caustic potash to raise the pH and increase the effectiveness when cleaning painted surfaces.

**Suez Canal rudder** *n.* An extension on a rudder to increase its power when maneuvering in tight quarters.

**sufferance wharf** *n.* A pier established by customs on which dutiable goods are allowed to be off-loaded and loaded under given conditions without paying duty.

**sugarloaf sea** *n.* A sea with waves formed into conical shapes, usually the result of intersecting waves.

**sugg** *v.* To roll heavily when aground.

**suitcase** *n.* A small wire drum on the side of a towing winch.

**suit of sails** *n.* The full complement of a vessel's sails.

**sumatra** *n.* A strong southwesterly thunderstorm found in the Strait of Malacca during the southwest monsoon; named for the island.

***Summary of Corrections*** *n.* A five-volume semiannual listing summarizing the corrections to charts, *Sailing Directions,* and *United States Coast Pilots* previously published in *Notice to Mariners.*

**summer tank** *n.* A compartment on a tanker in which extra oil can be carried during summer months to load the ship to the summer load line, which is above the winter load line.

**Sumner line** *n.* A line of position obtained from a single altitude observation. Named for Capt. Thomas H. Sumner, who, in 1837, developed a method of working out a line of position on a Mercator projection using a single celestial body. The Sumner method is rarely used today; an adaptation of the Sumner method, the Marcq St. Hilaire Method is favored.

**sump** *n.* A low point or well in a bilge where the water collects to be pumped out.

**Sun** *n.* The most frequently observed body in celestial navigation and the center of the Solar System around which the planets revolve. The **apparent** or **true Sun** is the Sun visible in the sky to an observer on Earth. The **mean** or **astronomical mean Sun** is a "fictitious" Sun understood to move eastward along the celestial equator at a rate that provides a uniform measure of time equal to the average apparent time. The Sun appears to rise and set in a different place every day. The summer solstice is that point on the ecliptic occupied by the Sun at the maximum northerly declination of 23°N (the Tropic of Cancer). The winter solstice is that point on the ecliptic occupied by the Sun at maximum southern declination of 23°S (the Tropic of Capricorn).

**sun deck**   n. The highest exposed deck on a passenger liner. It is used for shuffleboard and other deck games, and it is often the location for the radio room and officers' staterooms.

**sundowner**   n. An excessively strict officer; a bully. It is thought to have applied originally to captains who required all personnel to return from liberty by sundown.

**Sun line**   n. A line of position (LOP) determined from a sextant observation of the Sun. See SIGHT; SUMNER LINE.

**sun over the yardarm**   phr. An expression meaning that, judging from the sun's position relative to the yardarm—traditionally the foreyard, as seen from the quarter deck—it is time for a drink, about 1100 in the high latitudes.

**sunrise**   n. The crossing of the visible horizon by the upper limb of the rising Sun.

**sunset**   n. The crossing of the visible horizon by the upper limb of the setting Sun.

**supercargo**   n. An officer appointed by the owners of the cargo on a merchant ship who is charged with the responsibility of the cargo, its purchase, and its sale.

**superheat**   n. Steam that has been heated above the temperature necessary to create steam under the prevailing conditions. This is done by **superheat-**

ers to develop greater efficiency and speed.

**superior mirage**   n. The optical phenomenon observed occasionally when the sea surface temperature is unusually low and an inverted image is seen above the real object.

**superstructure**   n. A deck house, pilothouse, forecastle, or a decked structure on the freeboard deck of a vessel.

**superstructure deck**   n. A partial deck above the main deck.

**supertanker**   n. Fuel carrier in excess of 300,000 gross tons. See VERY LARGE CRUDE CARRIER.

**supplementary arc**   n. An extra arc fastened to the limb inside the curve of the regular arc of a sextant. It is used for taking two or three land bearings quickly.

**surf**   n. Waves breaking on a shoreline or reef; a series of breakers.

**surface**   v. To rise to the surface of the water.

**surface current**   n. A current on the surface of the water that extends only a few feet deep. See SUBSURFACE CURRENT; WIND CURRENT.

**surface effect ship (SES)**   n. A vehicle such as a hovercraft designed to move across either water or earth by means of a downward blast of air.

**surface warfare**   n. A naval officer specialty exclusive of submariners and naval aviators that embraces a career in surface ships.

**surfboat**   n. A long heavy boat that can be launched in the surf, used by refuge houses for rescue work.

**surf days**   n. Charter party term for days when cargo cannot be loaded by lighters because the state of the sea is such as to make it impractical.

**surf zone** *n.* The relatively narrow area along a shoreline in which the energy of the waves is expended.

**surge** *n.* (1) That part of a windlass into which a cable surges. (2) The difference between predicted wave height and observed wave height. (3) The slack or bight of a rope. (4) The swell of the sea. (5) Uncontrolled forward and/or aft motion of a hull, longitudinal bodily motion; one of the six principal motions of a vessel. A vessel might surge while moored at a pier as a result of tide or seiche. (6) See STORM SURGE.

**surge** *v.* (1) To slip around a windlass, said of a cable. (2) To rise and fall at anchor, usually associated with significant wave energy. (3) To vary in speed forward as a ship moves through waves. (4) To loosen or ease a cable.

**surveillance radar** *n.* A primary radar installation at a land station used to display at that station the position of vessels within radar range, usually for advisory purposes.

**survey** *n.* (1) A detailed inspection or investigation of a vessel or its cargo for insurance or other purposes: "The sale of the vessel will be subject to an acceptable survey." (2) The official U.S. Navy procedure to get expendable material off the accountability list.

**survey** *v.* (1) To thoroughly examine any vessel to determine its seaworthiness. Insurance companies insist on surveys of even the smallest boats for which they accept liability. U.S. Navy slang uses the same term for reviewing the fitness of personnel: "It's time to survey the old chief gunner's mate." (2) To examine a ship or its cargo to determine its condition, especially to establish a basis for claims in the event of damage to the vessel or its cargo due to heavy weather. (3) To measure an area in detail.

**surveying** *n.* That branch of mathematics that deals with the art of determining accurately the area of any part of the Earth's surface, the lengths and directions of the bounding lines, the contours of the surface, and so on.

**surveying ship (AGS)** *n.* A vessel that is assigned to hydrographic survey duty.

**surveyor** *n.* (1) A person certified to examine vessels for insurance purposes or prior to purchase. (2) A person who makes land or ocean surveys.

**swab** *n.* (1) Any mop used to wet down and clean a deck or a floor. A deck mop is a mop made on the mopstick, and a mophead is a detachable mop. Both are used as swabs. (2) A nickname for a sailor. Also *swabbie; swab jockey.*

**swage** *v.* To secure wire rope by compressing the metal of a fitting around the wire. You swage the shrouds and stays into the deck fittings that hold them. The tool used to accomplish this is also called a swage.

**swallow** *n.* (1) Larger opening in a block above or below the sheave. See BLOCK. (2) The round opening in a chock.

**swallow the anchor** *v.* To retire from the naval service or from the sea.

**swamp** *v.* To cause a vessel to be filled with water to the point of sinking, not from a leak but from water coming over the side. "With our built-in buoyancy, we could not be sunk even though we were swamped and our gunnels were level with the sea."

**swash** *n.* (1) Sandbar over which water washes. (2) The rush of water up onto a shore.

**swash bulkhead** *n.* A midline bulkhead with or without lightening holes, used in tanks as baffles to reduce the action of the liquid in the tank in big seas. Also *baffle plate* or *swash plate.*

**swash channel**    *n.* Relatively narrow tidal channel, often deep enough for boats, between land and a sandbar, between two sandbars, or between land and a small island.

**sway**    *n.* Lateral or side-to-side motion of a vessel. One of the six principal motions of a vessel.

**sway**    *v.* To hoist or raise, especially masts and spars, but also applied to cargo. A topmast is swayed to remove the fid before being struck below. Swaying has the connotation of lifting and lowering rather than lateral pulling as with warping a vessel. Also *sway away.*

**sweat**    *v.* (1) To haul as tightly as possible. To sweat a line is to take as much slack out of it as possible.

**sweat boards**    *n.* Plywood lining on the interior sides of a ship to protect personnel against the condensate from the steel hull.

**sweep**    *n.* (1) An electronics term referring to the sweep of the radar antenna or the sonar transducer. (2) A mine sweeping term meaning the action of clearing a harbor or channel of mines. (3) A long oar.

**sweep**    *v.* (1) To drag for rocks, anchors, and other objects; to search for something underwater. (2) To clear a harbor or channel of mines.

**sweep rate**    *n.* The number of times a radar radiation pattern rotates during 1 minute.

**swell**    *n.* A wave that continues after the wind has ceased or changed direction, or a long wave that moves continuously without breaking.

**swift (or swifter)**    *v.* To pull two shrouds or stays together, especially when

pulling two shrouds tight before putting on ratlines. The rope used for swiftering is called a **swiftering line.**

**swift boat**    See PATROL CRAFT, FAST.

**swifter**    *n.* (1) The aftermost shroud on either side of each mast. At the time of Sir Francis Drake and the Spanish Armada, the swifter consisted of a pendant with a double block and fall and served with a preventer for the mast forward of the shrouds. (2) A strong rope that was led around a fighting sailing ship just below the gunwale to strengthen the hull in case another ship came alongside in the heat of battle. (3) A rope used to hold the bars of a capstan in their apertures. It was passed through holes in the bars at their outer ends and made tight, to hold them as spokes of a wheel.

**swig**    *v.* To haul at the bight of a line that is fixed at one end and made fast to a movable object at the other end. You haul a sail aloft in this manner. Also *swig off.*

**swing**    *v.* (1) To ride at anchor with the bow pointing in different directions depending on the tide and wind; said of a ship at anchor. "We spent the next four days swinging at anchor while the front passed through." To **swing clear** is to ride at anchor without danger of colliding with another ship or object. (2) To bring a ship's head to a number of different headings to adjust the magnetic compass. An important part of every shakedown cruise is swinging the ship to adjust the compass. Some harbors have **swinging buoys** with carefully determined coordinates to assist ships in adjusting their compasses. Also *swinging the compass.*

**swinging booms**    See BOAT BOOM.

**swinging mooring**    *n.* A mooring with a single anchor chain; such a mooring swings with the ship with tide, wind, and current. See SINGLE-POINT MOORING.

**swing the arc**   *v.* To rock a sextant along the line of sight to make sure that the reading is with the celestial body at the bottom of the arc and that the sextant is vertical.

**swing out**   *v.* To move an anchor or small boat on davits out over the ship's side. "Swing out the lifeboats before we list any further."

**swivel**   *n.* A shackle or link with a shank that turns freely in a circular plane to make it possible for one chain to rotate without the other cable or chain turning; swivels are used on anchor chains, blocks, and so on.

**sword (or sword arm)**   *n.* A part of a pitot tube that resembles a blade that is lowered through the hull to determine the ship's speed through the water. Also *pit sword.*

**sword mat**   *n.* Antichafing mat made of woven rope-yarns.

**synchronous lights**   *n.* Lights with phase characteristics of the same frequency.

**synchronous rolling**   *n.* The condition that obtains when a vessel's rolling period coincides with the ambient wave period. This condition results in excessive motion, but can be corrected by a change of speed or course.

**synoptic chart**   *n.* In meteorology, any chart or map on which data and analyses are presented that describe the state of the atmosphere over a large area at a given moment.

**sypher**   *v.* To overlap plank edges for a bulkhead.

**systematic error**   *n.* One that follows a pattern and can be predicted, such as the index error of a marine compass or the error in a chronometer. See RANDOM ERROR.

**syzygy**   *n.* (pron. sizigee) Either of two points in the orbit of a celestial body when the body is in either conjunction or opposition to the Sun. Syzygy between Moon and Earth occurs twice each lunar month. See SPRING TIDE.

# T

**T**   See TANGO.

**tabernacle**   *n.* Any device at the base of a deck-stepped mast that holds the base of the mast in place and can be adjusted to lower and raise the mast at bridges. Also *mast pedestal; mast trunk.*

**table**   *n.* The outer part of a keel, stem, or sternpost that projects beyond the rabbet line.

**table**   *v.* To make a broad, stiffening hem in a sail at the head, leeches, and foot to accommodate the boltrope.

**tabling**   *n.* The reinforcing hem to which the boltrope is sewn.

**tabling needle**   *n.* Name given to the needle used to sew the leather used at the head, clew, and tack to protect those points from chafing against the shrouds and stays.

**tabular berg**   *n.* A flat-topped iceberg that has broken loose from an ice barrier; the length-to-height ratio is greater than 5:1.

**tabulated azimuth**   *n.* The azimuth taken from the tables before interpolation.

**tachometer** *n.* An instrument that measures the number of revolutions per minute (RPMs) that a propeller shaft turns.

**tack** *n.* (1) The forward lower corner of a fore-and-aft sail whether three- or four-sided. (2) The direction a vessel takes with relation to the wind and the placement of the sails. A vessel is on a starboard tack when the wind comes over the starboard side and the main boom is on the port side. (3) A sailing course: "We took the windward tack as far as Grand Turk." (4) A line led forward from the clew of a course on a square-rigged vessel.

**tack** *v.* To change course so as to necessitate shifting the main boom from one side to the other; to change from port tack to starboard tack, or vice versa, bringing the vessel's bow through the wind. See JIBE; POINTS OF SAILING.

**tack bolt** *n.* A temporary holding bolt.

**tack bumkin** *n.* An iron bracket that extends a few feet before the bow of a square rigger on which the tack of a foresail is set.

**tack cringle** *n.* The steel or bronze ring sewn into a fore-and-aft sail at the point where the luff and foot come together.

**tack downhaul** *n.* A line or tackle used to put a downward strain on the luff of a sail. See CUNNINGHAM; TACK LINE.

**tack hook** *n.* A hook fitted on the bowsprit or a stem fitting for securing the tack of the headsail; it is usually accompanied by a **keeper** that holds the tack on the hook when the sail is lowered.

**tack-jigger** *n.* Gear used for hauling down the weather tack of a foresail or mainsail. See BOARD THE TACK.

**tackle** *n.* Any combination of ropes and blocks that form a purchase providing a mechanical advantage.

**tackle upon tackle** *n.* A purchase with a luff tackle applied to the fall of another. See SPANISH BURTON.

**tack line** *n.* (1) A line used to haul down the tack of a gaff topsail. (2) A line spliced into the eye at the bottom of the tabling for securing a signal flag to the halyard. Also *tack of the flag.* (3) A length of line in a signal halyard that separates each group of flags when there is more than one group. See TACK DOWNHAUL.

**tackling** *n.* (1) The rigging or tackle of a ship. (2) The furnishings of a ship. Falconer pronounced the term obsolete in 1769.

**tack pin** *n.* A belaying pin.

**tack rag** *n.* A sticky cloth used to clean lint off a surface before painting or varnishing.

**tack tackle** *n.* The tackle used to haul down and tighten sails on fore-and-aft-rigged vessels. Also *downhaul.*

**tack trice** *n.* The tricing line used on gaff-rigged fore-and-aft sails to draw the tack of the gaff upward to spill the wind without lowering the gaff. Short for **tack tricing line.**

**tactical command ship (CC)** *n.* A U.S. Navy vessel designed as a command ship for a fleet/force commander. Such a ship is provided with extensive communication equipment.

**tactical diameter** *n.* The perpendicular distance a ship travels from the original course to the position where the ship has turned through 180° after the helm is put over.

**tactical range recorder** *n.* Equipment used in analyzing visual presenta-

# Tackle

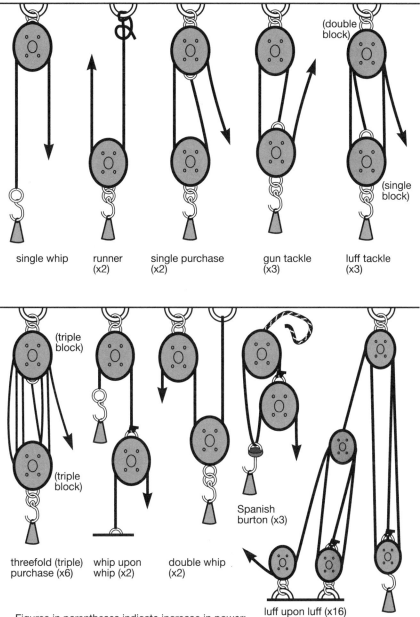

single whip

runner (x2)

single purchase (x2)

gun tackle (x3)

luff tackle (x3)

(double block)

(single block)

(triple block)

(triple block)

threefold (triple) purchase (x6)

whip upon whip (x2)

double whip (x2)

Spanish burton (x3)

luff upon luff (x16)

Figures in parentheses indicate increase in power; all blocks are single sheave except where noted.

tions of ranging echoes from submarine targets.

**taffrail**   *n.* The rail farthest aft on a vessel. On small boats it is also called a **stern pulpit.**

**taffrail log**   *n.* A patent log attached to the taffrail consisting of a rotator and sinker attached to a registering meter. The rotator is towed far enough astern to avoid the turbulence of the wake, and as the rotator turns, the line connecting it to the counter on the taffrail signals the speed with which the rotator is turning. This is translated into knots through the water. See PATENT LOG.

**tag line**   *n.* A rope used to steady a load being swayed aboard or lowered, such as a lifeboat.

**tail**   *n.* (1) The long end of a block strap that is used instead of a hook to secure the block. (2) The tapered end of the clew rope, head rope, or tack rope that extends a short length beyond the cringle. (3) The direction a ship tends from its anchor. The vessel is said to **tail downstream** or to **tail offshore.**

**tail**   *v.* (1) To taper the end of a rope by unlaying it a short length and tapering the strands with a knife. You then re-treat the strands with wax or other sealant and re-lay them. (2) To control a halyard or sheet as it is cranked after it has cleared the winch drum. "You crank the winch handle, and I'll tail." By so doing, the speaker will keep the hauling part clear and prevent fouling.

**tail block**   *n.* A single block having a short piece of line by which it can be secured to a piece of gear. Also *tall block.*

**tail chain**   *n.* A short length of chain with a hook attached at one end and used on a winch line so that it can be fastened to ropes or parts of rigging.

**tailhook**   *n.* A hook lowered from the after part of an aircraft to engage the arresting gear on a carrier when landing.

**tail off**   *v.* To pick up the end of a line and haul it.

**tail on**   *v.* To take a line and haul away on a winch or other device. Also *tally on,* when used as a command.

**tail shaft**   *n.* The shaft by which the motion of the engines is transmitted to the propellers. The rotational motion is communicated by means of sections of shafting carried by bearings and secured to each other by couplings that are usually flanged. The after section that carries the propeller is called the propeller shaft of the tail shaft.

**tail splice**   *n.* A splice used to connect fiber rope to wire rope.

**taint damage**   *n.* Damage to goods when cargo has become wet by seawater in heavy weather. In maritime law this is considered one of the perils of the sea.

**take a strain**   *phr.* To place tension on a line or cable.

**take a turn**   *phr.* To put a line around a winch or belaying pin and hold on. "We'll have to take at least three turns around the winch before it will hold the line in this blow."

**take charge**   *phr.* Said of a rope or cable when it goes out of control and runs out on its own momentum: "The cable will take charge if you don't set the brake first."

**take departure**   See TAKING DEPARTURE.

**take in**   *v.* (1) To lower and furl a sail: "Don't take in the headsail until the spinnaker is aloft and flying." (2) To pull in on a sheet, hawser, or other working rope. To **take in slack** is to pull a line taut. Also *tally.* See CAST OFF; PUT OUT.

**Take the bottom** *phr.* To go aground. See STRAND.

**take the ground** *phr.* Said of a vessel when the tide leaves it aground.

**taking departure** *phr.* The point at which a voyage is reckoned to begin. It is usually established by taking bearings of prominent landmarks as the ship clears harbor and proceeds to sea. When the navigator establishes this point, he is said to take departure. This point is also called the **point of departure.**

**takings at sea** *n.* Marine underwriter's term for the detention and taking into port of a neutral merchant ship for an examination when it is suspected of carrying contraband to the enemy in time of war.

**Taku wind** *n.* A strong, gusty wind from the east-northeast that occurs in the vicinity of the Taku River of Juneau, Alaska, during winter months.

**tall ship** *n.* A large sailing ship.

**tally** *n.* An accounting of the cargo being loaded or off-loaded.

**tally stick** *n.* A bamboo stick used by Chinese longshoremen in tallying cargo. They gave the mate a stick for each piece of freight as it was discharged.

**tampion** *n.* (pron. tampyen or tomkin) A plug placed in the muzzle of a cannon to keep out dirt and water when not in use. From the Old French *tampon,* a cotton plug. Also *tompion.*

**tan** *v.* To preserve sailcloth by soaking it in water and tannin derived from the **tanbark** of various trees. The English used oak and the Chinese used mangrove. See TANNED SAIL.

**tang** *n.* The metal fitting on the mast of a sailing vessel to which the shrouds and stays are attached. It is usually a mast band that encircles the masts.

**tangent** *n.* (1) The trigonometric concept of a line bearing on the edge of a circle. (2) A line bearing on the edge of an island is called the island's right or left tangent.

**tangent method** *n.* A method of determining a ship's position that consists of working a time sight by using the dead-reckoning latitude and taking the azimuth from the tables in Bowditch to establish a Sumner line.

**Tango** *n.* Phonetic word for "T." Used as a single-letter signal it means "Keep clear of me."

**tank** *n.* (1) A term used on nautical charts for a water tank elevated high above the ground on a skeleton structure. (2) A compartment for liquids.

**tanker** *n.* A vessel designed and built to carry bulk liquid such as crude oil, fuel, or liquefiable cargo (such as frozen orange juice concentrate), usually with no space for general cargo. The bridge and propulsion units are usually placed aft, and there are specific requirements for insulating flammable cargo from engine spaces. **Handy-size crude carriers** are 6,000 to 35,000 DWT; **medium crude carriers (MCC),** 35,000 to 160,000 DWT; **very large crude carriers (VLCC),** 160,000 to 300,000 DWT; **ultralarge crude carriers (ULCC),** 300,000 DWT and up. Also *tank ship.* See SHIP.

**tanker terminal** *n.* A mole or pier equipped to load and unload oil tankers.

**tank landing ship (LST)** *n.* A naval landing ship designed to transport and land amphibious vehicles, tanks, combat vehicles, and equipment in an amphibious assault.

**tank top**   *n.* The plating placed on the bottom floors of a ship; the plating forms the top side of the tank sections or double bottoms.

**tank vessel**   *n.* A vessel that is specially constructed or converted to carry liquid bulk cargo in tanks, as a non-self-propelled **tank barge** or machinery- or sail-powered tanker or **tank ship.**

**tanned sail**   *n.* A canvas sail that has been soaked in the bark of a tree, such as oak, that contains heavy concentrations of tannin, which slows the development of mildew and rot-causing bacteria.

**tar**   *n.* (1) A dark or black viscid substance produced by the destructive distillation of wood, coal, or peat. The tar used for tarring wooden ships' bottoms, caulking material, and rigging was usually made from pine tar. See NAVAL STORES. (2) A sailor. See TARPAULIN.

**tar**   *v.* To cover with tar. The standing rigging in sailing ships is tarred to protect it from the elements.

**TAR**   *n.* Acronym for Training and Administration of the Naval Reserve, the designation of a Naval Reserve officer or enlisted person on active duty and assigned to TAR.

**tare**   *n.* (rhymes with care) The weight of an empty container in which cargo is shipped; it is deducted from the gross weight to get the net weight of its contents.

**tarpaulin**   *n.* Heavy canvas or other material treated with tar or other waterproofing material for protection against the weather. Although tarpaulins, or **tarps,** are used for covering items exposed to the weather, originally they were the material from which sailors made waterproof clothing, for which reason sailors became known as tars.

**tarred rope**   *n.* A rope of natural fibers treated with coal tar when it is to be exposed to the weather; the tar makes it last longer in the weather, but at the same time, the tar, being a petroleum product, weakens the vegetable fibers.

**tartana**   *n.* A single-masted vessel with a lateen sail and a headsail, seen in the western Mediterranean along the African coast.

**task force**   *n.* (1) A temporary assignment of naval units under one commander for the purpose of carrying out a specific task. (2) A semipermanent group of naval units under one commander, formed for the purpose of carrying out a continuing task. (3) A major fleet subdivision of an independent U.S. Naval command that is assigned a specific and continuing task.

**task organization**   *n.* A fleet, force, group, element, or unit. The standard operating organization format of the U.S. Navy.

**tatoo**   *n.* Preparatory bugle call for taps. From the Dutch *taptoe,* the shutting of the taps (in the taverns before closing).

**taut**   *adj.* Tight, with no slack. Also said of a highly disciplined ship, "a taut (or tight) ship."

**taut bowline**   *n.* A close-hauled tack, to be sailing on a taut bowline is to be sailing close-hauled.

**taut-o**   *adj.* From the phrase all-a-taut-o, which meant that all the rigging was in place, tuned, and shipshape.

**teeth**   *n.* In the direction from which the wind is coming. "Our course took us into the teeth of the gale."

**telegraph block**   *n.* A block with several sheaves, one on top of the other, used for making signals with several halyards at one time.

**telegraph buoy**  *n.* A buoy that marks the position of a submarine telegraph cable.

**telemotor**  *n.* A hydraulic device by which the steering wheel controls the rudder and at the same time indicates to the helmsman the position of the rudder.

**telepher conveyor**  *n.* An electric hoist system, used for transferring cargo on a wharf.

**telescope**  *n.* A long optical instrument that magnifies a small area many times to make details visible at a distance; when not in use it can be slid into itself to become less cumbersome. See LONG GLASS.

**telescope mast**  *n.* One that has a top mast that slides down into a hollow lower mast.

**telescope shade**  *n.* A filter that can be screwed onto the eyepiece of a sextant telescope to keep out some Sun rays or to better penetrate, or see through, a fog.

**telescopic alidade**  *n.* A bearing circle employing a telescope instead of sight vanes. A prism reflects the bearings while the telescope enlarges the image of the object being sighted. When the alidade is mounted on a gimballed compass card that relays gyrocompass readings, the problem of the ship's motion is largely negated. This instrument is called a pelorus. The assembly is used for getting the compass bearings of other ships and objects.

**telltale**  *n.* (1) A length of yarn tied to the rigging, mast, or sail, so that the helmsman can determine the relative wind direction. Telltales mounted through the sail so that one end is on one side and the other on the other side of the sail will tell the helmsman whether the sails are properly trimmed. Also *tickler.* (2) A device used in shipyards that tells the shipwrights about the keel settlement

or the crushing of the crushing strips during a vessel's launching.

**telltale compass**  *n.* (1) A remote reading compass either acting off the gyro or independent magnetic compasses placed in the captain's sea cabin and stateroom and often the executive officer's stateroom and the navigator's stateroom. (2) A course recorder. (3) An inverted compass read from beneath, such as one over the navigator's bunk.

**Tellurometer**  *n.* The registered trademark for a system used for short-range, line-of-sight, distance measuring in hydrographic surveys.

**temperature chimneys**  *n.* Pipes leading down into bulk cargo through which thermometers can be lowered to determine if heat is being generated that might cause a fire.

**template**  *n.* A mold or pattern as of a ship's members, made to full size.

**temporales**  *n.* A strong southwesterly to westerly wind and heavy rain during July and August along the west coast of Nicaragua and Costa Rica.

**temporary light**  *n.* A light put into service for a limited time to replace an aid to navigation that is out of commission.

**temporary magnet**  *n.* Soft ferrous metal that loses its magnetism as soon as the source of magnetism is removed. All ships are temporary magnets to a slight degree, and each change in a ship's heading will change the temporary magnetism as a result of the change in the ship's position in the Earth's magnetic field; this is also called **transient magnetism.**

**tend**  *v.* (1) To man, to attend to, to do what is necessary on a specific task. "The deck gang is responsible for tending deck lines when mooring the ship." You speak of tending the mainsheet. See

SELF-TENDING SAIL. (2) To lead off in a given direction. "The anchor cable is tending aft in spite of the wind direction." To **tend ship** is to watch the swinging of a vessel at anchor and to use whatever means are available, especially the helm, to try to keep a clear hawse.

**tender**  *n.* (1) A repair vessel capable of sailing with a fleet for the purpose of doing maintenance work as necessary. (2) A vessel in a port, especially a foreign port, that is capable of accomplishing repairs that ships' personnel are not ordinarily expected to handle. "When we reach Malta, we have been assigned three days with a tender to repair the propeller shaft." (3) A destroyer tender is one that accompanies several destroyers to render various services, such as repair tenders and supply tenders. (4) A small boat or dinghy that transfers guests and supplies or that can be used to do repair work and painting on larger boats.

**tender**  *adj.* Describes a vessel that is tippy or crank. This is not necessarily a flaw in design, especially with racing boats. See STIFF.

**tender clause**  *n.* A stipulation in a marine underwriter's policy that enables the underwriter to determine where repairs can be made.

**tenon**  *n.* A mast heel fitted to go in a step.

**tensiometer**  *n.* A gauge used to determine the tension applied to a cable.

**tent an awning**  *v.* To cast off the stops of an awning and so rig it that it will catch rainwater.

**teredo**  *n.* A genus of mollusks especially harmful to wood-hulled vessels in warm waters. See SHIPWORM.

**tern schooner**  *n.* A three-masted, fore-and-aft-rigged sailing vessel common in the maritime provinces of Canada during the early part of the 20th century.

**terrestrial equator**  *n.* The great circle on the Earth's surface that is equidistant from both poles and has a plane perpendicular to the Earth's axis. Ordinarily it is called simply the equator, unless a distinction is being made between the terrestrial equator and the celestial equator.

**terrestrial magnetism**  *n.* The lines of magnetic force on the Earth's surface that give the compass needle its direction and also cause it to dip.

**terrestrial meridian**  *n.* The great circle on the Earth's surface that passes through both poles and the observer's position.

**territorial sea**  *n.* The zone off the coast of a nation or state immediately seaward from a baseline that is subject to the sovereignty of that state or nation. Traditionally the width of this zone was 3 nautical miles, or about the distance a cannon could be shot from land. Under the 1982 Conventions adopted at the Third UN Conference on the Law of the Sea (UNCLDS III), every state has the right to establish the width of its territorial sea up to a limit not exceeding 12 nautical miles measured from baselines as determined and defined by the conventions. Complete sovereignty is maintained over the coastal zone by that coastal nation, subject to the right of innocent passage of ships of all nations. Also *territorial waters.*

**territorial straits**  *n.* Straits that are 6 miles wide or less. When such a strait divides two countries, it is usually agreed that the dividing line between the two countries will run down the middle of the strait.

**TEU**  *n.* Acronym for twenty-foot equivalent unit, used to describe the cargo-carrying capacity of a container ship. A TEU is 20 feet by 8 feet by 82 feet or the equivalent.

**Texas deck**  *n.* The deck of an inland steamer adjacent to the pilot house and officers' quarters.

**Texas tower light station**  *n.* A light tower with a radar or microwave platform, supported on caissons anchored to the seabed, and that resembles the oil-drilling platforms first developed in the Gulf of Mexico off Texas. A typical tower may have a helicopter landing pad, living quarters for the crew, radio beacon, fog signals, the light itself, and oceanographic equipment.

**thalweg**  *n.* (pron. tholwaig or tallvek) (1) The middle of the deepest part of a river, channel, or stream. (2) When a channel separates two political areas, the main navigable channel is the thalweg as interpreted in international law. From the German *thal,* valley, and *weg,* way.

**Thames measurement**  *n.* (pron. temz) A yacht racing handicap developed and adopted in 1855 by the Royal Thames Yacht Club and still used extensively in Great Britain. It is also used for estimating the cost of building a yacht and for computing insurance premiums. The formula is as follows:

$$\frac{(L - B) \times B \times \frac{1}{2}B}{94},$$

where L is length on deck and B is maximum beam. The measurement is used by Lloyd's Underwriters in figuring premiums. Because American boats are generally beamier, they are at a disadvantage when this formula is used.

**theft**  *n.* In maritime tradition and in marine insurance, theft is large-scale stealing, or the taking of a whole thing and not just one of its parts. See PILFERAGE.

**theodolite**  *n.* A surveying and charting instrument that measures horizontal and vertical angles with a telescope that

moves in both horizontal and vertical planes.

**theory of infection**  See INFECTION, THEORY OF.

**thermocline**  *n.* A zone of rapid temperature decrease in the ocean. The surface temperature extends to about 125 meters in the Tropics; the deep ocean temperature begins at depths greater than 200 fathoms where the temperature everywhere is below 60°F. In the Arctic and Antarctic where the cooled water sinks from the surface to the depths, temperatures of 28.5°F exist. Because these layers refract sound waves, they cause a serious problem in locating submarines.

**thick-and-thin block**  *n.* A block designed to take two ropes of different diameters.

**thick strake**  *n.* Heavy ceiling timbers worked over the heads of the floor timbers and the first futtocks to prevent the heads and heels from becoming misshapen.

**thick weather**  *n.* Weather that is misty, foggy, rainy, or snowy; weather with reduced visibility.

**thieves' knot**  *n.* An especially painful addition to the cat-o'-nine tails used for thieves.

**thieving paste**  *n.* A coating applied to a rod that is used to determine the level of liquid in a tank. The coating changes color or dissolves, thus indicating what the level is. Caramel used to be used because it would dissolve, but more sophisticated coatings have been developed for different mediums.

**thimble**  *n.* (1) A round or oval device, usually made of galvanized iron or stainless steel, U-shaped in cross section, set in an eye-splice to protect the rope or wire from chafing by chains and fittings that are run through the eye-splice.

(2) A ring that prevents chafing in the eye or cringle of a sail through which lines are rove. (3) A metal ring around which a rope is spliced to prevent chafing of the rope when other ropes, chains, or cables are attached.

**thimble trysail**   *n.* A triangular fore-and-aft boomless storm sail.

**third deck**   *n.* The second deck below the main deck. Decks are numbered down from the main deck: main deck, second deck, third deck, and so on.

**thirty days clause**   *n.* Term used in marine insurance to allow 30 days after a vessel has reached its final destination before the policy is canceled.

**thirty-two point light**   *n.* A light showing an unbroken light over an arc of the horizon of 360°, or 32 points; an "all-round light." See NAVIGATION LIGHTS.

**thole (pin)**   *n.* A wooden peg driven into a hole in the gunwale of an oared boat against which the oar bears when pulled.

**thoroughfare (or thorofare)**   *n.* A public waterway such as a river or strait.

**thoroughfoot**   *n.* The fall of a tackle that has been twisted or a block that has been capsized.

**thoroughfoot**   *v.* To coil rope against its lay with the lower end coming up through the middle, pulling it through, and then coiling down with the lay; this is done to remove the kinks.

**thread**   *n.* The smallest component of a rope fiber, spun into yarn. Also *fiber.*

**three-figure compass card**   *n.* A compass card on a gyrocompass that uses three figures all the way around the card starting with 000° and ending with 359° or 360°; the ship's heading is always given in three figures, such as "Come to course zero zero five," not "five degrees."

**threefold block**   *n.* A block having three sheaves.

**threefold purchase**   *n.* A purchase consisting of two threefold blocks with the line rove off. See TACKLE.

**three-island steamer**   *n.* A steamer with a forecastle, midship house, and a poop.

**three-letter point**   *n.* The points of the compass cards between the cardinal points—north, south, east, and west—and the intercardinal points—northeast, southeast, southwest, and northwest. The eight three-lettered points (north northeast, east northeast, and so on) are abbreviated NNE, ENE, ESE, SSE, SSW, WSW, WNW, and NNW. See COMPASS CARD.

**three-letter signal**   *n.* Flag combinations enumerated in the *International Code of Signals.* These include descriptions, diagnoses, points of the compass and relative bearings, as opposed to four-letter hoists indicating ship's identification signal and tactical signals found in the *General Signal Book.*

**three sheets to the wind**   *adj.* Drunk and confused, as a ship might be with none of its sheets sheeted home.

**three-sixty/seven-twenty rule (360/720)**   *n.* In some racing rules, an alternative to being disqualified under which a boat can take a penalty of sailing once or twice around in a tight circle.

**three-star problem**   *n.* A position established by using three Sumner lines derived from three stars.

**three-twelve**   *n.* A nickname for early diesel-powered oil tankers. They were of about 12,000 tons deadweight, had a speed of 12 knots, and consumed 12 tons of fuel per day.

**throat**   *n.* (1) The midship part of a floor timber over the deepest part of the keel. (2) The upper forward corner of a gaff-rigged sail at the point where the head and luff join. Also *nock.* See GAFF. (3) The enlarged part of the anchor shank where it joins the arms. (4) That part of the shell of a block that is close to the eye or the hook.

**throat bolt**  *n.* Eyebolt at the inboard end of a gaff.

**throat brails**  *n.* Ropes from the leech to the gaff used to gather a sail.

**throat halyards**  *n.* Ropes and tackles used to hoist the inboard end of the gaff.

**throat seizing**  *n.* A seizing made without cross turns at the point where two lines cross.

**throttleman**  *n.* A member of the engine room crew who handles the throttles that control the speed of a ship.

**throttle watch**  *n.* An engineering watch necessitated by bad weather when someone must constantly operate the throttle to prevent the propeller from racing when the stern lifts out of the sea.

**through fastening**  *n.* A hull fitting that is bolted instead of being screwed.

**through hull**  *adj.* Describes a fitting that goes through the hull such as a drain, a bilge pump outlet, or a saltwater intake.

**through the cabin windows**  *phr.* A phrase used derisively to describe a person who reaches command without coming up through the ranks, or through the hawsepipe.

**through the hawsepipe**  *phr.* A term that describes an officer who has come up through all grades.

**throw off**  *v.* To take a line off a pin or to uncleat a line to let it run free. "Throw off the leeward lines first before

we throw off the windward lines and leave our slip."

**thrum mat**  *n.* An antichafing mat placed over the side to protect the hull from the "spur shore shoe" or to muffle oars. It is made by sticking a **thrum,** or short piece of rope, through a mat.

**thrust bearing (principal)**  *n.* A type of bearing installed in the reduction gear or on a line shaft to absorb the driving force of the propeller. Also *thrust block.*

**thrust collar**  *n.* One of the flanges on a propeller shaft that transfers the thrusting force of the propeller to the thrust bearing.

**thrust deduction**  *n.* The lost energy resulting from the suction caused by the stern of a vessel as it moves through the water. The thrust deduction coefficient is the ratio of the loss to the total thrust of the propeller.

**thruster**  *n.* A propeller, usually in an athwartships tunnel, located at either the bow or the stern that assists a vessel in moving the bow or stern sideways, frequently eliminating the need for assisting tugs.

**thumb cleat**  *n.* A cleat located near the end of a yardarm that prevents the reef earings from sliding in.

**thunderstorm**  *n.* A local disturbance associated with cumulonimbus clouds and accompanied by thunder and lightning with heavy rain and high winds. See CLOUDS; WEATHER.

**thwart**  *n.* An athwartships seat in a small boat.

**thwartship tackles**  *n.* Purchases used for rigging in davits that can be swung out.

**thwart stanchion**  *n.* A vertical brace that supports the thwarts in a small boat.

**ticket** *n.* Slang for merchant marine license, for instance, a master's ticket or a mate's ticket.

**tickler**  See TELLTALE.

**tidal basin**  *n.* A tidal harbor in which the water is kept at a constant level by means of floodgates. British term.

**tidal bore**  *n.* An initial wave created by tidal pressure when it overcomes a river current in a restricted area. The bore moves upstream. Bores are found in many places of the world; one of the more dramatic examples is created in the tributaries and rivers flowing into the Bay of Fundy between New Brunswick and Nova Scotia, Canada.

**tidal bulge**  See PRIMING OF THE TIDE.

**tidal constants**  *n.* Those tidal factors in an area that remain essentially constant, such as spring ranges and mean rise.

**tidal current**  *n.* The horizontal movement of water caused by the Sun and the Moon. Tidal currents are part of the tidal system of the sea. British usage is **tidal stream.**

*Tidal Current Charts*  *n.* A set of 12 charts published by the National Ocean Survey that depict by means of arrows and figures the direction and speed (velocity) of the tidal current for each hour of the tidal cycle.

**tidal current diagrams**  *n.* A set of 12 diagrams, one for each month, published annually by the National Oceanic Service, showing the 12 monthly computer constructed diagrams used in conjunction with the *Tidal Current Charts* for a particular area.

*Tidal Current Tables*  *n.* Tables giving the heights and times of tides, published by the National Ocean Service, that cover the Atlantic Coast of North America including the Gulf of Mexico and the Pacific Coast of North America and Asia.

**tidal datum**  *n.* The level from which heights and depths are measured and predicted. The most important datum is the chart sounding datum, the level used and indicated on the chart in the tide box. It is the level of water hydrographers use when making up charts and is the lowest level to which tides fall under normal circumstances.

**tidal day**  *n.* Equal to a lunar day of about 24 hours 50 minutes, the period of a complete tide cycle.

**tidal fall**  *n.* The difference between a high water and the following low water. See TIDAL RISE.

**tidal harbor**  *n.* A harbor in which the tides have a direct effect on the depth of water and in which the level in the harbor is not maintained by a water gate. See TIDAL BASIN; TIDAL RANGE.

**tidal oscillation**  *n.* One high tide and the succeeding low tide, or vice versa.

**tidal prism**  *n.* An engineering term for the amount of water that moves in and out of a harbor or channel.

**tidal quay**  *n.* A quay in an open harbor that offers sufficient depth for vessels to stay afloat during all tides.

**tidal range**  *n.* The average of the differences between successive high tides and low tides. It is different from the tidal fall, which is only one tidal oscillation. See METONIC CYCLE.

**tidal rise**  *n.* The difference between low water and the succeeding high water.

**tidal waters**  *n.* All water, including freshwater, that is affected by the ebb and flow of the tides. Rivers and tributaries that are affected by tides that "back up" into the freshwater area, causing the flow

## Tidal Levels and Charted Data

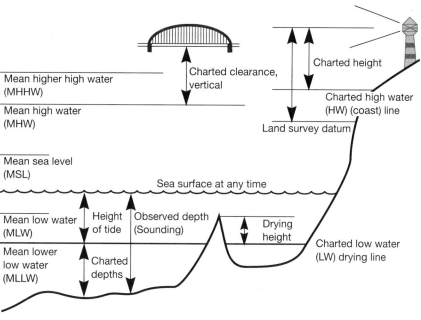

of fresh water to go upstream, have been defined by the courts as tidal waters.

**tidal wave**   See STORM SURGE; TSU-NAMI.

**tide**   *n.* The periodic rise and fall of the oceans of the world as they react to the gravitational attraction between the Earth and the Sun and the Moon. The vertical movement of a tide is the rise or fall, while the horizontal movement is the flood or ebb. Also *astronomical tide*. See BARY-CENTER; METEOROLOGICAL TIDE; SYZYGY.

**Tide and Current Glossary**   *n.* A publication of the National Ocean Service that includes tide and current terms as well as definitions peculiar to the work of the NOS.

**tide box**   *n.* Information on tide and tide constants listed on marine charts.

**tide-bound**   *adj.* Describes a ship unable to move because of low tide—not necessarily aground, but surrounded by low water through which it cannot move toward its destination.

**tide crack**   *n.* An ice navigation term that denotes the line between an immovable ice foot and fast ice that moves with the tide.

**tide gate**   *n.* (1) A place where the tide runs with great speed. (2) An opening through which the water can flow freely when the tide sets in one direction, but that closes automatically to prevent the water from flowing in the other direction when the flow reverses.

**tide gauge**   *n.* Any device used for recording tides, whether a stick against a seawall, or a more sophisticated damped instrument with a readout in a remote location.

**tidehead**   *n.* Inland limit of water affected by tides.

**tideland**   *n.* (1) Land submerged during high water, but uncovered during low water. (2) That part of the continental shelf between the shore and the boundaries on land claimed by the state government.

**tide mark**   *n.* The line along the shore reached by high water.

**tide notes**   *n.* Notes on marine charts regarding the tides.

**tide prediction**   *n.* The predetermination of times and heights of tides based on lunar cycles. Predicted tides are published annually in the *Tidal Current Tables* by the National Oceanic and Atmospheric Administration.

**tide race**   *n.* A divergent current produced by a tidal current when it flows against or over a rock or promontory in the sea. This can be quite formidable for the unsuspecting mariner in areas where the tidal range is several feet. They are well charted and should be carefully noted.

**tide rip**   *n.* A stretch of water that ripples as a result of two tides or currents meeting. See RIP CURRENT.

**tide rode**   *adj.* Describes an anchored vessel that swings with the tide. "Because of her deep, full-length keel, she could be expected to be tide rode." See WIND RODE.

**tide signals**   *n.* Semaphores, flags, and lights used at entrances to harbors to indicate the depth of water, the stage of the tide, and the velocity of the current. These are seen much more frequently in Britain and France than in the United States.

**Tide Tables**   *n.* Tabular presentations of time and height of tides at various locations published by the National Ocean Service. These cover most areas of the world except the United States, which is covered in the *Tidal Current Tables.*

**tidewater**   *n.* Freshwater affected by tides. See TIDAL WATERS.

**tideway**   *n.* (1) A waterway with a tidal current. (2) That part of a waterway in which the tide ebbs and flows.

**tie**   *n.* (1) Part of a purchase used for hoisting yards on square-rigged ships; it is the rope that is attached to the middle of an upper topsail. (2) A band or bungee cord used to furl sails.

**tie beam**   *n.* Heavy bar secured in place over hatch covers for security after waterproof tarpaulins have been placed over the hatches.

**tie block**   *n.* (1) A single steel block on a topsail or topgallant yard through which the tie of the halyard is rove. (2) The gin block through which a halyard runner is rove.

**tie-downs**   *n.* Deck fittings used to secure aircraft on deck. See PAD EYE; RINGBOLT.

**tie off**   *v.* To secure, as in "to tie off to a buoy." See TIE UP.

**tie plates**   *n.* Long narrow plates used to secure deck beams where there is no steel plating.

**tier**   *n.* (1) A single loop of anchor cable or chain in a chain locker. (2) A layer of casks.

**tier**   *v.* To stow an anchor chain in layers in the chain locker.

**tie up**   *v.* To secure, one "ties up to a buoy."

**tight**   *adj.* (1) Describes a wooden vessel that is well maintained and does not leak; staunch. (2) A **tight ship** is one that is strict about matters of decorum and efficiency. See TAUT.

**tiller**   *n.* (1) In both ships and small boats, the wood or steel rod connected directly to the rudderhead or rudder post and usually led forward. The quadrant is the tiller when a wheel is used. See MARCONI RIG. (2) An electric lever control of the follow-up type, used in place of wheel steering on large modern ships.

**tiller head** *n.* The end of a tiller to which the chains and ropes are attached, which make it possible to control the rudder from a remote position such as the bridge. The end opposite the tiller head fits into the rudder.

**tiller lines** *n.* Lines connected to a tiller used to control the rudder from a remote position. The friction of the line on the fairleads helps hold the tiller.

**tiller ropes** *n.* Rope or wires led from the tiller to the steering wheel axle.

**tiller telltale** *n.* A device that moves with the tiller to keep the helmsman and officer of the watch informed as to the position of the helm.

**timber head** *n.* Timbers that come through the deck for the purpose of providing bitts on deck.

**timbers** *n.* Large pieces of wood used in ship construction, especially the frames.

**time (of day)** *n.* The interval since the day began, measured by the mariner in mean solar time beginning at 0000 and ending at 2359:59.

**time charter** *n.* A charter party that places a vessel in the possession of a charterer for a specific time.

**time courses** *n.* A method of navigation using a series of courses for a given number of minutes before changing to the next.

**time difference (TD)** *n.* A Loran C term for the difference between the reception of two radio signals from which a position is computed.

**time freight** *n.* Periodic payment for a charter rather than a lump payment.

**time meridian** *n.* Any meridian used as the reference for reckoning time, especially a zone or standard meridian.

**timenoguy** *n.* (pron. timmino-guy): A line or guy from the foreshrouds to the anchor stock that prevents the foresheet from becoming tangled in the ground tackle.

**time notation** *n.* The method used by navigators to note the time of day so that the next watch will have no question about what is meant. This is done by counting out 24 hours in a day instead of 12 hours twice (A.M. and P.M.); the 24-hour period begins at midnight, 2400 hours, which is followed by 0001 as 1 minute after midnight. For example, 8:35 A.M. is expressed as 0835, and 8:35 P.M. as 2035. When the navigator writes down a time, he usually writes in six figures the hours minutes and seconds, separated by dashes. Thus, the previous examples would be written as 08–35–00 and 20–35–00. When a day of the month is needed, it is expressed ahead of the hour, as 04–08–35–00 which means 8:35 A.M. on the fourth day of the month.

**time penalty clause** *n.* A clause in marine insurance that relieves the insurer of liability arising from claims as a result of peril of the sea or other claims.

**time scale** *n.* Any one of the three fundamental systems of dating events. They are (a) **ephemeris time,** based on the rotation of the Earth and atomic time, or time obtained by counting the cycles of a signal in resonance with certain kinds of atoms; (b) **universal time** (UT), determined by the average rate of the apparent daily motion of the Sun related to the prime meridian at Greenwich; for practical purposes, UT is computed from sidereal time; (c) **universal coordinated time** (UTC) is UT adjusted to compensate for the small, unpredictable changes in the Earth's rotational speed.

**time sight** *n.* Originally, this was an observation of the altitude of a celestial body, made to determine longitude. The expression more frequently refers to the common method of reducing such observations.

**time zones** *n.* The 24 geographical divisions of the world into roughly 15°-wide zones starting at Greenwich, England, and proceeding westward (+) 12 zones and eastward (−) 12 zones.

**tin can** *n.* Slang term in the U.S. Navy for a destroyer; destroyers have comparatively thin, highly armored hulls.

**tinclad** *n.* Name given to assorted sternwheel riverboats converted to lightly armoured gunboats by the Union Army for operations on the Western Rivers during the Civil War.

**tin fish** *n.* Slang for a torpedo.

**tingle** *n.* Thin metal sheeting used to make temporary hull repairs.

**tip clearance** *n.* The least clearance between propeller and hull.

**tjalk** *n.* (pron. tyolk) A Dutch sailing vessel, of about 60 tons and usually single-masted, used for sea and river navigation.

**toad's back** *n.* Octagonal metal fitting used to step a trysail mast. See MAST STEP.

**toe rail** *n.* A low railing, perhaps no more than an inch high, along the deck edge of a small boat.

**toggle** *n.* Wood (typically *lignum vitae*) or metal pin with small line spliced around a scored midsection, used to secure the eye or becket of a rope that might have to be released quickly. Used on bunt whips, life buoys, and signal flags.

**tom (down)** *v.* (1) The opposite of shore up, to steady cargo or a bulkhead

by placing timbers above to oppose shoring. (2) To lay barrels in line to be held in place; barrels so stowed are said to be "tommed down."

**ton** See TONNAGE.

**ton burden** *n.* The difference in tons deadweight between a ship's light load line and the load line, expressed either in weight (2,240 pounds per ton) or volume (35 cubic feet per ton).

**tong boat** *n.* Open boat used in harvesting oysters and clams, used extensively on Chesapeake Bay and San Francisco Bay. Oysters and clams are gathered with long-handled tongs.

**tongue** *n.* (1) Small wooden block placed between the jaws of a gaff to facilitate sliding up and down the mast. (2) A submerged mass of ice projecting from a floe or iceberg. See FJORD.

**ton-mile** *n.* A measure of sea trade equivalent to one ton of cargo carried one nautical mile.

**tonnage** *n.* (1) A term with a variety of specific meanings pertaining to the measurement of a vessel's carrying capacity or its actual weight. As a unit of volume, 1 ton is generally taken to be the equivalent of 100 cubic feet; as a unit of weight, the long ton (or **freight ton**) of 2,240 pounds is meant. See DEADWEIGHT CAPACITY; DISPLACEMENT TONNAGE; REGISTERED TONNAGE. (2) In measuring racing boats, the product of one of several elaborate formulas having little or nothing to do with either weight or capacity.

**tonnage certificate** *n.* Document issued by a government or other recognized authority detailing a vessel's dimensions, name, and registry. In the United States, certificates of tonnage are issued by the Department of Commerce. Generally taxes and fees against vessels are levied on a basis of net registered tons. The gross tonnage and net tonnage shown on a vessel's certificate of documentation are recognized internationally except by the Suez Canal and the Panama Canal. Tolls for transiting the Panama and Suez canals are based on tonnage, but the respective authorities employ their own systems of measurement, which differ both from one other and from international tonnages.

**tonnage deck**   *n.* The deck from which tonnage measurements are taken. On vessels with more than one deck, the tonnage deck is the second deck from the keel; otherwise it is the upper deck.

**tonnage depth**   *n.* For tonnage measurement, the depth of the hold. In vessels with transverse framing, it is taken from the top of the tank top or hold ceiling at centerline to the lower side of the tonnage deck.

**tonnage length**   *n.* The length of a vessel measured along the centerline of the upper surface of the tonnage deck the extremities of which are where the inside lines of the framing ceiling or cargo battens meet.

**tonnage opening**   *n.* A nonwatertight opening above the freeboard deck that makes it possible to exempt shelter deck space from gross tonnage measurement.

**tonnage tax**   *n.* A U.S. tax on commercial vessels for entering, leaving, trading, and waiting in port. Also *tonnage dues.* See TONNAGE CERTIFICATE.

**tons per inch of immersion**   *n.* The weight in long tons required to increase a vessel's draft by one inch. The tons per inch at a given draft can be approximately determined by dividing the square footage of the water plane at that draft by 420.

**top**   *n.* A platform that rests on the trestletrees at the head of the lower masts of square-rigged ships. It spreads the topmast shrouds. The tops are named after the masts on which they belong,

such as mizzentop, maintop, and so on. Larger tops in warships are called **fighting tops,** and during close engagements marines stationed in the fighting tops were responsible for picking off individuals, usually officers, on the deck of the enemy ship. See CROW'S NEST; LUBBER'S HOLE.

**top**   *v.* (1) To lift, as a boom; "to top a boom" is to lift its after end into place. (2) To top a yard is to brace it a-cockbill.

**top around**   *v.* Western rivers usage meaning to turn 180°.

**top block**   *n.* A single block used for handling a topmast.

**top burton**   *n.* A long tackle used for raising and lowering yards, sails, and other rigging. It is made up with a double block and a single block. The double block has a hook; the single block, a long strap, hook, and thimble. The upper block is hooked on a pendant from the topmast head. The fall must be long enough to allow the lower block and hauling part to reach the deck.

**topgallant**   *n.* (pron. tuhgahlent) A square sail, or its associated mast and rigging, located above the topsail. It is often written **t'gallant.** Also pronounced **to'gar'ns** by British sailors. See SQUARE-RIGGED VESSEL.

**topgallant forecastle**   *n.* An elevated deck in the bow of a ship.

**top gun**   *n.* An advanced U.S. Naval aviation school for carrier-based strike and fighter pilots.

**top hamper**   *n.* Superstructure and spars, antennae, and rigging above the deck. Originally a sailing ship term, it is also used on modern naval and merchant vessels.

**top keel**   *n.* The uppermost beam of the keel in a ship where, to obtain the necessary molded size, the keel is made up of two timbers.

**top lining**   *n.* The reinforced backing for the after surface of the head of a square sail to reduce chafing.

**topmarks**   *n.* Cones, spheres, and other shapes that help facilitate the identification of buoys in both the uniform lateral system and the uniform cardinal system.

**topmast**   *n.* A mast between the topgallant mast and the lower mast. See SQUARE-RIGGED VESSEL.

**topmast rigging**   *n.* The shrouds and stays that support the topmast.

**topmast shrouds**   *n.* Lines running from crosstrees to the deck on fore-and-aft-rigged vessels.

**topman**   *n.* A sailor who works aloft on sailing ships.

**top off**   *v.* (1) To stow cargo, usually bagged, on top of other cargo, for the purpose of filling empty spaces and to help hold cargo in place. (2) To fill partially full water tanks, fuel tanks, and other vessels. "Be sure we top off the bunker C before we leave port." Also *top out.*

**topping lift**   *n.* (1) A part of the running rigging used to raise and support a boom. (2) A part of the standing rigging that supports a boom, but is not necessarily used to adjust its position. See GAFF.

**topping lift bull rope**   *n.* A wire rope for topping a cargo boom using a yoke at the boom; the hauling part is taken to a deck winch.

**top rail**   *n.* A rail on the platform at the top of a mast.

**top-rope**   *n.* A rope used to sway a topmast or topgallant mast into place; because of the weight of masts, a **top**

**tackle** hooked to the lower end of the mast is used with the top-rope.

**topsail**   *n.* (pron. topsle): In square-rigged vessels, a square sail set above the course. To increase ease of handling, topsails are frequently divided to make a **double topsail,** or an **upper topsail** and **lower topsail.** (2) A triangular or quadrilateral sail set above the gaff on a fore-and-aft-rigged ship. See SQUARE-RIGGED VESSEL.

**topsail schooner**   *n.* Fore-and-aft-rigged sailing vessel with one or more square topsails set on the foremast. Schooners with gaff topsails are rarely referred to as topsail schooners, schooners without gaff topsails being known often as **bald-headed schooners.** For absolute clarity, topsail schooners can be called **square topsail schooners.** See RIG.

**topsail tye**   *n.* A wire rope led from a yard up through a sheave under the trestletrees and down abaft the mast where a gin-block is spliced in the end.

**topside**   *adv.* Above-deck spaces and area. "Now hear this, all hands not on duty, lay topside for liberty inspection." See TOPSIDES.

**topsides**   *n.* A vessel's sides from the water line to the rail. "When we have finished topping off the fuel tanks, have the bunker C rinsed off the topsides as soon as possible." See TOPSIDE.

**topside tanks**   *n.* Ballast tanks placed at a ship's sides beneath the weather deck and aft to (a) minimize the propeller's racing, and (b) to reduce excessive initial stability when light, or to reduce metacentric height. Also *gunwale tank.* See STABILITY.

**top timbers**   *n.* The uppermost part of a vessel's frames.

**torpedo**   *n.* (1) Elongated, self-propelled, waterborne projectile designed to detonate near or on contact with its target. Also *fish; tin fish.* (2) An older term for a mine. When Adm. David Glasgow Farragut said, "Damn the torpedoes. Full speed ahead," at the Battle of Mobile Bay, he was referring to mines, not self-propelled projectiles.

**torpedoman's mate (TM)**  *n.* A petty officer in the U.S. Navy who maintains torpedoes, mines, and antisubmarine warfare ordnance.

**torpedo range**  *n.* The distance a torpedo is capable of running with the available fuel.

**torpedo retriever**  *n.* A high-speed boat used to recover practice torpedoes.

**torpedo run**  *n.* The distance a torpedo travels to its target.

**torpedo tube**  *n.* Launching cavity in the hulls of some naval vessels, especially submarines, from which torpedoes are fired.

**torpedo tube shutters**  *n.* Movable ports at the outboard ends of torpedo tubes that preserve the form of the hull.

**torsiometer**  *n.* A device that measures the twisting moment of a propeller shaft from which the power developed by the turbines is calculated.

**toss oars**  *phr.* To raise oars straight up in the air with the handles resting in the bottom of a boat, done as a salute or to prepare to take the boat aboard ship.

**tot**  *n.* A drinking cup with less capacity than a half pint, formerly used for the spirit ration aboard naval ships.

**total current**  *n.* A combination of tidal and nontidal currents; called flow in Britain.

**total loss**  *n.* An insurance underwriter's term that describes a vessel that is an actual total loss destroyed by fire or

perils of the sea or damaged so extensively that it cannot be put back into service for the purpose the insured party had contracted for. Underwriters frequently limit their liability to total loss only to exempt themselves from a partial loss.

**touch and go**  *phr.* (1) To scrape over a shoal without actually stopping. (2) In aircraft, to touch down and take off without stopping, a more common procedure on aircraft carriers than on land.

**tow**  *n.* One or more vessels, usually barges, being towed or pushed. "Our tow included three fuel barges and two garbage barges."

**tow**  *v.* (1) To pull one or more vessels through the water; to take a vessel in tow. (2) On the western rivers, tow can have the same meaning as push. See TOWBOAT.

**towage**  *n.* Port fees levied against a vessel using towing vessels.

**towage service**  *n.* The use of tugboats to facilitate harbor movements of another vessel when no peril is involved.

**towboat**  *n.* A flat-bowed vessel used exclusively for "towing by pushing ahead." These are used on western rivers to push tows of rafted barges—as many as 50 or more—at one time.

**tower**  *n.* A notation on a marine chart that indicates a structure that has its base on the ground and is high in proportion to the base.

**tower crane**  *n.* A tower mounting a derrick, usually with a house at the top for machinery and operator.

**towing and salvage clause**  *n.* A charter party term under which a chartered vessel may tow or be towed or to otherwise deviate from the terms of the charter for the purpose of assisting vessels in distress or saving life and property.

**towing bitts** *n.* Afterdeck bitts on tugboats to which the towline or hawser is led from the dutch bar, towing chock, gob rope, or norman pins.

**towing bows** *n.* (bows rhymes with toes) Girders across the caprail on the stern of a tug that keep the towline above the deck equipment and crew. Also *dutch bar.*

**towing bridle** *n.* (1) A span of cable or chain from the bow of a towed vessel permitting the towing strain to be taken from two separate strong points on the towboat to reduce yawing. (2) A length of cable with ends secured across the transom of a vessel with the towing strain placed amidships, used for towing another vessel astern.

**towing hawser** *n.* A rope used for pulling, made of three-strand nylon when maximum strength and elasticity are desired, otherwise made of double-braid nylon or plaited nylon.

**towing light** *n.* A yellow light having the same characteristics as a sternlight, that is, being placed as nearly as practicable at the stern and showing an unbroken light over an arc of the horizon of 135° and so fixed as to show the light 67.5° from right aft on each side of the vessel.

**towing line** *n.* An old term for cordage made from **best boltrope** (Manila), 5 inches or more, that runs 200 fathoms to the coil. The wire used for pulling a vessel is called a hawser. See TOWING HAWSER; TOWING WIRE.

**towing machine** *n.* A towing winch that keeps a safe tension on a towing hawser. The machine slacks the wire when a preset level of tension is reached and retrieves the same amount of wire that was let out when the tension is reduced.

**towing spar** *n.* A wooden buoy towed behind a ship when visibility is poor, to assist a following ship in keeping station.

**towing winch** *n.* A winch at the stern of a tugboat onto which the tow wire or hawser is reeled. See TOWING MACHINE.

**towing wire** *n.* Wire with wire core, generally made from extra improved plow steel used for towing. Also *tow wire.*

**tow rail** *n.* Steel beam at the stern of a tugboat on which the tow wire rides and that prevents the line from damaging deck gear. See TOE RAIL; TOWING BOWS.

**tracer** *n.* (1) A colored yarn in rope to identify it. (2) A marker on electrical wire that identifies certain strands. (3) A projectile trailing smoke or showing a light to assist in aiming a gun, usually with machine-gun ammunition.

**track (TR)** *n.* (1) The intended (anticipated, desired) horizontal direction of travel with respect to the Earth; a vessel's track in degrees of the compass may be different from the actual course due to such factors as current, seas, or steering. See DRIFT. (2) The path of intended travel with respect to the Earth as drawn on a chart. This is also called the **intended track** or **track-line.** (3) The actual path of a vessel over the ground such as may be determined by tracking. (4) A metal guide on a mast along which the sail slides when being raised or lowered. Also *sail track.*

**track** *v.* (1) To mark the course of another vessel on a radarscope or maneuvering board. (2) To follow a target as a patrol craft or submarine tracks an enemy convoy by observing its course and speed. (3) To tow a vessel, usually through a lock or along a canal, by means of land lines pulled by small railroad locomotives or mules. (4) A term for a vessel's ability to maintain a course with minimum rudder. A vessel is said to track well if the rudder can be left untended for a few minutes and continue in a straight line. Also *course stability; yaw stability.*

**track angle** *n.* The angle between a target's course and the reciprocal of a torpedo's course to intercept the target, measured clockwise through 360°.

**tracker** *n.* A member of a ship's company or a staff who keeps tabs on the location, capability, and availability of logistic support vessels.

**track made good** *n.* The single resultant direction from a point of departure to a point of arrival at any given time. See COURSE MADE GOOD.

**trader** *n.* A vessel that barters one cargo for another when moving from port to port. All but obsolete today.

**trade winds** *n.* A consistent pattern of air currents that move northeast in the tropics of the Northern Hemisphere and southeast in the tropics of the Southern Hemisphere. The term did not originate as meaning winds facilitating commerce as has been suggested, but derives from the archaic use of trade meaning a track or course because they blow regularly in a given direction. The trades of the Northern Hemisphere are call the **northeast trades** and those of the Southern Hemisphere are called the **southeast trades.**

**trading voyage** *n.* A term used in marine insurance that allows a vessel to off-load merchandise for trade and to reload it if not sold.

**trading warranties** *n.* Charter party clause that specifies the geographical boundaries within which a vessel must stay for the duration of the charter.

**traffic separation scheme (TSS)** *n.* Shipping corridors or **traffic lanes** marked by buoys that separate incoming traffic from outgoing vessels. Straits with exceptionally heavy traffic, such as the English Channel and the Strait of Gibraltar, are made a little less hair-raising by such schemes.

**traffic signals** *n.* Port and river signals that indicate upstream and downstream traffic, bridge information, locking information, and docking instructions.

**trail boards** *n.* Boards with an ornamental scroll bolted on either side of the stem from abaft the hawsehole to the figurehead. Also *headboard.* See BILLET-HEAD; FIDDLEHEAD.

**trailerable** *adj.* Said of the boat small enough and light enough to be towed on a light trailer behind a car or truck and unloaded at a ramp or hoist.

**trail oars** *phr.* To allow oars to swing in their locks without being held by a crew member.

**train** *v.* To control a gun, a searchlight or radar antenna horizontally: "Train right 45 degrees." See ELEVATE; LAY; POINT.

**train ferry** *n.* A ferry fitted with rails to take railroad cars, both freight and passenger, from one port to another, such as are used in service between England and Continental ports. See SHIP.

**training wall** *n.* A wall or jetty often submerged, built to direct the flow of a river or tidal current.

**train tackle** *n.* A combination of single- and double-hooked blocks with the latter being fastened to a ringbolt in the deck and the single-hook block being fastened in the train of a gun carriage (the reinforced channel along which it travels) to prevent the gun from running out through the port while being loaded.

**tramontana** *n.* (1) A chilly northerly day wind on the Adriatic. (2) Any cold wind coming down from a mountain. Also *tramontane.* See BORA.

**tramp**   *n.* Cargo vessel that does not have an established schedule but delivers and picks up freight as the opportunity arises. A tramp usually takes full cargoes of such items as grain, ore, or lumber. The word is also used as a verb.

**TRANSAT**   *n.* The U.S. Navy Navigational Satellite System for obtaining position fixes that became operational in 1964 and available for civilian use in 1967. This is a system of five or six satellites (often known as **birds**) in polar orbit that transmit on two frequencies, 150 MHz (military) and 400 MHz (civilian). The global positioning system (GPS or Navstar) will eventually replace TRANSAT, which is generally called SATNAV.

**transceiver**   *n.* A combination of transmitter and receiver in a single housing with some components used by both parts and that does not provide for simultaneous transmission and reception.

**transducer**   *n.* (pron. transdooser) A device that converts one type of energy to another, such as a loudspeaker that changes electrical energy into acoustical energy or a device that converts pressure from water movement to electrical energy to activate a speed indicator.

**transfer**   *n.* The distance a vessel moves perpendicular to its initial course in making a 90° or smaller turn using a constant rudder angle.

**transire**   *n.* (rhymes with transpire) A warrant furnished by the customhouse permitting the passage of merchandise for a vessel voyaging coastwise in lieu of the usual forms.

**transit**   *n.* The meridian passage of a heavenly body across an observer's meridian. The **lower transit** is the meridian passage of a celestial body below the pole; the **upper transit** is the meridian passage of a celestial body above the pole. Except for stars that are permanently above an observer's horizon, only

the upper transit can be observed. Also *culmination.*

**transit, meridian**   *n.* The passage of a celestial body across the observer's celestial meridian. When the passage is across the meridian above the observer (where it can be seen), it is known as the **superior** or **upper transit.** If the passage is across the meridian beneath the observer (on the other side of the Earth), it is the **inferior** or **lower transit.** The observer can only use a celestial body during superior or upper transit.

**transit cargo**   *n.* Merchandise not to be off-loaded at an intermediate port, but to continue on to its own destination. See TRANSIT SHED.

**transition buoy**   *n.* A buoy indicating the transition between the lateral system of marks, with buoys indicating the sides of the channel, and the cardinal system, with buoys indicating obstructions.

**transit passage, right of**   See RIGHT OF TRANSIT PASSAGE.

**transit port**   *n.* Port where cargo is off-loaded to continue to further destination via another carrier, usually another mode of transportation, as from a deepwater ship to a barge or a train.

**transit shed**   *n.* A quayside warehouse used for transit cargo.

**transmitting magnetic compass**   *n.* An electrically relayed compass reading that makes it possible to read the magnetic compass at remote stations. The gyro has largely replaced this once-valuable aid.

**transom**   *n.* (1) The main frame at the rudder stock; the aftermost transverse frame. (2) The stern above the counter. (3) A stationary couch in a stateroom or wardroom. In the days of square-rigged ships, the captain's cabin, as a rule, was at the stern with a long couch built into the transom. Thus, the couch became known as a "transom."

**transom stern**  *n.* A flat, vertical (or nearly so) stern, most often seen in small rowboats.

**transponder**  *n.* A component of a radar recognition system that accepts the interrogating radar signal and responds with a signal that identifies the transponding station.

**transport**  *n.* A vessel owned or chartered by a government to carry military troops and supplies.

**transship**  *v.* To transfer cargo from one carrier to another.

**transshipment**  *n.* The substitution of one vessel for another in shipping cargo. Unless specifically allowed in a shipping contract, transshipment is considered a serious breach of contract. Unless transshipment is covered in the marine insurance policy, the underwriters are discharged of their exposure when it occurs.

**transverse**  *adj.* At right angles to the keel; athwartship.

**transverse construction**  *n.* Longitudinal system of ship construction. The frames are notched to allow continuous longitudinals to pass through them.

**transverse framing**  *n.* The structural parts of a ship that contribute to the athwartships strength.

**transverse Mercator projection**  *n.* A Mercator projection using a cylinder tangent along a meridian instead of the equator; it is the most common of mariners' charts.

**transverse metacenter (M)**  *n.* The intersection of the vertical through the center of buoyancy when a vessel is in an upright position; with the vessel in-

clined, the vertical is through a different center of buoyancy. See STABILITY.

**transverse waves**  *n.* The waves caused by a vessel going through the water; one set of waves is created transverse to the bow, and a second set is created transverse to the stern. Their length relates to the speed of the vessel.

**traveler**  *n.* (1) A metal ring for the sheet blocks of staysails and fore-and-aft sails that slide athwartships along a metal rod. (2) A track bolted to the deck along which a car or slide that holds the sheet can ride when a boom is shifted.

**traveling martingale**  *n.* A martingale that is bent on only when a jib is set.

**traverse**  *v.* (1) To brace a yard fore and aft. (2) To move in an athwartship direction. "The mainsheet traverses the traveler."

**traverse**  *adj.* Used to describe a boom or spar that lies athwartship, as a traverse spar or a traverse boom. **Traverse horses,** or jackstays, are ropes or rods for sails to traverse on.

**traverse board**  *n.* A wooden board used to record courses and speeds during a watch. It had a circle with all eight points of the compass marked with holes for pegs. The course for each half hour (or **glass**) was noted by placing a peg in the appropriate hole.

**traverse frames**  *n.* Athwartships members that comprise a vessel's ribs.

**traverse sailing**  *n.* A combination of plane sailing solutions when two or more courses are sailed. This method is used to determine the equivalent course and distance made good by a vessel sailing a series of rhumb lines.

**trawl**  *n.* A large conical net made to prevent the escape of fish under the net as it is dragged through the water or over the seafloor.

**trawl**  *v.* To use a trawl to catch fish. The *Navigation Rules* define trawling as "the dragging through the water of a dredge net or other apparatus used as a fishing appliance."

**trawler**  *n.* A boat used for trawling for fish.

**treble-fold block**  *n.* A block with three sheaves. Also *treble block.*

**treble purchase**  *n.* A tackle with two treble blocks. It is so rove that the standing and hauling parts come out of the center sheave in each block; the standing part is made fast to a becket in the tail of the block through which the hauling part is led.

**treenails**  *n.* Wooden pegs used to fasten a ship's planks to its timbers. A **treenail wedge** is used at either end of the treenail to give it more holding power. Also *trunnels.*

**trend**  *n.* (1) The junction of the shank and arm of an anchor. Also *throat.* (2) The angle made by the anchor cable with the vessel's centerline. See TEND. (3) The general direction of a coast or chain of islands.

**trend**  *v.* To angle away from the ship, said of an anchor cable. "How does the cable trend?" Also *tend.*

**trestletrees**  *n.* Two strong pieces of timber, such as oak, bolted to the sides of the lower mastheads to support a crosstree's top and the weight of the topmast.

**tret**  *n.* An allowance made by underwriters for depreciation of a vessel during a voyage. The origin of the word is obscure.

**trial trip**  *n.* Successive runs in opposite directions over a measured mile to determine the effectiveness and capabilities of a ship's propelling equipment under full power. See SHAKEDOWN.

**triatic stay**  *n.* A horizontal stay running from one mast cap to another, or from a mast to a stack, used for support and for signaling. Also *signal stay; spring stay.* See SCIATIC STAY.

**tributary**  *n.* A stream that flows into another stream, river, or lake.

**trice**  *v.* To haul up by means of ropes. "Trice the gaff ready to sail." Bedding was also triced up, and the term is used today in that sense on naval vessels.

**tricing line**  *n.* A rope used to raise an object to a position out of the way of the routine at hand.

**tricing stay**  *n.* A rope to which a fore-and-aft sail is hanked to be hauled up and down by the halyard.

**trick**  *n.* A period of duty for the helmsman at the wheel; the expression is heard more on pleasure boats than on commercial or naval vessels.

**trick wheel**  *n.* An emergency wheel located in the engine spaces in the after steering compartment.

**tricolored lantern**  *n.* A light carried on sailing vessels of less than 20 meters that combines in one lantern the port and starboard sidelights and the white sternlight.

**Trident**  *n.* A general descriptive term for the sea-based strategic weapon system consisting of the Trident submarine and the long-range Trident ballistic missile.

**trigger bar**  *n.* Device for releasing an anchor from the deck to allow it to go overboard.

**trim**  *n.* Fore-and-aft attitude of a vessel with regard to the designed waterline.

Mariners speak of a ship being **out of trim** or, more specifically, **trimmed by the stern** (with the stern a little lower than the head) or **trimmed by the head.** Most vessels sail better if they are a little by the stern. If a vessel is transversely unbalanced, it is said to be listing or to have a port or starboard list.

**trim** *v.* (1) To adjust sails so they draw at their designed optimum. "We need to trim the spinnaker before it begins to spill its air." (2) To arrange ballast, fuel, water, or other stores to achieve proper balance fore and aft. (3) To shovel or otherwise move bulk cargo such as coal or grain to assist in unloading by means of buckets or conveyors. "Have your **trimmers** ready to trim the grain to the middle of the hold where the conveyor can pick it up." (4) To adjust water in **trim tanks** or **variable ballast tanks** to achieve neutral buoyancy in a submarine.

**trim and stability booklet** *n.* The primary system for keeping track of a vessel's stability, trim, and longitudinal hull strength, required to be aboard all cargo vessels. It is endorsed by the U.S. Coast Guard by a **stability letter,** which must be kept under glass in the pilothouse. The booklet contains a table of principal characteristics, a trim table, the table of hydrostatic values, a table of free surface constants, a table showing gain in metacentric height (GM) by ballasting, the required GM curve, a loading table, a calculation of GM and drafts, and double-bottom tankage requirements in tons. See STABILITY.

**trim by the head** (or **stern**) *phr.* To become lower by the bow (or stern). A ship is said to trim by the head (or stern) when the draft forward (aft) is greater than the draft aft (forward). Also *trimmed by the head (stern).*

**trimaran** *n.* A boat with three hulls.

**trim dive** *n.* A dive made by a submarine to check and correct compensation of variable weights so as to maintain neutral buoyancy and stability when submerged.

**trimmer** *n.* (1) A member of the boiler room crew on a coal-fired ship who transfers coal from bunkers to firing platform. (2) One who helps trim the cargo when off-loading a ship.

**trimming system** *n.* The system of pipes, pumps, and valves that enable a submarine to compensate for expending variable weights so that it can maintain neutral buoyancy and stability while submerged.

**trimming tanks** *n.* Tanks at the bow and stern used to adjust a vessel's trim.

**trim tabs** *n.* (1) Adjustable steel projections from the stern of a powerboat that adjust the boat's trim. (2) Adjustable tabs on the trailing edge of keels on racing sailboats that allow the boats to point higher. (3) Adjustable tabs on aircraft.

**trim tanks** *n.* Variable ballast tanks placed forward and aft in a submarine. Auxiliary tanks, also part of the trimming system, are placed amidships.

**Trinity House** *n.* A British corporation, chartered by Henry VIII in 1514, and formally known as Trinity House Lighthouse Service. Trinity House was concerned at first with lights, buoys, and piloting; today they maintain all navigation aids in British waters. The board of directors, known as **Trinity Masters** (and the Elder Brethren), act as expert witnesses and assessors in Admiralty Courts. Two of the members are elected from the Navy and 11 from the Merchant Service.

**trinket** *n.* The top or topgallant of any mast in a square-rigged vessel.

**trip** *n.* A one-way passage between two ports, as distinct from a **round trip.** See PASSAGE; VOYAGE.

**trip** v. (1) To release or to loosen an anchor from the seabed by using a line previously attached to the crown or a fluke. Older usage included simply pulling an anchor loose from the bottom without a tripping line. (2) To release a hook; when the **keeper** of a pelican hook is released, it is said to be tripped. (3) To swing a spar or yard into position for lowering.

**trip charter** n. A charter party that covers only one trip with the owner operating the vessel.

**triple-expansion engine** n. A reciprocating steam engine in which the expansion takes place in two stages, one being in the high-pressure cylinder, one in the intermediate-pressure cylinder, and the third in one of two low-pressure cylinders.

**tripping line** n. (1) Line used to cause a sea anchor to capsize. (2) A line fastened to an anchor to help loosen the anchor from rocks.

**trip stopper** n. A short length of chain secured by eyebolts on a vessel's side to be used for positioning a stocked anchor to let go.

**troll** v. To fish by towing lines astern a vessel. Trolling vessels are specifically excluded from the *Navigation Rules* definition of "vessels engaged in fishing," however, because they are not considered to be restricted in maneuverability.

**tropic** n. Either of the two parallels of declination of the Sun approximately 23°27′ north or south of the celestial equator. The northern of these is the Tropic of Cancer, the southern is the Tropic of Capricorn.

**tropical cyclone** n. A cyclonic system originating in the tropics or subtropics with sustained winds in excess of 32 meters per second (72 mph).

**tropical depression** n. A meteorological depression with one or more isobars and some rotary circulation at the surface, with surface winds not more than 33 knots.

**tropical disturbance** n. A cyclonic weather system lasting at least 24 hours, without sufficient force to be called a storm, generally 100 to 300 miles in diameter with a nonfrontal migratory character.

**tropical load line** n. The upper edge of a line marked T on load line marks. The tropical freshwater load line is marked TF. The tropical load line delineates the freeboard required in the tropical zone. See PLIMSOLL MARK OR LINE.

**tropical storm** n. A weather system characterized by closed isobars with a distinct rotary system at the surface and sustained winds of 34 to 63 knots.

**tropical revolving storm (TRS)** n. Maritime name for a tropical cyclone, hurricane, or typhoon.

**Tropic of Cancer** n. The northern parallel of declination, approximately 23°27′N from the celestial equator, reached by the Sun at its maximum northerly declination at the summer solstice.

**Tropic of Capricorn** n. The southern parallel of declination, approximately 23°27′S from the celestial equator, reached by the Sun at its maximum southerly declination at the winter solstice.

**tropic current** n. Tidal currents that occur semimonthly at times of tropic tides when the effect of the Moon's maximum declination is greatest. At these times, the tendency of the Moon to produce a diurnal inequality in the current is at a maximum.

**tropic higher high water** n. The higher high water of a tropic tide.

**tropic lower low water**  *n.* The lower low water of a tropic tide.

**tropic speed**  *n.* The speed of the greater flood or the greater ebb at the time of tropic currents.

**tropic tides**  *n.* Tides (and currents) that occur when the Moon is at its maximum semimonthly declination (north or south) when the diurnal effect is at a maximum. See TROPIC CURRENT.

**trot**  *n.* A line of mooring buoys and moorings.

**trot line**  *n.* A long line anchored at both ends rigged with fishhooks or snoods every few feet, used for fishing.

**trough**  *n.* The low period in a wave formation whether it be water, radio, heat, pressure, or some other type, as opposed to the crest of a wave. The **trough of the sea** is the hollow between the crests of two waves or seas. To ride **in the trough** is to ride with the sea on the beam.

**truck**  *n.* (1) The top of the highest mast or of a flagstaff. The truck is distinguished by its mast, as **foretruck** or **maintruck.** Lower masts have caps. (2) See SPUR SHORE.

**true altitude**  *n.* The altitude of a star or planet above the apparent horizon corrected for refraction, semidiameter, and/or parallax.

**true azimuth**  *n.* The true bearing of a celestial body as observed by compass and corrected for instrument error.

**true bearing**  *n.* Bearing of an object from a vessel using the ship's compass as the basis of the bearing rather than the ship's heading. An object on the starboard bow of a ship with a heading of 180° might have a true bearing of 200° but a relative bearing of 020°. See DIRECTION.

**true course**  *n.* The course based on the true or geographic north rather than the magnetic compass course. On a course line, it is marked either 063° True or 063° PGC (per gyro compass).

**true direction**  *n.* The direction from one point to another on the Earth's surface relative to true (geographic) north pole rather than magnetic north and is expressed in three numbers: 8° is expressed as "zero zero eight" and written as 008. The outer ring of the compass rose represents true compass points, while the inner ring, if present, represents the magnetic compass points.

**true north**  *n.* The geographic north as opposed to the magnetic north. See DIRECTION.

**true position**  *n.* The position of a vessel established from bearings or objects of known positions. See FIX.

**true slip**  *n.* The difference between the velocity of water approaching a propeller and that which is projected from the propeller, relative to the speed of the vessel.

**true time**  *n.* The time lapse between two consecutive crossings of a given meridian by the Sun.

**true wind**  *n.* The direction of the wind as observed from a stationary position, as opposed to the relative wind or apparent wind of a moving object, usually a ship or airplane. A ship sailing due north at 15 knots against a south wind of 5 knots true, experiences a relative wind of 20 knots, but the true wind is still 5 knots. See APPARENT WIND.

**trundle head**  *n.* The part of a capstan in which the capstan bars are fitted.

**trunk**  *n.* (1) Enclosed well in sailboats for dagger boards and centerboards. (2) A casing through a deck for ladders or for ventilation. (3) A vertical shaft through a deck.

**trunk, expansion** *n.* A small tank situated above a much larger tank and into which liquid can flow from the lower tank if its contents expand.

**trunk bulkhead** *n.* A partition or enclosure that runs from deck to deck and surrounds a hatch opening.

**trunk cabin** *n.* A cabin with part above a deck and part below. Trunk cabins are popular on small boats and motor yachts.

**trunnel** See TREENAILS.

**trunnion** *n.* A pin or gudgeon on which a gun pivots as it is elevated. Trunnions on the cannons of sailing ships were part of the gun; today, the trunnion is a part of the mount.

**trunnion hoop** *n.* A hinged device fitted on a mast cap to receive the next mast.

**truss** *n.* (1) A rope used to control lower yards to hold them closer or to slacken them from their masts. (2) A metal forging designed to support a lower yard; it is hinged in such a manner as to allow it to move vertically and horizontally. See TRUSS YOKE.

**truss tackle** *n.* A tackle used to hold a lower yard to its mast.

**truss yoke** *n.* A fixture on a yard to which a bracket, the truss, is fitted.

**try** *v.* (1) To lie to, to keep the head of a vessel into the sea rather than allow a vessel to wallow in the troughs. Rarely used today. (2) A joinery term meaning to plane a piece of wood until it has a perfectly flat surface.

**try cocks** *n.* Faucets on a steam drum used to determine water level when the gauge fails.

**trysail** *n.* (pron. trysl) (1) Small three-cornered sail lashed to the mast and se-

cured at the clew and used in heavy weather. Also *storm trysail.* (2) Three-cornered fore-and-aft sail used on ketches and yawls to balance the helm on beam reaches and when close-hauled. See TRY.

**try works** *n.* The brick oven works on whaling ships used for processing blubber for whale oil.

**tsunami** *n.* Enormous waves produced by sudden motion of a portion of the seafloor or the shore in the case of volcanic eruptions and earthquakes. Tsunamis, by definition, are never the result of storms or tides, even though they are frequently called tidal waves, a misnomer. The word is of Japanese origin and means "port wave."

**Tsushima Current** *n.* Part of the Koroshio that flows through the Tsushima Strait between Japan and Korea and through the Sea of Japan. See OCEAN CURRENT.

**tub** *n.* (1) An old, slow-moving vessel. (2) A container in which line is coiled down, especially aboard fishing vessels and whale boats.

**tub oarsman** *n.* The second oar in a whaleboat's crew. His thwart is beside the harpooner's tub and he tends the harpoon line.

**tuck** *n.* The point at which the sides of a vessel meet the bottom. See CHINE.

**tuck plate** *n.* A flat plate fitted over the stern frame bridge piece in designs where the body of the hull is some distance above the arch.

**tufa** *n.* A porous, rocky, calcareous or siliceous deposit found in streams and oceans near the mouths of rivers. It is marked T on nautical charts.

**tugboat** *n.* A small, mechanically propelled vessel used for getting ships in and out of harbors and for pulling barges, tows, dry docks, oil rigs, bridge sections, and ships. See TOWBOAT.

**tugboat stern** *n.* An elliptical stern with pronounced tumble home.

**tumble** *v.* To lose stability, said of a gyroscope.

**tumble home** *n.* The inward (and upward) curve of the sides of a vessel from the turn of the bilge to the upper deck. Sailing men-of-war had tumble homes to make it possible to be alongside the enemy's ship with the guns still run out. Also *falling home.* Vessels with vertical sides are said to be **wall-sided,** while vessels with the sides leaning out are said to be **flared-sided.**

**tumbler** *n.* A deck device used for tripping a stocked anchor. It is a revolving iron bar set on deck and fitted with a handle, two horns, and a pin.

**tumbler pin** *n.* A pin that prevents the trigger bar from turning when the anchor is on the billboard.

**tune** *v.* (1) To adjust a vessel's rigging and sails for optimal efficiency. (2) To adjust the frequency of circuit to optimal performance.

**tunnel frame** *n.* A frame that supports the plating of the access tunnel housing a shaft.

**tunnel shaft propeller** *n.* A propulsion system for shallow-draft vessels in which the hull forms a tunnel through which water flows when the vessel is under way by force of the propeller in the tunnel.

**tunnel stern** *n.* A powerboat design in which the propeller is housed in a tunnel in the hull to protect it in the event of grounding.

**turbidity currents** *n.* Avalanche currents on the ocean floor that are strong enough to carry heavy masses of sediment far out to sea. These can be strong enough to cause ocean cables to part.

**turbine** *n.* Any machine capable of converting the kinetic energy of a moving fluid to mechanical energy when the fluid impinges on blades, paddles, or other devices arranged around an axis. In a **steam turbine,** the steam enters the turbine through nozzles that direct the steam on to blades on a rotor enclosed in a casing. The steam turns the blades and then passes on to a row of stationary blades on the casing, which then turn the steam against a second row of moving blades on the same rotor. Each set of moving turbines is called a **turbine stage.** A **gas turbine** is a heavy-fuel, high-speed ship propulsion system that utilizes gases produced in a combustion chamber to turn turbines similar to the action of steam turbines.

**turboblower** *n.* (1) A blower used to complete the evacuation of water from a submarine's ballast tanks when the boat has surfaced. (2) Used on diesels to increase efficiency by increasing the air content per stroke.

**turbulence** *n.* Agitated and irregular motion in seawater or in the atmosphere. Its occurrence is often due to the water or air currents meeting.

**Turk's head** *n.* A turbanlike round knot used for ornamentation of rails, stanchions, awnings, and so on.

**turn** *n.* (1) The change of tide from ebb to flow, and vice versa, same as slack tide or slack water. (2) Rotation of ships waiting to use a lock or canal. (3) A maneuver similar to a flank turn in marching, as opposed to a column turn. All ships turn simultaneously. While battle lines are no longer used, the maneuver is still used with ships in convoy.

**turn around** *v.* To go through the procedures necessary to entering port, unloading and/or loading, and returning to sea. "By using the more modern equipment, we were able to turn around in less than four days where it used to take better than a week.''

**turnbuckle**   *n.* A threaded rigging fitting used to tighten or loosen shrouds, stays, and life lines. Because the two screws at opposite ends of the turnbuckle have opposite threading, when the turnbuckle is turned and the screws at the ends hold firm, the rigging is either tightened or loosened. Also *rigging screw.*

**turn count masking**   *n.* The practice of surface ships to change screw revolutions at random to preclude a submarine's being able to estimate its speed.

**turn in**   *v.* To secure a block or deadeye. You turn in a block when you place the strap on it. You turn in a deadeye by seizing the end of a shroud or stay around it.

**turn in**   *v.* To go to bed. To **turn in all standing** is old sailor slang for turning in with all one's clothes on. See TURN OUT.

**turning basin**   *n.* A wide area in a channel or at the end of a channel that can be used for turning vessels around.

**turning buoy**   *n.* A buoy marking a turn in a channel.

**turning circle**   *n.* The smallest possible circle a vessel's **pivot point** can make with the rudder hard over, the pivot point being the point about which the ship turns when the rudder is hard over. On a lightly loaded vessel, the pivot point is well aft because of the weight of the engines; if the same vessel is trimmed by the head with a load forward, the pivot point will move forward.

**turn of the bilge**   *n.* The outer hull at the top of the bilge where the bottom turns upward for the rise of the sides. Also *Chine.*

**turn out**   *v.* To untie reef points in a sail, to **shake out** the reef. "As soon as the storm had passed, we turned out the reef and continued with full canvas.'' (2) To awaken.

**turn to**   *interj.* Command to begin work. "O.K. deck gang, turn to!''

**turn turtle**   *v.* To capsize.

**turret**   *n.* A low, heavily armored structure enclosing heavy guns of the main battery on warships, constructed to revolve around a vertical axis. The turret has come to be the entire rotating mount inside the stationary barbette that supports it.

**turtle deck**   *n.* A deck with a pronounced camber, like a turtle's back.

**'tween deck bunker**   *n.* A fuel bunker located between two decks.

**'tween decks**   *n.* A deck or decks between the upper deck and the hold. Most often it refers to the space between the main deck and the next lower deck or the space between any continuous decks.

**'tween deck tank**   *n.* A tank located between the main deck and the next deck below.

**twice-laid rope**   *n.* Rope made from recycled yarn.

**twiddling line**   *n.* Rope or shock cord used to hold a tiller or wheel when the helmsman wants to leave the tiller or wheel.

**twig**   *v.* In square-rigged ships, to secure sails and square the yards.

**twilight**   *n.* Period of incomplete darkness following sunset and again just before sunrise. **Civil twilight** is the point at which the center of the Sun is 6° below the celestial horizon. **Nautical twilight** is when the center of the Sun is 12° below the horizon. **Astronomical twilight** begins when the center of the Sun is 18° below the celestial horizon. Most navigators agree that the best time to take star sights is when the center of the sun is 10° below the horizon, between the beginning of nautical twilight and civil twilight in the morning, and after civil twilight but before nautical twilight in the evening.

**twin bulkhead tanker**  *n.* A tank vessel in which the summer tanks have been replaced by two fore-and-aft bulkheads placed midway on both sides of a vessel's centerline.

**twine**  *n.* Coarse thread made up of a number of fibers.

**twing**  *n.* An adjustable control line at the outer end of a rigged spinnaker pole that prevents its rising; usually called a *foreguy.*

**twins**  *n.* Double headsails, one flown on one side and one on the opposite side, used going downwind. See WING AND WING.

**twin-screw**  *adj.* Used to describe a vessel propelled by two shafts and propellers. The shafts can be inboard- or outboard-turning, depending on the requirements of the vessel. Inboard-turning propellers have greater power, while outboard-turning propellers have greater maneuverability.

**twist**  *n.* The tendency of a sail's leech to turn more to leeward toward the head.

**two-block**  *n.* The condition when two blocks of a tackle have been hauled together as closely as possible by the fall.

**two-block**  *v.* (1) To bring the two blocks of a tackle together by hauling on the fall. "Two-block the cargo hoist." (2) It is frequently used to mean to haul a flag or a sail to the top of the mast or staff. (3) To tighten the knot of a necktie so that the collar doesn't show. "Two-block that necktie, Midshipman."

**twofold purchase**  *n.* A tackle with two double blocks yielding a 4:1 advantage.

**two-leg mooring**  *n.* A permanent mooring buoy with two anchors connected by a suitable length of chain; the center of the span is fitted with a swivel to which the riding chain and buoy are connected.

**two-topsail schooner**  See MAIN TOPSAIL SCHOONER.

**two-way route**  *n.* A route within defined limits inside which two-way traffic is established. Such routes are designed to provide safe passage of ships through waters where navigation is difficult or dangerous.

**tye (or tie)**  *n.* A halyard used to convey the effort on a tackle to hoist upper yards and gaffs.

**type commander**  *n.* A flag officer in command of all U.S. Navy ships of a given type. For example, COMDESLANT (*commander, destroyers, Atlantic*) is the type commander for all destroyers in the Atlantic fleet, called DESLANT.

**typhoon**  *n.* A weather system characterized by low barometric pressure, a strong and very pronounced rotary circulation, and sustained surface wind speeds of 64 knots or higher. The word is interchangeable with hurricane, but is used in the western North Pacific and in the South Pacific. From the Cantonese *tai fung,* great wind. It is more severe than a tropical storm.

# U

**U**   See UNIFORM.

**U-boat**   *n.* A German or Austrian submarine. It is a translation of *U-boot*, which is short for *Untersee Boot*, or undersea boat.

**U-clip**   *n.* A bolt cut in the shape of a "U" with nuts on both ends.

**ullage**   *n.* (pron. uhlidge) (1) The space in a tank above the liquid. To determine how much liquid is in a tank, the distance from the top of the tank to the liquid can be measured and the amount of ullage determined; from this the amount of the contents of the tank can be calculated. (2) The amount of liquid lost from a container such as a cask during shipment.

**ullage board**   *n.* A device used on tankers for determining the ullage in a tank or compartment.

**ullage hole**   *n.* A hole fitted with an **ullage plug** in hatch covers used for taking ullage. Also *sounding hole; sounding tube.* Sounding tubes are also used to measure bilges and double bottoms.

**ultralarge crude carrier (ULCC)**   *n.* A crude oil tanker of 300,000 DWT or more. See TANKER.

**ultra quick (UQ)**   *adj.* Light phase description indicating a flashing light with a repetition rate of 160 or more (usually 240 to 300) flashes per minute. Lights may be **continuous ultra quick** or **interrupted ultra quick.** See LIGHT PHASE CHARACTERISTICS.

**ultrasonic depth finder**   *n.* A direct-reading echo sounder that determines water depths by measuring the time lapse between the emission of the ultrasonic signal and the return of the echo. An audible depth finder is called a **sonic depth finder.**

**umbrella**   *n.* Cone-shaped shield at the top of a smokestack to keep out the weather.

**umiak**   *n.* A large open boat made of skins and used by the Eskimos.

**una boat**   *n.* A small craft used in the United Kingdom with a rig similar to a catboat.

**unattended light**   *n.* An aid to navigation that does not require a permanent attendant and that is only activated when sunlight fails.

**unbalanced rudder**   *n.* A rudder that does not extend forward of its axis of rotation. See BALANCED RUDDER.

**unballast**   *v.* To unload ballast from a vessel. Also *deballast.*

**unbitt**   *v.* To remove a rope or line from a bitt.

**UNCLOS**   *n.* U.N. Conference on the Law of the Sea. There have been three such conferences. UNCLOS I was held in 1958; UNCLOS II was held in 1960; UNCLOS III was held between 1974 and 1982.

**uncoil**   *v.* To remove cable or rope from its coil, starting from the middle of the coil.

**uncorrecting**   *n.* The term used for converting from true compass course to magnetic. When converting from magnetic compass to true, it is called correcting. See COMPENSATE.

**uncovered** *adj.* or *adv.* Not submerged; either afloat, as a buoy, or above the water level, as an island.

**undecked** *adj.* Said of an open boat.

**under bare poles** *phr.* Said of a vessel lying to or lying a-try with no sails set during a storm.

**under below** *interj.* A warning call for those below deck that the vessel is standing into danger.

**underbody** *n.* The hull below the waterline.

**under bow** *v.* To make use of a contrary tide when a vessel is under sail with the wind across the waterway by heading the vessel to place the tide against the lee bow when full and by. The vessel is then set to windward. Also *lee bowing.*

**under canvas** *phr.* Under sail. "By four bells in the first dog watch, the wind had veered and we were able to depart under canvas."

**undercanvassed** *adj.* A word meaning the vessel does not have enough sail in use, such as using a working jib when 140% genoa would be more appropriate. Also *underpowered.*

**undercurrent** *n.* A subsurface current when the surface has either no current or a contrary current. Also *underset.* See UNDERTOW.

**underdeck tonnage** *n.* The total capacity of a vessel below the tonnage deck, the deck from which the ship's tonnage is measured, without regard for the limitations necessary to arrive at net register tonnage.

**underfoot** *adj.* (1) Often used with regard to the anchor when the anchor is let go while the vessel is still under way; for the anchor to be underfoot it has to be under the vessel's hawsehole beneath the forefoot. (2) Said of a current when it is running with the vessel's course.

**under hack** *phr.* Said of a U.S. Navy officer who is confined to his quarters for a minor infraction of naval discipline. Also *in hack.*

**underhaul** *v.* To ride at an angle different from the surface current because of a subsurface current. "She was underhauled by an unseen current."

**underhauled** *adj.* Lying at anchor at an angle contrary to either the surface current or the wind direction as a result of an undercurrent or subsurface current. This will usually cause a vessel to **horse** or to **run.**

**underhung (rudder)** *adj.* Said of a spade rudder that is entirely supported from within the hull and not supported by the sternpost.

**underkeel clearance** *n.* Depth under the vessel's bottom deduced from charted depth with tide levels taken into consideration. Also *net bottom clearance.*

**underlay** *v.* To tack too soon when approaching a mark so that another tack is necessary to round the mark.

**undermanned** *adj.* (1) Said of a ship the crew of which is below the Inspection Certificate's manning schedule. (2) Insufficient crew to handle the assigned duties aboard a vessel.

**undermasted** *adj.* Vessel with insufficient sail area as a result of too few or too short masts to be able to sail at the designed hull speed. See UNDERRIGGED.

**under power** *phr.* The use of machinery to propel a vessel. If a vessel is under sail and under power, it must abide by the rules for vessels under power.

**underpowered**  *adj.* Said of a vessel that does not have enough power to push the hull as designed, either under sail or power.

**underrigged**  *adj.* Said of a vessel with rigging that is too light or otherwise insufficient to move the vessel efficiently or properly.

**under run (or underrun)**  *v.* (1) To take in line on one side of a vessel, run it across the deck, and pay it out on the other side. A fishing vessel under runs its gear when the operator starts on the leeward end of the line and takes fish off the line on the windward side, then pays it out baited on the leeward side. (2) Said of a log when the ship travels farther than the log indicates. The log is said to have under run. (3) To separate the several parts of a tackle so that it can run or be hauled free.

**under sail**  *adv.* Under way with sails set. "We proceeded through the strait under sail, barely ghosting along."

**underset**  See UNDERCURRENT.

**under the lee**  *phr.* To sail or to be in the lee of a shore or another vessel. "We sailed under the lee of the headland as long as possible before changing course and shortening sail."

**undertow**  *n.* A subsurface current caused by breaking waves on a beach. See UNDERCURRENT.

**underwater navigation**  *n.* Navigation for submarines, as distinct from **surface navigation** and **land navigation.**

**underwater terrain**  *n.* The terrain on the bottom of the oceans and channels as shown on the various charts to assist navigators, especially in anchoring. When you see that an area is covered with seaweed, it might be a good idea to move on if possible to a more hospitable anchorage. Anchoring over a wreck can also lead to problems.

**underway**  *adv.* Any vessel that is not at anchor, made fast, or aground is said to be underway.

**underway replenishment (UNREP)**  *n.* The operation of refueling and restocking vessels while under way.

**underway replenishment group**  *n.* A task group assigned to give logistic support to ships while under way by transfer at sea.

**underwrite**  *v.* To assume financial responsibility for a vessel in marine insurance policies by signing one's name to a policy either personally or as agent and to receive a premium in consideration.

**underwriter, marine**  *n.* An insurer of vessels and cargo. When a vessel seeks insurance, various underwriters underwrite a part of the total risk exposure.

**undock**  *v.* To take a vessel out of its dock, slip, or berth.

**undocumented vessel**  *n.* Any vessel that is not required to have, and does not have, a valid marine document issued by the U.S. Coast Guard.

**unfurl**  *v.* To spread out a flag or sail, to shake out a furled sail or flag, to cast loose a sail by removing the gaskets.

**unidentifiable cargo**  *n.* Cargo that reaches its destination damaged in such a manner that it is unidentifiable. U.S. underwriters take over the goods and settle for a total loss. In Britain they are considered particular average claims.

**Uniform**  *n.* Phonetic word for the letter "U." Used as a single-letter signal, it means, "You are standing into danger."

**uniform cardinal system**  *n.* One of two buoyage systems used since 1936 throughout the world (the other system is the uniform lateral system). All countries use one system or the other, but the cardinal system is always used in conjunction with the lateral system. The cardinal system is best suited to coasts with numerous rocks and shoals, while the lateral system is best for regions with many channels. The cardinal system employs markers that indicate the true bearing of the danger to navigation. See BUOYAGE; INTERNATIONAL ASSOCIATION OF LIGHTHOUSE AUTHORITIES.

**uniform lateral system**   *n.* One of two buoyage systems used since 1936 (the other system is the uniform cardinal system). The lateral system is best suited to regions with well-defined channels. The location and topmarks of the buoy indicate the direction of the danger it marks relative to the course that should be followed. It is the predominant buoyage system used in the United States. See BUOYAGE SYSTEMS; INTERNATIONAL ASSOCIATION OF LIGHTHOUSE AUTHORITIES.

**uniform of the day**   *n.* Uniform for U.S. Naval officers and enlisted personnel prescribed for a day or other fixed period. The uniform of the day can be prescribed to be undress khakis until 1200, but at 1300, all men and officers will be in dress whites for inspection before liberty sections are allowed to leave the ship.

**uniform pitch**   *n.* Describes the pitch of a propeller blade when the driving face lies in a true helical surface with no variation either radially or axially.

**Uniform State Waterway Marking System**   *n.* The buoyage system developed by the U.S. Coast Guard and the various state boating administrations to assist small-craft operators in state waters marked by participating states. The state system of aids to navigation is compatible with the Coast Guard lateral system. The regulatory markers warn operators of small craft of dangers or provide general information and direction.

**union**   *n.* A national flag or the inner upper corner of a flag if there is a separate device or field. The ensign of the United States has a blue union with 50 stars; the red and white stripes are in what is called the **fly.** A flag is flown **union down** as a sign of distress or surrender.

**union gear**   *n.* A gear with two falls secured to a single hook, used for cargo handling.

**Union Jack**   *n.* (1) A flag with only the union of the national ensign, flown at the bow by U.S. Naval vessels, U.S. Coast Guard vessels, and sometimes merchant vessels, but only when in port, anchored, or in the yard making repairs. The Union Jack is flown in boats carrying high officials and flown from the yardarm while a general court-martial or a court of inquiry is being conducted. (2) The flag of the United Kingdom.

**United States Coast and Geodetic Survey**   *n.* The agency in charge of the publication of coast and harbor charts and aeronautical charts of the 50 states, tide tables for U.S. and foreign waters, and publications regarding research in hydrography, cartography, and comparable matters.

**United States Coast Guard (USCG)**   *n.* A branch of the armed forces that operates as part of the Department of Transportation except when the nation is at war or as the President directs, the Coast Guard is in charge of a variety of activities such as inspection of merchant vessels, licensing merchant officers, maintenance of aids to navigation from unmarked buoys to lighthouses, publication of light lists, and chasing smugglers; it is the principal federal agency for the enforcement of maritime law and marine safety. The U.S. Coast Guard was organized in 1790 as The Revenue Marine. See LIFESAVING SERVICE; LIGHTHOUSE SERVICE.

**United States Coast Guard Academy**   *n.* A military institution of higher learning maintained by the federal government and under the auspices of the

Treasury Department for the education and training of U.S. Coast Guard officers. It was founded by the Congress in 1876 and is located at New London, Connecticut. In addition to receiving instruction in the regular curriculum, each cadet makes a cruise aboard the three-masted bark *Eagle* and escort cutters.

**United States Coast Guard Auxiliary**   *n.* A volunteer civilian organization of owners of boats, aircraft, and shore radio stations, administered by the U.S. Coast Guard, that promotes safety in boat operation through education, boat examinations, and operational activities.

*United States Coast Pilot*   *n.* A nine-volume series published by the National Ocean Survey that covers the coastline of all 50 states and includes information on bridges and cables, cable ferries, currents, depths alongside wharves, distances from port to port, depths in channels often not shown on charts, ranges, radio aids to navigation, and a wealth of other information.

**United States controlled shipping**   *n.* Shipping under the U.S. flag as well as selected ships under foreign flags that can reasonably be expected to be made available to the United States in time of national emergency.

**United States ensign**   *n.* The national flag, with 13 stripes and 50 stars, may be flown on any U.S. yacht or ship. It is flown from the stern at anchor and from the stern of powerboats and sailboats under power while under way. Sailing vessels under way and sailing with no power customarily fly the national ensign from the leech of the aftermost sail about one-third of the way down from the head. See UNION JACK; UNITED STATES YACHT ENSIGN.

**United States Hydrographic Office**   *n.* The federal agency involved with work similar to the U.S. Coast and Geodetic Survey, but in international waters and foreign shores in cooperation with foreign government agencies.

**United States Marine Corps**   *n.* A branch of the United States Armed Forces composed chiefly of amphibious troops under the authority of the Secretary of the Navy.

**Unites States Merchant Marine Academy (USMMA)**   *n.* A federal service academy established in 1943 at Kings Point, New York, to prepare cadets to serve as officers in the merchant marine. After the four-year, college-level program, its graduates receive a bachelor's degree and are licensed as deck officers or engineer officers. They are also commissioned as ensigns in the U.S. Naval Reserve.

**United States Naval Academy**   *n.* A federal service academy for the academic training of Navy and Marine Corps officers. The Academy was established at Annapolis, Maryland, in 1845 by Secretary of the Navy George Bancroft. After four years, midshipmen receive a bachelor's degree and a commission as an ensign in the U.S. Navy or as second lieutenant in the U.S. Marine Corps.

**United States Naval Institute (USNI)**   *n.* A professional society with a primary interest in keeping its members informed on matters of interest to the Navy through its *Proceedings* magazine and *Naval History* magazine and book publishing program. The USNI is a self-supporting, nonprofit organization located in Annapolis, Maryland.

**United States Naval Observatory**   *n.* The federal agency that promulgates time signals, nautical and air almanacs, and so on, located in Washington, D.C.

**United States Naval ship (USNS)**   *n.* A vessel that is owned by the U.S. Navy. It is not commissioned as a part of the Navy, but is usually manned by civilians and operated under the Military Sealift Command.

**United States Navy (USN)**   *n.* The military organization of the United States for sea warfare and defense, including vessels, personnel, and shore establishment.

**United States Navy Regulations** *n.* A book published by the Secretary of the Navy that contains the principles for guiding the Navy establishment; it includes duties, responsibilities, and authority of all offices and individuals in the Navy. Often referred to as Navy Regs.

**United States Power Squadron (USPS)**   *n.* A private organization that promotes boating safety, education, and good seamanship.

**United States Sailing Association** *n.* The national governing body for the sport of sailing in the United States; formerly the U.S. Yacht Racing Union (USYRU).

**United States ship (USS)**   *n.* The designation before the name of a vessel commissioned as a part of the United States Navy. For example, USS *Arleigh Burke* (DDG-51).

**United States yacht ensign**   *n.* A 13-star flag with a fouled anchor in the center. In earlier days it was the custom for only documented yachts to fly the yacht ensign, but today all yachts may fly it. In international waters, however, the national ensign should be flown. See UNION JACK; UNITED STATES ENSIGN.

**unitized cargo**   *n.* Containerized, palletized, or standard timber units of otherwise loose cargoes so packaged to facilitate handling and stowing.

**unit loading**   *n.* The handling of unitized cargo between ship and shore.

**universal joint**   *n.* A coupling of two shafts not directly in line that allows one shaft to transmit rotation to another.

**universal plotting sheet (UPS)**   *n.* Form plotting sheets that are not specific for latitude or scale. These are different from standard plotting sheets that are printed for specific latitudes and scales. See SMALL-AREA PLOTTING SHEET.

**universal time (UT)**   *n.* In concept, time determined from the apparent diurnal motion of a fictitious mean Sun that moves uniformly along the celestial equator at the average rate of the apparent sun. In practice, UT is related to the rotation of the Earth with relation to sidereal time. Universal time at any given instant is derived from observations of the diurnal motion of the stars and depends somewhat on the place of observation; thus it is called UTO (with "O" referring to observation).

**unlash**   *v.* To loosen or untie something that has been previously secured by rope or lashing.

**unlay**   *v.* Unravel or untwist strands of rope, as for splicing or whipping.

**unlighted buoy**   *n.* A buoy not fitted with a light. A buoy with a light that is not functioning is described as inoperative.

**unmanned buoy**   *n.* A light that is operated automatically.

**unmoor**   *v.* (1) To free a vessel from its moorings. (2) To raise one anchor, but leave the other down.

**unneutral service**   *n.* The breach of neutrality by a merchant vessel when it carries contraband to a nation at war or runs a blockade.

**unreeve**   *v.* To pull a rope out of a block or fairlead. Past tense and past participle: unrove.

**unrig**   *v.* To remove both standing and running rigging from a vessel.

**unship** *v.* To remove a mast or other object from its accustomed place or fitting.

**unstable equilibrium** n. The condition that exists when the center of gravity (G) is above metacenter (M). In this condition, a vessel does not tend to return to an upright position after being inclined, but tends to continue inclining. See STABILITY.

**unstep** *v.* To remove a mast or other spar from its step.

**unstow** See BREAK OUT.

**unvalued policy** n. An open policy in maritime insurance in which the value is not specified but leaves the value to be determined if the need arises, subject to the face value or limits of the policy.

**unwatched (U)** *n.* A light list term for an unmanned automatic light.

**up anchor** *v.* To raise the anchor. "Let's up anchor and get out of here before the fog rolls in." See HEAVE.

**up and down** *adj.* Said of the anchor cable when it is under the forefoot, but the anchor has not broken loose from the bottom; the anchor is then atrip but not aweigh. See SHORT STAY.

**up behind** *interj.* To slacken a line to make cleating possible.

**up-current** *adv.* or *adj.* In the direction from which the current is flowing.

**up-current tack** *n.* A tack more in the direction from which the water is flowing.

**up helm** *v.* To push the tiller to windward so that the rudder goes to leeward and the vessel will go downwind.

**uphill** *adj.* or *adv.* Windward, as in the **uphill leg** of a race, or to windward.

**uphroe** *n.* (pron. yewfroh) An oblong block without sheaves used to suspend an awning; it has several holes through the middle through which small lines are passed to hold the awning and a groove around the outside to receive the line by which it is suspended. Also *euphroe.*

**upper deck** *n.* A deck above the main deck of a merchant ship. In general, it is held to be a continuous deck on passenger ships, but a partial deck on cargo vessels.

**upper limb** *n.* That half of the outer edge of a celestial body having the greater altitude.

**upper mast** *n.* Any mast above a lower mast.

**upper shroud** *n.* A transverse guy from the chain plate to the masthead on a one-part mast, as distinguished from a lower shroud that extends only partway up the mast, usually to a set of spreaders.

**upper topsail** *n.* A topsail above a lower topsail.

**upper works** *n.* (1) The hull from normal loaded draft to upper deck. Also *deadworks; freeboard; topsides.* (2) All components of a vessel above the waterline. (3) The superstructures on a vessel's weather deck.

**upsetting angle** *n.* The angle of heel of a vessel at which point the righting moment becomes zero.

**upsetting moment** *n.* The product of displacement in tons multiplied by the upsetting arm (or lever) in feet, expressed in foot-tons.

**upstream** *n.* Against the current of a river or a channel.

**uptake ventilator** *n.* Forced-draft ventilators that remove stale or hot air from the various compartments of a ship.

**upwell**  *v.* Said of seawater when a cold, nutrient-rich mass rises to the surface from deep down. This is observed along coasts on which winds constantly drive water seaward.

**upwind**  *adj.* or *adv.* To windward of another vessel or an object. "We were upwind of the garbage scow and could not smell it."

**upwind**  *v.* To maneuver a sailboat to windward of another so as to take the leeward boat's wind. Also *cover.*

**upwind end**  *adj.* The end of a starting or finishing line that is to windward.

**useful deadweight**  *n.* The amount of cargo (expressed in deadweight tons) a vessel can carry to bring her to the summer, saltwater load marks. Also *net capacity.* See PLIMSOLL MARK OR LINE.

**useful load**  *n.* That part of the total displacement available for the intended purpose of the ship when it is floating at the designed draft. The term refers exclusively to weight and not volume. Also *dead load; net capacity.*

# V

**V**  See VICTOR.

**vail**  *v.* To haul down a sail or banner, especially to salute by hauling down sails.

**valuation clause**  *n.* An underwriter's clause in maritime insurance policies in which it is agreed that the insured value shall be taken as the repaired value in determining if a constructive loss has taken place.

**valued policy**  *n.* In marine insurance, a policy that specifies the agreed value of the insured.

**valve chest**  *n.* A steel box with valves and piping leading to various tanks and compartments making it possible to pump the contents from one space to another to maintain trim. See MANIFOLD.

**van**  *n.* The forward part of a formation of vessels; the opposite is the rear. "The van consisted of five frigates in the screen."

**vane**  *n.* A piece of yarn (a **telltale**) or a piece of sheet metal on a spindle (**weathercock**) used to tell the apparent wind direction. The arrow on a metal wind vane is always designed to point in the direction from which the wind is coming instead of the direction in which it is blowing; the same is true with a cock on the vane—he faces the direction from which the wind is blowing. This is consistent, however, with the accepted practice of calling a wind out of the North a north wind, and so on.

**vang**  *n.* (1) A steadying line or bar that prevents a boom from lifting or accidentally jibing when sailing off the wind, or that prevents the peak of a gaff from falling off to windward. See MARCONI RIG; SQUARE-RIGGED VESSEL. (2) A heavy tackle used to steady a spar in the desired position.

**vanishing point**  *n.* That angle at which a listing ship no longer returns to an upright position.

**vanishing tide**  *n.* One high and one low water during a day. The other high and low have insufficient difference to become tides.

**vapor cock** *n.* An escape valve fitted on oil tanker hatches to allow gases to escape and equalize pressure.

**vapor pressure** *n.* The pressure of water vapor in the air; that part of the total atmospheric pressure that is due to water vapor.

**vaps** *n.* U.S. Navy slang for evaporators or desalinization plants. Also *evaps.*

**Vardar** *n.* A cold fall wind that blows from the northeast down the Vardar Valley of Greece to the Gulf of Salonica.

**variable range marker** *n.* A luminous range ring on a plan position indicator with an adjustable radius. The range setting of the marker is read on the range counter of the radar indicator.

**variable tanks** *n.* The trimming tanks of a submarine that include trim tanks and ballast tanks.

**variable winds** *n.* Winds of varying strength.

**variation** *n.* The angular difference between the direction a magnetic compass points and the direction in which the geographic north or south will be found, or the difference between true and magnetic north at any given point on the Earth's surface. Variation can be plotted by means of isogonic lines along which the difference is the same. Variation is said to be **easterly** if the compass card of a magnetic compass points east of true north and **westerly** if it points west of true north. See DEVIATION.

**V-bottom hull** *n.* Hull with V-shaped configuration when observed longitudinally. A **deep V** has more pronounced angle at the keel. Dinghies with V-bottoms and hard chines are more stable than dinghies with rounded chines.

**V-butt weld** *n.* Two plates butted together and welded after the edges have been beveled or chamfered to form a "V."

**V-depression** *n.* A weather system within which the isobars are V-shaped. The circulating winds blow according to the usual law down one side of a central zone and up the other. See BUYS BALLOT'S LAW.

**V-drive** *n.* An engine mounted with the drive shaft extending forward to the gear box and reversing its direction to come out under the hull in the normal manner.

**vector** *n.* A graphic presentation of a force acting over a distance on an object; the direction of the line (vector) indicates the direction of the force, and the length of the line indicates the strength of the force. In a maneuvering board or radar problem, vectors represent the headings and speeds of various vessels relative to a guide, the vessel in which the observer is riding, or another vessel.

**vector** *v.* To follow a compass direction to a beach; used in amphibious landings.

**veer** *v.* (1) Used to describe a change in wind direction in a clockwise direction in the Northern Hemisphere and a counterclockwise direction in the Southern Hemisphere. The opposite of veering is backing. A wind that veers is also said to **clock.** See LEFT SEMICIRCLE; RIGHT SEMICIRCLE. (2) If the wind changes direction aft relative to a given vessel, it is said to veer, while a wind that moves forward (usually from the beam) is said to haul (forward). (3) To pay out a line or rope, especially an anchor cable. "As the wind picked up, it seemed prudent to veer the anchor cable from our initial 3:1 scope to a scope of 5:1," that is, to let the cable out from three times the depth of the water to five times the depth of the water. A cable or line is also said to be **veered away.**

**veer and haul**  *v.* To slacken and pull a rope alternately.

**velocity of current**  *n.* Speed and direction of current.

**velocity of translation**  *n.* The speed with which a storm center moves in a given direction.

**vendaval**  *n.* (pron. vendavol): A stormy period accompanied by rain, thunder, and lightning, on the coast of Mexico during autumn months.

**vent**  *n.* (1) A valve in a tank or compartment that allows air to escape when the trunk or compartment is being filled or when pressure builds for any other reason, such as heat. Also *pressure vacuum (PV) valve.* See VAPOR COCK. (2) The hole at the base of the bore of a muzzle-loaded gun through which the charge was lighted to fire the gun. When a gun was "spiked," a spike was rammed into the vent.

**vent**  *v.* To allow air into a cargo tank or to release air from a cargo tank.

**vent header**  *n.* The top of a venting pipe system that rises above the weather deck of a tanker. When light and volatile oils are carried, a pressure vacuum relief valve is sometimes fitted.

**ventilating funnel**  *n.* A system of ducts built in a stack where the hot air forms a draft.

**ventilating trunk**  *n.* A space between two closed frames to form an air duct to ventilate bilges.

**ventilation**  *n.* The distribution of fresh air to below-deck spaces.

**ventilator**  *n.* A cylindrical tube leading from below to well above the deck where the **ventilator cowls** catch the wind and force it below. A **gooseneck** or **swan-neck** ventilator is curved downward at its upper end. A **mushroom** ventilator is one that is protected from the weather at the upper end by a mushroom top.

**ventilator coaming**  *n.* A ventilator duct that extends above the weather deck and to which a cowl is secured. In foul weather, the ventilator coaming is plugged and a **ventilator cover** placed over it.

**vent line**  *n.* A ventilating system on tankers carrying highly flammable material.

**verification of flag**  *n.* A procedure recognized under international law that allows a warship to stop another vessel suspected of sailing under false colors. The warship must first display its own colors.

**vernier**  *n.* On a sextant, a small, graduated scale meshed with a larger one to make finer adjustments than are possible with the larger one alone. The vernier has been largely replaced by a micrometer drum tangent screw for ease of reading and reduced chance of error.

**vertical axis**  *n.* A line through the center of gravity of a vessel, perpendicular to both the longitudinal and lateral axes around which a vessel yaws.

**vertical center of gravity (VCG)**  *n.* (1) The center of gravity of a vessel above the keel. See STABILITY. (2) The vertical height of the center of gravity of a compartment above its own bottom.

**vertical-cut sails**  *n.* A cut popular with square-rig sails and gaff rig sails when the heaviest strain is from luff to leech.

**vertical danger angle**  *n.* The use of a landmark of known elevation to avoid a danger area. The angle of the top landmark from the observer is predetermined so that the conning officer knows to keep inside or outside the given angle as the situation requires.

**vertical keel**   *n.* A row of vertical plates extending along the center of the flat keel plate. Also *center keelson.*

**vertical loading**   *n.* A type of loading whereby items of like character are vertically tiered throughout the holds of a ship so that selected items are available at any stage of the unloading. See HORIZONTAL LOADING.

**vertical replenishment (VERT-REP)**   *n.* The transfer of supplies between naval ships by helicopter to reduce the time required in a dispersed formation.

**vertical ring**   *n.* The ring in which a free gyro is placed when converting it to a gyrocompass. The rotor is mounted in a sphere, and the sphere is supported by the vertical ring.

**very close pack ice**   *n.* Pack ice from ⅞ to less than ⅞ concentration. See VERY OPEN PACK ICE.

**very high frequency (VHF)**   *n.* The most prevalent radio for all vessels at sea. Smaller recreational vessels are not required to have any radio, but if they do it must be a VHF set with frequencies between 156 and 163 MHz, the band allocated for marine use by international agreement.

**very high sea**   *n.* Douglas scale reading of 7, indicating wave heights between 23 and 36 feet with a heavy swell.

**very large crude carrier (VLCC)**   *n.* A crude oil tanker of 160,000 to more than 400,000 DWT. See TANKER.

**Very lights**   *n.* (pron. veery) Pyrotechnic signals fired from a hand-held gun invented by Edward W. Very for signaling at night. The cartridges are arranged so that the various colors and patterns are identifiable in the dark.

**very open pack ice**   *n.* Pack ice ⅛ to less than ⅜ concentration.

**very quick (VQ)**   *adj.* Light phase description indicating a flashing light with a repetition rate of 80 to 159 (usually 100 or 120) flashes per minute. Lights may be **continuous very quick, group very quick,** or **interrupted very quick.** See LIGHT PHASE CHARACTERISTICS.

**very rough sea**   *n.* Douglas scale reading of 5, indicating wave heights between 9 and 15 feet with a long, moderate swell.

**very well**   *interj.* In the U.S. Navy the response of a senior to a report by a junior. A junior never responds with either phrase, but with "Aye, aye, Sir." Also *very good.*

**vessel**   *n.* Any water craft, including nondisplacement craft and seaplanes whether self-propelled or not, that can be used as a means of transportation on the water. See POWER-DRIVEN VESSEL; SAILING VESSEL.

**vessel constrained by her draft**   *n.* In the *Navigation Rules,* a power-driven vessel that, because of its draft in relation to the available depth and width of navigable water, is severely restricted in its ability to deviate from the course it is following.

**vessel engaged in fishing**   *n.* In the *Navigation Rules,* any vessel fishing with nets, lines, trawls or other fishing apparatus that restricts maneuverability. Vessels fishing with trolling lines or other fishing apparatus that does not restrict maneuverability are not considered to be engaged in fishing.

**vessel not under command**   *n.* According to the *Navigation Rules,* any vessel "which through some exceptional circumstance is unable to maneuver . . . and is therefore unable to keep out of the way of another vessel." A vessel not under command usually is one with an engine breakdown or a rudder failure.

**vessel restricted in her ability to maneuver**  n. According to the *Navigation Rules,* any vessel "which from the nature of her work is restricted in her ability to maneuver . . . and is therefore unable to keep out of the way of another vessel." This includes vessels "laying, servicing, and picking up navigation marks, or laying submarine cable; vessels transferring persons, provisions, or cargo while underway; vessels launching or recovering aircraft; and vessels engaged in mineclearance operations; vessels engaged in towing such as to severely restrict their ability to deviate from course."

**Vessel Traffic Services (VTS)**  n. A wide range of vessel trafficking schemes primarily aimed at preventing vessel collisions, rammings, and groundings in ports and waterways, and designed also to expedite ship movements, increase system capacity, and improve all-weather operating capability. Such services vary with the locality based on local needs and safety requirements. They can be passive systems such as traffic separation schemes and regulated navigation areas or manned services with communications, electronic surveillance, and automated capabilities. The public laws governing VTS include the Ports and Waterways Safety Act of 1972 and the St. Lawrence Seaway Act. Recreational boats are not customarily subject to the VTS, but they should be aware of the restrictions the VTS places on the larger ships.

**viaduct**  n. Chart term meaning a structure consisting of a series of arches or towers that supports a roadway or waterway across a depression, highway, railway, or waterway.

**vibrating needle**  n. A magnetic needle used by compass adjusters to determine the relative intensity of the horizontal component of a ship's magnetism.

**vibrational period**  n. Compass adjuster's term for the time required for a magnetic compass card to perform a complete oscillation when it is deflected not more than 40°.

**vice admiral (VAdm.)**  n. A flag officer in the U.S. Navy or Coast Guard ranked below admiral and above rear admiral.

**vice commodore**  n. Second in command of a convoy. See COMMODORE.

**Victor**  n. Phonetic word for "V." When used in a single-letter signal, it means "I need assistance."

**Victory ship**  n. Either of two types of ships, designated AP2 and AP3, built by the U.S. Maritime Commission from 1942 on. They were essentially an improved version of the earlier Liberty ships, with a similar hull shape but larger and faster. The Victorys had a length of 460 feet, a beam of 42 feet, and a loaded draft of 28.5 feet. The deadweight capacity was 10,700 tons and the load displacement 15,200 tons. The AP2 had a speed of 15 knots, and the AP3 could make 16 knots.

**victualing bill**  n. (pron. vittling) A list of all bonded goods taken on board for use as ship's stores during a cruise; when signed by customs, it becomes one of the master's clearance documents.

**vigia**  n. (pron. veejeea) A warning on a chart denoting a hazard to navigation of doubtful position. From the Spanish *vigia,* a lookout.

**viol**  n. A messenger made fast to the anchor cable and brought to the capstan.

**viol block**  n. (1) A block similar to a snatch block, but without a hinge, into the sheave of which the bight of a rope may be dropped. (2) A large rope, that acts as a messenger when weighing anchors, by transmitting the effort of the capstan to the cables. See NIPPER.

**violent storm** *n.* Wind of Beaufort force 11 (56–63 knots).

**virtual plan position indicator reflectorscope (VPR)** *n.* Navigation chart fitted on the display of a radar console for comparing the presentation on the scope with the chart of the area.

**viscosity** *n.* Resistance to flow. Seawater is more viscous than freshwater. Viscosity increases with increasing salinity to a far less degree than it does with decreasing temperature. Viscosity of oil has been standardized by the Society of Automotive Engineers (SAE). An oil with the viscosity of SAE 30 takes 30 seconds for a standard volume to pass through a standard orifice.

**visibility** *n.* That property of the atmosphere that determines the ability of an observer to see and identify objects by day or lights and lighted objects by night.

**visitation, right of** See RIGHT OF VISITATION.

**visor** *n.* An awning just forward of the pilothouse designed to give protection from the Sun's glare and the rain. See EYEBROW; WRIGGLE.

**visual aid to navigation** *n.* An aid to navigation, either lighted or unlighted, that transmits information through observation.

**visual distress signals** *n.* Approved devices that can be used to attract attention when emergencies arise. These are required on all vessels of any size operating at night or operating for hire, and on all vessels 16 feet or more operating any time.

**visually in sight** *phr.* Something that can be seen by the eye directly and not only by electronic means.

**visual range** *n.* The maximum distance at which a given object can be seen

by day in any circumstances, as limited by atmospheric conditions. See VISIBILITY; VISUAL RANGE OF A LIGHT.

**visual range of a light** *n.* The predicted distance at which a light can be observed, either the luminous or geographic range. If the geographic range is less than the luminous range, then it is the limiting range, and vice versa. The **luminous range** is the maximum range at which a light can be seen under existing conditions of visibility and the given luminous intensity and does not take into account the elevation of the light, the observer's height of eye, the curvature of the Earth, or background interference. The **nominal range** is the maximum distance at which a light can be seen in clear weather without regard to the curvature of the Earth, height of eye, or height of light. The **geographic range** is the maximum distance at which the curvature of the Earth and terrestrial refraction permit a light to be seen without regard for luminous intensity. The geographic range sometimes printed on charts and in light lists is the maximum range at which the curvature of the Earth and refraction permit a light to be seen from a height of eye of 15 feet above the water when the elevation of the light is taken above the height datum of the largest scale chart of the area.

**voice tube** *n.* A hollow brass tube for voice communication for short distances on a ship. They have almost all been replaced by sound-powered telephones.

**void** *n.* A compartment designed to be left empty.

**volatile fuel** *n.* A classification of fuels such as propane, naphtha, and gasoline, but not diesel fuel. Any vessel with volatile fuel aboard is required to have a bilge ventilation system. Diesel-fueled vessels are exempted.

**volume coefficient** *n.* The difference in volume of a liquid such as oil caused by a 1° change in temperature expressed as a percentage of the total volume. Volume coefficient must be accounted for to allow sufficient ullage to prevent overflowing when a liquid warms and expands.

**volume of displacement**   *n.* The volume of water in cubic feet, displaced by a vessel, equal to 35 times the displacement of saltwater in tons or 36 times the displacement of freshwater in tons.

**voluntary stranding**   *n.* The intentional beaching of a boat to avoid greater danger and harm. In underwriters' terms, this is a case of general average, a loss to be made good by contribution from all interested parties.

**volute**   *n.* The sleeve in which a pump impeller revolves. From the Latin *volvere*, to turn.

**vortex**   *n.* The center of a tropical cyclone where the pressure is lowest, where the winds are relatively calm, and the seas are confused; the eye of a storm.

**voyage**   *n.* A trip from one port to another, usually involving a foreign port. Marine underwriters use voyage specifi-

cally to mean a trip by water from one port to another. See PASSAGE; TRIP.

**voyage charter**   *n.* An agreement to hire a vessel for a round-trip voyage. The voyage charter starts when the vessel begins to load cargo and ends when the return cargo is unloaded at the same port when the ship arrives back at the original port. The charter covers the two cargos and any intermediate passages.

**voyage policy**   *n.* Insurance coverage for a single voyage as specified by the underwriter.

**voyage repair**   *n.* (1) Emergency work required by a naval vessel so managed that the repair does not affect the vessel's operating commitment. (2) Repairs that result from damage caused by the normal wear and tear of operating a vessel at sea. See DAMAGE REPAIR.

**vulgar establishment**   *n.* The establishment of a port, high water full and change (HWF&C), or **common establishment**. It is the time lag between the Moon's transit across the meridian on the day of a new Moon or a full Moon and the following high water.

# W

**W**   See WHISKEY.

**wack**   *n.* A sailor's food ration. Origin unknown. Also *whack*.

**waft**   *n.* A flag tied in the middle or a flag flown with the fly fastened to the staff. It was used at one time as a request for customs, but has been replaced by the "Q" flag. Also *weft; wheft*.

**waft**   *v.* To convoy merchant ships, used in the days of sailing merchant ships.

**wager policy**   *n.* A type of marine insurance policy that leaves many clauses and phrases undefined but enforceable. In the event of a loss, the insured is exempt from having to prove his interest. These are also called **honor policies,** and they are enforceable in admiralty courts around the world.

**waif**   *n.* A buoy on a whale line used to retain title to a harpooned whale while it was abandoned to go after other whales.

**waist**   n. (1) The portion of the deck between the forecastle and the quarterdeck. (2) The central part of a vessel. (3) The upper deck between poop and forecastle. (4) Midships between bow and stern.

**waist anchor**   n. A sheet anchor.

**waister**   n. An incompetent or worn-out sailor. The term probably derives from the practice of employing in the waist of the ship old sailors or youngsters and landlubbers with insufficient experience to work aloft.

**waiver clause**   n. A clause in marine insurance policies that allows either party to take such action or incur such expense as to minimize losses without prejudice.

**wake**   n. Turbulence caused by something moving through water. It includes the bow wave as well as other waves caused by a vessel passing through the water and visible long after a ship has passed a particular spot. Ships' wakes vary depending on the size, mode of propulsion (sail, single-propeller, or multipropeller), and speed of the vessel.

**wake current**   n. The motion of water that follows a vessel as a result of the friction of the hull against the water.

**wake of a hatch**   n. That part of a hatch immediately beneath the opening.

**wake light**   n. A light focused on the wake behind a ship to assist a following ship in keeping station.

**wale**   n. The heavy longitudinal strake below the gunwale. Also *rubbing strake.*

**wale piece**   n. A heavy timber on a wharf for the protection of the wharf from ships tied up to it.

**wale shore**   n. A spar wedged into a vessel's side in dry dock to keep the vessel upright.

**walk**   v. (1) To make a steady haul instead of a succession of short pulls while standing in one place. (2) To move dividers or pointers end over end to determine distances along a course on a chart.

**walk back**   v. To reverse the capstan to ease the strain on a rope.

**walking beam**   n. The oscillating beam on the beam engine of a sidewheeler that converts the reciprocal motion from the engine to rotary motion for the wheels.

**walk pointers**   v. To use dividers or pointers in such a way that the spacing along a course line will yield the distance from point to point.

**wall and crown**   n. A wall knot finished with a crown by leading the ends of two strands over each other and by tucking the third one under.

**Wallis brake**   n. A wire brake used to maintain tension on a wire rope being wound on a drum.

**wall knot**   n. An ornamental stopper knot raised at the end of a rope by unlaying the strands and interweaving them among one other.

**wall-sided**   adj. Perpendicular sides, said of a hull.

**wander**   v. To stray from course, usually used with reference to a vessel that tends to wander from course if not carefully steered.

**waning Moon**   n. The phase of the Moon between full and new.

**wardroom**   n. Commissioned officers' mess and sitting area located in ''officers' country'' on U.S. Navy vessels and almost always contiguous with officers' staterooms.

**warehouse-to-warehouse   clause**
n. A stipulation in marine insurance pol-

icies that covers goods from one warehouse through transit to the final warehouse named in the policy.

**warm air mass**   *n.* An air mass that is warmer than the surrounding air; the term usually implies that the air mass is warmer than the surface over which it is moving.

**warm front**   *n.* The frontal wave of an air mass that replaces colder air; the trailing edge is the cold front.

**warning light**   *n.* An obsolete term for a lighthouse, lightship, lighted buoy, or beacon that marks an obstruction or hazard to navigation.

**warning radio beacon**   *n.* An auxiliary radio beacon located at a lightship to warn vessels of their proximity to the lightship. It is of short range and sounds a warbling note for one minute immediately following the main radio beacon transmission on the same frequency.

**warp**   *n.* (1) A heavy rope used to move vessels short distances in a harbor. (2) Rope used in a bight behind a small boat to slow its speed in heavy seas. "We were able to keep to our downwind course by reducing sail and streaming warps." (3) Lengthwise strands of yarn or thread in cloth or canvas. Also *weft; wheft.* See WOOF.

**warp**   *v.* To move a vessel within its dock or along a quay by using warping lines. "Rather than call a tug, we warped her into place with a dockside donkey engine." In the days of sailing ships, a kedge was often put in a longboat and rowed out to open water where it was dropped over the side. The anchor line was then hauled to warp the vessel out to the open water. This is still a practical way of maneuvering a boat into deep water after grounding.

**warping bridge**   *n.* A bridge at the stern of a ship used only for docking.

**warping buoy**   *n.* A buoy so placed that lines can be fastened to it to move ships from place to place within a harbor.

**warping capstan**   *n.* A power capstan used for handling mooring lines or tow lines. A gipsy can be used for same purpose.

**warping chock**   *n.* Chock used for hauling lines during a warping operation.

**warping tug**   *n.* A tug made from pontoon sections used by amphibious construction teams.

**warping winch**   *n.* A steam or electric winch used for warping a vessel from place to place along a quay or within a harbor.

**warp-laid rope**   *n.* The same as cable-laid but with the primary strand and the finished rope having a shorter lay or tighter twist.

**warrant officer**   *n.* An officer in the U.S. Navy who is senior to all chief petty officers and junior to all commissioned officers. His authority derives from a warrant issued by the Secretary of the Navy. A commissioned warrant officer is the highest grade of warrant officer whose commission is under the authority of the President and confirmed by Congress.

**warranty**   *n.* The assurance by a seller that the goods are exactly as represented or that the goods will be as promised in a contract. In a marine insurance policy, an insurer's obligation is discharged if the conditions are breached.

**warranty of legality**   *n.* An implied warranty in a charter party that the contracted service is a legal one.

**warranty of neutrality**   *n.* An implied warranty in a marine insurance policy, that the ship and cargo have a neutral character and that such character will be sustained during the life of the risk.

**war risk clause** *n.* A clause in marine insurance policies dealing with the risk arising from the consequences of hostilities or belligerent operations. The perils insured under war risks must be due directly to some hostile action. If the peril is a marine risk and is only aggravated by hostile action, the risk is not held to be a war risk.

**warship** *n.* Under international law, a ship that belongs to the armed forces of a state and bears the external marks that distinguish such ships of its nationality, is under the command of an officer duly commissioned by the government of the state and whose name appears in the appropriate service list or its equivalent, and is manned by a crew that is under the discipline of regular armed forces.

**wash** *n.* (1) The heavy turbulence left in the water by a passing vessel; more damaging to nearby property than a wake. (2) The dry bed of an intermittent stream.

**washboard** *n.* (1) A plank above the gunwale around the cockpit of a small open boat that serves to increase the freeboard and reduce the spray. (2) Board in a companionway hatch. Also *washstrakes.*

**wash-deck hose** *n.* A hose connected to a shipboard fireplug and used to wash down the decks.

**wash plates** *n.* Plating fitted in deep tanks and peak tanks to reduce the movement of the water or fuel in them. Also *baffles.*

**wash port** *n.* An opening in a ship's side that allows seawater to drain from the deck. See SCUPPERS.

**washstrake** *n.* A plank that forms the lower part of a bulwark and rests on the covering board.

**waste** *n.* Cotton yarn used for cleaning purposes, usually around the deck gear, machinery, and guns.

**waste heat boiler** *n.* A boiler that uses waste engineering heat for heating water and for heating spaces.

**waste-water boiler** *n.* An auxiliary boiler that provides steam for auxiliary equipment.

**watch** *n.* (1) A period of time on duty; in the U.S. Navy, this usually is 4 hours, though it can vary from ship to ship as conditions warrant. (2) That part of the ship's company that is on duty at any given time. (3) A buoy that marks the anchor so that its position will be known to the anchor watch. The watch schedule used on most U.S. Navy ships is

| | |
|---|---|
| first (evening or night) watch | 2000–2400 |
| midwatch | 0000–0400 |
| morning watch | 0400–0800 |
| forenoon watch | 0800–1200 |
| afternoon watch | 1200–1600 |
| first dog watch | 1600–1800 |
| second dog watch | 1800–2000 |

**watch, quarter, and station bill** *n.* The duty list and billet assignments for the crew of a U.S. Navy ship. The names are listed with the battle stations, cleaning stations, emergency stations, and so on, opposite each name.

**watch and watch** *adj.* A duty schedule that calls for being off only one watch and then back on again. "We'll have to stand watch and watch until the mate is back on his feet." Also *heel and toe.*

**watch below** *n.* The duty section(s) not on watch.

**watch buoy** *n.* An unlighted buoy that marks the position where a lightship should be in case it has wandered from its position.

**watch cap**   *n.* (1) Canvas cover secured over a funnel when not in use. (2) A navy blue knitted wool cap, full enough on the sides that it can be pulled down as far as possible without obscuring vision.

**watch error**   *n.* The difference between the time indicated by a deck or hack watch and Greenwich mean time (GMT) or (UT1) or zone time and labeled F or S for fast or slow.

**watching properly**   *phr.* Said of an aid to navigation that is on station and exhibiting its charted characteristics.

**watch officer**   *n.* The officer taking his turn as officer of the watch, officer of the deck, or engineering officer of the watch. The watch officer is responsible for the safe conduct of the vessel while he has the duty.

**watch stander**   *n.* Any person on watch with a regular assigned duty.

**watch tackle**   *n.* A tackle with a single and double block; the standing part is fastened to the hook on the single block. Also *jigger tackle; luff tackle.*

**watch time (WT)**   *n.* Time indicated by the watch, or hack, used on the bridge by the navigator. It is usually set to zone time or Greenwich mean time.

**water bailiff**   *n.* The British equivalent of the U.S. port authority responsible for the collection of fees and enforcement of shipping regulations.

**water ballast**   *n.* Seawater used as ballast in various tanks about a vessel as a means of maintaining proper trim and draft. See STABILITY.

**water boat**   *n.* Tank vessel used in harbors to deliver fresh water to vessels without desalinization plants or without sufficient desalinization capacity to sustain a voyage. See HOY.

**waterborne**   *adj.* (1) Supported by water and not aground. "As soon as the tide had risen, and we were waterborne, we were underway again." (2) Carried by water, said of cargo and other commercial traffic. (3) Used with regard to goods placed aboard a vessel.

**water bottom**   *n.* A ballast tank located between the tank top plating and the outer bottom.

**water butt**   *n.* A water cask or scuttlebutt.

**watercourse**   *n.* (1) A stream of water. (2) A natural channel through which water runs. (3) Limber holes and waterways in the lower compartments of a ship.

**watercraft**   *n.* General term for all boats and vessels capable of being used for transportation. See VESSEL.

**water drum**   *n.* A round tank at the base of a boiler. Also *mud drum.*

**water hammer**   *n.* A section of condensed steam in a steam line that causes the piping to hammer at the elbows and valves.

**water hole**   *n.* A hole cut in the lower end of a water sail to prevent damage by the sea.

**water-laid rope**   *n.* A three- or four-strand left-hand laid hemp rope made by wetting the fibers with water instead of oil or tallow. It has lower tensile strength than plain-laid cordage, but is more elastic and was used for salvage work and for towing. Water-laid rope has been widely replaced by synthetic fiber.

**waterline (WL)**   *n.* (1) The painted line at or just above the designed waterline by which one can judge whether a vessel is sitting too low in the water or is otherwise out of trim. (2) The intersection of any horizontal plane with the molded form of a ship. See STABILITY.

**waterline model**   *n.* The model of a vessel that represents the external shape at the various levels used in drawing up the vessel's lines.

**waterlogged**   *adj.* (1) Said of a vessel, usually a tender, with too much water in the holds so as to make it sluggish. (2) Used to describe something that is filled or soaked with water but still afloat.

**waterman**   *n.* A boatman, one who works on or around boats, a very general term.

**watermarks**   *n.* Numbers at the bow and stern of ships denoting the draft at the bow and stern. See LOAD LINE MARKS.

**water plane**   *n.* The horizontal cross-sectional view of a vessel at the waterline. There are light water planes, load water planes, and so on.

**water sail**   *n.* A sail set below a lower studding sail boom or passaree boom. Because it frequently dragged in the water, a water hole was cut in the outer end.

**water seasoning**   *n.* A method of seasoning logs to extend their useful life by dissolving foreign matter, especially insects, and excluding the air. It is still done in many parts of the world, including the Pacific Northwest of the United States.

**water service pump**   *n.* A pump designed to circulate cooling water through shaft bearings and crosshead guides.

**watershed**   *n.* An awning or metal shed over a door that prevents spray and rain from entering. See DODGER.

**watersides**   *n.* The sides of boiler tubes where the feedwater is heated by the oil- or coal-fired firesides of the boiler tubing system.

**water sky**   *n.* Clouds in ice fields that reflect the water below on their under-sides. This is the darkest of the several types of sky for which the icebound mariner looks when searching for open water, others are land sky, ice sky, and snow sky.

**water spar**   *n.* A spar rigged in derrick fashion with a snatch block and a whip at the head and from which a bucket could be lowered to catch seawater for washing.

**waters specified by the Secretary**   *phr.* A phrase encountered on U.S. charts and meaning, under the *Navigation Rules,* the Tennessee-Tombigbee Waterway, the Tombigbee River, the Black Warrior River, the Alabama River, the Coosa River, the Mobile River above the Cochrane Bridge at St. Louis Point, the Flint River, the Chattahoochee River, and the Apalachicola River above its confluence with the Jackson River.

**waterspout**   *n.* Small, whirling storm over water; its chief characteristic is its funnel-shaped cloud. As it develops, the base extends from the water to the cumulus cloud with the water generally confined to the lower portion.

**waterstop ring**   *n.* A rubber fitting on the forward face of the propeller boss that prevents seepage of seawater into the after end of the shaft liner.

**water taxi**   *n.* Shore boat or tender available for hire.

**water tender**   *n.* A petty officer who directs the maintenance of necessary steam pressure and maintains the proper level of water in the boilers in steam-powered ships. He also supervises the engine room watch. See BOILER TECHNICIAN.

**watertight**   *adj.* Designed and constructed to withstand a constant stream of water without leakage. Watertight is not as tight as oiltight.

**watertight closure log**   *n.* A log-book in which the openings of watertight closures are recorded. The opening of watertight closures is only done with the permission of the officer of the deck.

**watertight compartment**   *n.* Spaces protected by watertight bulkheads and doors. Water entering one compartment cannot enter the next watertight compartment.

**watertight door**   *n.* A heavily constructed door that is fitted with a gasket and dogs and special closure equipment; when it is dogged, water cannot pass through it even when under pressure. Watertight doors can either be hinged or mounted on slides for being opened either vertically or horizontally.

**watertight hatch**   *n.* A hatch with a steel cover that fits into a gasket on the hatch frame and is dogged to make a tight seal.

**water tower**   *n.* A chart term to indicate a structure that encloses a tank or standpipe.

**watertube boiler**   *n.* A steam plant in which the water is carried in tubes that pass through hot gases. Watertube boilers are lighter and take less space than fire-tube or Scotch boilers.

**waterway**   *n.* (1) A gutter or narrow passage along the edge of a deck for deck drainage. The waterway, in turn, drains into the scuppers. (2) Navigable river, channel, or canal system such as the 3,100-mile Intracoastal Waterway from Anisquam, Mass., to Brownsville, Tex.

**waterway bar**   *n.* Angle iron at the upper deck stringer plate running longitudinally with the gunwale bar to form the waterway. It serves as an abutment for wood deck planking.

**water whip**   *n.* A purchase used from yards to sway aboard loads of moderate weight.

**water wings**   *n.* Derisive nickname for the U.S. Navy's surface warfare insignia.

**wave**   *n.* (1) An undulation of the sea that results in the rise and fall of the water, but not the horizontal movement of the water. Waves result from the local wind, while swells result from more remote conditions. The **wave period** is the time interval between one crest and the next. **Wave height** is measured from the trough to the crest. Waves are named for the direction from which they come; northerly waves move from north to south. See DOUGLAS SCALE. (2) A line of amphibious craft headed for a beach.

**wave, internal**   *n.* A wave along a plane separating two water masses such as are found in a thermocline.

**wave amplitude**   *n.* One-half the distance from the crest of a wave to the trough.

**wave attenuation**   *n.* The diminution of the form or height of a wave with the distance from the wave source.

**wave basin**   *n.* A basin close to an inner harbor entrance in which the waves of the outer harbor are absorbed.

**wave crest**   *n.* The highest part or top of a wave.

**wave height**   *n.* The vertical distance from the trough of a wave and the succeeding crest.

**wavelength**   *n.* The distance between two consecutive crests or troughs, whether of sea or other waves.

**wave period**   *n.* The time between two wave crests.

**wave profile**   *n.* The outline of a wave generated by a vessel traveling a given speed. The wave is fairly constant and important in calculations of hull strength when designing a vessel or in computing its vulnerability to anticipated stresses.

**wave refraction**   *n.* The tendency of a wave to become more parallel to the shoreline as it approaches the shore, caused by the drag of the lower portion of the wave over the ground on that end of the wave closest to the shore.

**wave resistance**   *n.* The drag on the ship's hull caused by formation of waves; the energy so expended is second only to the frictional resistance between hull and water.

**wave velocity**   *n.* The speed with which a wave crest (or trough) travels in a horizontal direction. This can be calculated by dividing the wavelength by the wave period.

**waxing moon**   *n.* Moon in the half-cycle between new and full as the lighted portion increases. See WANING MOON.

**way**   *n.* Speed or progress of a vessel through the water. To **make way** through the water means simply to move through the water; **gathering way** or **losing way** means increasing or decreasing speed through the water. A ship that is **under way** with **no way on** is one that is not aground, not tied to a pier, and not anchored, but that is making no progress through the water.

**way-end pressure**   *n.* Pressure at the ends of the ground ways, both on the ways and against the hull during launching.

**way enough**   *interj.* Order to boat's crew from the coxswain to take one more stroke and then cease rowing because there is sufficient way on to make the destination.

**waypoint**   *n.* A reference point on a track or sea route, especially one where a course or speed change is planned.

**ways**   *n.* Timbers upon which ships are constructed and repaired.

**ways end**   *n.* The lower end of launching ways; the end at the water.

**W − C**   *n.* The time difference between the navigator's watch (W) and the chronometer (C). The difference subtracted or added to the watch equals the chronometer time.

**weapons officer**   *n.* An officer in the U.S. Navy charged with responsibility for a ship's armament. Formerly known as the gunnery officer or gun boss.

**wear**   *v.* To bring a square-rigged ship to the opposite tack by bringing the wind across the ship's stern, the equivalent of jibing a fore-and-aft-rigged vessel.

**weather**   *n.* (1) The state of the atmosphere with regard to clouds, humidity, pressure, temperature, barometric pressure, and other meteorological characteristics. See CLIMATE. (2) The windward side of a vessel. "She sails to weather better than most boats in her class."

**weather**   *v.* (1) To survive, as a storm, with minimal damage. (2) To pass a buoy, landmark, or other object to windward. (3) To place a ship to windward of another when on parallel course so as to steal the wind from the leeward vessel. Also *blanket; cover.*

**weather**   *adj.* (1) Used to describe something exposed to the elements, as a **weather deck**. (2) Of or pertaining to something to windward of a point of reference, as the **weather end** of a starting line, or a vessel's weather quarter.

**weather advisory**   *n.* Warning issued by the U.S. Weather Service and other agencies predicting a change in weather or advising of current conditions. Specific advisories are small-craft advisory, and tornado advisory.

**weatherboards**   *n.* (1) Storm boards placed over outside doors on the weather deck during stormy weather, especially

# Weather Symbols

| | | |
|---|---|---|
| aurora | halo, lunar | sandstorm |
| corona, solar | halo, solar | showers |
| dew | haze, damp | sleet |
| drizzle | haze, dry | smoke |
| dust | ice crystals | snow |
| duststorm | ice fog | snow, blowing |
| fog | lightning, distant | snow, drifting |
| fog, light | rain | snow grains |
| frost | rain and snow, mixed | snow pellets |
| glaze | rainbow | thunderstorm |
| hail | rime, hard | thunderstorm, distant |
| hail, small | rime, soft | visibility exceptional |

## Weather Chart Symbols and Color Code

| Type of front | Symbol | Coloring |
|---|---|---|
| cold front | | blue line |
| warm front | | red line |
| occluded front | | purple line |
| stationary front | | alternate red and blue line |
| upper cold front | | dashed blue line |
| upper warm front | | dashed red line |

on passenger liners. (2) Boards that slide in grooves in a hatch on small craft. See WASHBOARD. (3) Planks placed above the rail of an open boat.

**weather-bound**  *adj.* Held over in port because of unfavorable weather.

**weather breeder**  *n.* A fair day that has the appearance of bad weather to come.

**weather clew**  *n.* (1) The tack of a fore-and-aft sail. (2) The windward clew at the bottom of a square sail.

**weather cloth**  *n.* Shield or awning used to protect crew from weather at lookout stations or before the pilothouse.

**weather deck**  *n.* The uppermost deck of a vessel exposed to the elements.

**weathered**  *adj.* Wind- and seawater-damaged, said of timbers, canvas, and old sailors.

**weathered berg**  *n.* An irregularly shaped iceberg.

**weather end**  *n.* The windward end of a starting line.

**weather eye.**  *n.* An alert eye for change in weather or, by extension, any other situation.

**weatherfax**  *n.* Radio equipment that prints weather maps at sea and elsewhere. This application of the fax machine was common aboard ships long before faxes became popular on land.

**weather gauge**  See GAUGE.

**weather gleam**  *n.* A clearing to windward in storm clouds.

**weather-going current**  *n.* The motion of the water when it flows contrary to the direction of the wind. **Wind over tide** causes a nasty chop.

**weather helm**  *n.* (1) The tendency of a sailing vessel to turn to windward. A vessel with a weather helm is described as **ardent.** (2) The helm necessary to prevent a vessel from going to windward. See LEE HELM.

**weatherliness**  *n.* The capability of a sailing vessel to carry sufficient sail in heavy air to enable it to go to windward. The weatherliness of a vessel is greatest when the center of effort is abaft the center of lateral resistance.

**weatherly**  *adj.* A word of ambiguous meaning used to describe both a vessel (a) able to sail close to the wind against heavy seas without drifting to leeward, and (b) unable to make significant headway against heavy seas when close-hauled. See SEAWORTHY.

**weather main and lee crossjack braces**  *interj.* A square-rigger order to man the gear of the after yards when the helm was put up. The crossjack was the square sail extended below the lowest yard on a mizzenmast. The phrase was associated in most sailors' minds with a close call with a lee shore.

**weather mark**  *n.* The mark that ends the weather leg of a race. See WINDWARD MARK.

**weather permitting**  *phr.* Charter party expression that specifies that lay days do not count against the specified time if they are due to weather conditions that preclude working cargo.

**weather routing**  *n.* The science of routing shipping using weather forecasting directed at minimizing time and damage. The distance sailed may be longer, but storms and high wind and sea action are more apt to be avoided or lessened.

**weather signal**  *n.* A flag hoist and other visual displays on shore that indicate the weather forecast. These are no longer used officially in the United States.

**weather tide**  *n.* (1) A tide that sets to windward. (2) A tide going in the same direction as the wind.

**weathertight**  *adj.* Said of an object that water cannot penetrate in any sea condition.

**weather working days**  *n.* Days on which cargo can be safely handled without being damaged by weather; the term applies only in situations in which cargo is involved that might be damaged by weather.

**weave**  *v.* To zigzag; to make small changes in course for short distances.

**web**  *n.* (1) The vertical portion of a beam. (2) The athwartship portion of a frame.

**web belt**  *n.* A broad cotton belt worn to carry a canteen or handgun. Web belts are also worn by sentries and messengers and other naval personnel as part of their badge of office.

**web frame.**  *n.* A frame with a deep web or flange composed of web plates used for supports at the forward and after ends of hatches. See WEB PLATE.

**web frame system**  *n.* A system of strengthened framing in which every sixth frame is of extra heavy construction.

**web plate**  *n.* A wide girder usually reinforced with angle iron on both sides.

**web sling**  *n.* A cargo sling with sides connected by rope webbing or heavy canvas, used for bagged cargo that would be broken open with ordinary rope slings.

**wedge ram**  *n.* Heavy timber fitted with a steel cap that is used for driving the launching cradle against a ship's hull to assist in knocking out the shores and keel blocks before launching.

**wedge riders**  *n.* Timbers of a launching cradle laid on driving-up wedges.

**wedges**  *n.* Pie-shaped pieces of wood used for driving up or easing the weight of a hull on shores or for tightening a batten against the coaming when battening hatches.

**weep**  *v.* To leak slowly.

**weft**  See WARP.

**weigh**  *v.* To raise, as an anchor or a mast. Once the anchor is clear of the ground, the anchor detail reports to the bridge "Anchor's aweigh." This means that the anchor is clear of the bottom, but not necessarily that it is out of the water.

**weighing line**  *n.* A wire made fast to the crown of an anchor so that the anchor can be recovered if the cable should part, or if the flukes are caught under a rock.

**weir**  *n.* (1) An open fence in a stream or close to shore used to prevent people or sea creatures from going into a place, or to prevent people or sea creatures from leaving a place. They are also used for catching fish. When spoil banks are formed, the spoil can be put in a basin formed in the center of an above-sea-level island. A weir allows the water to drain, but keeps the sediment in the basin. (2) A dam or shunt that forms a millrace.

**welded hull**  *n.* Hull construction in which the greater part of the plating is welded instead of riveted.

**Welin davit**  *n.* A davit whose lower end is in the form of a cogged arc. It is swung out and in by the use of cranks to operate the gears.

**well**  *n.* (1) A cofferdam or a sump in the double bottom to facilitate pumping the bilge. (2) The part of the weather deck between the pilothouse and forecastle. (3) An open space in a landing craft where cargo or personnel are carried.

**well** *interj.* Used as a command to indicate than an order has been done sufficiently and to stand by for further orders. "Well the main halyard" would mean to stop hauling on the halyard, but not necessarily to make it off.

**well deck** *n.* (1) A weather deck fitted with solid bulwarks that impede the drainage of water over the sides. (2) An exposed recess in the weather deck extending one-half or more of the length of the vessel measured over the weather deck.

**well-found** *adj.* Describes a vessel that is well-built, well-supplied, and well-equipped.

**West Australia Current** *n.* A counterclockwise ocean current that flows northward along the west coast of Australia during the Southern Hemisphere's summer. During other times of the year, it becomes unstable and less defined.

**westerly** *n.* (1) An ocean current flowing *toward* the west. (2) A wind blowing *from* the west. See WIND.

**Western Ocean** *n.* British name for North Atlantic.

**Western Rivers** *n.* In the *Navigation Rules,* the Western Rivers refers to the Mississippi River, its tributaries, (including the Missouri and Ohio rivers) South Pass, and Southwest Pass, to the navigational demarcation lines dividing the high seas from harbors, rivers and other inland waters of the United States; the Port Allen-Morgan City Alternate Route; and that part of the Atchafalaya River above its junction with the Port Allen-Morgan City Alternate Route including the Old River and Red River.

**West Greenland Current** *n.* An ocean current that flows from the southern tip of Greenland at Cape Faval northwest along the coast of Greenland.

**westing** *n.* The distance a vessel makes good to the west. See EASTING.

**West Wind Drift** *n.* The ocean current that flows eastward through all the oceans around Antarctica. On its northern edge it is coextensive with the South Atlantic Current, the South Pacific Current, and the South Indian Current. See OCEAN CURRENT.

**wet compass** See SPIRIT COMPASS.

**wet dock** *n.* An enclosed docking area with water gates tight enough to keep the water in and the vessels afloat during periods of low water. When the water rises, the gates are again opened and vessels can go and come at will. Also *wet basin.*

**wet locker** *n.* A closet used for stowing wet foul weather gear and damp clothes.

**wet storage** *n.* A slip in which a boat is stored, as distinct from dry storage in which boats are set up on banks or trailers on land.

**wetsuit** *n.* Tightly fitting foam rubber suit that retains body heat and is worn by divers, surfers, and sailors when working in cold, wet weather or in cold water. The body temperature raises the temperature of the water in the suit to keep the user relatively warm. See DRY SUIT.

**wetted surface** *n.* The total surface of a vessel below the waterline, measured in square feet and used in calculating horsepower and hull resistance.

**whaleback** *n.* (1) Small structure on the stern to protect personnel from breaking seas. (2) A vessel with a humped or rounded topside like the back of a whale, with the engine at the stern; it was popular on the Great Lakes. See CAMBER.

**whaleboat** *n.* A double-ended open rowboat originally used for whaling. Boats similar to those used for whaling are carried aboard merchant ships and naval ships and are generally propelled by a small diesel plant.

**whaler** *n.* (1) A ship engaged in whaling. (2) A temporary brace for a bulkhead or deck section.

**wharf** *n.* A concrete, wood, or steel structure to which vessels can tie up, and built parallel or at an angle to the land. See DOCK; MOLE; PIER; QUAY.

**wharfage** *n.* A fee charged for a vessel to be tied up at a wharf and/or for goods loaded and unloaded.

**wharf boat** *n.* A floating office or warehouse but without self-propelling machinery.

**wharf demurrage** *n.* A fee charged against a vessel or its cargo when either is at the wharf beyond contract time.

**wharfinger** *n.* (pron. wharf-injure) Owner or manager of a wharf.

**wharfman** *n.* A laborer at a wharf who catches lines, ties ships to bollards, secures ladders and gangways, but does not handle cargo. See LONGSHOREMAN.

**wharf superintendent** *n.* A shipping line's representative in charge of the company's wharf.

**wheel** *n.* (1) A ship's steering wheel. (2) The handwheel of a capstan. (3) A propeller.

**wheel** *v.* To turn a fleet of ships so that all ships stay in the same relative position. The ships on the outside go at flank speed, while the ones at the axis only maintain steerage.

**wheel chain** *n.* A chain used for connecting the steering wheel or steering engine with the helm.

**wheelhouse** *n.* A structure built around the helmsman's station; a pilothouse. It contains the various controls for speed and steering, compass, communication equipment for talking with personnel in other parts of the ship as well as radios for communicating with other ships, tugs, and pilots. See BRIDGE.

**wheel rods** *n.* Iron rods that form part of the line of the wheel ropes and chains.

**wheel ropes** *n.* Ropes or cables connecting the steering wheel to the yoke of the rudder.

**wheft** See WAFT.

**whelp** *n.* (1) A rib on a winch barrel or capstan barrel. See CAPSTAN. (2) A tooth of a sprocket wheel.

**where away** *interj.* The answer to a lookout who has reported seeing something of note. "Sail, Ho!" "Where away?" "Broad starboard."

**wherry** *n.* A ship's small rowboat usually fitted for two pairs of oars. Before motor whaleboats, the U.S. Navy used them principally for officers.

**whip** See SCHOONER STAY.

**whip** *v.* To wrap a line with small stuff to prevent raveling or chafing.

**whip and runner** *n.* A whip with a block and pendant; the pendant is rove through a single block.

**whip staff** *n.* A pivoted vertical spar attached at the base to the tiller to give the helmsman some mechanical advantage in steering a ship.

**whip-upon-whip** *n.* A whip clapped on the fall of another whip. See TACKLE.

**whirlpool** *n.* An eddy in a river or in a channel caused by the configuration of the land under it or the land close by. Whirlpools are frequently caused by tide and therefore increase and decrease in magnitude with the tides.

## Whipping

a

a

(a) whipping

**whirlwind**   *n.* A mass of air moving in a circle and spiraling upward. The eye of the whirlwind moves across the water at varying speeds. See WATERSPOUT.

**whisker**   *n.* One of a pair of horizontal spars used on both sides of the bowsprit to spread the jibboom guys. Also *whisker boom.*

**whisker pole**   *n.* A spar used on sailboats to hold the headsail to windward when sailing wing and wing.

**whiskers**   *n.* Crosstrees on a bowsprit.

**Whiskey**   *n.* Phonetic word for the letter "W." Used as a single-letter signal, it means "I require medical assistance."

**whistle**   *n.* A signaling device required on commercial vessels. The frequency, intensity, range of audibility, and other characteristics are determined by the vessel's size and use. See PROLONGED BLAST; SHORT BLAST.

**whistle buoy**   *n.* A navigation buoy fitted with a horn so that it whistles with the wave action. It sounds more like a groan than a whistle and can be quite startling to the watch section if they are not expecting it. Also *whistler; whistling buoy.*

**whitecap**   *n.* Foamy crest of a wave caused by action of the wind at Beaufort force 3. Also *horses' manes; white horses.*

**white hat**   *n.* Slang for enlisted personnel in the U.S. Navy below chief petty officer.

**white ice**   *n.* Same as thin first-year ice.

**white oakum**   *n.* Oakum made from untarred hemp.

**white rope**   *n.* Rope made from untarred hemp used for logs and lead lines.

**white squall**   *n.* Whirlwind of small radius and heavy rain with low visibility but without the usual clouds; peculiar to the tropics. Bowditch doubts the existence of a white squall.

**white water**   *n.* Swiftly flowing, frothy water in river rapids.

**whole gale**   *n.* Beaufort scale reading of 10, with winds of 48–55 knots.

**wickie**   *n.* A U.S. Coast Guard nickname for the crew member responsible for trimming the wicks in aids to navigation in the days of oil-fired aids. Today the lightkeepers in the last of the manned lights are still so called. The name is also used in a pejorative sense for anyone charged with a job that does not require a great deal of intelligence.

**wide berth**   *n.* Ample room. "We need to give the cape a wide berth to avoid the rocks and shoals at the base."

**wigwag**   *n.* Use of hand-held flags for communicating by use of a code; more formally called semaphore. Also used as a verb or adjective; so "We used wig-wag"; "We wigwagged them"; and "We sent a wigwag message."

**wilco**   *interj*. A term that means the message has been received, understood, and will be complied with (*will* comply). See ROGER.

**wild**   *adj*. Out of control, applied to a vessel that is steering with difficulty or to gear that is adrift and rolling about the deck.

**wildcat**   *n*. The sprocket wheel on a windlass for taking links of a chain. See CAPSTAN.

**Williamson turn**   *n*. A maneuver used to recover someone lost over the side. The evolution gives the ship time to turn, stop engines, and arrive at the approximate position it was in when the "Man overboard" alarm was sounded. When the alarm is heard, the helm is put hard over to the side from which the victim fell; the engine speed is maintained until approximately 60° from the original heading. At that point, the rudder is put hard over to the opposite side until the vessel is on the reciprocal course of the original heading. The engines are then stopped and the vessel allowed to drift down to the victim's position dead ahead. Experience has shown that this takes about 5 minutes longer than simply using the standard turning circle, and it has gone into disuse by most captains who prefer to eyeball the situation and keep the man in sight. It was named for World War II Capt. John A. Williamson, USNR. Widely endorsed by the Navy, the maneuver was almost unknown in the merchant service. See MAN OVERBOARD MANEUVER.

**williwaw**   *n*. A sudden, violent gust of wind blowing out to sea from the mountains of the Patagonian Channel and Magellan Strait.

**winch**   *n*. An engine mounted on deck and fitted with one or more drums or gipsies for hauling cable, chain, and so on.

**winch platform**   *n*. A heavily built mast table that serves as the base for cargo winches around a mast.

**wind**   *n*. (rhymes with pinned) A moving air mass with variable speed and direction. Winds are named for the direction from which they blow. A southwesterly wind blows from southwest to northeast.

**wind**   *v*. (pron. wined) To turn a ship around by using mooring lines. "I want to wind her around so that the bow will be heading out of her berth."

**windage**   *n*. (1) Frictional resistance of a boat to the airflow above the surface of the water. (2) Sail area presented to the wind.

**wind bird**   *n*. Nickname for an anemometer.

**windbound**   *adj*. Held in port or at anchor because of adverse winds. See WEATHER-BOUND.

**wind catcher**   *n*. A sheet metal scoop that can be turned to face forward to catch the wind and force it below decks. See WINDSAIL; WIND SCOOP.

**wind current**   *n*. An ocean current caused by an air mass moving steadily across the sea for at least 12 hours. It is also called **Ekman wind current** for Swedish oceanographer and physicist Vagn Walfrid Ekman (1874–1954).

**wind drift**   *n*. General direction of wind disregarding minor shifts.

**wind galls**   *n*. Portions of rainbows.

**wind indicator**   *n*. A device that indicates the wind direction. See ANEMOMETER.

**winding pennant**   *n*. (rhymes with minding) A heavy device made fast to

# Wind Systems

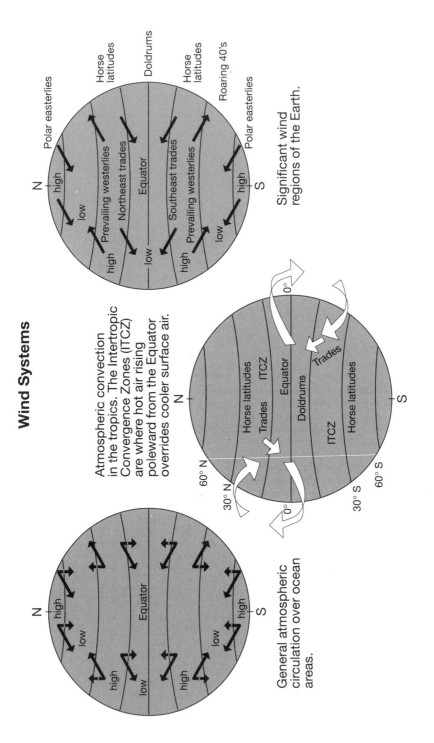

Atmospheric convection in the tropics. The Intertropic Convergence Zones (ITCZ) are where hot air rising poleward from the Equator overrides cooler surface air.

General atmospheric circulation over ocean areas.

Significant wind regions of the Earth.

the lower masthead and then to the yardarm; it is seized to a lizard, which acts as a fairlead. The hoisting tackle is placed in the winding pennant and is used to handle heavy weights.

**winding tackle**   *n.* Tackle formed with one triple block and one double or triple block. It is used to hoist heavy equipment aboard. Rarely heard today.

**wind interference**   *n.* A racing term for the effect of the sails of one boat on the airflow toward the sails of another boat, resulting in a disadvantage to the latter.

**windjammer**   *n.* Large sailing ship, not necessarily a square rigger, but often it is. The term is used today for a sort of seagoing dude ranch for people who want to experience the sailing life with a crew to do the unpleasant stuff.

**windlass**   *n.* A deck engine used for heaving in ground tackle or to warp a ship in port. A drum fitted with ratchet and brake can be worked to hold or haul the chain as desired. Also *capstan.*

**windlass bitts**   *n.* Projecting timbers that support and rise above older model windlasses. Also *carrick heads.*

**windlop**   *n.* Short waves caused by local wind, as distinguished from ocean waves.

**wind over tide**   See WEATHER-GOING CURRENT.

**window**   *n.* An opening in a sail covered with clear material that makes it possible to see through the sail, used especially in small racing boats.

**wind rode**   *adj.* Said of a vessel at anchor that is riding head to the wind and not affected by tidal currents. See TIDE RODE.

**wind rose**   *n.* Any of several meteorological diagrams depicting the average direction and force of the wind for a given period of years. On U.S. pilot charts, the arrows in the rose have chevrons or feathers showing the wind force; the number of chevrons coincide with the Beaufort scale wind speed.

**windsail**   *n.* A fabric funnel used at hatches and ports to catch the wind and shunt it below. See SQUARE-RIGGED VESSEL; WIND CATCHER.

**wind scoop**   *n.* A metal funnel that can be turned in various directions to catch the wind if the ship is in port, or forward if under way. See WIND CATCHER.

**windseeker**   *n.* A lightweight headsail used in light air. Also *drifter.*

**wind's eye**   *n.* ·The direction from which the wind comes. Winds are named for the direction from which they blow, so a south wind is a wind the eye of which is to the south of the observer.

**wind shear**   *n.* (1) Difference in the speed and direction of the wind between the deck and the masthead. (2) The difference in wind speed or direction or both in either a vertical or horizontal plane that results in a shearing effect. This difference can be strong enough to tear the wings off an aircraft.

**wind speed**   *n.* The rate of motion of air. See APPARENT WIND.

**Windsurfer**   *n.* A trade name for a type of sailboard.

**wind vane**   *n.* A device for indicating wind direction. See ANEMOMETER.

**wind velocity**   *n.* The speed and direction of the wind.

**windward.**   *n.* The direction from which the wind blows, upwind. Also used as an adjective and, rarely, an adverb.

**windward flood**   *n.* A flood tide contrary to the wind.

**windward great circle sailing**   *n.* Sailing great circle routing against the wind so that small adjustments from the great circle have to be made to accommodate the wind direction.

**windward mark**   *n.* The mark that ends a windward leg of a race. See WEATHER MARK.

**windward sailing**   *n.* Sailing in an upwind direction, beating as close to the wind as possible.

**windward tide**   *n.* A tide that sets a vessel to windward.

**wind-wave**   *n.* Sea wave produced by the action of wind on the ocean. The size of the wave and the velocity are determined by the velocity of the wind, the duration, and the fetch.

**wing**   See BRIDGE WINGS.

**wing and wing**   *adv.* Describes a vessel with fore-and-aft sails running before the wind, or almost so, with the mainsail on one side and the headsail held out on the other side usually by a whisker pole. Also *wing on wing.*

**wing boards**   *n.* Boards built at an angle and extending down into a coal bunker to prevent shifting.

**wing bracket**   *n.* A large bracket used to fasten a margin plate to a lower frame end. Also *bilge bracket.*

**winger**   *n.* A tier of barrels stowed in the wings of a ship's hold.

**winghouse**   *n.* A small deckhouse at the side of the upper deck that serves as a utility storage area.

**winging**   *n.* The distribution of weights or cargo toward the sides of a vessel to increase the transverse moment of inertia and lengthen the period of roll without jeopardizing the vessel's stability.

**wing passage**   *n.* A passageway along the hull below the waterline on a warship, used for repairs and inspection.

**wings**   *n.* The parts of a hold or a bridge deck near the sides of a ship. See WINGING.

**wing tanks**   *n.* Ballast tanks constructed outboard and beneath the weather deck.

**Winter   Coastal   Countercurrent**   See DAVIDSON CURRENT.

**winter light**   *n.* A light that is maintained during the winter months when the regular light is extinguished. It is of lower candlepower than the regular light, but usually exhibits the same characteristics.

**winter load line**   *n.* A load line with extra freeboard for winter weather conditions. See PLIMSOLL MARK OR LINE.

**winter marker**   *n.* A lighted or unlighted buoy without a sound signal used as a replacement during winter months when other aids are closed or withdrawn.

**wiping**   *n.* The process of reducing the amount of permanent magnetism in a vessel by placing a single energized coil horizontally around the vessel and moving it up and down the sides.

**wire drag**   *n.* Instrument used to survey an uncharted area of the sea for shoals and other impediments. It consists of a weighted wire dragged at a fixed depth.

**wireless**   *n.* Early name for radio.

**wire luff**   *n.* A luff in which a wire rope is used in place of a boltrope when the sail is not bent to a stay.

**wire netting**   *n.* Heavy netting woven from wire and rope used for cargo.

**wire rope** *n.* Rope made of twisted strands of wire. Spring lay wire rope is made with a filler of hemp or synthetic material to increase flexibility and to absorb and disperse lubrication.

**wire sling** *n.* A cargo sling made from wire rope.

**wire stopper** *n.* (1) A deck device used for securing a wire hawser; it consists of two jaws that obviate the use of bitts that would not be appropriate for wire rope. (2) A length of chain shackled to a strong point.

**wishbone** *n.* (1) A supporting rod for the upper platform of an accommodation ladder. (2) A sprit or boom consisting of two spars connected to the mast with goosenecks and to each other, at the after ends, by a crosspiece. The sail is hauled out between the two spars, and the clew is secured to the crosspiece. Designed by N. G. Herreschoff in 1933, the wishbone has been revived for use on sailboards.

**with average** *phr.* Marine underwriter's term that means both particular and general average claims are included. The opposite is free of average.

**withdrawn** *adj.* Said of a floating aid taken out of service during severe ice conditions or for the season.

**withe** *n.* (pron. with) A band on a yard with a fitting for another spar to be run through, such as a studding sail boom. Also *wythe.*

**with-the-sun** *adj.* Clockwise, or from east to west, used to describe right-hand lay rope. From lower left to upper right. See Z-TWIST.

**wolf pack** *n.* A coordinated attack team of two or more submarines.

**woodlock** *n.* Wood plug tightly inserted below a pintle to keep the rudder from unshipping.

**woof** *n.* The transverse strand of yarn or thread in cloth or canvas. See WARP.

**woold** *v.* (rhymes with cold) (1) To wrap chain or rope around a scarf to make the union more secure. (2) To repair a broken spar by lashing it together at the break. The lashing—or **woolding**—is tightened by using a small pin called a **woolder** to twist the lashing.

**wooldlock** *n.* A wooden block beneath the pintles of a rudder to prevent it from unshipping.

**work** *v.* (1) To loosen at the seams or between plates, causing leaks and squeaks, usually the result of strain in heavy seas. (2) Used to describe the action of cargo that is not sufficiently secure under similar circumstances. (3) To beat to windward, as in to work to windward. (4) To handle a ship by engines or by sails without relying on the rudder, or in conjunction with the rudder. **Working ship** is usually only necessary in very tight situations.

**workaway** *n.* A laborer who signs on to work his passage from one port to another.

**workboat** *n.* A small vessel used for harbor and nearby offshore chores.

**working anchorage** *n.* An anchorage where ships lie to discharge cargoes overside to coasters or lighters.

**working canvas** See WORKING SAILS.

**working jib** *n.* A general-purpose headsail with minimum overlap to slow down tacks and the area of which occupies about 100% of the foretriangle.

**working lights** *n.* Lights used on deck while working at night. See DECK LIGHTS.

**working lines** *n.* Another name for mooring lines or docking lines.

**working party** *n.* A detail assigned to a special job.

**working pool** *n.* An area of navigable water in a field of ice.

**working sails** *n.* Sails used in ordinary weather for a particular area. They are not as heavy as storm sails, nor as light as light air sails. Working sails for a boat that sails on San Francisco Bay would be heavier than those used on a similar boat in the Gulf of Mexico. See WORKING JIB.

**working topsail** *n.* A topsail that is carried in a fresh breeze on fore-and-aft-rigged vessels.

**working to windward** *n.* Working toward the direction from which the wind is coming by using a series of tacks. See BEAT; TACK.

**World Geographic Reference System (GEOREF)** A reference system for reporting and plotting the positions of ships and aircraft. GEOREF can be applied to any map or chart marked in latitude and longitude with Greenwich as the prime meridian, regardless of the projection.

**World Marine Weather Broadcast** *n.* A joint publication of the National Weather Service and the Naval Weather Service Command that provides information on marine weather broadcasts in all areas of the world.

**Worldwide Navigational Warning Service (WWNWS)** *n.* An agency established by the International Hydrographic Organization and the Intergovernmental Maritime Consultative Organization to broadcast by radio information on hazards to navigation that might endanger international shipping.

**worm** *v.* To fill the spiral contlines of a rope with tarred small stuff, called **worming,** to make the rope more water-resistant. See PARCEL; SERVE; WHIP.

**worm gear** *n.* A gear that consists of a large screw that turns another gear by intermeshing the screw threads with the slots of the second gear. A worm gear is quieter in operation and usually faster than most other types of gears. Often used on deck winches for hauling ground tackle.

**wreck** *n.* A vessel that has been badly damaged, sunk, or cast up on a shore. In admiralty law, a wreck is a part of a vessel or its cargo thrown up on the land by the sea. Marine underwriters consider a vessel a wreck when it has been so disabled as to be unmanageable and unnavigable.

**wreckage** *n.* Debris from a wreck. Goods thrown up on shore from a wreck. See FLOTSAM; JETSAM.

**wreck buoy** *n.* A buoy painted with red and white stripes and marking a wreck. Abbreviated Wrk on charts.

**wrecker** *n.* (1) One who makes a practice of illegally moving lights along the shore to mislead mariners and to cause them to wreck their ships—a practice common in the 19th-century Florida Keys, and similar areas of the world. (2) One who makes a living legally salvaging vessels. Also *salvor.*

**wrecking cable** *n.* Hawser-laid cable 14 to 16 inches in circumference.

**wrecking tug** *n.* Vessel with heavy engines, pumps, hull structure, associated beach gear, and so on, used for salvage work.

**wreck master** *n.* Person in charge of a salvaging operation. Commonly called a **salvage master.**

**wriggle** *n.* Metal lip over a port to shield it from water coming down the sides of a vessel; an eye brow.

**writ of prohibition** *n.* Admiralty term that refers to a higher court's advising a lower court to cease proceeding in a case outside its jurisdiction.

**wrong direction alarm**   *n.* A device that signals that the engine order telegraph and the hand throttle are not going in the same direction. The alarm is sounded if the hand throttle is in the AHEAD position and the engine order telegraph is in the ASTERN position, or vice versa.

**wrought mat**   See PAUNCH.

**wythe**   See WITHE.

# X

**X**   See X-RAY.

**x-axis**   *n.* (1) A horizontal axis in a system of coordinates. (2) A reference line on a map, chart, or graph on which distances to the right and left, or east and west, are marked.

**xebec**   *n.* (pron. zeebeck) A type of three-masted Mediterranean coaster that was used by the Barbary corsairs. They ranged from 30 to 60 tons.

**X-ray**   *n.* Phonetic word for the letter "X." Used in a single-letter signal, it means "Stop carrying out your intentions and watch for my signals."

# Y

**Y**   See YANKEE.

**yacht**   *n.* (pron. yot) Generic term for any vessel used exclusively for the personal pleasure of the owner or charter. It comes from the Dutch word *jaghtschip* or chase ship, a workboat and not a pleasure craft. Yachts first appeared in English waters as pleasure craft in 1660 when two such Dutch vessels were presented to Charles II. See CORINTHIANS.

**yacht canvas**   See SAIL CLOTH.

**yacht club**   *n.* A private organization of people interested in boating and socializing with others of similar interests.

**yacht ensign**   *n.* A flag used on United States yachts that has the red and white stripes of the national ensign, but with a fouled anchor in the center of a circle of 13 stars in the union. The yacht ensign was adopted by the United States Congress and may be saluted upon departure from the yacht; when dipped as a salute, warships will return the salute. When a yacht is taken beyond the continental limits of the United States, the national ensign should be flown instead of the yacht ensign.

**yachtsman's anchor**   *n.* See ANCHOR.

**Yankee**   *n.* Phonetic word for the letter "Y." Used as a single-letter signal, it means "I am dragging anchor."

**yankee jib topsail**   *n.* A racing topsail with a luff that extends from bowsprit to masthead. When in vogue, it was cut on the diagonal, had a wire luff, and was set on a topmast stay. See GOLLY-WOBBLER.

**yard**  *n.* A spar set perpendicular to the mast for setting square sails. Yards are moved up and down the mast by slings and lifts, and crew work out along the yard while standing on rope harnesses suspended from the yard by stirrups. See SQUARE-RIGGED VESSEL.

**yard-and-stay method**  *n.* A method of handling cargo in which the **hatch boom** is fixed or spotted over the hatch, and the **yard boom** is spotted over the pier; the cargo whips are shackled to one hook. The guys and preventers and the midship guy between the two boom ends or **link bands** are set up and made fast. The cargo handling can then begin. The yard boom was originally a yardarm tackle over the side, and the stay tackle was on the mainstay or preventer.

**yardarm**  *n.* The tapered end of a yard on a square-rigged vessel, as distinct from the entire yard.

**yardarm sling**  *n.* The attachment that holds a yard to a mast.

**yardarm-to-yardarm**  *phr.* Said of ships tied up alongside each other with yardarms all but touching.

**yard becket**  *n.* A grommet fastened to a yard used as a handhold or foothold by men working aloft.

**yardbird**  *n.* (1) A shipyard worker, usually a retired seaman who has swallowed the anchor. (2) Slang for a low-ranking enlisted man who shows little aptitude for his work.

**yard boom**  *n.* A cargo boom that is swung over the sides for handling cargo.

**yard craft**  *n.* Tugs, barges, tenders, and other vessels used in a dockyard.

**yard crane**  *n.* A steel arm at the forepart of a mast or mast cap that is hinged to move horizontally; it is used to support lower topsails or lower topgallant yards.

**yardmaster**  *n.* A dockyard foreman who supervises material-handling equipment and operations.

**yard rope**  *n.* A rope used for handling yards and kept rove off at the masthead.

**yard tackle**  *n.* Equipment used to hoist boats and other heavy gear in and out. Yard tackles were used in conjunction with a stay tackle and fastened to a lower yard when the lower yard was used as a derrick.

**yard whip**  *n.* A cargo whip attached to the end of a yard of a derrick boom, used for swinging a cargo sling in and out.

**yare**  *adj.* (rhymes with care) Easily maneuverable, responsive, lively, said of a vessel.

**yarn**  *n.* Fibers of a material loosely twisted together. Yarn differs from **thread** in that yarns are loosely twisted. See ROPE.

**yaw**  *v.* One of the six motions of a vessel, to yaw is to deviate from course because of poor helmsmanship, waves, or poor sail management. Yawing can be especially difficult to prevent when running before the wind or quartering seas. "Heavy seas caused us to yaw badly."

**yawl**  *n.* (1) A sailing vessel with two masts, the after mast being much shorter and stepped abaft the rudder stock. Easily confused with a ketch, which has the after mast stepped forward of the rudder stock. The after mast is called a jigger, mizzen, or a dandy. See RIG. (2) A double-ended rowboat such as a lifeboat with pointed bow and stern, or a Norway yawl with flat bow and stern. (3) A warship's boat, carvel-built and resembling a pinnace.

**yellow jack**   n. Nickname for the "Q" flag, the quarantine flag.

**yeoman (YN)**   n. A petty officer in the U.S. Navy trained for ship's clerical and secretarial work. In the Royal Navy, the yeoman for signals is the equivalent of a quartermaster in the U.S. Navy.

**yoke**   n. (1) A frame or bar connected to the rudderhead usually by a key; cables connect the yoke and rudderhead to the steering mechanism on deck. (2) A U-shaped metal bar secured to the center of a yard and the corresponding truss.

**yoke line**   n. One of the cables attached to the end of the yoke by which the rudder is moved in small boats.

**York-Antwerp Rules**   n. The first uniform basis for adjusting general average marine insurance claims. The first meeting was held in York in 1864, followed by one in Antwerp in 1877. Later revisions took place at conferences in Liverpool (1890), Genoa (1892), Antwerp (1903), and Stockholm (1924). Adjustments to general average claims are usually made according to the 1924 revisions. The maritime nations continue to update the York-Antwerp Rules from time to time.

**young coastal ice**   n. The initial stage of fast ice formation with nilas or young ice, its width varying from a few meters up to 100 or even 200 meters from the shoreline.

**young ice**   n. Sea ice that has attained a thickness of from 10 to 30 centimeters and is in transition between nilas and first-year ice.

# Z

**Z**   See ZULU.

**Z-bar**   n. A structural shape for which the cross section resembles the letter "Z." It is used as a stiffener for plating and bulkheads.

**Z-card**   See   MERCHANT   MARINER'S DOCUMENT; SEAMAN'S PASSPORT.

**zenith (Z)**   n. The point on the celestial sphere directly above the observer. The point 180° from the nadir.

**zenith distance**   n. The complementary angle to the altitude; that is, 90° minus the altitude equals the zenith. The angular distance from the center of a heavenly body to the zenith.

**zephyr**   n. A gentle west wind.

**zero**   v. (1) To reset the index on an instrument or a piece of machinery. (2) To adjust a compass's compensating magnets so that they have no effect on the compass, and any effect must come from external forces. This is done well away from the vessel and other iron work. Compasses are usually shipped with the magnets already set at zero or zeroed.

**zigzag**   adj. Describes a course using a series of short variations from the base course. Zigzagging is a form of evasive steering used to confuse submarines.

**zigzag riveting**   n. Two or more rows of rivets spaced so that the rivets of one row are offset against those of the next.

**zigzag stitching**   n. A method of sewing strong lap joints of cloth.

**zincs**   *n.* The zinc rings or plates placed on the propeller shaft or hull outboard of the vessel to prevent its being eaten away by galvanic action. If there are stray electric charges in the vessel or near the vessel that would cause such corrosive action, the zincs are sacrificed instead of the propeller, bearings, hull, engine, or valves. See SACRIFICIAL ANODE.

**zodiac**   *n.* (1) A band of the celestial sphere extending 9° on either side of the ecliptic and divided into 12 equal parts called by the signs of the zodiac; this is the path of the Sun, Moon, and navigational planets. (2) The trade name for an especially heavy-duty inflatable raft; always capitalized.

**zonda**   *n.* A hot wind off the pampas of Argentina.

**zone description (ZD)**   *n.* The correction applied to an observer's time to obtain the corresponding Greenwich mean time, now called UT1 or UTC. See UNIVERSAL TIME.

**zone inspection**   *n.* The practice of assigning a zone of a large, modern ship to an officer and an inspection party. Frequently the commanding officer will join one of the zone inspection parties. On smaller ships, the captain inspects the entire ship, but that is not practicable on larger ships.

**zone meridian**   *n.* The meridian used for reckoning zone time. This is usually the nearest meridian divisible by 15°. The daylight saving meridian is 15° east of the standard zone meridian.

**zone noon**   *n.* The local mean time of a reference or zone meridian with time kept throughout a designated zone. See LOCAL APPARENT NOON.

**zone time**   *n.* The time used by all ships at sea within 7.5° on each side of a meridian. Each contiguous zone differs by exactly 1 hour from the next. Ship's clocks are set to zone time, which is based on the number of zones away from Greenwich meridian. Greenwich mean time (GMT) or universal time (UT) is the zone time of Greenwich, England, the 0° meridian.

**Z-twist**   *n.* Another name for right-hand lay, the commonest lay in which stranded rope is twisted; the opposite of S-twist. See WITH-THE-SUN; ROPE.

**Zulu**   *n.* Phonetic word for letter "Z." Used as a single-letter signal, it means "I require a tug" or "Fishing: shooting nets."

**Zulu time**   *n.* Greenwich mean time (GMT). Each time zone of the world is assigned a phonetic alphabet word. Instead of starting with Greenwich as Alfa zone, the system ends with Greenwich as Zulu zone.

# ABBREVIATIONS

| | |
|---|---|
| AB | able seaman |
| ACB | amphibious construction battalion; ice breaker |
| ACDS | advanced combat direction system |
| ADAC | Acoustic Data Analysis Center |
| ADCOM | administrative command |
| ADM | admiral |
| AGS | surveying ship |
| AH | hospital ship |
| AIP | air-independent propulsion system |
| ALNAV | all-Navy message |
| AMVER | Automated Mutual-Assistance Vessel Rescue System |
| AO | fuel tanker, oiler |
| ARPA | automatic radar plotting aids |
| ARPD | automatic radar plotting discs |
| ASDIC | Antisubmarine Detection Investigation Committee |
| ASK | automatic station keeping system |
| ASW | antisubmarine warfare |
| ATL | actual total loss |
| AWOL | absent without leave |
| | |
| B/L | bill of lading |
| BARCAP | barrier combat air patrol |
| BB | battleship |
| BHP | brake horsepower |
| BTU | British thermal unit |
| BUSANDA | Bureau of Supplies and Ships |
| | |
| C | centigrade; course |
| CA | heavy cruiser |
| CAPT | captain |
| CB | construction battalion (seabee) |
| CBT | clean ballast tanks |
| CC | tactical command ship |
| CDR | commander |
| CE | center of effort |
| CEP | circular probable error |
| CG | center of gravity; guided-missile cruiser |
| CGN | guided-missile cruiser, nuclear-powered |
| CIC | combat information center |
| CIF | cost, insurance, freight |
| CINC | commander-in-chief |
| CINCLANT | commander-in-chief Atlantic Fleet |
| CINCPAC | commander-in-chief Pacific fleet |
| CL | light cruiser |
| CLG | guided-missile light cruiser |

| | |
|---|---|
| CLR | center of lateral resistance |
| CMDR | commander |
| CMG | course made good |
| Cn | course |
| CNO | Chief of Naval Operations |
| CO | commanding officer |
| COLREGS | Convention on the International Regulations for Preventing Collisions at Sea |
| COM | commander (of a specific command) |
| COMMO | commodore |
| COS | central operating system |
| CPA | closest point of approach |
| CPE | circular probable error |
| CPO | chief petty officer |
| CQR | secure (anchor type) |
| CTL | constructive total loss |
| CV | aircraft carrier |
| CVA | attack aircraft carrier |
| CVAN | attack aircraft carrier, nuclear-powered |
| CVS | ASW-support aircraft carrier |
| | |
| DD | destroyer |
| DDG | guided-missile destroyer |
| DE | destroyer escort |
| DISP | displacement |
| DIW | dead in the water |
| DR | dead reckoning |
| DRT | dead-reckoning tracer |
| DSRV | deep-submergence rescue vehicle |
| DTG | date-time group |
| DWL | design water line |
| DWT | deadweight tonnage |
| | |
| ECM | electronic countermeasures |
| EDO | engineering duty officer |
| EEOW | engineering officer of the watch |
| EEZ | exclusive economic zone |
| EFPH | equivalent full-power hours |
| EFZ | exclusive fishing zone |
| EHP | effective horsepower |
| ENS | ensign |
| EOOW | engineering duty officer of the watch |
| EPIRB | emergency positioning indicating radio beacon |
| EqT | equation of time |
| ET | electronics technician |
| ETA | estimated time of arrival |
| ETC | estimated time of completion |
| ETD | estimated time of departure |
| | |
| F | Fahrenheit; freshwater load line |
| FADM | fleet admiral |
| FBM | fleet ballistic missile |
| FCC | Federal Communications Commission |

| | |
|---|---|
| FFG | guided missile frigate |
| FFR | radar picket frigate |
| FIFO | first-in—first-out |
| FOB | free on board |
| FOC | flag of convenience |
| FP | shipfitter |
| FRAM | fleet modernization and repair program |
| FRP | fiber-reinforced plastic |
| FT | fire control technician |
| FWE | finished with engines |
| | |
| G | center of buoyancy |
| GARP | Global Atmospheric Research Program |
| GAT | Greenwich apparent time |
| GCLWD | Gulf Coast low-water datum |
| GCT | Greenwich civil time |
| GEOREF | World Geographic Reference System |
| GHA | Greenwich hour angle |
| GLORIA | geographic long-range inclined ASDIC |
| GM | gunner's mate; metacentric height |
| GMT | Greenwich mean time |
| GPS | global positioning system |
| GRT | gross registered tonnage |
| GZ | upsetting arm |
| | |
| HHW | higher high water |
| HLW | higher low water |
| Ho | observed altitude |
| H.O. | Hydrographic Office |
| HP | horsepower; boiler horsepower |
| HT | hull technician |
| HUK | hunter-killer force |
| HW | high water |
| HWF&C | high-water full and change |
| | |
| IALA | International Association of Lighthouse Authorities |
| ICW | intracoastal waterway |
| IFS | fire support ship, inshore |
| IHB | International Hydrographic Bureau |
| IHO | International Hydrographic Organization |
| IHP | indicated horsepower |
| IMCO | Intergovernmental Maritime Consultative Organization |
| IMO | International Maritime Organization |
| IMS | international measurement system |
| INM | international nautical mile |
| INS | integrated navigation system |
| IOR | International Offshore Rule |
| ITCZ | intertropical convergence zone |
| ITU | International Telecommunication Union |
| IYRU | International Yacht Racing Union |
| | |
| JAN grid | joint Army and Navy grid system |
| JOOD | junior officer of the deck |

| | |
|---|---|
| K | Kelvin scale |
| km | kilometer |
| kHz | kilohertz |
| KM | height of metacenter |
| | |
| LAN | local apparent noon |
| LASH | lighter aboard ship |
| LAT | local apparent time |
| LCC | amphibious command ship |
| LCDR | lieutenant commander |
| LDO | limited duty officer |
| LHA | local hour angle; amphibious assault ship (general purpose) |
| LHW | lower high water |
| LIEUT | lieutenant |
| LKA | attack cargo ship |
| LLW | lower low water |
| Lm | middle latitude |
| LMT | local mean time |
| LNB | large navigational buoy |
| LNG | liquefied natural gas |
| LOA | length overall |
| LOP | line of position |
| LORAD | long-range activation detection system |
| LORAN | long-range navigation system |
| LOT | load on top |
| LPD | amphibious transport dock |
| LPH | amphibious assault ship |
| LSD | dock landing ship |
| LSMR | rocket ship |
| LST | tank landing ship |
| LT | lieutenant |
| LCDR | lieutenant commander |
| LTJG | lieutenant, junior grade |
| LW | lower water |
| LWD | lower water datum |
| LWL | waterline length; load waterline |
| | |
| M | metacenter; transverse metacenter |
| MAA | master-at-arms |
| MAD | magnetic airborne detector |
| MARPOL | International Convention on the Prevention of Marine Pollution by Dumping of Wastes and Other Matter |
| Mb | millibar |
| MCB | mobile construction battalion |
| MCPO | master chief petty officer |
| MCPON | Master Chief Petty Officer of the Navy |
| MCS | mine countermeasures ship |
| MEREP | merchant ship report |
| MERINT | merchant intelligence report |
| MGB | motor gunboat |
| MHW | mean high water |
| MHWN | mean high-water neaps |
| MHWS | mean high-water springs |

| | |
|---|---|
| MHz | megahertz |
| MIDAS | maritime industrial development area |
| MLLW | mean lower low water |
| MLS | military sealift command |
| MLW | mean low water |
| MLWN | mean low-water neaps |
| MLWS | mean low-water springs |
| MM | machinist's mate |
| MMD | merchant mariner's document |
| MOS | military occupational specialty |
| MRC | movement report center |
| MRO | movement report office |
| MRS | movement report system |
| MSB | minesweeping boats |
| MSC | Military Sealift Command |
| MSD | marine sanitation device |
| MSL | mean sea level |
| MSTS | Military Sea Transport Service |
| MTB | motor torpedo boat |
| | |
| NAF | naval air facility |
| NAS | naval air station |
| Navicert | navigation certificate |
| NAVSTAR | Navy Navigation Satellite System |
| NAYRU | North American Yacht Racing Union |
| NCO | noncommissioned officer |
| NEC | Navy enlisted classification code |
| nm | nautical mile |
| NOAA | National Oceanic and Atmospheric Administration |
| NOMAD | Navy oceanographic and meteorological automatic device |
| NOS | National Ocean Service |
| NRT | net registered tonnage |
| NSFO | Navy standard fuel oil |
| NUC | Navy Unit Commendation |
| NWS | National Weather Service |
| | |
| OBO | ore-bulk-oil carrier |
| OC | officer candidate |
| OD | ordinary seaman |
| OOD | officer of the deck |
| OOW | officer of the watch |
| OPNAV | naval operations staff under CNO |
| OTSR | optimum track ship routing |
| | |
| PA | position approximate |
| PC | submarine chaser |
| PD | position doubtful |
| PDL | pass down the line |
| PFD | personal flotation device |
| PGC | per gyrocompass |
| PGR | precision graphic recorder |
| PHRF | performance handicap racing fleet |
| PIM | point of intended movement |

| | |
|---|---|
| PO | petty officer |
| PPI | plan position indicator |
| PPT | parts per thousand |
| PSC | per standard compass |
| PSI | pounds per square inch |
| | |
| QM | quartermaster |
| | |
| RACON | radar beacon |
| RADM | rear admiral |
| RATAN | radio and television aids to navigation |
| RDF | radio direction finder |
| RO–RO | roll on–roll off |
| ROC | Reserve Officer Candidate program |
| ROTC | Reserve Officer Training Corps |
| RPM | revolutions per minute |
| RT | radiotelephone |
| RTTY | radioteletype |
| | |
| S | summer load line, seawater |
| SA | sail area; seaman apprentice |
| SAE | Society of Automotive Engineers |
| SAR | search and rescue |
| SATNAV | satellite navigation |
| SBM | single-buoy mooring |
| SC | submarine chaser |
| SCPO | senior chief petty officer |
| SEBS | submarine emergency buoyancy system |
| SECNAV | Secretary of the Navy |
| SELF | submarine extremely low frequency radio |
| SERVFOR | service force |
| SES | surface effect ship |
| SHA | sidereal hour angle |
| SHIPALT | ship alteration |
| SHOPAT | shore patrol |
| SHORAN | short-range navigation system |
| SHP | shaft horsepower |
| SINS | ship's inertial navigation system |
| SIU | Seamen's International Union |
| SIV | special interest vessel |
| SK | storekeeper |
| SLEP | Service Life Extension Program |
| SMG | speed made good |
| SN | seaman |
| SOA | speed of advance |
| SOFAR | sounding, fixing, and ranging signal |
| SOG | speed over the ground |
| SOLAS | International Convention for the Safety of Life at Sea |
| SONAR | sound navigation and ranging |
| SOPA | senior officer present afloat |
| SORD | submerged ordnance recovery device |
| SOSSUS | sound surveillance system |
| SP | shore patrol |

| SPM | single-point mooring |
| SR | seaman recruit |
| SRM | speed of relative movement |
| SS | steamship; submarine |
| SSBN | fleet ballistic-missile submarine |
| SSG | guided-missile submarine |
| SSGN | guided-missile submarine, nuclear powered |
| SSN | submarine, nuclear-powered |
| SWL | safe working load |

| T | tropical load line, seawater |
| TAI | international atomic time |
| TAR | Training and Administration of the Naval Reserve |
| TD | time difference |
| TEU | twenty-foot equivalent unit |
| TF | tropical load line, freshwater |
| TM | torpedoman's mate |
| TO | table of organization |
| TRS | tropical revolving storm |
| TSS | traffic separation scheme |

| U | unwatched (buoy) |
| ULCC | ultralarge crude carrier |
| UNCLOS | United Nations Conference on the Law of the Sea |
| UNREP | underway replenishment |
| UPS | universal plotting sheet |
| USCG | United States Coast Guard |
| USMMA | United States Merchant Marine Academy |
| USN | United States Navy |
| USNI | United States Naval Institute |
| USNR | United States Naval Reserve |
| USNS | United States Naval ship |
| USPS | United States Power Squadron |
| USS | United States ship |
| USYRU | United States Yacht Racing Union |
| UT | universal time |
| UTC | universal coordinated time |

| VADM | vice admiral |
| VCG | vertical center of gravity |
| VERTREP | vertical replenishment |
| VHF | very high frequency |
| VLCC | very large crude carrier |
| VPR | virtual plan position indicator reflectorscope |
| VTS | vessel traffic services |

| W | winter load line |
| WL | waterline |
| WNA | winter load line, North Atlantic |
| WT | watch time |
| WWNWS | World Wide Navigational Weather Warning Service |

| XO | executive officer |

| YN | yeoman |
|----|--------|
| z  | zenith distance |
| Z  | azimuth angle; zenith |
| ZD | zone description |
| Zn | azimuth; true azimuth |
| ZT | zone time |

# BIBLIOGRAPHY

*American Heritage Dictionary of the English Language.* Boston, Massachusetts: Houghton Mifflin Company, 1981.

Ashley, Clifford W. *The Ashley Book of Knots.* Garden City, New York: Doubleday & Company, 1944.

Biddlecombe, George, Captain R.N. *The Art of Rigging.* London, England: Norrie & Wilson, 1848. Based on an earlier work by David Steele in 1794. In 1969 "Biddlecombe" was reprinted by Edward L. Sweetman Company, New York.

Blackburn, Graham. *The Overlook Illustrated Dictionary of Nautical Terms.* Woodstock, New York: The Overlook Press, 1981.

Bowditch, Nathaniel. *American Practical Navigator,* Volumes I and II. Washington, D.C.: Defense Mapping Agency's Hydrographic/Topographic Center, 1975 and 1981.

Bradford, Gershom. *A Glossary of Sea Terms.* New York, New York: Yachting, Inc., 1927.

Brittin, Burdick H. *International Law for Seagoing Officers,* 4th edition. Annapolis, Maryland: Naval Institute Press, 1984.

*\*Bulletin,* the U.S. Coast Guard magazine, various monthly editions.

Chapman, Charles F. *Piloting, Seamanship, Small Boat Handling,* 54th edition. New York, New York: Hearst Books, 1979.

Cope, Harley, RAdm USN (Ret.). *The Naval Officer's Manual.* Harrisburg, Pennsylvania: Military Service Publishing Company, 1951.

Daniels, Edwin H., Jr., Lt. U.S.C.G. *Eagle Seamanship, A Manual for Square-Rigger Sailing,* 3rd edition. Originally written by William I. Norton, U.S.C.G.R., 1969. Annapolis, Maryland: Naval Institute Press, 1990.

DeKerchove, René. *International Maritime Dictionary.* Princeton, New Jersey: D. Van Nostrand Company, Inc., 1961.

Dunlap, G. D. and H. H. Shufeldt. *Dutton's Navigation and Piloting,* 12th edition. Annapolis, Maryland: United States Naval Institute, 1969.

Falconer, W. *An Universal Dictionary of the Marine.* A new corrected edition. London, England: 1780. Reprinted by Newton Abbot, 1970.

Farnsworth, B. A. and Larry C. Young. *Nautical Rules of the Road, the International and Inland Rules,* 3rd edition. Centreville, Maryland: Cornell Maritime Press, 1990.

Farrar, Frank F., Captain. *A Ship's Log Book,* edited by Dorothy Maxwell. St. Petersburg, Florida: Great Outdoors Publishing Co., 1988.

Forester, C. S. *The Captain from Connecticut.* Boston, Massachusetts: Little, Brown and Company, 1941.

Garyantes, H. F. *Handbook for Shipwrights.* New York, New York: McGraw-Hill, 1944.

Illingworth, Valerie. *The Facts on File Dictionary of Astronomy.* New York, New York: Facts On File, 1986.

Knight, Austin. *Modern Seamanship,* 10th edition. New York, New York: D. Van Nostrand Company, Inc., 1942.

La Dage, John. *Stability and Trim for the Ship's Officer,* 3rd edition, edited by William E. George. Centreville, Maryland: Cornell Maritime Press, 1983.

Langenkamp, R. D. *Handbook of the Oil Industry Terms and Phrases,* 3rd edition. Tulsa, Oklahoma: PennWell Publishing Company, 1981.

Lowry, Lt. Comdr. R.N. *The Origins of Some Naval Terms and Customs.* Paulton (Somerset) and London, England: Purnell & Sons, 1918.

Maloney, Elbert S. *Chapman, Piloting Seamanship and Boat Handling,* 58th edition. New York, New York: Hearst Marine Books, 1987.

Maloney, Elbert S. *Dutton's Navigation & Piloting,* 13th edition. Annapolis, Maryland: Naval Institute Press, 1978.

Martin, Ben. *Shipmaster's Handbook on Ship's Business.* Centreville, Maryland: Cornell Maritime Press, 1969.

McEwen, William A., Captain and Alice Lewis. *Encyclopedia of Nautical Knowledge.* Centreville, Maryland: Cornell Maritime Press, 1985.

Morison, Samuel Eliot, RAdm USNR (Ret.). *Admiral of the Ocean Sea.* Boston, Massachusetts: Little, Brown and Company, 1942.

National Oceanic and Atmospheric Administration, *Chart No. 1, United States of America: Nautical Chart Symbols, Abbreviations and Terms,* 9th edition. Washington, D.C.: U.S. Department of Commerce, 1990.

Newport News Shipbuilding and Dry Dock Company, *Blueprint Reading for Hull Trades,* self-published, no date.

Noel, John V., Jr., Captain, USN (Ret.), ed. *Knight's Modern Seamanship,* 16th edition. New York, New York: Van Nostrand Reinhold Company, 1977.

Noel, John V., Jr., Captain, USN (Ret.). *The VNR Dictionary of Ships and the Sea.* New York, New York: Van Nostrand Reinhold Company, 1981.

Noel, John V., Jr., Captain, USN (Ret.) and Edward L. Beach, Captain, USN (Ret.). *Naval Terms Dictionary,* 5th edition. Annapolis, Maryland: Naval Institute Press, 1988.

Office of the Federal Register, *Code of Federal Regulations, Title 46: Shipping.* Washington, D.C.: National Archives and Records Administration, 1992.

*One-Design & Offshore Yachtsman* editors. *Encyclopedia of Sailing.* New York, New York: Harper and Row, Publishers, 1971.

*Oxford English Dictionary.* Oxford, England: Oxford University Press, Compact Edition, 1971.

Parks, Alex L. *Law of Tug, Tow and Pilotage.* Centreville, Maryland: Cornell Maritime Press, 1971.

Patterson, W. B. *Red Book of Marine Engineering, Steam and Power,* 4th edition, Eighth Printing. Centreville, Maryland: Cornell Maritime Press, 1981.

Rousmaniere, John. *A Glossary of Modern Sailing Terms,* revised and updated. New York, New York: G. P. Putnam's Sons, 1989.

Royce, Patric M. *Royce's Sailing Illustrated,* Sacramento, California: Spilman Printing, 1988.

Shafritz, Jay M., Todd J. A. Shafritz, and David Robertson. *The Facts On File Dictionary of Military Science.* New York, New York: Facts On File, 1989.

Soule, C. C. *Naval Terms and Definitions.* New York, New York: D. Van Nostrand Company, Inc., 1923.

Szczurek, Greg. *Unified Rules,* 3rd edition. Kenner, Louisiana: Houston Marine Consultants, 1990.

*The Times Atlas of the Oceans,* edited by Alastair Dougal Cooper. New York, New York: Van Nostrand Reinhold Company, 1983.

Turpin, Edward A. and William A MacEwen. *Merchant Marine Officers' Handbook,* 5th edition, edited by William B. Hayler. Centreville, Maryland: Cornell Maritime Press, 1989.

Tver, David F. *The Norton Encyclopedic Dictionary of Navigation.* New York, New York and London, England: W. W. Norton & Company, 1987.

United States Coast Guard. *Coastguardsman's Manual, The.* Annapolis, Maryland: United States Naval Institute.

United States Navy. *Bluejackets' Manual, The.* Annapolis, Maryland: United States Naval Institute.

U.S. Department of Commerce, National Oceanic and Atmospheric Administration, *United States Coast Pilot,* Washington, D.C.: National Ocean Service.

U.S. Department of Transportation, U.S. Coast Guard, *Light List,* Volume II, *Atlantic and Gulf Coasts.* Washington, D.C.: Superintendent of Documents, U.S. Government Printing Office.

U.S. Department of Transportation, U.S. Coast Guard, *Navigation Rules, International-Inland.* Washington, D.C.: Superintendent of Documents, U.S. Government Printing Office, 1990.

U.S. Department of Transportation, U.S. Coast Guard, *A Manual for the Safe Handling of Flammable and Combustible Liquids and Other Hazardous Products.* Washington, D.C., 1976.

U.S. Naval Institute *Proceedings,* Washington, D.C.: United States Naval Institute, Various issues, 1988, 1989.

Walker, Stuart. *Advanced Racing Tactics.* New York, New York: W. W. Norton & Company, Inc. 1976.

Walker, Stuart. *The Tactics of Small Boat Racing.* New York, New York: W. W. Norton & Company, Inc. 1966.

*Webster's Dictionary of English Usage,* Springfield, Massachusetts: Merriam-Webster Inc. 1989.